T0320523

Deep Learning Techniques and Optimization Strategies in Big Data Analytics

J. Joshua Thomas
KDU Penang University College, Malaysia

Pinar Karagoz
Middle East Technical University, Turkey

B. Bazeer Ahamed
Balaji Institute of Technology and Science, Warangal, India

Pandian Vasant
Universiti Teknologi PETRONAS, Malaysia

A volume in the Advances in Systems Analysis,
Software Engineering, and High Performance
Computing (ASASEHPC) Book Series

Published in the United States of America by
    IGI Global
    Engineering Science Reference (an imprint of IGI Global)
    701 E. Chocolate Avenue
    Hershey PA, USA 17033
    Tel: 717-533-8845
    Fax: 717-533-8661
    E-mail: cust@igi-global.com
    Web site: http://www.igi-global.com

Library of Congress Cataloging-in-Publication Data

Names: Thomas, J. Joshua, 1973- editor.
Title: Deep learning techniques and optimization strategies in big data
  analytics / J. Joshua Thomas, Pinar Karagoz, B. Bazeer Ahamed, Pandian
  Vasant, editors.
Description: Hershey, PA : Engineering Science Reference, [2020] | Includes
  bibliographical references and index. | Summary: "This book examines the
  application of artificial intelligence in machine learning, data mining
  in unstructured data sets or databases, web mining, and information
  retrieval"-- Provided by publisher.
Identifiers: LCCN 2019025566 (print) | LCCN 2019025567 (ebook) | ISBN
  9781799811923 (hardcover) | ISBN 9781799811930 (paperback) | ISBN
  9781799811947 (ebook)
Subjects: LCSH: Big data. | Quantitative research.
Classification: LCC QA76.9.B45 D44 2020 (print) | LCC QA76.9.B45 (ebook)
  | DDC 005.7--dc23
LC record available at https://lccn.loc.gov/2019025566
LC ebook record available at https://lccn.loc.gov/2019025567

This book is published in the IGI Global book series Advances in Systems Analysis, Software Engineering, and High Performance Computing (ASASEHPC) (ISSN: 2327-3453; eISSN: 2327-3461)

British Cataloguing in Publication Data
A Cataloguing in Publication record for this book is available from the British Library.

For electronic access to this publication, please contact: eresources@igi-global.com.

Advances in Systems Analysis, Software Engineering, and High Performance Computing (ASASEHPC) Book Series

Vijayan Sugumaran
Oakland University, USA

ISSN:2327-3453
EISSN:2327-3461

MISSION

The theory and practice of computing applications and distributed systems has emerged as one of the key areas of research driving innovations in business, engineering, and science. The fields of software engineering, systems analysis, and high performance computing offer a wide range of applications and solutions in solving computational problems for any modern organization.

The **Advances in Systems Analysis, Software Engineering, and High Performance Computing (ASASEHPC) Book Series** brings together research in the areas of distributed computing, systems and software engineering, high performance computing, and service science. This collection of publications is useful for academics, researchers, and practitioners seeking the latest practices and knowledge in this field.

COVERAGE

- Computer Networking
- Performance Modelling
- Engineering Environments
- Software Engineering
- Network Management
- Virtual Data Systems
- Storage Systems
- Enterprise Information Systems
- Distributed Cloud Computing
- Computer Graphics

IGI Global is currently accepting manuscripts for publication within this series. To submit a proposal for a volume in this series, please contact our Acquisition Editors at Acquisitions@igi-global.com or visit: http://www.igi-global.com/publish/.

Titles in this Series

For a list of additional titles in this series, please visit:
https://www.igi-global.com/book-series/advances-systems-analysis-software-engineering/73689

Crowdsourcing and Probabilistic Decision-Making in Software Engineering Emerging Research and Opportunities
Varun Gupta (University of Beira Interior, Covilha, Portugal)
Engineering Science Reference • © 2020 • 182pp • H/C (ISBN: 9781522596592) • US $200.00 (our price)

Metrics and Models for Evaluating the Quality and Effectiveness of ERP Software
Geoffrey Muchiri Muketha (Murang'a University of Technology, Kenya) and Elyjoy Muthoni Micheni (Technical University of Kenya, Kenya)
Engineering Science Reference • © 2020 • 391pp • H/C (ISBN: 9781522576785) • US $225.00 (our price)

User-Centered Software Development for the Blind and Visually Impaired Emerging Research and Opportunities
Teresita de Jesús Álvarez Robles (Universidad Veracruzana, Mexico) Francisco Javier Álvarez Rodríguez (Universidad Autónoma de Aguascalientes, Mexico) and Edgard Benítez-Guerrero (Universidad Veracruzana, Mexico)
Engineering Science Reference • © 2020 • 173pp • H/C (ISBN: 9781522585398) • US $195.00 (our price)

Architectures and Frameworks for Developing and Applying Blockchain Technology
Nansi Shi (Logic International Consultants, Singapore)
Engineering Science Reference • © 2019 • 337pp • H/C (ISBN: 9781522592570) • US $245.00 (our price)

Human Factors in Global Software Engineering
Mobashar Rehman (Universiti Tunku Abdul Rahman, Malaysia) Aamir Amin (Universiti Tunku Abdul Rahman, Malaysia) Abdul Rehman Gilal (Sukkur IBA University, Pakistan) and Manzoor Ahmed Hashmani (University Technology PETRONAS, Malaysia)
Engineering Science Reference • © 2019 • 381pp • H/C (ISBN: 9781522594482) • US $245.00 (our price)

Interdisciplinary Approaches to Information Systems and Software Engineering
Alok Bhushan Mukherjee (North-Eastern Hill University Shillong, India) and Akhouri Pramod Krishna (Birla Institute of Technology Mesra, India)
Engineering Science Reference • © 2019 • 299pp • H/C (ISBN: 9781522577843) • US $215.00 (our price)

Cyber-Physical Systems for Social Applications
Maya Dimitrova (Bulgarian Academy of Sciences, Bulgaria) and Hiroaki Wagatsuma (Kyushu Institute of Technology, Japan)
Engineering Science Reference • © 2019 • 440pp • H/C (ISBN: 9781522578796) • US $265.00 (our price)

701 East Chocolate Avenue, Hershey, PA 17033, USA
Tel: 717-533-8845 x100 • Fax: 717-533-8661
E-Mail: cust@igi-global.com • www.igi-global.com

Editorial Advisory Board

Table of Contents

Detailed Table of Contents

Chapter 1

An electrocardiogram (ECG) is used as one of the important diagnostic tools for the detection of the health of a heart. An automatic heart abnormality identification methods sense numerous abnormalities or arrhythmia and decrease the physician's pressure as well as share their workload. In ECG analysis, the main focus is to enhance degree of accuracy and include a number of heart diseases that can be classified. In this chapter, arrhythmia classification is proposed using hybrid features of T-wave in ECG. The classification system consists of majorly three phases, windowing technique, feature extraction, and classification. This classifier categorizes the normal and abnormal signals efficiently. The experimental analysis showed that the hybrid features arrhythmia classification performance of accuracy approximately 98.3%, specificity 98.0%, and sensitivity 98.6% using MIT-BIH database.

Chapter 2

Artificial intelligence (AI) is going through its golden era. Most AI applications are indeed using machine learning, and it currently represents the most promising path to strong AI. On the other hand, deep learning, which is itself a kind of machine learning, is becoming more and more popular and successful at different use cases and is at the peak of developments by enabling more accurate forecasting and better planning for civil society, policymakers, and businesses. As a result, deep learning is becoming a leader in this domain. This chapter presents a brief review of ground-breaking advances in deep learning applications.

    Jahedul Islam, Universiti Teknologi PETRONAS, Malaysia

    Pandian M. Vasant, Universiti Teknologi PETRONAS, Malaysia

    Berihun Mamo Negash, Universiti Teknologi PETRONAS, Malaysia

    Moacyr Bartholomeu Laruccia, Independent Researcher, Malaysia

    Myo Myint, Universiti Teknologi PETRONAS, Malaysia

Well placement optimization is one of the major challenging factors in the field development process in the oil and gas industry. This chapter aims to survey prominent metaheuristic techniques, which solve well the placement optimization problem. The well placement optimization problem is considered as high dimensional, discontinuous, and multi-model optimization problem. Moreover, the computational expenses further complicate the issue. Over the last decade, both gradient-based and gradient-free optimization methods were implemented. Gradient-free optimization, such as the particle swarm optimization, genetic algorithm, is implemented in this area. These optimization techniques are utilized as standalone or as the hybridization of optimization methods to maximize the economic factors. In this chapter, the authors survey the two most popular nature-inspired metaheuristic optimization techniques and their application to maximize the economic factors.

    Md. Shokor A. Rahaman, Universiti Teknologi PETRONAS, Malaysia

    Pandian Vasant, Universiti Teknologi PETRONAS, Malaysia

Total organic carbon (TOC) is the most significant factor for shale oil and gas exploration and development which can be used to evaluate the hydrocarbon generation potential of source rock. However, estimating TOC is a challenge for the geological engineers because direct measurements of core analysis geochemical experiments are time-consuming and costly. Therefore, many AI technique has used for TOC content prediction in the shale reservoir where AI techniques have impacted positively. Having both strength and weakness, some of them can execute quickly and handle high dimensional data while others have limitation for handling the uncertainty, learning difficulties, and unable to deal with high or low dimensional datasets which reminds the "no free lunch" theorem where it has been proven that no technique or system be relevant to all issues in all circumstances. So, investigating the cutting-edge AI techniques is the contribution of this study as the resulting analysis gives top to bottom understanding of the different TOC content prediction strategies.

    *Rajalakshmi R., School of Computing Science and Engineering, Vellore Institute of
        Technology, Chennai, India*
    *Hans Tiwari, School of Electronics Engineering, Vellore Institute of Technology, Chennai,
        India*
    Jay Patel, School of Electronics Engineering, Vellore Institute of Technology, Chennai, India
    *Rameshkannan R., School of Computing Science and Engineering, Vellore Institute of
        Technology, Chennai, India*
    Karthik R., Vellore Institute of Technology, Chennai, India

The Gen Z kids highly rely on internet for various purposes like entertainment, sports, and school projects. There is a demand for parental control systems to monitor the children during their surfing time. Current web page classification approaches are not effective as handcrafted features are extracted from the web content and machine learning techniques are used that need domain knowledge. Hence, a deep learning approach is proposed to perform URL-based web page classification. As the URL is a short text, the model should learn to understand where the important information is present in the URL. The proposed system integrates the strength of attention mechanism with recurrent convolutional neural network for effective learning of context-aware URL features. This enhanced architecture improves the design of kids-relevant URL classification. By conducting various experiments on the benchmark collection Open Directory Project, it is shown that an accuracy of 0.8251 was achieved.

    Anoop Balakrishnan Kadan, Vimal Jyothi Engineering College, India
    Perumal Sankar Subbian, Toc H Institute of Science and Technology, India
    Jeyakrishnan V., Saintgits College of Engineering, India
    Hariharan N., Adi Shankara Institute of Engineering and Technology, Ernakulam, India
    Roshini T. V., Vimal Jyothi Engineering College, India
    Sravani S. Nath, Vimal Jyothi Engineering College, India

Diabetic retinopathy (DR), which affects the blood vessels of the human retina, is considered to be the most serious complication prevalent among diabetic patients. If detected successfully at an early stage, the ophthalmologist would be able to treat the patients by advanced laser treatment to prevent total blindness. In this study, a technique based on morphological image processing and fuzzy logic to detect hard exudates from DR retinal images is explored. The proposed technique is to classify the eye by using a neural network approach (classifier) to predict whether it is affected or not. Here, a classifier is added before the fuzzy logic. This fuzzy will tell how much and where it is affected. The proposed technique will tell whether the eye is abnormal or normal.

Applying deep learning to the pervasive graph data is significant because of the unique characteristics of graphs. Recently, substantial amounts of research efforts have been keen on this area, greatly advancing graph-analyzing techniques. In this study, the authors comprehensively review different kinds of deep learning methods applied to graphs. They discuss with existing literature into sub-components of two: graph convolutional networks, graph autoencoders, and recent trends including chemoinformatics research area including molecular fingerprints and drug discovery. They further experiment with variational autoencoder (VAE) analyze how these apply in drug target interaction (DTI) and applications with ephemeral outline on how they assist the drug discovery pipeline and discuss potential research directions.

# Chapter 8

Multimedia application is a significant and growing research area because of the advances in technology of software engineering, storage devices, networks, and display devices. With the intention of satisfying multimedia information desires of users, it is essential to build an efficient multimedia information process, access, and analysis applications, which maintain various tasks, like retrieval, recommendation, search, classification, and clustering. Deep learning is an emerging technique in the sphere of multimedia information process, which solves both the crisis of conventional and recent researches. The main aim is to resolve the multimedia-related problems by the use of deep learning. The deep learning revolution is discussed with the depiction and feature. Finally, the major application also explained with respect to different fields. This chapter analyzes the crisis of retrieval after providing the successful discussion of multimedia information retrieval that is the ability of retrieving an object of every multimedia.

# Chapter 9

Construction of a neural network is the cardinal step to any machine learning algorithm. It requires profound knowledge for the developer in assigning the weights and biases to construct it. And the construction should be done for multiple epochs to obtain an optimal neural network. This makes it cumbersome for an inexperienced machine learning aspirant to develop it with ease. So, an automated neural network construction would be of great use and provide the developer with incredible speed to program and run the machine learning algorithm. This is a crucial assist from the developer's perspective. The developer can now focus only on the logical portion of the algorithm and hence increase productivity. The use of Enas algorithm aids in performing the automated transfer learning to construct the complete neural network from the given sample data. This algorithm proliferates on the incoming data. Hence, it is very important to inculcate it with the existing machine learning algorithms.

# Chapter 10

Natural data erupting directly out of various data sources, such as text, image, video, audio, and sensor data, comes with an inherent property of having very large dimensions or features of the data. While these features add richness and perspectives to the data, due to sparsity associated with them, it adds to the computational complexity while learning, unable to visualize and interpret them, thus requiring large scale computational power to make insights out of it. This is famously called "curse of dimensionality." This chapter discusses the methods by which curse of dimensionality is cured using conventional methods and analyzes its performance for given complex datasets. It also discusses the advantages of nonlinear methods over linear methods and neural networks, which could be a better approach when compared to other nonlinear methods. It also discusses future research areas such as application of deep learning techniques, which can be applied as a cure for this curse.

# Chapter 11

The engendering of uncertain data in ordinary access news sources, for example, news sites, web-based life channels, and online papers, have made it trying to recognize capable news sources, along these lines expanding the requirement for computational instruments ready to give into the unwavering quality of online substance. For instance, counterfeit news outlets were observed to be bound to utilize language that is abstract and enthusiastic. At the point when specialists are chipping away at building up an AI-based apparatus for identifying counterfeit news, there wasn't sufficient information to prepare their calculations; they did the main balanced thing. In this chapter, two novel datasets for the undertaking of phony news locations, covering distinctive news areas, distinguishing proof of phony substance in online news has been considered. N-gram model will distinguish phony substance consequently with an emphasis on phony audits and phony news. This was pursued by a lot of learning analyses to fabricate precise phony news identifiers and showed correctness of up to 80%.

    Anongpun Man-Im, Asian Institute of Technology, Thailand
    Weerakorn Ongsakul, Asian Institute of Technology, Thailand
    Nimal Madhu M., Asian Institute of Technology, Thailand

Power system scheduling is one of the most complex multi-objective scheduling problems, and a heuristic optimization method is designed for finding the OPF solution. Stochastic weight trade-off chaotic mutation-based non-dominated sorting particle swarm optimization algorithm can improve solution-search-capability by balancing between global best exploration and local best utilization through the stochastic weight and dynamic coefficient trade-off methods. This algorithm with chaotic mutation enhances diversity and search-capability, preventing premature convergence. Non-dominated sorting and crowding distance techniques efficiently provide the optimal Pareto front. Fuzzy function is used to select the local best compromise. Using a two-stage approach, the global best solution is selected from many local trials. The discussed approach can schedule the generators in the systems effectively, leading to savings in fuel cost, reduction in active power loss and betterment in voltage stability.

    Timothy Ganesan, Royal Bank of Canada, Canada
    Pandian Vasant, Universiti Teknologi PETRONAS, Malaysia
    Igor Litvinchev, Nuevo Leon State University, Mexico

As industrial systems become more complex, various complexities and uncertainties come into play. Metaheuristic-type optimization techniques have become crucial for effective design, maintenance, and operations of such systems. However, in highly complex industrial systems, conventional metaheuristics are still plagued by various drawbacks. Strategies such as hybridization and algorithmic modifications have been the focus of previous efforts to improve the performance of conventional metaheuristics. This work tackles a large-scale multi-objective (MO) optimization problem: biofuel supply chain. Due to the scale and complexity of the problem, the random matrix approach was employed to modify the stochastic generator segment of the cuckoo search (CS) technique. Comparative analysis was then performed on the computational results produced by the conventional CS technique and the improved CS variants.

    Saravanan Radhakrishnan, Vellore Institute of Technology, India
    Vijayarajan V., Vellore Institute of Technology, India

Deep learning opens up a plethora of opportunities for academia and industry to invent new techniques to come up with modified or enhanced versions of standardized neural networks so that the customized technique is suitable for any specialized situations where the problem is about learning a complex mapping from the input to the output space. One such situation lies in a farm with huge cultivation area, where examining each of the plant for any anomalies is highly complex that it is impractical, if not impossible, for humans. In this chapter, the authors propose an optimized deep learning architectural model, combining various techniques in neural networks for a real-world application of deep learning in computer vision in precision farming. More precisely, thousands of crops are examined automatically and classified as healthy or unhealthy. The highlight of this architecture is the strategic usage of spatial and temporal features selectively so as to reduce the inference time.

Chapter 15

Fawaz H. H. Mahyoub, School of Computer Sciences, Universiti Sains Malaysia, Malaysia
Rosni Abdullah, School of Computer Sciences, Universiti Sains Malaysia, Malaysia

The prediction of protein secondary structure from a protein sequence provides useful information for predicting the three-dimensional structure and function of the protein. In recent decades, protein secondary structure prediction systems have been improved benefiting from the advances in computational techniques as well as the growth and increased availability of solved protein structures in protein data banks. Existing methods for predicting the secondary structure of proteins can be roughly subdivided into statistical, nearest-neighbor, machine learning, meta-predictors, and deep learning approaches. This chapter provides an overview of these computational approaches to predict the secondary structure of proteins, focusing on deep learning techniques, with highlights on key aspects in each approach.

Chapter 16

BURCU YILMAZ, Institute of Information Technologies, Gebze Technical University
Hilal Genc, Department of Computer Engineering, Gebze Technical University, Turkey
Mustafa Agriman, Computer Engineering Department, Middle East Technical University, Turkey
Bugra Kaan Demirdover, Computer Engineering Department, Middle East Technical University, Turkey
Mert Erdemir, Computer Engineering Deptartment, Middle East Technical University, Turkey
Gokhan Simsek, Computer Engineering Department, Middle East Technical University, Turkey
Pinar Karagoz, Computer Engineering Department, Middle East Technical University, Turkey

Graphs are powerful data structures that allow us to represent varying relationships within data. In the past, due to the difficulties related to the time complexities of processing graph models, graphs rarely involved machine learning tasks. In recent years, especially with the new advances in deep learning techniques, increasing number of graph models related to the feature engineering and machine learning are proposed. Recently, there has been an increase in approaches that automatically learn to encode graph structure into low dimensional embedding. These approaches are accompanied by models for machine learning tasks, and they fall into two categories. The first one focuses on feature engineering techniques on graphs. The second group of models assembles graph structure to learn a graph neighborhood in the machine learning model. In this chapter, the authors focus on the advances in applications of graphs on NLP using the recent deep learning models.

Chapter 17

Kallol Biswas, Universiti Teknologi PETRONAS, Malaysia
Pandian M. Vasant, Universiti Teknologi PETRONAS, Malaysia
Moacyr Batholomeu Laruccia, Independent Researcher, Malaysia
José Antonio Gámez Vintaned, Universiti Teknologi PETRONAS, Malaysia
Myo M. Myint, Universiti Teknologi PETRONAS, Malaysia

Due to a variety of possible good types and so many complex drilling variables and constraints, optimization of the trajectory of a complex wellbore is very challenging. There are several types of wells, such as directional wells, horizontal wells, redrilling wells, complex structure wells, cluster wells, and extended reach wells. This reduction of the wellbore length helps to establish cost-effective approaches that can be utilized to resolve a group of complex trajectory optimization challenges. For efficient performance (i.e., quickly locating global optima while taking the smallest amount of computational time), we have to identify flexible control parameters. This research will try to develop a review of the various (particle swarm optimization) PSO algorithm used to optimize deviated wellbore trajectories. This chapter helps to find out optimal wellbore trajectory optimization algorithms that can close the technology gap by giving a useful method. This method can generate a solution automatically.

Foreword

Artificial Intelligence and Machine Learning have started to change the global economy. They can be seen as new industries which produce new business models across all sectors. They constitute a major component of the Industry 4.0 transformation, for accelerating of operation efficiency and enterprise-wide growth. They also have a major role in the Society 5.0 transformation, merging the physical and cyber space and analyzing big data volumes collected by sensors and devices.

Deep learning techniques and optimization strategies have been the main driving force in recent developments and achievements in the analysis of big data. Major improvements, related to classification, regression, prediction and uncertainty estimation, have been achieved, reaching, or even exceeding respective results provided by humans. This has been shown in most important application fields, including vision, image analysis and synthesis, speech and emotion recognition, text analysis and natural language processing, healthcare, robotics, energy consumption, smart agriculture and agri-food.

It is therefore necessary to produce diverse strategies and applications of deep learning and optimization, which will form the basis of further development of the field, enhancing transparency, explainability and trustfulness of the derived approaches in human-centric frameworks.

This book comes to contribute to this generation of diverse deep learning and optimization strategies in the big data analytics field. The editors, J. Joshua Thomas, Pinar Karagoz, B. Bazeer Ahamed and Pandian Vasant, have managed to generate a remarkable number of different contributions to both technology and application development in the field. The book will be of great assistance to researchers who wish to get informed about new developments and applications of deep learning, as well as to researchers that are already active in the field and find further information about the usage of deep learning and optimization methodologies in their own or other application fields.

The 17 chapters cover a variety of strategies and applications. There are two reviews on deep learning and optimization methods and on their applications, as well as three papers on transfer learning in deep neural networks, on natural language processing and on data dimensionality reduction. Three papers refer to information analysis on the Web, focusing on fake news detection, on monitoring kids' surfing and on multimedia information retrieval. Five papers focus on healthcare, biological and agricultural prediction; specifically, on detection of diabetic retinopathy and arrhythmia, on graph networks for drug discovery, on protein prediction and on crop health classification. Seven papers focus on optimization and energy related problems. In particular on optimization of drilling operations, of wellbore trajectories, of well placement in the oil and gas industrial operation, of biofuel supply, on power system scheduling, on prediction of total organic carbon and on energy efficiency in IoT based on wireless sensor networks.

The editors of IGI Global have done their best to include contributions to deep learning and optimization strategies in a variety of important technological and application fields in the book and we thank them very much for this.

Stefanos Kollias
School of Computer Science, University of Lincoln, UK

Stefanos Kollias *has been Founding Professor of Machine Learning in the Computer Science School of the University of Lincoln, UK, since September 2016, leading the mlearn Research Group (mlearn.lincoln.ac.uk). He also holds a Professorial in the Computer Science Division of ECE School, National Technical University of Athens, since 1997. He has been Fellow of the IEEE since 2015, Member of the Executive Committee of the European Neural Network Society, 2007-2016. He has published 110 papers in journals and 310 papers in Conferences. He has been Co-Editor of the book 'Multimedia and the Semantic Web', Wiley, 2005. His research work has about 10,000 Citations, h-Index 46 (Google Scholar). He has supervised 42 Ph.D. students, having obtained many best paper awards. He has been General Chair in 6 Conferences and Program Committee Member in 50 Conferences. He has served as National Representative in the EC Member State Expert Group for Content Digitization and in the EUREKA High Level Group. He has coordinated his Group participation in 100 European research projects with funding of 20MEuro.*

Preface

We are living in the era of big data. Almost all activites, whether in business life or daily life, involve with production of data. The number is resources for such data is countless and they come from a rich variety of activities: financial transactions, sensor data flowing from almosot all types of machinery and plants, and survellience devices, web search activities, social media activites, etc.

In addition to the increase in the amount of data produced, there is an increase in capability to store and process data, as well. Thanks to advancement in data storage devices, and data storage models such as the cloud storage services, it is possible to store the high amount of data being produced. This capability further triggered the need and demand for obtaining useful information stored data, and paved the way for big data analytics capabilities.

Big data analytics involve a variety of artificial intelligence and machine learning techniques, as well as descriptive analytics approaches. In this book, among these, we particularly focus on deep learning and optimization strategies. Deep learning, which involves multi-layered neural architectures and focus on feature learning as a core step of the learning process, is a comparatively new technique, providing successful results for well-known analytics and learning problems in a set of domains such as face recognition and natural language processing. Hence, it is considered as the basis for new generation artificial intelligence. It is closely related with big data in the sense that deep learning techniques perform better particularly under high amount of observations.

On the other hand, optimization is a very well-known area with a vast number of applications, from route finding problems to medical treatment and maintenance schedules in plants. Under the high amount of data, conventional linear programming-based solutions and earlier heuristics fall short for the big data era. Therefore, new optimization strategies adaptive to increasing amount of data have emerged.

OBJECTIVE OF THE BOOK

Being two important aspects in big data analytics, deep learning techniques and optimization strategies have been studied intensely in the academia, and various solutions are available and in use. In this book, gathering the recent advancements on these two important aspect, we aim to provide a resource for the audience. Another important objective of the book is to present a variety of domains in which deep learning techniques and optimization strategies are used. The techniques and strategies need adaptations and tunings according to the nature of the data available in the domain. Hence, the book aims to provide a reference and guidence for the use of deep learning and optimization for various domains. Additionally, this providence a guidence as to how these techniques and tunings can be applied in other domains in the future.

In terms of deep learning techniques, the book covers a wide range of neural models including Convolutional Neural Networks (CNN), Recurrent Neural Networks (RNN), Recursive RNNS, Bidirectional Generative Neural Networks (BGNN), Graph Neural Networks. These technques are described in terms of features and structure, and also domains in which they are successfully applied. For optimization strategies, various metaheuristic algorithms are covered including Genetic Algorithm, Particle Swarm Optimization (PSO), Cuckoo Search (CS), and their variants.

In terms of domains in which deep learning techniques and optimization strategies are applied, the book includes a variety of areas. The audience can find recent advancements of these techniques and strategies in a wide coverage of areas including healthcare, biology and chemistry, enery and power systems, information retrieval, natural language processing and agriculture.

TARGET AUDIENCE

The book intends to provide useful information for audience with various background and with various data analytics expertise level. The book includes chapters offering overview of deep neural models and their applications, which would be useful for audience from any background. The details for specific neural models and their adaptation in various domains are also available, which would address the audience with data analytics background or with domain knowledge on areas, such as geology, power systems, healtcare, agriculture or natural language processing. Similarly several optimization strategies are described in more detail, which would be informative to those who are interested in domain specific optimization problems.

The book includes 17 chapters, presenting recent advancements on deep learning techniques and optimization strategies on a variety of models, algorithms and application domains.

In Chapter 1, in healthcare domain, the use of deep learning for automatic heart abnormality identification is presented. Electrocardiogram (ECG) is one of the most important diagnostic tools for the health status analysis of a heart. Sense numerous abnormalities or arrhythmia automatically facilitates the diagnosis process for the physicians. In ECG analysis, the main objective is to enhance the degree of accuracy and to include a number of heart diseases that can be classified. The authors propose an auto-encoder based deep neural network solution for arrhythmia classification by hybrid features of T-wave in ECG. The experimental analysis shows that the proposed arrhythmia classification technique has accuracy of approximately 98.3%, specificity of 98.0% and sensitivity of 98.6% using MIT-BIH database.

Chapter 2 focuses on the use of deep learning techniques successfully in a wide range of cases, and presents a review of deep learning applications. From speech recognition and computer vision to virtual assistans, healthcare and self-driving cars, ground breaking advances in deep learning applications are described.

In Chapter 3, well placement optimization problem is studied. It is one of the major factors to be considered in the field development process in the oil and gas industry. The well placement optimization problem is considered as a high dimensional, discontinuous and multi-model optimization problem with high computational complexity. The authors focus on two popular nature-inspired metaheuristic optimization techniques, Particle Swarm Optimization and Genetic Algorithm, and describe how well placement optimization problem can be specified and solved bu using these two techniques. The chapter further discusses the use of other metaheuristic optimization techniques for the problem.

In Chapter 4, AI based solutions for the shale reservoir analysis is presented. The challenged problem is the Total organic carbon (TOC) content prediction, as TOC is the most significant factor for shale oil and gas exploration and development. In this domain, direct measurements of core analysis and geo-chemical experiments are reported to be time-consuming and costly. Hence AI techniques facilitate the process considerably. The problem has several performance aspects such as handling high dimensional data and providing time efficiency. The authors invesgate the performance of various AI techniques through various aspects, and provide an understanding of the different TOC content prediction strategies.

In Chapter 5, the use of deep learning for web page classification problem is elaborated on. More particularly, the addressed problem is URL classification for parental control of web access. The objective is to to block the content before downloading the page. To this aim, Convolutional Neural Network (CNN) is combined with Bidirectional Gated Recurrent Unit (BGRU) in order to extract rich context-aware features as well as to preserve to sequence information in the URL. Additionally, attention mechanism is incorporated in the neural architecture in order to retain significant URL features. On the benchmark data collection, 82.2% accuracy was reported.

Chapter 6 is on another important detection/classification problem in healthcare domain, Diabetic Retinopathy (DR) detection. DR, which affects the blood vessels of the human retina, is considered to be the most serious complication prevalent among diabetic patients. If detected successfully at an early stage, the ophthalmologist would be able to treat the patients by advanced laser treatment to prevent total blindness. In the chapter, authors propose a hybrid approach, which is a combination of a supervisde neural model and fuzzy logic, in order to detect hard exudates from DR retinal images.

In Chapter 7, the authors study graph neural networks, as in Chapter 16. However, this time the focus is on two particular neural models, Graph Convolutional Networks, and Graph Autoencoders. The chapter elaborates on the use of these two techniques on chemoinformatics, including the tasks of molecular fingerprints, and drug discovery. Experiments with variational Autoencoder (VAE) demonstrate how such neural models can be used in chemoinformatics research. Potential research directions are also discussed.

Chapter 8 is on another important domain, multimedia information retrieval, in which deep learning techniques have a crucial role. Multimedia information retrieval is the process of retrieving multimedia objects fulfilling the given query. Multimedia retrieval has been involved in a wide range of applications, resulting with a need of efficient multimedia information processing, access, and analysis solutions. Deep learning is an emerging technique in the sphere of multimedia information processing, which solves the shortcomings of the conventional techniques. In the chapter, the authors discuss the deep learning revolution describing the main features and techniques of deep learning. Then, use of deep learning techniques for multimedia information retrieval tasks are described.

Chapter 9 is about the problem of neural model construction in deep learning. It requires profound knowledge for the developer in assigning the weights and biases. Since the training involves multiple epochs, it is a cumbersome process for an inexperienced machine learning practitioner to decide for the optimal structure. In the chapter, the authors focus on Convolutional Neural Networks (CNN) and describes how Transfer Learning can be used to facilitate the neural model construction for the given problem. The process starts with a pretrained architecture, by reusing the network weights and archi-tecture, and the network model is trained on the user's dataset through Efficient Neural Architecture Search (ENAS) algorithm. The performance of the approach is analyzed on a task of learning graph analysis against baseline methods.

In Chapter 10, the problem of handling high number of dimensions in the data is studied. In addition to the high amount of data, high dimensionality in the data poses a challenge for analytics. The chapter initally discusses about the conventional methods employed for curse of dimensionality, and analyzes the performance for a complex benchmark data set. Following this, advantages of nonlinear methods, especially neural network techniques, over linear methods for the problem are discussed. The authors elaborate on the use of deep learning techniques as a cure for this curse as future research areas, as well.

In Chapter 11, fake news detection problem is focused on. Due to increase in online news sources and uncertainity in the quality of the online content, the need for computational instruments to measure the quality of the content and the credibility of the source has been increasing. In the chapter, the authors summarize various neural models that can be utilized in fake news detection problem, and then present a solution that incorporates semantic similarity. The experiments conducted two benchmark data sets show that the proposed approach provides fake news detection accuracy up to about 80%.

In Chapter 12, power system scheduling optimization problem is elaborated on. The effective scheduling is important for fuel cost saving, reducing power loss and having better voltage stability index. The authors describe the use of a variant of Particle Swarm Optimization (PSO), which is stochastic weight trade-off chaotic mutation based non-dominated sorting particle swarm optimization algorithm, for power system scheduling. The algorithm makes use of chatoic mutation in order to enhance diversity and search capability, and employs non-dominant sorting and crowding distance techniques in order to provide the optimal Pareto front efficiently. Using a two-stage approach, the global best solution is selected from many local trials.

In Chapter 13, a large-scale multiobjective optimization problem, biofuel supply chain optimization, is presented. Metaheuristic-type optimization techniques have become crucial for effective design, maintenance and operations of such systems. Strategies such as hybridization and algorithmic modifications has been the focus of previous efforts to improve the performance of conventional metaheuristics. In the chapter, the authors propose a modification on Cuckoo Search (CS) technique, such that, due to the scale and complexity of the problem, the random matrix approach is employed to modify the stochastic generator segment. Comparative analysis of the improved CS variant is presented against the conventional CS technique.

Chapter 14 focuses on the use of deep learning in agriculture domain. Precision farming is one of the subdomains where deep learning has high potentional for improving the efficiency. One of the important problems studied under precision farming is that, in a farm with huge cultivation area, examining each of the plants for any anomalies is highly complex, and it is impractical for humans. The authors propose an optimized deep learning architectural model, combining various techniques in neural networks for precision farming. More precisely, thousands of crops are examined automatically through the proposed neural model, and classified as healthy or unhealthy. The novelty of the proposed architecture lies in the strategic usage of spatial and temporal features selectively in order to reduce the inference time.

Chapter 15 discusses the use of deep learning techniques for the prediction of protein secondary structure from a protein sequence. Such a prediction provides useful information for predicting the three-dimensional structure and function of the protein. In recent decades, protein secondary structure prediction systems have been improved benefiting from the advances in computational techniques as well as the growth and increased availability of solved protein structures in protein data banks. The authors provides an overview of the existing computational approaches to predict the secondary structure of proteins, focusing on deep learning techniques, with highlights on key aspects in each approach.

In Chapter 16, the authors focus on graph neural models and their use in Natural Language Processing (NLP) problems. Since graphs are powerful data structures that allow us to represent varying kinds of relationships within data, neural models for graph processing are arising. The graph neural models in the literature basically aim to perform feature engineering and to learn graph neighborhood. Among various domains, in which such graph models are employed, NLP applications present considerable advancement. The authors firstly describe the graph neural models in the literature, and then present the use of such models in various NLP applications, including machine translation, visual question answering, reasoning and text classification.

In Chapter 17, trajectory of a complex wellbore is studied as an optimization problem. The reduction of the wellbore length is important in order to provide cost efficency. However, the existance of a variety of drilling variables and constraints make specifying wellbore trajectory a complex optimization problem. The chapter focuses on the use of Particle Swarm Optimization (PSO) algorithm for wellbore trajectory optimization, and reviews variations of PSO fort he problem.

We aim to provide a rich selection of recent advancements in big data analytics in the aspects of deep learning techniques and optimization strategies in terms of both algoritms and models, and also application areas. We belive that the book will be a useful resource for a wide range of audience, including artificial intelligence researchers, physicians, geological engineers, energy and agriculture specialist. It provides useful cases for municipalities, ministeries and other organizations involving a variety of areas agriculture, energy, healthcare. The improvements in learning and optimization tasks will be of interest to IT companies especially on natural language processing, information retrieval and social media analytics.

J. Joshua Thomas
KDU Penang University College, Penang, Malaysia

Pinar Karagoz
Middle East Technical University, Turkey

B. Bazeer Ahamed
Balaji Institute of Technology and Science, Warangal, India

Pandian Vasant
Universiti Teknologi PETRONAS, Malaysia

Acknowledgment

The editors would like to acknowledge the efforts of all the people, which were involved in the activity on creation of this book. Particularly they would like to thank each one of the authors for their contributions. Our sincere gratitude goes to the chapters' authors who contributed the time and expertise to this book. Special gratitude should be given to the people which besides the preparing their chapters took part in the reviewing process. Without invaluable support of all of them, this book would not have become a reality.

A lot of thanks to the editorial advisory board members which have made a lot for making the high quality of the book. Specially needs to underline essential role of Editorial Board member, Professor Stefanos Kollias for excellent forward and precious assistance. The editors are confident that this book will certainly be useful to readers, because, among other things, it gives them the opportunity to be acquainted with the results of research that has published. It would be reference the enormous role that IGI Global publishing house has played in order for this information to publish.

Finally, many thanks the editors would like to express to the entire staff of IGI Global publishing houses who helped the editors and authors in preparing the manuscript of this book professionally and extremely friendly, and have made a lot to make this book the edition of exceptional quality.

J. Joshua Thomas
KDU Penang University College, Malaysia

Pinar Karagoz
Middle East Technical University, Turkey

B. Bazeer Ahamed
Balaji Institute of Technology and Science, Warangal, India

Pandian Vasant
Universiti Teknologi PETRONAS, Malaysia

Chapter 1
Arrhythmia Detection Based on Hybrid Features of T–Wave in Electrocardiogram

Raghu N.
ⓘ https://orcid.org/0000-0002-2091-8922
Jain University, India

ABSTRACT

An electrocardiogram (ECG) is used as one of the important diagnostic tools for the detection of the health of a heart. An automatic heart abnormality identification methods sense numerous abnormalities or arrhythmia and decrease the physician's pressure as well as share their workload. In ECG analysis, the main focus is to enhance degree of accuracy and include a number of heart diseases that can be classified. In this chapter, arrhythmia classification is proposed using hybrid features of T-wave in ECG. The classification system consists of majorly three phases, windowing technique, feature extraction, and classification. This classifier categorizes the normal and abnormal signals efficiently. The experimental analysis showed that the hybrid features arrhythmia classification performance of accuracy approximately 98.3%, specificity 98.0%, and sensitivity 98.6% using MIT-BIH database.

INTRODUCTION

The digitalised electrocardiogram accession techniques form an important part of the contemporary framework in recognising and saving the signals at real time in order to assist in acknowledging the cardiac conditions.

This method does not incorporate dissection of the body or use of any insertion instruments. This technique is non-invasive and caters to a wide range of heart conditions like arrhythmia, heart rate variability, etc. that can be diagnosed with ease by employing the classifiers techniques in discussion system (Senapati, Senapati, and Maka, 2014). The process of analysing ECG signals is time consuming and very laborious for the cardiologists and the possibility of omission of vital information due to human error is high and thereby computerized techniques for the determination of arrhythmia from the

DOI: 10.4018/978-1-7998-1192-3.ch001

various available medical data is much required (Dong, Wang, and Si, 2017 & Jadhav, Nalbalwar, and Ghatol, 2014). Many a times the medical practitioner are in a situation where in the signals obtained are; two signals having same patterns but indicate non-identical diseases and also the vice-versa where in the two signals with dissimilar patterns but revealing the same disease thus, complicating the task of ailment diagnosis for the doctor with . Hence, it can be noted that the appearances of the ECG signals are not completely accurate for the identification of the diseases. Therefore, employing the different characteristics of these signals would aid to corroborate the analyzing the respective heart conditions (Hassan, Saleem, and Habib, 2017). Many methods are used to identify and categorize the diseases interconnected to heart like abnormal and normal sinus rhythm etc.

Numerous methods for heart disease detections and ECG analysis have been discovered/developed in past few years for improvised classification of heart abnormality. P, Q, R, T and U are the five basic waves of an ECG waveform. Atrial depolarization is indicated by the P wave, ventricular depolarization is indicated by the QRS complex and repolarization of ventricle is indicated by T wave. The shape of the QRS complex is the most important and plays an integral role in the ECG signal analysis (Alickovic and Subasi, 2016).

The electrocardiogram signals are similar for different types of heartbeats as well as differ for the same person. Heart abnormality classification can be can be carried out by various existing techniques like; Support Vector Machine (SVM), Radial Basis Function (RBF), Linear Discriminant Analysis (LDA), Principle Component Analysis (PCA) (Elhai et. al, 2016). The method of using ECG signals for the detection of heart abnormality has major drawbacks due to the variations in signals depending on individual persons based on gender, age, etc. Another drawback includes the variations of the signals for the same person caused by few physical conditions. And due to these limitations following a single permanent method to carry out the detections seems inappropriate (Shadmand and Mashoufi, 2016).

In this chapter, characteristics based on both DWT coefficient and Time domain based features such as DE, peak magnitude RMS ratio, Auto regressive features like Yule-Walker Method, and Burgs method are used for the ECG signal feature extraction The improvisation of the ECG signal categorization is performed based on the above mentioned features and the two abnormalities of the heart can be identified using the SVM classifier.

LITERATURE SURVEY

A. Daamouche, L. Hamami, N. Alajlan, and F. Melgani (2012) presented a wavelet optimization strategy depends on the mixture of the poly phase representation of wavelets and PSO. This strategy finds the wavelets that indicate the beats of discrimination capability calculated through an empirical measure of the classifier efficiency. The SVM classifier illuminates the accuracy and stability of the proposed method and poly phase permits the wavelet filter bank from angular parameter. The wavelet method for ECG signal improves the classification accuracy but, this proposed technique not suitable for all datasets.

P. Kora and K.S.R. Krishna (2016) presented Wavelet Coherence (WTC) method for ECG signal investigation. The WTC measures the similarity among two waveforms in the frequency domain. The features are extracted from ECG signal after that optimized with the help of Bat algorithm. The optimized features are classified using Levenberg Marquardt neural network classifier. These techniques select the relevant features and reduce the feature redundancy as well as improve the classification accuracy but, this architecture is a bit time consuming.

V.H.C. de Albuquerque et. al (2016) illustrated the arrhythmia identification in ECG signal using supervised machine learning methods of Optimum Path Forest (OPF) classifier. The proposed method's efficiency and effectiveness are compared with the different feature extraction methods and classifiers. The OPF discovered more skills to generalize data. This technique is more efficient in terms of computation time of testing and training. But, sometimes possibilities of miss prediction activities were occurring.

S.S. Kumar, and H.H. Inbarani (2016) proposed Multi-granulation rough set based classification approaches are applied for ECG cardiac arrhythmia categorization. The classifier was verified ECG signals of 24 channels were recorded from the database. The Pan-Tomkins's and Wavelet Transform (WT) methods have been decided on to gain a compact set of features. The classifier improves the classification accuracy. In this work, only a limited number of ECG channels are taken for the experiment and all channels are not taken.

D. Ai et. al (2015) evaluated Fast feature fusion technique of Generalized-N-Dimensional (GND)-ICA for ECF heartbeat classification based on multi-linear subspace learning. In feature fusion, all extracted feature of ECG signal heartbeat was arranged as a two-way tensor, in which feature-fusion procedure was implemented using a multi-linear subspace-learning method, GND-ICA. The SVM classifier was used for classification, which classified the heartbeats. This classifier decreased the classification time and removed the redundant features. This work achieved high accuracy, but limited number of ECG channels are used.

PROPOSED METHODOLOGY

ECG is one of the most important clinical tool for cardiologists which records the rhythm and function of the heart which further helps in diagnosis of different heart related diseases .The abnormalities can be detected by this information. The input signals are compiled from MIT-BIH database, IIR filter is used for the preprocessing of the input signals. The time and frequency domain factors are obtained through DWT. Methods used for obtaining the attributes of time domain, statistical based and morphology include peak-magnitude-RMS ratio, DE, Yule Walker method, Burgs method and auto aggressive feature. In the end the signals are classified under normal signals and abnormal signals, if the signals are classified under abnormal signals they are further classified based on the different heart diseases. In Figure 1 shows the proposed architecture diagram and description.

Signal Data Accession

Heart rate, diseases, and heart related information and details could be detected with the help of accession of an ECG signal. Personal Health Record (PHR) dataset, MIT-BIH sinus arrhythmia and Normal Sinus Rhythm (NSR) dataset, etc. are the significant ECG database. In which the input ECG signals are taken from MIT-BIH Arrhythmia database for detecting the normal and abnormal signals. It contains 48 half hour excerpts of two channel ambulatory ECG data taken from around 47 subjects researched by the BIH arrhythmia Laboratory between 1975 and 1979. At Boston's Beth Israel Hospital, twenty three recordings were randomly taken from a set of 4,000 twenty four hour ambulatory ECG data collected from a mixed population inclusive of both inpatients (approximately 60%) and outpatients (approximately 40%). The Remaining 25 recordings were chosen from the same set to add less common but clinically

Figure 1. Proposed architecture of arrhythmia classification

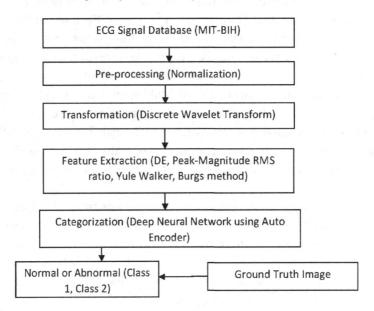

significant arrhythmias. The ECG soundtracks are experimented at 360 Hz. Per channels with 11-bit resolution over 10 mV ranges.

Noise in ECG Signal and Filtering

The ECG signal is a very sensitive signal to the noise due to its low frequency-band having frequency range of 0.5-150 Hz (Abhinav-Vishwa, Lal, and Vardwai, 2011). The signal characteristics changes during recording due to the interference of different source of noises and artifacts. Therefore, it is a challenging task to extract useful information from the ECG signal for accurate detection of cardiac arrhythmias. The common noises are baseline wander, power line noise, and 11 muscular interference and these noises can be removed with appropriate filters (Kim, Min, and Lee, 2011 & Kora and Krishna, 2016 & Jadhav, Nalbalwar, and Ghatol, 2011). The preprocessing step is used to eliminate the noise and enhances the wanted signal components in ECG signal. The major source of noises in ECG signal is shown in Fig. 1.7 and is explained as:

i) **Power Line Interferences**: The power-line can cause 60 Hz sinusoidal interference due to electro-magnetic fields which may appear as additional spikes in the recorded signal as shown in Figure 3b. This noise content, frequency of 60 Hz/50 Hz with an amplitude about 50 percent of peak-to-peak amplitude of electrocardiogram (ECG) signal (Shadmand and Mashoufi, 2016). The power line interferences are eliminated with 60 Hz notch filter.

ii) **Baseline Wander**: It is a low-frequency of 0.5 Hz and high-bandwidth components, caused due to electrode-skin impedance, respiration and body movements. Sometimes this noise is generated due to variations in temperature and biasing in instrumentation amplifiers as shown in Figure 2 and Figure 3 (c). A high-pass filter with 0.5 Hz cutoff frequency is used to remove the baseline

Figure 2. ECG signal without baseline wander, with baseline wander and baseline

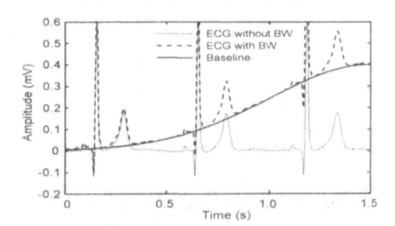

drift. This may cause problems in analysis, especially during examining the low-frequency ST-T segment. High-pass filtering is apprehended in hardware or software to remove these noises.

iii) **Motion Artifacts**: A Motion artifact occurs due to the movement of skin electrode that changes the in ECG waveforms and makes ECG interpretation difficult. It generates larger signal amplitude of 500 percent of Peak to Peak amplitude of ECG signal and its duration is about 100-500 milliseconds as shown in Figure 3 (d). This interference of motion artifacts can be removed with an adaptive filter.

iv) **Muscle Contraction (EMG)**: EMG is the electrical activity produced by contraction of skeletal muscle as shown in Figure 3 (e). The signals amplitude is 10% of ECG and bandwidth of 20 - 1000 Hz with duration is 50 ms. It generates rapid fluctuation in ECG wave and is eliminated by morphological filter of a unit square-wave structure.

Electrocardiogram Data

i. The raw data available from MIT-BIH database is in the form of sample numbers corresponding to time (360 Hz sampling) and sample values corresponding to millivolts, (unipolar, 11 bit ADC over ± 5mV range) we have retained the same values instead of converting these into seconds and millivolts, but using the units as seconds and mV respectively, keeping in mind the conversion factor.

ii. Eighteen varieties of two sets (Abnormal and Normal) heartbeats have been identified for the classification purpose.

iii. The Arrhythmia benchmark database from Physionet Massachusetts Institute of Technology-Beth Israel Hospital (MIT-BIH): Abnormal ECG record numbers 111, 113, 114, 117, 118, 119, 121, 200, 203, 207, 208, 210, 212, 213, 214, 217, 222, 228 and normal ECG record numbers 105, 106,

Figure 3. (a) Normal ECG signal without interferences; (b) ECG signal with powerline interference; (c) ECG signal with baseline wander; (d) ECG signal with muscle artifacts; (e) ECG signal with motion artifacts

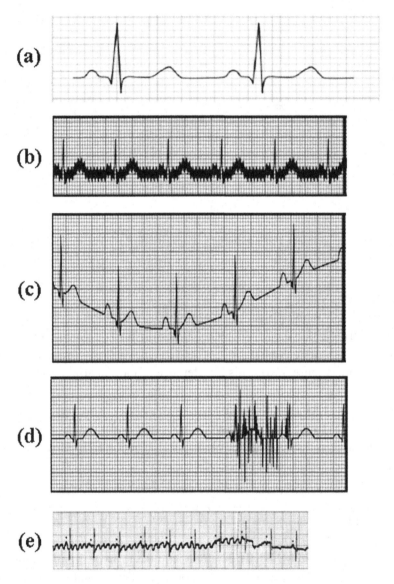

107, 108, 109, 112, 115, 116, 122, 123, 124, 201, 202, 205, 209, 215, 219, 220 are used for guidance, cross-confirmation and trail purposes. This dataset involve forty eight half-hour excerpts of 2 channel ranging electrocardiogram recordings, secured from forty seven subjects studied by the BIH Arrhythmia Laboratory.

iv. Morphological changes are considered for diagnosing, the only temporal aspect considered is R-R interval.

Signal Preprocessing

With the help of databases ECG signals are obtained. Baseline wandering and power line interference is the chief noises comprised in it. They are the most considerable noises in ECG signal analysis. Finite Impulse Response (FIR), Median Filter, Savitzky - Golay Filtering, Polynomial Filtering, etc. are the usual preprocessing procedures or techniques. Where the signal noise is removed using Infinite Impulse Response (IIR) filter. Baseline wandering that result from respiration deceits between 0.15Hz and 0.3 Hz.

The power-line interference is a narrow-band noise positioned at 60 Hz having a bandwidth of less than 1 Hz. Many factors can affect Amplitude and baseline potential of ECG signal propagating from same, which will prominently alter the accurateness of recognition and classification. Normalization must be done to ECG signals in order to advance and improvise the accuracy of recognition and classification. This method involves setting up the baseline to 0, and the maximum amplitude to 1 or -1. Here, remove the features of R peak location as the major peaks. Next move certain sample of left side and some sample of right side to find PQST and R peaks to obtain that particular portion using windowing method.

Transformation

Shifting the signals from time domain to frequency domain can be carried out by a mathematical device, transformation. The representation of signal can be changed by transforms by projecting it into a set of basic functions but they do not alter the signal information. Discrete Wavelength Transform (DWT), Fast Fourier Transform (FFT), Walsh-Hadamard Transform (WHT), etc. are the chief transforms that are employed in peak recognition.

Discrete Wavelet Transform

The DWT is offering greater time resolution and frequency resolution. DWT can disclose the indigenous features of the input signal and helps to decrease the feature degradation with the help of its time and frequency localization ability. Information of signals in both time and frequency domain can be conveyed by Wavelet transform (WT). In wavelet transform, time-domain signals are circulated through numerous low cut and averaging filters, then, both are taken. This procedure is termed as signal decomposition. This process continues until the signal predefined level is reached. The subsequent signals contain both higher and lower frequencies, where the higher frequencies are better determined in time domain and lesser frequencies are improved by frequency. Continuous wavelet transform can be defined with the help of the below equation (1),

$$w(a,b) = \int_{-\infty}^{\infty} x(t) \frac{1}{\sqrt{a}} \Psi\left(\frac{t-b}{a}\right) dt \ldots\ldots\ldots\ldots \tag{1}$$

Where a and b are the scale and translation parameters, respectively. ψ is wavelet family (mother wavelet). As the parameters (a, b) are constantly valued, the transform is known as continuous wavelet transform. Sufficient information for the exploration and synthesis of the raw ECG signal is offered by

7

discrete wavelet transform. The DWT decompose the signals at numerous bands with multi-resolutions to summon signals approximation and detail coefficient. The Discrete wavelet transform can be defined using the below equation (2),

$$\varphi_{m,n} = \frac{1}{\sqrt{a^m}} \varphi \left(\frac{t - nba^m}{a^m} \right) dt \dots\dots\dots\dots\dots \tag{2}$$

Where m and n are the integers for managing the dilation and translations correspondingly, φ is a wavelet function and a is the parameter. Later the DWT based transformation signal is relocated to the feature extraction stage using distinctive features.

Feature Extraction

Wavelet Transform can provide the particular regularity of definite pattern and disintegrate signal into elementary building blocks, which are well, confined both in time and frequency domain. Important features from the ECG signal are obtained using the Wavelets coefficients. Various feature like, Time Domain features, Morphological features, and Statistical Features are involved in this system, in order to improvise heart related disease categorization.

Differential Entropy

The complexity of a continuous random variable, which is associated to the least description length, can be measured using differential entropy. The features of DE are most suitable for recognizing drowsiness. The average energy of ECG signals in frequency bands is the energy spectrum. DE is initially defined by equation (3),

$$h(X) = \int_x f(x) \log(f(x)) dx \dots\dots\dots\dots\dots \tag{3}$$

Here, X is a random variable, $f(x)$ is the probability density function of X. For the time series X obeying the Gauss distribution $N(\mu, \sigma^2)$ and the length of ECG sequence is static. Hence, DE is estimated by equation (4),

$$h(X) = -\int_{-\infty}^{\infty} \frac{1}{\sqrt{2\pi\sigma^2}} e^{\frac{-(x-\mu)^2}{2\sigma^2}} \log \left(\frac{1}{\sqrt{2\pi\sigma^2}} e^{\frac{-(x-\mu)^2}{2\sigma^2}} \right) dx \dots\dots\dots\dots \tag{4}$$

It can be found that ECG signals are exposed to Gaussian distribution though the original ECG signals do not follow a definite fixed distribution. In a certain frequency band DE is equal to the logarithm energy spectrum. Logarithm energy spectrum is frequently utilized by investigators and the ability of discriminating ECG pattern can be balanced between high and low frequency energy as the low frequency energy is higher than the high frequency energy in ECG, so after the logarithm of energy.

Peak-Magnitude to Root Mean Square Ratio

To determine the positive peak and negative peak values of the single transition waveform or the single pulse waveform consider the minimum peak value as the low or first state level and the maximum peak value as the high or second state level. The mathematical equations of Peak-Magnitude to Root Mean Square Ratio (PRMS) is defined in equation (5),

$$PRMS = \frac{X_\infty}{\sqrt{\frac{1}{N}\sum_{n=1}^{N}|X_n|^2}} \dots\dots\dots\dots\dots \quad (5)$$

The waveforms with state levels of negligible or relatively short duration can be analysed by using this procedure.

Morphological Features

P wave, QRS complex and T wave are the three waveform components of one heartbeat of ECG. These ECG signals are biomedical signals and they are non-stationary in nature. Non-stationary nature is nothing but the presence of some statistical features. These signals are altered over position or time. MATLAB functions are used to detect the peaks and locations of several ECG signal parameters like P Q R S T waves to detect its amplitude and duration of the required parameter. Here, R peak, Tmin and Tmax peaks are used for feature extraction in order to efficiently calculate the normal and abnormal signals. T peaks are more effected to the abnormal signals compare to the other peaks, so Tmin and Tmax features are used.

Auto Regressive Feature

Power Spectrum Density (PSD) of the signal can be estimated by Autoregressive (AR) methods using a parametric approach. Hence, AR methods will not have any problems like spectral leakage and thus give better frequency resolution unlike nonparametric approach. The AR model is a depiction of a type of casual technique; which is used to describe the time varying progressions in nature. The AR model stipulates that the output variable depends linearly on its own previous values and on a stochastic term (an imperfectly predictable term); hence the model is in the form of a stochastic difference equation. By calculating the coefficients, that is, the parameters of the linear system under consideration we can estimate PSD. The following methods are used to estimate AR models,

Yule-Walker Method

This method involves estimation of AR parameters or coefficients utilizing the resulting biased approximate of the autocorrelation data function. This is carried out by subsequently finding the minimization of the least squares of the forward prediction error calculation given in the equation (6),

$$
\begin{bmatrix} r(0)_{xx} & \cdots & r(-p+1)_{xx} \\ \vdots & \ddots & \vdots \\ r(p-1)_{xx} & \cdots & r(0)_{xx} \end{bmatrix} \times \begin{bmatrix} a(1) \\ \vdots \\ a(p) \end{bmatrix} \dots\dots\dots\dots\dots\dots\dots \tag{6}
$$

Where r_{xx} can be determined by the equation (7),

$$
r_{xx}(m) = \frac{1}{N} \sum_{N=0}^{N-m-1} x^{*}(n) \, x(n+m), \, m \geq 0 \dots\dots\dots\dots\dots \tag{7}
$$

Calculating the above set of $(p+1)$ linear equations, the AR coefficients can be obtained in equation (8),

$$
P_{xx}^{BU} = \frac{\sigma_{wp}^{2}}{\left| 1 + \sum_{k=1}^{P} \hat{a}_{p}(k) e^{-j2\pi fk} \right|^{2}} \dots\dots\dots\dots\dots\dots\dots\dots\dots \tag{8}
$$

While $\hat{\sigma}wp$ gives the approximated lowest mean square error of the pth-order predictor given as equation (9),

$$
\sigma_{wp}^{2} = E_{p}^{f} = r_{xx}(0) \prod_{k=1}^{P} [1 - |a_{k}(k)|^{2}] \dots\dots\dots\dots\dots \tag{9}
$$

Burg's Method

The principle behind this method is AR spectral estimation which is based on reducing the forward and backward prediction errors to satisfy Levinson-Durbin recursion. The reflection coefficient can be estimated directly by Burg's method without calculating the autocorrelation function. Following are the merits of this method:

1. PSD's data records can be estimated to look exactly like the original data value by Burg's Method.
2. It can yield intimately packed sinusoids in signals once it contains minimal level of noise.

The major difference between the method of Yule-Walker and Burg's method is in the methodology of calculating the PSD. For Burg's method, the PSD is estimated using equation (10),

$$P^{BU}_{xx}\left(f\right) = \frac{\widehat{E}_P}{\left|1 + \sum_{k=1}^{P} \widehat{a_P}\left(k\right) e^{-j2\pi fk}\right|^2} \quad \dots\dots\dots\dots\dots\dots \quad (10)$$

Parametric methods like autoregressive one reduce the spectral leakage issues and yield better frequency resolution. The main advantages of the Burg method are resolving closely spaced sinusoids in signals with low noise levels, and estimating short data records, in which case the AR power spectral density estimates are very close to the true values. In addition, the Burg method ensures a stable AR model and is computationally efficient. After the feature extraction the signals are go through the classification step, here DNN classifier is used and described in below section.

Classification

After obtaining the features from pre analyzed data, the ECG data are used to predict abnormal and normal signal. The classification used is DNN, which create compositional models in which the object is expressed as a layered composition of primitives. The DNN, minimize the cross entropy or noise between the actual and predicted outcomes. Neural layers learning on huge dataset is involved in it. Hypothetically additional layers allow configurations of lower layer features constructing complex data.

Deep Neural Network Using Auto Encoder

The DNNs works like feed forward networks. where, the data flows from input layer to the output layer with no looping back. The main advantage of DNN classifier being, the possibilities of missing some signals in this situation the classifier will automatically take the signal and is used further process. The DNN assigns a classification score $f(x)$ during estimate time. To every input data sample $x=[x_1,\dots,x_N]$ via a forward pass. Typically, f is the function, which involves a series of layers of computation, which is signified in the equation (11),

$$Z_{ij=}x_i w_{ij}; Z_j = \sum_i Z_{ij} + b_j; X_j = g\left(Z_j\right) \quad \dots\dots\dots\dots\dots \quad (11)$$

Where, input of the layer is x_i, its output is $x_j w_{ij}$ are the model parameters and $g(.)$ realizes the mapping or pooling function.

Layer-wise Relevance Propagation decomposes the classifier output $f(x)$ in terms of relevance's r_i attaching to each input component x_i its share with which it contributes to the cataloging decision described in equation (12),

$$f\left(x\right) = \sum_i r_i \quad \dots\dots\dots\dots\dots\dots \quad (12)$$

Where, $r_i>0$ indicates the positive indication supporting the classification decision and $r_i>0$ negative evidence of the classification, otherwise neutral indication.

Unknown feature coherences of input signals can be investigated by DNN. The DNN provides a hierarchical feature-learning tactic. So, the high level features are derived from the low level feature with a greedy layer wise unsupervised pre-training data. Therefore, the fundamental objective of DNN is to handle complex functions that can represent high-level abstraction.

Stacked Auto Encoder

The auto encoder neural network comprises various layers of sparse auto encoders. Every layer output support to the input of the successive layers. An auto encoder attempts to learn an approximation to the identity function, shown in the equation (13),

$$x = h_{w,b}(x) \approx x \dots\dots\dots\dots\dots\dots \tag{13}$$

The DLN exploits the unsupervised pre-training technique with greedy layer wise training. This technique executes at time one layer in unsupervised pre training, beginning from input to output layer. The first sparse auto encoder (1st hidden layer) is trained on the raw inputs (x) to learn primary features $h^{(1)}$ on the inputs.

Figure 4 shows the structure of an auto encoder. In the pre-training process, we can lessen the cost function by using all of weight and bias parameters. The Figure.5 depicts the Softmax classifier using auto encoder. Forward propagation is used by the input data to train sparse auto encoder to achieve the basic features.

In the next concealed layer of pre training data, the auto encoder technique calculates its features using the same method from the preceding hidden layers. Equation (14) defines auto encoder,

$$cost = \frac{1}{2n}\sum_{i=1}^{n}(x_i - x_i)2 + \beta\sum_{j=1}^{m}KL\left(p|\widehat{p_J}\right) + \frac{\lambda}{2}\sum_{i=1}^{n}\sum_{j=1}^{m}\theta_{ij}^2 \dots\dots \tag{14}$$

Figure 4. Structure of an auto encoder

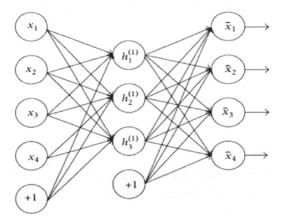

Figure 5. Stacked auto encoder with softmax classifier

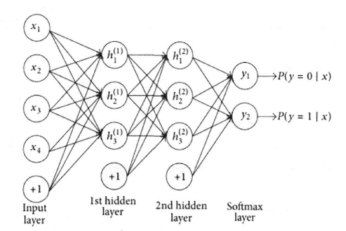

Where, concealed nodes are signified in m, inputs are n, weight of sparsity penalty as β, the probability of firing activity indicated as $\hat{p}_j$, the sparsity parameter is represented as ρ, λ is used to represent weight delay, Kullback-Leibler divergence function is denoted by KL, and θ is the weight of concealed nodes. By DNN classifier, the ECG signal is classified successfully whether the signal is normal or abnormal. Output images are validated with ground truth images after the classification, whether the DNN classifier is properly classified or not, the ground truth images verify the output signals. Arrhythmia classification's experimental analysis and functioning calculations of existing and proposed techniques are described in the below segments.

Experimental Result and Discussion

This segment indicates the experimental results obtained during the process of the study. The experiments were executed on PC with 1.8GHz Pentium IV processor by using MATLAB (version 6.5). Here, the several permutations of features were tested and qualified by using DNN of ECG signal from MIT-BIH database. This dataset involve 48 half-hour excerpts of two channel ambulatory ECG recordings, obtained from 47 subjects studied by the BIH Arrhythmia Laboratory. Two sets of signals are taken in this study, such that 18 normal signals and 18 abnormal signals, so total 36 signals are considered in same training and testing cases. The proposed architecture recognize the normal or SNR and abnormal or Arrhythmia using ECG signal. The performance evaluation of the proposed system is defined further in the below segments.

Unsupervised pre-training techniques are deployed by DNN with greedy layer wise training, beginning from the input layer to the soft max layer. To learn the primary features on inputs, firstly sparse auto encoder is trained on the features. The DNN parameter settings based on ECG signal are given in Table 1. The performance evaluation proposed method is explained in below sector.

The ECG factors along with their explanation and normal durations are portrayed in the Table 2. Usually, P wave, QRS complex, and T wave are the components of an ECG beat. Each peak (P, Q, R, S, T, and U), intervals (PR, RR, QRS, ST, and QT) and segments (PR and ST) of ECG signals will have their standard amplitude or duration values. These peaks, intervals, and segments are termed as ECG

Table 1. DNN parameter settings

Specification	Values
Maximum iterations: SAE learning	400
Maximum iterations: Softmax learning	1000
Hidden layer size	100, 50
L2Weight Regularization	0.004
Sparsity Regularization	4
Sparsity Proportion	0.15
Scale Data	False

Table 2. ECG factors and their normal durations

Features	illustrations	Time Scale
P	First short upward movement of the ECG	80ms
PR	Measured from the beginning of the P wave to the beginning of the QRS complex	120-200ms
QRS	Normally begins with a downward deflection Q, a larger upwards deflection R and ends with a downward S wave	80-120ms
PR	Connects the P wave and the QRS complex	50-120ms
ST	Connects the QRS complex and the T wave	80-120ms
T	Normally a modest upward waveform	160ms
QT	Measured from the beginning of the QRS complex to the end of the T wave	420ms

features. Thousands of such beats are comprised in a single ECG signal. The categorization of ECG signals plays a vital role in clinical diagnosis of heart disease. The normal ECG may differ from one person to another and sometimes a particular disease can have dissimilar signs on the ECG signals of different patients. This happens to be the main issue problem in detecting heart disease using ECG. Also, two different diseases can approximately show similar outcomes on normal ECG signals. Heart disease diagnose will get complicated because of these problems. Therefore, the implementation the method with the DNN classifier can refine the diagnoses of the new patients with ECG arrhythmia diagnoses.

Performance Evaluation

From the proposed combined features of time domain, morphological and statistical features such as DE, Peak magnitude RMS, Yule walker (YM) method, and Burgs (BR) method ECG signals are obtained. Normal (SNR) or abnormal (Arrhythmia) signals are resolved by the DNN classifier. Neural Network (NN), Support Vector Machine (SVM), in terms of Accuracy, Specificity, and Sensitivity are some of the existing classifiers that are compared with the proposed DNN classifier performance in this experimental analysis. Using the values of TP, FP, FN, and TN estimation is done for these parameters, where TP refers to true positive, TN is true negative, FP is false positive and FN is false negative. The calculation of parameters is shown below,

i)   i) **Accuracy:** Accuracy is nothing but the most instinctive performance measure and it is simply a ratio of correctly predicted observation to the total observations. It is directly proportional to true results considering both true positives and true negatives among the total number of cases scrutinized. The parameter of accuracy can be calculated using equation (15),

$$Accuracy = \frac{(TP+TN)}{(TP+TN+FP+FN)} \times 100 \dots\dots\dots\dots\dots \tag{15}$$

ii)   ii)   **Specificity:** The measures of the amount of negatives that are accurately identified and specificity is shown in equation (16).

$$Specificity = \frac{TN}{(TN+FP)} \dots\dots\dots\dots\dots\dots\dots\dots.. \tag{16}$$

iii)   iii)   **Sensitivity:** The sensitivity calculates the ratio of positives that are appropriately recognized signals and mathematical equation of sensitivity is described in equation (17).

$$Sensitivity = \frac{TP}{(TP+FN)} \dots\dots\dots\dots\dots\dots\dots\dots. \tag{17}$$

In experimental analysis, the ECG signal based prediction of normal and abnormal signals. In below section, the Arrhythmia disease signal and Normal signals are shown below.

The Figure 6 explains the Arrhythmia disease ECG signal. Here, the black star is the P and T peak. Blue star is the R peak, pink star is the S peak and green peak is the Q peak. The T peak represents the high voltage effecting the disease signal. The T peak is much affected on the abnormal signals.

Figure 6. ECG signal of arrhythmia disease

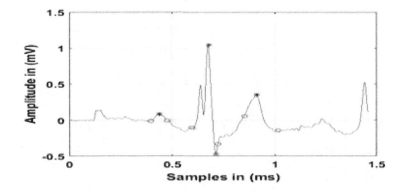

The Figure 7 shows the normal and abnormal ECG signals. The signals shown in the graph indicate X-axis of the sample in time (ms) and Y-axis is the Amplitude in mV. Name the figures – fig a is the input of normal signal and abnormal signals. In fig b represents the applied normalization techniques and detected R peaks. All R peaks are detected and based on R peak P, Q and T peaks are detected. Fig c represents the applied windowing technique. The windowing techniques to detected both normal and abnormal signal is as shown in third row.

The Table 3 represents signal based performance of the pre-existing classifiers and the proposed classifiers with various features such as DE, PRMS, BR, YM, Max, Min and, also a set of proposed

Figure 7. Normal ECG signals

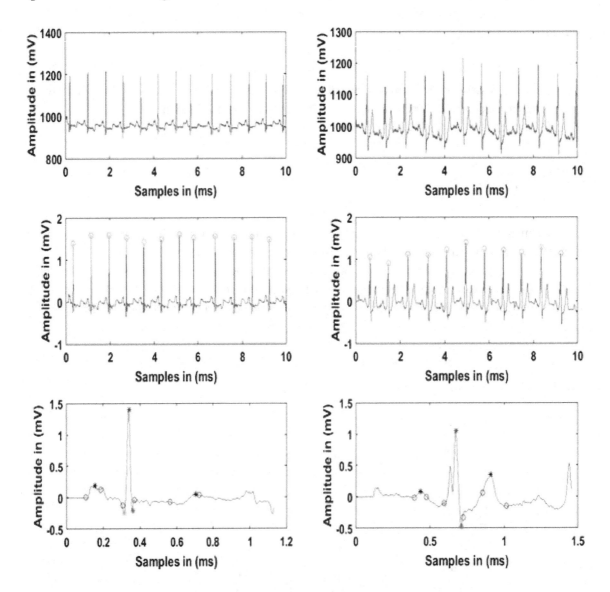

Table 3. Signal based performance evaluation of different classifiers and features

Classifiers	Features	Sensitivity	Specificity	Accuracy (%)
NN	DE	67.50	58.61	63.06
	PRMS	55.56	57.78	56.67
	BR	69.70	63.61	66.67
	YM	60.83	64.17	62.50
	Max	65.00	60.00	62.50
	Min	65.83	63.33	64.58
	Proposed	75.83	78.33	77.08
SVM	DE	77.78	55.56	66.67
	PRMS	55.56	94.44	75.00
	BR	38.89	83.33	61.11
	YM	66.67	66.67	66.67
	Max	88.89	72.22	80.56
	Min	66.67	72.22	69.44
	Proposed	88.89	83.33	86.11
DNN	DE	75.28	65.83	70.56
	PRMS	68.06	96.39	82.22
	BR	89.17	87.78	88.47
	YM	94.72	11.67	53.19
	Max	85.56	76.67	81.11
	Min	74.17	65.56	69.86
	Proposed	98.61	98.06	98.33

combined features. The accuracy achieved in the combined feature comparison; NN classifier achieved 77.085, SVM classifier achieved 86.11% and the proposed DNN classifier achieved 98.33%. The training and testing performance of the window based method

of Arrhythmia disease and Supraventricular Arrhythmia prediction is described below.

The Table 4 indicated as the training and testing performance of the Arrhythmia diseases and Supraventricular Arrhythmia disease. A comparative performance study of the proposed DNN classifier with the existing classifiers such as NN and SVM is given in table -3. The training and testing performances are classified into three sections with 20 training samples-80 testing samples, 40 training samples- 60 testing samples and 80 training samples-20 testing samples. It is seen that the training and performance of the Supraventricular Arrhythmia disease training and testing performance is lower than that of the arrhythmia classification. The below section represents the comparative analysis of the existing and proposed work.

The Table 5 elaborated the study conducted to formulate a parallel performance analysis of the pre-existing work and that of the proposed work. Using machine-learning techniques the existing work of arrhythmia classification is achieved 96.21% of accuracy. Reducing the input space dimension or ap-

Table 4. Training and testing performance of arrhythmia disease and supraventricular arrhythmia disease

Arrhythmia Diseases			
Classifiers	Training and Testing		
	20-80	40-60	80-20
NN	62.8	66.67	76.5
SVM	60	71.90	74.67
DNN	63.9	72.85	77.33
Supraventricular Arrhythmia Disease			
Classifiers	Training and Testing		
	20-80	40-60	80-20
NN	20-80	40-60	80-20
SVM	53.8	62.4	71.9
DNN	59	68.4	72.8

Table 5. Comparative study of prosed and existing work

Existing Work	Accuracy
Artificial Neural Network techniques of arrhythmia classification using ECG signals (Abhinav-Vishwa, Lal, and Vardwai, 2011)	96.21%
An arrhythmia classification algorithm using a dedicated wavelet adapted to different subjects (Kim, Min, and Lee, 2011)	97.94%
Arrhythmia disease detection of wavelet coherence and bat technique using ECG signals (Kora and Krishna, 2016)	94.07%
Modular NN based arrhythmia classification (Jadhav, Nalbalwar, and Ghatol, 2011)	93.95%
The Proposed work	98.33%

propriately describing the input features are some the vital data operating and post operational steps. Continuous Wavelet Transform (CWT) technique is used for various fields in arrhythmia classification.

In this section the, the execution of both Supraventricular ectopic beat class (S) and Ventricular ectopic beat class (V) on few of the subjects' indicates stunted performance and an elevated load in computing. There by making the total precision of the CWT technique used for arrhythmia classification a 97.94%. The arrhythmia detection technique using the bat technique based screens for other additional features by overlooking features like the noise and unneeded components. Accuracy of the order 94.07% is achieved by other researcher, but the experiment uses less number of sampling signals. An accuracy of 93.95% is achieved in modular NN based arrhythmia classification technique inspite of limited sampling data available for the experiment. In the proposed work the experiment adopts both normal and abnormal samples and results in an accuracy of 98.33% which is greater than any of the pre-existing works.

CONCLUSION

An ECG signal based Arrhythmia classification is one of the most significant research areas in computer-aided diagnosis. There are many types of heart arrhythmias which can be detected by analysis of the ECG signals. ECG signals have well defined P, T waves and QRS complexes. In this research windowing technique, various feature extraction methods and classification methods are used. A DNN classifier, categorize the signal as normal or abnormal after classification output data are verified with ground truth images. The experimental result demonstrated that existing classifiers as NN and SVM shows the lower result than proposed classifier and MIT-BIH database is taken for experiment. In 100th iteration the proposed DNN classifier has achieved approximately 98.33% accuracy. Here, performance is measured in various evaluation metrics such as Accuracy, Sensitivity, and Specificity. In the future work, for further improving the classification accuracy, a multi-objective classification method is used along with appropriate features.

REFERENCES

Abhinav-Vishwa, M. K., Lal, S. D., & Vardwaj, P. (2011). Clasification of arrhythmic ECG data using machine learning techniques. *International Journal of Interactive Multimedia and Artificial Intelligence*, *1*(4), 67–70. doi:10.9781/ijimai.2011.1411

Ai, D., Yang, J., Wang, Z., Fan, J., Ai, C., & Wang, Y. (2015). Fast multi-scale feature fusion for ECG heartbeat classification". *EURASIP Journal on Advances in Signal Processing*, *1*(1), 46. doi:10.118613634-015-0231-0

Alickovic, E., & Subasi, A. (2016). Medical decision support system for diagnosis of heart arrhythmia using DWT and random forests classifier. *Journal of Medical Systems*, *40*(4), 108. doi:10.100710916-016-0467-8 PMID:26922592

Daamouche, A., Hamami, L., Alajlan, N., & Melgani, F. (2012). A wavelet optimization approach for ECG signal classification. *Biomedical Signal Processing and Control*, *7*(4), 342–349. doi:10.1016/j.bspc.2011.07.001

de Albuquerque, V. H. C., Nunes, T. M., Pereira, D. R., Luz, E. J. D. S., Menotti, D., Papa, J. P., & Tavares, J. M. R. (2016). Robust automated cardiac arrhythmia detection in ECG beat signals". *Neural Computing & Applications*, 1–15.

Dong, X., Wang, C., & Si, W. (2017). ECG beat classification via deterministic learning". *Neurocomputing*, *240*, 1–12. doi:10.1016/j.neucom.2017.02.056

Elhaj, F. A., Salim, N., Harris, A. R., Swee, T. T., & Ahmed, T. (2016). Arrhythmia recognition and classification using combined linear and nonlinear features of ECG signals. *Computer Methods and Programs in Biomedicine*, *127*, 52–63. doi:10.1016/j.cmpb.2015.12.024 PMID:27000289

Hassan, W., Saleem, S., & Habib, A. (2017). Classification of normal and arrhythmic ECG using wavelet transform based template-matching technique". *JPMA. The Journal of the Pakistan Medical Association*, *67*(6), 843. PMID:28585579

Jadhav, S., Nalbalwar, S., & Ghatol, A. (2014). Feature elimination based random subspace ensembles learning for ECG arrhythmia diagnosis. *Soft Computing*, *18*(3), 579–587. doi:10.100700500-013-1079-6

Jadhav, S. M., Nalbalwar, S. L., & Ghatol, A. A. (2011). Modular neural network based arrhythmia classification system using ECG signal data. *International Journal of Information Technology and Knowledge Management*, *4*(1), 205–209.

Kim, J., Min, S. D., & Lee, M. (2011). An arrhythmia classification algorithm using a dedicated wavelet adapted to different subjects". *Biomedical Engineering Online*, *10*(1), 56. doi:10.1186/1475-925X-10-56 PMID:21707989

Kora, P., & Krishna, K. S. R. (2016). ECG based heart arrhythmia detection using wavelet coherence and bat algorithm". *Sensing and Imaging*, *17*(1), 1–16. doi:10.100711220-016-0136-5

Kumar, R., Kumar, A., & Singh, G. K. (2015). Electrocardiogram signal compression based on singular value decomposition (SVD) and adaptive scanning wavelet difference reduction (ASWDR) technique". *AEÜ. International Journal of Electronics and Communications*, *69*(12), 1810–1822. doi:10.1016/j.aeue.2015.09.011

Kumar, S. S., & Inbarani, H. H. (2016). Cardiac arrhythmia classification using multi-granulation rough set approaches. *International Journal of Machine Learning and Cybernetics*, 1–16.

Kumar, S. U., & Inbarani, H. H. (2017). Neighborhood rough set based ECG signal classification for diagnosis of cardiac diseases. *Soft Computing*, *21*(16), 4721–4733. doi:10.100700500-016-2080-7

Paulter, N. G., Larson, D. R., & Blair, J. J. (2004). The IEEE standard on transitions, pulses, and related waveforms, Std-181-2003. *IEEE Transactions on Instrumentation and Measurement*, *53*(4), 1209–1217. doi:10.1109/TIM.2004.831470

Senapati, M. K., Senapati, M., & Maka, S. (2014). Cardiac Arrhythmia Classification of ECG Signal Using Morphology and Heart Beat Rate. *Proc. of Fourth International Conf. on Advances in Computing and Communications (ICACC)*, 60-63. 10.1109/ICACC.2014.20

Shadmand, S., & Mashoufi, B. (2016). A new personalized ECG signal classification algorithm using block-based neural network and particle swarm optimization. *Biomedical Signal Processing and Control*, *25*, 12–23. doi:10.1016/j.bspc.2015.10.008

Wang, J. S., Chiang, W. C., Yang, Y. T. C., & Hsu, Y. L. (2011). An effective ECG arrhythmia classification algorithm. *Proc. of International Conf. on Intelligent Computing*, 545-550.

Chapter 2
A Review on Deep Learning Applications

Chitra A. Dhawale
P. R. Pote College of Engineering and Management, India

Kritika Dhawale
Indian Institute of Information Technology, Nagpur, India

Rajesh Dubey
Mohanlal Sukhadia University, India

ABSTRACT

Artificial intelligence (AI) is going through its golden era. Most AI applications are indeed using machine learning, and it currently represents the most promising path to strong AI. On the other hand, deep learning, which is itself a kind of machine learning, is becoming more and more popular and successful at different use cases and is at the peak of developments by enabling more accurate forecasting and better planning for civil society, policymakers, and businesses. As a result, deep learning is becoming a leader in this domain. This chapter presents a brief review of ground-breaking advances in deep learning applications.

INTRODUCTION

Artificial intelligence (AI) is omnipresent, our daily life is mostly influenced by it in one way or the other. In recent years, most of the researchers are getting attracted towards AI domain due to its major applications including multimedia (text, image, speech, video) recognition, social network analysis, data mining, natural language processing, driverless car and so forth are using machine learning which leads this sub domain to the top of popularity amongst researchers and industrialist. Most AI applications are indeed using Machine learning and it currently represents the most promising path to strong AI. Machine-learning technology has a potential which influenced our modern society in all dimensions

DOI: 10.4018/978-1-7998-1192-3.ch002

like content mining social media networks to e-commerce websites, it has converted our simple calling phone to smart phone, normal camera to smart cameras. Apart from this Machine-learning are used in image identification, speech recognition and its translation to text, extraction of specific news, customer sentiment analysis for business growth etc .

Till now machine learning was implementing all above tasks in traditional way by processing raw data and then applying feature extraction techniques followed by matching and labeling. To execute these steps machine-learning system needed a significant skillful domain wise expertise to construct a feature extractor which can represent the raw data into specific feature vector which can be used by machine learning algorithm often a classifier, which can identify and classify input data. Machine learning uses single level at each stage of processing raw data to suitable representation for detection, recognition and classification. Due to this single level of processing between input and output, may lead to less accurate result, On the other hand recently to increase accuracy and speed of processing, Deep-learning methods are used which uses learning methods but with multiple intermediate layers of representation. These layers are incorporated by non-linear modules which modify the representation at one level into a more conceptual representation at next level. Complex functions are built using such simple transformation at each layer which can lead to decrease the variations and discriminations. Unlike machine learning feature extracting layers are not designed by human experts: they are learned from data using a general-purpose learning procedure.

Deep learning is making a significant contribution for achieving more and more strong and accurate decision . Deep learning has changed the entire landscape over the past few years. Every day, there are more applications that rely on deep learning techniques in fields as diverse as healthcare, finance, human resources, retail, earthquake detection, and self-driving cars. In Overall dimensions in development DL is at the peak and hence DL is becoming a leader in this domain (LeCun, Bengio, and Hinton, 2015).

This chapter presents a brief review of pioneering advances in deep learning applications.

APPLICATIONS OF DEEP NEURAL NETWORKS

Here we will take a general review of several selected applications of the deep networks.

Speech Recognition

During the past few decades, machine learning algorithms have been widely used in areas such as automatic speech recognition (ASR) and acoustic modeling (Jaitly and Hinton, 2011 & Mohammed, Dahl, and Hinton, 2012 & Mohamed, Yu, and Deng, 2010 & Padmanaban and Premkumar, 2015). The ASR can be regarded as a standard classification problem which identifies word sequences from feature sequences or speech waveforms.

Many issues have to be considered for the ASR to achieve satisfactory performance, for instance, noisy environment, multi-model recognition, and multilingual recognition. Normally, the data should be pre-processed using noise removal techniques before the speech recognition algorithms are applied. Singh, Tripathy, and Anand (2014) reviewed some general approaches for noise removal and speech enhancement such as spectral subtraction, Wiener filtering, windowing, and spectral amplitude estimation.

Traditional machine learning algorithms, such as the SVM, and NNs, have provided promising results in speech recognition (Hinton et. al, 2012). For example, Gaussian mixture models (GMMs) have been used to develop speech recognition systems by representing the relationship between the acoustic input and the hidden states of the hidden Markov model (HMM) (Baker et. al, 2009).

Since 2006, deep learning has emerged as a new research area of machine learning. As we just mentioned, deep learning algorithms can bring satisfactory results in feature extraction and transformation, and they have been successfully applied to pattern recognition. Compositional models are generated using DNNs models where features are obtained from lower layers. Through some well-known datasets including the large vocabulary datasets, researchers have shown that DNNs could achieve better performance than GMMs on acoustic modeling for speech recognition. Due to their outstanding performance in modeling data correlation, the deep learning architectures are now replacing the GMMs in speech recognition (Deng et. al, 2013 & Hinton et. al, 2012). Early applications of the deep learning techniques consist of large vocabulary continuous speech recognition (LVCSR) and phone recognition (Dahl et. al, 2012).

Computer Vision and Pattern Recognition

Computer vision aims to make computers accurately understand and efficiently process visual data like videos and images (Mohamed, Dahl, and Hinton, 2010 & Mohamed et. al, 2011). The machine is required to perceive real-world high-dimensional data and produce symbolic or numerical information accordingly. The ultimate goal of computer vision is to endow computers with the perceptual capability of human. Conceptually, computer vision refers to the scientific discipline which investigates how to extract information from images in artificial systems.

Recently, the development in deep learning architectures has provided novel approaches to the problem of pattern recognition, which will be discussed in what follows.

1) Recognition: During the past few years, deep learning techniques have achieved tremendous progress in the domains of computer vision and pattern recognition, especially in areas such as object recognition (Ballard and Brown, 1982).

2) Detection: Detection is one of the most widely known sub-domains in computer vision. It seeks to precisely locate and classify the target objects in an image. In the detection tasks, the image is scanned to find out certain special issues (Sonka, Hlavac, and Boyle, 2014).

3. Other Applications: Face alignment plays an important role in various visual applications such as face recognition. However, for the extreme situations where the face images are taken, face alignment may lead to difficulties during the analyzing process. Therefore, different models for shape and appearance variation have been considered to solve this problem. Based on the model used, the standard approaches can be roughly divided into three groups: the active appearance model, the constrained local model and the regression. Compared with the normal regression based methods, the adaptive cascade deep convolution neural networks (ACDCNN), proposed by Dong for facial point detection, have dramatically reduced the system complexity (Dong and Wu, 2015). Dong et al. improved the basic DCNNs by exploiting an adaptive manner for training with different network architectures. Experiment results showed that their networks can achieve better performance than the DCNNs or other start-of-the-art methods. It should be noted that the multi label image annotation is a hot topic in the field of computer vision (Zhu et. al, 2015). Furthermore, deep learning techniques have recently been applied

to the content-based image retrieval applications (Emad, Yassine, and Fahmy, 2015). More specifically, to address the cross-modal retrieval tasks, a correspondence AE (Corr-AE) was introduced by correlating the hidden representations of two uni-modal AEs (Feng, Wang, and Li, 2014).

Virtual Assistants

The most popular application of deep learning is virtual assistants ranging from Alexa to Siri to Google Assistant. Each interaction with these assistants provides them an opportunity to learn more about your voice and accent, thereby providing you a secondary human interaction experience (López, Quesada, and Guerrero, n.d.). Virtual assistants use deep learning to know more about their subjects ranging from your dine-out preferences to your most visited spots or your favorite songs. They learn to understand your commands by evaluating natural human language to execute them (Chung, Iorga, and Lee, n.d.). Another capability virtual assistants are endowed with is to translate your speech to text, make notes for you, and book appointments. Virtual assistants are literally at your beck-and-call as they can do everything from running errands to auto-responding to your specific calls to coordinating tasks between you and your team members. With deep learning applications such as text generation and document summarizations, virtual assistants can assist you in creating or sending appropriate email copy as well (Tulshan et. al, 2019).

Deep Learning is going to transform the worksplace, but often in ways that pose a threat to jobs. There's a widespread notion that many tasks will be automated, and there'll be no place for humans.

Healthcare

According to NVIDIA, "From medical imaging to analyzing genomes to discovering new drugs, the entire healthcare industry is in a state of transformation and GPU computing is at the heart. GPU-accelerated applications and systems are delivering new efficiencies and possibilities, empowering physicians, clinicians, and researchers passionate about improving the lives of others to do their best work." Helping early, accurate and speedy diagnosis of life-threatening diseases, augmented clinicians addressing the shortage of quality physicians and healthcare providers, pathology results and treatment course standardization, and understanding genetics to predict future risk of diseases and negative health episodes are some of the Deep Learning projects picking up speed in the Healthcare domain (Miotto et. al, 2017). Read missions is a huge problem for the healthcare sector as it costs tens of millions of dollars in cost. But with the use of deep learning and neural networks, healthcare giants are mitigating health risks associated with readmissions while bringing down the costs (Pitoglou, 2018). AI is also being exceedingly being used in clinical researches by regulatory agencies to find cures to untreatable diseases but physicians skepticism and lack of a humongous dataset are still posing challenges to the use of deep learning in medicine.

Self-Driving Cars

Deep Learning is the force that is bringing autonomous driving to life. A million sets of data are fed to a system to build a model, to train the machines to learn, and then test the results in a safe environment. The Uber AI Labs at Pittsburg is not only working on making driverless cars humdrum but also integrating several smart features such as food delivery options with the use of driverless cars. The major concern for autonomous car developers is handling unprecedented scenarios (Bojarski et. al, 2017a). A regular cycle of testing and implementation typical to deep learning algorithms is ensuring safe driving with more and more exposure to millions of scenarios. Data from cameras, sensors, geo-mapping is helping create succinct and sophisticated models to navigate through traffic, identify paths, signage, pedestrian-only routes, and real-time elements like traffic volume and road blockages. According to Forbes, MIT is developing a new system that will allow autonomous cars to navigate without a map as 3-D mapping is still limited to prime areas in the world and not as effective in avoiding mishaps (Bojarski et. al, 2017b). CSAIL graduate student Teddy Ort said, "The reason this kind of 'map-less' approach hasn't really been done before is because it is generally much harder to reach the same accuracy and reliability as with detailed maps. A system like this that can navigate just with onboard sensors shows the potential of self-driving cars being able to actually handle roads beyond the small number that tech companies have mapped" (Bojarski et. al, 2016).

News Aggregation and Fraud News Detection

Extensive use of deep learning in news aggregation is bolstering efforts to customize news as per readers. While this may not seem new, newer levels of sophistication to define reader personas are being met to filter out news as per geographical, social, economical parameters along with the individual preferences of a reader. Fraud news detection, on the other hand, is an important asset in today's world where the internet has become the primary source of all genuine and fake information. It becomes extremely hard to distinguish fake news as bots replicate it across channels automatically. The Cambridge Analytica is a classic example of how fake news, personal information, and statistics can influence reader perception (Bhartiya Janta Party vs Indian National Congress), elections (Donald Trump Digital Campaigns), and exploit personal data (Facebook data for approximately 87 million people was compromised). Deep Learning helps develop classifiers that can detect fake or biased news and remove it from your feed and warn you of possible privacy breaches. Training and validating a deep learning neural network for news detection is really hard as the data is plagued with opinions and no one party can ever decide if the news is neutral or biased (Najafabadi et. al, 2015 & Wang and Xu, 2018).

Entertainment

Wimbledon 2018 used IBM Watson to analyse player emotions and expressions through hundreds of hours of footage to auto-generate highlights for telecast. This saved them a ton of effort and cost. Thanks to Deep Learning, they were able to factor in audience response and match or player popularity to come up with a more accurate model (otherwise it would just have highlights of the most expressive or aggressive players). Netflix and Amazon are enhancing their deep learning capabilities to provide a personalized experience to its viewers by creating their personas factoring in show preferences, time of access, history, etc. to recommend shows that are of liking to a particular viewer. VEVO has been using deep learning to create the next generation of data services for not only personalized experiences for its users and subscribers, but also artists, companies, record labels, and internal business groups to generate insights based on performance and popularity. Deep video analysis can save hours of manual effort required for audio/video sync and its testing, transcriptions, and tagging. Content editing and auto-content creation are now a reality thanks to Deep Learning and its contribution to face and pattern recognition. Deep Learning AI is revolutionizing the filmmaking process as cameras learn to study human body language to imbibe in virtual characters (Thomas et, al, 2018 & Yang, Yao, Wang, 2018 & Aznan et. al, 2018).

Fraud Detection

Another domain benefitting from Deep Learning is the banking and financial sector that is plagued with the task of fraud detection with money transactions going digital. Autoencoders in Keras and Tensorflow are being developed to detect credit card frauds saving billions of dollars of cost in recovery and insurance for financial institutions (El Bouchti, Chakroun, and Okar, 2017). Fraud prevention and detection are done based on identifying patterns in customer transactions and credit scores, identifying anomalous behavior and outliers. Classification and regression machine learning techniques and neural networks are used for fraud detection. While machine learning is mostly used for highlighting cases of fraud requiring human deliberation, deep learning is trying to minimize these efforts by scaling efforts (Moro, Cortez, and Rita, 2015).

Personalizations

Every platform is now trying to use chatbots to provide its visitors with personalized experiences with a human touch. Deep Learning is empowering efforts of e-commerce giants like Amazon, E-Bay, Alibaba, etc. to provide seamless personalized experiences in the form of product recommendations, personalized packages and discounts, and identifying large revenue opportunities around the festive season. Even race in newer markets is done by launching products, offerings, or schemes that are more likely to please the human psyche and lead to growth in micro markets. Online self-service solutions are on the rise and reliable workflows are making even those services available on the internet today that were only physically available at one time. Robots specialized in specific tasks are personalizing your experiences real-time by offering you the most suited services whether it is insurance schemes or creating custom burgers (Schneider and Handali, 2019).

Autism Detection

Speech disorders, autism, and developmental disorders can deny a good quality of life to children suffering from any of these problems. An early diagnosis and treatment can have a wonderful effect on the physical, mental, and emotional health of differently-abled children. Hence, one of the noblest applications of deep learning is in the early detection and course-correction of these problems associated with infants and children (Tariq et. al, 2019). This is a major difference between machine learning and deep learning where machine learning is often just used for specific tasks and deep learning on the other hand is helping solve the most potent problems of the human race. Researchers at the Computer Science and Artificial Intelligence Laboratory at MIT and Massachusetts General Hospital's Institute of Health Professions have developed a computer system that can identify language and speech disorders even before kindergarten when most of these cases traditionally start coming to light. The researchers evaluated the system's performance using a standard measure called area under the curve, which describes the tradeoff between exhaustively identifying members of a population who have a particular disorder. They use residual analysis that identifies the correlation between age, gender, and acoustic features of their speech to limit false positives (Heinsfeld et. al, 2018). Autism is often detected by combining it with cofactors such as low birth weight, physical activity, body mass index, learning disabilities, etc.

CHALLENGES

In the above section we took the review of various luring applications of deep learning. These applications are exciting people about the opportunities this field brings. Although it seems to be attracting the industries, but researcher are facing challenging problems to handle the exponentially growing data, overfitting issues in neural networks, minimization of hyper-parameter, lack of highly configured processors, processing in hidden layers etc etc (Shrivataya, n.d.).

Voluminous Data

To increase the accuracy for getting desired result, Deep learning algorithms are trained on large data set like a human brain needs a lot of experiences to learn and deduce information. Researchers feed terabytes of data for the algorithm to learn which is really a time-consuming process and requires tremendous data processing capabilities. The neural network becomes more complicated as the number of parameters used in training goes on increasing.

Overfitting Problem

At times, there is a sharp difference in error occurred in training data set and the error encountered in a new unseen data set. It occurs in complex models, such as having too many parameters relative to the number of observations. The efficacy of a model is judged by its ability to perform well on an unseen data set and not by its performance on the training data fed to it.

Minimisation of Hyperparameter

Hyperparameters are the parameters whose value is defined prior to the commencement of the learning process. Changing the value of such parameters by a small amount can cause a large change in the performance of your model.

Relying on the default parameters and not performing Hyperparameter Optimization can have a significant impact on the model performance. Also, having too few hyperparameters and hand tuning them rather than optimizing through proven methods is also a performance driving aspect.

High-Performance Hardware

Deep learning algorithms requires a lot of data for training models. To perform a task to solve real world problems, the machine needs to be equipped with adequate processing power. To ensure better efficiency and less time consumption, data scientists switch to multi-core high performing GPUs and similar processing units. These processing units are costly and consume a lot of power.

Industry level Deep Learning systems require high-end data centers while smart devices such as drones, robots other mobile devices require small but efficient processing units. Deploying Deep Learning solution to the real world thus becomes a costly and power consuming affair.

Neural Networks: Blackbox

We know our model parameters, we feed known data to the neural networks and how they are put together. But we usually do not understand how they arrive at a particular solution. Neural networks are essentially Blackboxes and researchers have a hard time understanding how they deduce conclusions.

The lack of ability of neural networks for reason on an abstract level makes it difficult to implement high-level cognitive functions. Also, their operation is largely invisible to humans, rendering them unsuitable for domains in which verification of process is important.

Lack of Flexibility and Multitasking

Deep Learning models, once trained, can deliver tremendously efficient and accurate solution to a specific problem. However, in the current landscape, the neural network architectures are highly specialized to specific domains of application.

CONCLUSION

In this Chapter, we have touched most of the sensitive applications of deep learning including computer vision, pattern recognition, speech recognition, virtual assistant, driverless car, personalisation, etc. Along with applications we also put light on the challenges in deep learning for the successful implementation of these applications. With the fast development of hardware resources and computation technologies, we are confident that deep neural networks will receive wider attention and find broader applications in the future. Still there is vast scope for further extensive research. In particular, more work is necessary on how we can adapt Deep Learning algorithms for problems associated with Big Data with high dimensionality, sparcity, streaming data analysis, scalability of Deep Learning models, improved formulation of data abstractions, distributed computing, semantic indexing, data tagging, information retrieval, criteria for extracting good data representations, and domain adaptation. Future works should focus on addressing one or more of these problems often seen in Big Data.

REFERENCES

Baker, J. M., Deng, L., Glass, J., Khudanpur, S., Lee, C. H., Morgan, N., & Shaughnessy, D. O. (2009). Developments and directions in speech recognition and understanding, part 1 [dsp education]. *IEEE Transactions on Signal Processing Magazine, 26*(3), 75–80. doi:10.1109/MSP.2009.932166

Ballard, D. H., & Brown, C. M. (1982). *Computer vision*. Englewood Cliffs, NJ: Prenice-Hall.

Bojarski, Asa, Colak, & Czarkowski. (2017). Analysis and control of multiphase inductively coupled resonant converter for wireless electric vehicle charger applications. *IEEE Transactions on Transportation Electrification, 3*(2), 312-320.

Bojarski, M., Choromanska, A., Choromanski, K., Firner, B., Jackel, L., & Muller, U. (2016). *Visualbackprop: visualizing cnns for autonomous driving.* arXiv preprint arXiv:1611.05418

Bojarski, M., Yeres, P., Choromanska, A., & Choromanski, K. (2017). *Explaining how a deep neural network trained with end-to-end learning steers a car.* arXiv preprint arXiv:1704.07911

Dahl, G. E., Yu, D., Deng, L., & Acero, A. (2012). Context-dependent pre-trained deep neural networks for large-vocabulary speech recognition. *IEEE Transactions on Audio, Speech, and Language Processing, 20*(1), 30–42. doi:10.1109/TASL.2011.2134090

Deng, L., Li, J., Huang, J. T., Yao, K., Yu, D., Seide, F., . . . Acero, A. (2013). Recent advances in deep learning for speech research at Microsoft. *Acoustics, Speech and Signal Processing (ICASSP), 2013 IEEE International Conference on*, 8604–8608. 10.1109/ICASSP.2013.6639345

Dong, Y., & Wu, Y. (2015). Adaptive cascade deep convolutional neural networks for face alignment. *Computer Standards & Interfaces, 42*, 105–112. doi:10.1016/j.csi.2015.06.004

El Bouchti, A., Chakroun, A., Abbar, H., & Okar, C. (2017). Fraud detection in banking using deep reinforcement learning. *Seventh International Conference on Innovative Computing Technology (INTECH)*, 58-63. 10.1109/INTECH.2017.8102446

Emad, O., Yassine, I. A., & Fahmy, A. S. (2015). Automatic localization of the left ventricle in cardiac mri images using deep learning. *Engineering in Medicine and Biology Society (EMBC), 2015 37th Annual International Conference of the IEEE*, 683–686. 10.1109/EMBC.2015.7318454

Feng, F., Wang, X., & Li, R. (2014). Cross-modal retrieval with correspondence autoencoder. *Proceedings of the ACM International Conference on Multimedia*, 7–16.

Heinsfeld, A. S., Franco, A. R., Craddock, R. C., Buchweitz, A., & Meneguzzi, F. (2018). Identification of autism spectrum disorder using deep learning and the ABIDE dataset. *NeuroImage. Clinical, 17*, 16–23. doi:10.1016/j.nicl.2017.08.017 PMID:29034163

Hinton, G. E., Deng, L., Yu, D., Dahl, G. E., Mohamed, A. R., Jaitly, N., ... Sainath, T. N. (2012). Deep neural networks for acoustic modeling in speech recognition: The shared views of four research groups. *IEEE Signal Processing Magazine, 29*(6), 82–97. doi:10.1109/MSP.2012.2205597

Hinton, G. E., Deng, L., Yu, D., Dahl, G. E., Mohamed, A. R., Jaitly, N., ... Sainath, T. N. (2012). Deep neural networks for acoustic modeling in speech recognition: The shared views of four research groups. *IEEE Signal Processing Magazine, 29*(6), 82–97. doi:10.1109/MSP.2012.2205597

Jaitly, N., & Hinton, G. (2011). Learning a better representation of speech soundwaves using restricted Boltzmann machines. *Acoustics, Speech and Signal Processing (ICASSP), 2011 IEEE International Conference on*, 5884–5887. 10.1109/ICASSP.2011.5947700

LeCun, Y., Bengio, Y., & Hinton, G. (2015). Deep learning. *Nature, 521*(7553), 436–444. doi:10.1038/nature14539 PMID:26017442

Miotto, Wang, Wang, Jiang, & Dudley. (2017). Deep learning for healthcare: Review, opportunities and challenges. *Briefings in Bioinformatics*, 1–11.

Mohamed, A., Dahl, G. E., & Hinton, G. E. (2012). Acoustic modeling using deep belief networks. *IEEE Transactions on Audio, Speech, and Language Processing*, *20*(1), 14–22. doi:10.1109/TASL.2011.2109382

Mohamed, A., Sainath, T. N., Dahl, G., Ramabhadran, B., Hinton, G. E., & Picheny, M. A. (2011). Deep belief networks using discriminative features for phone recognition. *IEEE International Conference on Acoustics, Speech and Signal Processing (ICASSP)*, 5060–5063. 10.1109/ICASSP.2011.5947494

Mohamed, A., Yu, D., & Deng, L. (2010). Investigation of full-sequence training of deep belief networks for speech recognition. INTERSPEECH, 2846–2849.

Mohamed, Dahl, & Hinton. (2009). Deep belief networks for phone recognition. *Nips workshop on deep learning for speech recognition and related applications, 1*(9), 39.

Mohamed, Yu, & Deng. (2010). Investigation of full-sequence training of deep belief networks for speech recognition. *INTERSPEECH*, 2846–2849.

Moro, S., Cortez, P., & Rita, P. (2015). Business intelligence in banking: A literature analysis from 2002 to 2013 using text mining and latent Dirichlet allocation. *Expert Systems with Applications*, *42*(3), 1314–1324. doi:10.1016/j.eswa.2014.09.024

Najafabadi, Villanustre, Khoshgoftaar, Seliya, Wald, & Muharemagic. (2015). Deep learning applications and challenges in big data analytics. *Journal of Big Data, 2*(1). doi:10.118640537-014-0007-7

Nik, K. N. A., Bonner, S., Connolly, J., Al Moubayed, N., & Breckon, T. (2018). On the Classification of SSVEP-Based Dry-EEG Signals via Convolutional Neural Networks. *Systems Man and Cybernetics (SMC) 2018 IEEE International Conference on*, 3726-3731.

Padmanabhan, J., & Johnson Premkumar, M. J. (2015). Machine learning in automatic speech recognition: A survey. *IETE Technical Review*, *32*(4), 240–251. doi:10.1080/02564602.2015.1010611

Pitoglou. (2018). Machine Learning in Healthcare, Introduction and Real World Application Considerations. *International Journal of Reliable and Quality E-Healthcare, 7*(2), 27-36.

Schneider & Handali. (2019). Personalized explanation in machine learning. *CORR Journal*.

Shrivatava, P. (n.d.). *Challenges in Deep Learning*. Retrieved from https://hackernoon.com/challenges-in-deep-learning-57bbf6e73bb

Singh, M. T., & Anand, R. (2014). Subjective and objective analysis of speech enhancement algorithms for single channel speech patterns of indian and english languages. *IETE Technical Review, 31*(1), 34–46. doi:10.1080/02564602.2014.890840

Sonka, M., Hlavac, V., & Boyle, R. (2014). *Image processing, analysis, and machine vision*. Cengage Learning.

Tariq, Fleming, Schwartz, Dunlap, Corbin, Washington, … Wall. (2019). Works citing "Detecting Developmental Delay and Autism Through Machine Learning Models Using Home Videos of Bangladeshi Children: Development and Validation Study. *J Med Internet Res., 21*(4).

Thomas, J., Comoretto, L., Jin, J., Dauwels, J., Cash, S. S., & Westover, M. B. (2018). EEG CLassification Via Convolutional Neural Network-Based Interictal Epileptiform Event Detection. *IEEE Engineering in Medicine and Biology Society (EMBC) 2018 40th Annual International Conference of the*, 3148-3151. 10.1109/EMBC.2018.8512930

Tulshan, A., & Dhage, N. (2019). Survey on Virtual Assistant: Google Assistant, Siri, Cortana, Alexa. *4th International Symposium SIRS 2018*, Bangalore, India. 10.1007/978-981-13-5758-9_17

Wang, Y., & Xu, W. (2018). *Leveraging deep learning with LDA-based text analytics to detect automobile insurance fraud. In Decision Support Systems*. Elsevier.

Yang, J., Yao, S., & Wang, J. (2018). Deep Fusion Feature Learning Network for MI-EEG Classification. *Access IEEE*, *6*, 79050–79059. doi:10.1109/ACCESS.2018.2877452

Zhu, S., Shi, Z., Sun, C., & Shen, S. (2015). Deep neural network based image annotation. *Pattern Recognition Letters*, *65*, 103–108. doi:10.1016/j.patrec.2015.07.037

Chapter 3
A Survey of Nature–Inspired Algorithms With Application to Well Placement Optimization

Jahedul Islam
Universiti Teknologi PETRONAS, Malaysia

Pandian M. Vasant
Universiti Teknologi PETRONAS, Malaysia

Berihun Mamo Negash
Universiti Teknologi PETRONAS, Malaysia

Moacyr Bartholomeu Laruccia
Independent Researcher, Malaysia

Myo Myint
Universiti Teknologi PETRONAS, Malaysia

ABSTRACT

Well placement optimization is one of the major challenging factors in the field development process in the oil and gas industry. This chapter aims to survey prominent metaheuristic techniques, which solve well the placement optimization problem. The well placement optimization problem is considered as high dimensional, discontinuous, and multi-model optimization problem. Moreover, the computational expenses further complicate the issue. Over the last decade, both gradient-based and gradient-free optimization methods were implemented. Gradient-free optimization, such as the particle swarm optimization, genetic algorithm, is implemented in this area. These optimization techniques are utilized as standalone or as the hybridization of optimization methods to maximize the economic factors. In this chapter, the authors survey the two most popular nature-inspired metaheuristic optimization techniques and their application to maximize the economic factors.

DOI: 10.4018/978-1-7998-1192-3.ch003

INTRODUCTION

Metaheuristics are generally implemented to tackle problems when no satisfactory problem-specific algorithm is available to solve them. "Conventional" mathematical programming methods such as gradient-based methods have not provided satisfactory results in solving optimization problems which comprise of multi-modality, discontinuity, and non-smooth cost function. **So, Metaheuristic has emerged as an alternative to traditional methods.** In recent years Stochastic algorithms are widely used in different complex problems in the real world.

In the current epoch, the Well placement optimization problem has become a major concern in the field development process in the Oil and gas industry. This optimization problem is viewed as a challenging problem cause the objective function is **multimodal, nonconvex and discontinuities** (J. E. Onwunalu & Durlofsky, 2010). Previously Classical methods had been utilized to tackle well placement optimization problems(Rosenwald & Green, 1974), (Ma, Plaksina, & Gildin, 2013), (Pan & Horne, 1998), (Li & Jafarpour, 2012),(Jansen & Fluids, 2011), (Bangerth, Klie, Wheeler, Stoffa, & Sen, 2006),(Zhang et al., 2016) . On the other hand, **Non-classical** derivative-free stochastic techniques do not require the calculation of derivatives and they are less likely to get stuck in local optimal (Isebor, Durlofsky, & Ciaurri, 2014), (Giuliani & Camponogara, 2015), (Fahim Forouzanfar, Reynolds, & Engineering, 2013). Derivative-free stochastic techniques have the capacity to avoid local optima due to their inherent stochasticity. Meta-heuristics approaches are probabilistic in nature and controlled by parameters, e.g., population, elite population size, the number of generations, etc. It is true that the performance of Metaheuristic is largely dependent on parameter tuning. Due to computational expenses, proper tuning of parameters for Well placement optimization is challenging and improper tuning may result in increased computation expenses or local optima. The Recent attention from the researcher in well placement optimization is summarized in the Table 1.

The motivation for this work is to consider a metaheuristic algorithm to tackle the well placement problem. Resolving placement optimization problems is a daunting task, despite evolution and improved computing power. The purpose of this chapter is to review the use of particle placement optimization algorithms and genetic algorithms for well placement optimization problems and to evaluate their contribution in the solution of well placement optimization problems. PSO, GA, and its hybridization are used in many types of research.

This chapter consists of eight major units that explore various aspects of the paradigm of this study. In the first part, the author gives an overview of the optimization of well placement. The problem statements in the next section, on the other hand, illustrate different forms of the objective function. The third section represents different optimization techniques used for well placement optimization problems. The next section will focus on quantitative analysis of various metaheuristic algorithms and the author's opinion on future optimization methods. The final section provides a final comment on the optimization of well placement. Sections 6, 7and 8 provide the acknowledgment, references and nomenclature respectively.

WELL PLACEMENT OPTIMIZATION - RESEARCH CHALLENGE

The objective function NPV, can be represented as Equation 1 taking into account the price of oil sold, the cost of water production and injection, and the cost of drilling.

Table 1. Recently applied methods on well placement optimization

No.	Reference work	Year	Diligence
1.	(S. Ding et al., 2019)	2019	Incorporated DMPP technique with PSO.
2.	(Redouane, Zeraibi, & Nait Amar, 2018)	2019	An intelligent neighborhood search mechanism is combined with GA to improve the quality of proxy models.
3.	(Janiga, Czarnota, Stopa, & Wojnarowski, 2019)	2019	Authors developed a clustering approach that significantly reduces the convergence time of the particle swarm optimization algorithm.
4.	(Miyagi & Yamamoto, 2018)	2018	CMA-ES is included with mixed-integer support for Well Placement optimization.
6.	(Jang, Oh, Kim, Park, & Kang, 2018)	2018	The search space is successively refined using an artificial neural network.
7.	(Chen et al., 2018)	2018	Combined cat swarm optimization (CSO) algorithm, particle swarm optimization (PSO) mesh adaptive direct search (MADS) algorithm.
8.	(Chen et al., 2017)	2017	An analytical expression used to calculate the cost function using the cat swarm optimization (CSO) algorithm.
9.	(Hamida, Azizi, & Saad, 2017)	2017	PUNQ-S3 and Brugge field datasets are used to test the robustness of the Genetic Similarity Algorithm (GSA).
10.	(Pouladi, Keshavarz, Sharifi, & Ahmadi, 2017)	2017	By combining FMM-based methods with Particle Swarm Optimization algorithms, authors introduced a surrogate model that includes cost functions.
11.	(Sayyafzadeh, 2017)	2017	Development of a computationally cheaper self-adaptive model management strategy using a proxy support algorithm.
12.	(Jesmani, Jafarpour, Bellout, Hanea, & Foss, 2016)	2016	Authors adopted the Simultaneous Perturbation Stochastic Approximation (SPSA) algorithm using an efficient stochastic gradient approximation.

$$NPV = \sum_{i=1}^{T} \frac{Q_O P_O + Q_W C_W - OPEX}{(1+D)^i} - CAPEX \tag{1}$$

Here Qo, Qw, Po is accumulative oil production, accumulative water production, oil's cost respectively. OPEX is the operational cost, D is the discount rate, NPV is net present value, CAPEX is the capital expenditure, Cw is the cost per unit volume of produced water, and T is the number of years passed since the production has started. **Table 2.** Shows different cost function consideration in Well placement optimization problem.

METAHEURISTIC TECHNIQUES

In real-world engineering problems optimization techniques based on meta-heuristic techniques are more prevalent as they are gradient-free, easy to implement and can be employed in a vast range of problems. Metaheuristic techniques can be divided in three large groups: Evolutionary based algorithm (e.g. GA, DE etc.), physics-based algorithm (e.g. Cuckoo search, GSA etc.), and population-based algorithm (e.g. PSO, ACO etc.). Especially, metaheuristic algorithms work well on surfaces which are populated with many local optima. In this section Authors briefly discusses some well know methods and their variants.

Table 2. Consideration of different objective functions for well placement optimization

No	Reference(s)	Year	Cost Function
1.	(Cheng, An, Wang, & Zhu, 2012)	2012	Conventional net profit value.
2.	(Chen et al., 2017)	2017	Objective function based on an analytic expression.
3.	(Awotunde, Sibaweihi, & Management, 2014)	2014	NPV and Voidage Replacement Ratio both are objective function.
4.	(Hutahaean, Demyanov, Arnold, & Vazquez, 2014)	2014	**A multi-objective approach** minimizing scale risk and maximizing oil recovery.
5.	(Chen et al., 2018)	2018	Replaced the traditional objective function with a minimal Theil index.

The success of a metaheuristic approach on a given problem depends on the balance between exploration and exploitation. In Exploitation mode, metaheuristic approaches fine-tune the solution in a specific area. Many classical and non-classical Optimization techniques have been employed for well placement optimization techniques. In the following section, a review of some popular optimization techniques is given. To overcome the lacking of mathematical model based approaches, non-conventional methods like PSO, GA, BA, DE, CMA-ES, and many other techniques have been implemented on well placement optimization problem. The main differences between all these metaheuristics are in which way create a balance between exploration and exploitation. Among all the Meta-heuristic algorithms that have been used in this particular problem, GA is the most famous, naturally inspired algorithm and PSO is the most prevalent one. In this paper, authors mainly focus on surveying GA and PSO because these two are the most prevalent in this area. PSO and GA are presented in the following Section respectively.

Particle Swarm Optimization (PSO)

PSO is a swarm based computing technique developed by Kennedy and Eberhart (**Kennedy & Eberhart, 1995**). PSO has earned popularity because it is easy to implement and it has faster convergence. In PSO, Particles fly randomly and update their position according to its positon's equation to identify the optimum solution in a search space (Rahman, Vasant, Singh, & Abdullah-Al-Wadud, 2016). At first, particles of the swarm initialize velocity and position randomly. Then the fitness of the probable solutions calculates and adjusts its position. PSO combines global search techniques with local search techniques to balance exploration and exploitation. Steps of PSO algorithm for optimization of well placement problem given in **Fig. 1.** A commonly used method is to represent the particle as $1 \times n$ vector, where n is variables of the well placement optimization problem. Initially, a $m \times n$ position matrix is created, where m is the no. of particle The velocity of individual particles is updated using the following formula:

$$V_i^{k+1} = wV_i^k + c_1 rand_1\left(pbest_i^k - x_i^k\right) + c_2 rand_2\left(gbest^k - x_i^k\right) \dots\dots\dots\dots\dots \quad (2)$$

Here V_i is the velocity of individual i at iteration k, w is weight vector, $c_1 \, and \, c_2$ are acceleration constant, represents random numbers are represented by $rand_1 and \, rand_2$, x_i^k represents the particle i's position at iteration k, $pbest_i^k$ represents the optimal position of particle i up to k th iteration and $gbest^k$

Figure 1. Flow chart of particle swarm optimization

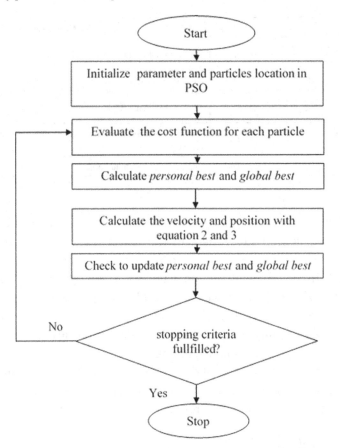

represents optimal position of the group up to k th iteration. Again, each particle uses the following formula to update the next position in the search space

$$x_i^{k+1} = V_i^{k+1} + x_i^k \dots\dots\dots\dots\dots\dots\dots\dots\dots\dots\dots\dots\dots \tag{3}$$

At first, Onwunalu in his study used PSO where he narrowed down the search space by gradually changing from the exploratory mode to exploitive mode (J. Onwunalu, 2010). But this gradual change may be sensitive to search space. **Feng Q. et al** implemented **Clerc's** proposed PSO algorithm which decreases the search process. (Feng, Zhang, Zhang, & Hu, 2012) **(Clerc, 1999)**. In the PSO algorithm, a neighborhood topology provides different swarm searches in the landscape by enabling different flying patterns among its particles. The neighborhood topology has effects on the PSO convergence. **Researchers utilized Random neighborhood with** PSO to tackle Well placement optimization problem (J. E. Onwunalu & Durlofsky, 2010) (Foroud, Baradaran, & Seifi, 2018). In this topology the behavior of particle such that each particle is connected to some of the particles in the swarm but not to the remaining particles. This solution provides better global optima and avoids local optima.

Niches are one of the primitive approaches developed to address multimodalities, but relatively few researchers have proposed a PSO-based niche approach. Cheng et al. A variant of the PSO named Niche PSO was applied to optimize the well position (Cheng et al., 2012) (Brits, Engelbrecht, & Van den Bergh, 2002). This new technique can handle many multidimensional variables. In this way, the flock is divided into smaller subgroups. This technology has improved herd exploration capabilities. Experimental results show that increasing the size of the flock reduces the number of iterations and the niche PSO outperforms the standard PSO. Ding et al. introduced time-of-flight coefficients, modified inertial weight, velocity, and position update equations and incorporated the proposed MPSO with quality map technique(S. W. Ding, Jiang, Li, & Tang, 2014). The result shows that the proposed method can find the best location over SPSO, Central Progressive PSO (CP-PSO) and MPSO

HYBRID PSO

The MPSO algorithm is used by Ding et al. to optimize the type, location and shape of the well (S. Ding et al., 2016). Isebar incorporated PSO and a local optimization method MADS search methods by hybridizing and to process nonlinear constraints filter-based methods is used (Isebor, Ciaurri, & Durlofsky, 2014). In the experiment, the performance of the new hybrid technique is superior to the independent PSO and MADS. Nwankwor et al. proposed the HPSDE algorithm, incorporation of DE and PSO to find the best well location (Nwankwor, Nagar, & Reid, 2013). The results show that the HPSDE algorithm is better than two independent algorithms.

Genetic Algorithm (GA)

Inspired by the theory that only strong and fit species survive in nature, John Holland developed the Genetic Algorithm (GA) in 1970 (Holland, 1992). The GA algorithm's population consist of a set of chromosomes. First, the process is started randomly and the crossover, mutation and recombination processes continue until a single optimal solution is reached. The general flow chart of the GA algorithm is shown in Figure 2.

Some of the Basic terms of Genetic Algorithm is described below:

1. Selection

According to Darwin's evolution theory, the fittest ones should survive and produce new offspring. Some selection methods are tournament selection, roulette wheel selection, rank selection and some others. In GA Chromosomes are selected as parents for crossover.

2. Crossover

Crossover picks genes from parent chromosomes and produces a new offspring. The least intricate way to do this is to pick a crossover point randomly and duplicate everything before this crossover point from a first parent and duplicate everything after this point from the second parent.

The crossover would then be able to resemble this

Figure 2. Flow chart of genetic algorithm

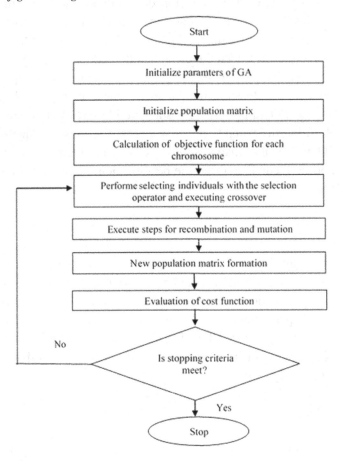

Chromosome 1 11011 | 00100111011
Chromosome 2 11000 | 11000011110
Offspring 1 **11011** | 11000011110
Offspring 2 11000 | **00100111011**

There are different ways how to make crossover, for instance, we can pick more crossover points. Crossover can be somewhat confused and very relies upon encoding of the chromosome. Explicit crossover made for a specific issue can improve execution of the genetic algorithm.

3. Crossover probability

Crossover probability indicates how regularly will be crossover executed. If the cross over is 0% then the offspring is exactly the same copy of the parent chromosomes from the old population. that does not mean that the offspring is the same. if crossover probability is 100%, at that point all-new generation is made by crossover. Crossover is made with the expectation that new chromosomes will have great pieces of old chromosomes and possibly the new chromosomes will be better.

4. Mutation

Mutation takes place after a crossover is performed. This is to tackle local optimum in the optimization problem. The mutation changes haphazardly the new generation. For binary encoding, we can toggle bits from 1 to 0 or from 0 to 1. Example of mutation is:

Original offspring 1 1100111000011110
Original offspring 2 1101101100110110
Mutated offspring 1 1101111000011110
Mutated offspring 2 1101100100110100

5. Mutation probability

Mutation probability indicates how regularly will be portions of chromosome muted. if Mutation probability is 100%, at that point all new generation is changed. If the Mutation probability is 0% then, nothing is changed. Mutation is made to avoid falling GA into local optimums, yet it should not happen very frequently, because then GA will become a random search.

Güyagülern and Horne implemented GA to optimize well location and injection rate, considering net present value (NPV) as the objective function (Guyaguler & Horne, 2001). Quality map is incorporated into genetic algorithms with nonlinear constraints (Emerick et al., 2009). The results show that the quality map helps determine the correct position for proper well placement. Lyons and Nasrabadi proposed combining pseudo-history matching and genetic algorithm (GA), indicating that the results reduced the computation time by a factor of four.**(Lyons & Nasrabadi, 2013).** Well placement optimization problem is considered as a multi-objective problem by Chang, Y.**(Chang, Bouzarkouna, & Devegowda, 2015)**. In this research work, the "non-dominant sorting genetic algorithm-II (NSGA-II)" has been implemented to solve the multi-objective well placement optimization problem. In this work, a polynomial-based approach is used to reduce the computational cost. The results show that NSGA II is an effective and robust method for dealing with multi-objective problems. Ariadji et al. claimed that GA method is effective and robust for accurately solving well location problems m (**Ariadji et al., 2012**). An important contribution of this technique is the formulation of the cost function.. **Overall, in well placement optimization problem, GA and its variants are one of the most popular technique for optimization purpose.** In general, GA can find global optima, but shows slow convergence rate.

OTHER ALGORITHMS

Taking into account NPV as an objective function, Ding uses CMA-ES to optimize well placement (D. Ding, 2008). The authors conclude that population size and parameters affect the performance of the algorithm. Forouzanfar et al. considered the well placement optimization problem as joint optimization problem and implemented the CMA-ES algorithm to solve the challenge (F. Forouzanfar, Poquioma, & Reynolds, 2016). Findings of the study suggest that the simultaneous optimization method produces better results than the sequential optimization method.

Naderi and Khamehchi have implemented the Bat algorithm to successfully solve well placement (Naderi & Khamehchi, 2017). The experimental results show that compared with PSO and GA, BA increased NPV by 7.5% and 21.7%, respectively Dossary and Nasrabadi implemented the **imperialist competitive algorithm(ICA)** and compared the results with PSO and GA (Al Dossary, Nasrabadi, & Engineering, 2016) (Al Dossary & Nasrabadi, 2015). The results obtained reveal a significant improvement in NPV and rapid convergence to global optimization. However, the three main ICA parameters are problem-specific and need to be adjusted for other search spaces.

DISCUSSION AND FUTURE WORKS

The authors conducted extensive searches in the Scopus and Web of Science databases. Figure 3 shows the number of papers that solved the well location optimization problem using meta-heuristics such as GA, PSO, CMA-ES and DE. The most commonly used algorithm can be seen in Figure 3. From this quantitative analysis, it is clear that researchers are interested in implementing an independent approach to solving WPO problems. In future research, a comparative study among Meta-heuristic algorithms on a common platform should be conducted for evaluation. Also, Future research should aim at reducing the computational time using surrogate approaches. There is a need for robust reliable optimization frameworks that are useful for a large scale optimization problem. Furthermore, The techniques that narrow downs the search space for extreme-scale systems should be implemented. In recent years many new techniques have been developed. For example, the nature-inspired algorithms such as Hunting Search Algorithm(HSA), Firefly Algorithm (FA), Roach Infestation Optimization (RIO), Artificial Fish School Algorithm (AFS), Eagle Strategy (ES), Artificial Plant Optimization Algorithm (APO), Gravitational Search Algorithm (GravSA), Eagle Strategy (ES), Glowworm Swarm Algorithm (GlowSA), Bacterial Evolutionary Algorithm (BEA), Krill Herd Algorithm (KHA), Flower Pollination Algorithm(FPA)

Figure 3. Number of papers by algorithms used for solving WPO problem

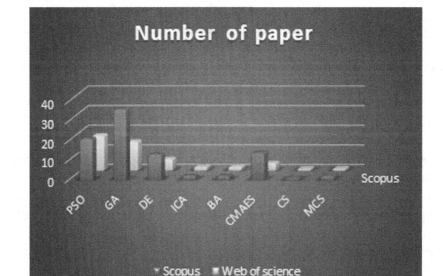

and others. These Novel algorithms may possess some novel characteristics which can help tackle well placement problem. These 3rd generation algorithms may offer incredible preferences as far as finding the global optimality in tremendous and complex search spaces. The implementation of these approaches is moderately direct and simple. They are likewise sensibly adaptable as parameters can be changed effectively for better execution.

The issue in Well placement optimization largely related to multimodality problem and high computational expense. Researches have tried to tackle the multimodality problem with high diversity. Exploration is empowered by high diversity but it does not necessarily mean that low diversity is exploitation as exploitation requires an extensive search in a small area. It is also true that adequate diversity does not guarantee to take care of the convergence issue since convergence is a much-complicated issue. Furthermore, a great balance between exploration and exploitation may make an approach work to its best ability, yet this does not really mean its convergence rate is high. Cunning exploitation at the right time at the right place can give fast convergence. But it is still an open issue. In this manner, appropriate diversity must be maintained during the searching procedure to tackle local optima, even with the cost of slower convergence. Also, hybridization has been a broadly worthy technique to advance exploration along the quest for the global optima. So, the future researcher may take interest in the hybridizing the meta-heuristic algorithms for well placement optimization. But some challenges arise concerning hybrid approaches also. For instance, most hybrid approaches will increase the number of parameters in the calculations, in this manner making it harder to tune their parameters. Moreover, hybrid approaches are somewhat harder to implement, and consequently increasingly inclined to blunders. Along these lines, care ought to be taken when translating results from hybrid approaches. Furthermore, hyper-heuristic approaches can be viewed as a sort of hybrid techniques. In hyper-heuristic strategies, parameters are chosen by a sub-algorithm or through a learning system.

Apart from multimodality problem, Well placement optimization problem creates another challenge by posing computationally expensive cost function. To tackle this problem many researchers have used surrogate model. The surrogate model intends to give a more straightforward, and thus quicker, model which imitates the actual behavior of the cost function. In talking about the application to Well Placement of this technique, we note that surrogate model's accuracy is largely dependent on data sampling; and some of the further developed surrogate strategies are yet to be implemented in the Well placement problem.

CONCLUSION

This chapter reviews the genetic algorithm and Particle swarm optimization implemented in the topic of well placement optimization. In the past decade, significant progress has been made in using the meta-heuristic algorithm to achieve proper well location with higher net profit value. Metaheuristic algorithms are usually slower than deterministic algorithms. Due to the nature of randomness, premature convergence can be avoided if properly adjusted. A lot of work is required to properly adjust these algorithms. In this study, the authors found that PSOs and their variants converge faster and provide high-quality solutions. These variants of PSO and GA also provide a better solution from standard algorithms, indicating that changes to specific problems lead to the right solution. The well placement optimization problem has proven to be very complex, multi-model and discontinuous. But the challenge for researchers is not just the complex surface. Since the cost function takes a long time to calculate, it is difficult to adjust the algorithm correctly. Therefore, the surrogate model can significantly reduce the calculations and help to tune the algorithm's parameters.

ACKNOWLEDGMENT

The authors would like to thank the Fundamental and Applied Science Department for their valuable support and Centre of Graduate Studies of Universiti Teknologi PETRONAS for funding this research project under Graduate Assistantship (GA) scheme.

REFERENCES

Al Dossary, M. A., & Nasrabadi, H. (2015). *Well placement optimization using imperialist competition algorithm.* Paper presented at the SPE reservoir characterisation and simulation conference and exhibition. 10.2118/175646-MS

Al Dossary, M. A., & Nasrabadi, H. J. J. o. P. S. (2016). Well placement optimization using imperialist competitive algorithm. *Engineering, 147*, 237-248.

Ariadji, T., Sukarno, P., Sidarto, K. A., Soewono, E., Riza, L. S., & David, K. J. J. o. E. (2012). Optimization of Vertical Well Placement for Oil Field Development Based on Basic Reservoir Rock Properties using a Genetic Algorithm. *Science, 44*(2), 106-127.

Awotunde, A. A., & Sibaweihi, N. J. S. E. (2014). Consideration of voidage-replacement ratio in well-placement optimization. *Management, 6*(1), 40-54.

Bangerth, W., Klie, H., Wheeler, M. F., Stoffa, P. L., & Sen, M. K. (2006). On optimization algorithms for the reservoir oil well placement problem. *Computational Geosciences*, *10*(3), 303–319. doi:10.100710596-006-9025-7

Brits, R., Engelbrecht, A. P., & Van den Bergh, F. (2002). A niching particle swarm optimizer. *Proceedings of the 4th Asia-Pacific conference on simulated evolution and learning*.

Chang, Y. Q., Bouzarkouna, Z., & Devegowda, D. (2015). Multi-objective optimization for rapid and robust optimal oilfield development under geological uncertainty. *Computational Geosciences*, *19*(4), 933–950. doi:10.100710596-015-9507-6

Chen, H. W., Feng, Q. H., Zhang, X. M., Wang, S., Ma, Z. Y., Zhou, W. S., & Liu, C. (2018). A meta-optimized hybrid global and local algorithm for well placement optimization. *Computers & Chemical Engineering*, *117*, 209–220. doi:10.1016/j.compchemeng.2018.06.013

Chen, H. W., Feng, Q. H., Zhang, X. M., Wang, S., Zhou, W. S., & Geng, Y. H. (2017). Well placement optimization using an analytical formula-based objective function and cat swarm optimization algorithm. *Journal of Petroleum Science Engineering*, *157*, 1054–1070. doi:10.1016/j.petrol.2017.08.024

Cheng, G., An, Y., Wang, Z., & Zhu, K. (2012). *Oil well placement optimization using niche particle swarm optimization.* Paper presented at the 2012 Eighth International Conference on Computational Intelligence and Security. 10.1109/CIS.2012.22

Clerc, M. (1999). The swarm and the queen: towards a deterministic and adaptive particle swarm optimization. *Proceedings of the 1999 congress on evolutionary computation-CEC99 (Cat. No. 99TH8406).* 10.1109/CEC.1999.785513

Ding, D. (2008). *Optimization of wellplacement using evolutionary algorithms, SPE Europec.* Paper presented at the EAGE Ann. Conf. & Exhibition, SPE.

Ding, S., Jiang, H., Li, J., Liu, G., & Mi, L. J. J. o. I. (2016). Optimization of well location, type and trajectory by a modified particle swarm optimization algorithm for the punq-s3 model. *Information, 4*(1).

Ding, S., Lu, R., Xi, Y., Wang, S., & Wu, Y. J. C. (2019). Well placement optimization using direct mapping of productivity potential and threshold value of productivity potential management strategy. *Engineering, 121*, 327-337.

Ding, S. W., Jiang, H. Q., Li, J. J., & Tang, G. P. (2014). Optimization of well placement by combination of a modified particle swarm optimization algorithm and quality map method. *Computational Geosciences, 18*(5), 747–762. doi:10.100710596-014-9422-2

Emerick, A. A., Silva, E., Messer, B., Almeida, L. F., Szwarcman, D., Pacheco, M. A. C., & Vellasco, M. M. B. R. (2009). *Well placement optimization using a genetic algorithm with nonlinear constraints.* Paper presented at the SPE reservoir simulation symposium. 10.2118/118808-MS

Feng, Q. H., Zhang, J. Y., Zhang, X. M., & Hu, A. M. (2012). Optimizing well placement in a coalbed methane reservoir using the particle swarm optimization algorithm. *International Journal of Coal Geology, 104*, 34–45. doi:10.1016/j.coal.2012.09.004

Foroud, T., Baradaran, A., & Seifi, A. (2018). A comparative evaluation of global search algorithms in black box optimization of oil production: A case study on Brugge field. *Journal of Petroleum Science Engineering, 167*, 131–151. doi:10.1016/j.petrol.2018.03.028

Forouzanfar, F., Poquioma, W. E., & Reynolds, A. C. (2016). Simultaneous and Sequential Estimation of Optimal Placement and Controls of Wells With a Covariance Matrix Adaptation Algorithm. *SPE Journal, 21*(2), 501–521. doi:10.2118/173256-PA

Forouzanfar, F., & Reynolds, A. J. J. o. P. S. (2013). Well-placement optimization using a derivative-free method. *Engineering, 109*, 96-116.

Giuliani, C. M., & Camponogara, E. (2015). Derivative-free methods applied to daily production optimization of gas-lifted oil fields. *Computers & Chemical Engineering, 75*, 60–64. doi:10.1016/j.compchemeng.2015.01.014

Guyaguler, B., & Horne, R. N. (2001). *Uncertainty assessment of well placement optimization.* Paper presented at the SPE annual technical conference and exhibition. 10.2118/71625-MS

Hamida, Z., Azizi, F., & Saad, G. (2017). An efficient geometry-based optimization approach for well placement in oil fields. *Journal of Petroleum Science Engineering, 149*, 383–392. doi:10.1016/j.petrol.2016.10.055

Holland, J. H. J. S. a. (1992). *Genetic algorithms*. Academic Press.

Hutahaean, J. J., Demyanov, V., Arnold, D., & Vazquez, O. (2014). *Optimization of Well Placement to Minimize the Risk of Scale Deposition in Field Development*. Paper presented at the Abu Dhabi International Petroleum Exhibition and Conference. 10.2118/171733-MS

Isebor, O. J., Ciaurri, D. E., & Durlofsky, L. J. (2014). Generalized Field-Development Optimization With Derivative-Free Procedures. *SPE Journal, 19*(5), 891–908. doi:10.2118/163631-PA

Isebor, O. J., Durlofsky, L. J., & Ciaurri, D. E. (2014). A derivative-free methodology with local and global search for the constrained joint optimization of well locations and controls. *Computational Geosciences, 18*(3-4), 463–482. doi:10.100710596-013-9383-x

Jang, I., Oh, S., Kim, Y., Park, C., & Kang, H. (2018). Well-placement optimisation using sequential artificial neural networks. *Energy Exploration & Exploitation, 36*(3), 433–449. doi:10.1177/0144598717729490

Janiga, D., Czarnota, R., Stopa, J., & Wojnarowski, P. (2019). Self-adapt reservoir clusterization method to enhance robustness of well placement optimization. *Journal of Petroleum Science Engineering, 173*, 37–52. doi:10.1016/j.petrol.2018.10.005

Jansen, J. J. C. (2011). Adjoint-based optimization of multi-phase flow through porous media–a review. *Fluids, 46*(1), 40-51.

Jesmani, M., Jafarpour, B., Bellout, M., Hanea, R., & Foss, B. (2016). *Application of simultaneous perturbation stochastic approximation to well placement optimization under uncertainty*. Paper presented at the ECMOR XV-15th European Conference on the Mathematics of Oil Recovery. 10.3997/2214-4609.201601873

Kennedy, J., & Eberhart, R. (1995). Particle swarm optimization. In *IEEE International of first Conference on Neural Networks*. Perth, Australia, IEEE Press.

Li, L. L., & Jafarpour, B. (2012). A variable-control well placement optimization for improved reservoir development. *Computational Geosciences, 16*(4), 871–889. doi:10.100710596-012-9292-4

Lyons, J., & Nasrabadi, H. (2013). Well placement optimization under time-dependent uncertainty using an ensemble Kalman filter and a genetic algorithm. *Journal of Petroleum Science Engineering, 109*, 70–79. doi:10.1016/j.petrol.2013.07.012

Ma, X., Plaksina, T., & Gildin, E. (2013). *Integrated horizontal well placement and hydraulic fracture stages design optimization in unconventional gas reservoirs*. Paper presented at the SPE Unconventional Resources Conference Canada. 10.2118/167246-MS

Miyagi, A., & Yamamoto, H. (2018). Well placement optimization for carbon dioxide capture and storage via CMA-ES with mixed integer support. *Proceedings of the Genetic and Evolutionary Computation Conference Companion*. 10.1145/3205651.3205706

Naderi, M., & Khamehchi, E. (2017). Application of DOE and metaheuristic bat algorithm for well placement and individual well controls optimization. *Journal of Natural Gas Science and Engineering*, *46*, 47–58. doi:10.1016/j.jngse.2017.07.012

Nwankwor, E., Nagar, A. K., & Reid, D. C. (2013). Hybrid differential evolution and particle swarm optimization for optimal well placement. *Computational Geosciences*, *17*(2), 249–268. doi:10.100710596-012-9328-9

Onwunalu, J., & Durlofsky, L. J. (2010). *Optimization of field development using particle swarm optimization and new well pattern descriptions*. Stanford University.

Onwunalu, J. E., & Durlofsky, L. J. (2010). Application of a particle swarm optimization algorithm for determining optimum well location and type. *Computational Geosciences*, *14*(1), 183–198. doi:10.100710596-009-9142-1

Pan, Y., & Horne, R. N. (1998). *Improved methods for multivariate optimization of field development scheduling and well placement design*. Paper presented at the SPE Annual Technical Conference and Exhibition. 10.2118/49055-MS

Pouladi, B., Keshavarz, S., Sharifi, M., & Ahmadi, M. A. (2017). A robust proxy for production well placement optimization problems. *Fuel*, *206*, 467–481. doi:10.1016/j.fuel.2017.06.030

Rahman, I., Vasant, P., Singh, B. S. M., & Abdullah-Al-Wadud, M. (2016). Hybrid Particle Swarm and Gravitational Search Optimization Techniques for Charging Plug-In Hybrid Electric Vehicles. In *Handbook of Research on Modern Optimization Algorithms and Applications in Engineering and Economics* (pp. 471–504). IGI Global. doi:10.4018/978-1-4666-9644-0.ch018

Redouane, K., Zeraibi, N., & Nait Amar, M. (2018). *Automated Optimization of Well Placement via Adaptive Space-Filling Surrogate Modelling and Evolutionary Algorithm*. Paper presented at the Abu Dhabi International Petroleum Exhibition & Conference. 10.2118/193040-MS

Rosenwald, G. W., & Green, D. W. J. S. o. P. E. J. (1974). *A method for determining the optimum location of wells in a reservoir using mixed-integer programming*. Academic Press.

Sayyafzadeh, M. (2017). Reducing the computation time of well placement optimisation problems using self-adaptive metamodelling. *Journal of Petroleum Science Engineering*, *151*, 143–158. doi:10.1016/j.petrol.2016.12.015

Zhang, L. M., Zhang, K., Chen, Y. X., Li, M., Yao, J., Li, L. X., & Lee, J. I. (2016). Smart Well Pattern Optimization Using Gradient Algorithm. *Journal of Energy Resources Technology-Transactions of the Asme, 138*(1). doi:10.1115/1.4031208

Chapter 4
Artificial Intelligence Approach for Predicting TOC From Well Logs in Shale Reservoirs:
A Review

Md. Shokor A. Rahaman
Universiti Teknologi PETRONAS, Malaysia

Pandian Vasant
Universiti Teknologi PETRONAS, Malaysia

ABSTRACT

Total organic carbon (TOC) is the most significant factor for shale oil and gas exploration and development which can be used to evaluate the hydrocarbon generation potential of source rock. However, estimating TOC is a challenge for the geological engineers because direct measurements of core analysis geochemical experiments are time-consuming and costly. Therefore, many AI technique has used for TOC content prediction in the shale reservoir where AI techniques have impacted positively. Having both strength and weakness, some of them can execute quickly and handle high dimensional data while others have limitation for handling the uncertainty, learning difficulties, and unable to deal with high or low dimensional datasets which reminds the "no free lunch" theorem where it has been proven that no technique or system be relevant to all issues in all circumstances. So, investigating the cutting-edge AI techniques is the contribution of this study as the resulting analysis gives top to bottom understanding of the different TOC content prediction strategies.

INTRODUCTION

For gas and oil exploration, it is critical to evaluate source rock property accurately. The abundance of organic carbon can be represented by Total organic carbon as a basic and important index (Passey, Creaney, Kulla, Moretti, & Stroud, 1990),(King, 2010). Generally, from core laboratory analysis, this

DOI: 10.4018/978-1-7998-1192-3.ch004

parameter is obtained which are time-consuming and expensive (Delvaux, Martin, Leplat, & Paulet, 1990; Hare et al., 2014; Johannes, Kruusement, Palu, Veski, & Bojesen-Koefoed, 2006). This constrains the quick advancement of unconventional oil and gas exploration.

Then again, permeability, thermally mature, total organic carbon (TOC) content, porosity, saturation, mechanical properties and rock mineralogy etc. define the productivity of shale quality. Further, reservoir properties which are critical can judge qualitatively of most productive shale reservoir which are commercially potential typically has at least 2% TOC and Ro (more than 1.4 in gas dry window). For a good oil and gas flow capability and storage, it needs under 40% saturation and 100 nano-darcy permeability and over 2% porosity. Further, low differential stress, a certain degree of natural fractures and over 40% quartz or carbonate in mineralogy is needed additionally for commercial shales (Sondergeld, Newsham, Comisky, Rice, & Rai, 2010). For basic and important index, TOC content is the one among the all factors representing the organic matter.

Well logging and direct geochemical analysis are utilized conventionally for TOC determination in the present petroleum industry. Whatever, core data for TOC are not available due to the time and cost required for testing and the difficulties related to gather occasion an intact and representative sample. Despite the fact that laboratory test of TOC is difficult, they are still the preferred and necessary techniques (Guangyou, Qiang, & Linye, 2003; Jarvie*, Jarvie*, Weldon*, & Maende*, 2015).

For further prediction, these lab results are regularly applied as references for the mathematical approaches. With the fast advancement of unconventional exploration of gas and oil, the accurate and continuous study on the TOC is vital. High longitudinal resolution portrays well logging. For the fact of giving continuous TOC profiles that cover the entire interval of interest when continuity of the information and log-based TOC prediction are all the more universally applicable. By comparing with surrounding rocks, some specific geophysical responses (e.g., resistivity, neutron, density, and gamma-ray) of the source rock can be recognized. During utilization of log-based TOC prediction the empirical mathematical equations are commonly utilized. Notwithstanding, equation quality are incredibly dependent by the estimation result by logging data. Meanwhile, the gamma-ray and uranium correlation technique are some of the time not reasonable for shale reservoir. Having radioactivity in phosphatic fish plates in shale reservoir elevated gamma-ray and uranium counts can't reflect TOC (Bessereau, Carpentier, & Huc, 1991; Passey et al., 1990).

A complicated non-linear function relationship is seen between the TOC content and the logging data. Between the logging data and the TOC content a complicated relationship is seen which are non-linear. By using simple linear regression, approximating the real function relationship is hard and utilizing the well log, it is impossible to predict the TOC content. Nowadays, most researchers have been attracted by AI. The real research demonstrates that AI strategies have extremely solid approximation abilities to non-linear implicit functions. On the other hand, the prediction of TOC content has been worked by AI strategies revealed by the current research result. Between TOC content and the logging parameters a correlation models have been established by utilizing the NN so as to accomplish a good prediction of TOC content. Indeed, the utilization of robust AI techniques approaches have been presented and effectively utilized in numerous engineering fields, for example, permeability estimation, lithology classification et al. (Shadizadeh, Karimi, & Zoveidavianpoor, 2010; Yuan, Zhou, Song, Cheng, & Dou, 2014; Zoveidavianpoor, Samsuri, & Shadizadeh, 2013). Table 1 abridge current TOC prediction strategies utilizing well logs.

Table 1. Summary of log-based TOC prediction models

Method	Parameters	Explanation and feature	Reference
LogR method	Resistivity and Porosity	(1) TOC foundation levels and Baseline shift territorially (2) LOM range varies in specific areas (3) Underestimates TOC in reservoir with a plenitude of pyrite	[1], [13]– [15]
Bulk density method	Density	(1) Suitable for reservoirs with similar consistent mineralogy and liquid phases. (2) Need a solid relationship amongst TOC and density.	(Schmoker, 1979; Schmoker & Hester, 1983)
Natural gamma method	Gamma intensity	(1) For non-radioactive or uranium content with phosphatic minerals has limitation. (2) Better for marine source rocks (with concentrated uranium)	(Beers, 1945; Hester & Schmoker, 1987)
Interval transit time method	Compressional transit-time	(1) Sonic velocities can be affected significantly by many variables. (2) Need a solid relationship between TOC and compressional transit time	(Autric, 1985; Decker, Hill, & Wicks, 1993)
Geochemical Laboratory measurements (Leco TOC and Rock Eval)	(1) Combust pulverized tock (2) S1, S2, S3 peaks in rock Eval technique	(1) Discrete data points (2) Direct measurements from core samples (3) Expensive	(Jarvie* et al., 2015; Peters, 1986)
Spectral gamma ray method	Uranium, potassium, uranium content	(1) Expensive and availability is less for all wells	(Nardon et al., 1991)
Volume model method	Water volume and Hydrocarbon, carbonate volume, Kerogen volume clay volume, and siliceous volume	(1) Organic carbon conversion factor (K) changes territorially (2) Composite well log integration	(Mendelzon & Toksoz, 1985)
Laser-induced breakdown spectrometry, chemostratigraphy, RockView	The carbon abundance of formation and carbonate mineral in spectroscopy	(1) International oil service companies (Schlumberger-Litho Scanner, Baker Huges-RockView services et al.) controls the Core technologies (2) The chemical contents can be determined directly	(Charsky & Herron, 2013; Pemper et al., 2009)
Multivariate fitting	Composite well logs	(1) Need database foundation (2) Hard to decide the significant parameters because of nonlinear connection between various well logs	(Heidari, Torres-Verdin, & Preeg, 2011)
Neural network methods	Composite well logs	(1) For over-fitting input issue data-pre-processing is essential (2) Suitable at the beginning time for TOC prediction. (3) Kernel functions are significant for SVR	(Huang & Williamson, 1996; Kamali & Mirshady, 2004; Tan, Song, Yang, & Wu, 2015)

BACKGROUND

It is evident in published literature that the utilization of AI acts to diminish the framework complexities to be modeled. For the overall framework AI can give a high level of simulated accuracy. To give some examples such studies, we note that the AI technique can be classified into these algorithms: ANNs, FL, generalized regression neural network, SVMs, radial basis function, convolutional neural networks (CNNs),

Genetic calculation (GA), PSO, Neuro Fuzzy (NF), Artificial intelligence system (AIS) et al. applied to optimize the whole modeling procedure (Ardabili, Mahmoudi, & Gundoshmian, 2016; Kalantari et al., 2018). Having the amazing capability of learning the patterns AI can perceive the complex behavior in such information for modeling the objective variable. Utilizing computer-based technique research demonstrates that for accomplishing a high level of accuracy, AI models can utilize significantly large volume of data. More importantly, AI methodologies with the assistance of computer assisted facilities can also enable a variety of decision-making alternatives modeled by realistic estimates of procedures that should be applied in practical life (O'Leary, 2013).

In the same way as other different fields, AI has achieved a decent spot in the optimization, production and evaluation of source rock in shale reservoir predominantly on the grounds that the generation potential of source rock involving large volume of information with several input parameters is relatively complex process. Those can be breaking down cautiously and predict Total Organic Carbon in shale reservoir. Wang, Alizadeh, Johnson, Mahmoud, and Shi et al. utilized ANN to evaluate TOC content in shale reservoir whereas Peng, Tahmasebi, Wang et al. developed a hybrid method using FL, GA, LSSVM, PSO et al. Whatever remains of the studies, as displayed in Table 2, can be sorted dependent on the particular I approach.

MAIN FOCUS OF THE CHAPTER

The goal of this review is to investigate the cutting-edge AI approaches utilized in TOC content prediction in shale reservoir as far as their setting of application, sensitivity and accuracy to the model's input datasets. For providing comprehensive data on the usage of AI in TOC content prediction, an extensive interpretation, review and analysis is expected where the researcher would be helped by optimizing their methodology. This review work has five stages where the first stage is about a comprehensive introduction of TOC content in shale reservoir and its prediction procedure. In second stage, an arrangement of studies dependent on the developed AI technique in a more prominent detail is provided. The next stage presents AI and TOC content prediction strategies. The criteria for assessment of models is characterized in stage four and the final stage builds up the comparison dependent on assessment criteria and the general conclusion and the synthesis of cutting-edge studies reached in the review paper in TOC prediction studies.

METHODOLOGY

Eight recent articles of AI technique are adopted in this review which are the cutting-edge methods for TOC content prediction from well logs data. This information is gathered from IEEE, Science Direct and Springer. TOC content prediction strategy, modeling technique and the obtained results are reviewed in this paper. A list of studies on AI technique are provided in Table 2.

Table 2. Publications on AI techniques in field of TOC content prediction between 2012 and 2019

Row	Published Year	Author (s)	Objective
Artificial neural network			
1	2019	Huijun, Wei, Tao, Xinjun, Guangxu	To predict TOC, S1 and S2 with high accuracy based on well logs.
2	2018	Yousef, Ali Moradzadeh; Mohammad Reza	To estimate one dimensionally the organic geochemical parameters in one well of the Canning basin, Western Australia
3	2018	Bahram, Khaled, Mohamad Hossein	To estimate TOC; To estimate S2 and HI factors; To distinct the kerogen types
4	2018	Lukman, Reza, Ali, Gregory, Hongyan	To predict continuous geochemical logs in wells with no or limited geochemical information. To predict TOC, S1, S2
5	2017	Ahmed Abdulhamid, Salaheldin, Mohamed, Mohamed, Abdulazeez, Abdulwahab	To determine the TOC for Barnett and Devonian shale formation based on conventional logs
6	2016	Maojin, Xiaodong, Xuan, Qingzhao	To estimate the TOC content in gas-bearing shale (to investigate log-based TOC prediction for organic shale using the SVR method)
SVM, GA, PSO, ELM, FUZZY, and other methods			
1	2018	Pan, Suping	To predict TOC from well logs data
2	2018	Pan, Suping, Taohua	To predict TOC from well logs data
3	2017	Linqi, Chong, Chaomo, Yang, Xueqing, Yuan, Yuyang, Le	To predict TOC from well logs data
4	2017	Pejman, Muhammad	To predict TOC and FI from well logs
5	2017	Vahid, Ali, Reza	To formulate TOC values in the absence of laboratory TOC measurements from conventional well log data.
6	2016	Xian, Jian, Gang, Liu, Xinmin,	To predict TOC from well logs data
7	2015	Sid-Ali, Leila	To predict TOC from well-logs data. To implant an intelligent system able to replace the Schmoke model in case of lack of measurement of the Bulk density.
8	2015	Maojin, Xiaodong, Xuan, Qingzhao	To estimate the TOC content in gas-bearing shale (to investigate log-based TOC prediction for organic shale using the SVR method)
9	2012	Ebrahim, Ali, Saeid	To predict TOC using intelligent systems

CHARACTERISTICS OF THE STUDIES

The characteristics of studies such as methodology, modeling technique, input and output criteria of every AI approaches presented in Table 3

Table 3. Modeling characteristics

No	Methodology	Modeling method/ classification method/ regression method/ clustering method	Input (s)/ objective functions (s)	Output (s)/ Criteria	References
1	First- We made a correlation between TOC, S1, S2 and well logs to determine the suitable inputs. Second- 125 core shale samples and well logging data of Shahejie Formation from Dongying Depression, Bohai Bay, China were randomly split into 100 training samples and 25 validating samples to develop the proposed CNN for predicting TOC, S1 and S2. Third- all logs and chosen logs were used as inputs respectively for comparison.	Six Layer CNN	Density (DEN), resistivity (RT), neutron (CNL), and sonic transit time (AC)	TOC, S1 and S2	Huijun et al (2019)
2	First, simulated annealing algorithm combined with the GA to analyze the fuzzy c-means clustering so as to classify sample data, and then to obtain the high-quality data. Then for the small sample data, LSSVM was established to predict TOC. Further, PSO-LSSVM was established to predict TOC content. At the same time, a BP-NN model for the contrastive analysis was established.	SAGA-FCM (Simulate annealing algorithm genetic algorithm-Fuzzy C mean clustering); LSSVM; PSO-LSSVM; BPNN	SP, GR, DTC, RT, U, KTH, TH, DEN, CNL	TOC	Pan et al (2018)
3	A multi-layer perceptron neural network used to predict S1, S2, S3 and TOC in presence of the petrophysical logs like GR, DT, SP, CAL, NPHI, FCNL, LLD, LLS, RHOB and MSFL as input variables. Then, the well-derived geochemical data were simulated by Sequential Gaussian Simulation (SGS) method.	MLP-NN and SGS (Sequential Gaussian Simulation)	GR, DT, SP, CAL, NPHI, LLD, LLS, RHOB, MSFL	TOC, S1	Yousef et al (2018)
4	ANN and ΔLogR techniques were used to make a quantitative and qualitative correlation between TOC content and wireline data. Then, Artificial Neural Network and mathematical relationship between geochemical factors were used to estimate S2 and HI factors. Furthermore, estimated parameters were used to distinct the kerogen types. Finally, geochemical and depositional properties of the Pabdeh Formation were evaluated to depict applicability of the method used.	ANN; ΔLogR techniques;	(1)ΔLogR technique, sonic log (DT), corrected resistivity log (Rt) and LOM factor; GR log; (2) TOC, Rt, DT, and LOM	(1) TOC; (2) S2	Bahram et al (2018)
5	The study investigates three types of models including PSO-LSSVM, LSSVM and ANN-BP for TOC prediction. Moreover, in this study, two cases of models will be designed. One takes the selected well logs as input, while the other takes all available well logs as input.	ANN-BP, LSSVM, PSO-LSSVM	Selected Log= (CNL, DTC, RT,U,GR,DEN)	TOC	Pan, Suping et al (2018)
6	ANN is utilized to predict organic geochemical data in two wells with no laboratory measured geochemical data, and four (4) wells with limited laboratory measured data. The distribution of these geochemical properties within the ~200m–300m thick Goldwyer 3 Shale member is subsequently modelled across the Broome Platform of the Canning Basin.The methods employed in this study can be subdivided into four main steps. a. Well log to geochemical data compilation b. Identification of relationship between well logs and geochemical property c. Network Training d. Geochemical Property Model	ANN	DTC; GR; CNL; DEN; KTH; TH; U	TOC	Lukman et al (2018)
7	Applied an ANN model with single hidden layer and 5 neurons to predict TOC in presence of the GR, R_{ILD}, Δt_b as input and TOC as output of process.	ANN	Gamma ray log, deep induction resistivity log, compressional transient time, and bulk density log	TOC	Ahmed et al (2017)
8	First, a method of data mining called stepwise regression for identifying the correlations between target (i.e., dependent) parameters- the TOC and FI and the available well log data (the independent variables). Then a hybrid machine-learning algorithm (FL-GA-ANN) is also presented that models more accurately the complex spatial correlations between the input and target parameters.	Multiple linear regression (MLR); Fuzzy Logic, Genetic algorithm, ANN, Hybrid Machine Learning (FL-GA-ANN)	GR, Rhob, Nphi, DT, PE, RT10, SP, Ur, Thor, K	TOC, Fracable Index (FI)	Pejman et al (2017)
9	First- Rock-Eval pyrolysis measurements on drill cutting samples. Second, Synthesis of TOC log from conventional well log data using FL and calculating TOC applying △ log R technique. Third, grouping the synthesized TOC log data into clusters using k-means algorithm. Fourth, Training SVM and ANN classifiers to predict the source rock class membership (zones) from well log data and finally, Correlation of estimated with the achieved source rock class membership (zones)	FIS; K-means algorithm; SVM; ANN	GR, RHOB, LLD	TOC	Vahid et al (2017)
10	Two methods are mainly used in the estimation of the total organic carbon from well logs data, the first one is called the Passey's method or ΔLogR, the second method is called the Schmoker's method, it requires a continuous measurement of the Bulk density. Then, comparison between the fuzzy logic and the artificial neural network in the prediction of the total organic carbon in case of the lack of measurement of the Bulck density were established.	Fuzzy Logic; MLP-NN	Gamma ray log, deep induction resistivity log, compressional transient time, and bulk density log	TOC	Ahmed et al (2017)
11	An integrated hybrid neural network (IHNN), as an improved method, is optimized on the basis of BPNN from the following aspects including weight optimization before iteration, network structure optimization and serial-parallel integration was established for evaluating the TOC using conventional logging curves (low feature dimensions).	BP_AdaBoost; KELM; SVM; DEN; ΔlogR; IHNN	PE, KTH, AC, CNL, RD, TH, K, U, DEN, GR, SP	TOC	Linqi et al (2017)

continued on the following page

Table 3. Continued

No	Methodology	Modeling method/ classification method/ regression method/ clustering method	Input (s)/ objective functions (s)	Output (s)/ Criteria	References
12	An Extreme Learning Machine (ELM) network is a single hidden-layer feed-forward network with many advantages over multi-layer networks was employed to predict TOC from well logs data Then The results and performance characteristics of the ELM technique are compared to those obtained by the ANN method to evaluate the efficiency of these two networks during the prediction process.	ELM; ANN	DTC; GR; CNL; DEN; KTH; TH; U	TOC	Xian et al (2016)
13	Three different regression algorithm (the Epsilon-SVR, Nu-SVR, and SMO-SVR) and four different kernel functions (Linear function, Polynomial function, Gaussian function, Multilayer perceptron) used in a packet dataset validation process and a leave-one-out cross-validation process. Then, for comparison, the SVR-derived TOC with the optimal model and parameters is compared with the empirical formula and the logR methods. Additionally, the radial basis network (RBF) is also applied to perform tests with different inputs; the results of these tests are compared with those of the SVR method.	Epsilon-SVR; Nu-SVR; SMO-SVR	CNL; K; GR; U; TH; AC; DEN; PE; LLD	TOC	Maojin et al (2015)
14	An Artificial Neural Network (ANN) was applied to predict the TOC form well-logs data in case of absence of measurement of the Bulk density log. Then, different methods that are used for the determination of the TOC had been explained. The implanted neural network machine is applied to two horizontal wells drilled in the Barnett shale.	MLP-ANN	Natural gamma ray, Neutron porosity, sonic P and S wave slowness	TOC	Sid-Ali et al (2014)
15	Firstly, petro physical data were clustered into distinct groups. This classification does not require any further subdivision of the dataset but follows naturally based on the unique characteristics of well log measurements reflecting mineral and lithofacies responses within the logged intervals. Then, using an intelligent model such as Neural Network (NN) the amount of the-TOC was estimated in each individual EF(Electro-facies).	SOM; K-means clustering; Hierarchical Cluster Analysis; BP-ANN;	thermal neutron porosity (TNPHI), sonic transit time (DT), GR, CGR, SGR, K and THOR logs	TOC	Ebrahim et al (2012)

AI APPROACH EVALUATION CRITERIA

The viability of past AI approach connected in an issue of TOC content prediction has been assessed dependent on a correlation of the output of the developed model and the target values, utilized for most precise forecast, discovery, and streamlining and observing of the procedure in term of their measurable execution exactness. Table 4 exhibits the evaluating factors that have been utilized for looking at the productivity of the AI approach. The second segment portrays the parameters utilized in the performance indices.

STATE-OF-THE-ART OF AI APPROACHES IN TOC PREDICTION

Artificial Neural Network (ANN)

For learning and analyzing information features and subsequently implementing non-linear approximation function ANNs have a decent capacity and are being considered as a standout amongst the most effective strategies contrasted with statistical models. By working based on the biological neural system ANNs has prompted their effective applications in numerous regions, for example, image analysis, pattern recognition, adaptive controls and so forth. Any initial assumption does not require for ANN for the nature of the information distribution or fitting function and making the model a primary advantage over the counterpart are statistical. Then again, experimental data can be trained by ANN. Importantly, complex frameworks can be demonstrated in an easy way by ANNs requiring no parametric form of complex physical equations, data assumption, and initial or on the other hand boundary conditions con-

Table 4. Model evaluation criteria

Accuracy and Performance Index	Description
$MSE = \dfrac{1}{N \times p} \sum\limits_{i=1}^{p} \sum\limits_{j=1}^{N} \left(T_{ij} - L_{ij}\right)^2$ $RMSE = \sqrt{\dfrac{1}{N \times p} \sum\limits_{i=1}^{p} \sum\limits_{j=1}^{N} \left(T_{ij} - L_{ij}\right)^2}$ $MAE = \dfrac{1}{N \times p} \sum\limits_{i=1}^{p} \sum\limits_{j=1}^{N} \left|T_{ij} - L_{ij}\right|$ $MAE = \dfrac{1}{N \times p} \sum\limits_{i=1}^{p} \sum\limits_{j=1}^{N} \left|T_{ij} - L_{ij}\right|$ $MAPE = 100 \times \dfrac{1}{N \times p} \sum\limits_{i=1}^{p} \sum\limits_{j=1}^{N} \left|\dfrac{T_{ij} - L_{ij}}{T_{ij}}\right|$ $AAD = \dfrac{1}{N} \sum\limits_{i=1}^{N} \left|T_{ij} - \overline{T_i}\right|$ $R = \dfrac{\sum\limits_{i=1}^{n} \left[\left(p_{Mi} - \overline{p_M}\right)\left(p_{pi} - \overline{p_p}\right)\right]}{\sum\limits_{i=1}^{n} \left[\left(p_{Mi} - \overline{p_M}\right)^2 \sum\limits_{i=1}^{n} \left(p_{pi} - \overline{p_p}\right)^2\right]}$	• P, the number of data set patterns • n is the number of the samples • N, the number of output units • T_{ij} and L_{ij} are target and output values • p_p is the output power • p_{Mi} is the target power • p_m is the average power

Figure 1.

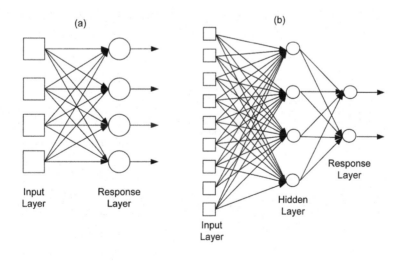

trasted with mathematical type models. ANN can be partitioned into single/multi-layer, self-organized and recurrent in terms of the topology of networks. In Figure 1 (Heiliö et al., 2016) a schematic of single and multi-layer networks is portrayed.

In Figure 2, the different attributes of ANNs of diverse categorization is summarized. Further the common activation function utilized in the design of ANNs structures have given in Table 3.

Depending on the classification of ANN and applied activation function on the input, different structure of ANN is conceivable (see Table 5 and Figure 5).

(Basheer & Hajmeer, 2000)displayed a summarization of popular networks in Table 6.

Support Vector Machine (SVM)

In 1960s, SVMs(Support Vector Machines) first introduced (Vapnik, 1963, 1964); nonetheless, the thought was revitalized (Cortes & Vapnik, 1995) later in 1990s when the SVM displayed better execution in various classification issues over the ANN approach, which had been acknowledged as an effective strategy. As being popular AI method SVM is applied as per statistical learning theory, has a wide application in numerous fields of science and engineering including regression and classification problem (Ebtehaj, Bonakdari, Shamshirband, & Mohammadi, 2016; Ghorbani et al., 2017). SVM prefer the generalized upper bound error for reducing than the local training error which is one of the main advantages contrasted with the traditional machine learning methods. Further, by utilizing SRMP and presenting a decent generalization capacity to conquer the deficiencies of the conventional ANN model that uses the empirical risk minimizing in modeling a given variable by SVM.

SVM can be demonstrated by the idea of classification considering a 2D simplest case input space containing class1 and class 2 data. Linearly classification can be possible with these data. SVM sim-

Figure 2. Attributes of ANN

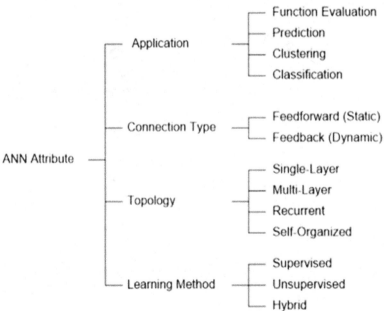

Table 5. Activation functions of ANN (Da Silva, Spatti, Flauzino, Liboni, & dos Reis Alves, 2017)

Activation function	Formula	Range of output
Bipolar step	$f\left(x\right) = \begin{cases} 1 & x < 0 \\ 0 & x = 0 \\ -1 & x > 0 \end{cases}$	[-1,1]
Step	$f\left(x\right) = \begin{cases} 1, & x \leq 0 \\ -1, & x > 0 \end{cases}$	[-1,1]
Linear	$f(x) = x$	[-∞,∞]
Unit step	$f\left(x\right) = \begin{cases} 1, & x \leq 0 \\ 0, & x > 0 \end{cases}$	[0,1]
Symmetric ramp	$f\left(x\right) = \begin{cases} a & x < a \\ x & -a \leq x \leq a \\ -a & x > a \end{cases}$	[-a,a]
Piecewise linear	$f\left(x\right) = \begin{cases} 1 & x < 0 \\ x + \dfrac{1}{2} & -\dfrac{1}{2} \leq x \leq \dfrac{1}{2} \\ -1 & x > 0 \end{cases}$	[0,1]
Bipolar sigmoid	$f\left(x\right) = \dfrac{1 - e^{-x}}{1 + e^{-x}}$	[-1,1]
Sigmoid	$f\left(x\right) = \dfrac{1}{1 + e^{-x}}$	[0,1]
Gaussian	$f\left(x\right) = \dfrac{1}{\sqrt{2\pi}\sigma} e^{\left[\frac{-\left(z-\mu\right)^2}{2\sigma^2}\right]}$	[0,1]
Tangent hyperbolic	$f\left(x\right) = \tanh\left(x\right) = \dfrac{e^x - e^{-x}}{e^x + e^{-x}}$	[-1,1]

ply illustrated in Figure 3 (Cortes and Vapnik, 1995). In Figure 3 circle and squares are recognized as class 1 and class 2 respectively in input space. Both Figure 3(a) and Figure 3(b) represents the smallest margin and largest margin of two classes. Further, both in Figure 3(a) and Figure 3(b), there are three

Table 6. A list of popular ANN design

ANN designs	Characteristics	Cons and pros	Application in engineering
Backpropagation (BP) (Rumelhart, Hinton, & Williams, 1985)	• Backpropagation error with feedforward network • Supervised learning • MLP with more than one layer •Sigmoid activation function	• Most widely, simple, and straightforward (Priddy & Keller, 2005) • Trapping in local optima and slow learning • complex non-linear mapping can be handled (Priddy & Keller, 2005)	Image processing (Hassoun, 1995) • Modelling and control (Hassoun, 1995) •Pattern recognition (Hassoun, 1995) • Forecasting and mapping (Hassoun, 1995)
Radial basis function (RBF)(Broomhead & Lowe, 1988)	• Feed forward with error BP(Back Propagation) •Gaussian activation function • MLPs with three layers	• Flexibility is less and slower compared to BP • Using two-step unsupervised-supervised hybrid training makes it faster in training stage than BP networks	• Function approximation (Wei, Saratchandran, & Narasimman, 1999) • Adaptive control (Wei et al., 1999) • Non-linear dynamic system identification (Wei et al., 1999)•Signal processing (Wei et al., 1999)
Recurrent (Williams & Zipser, 1989)	• Exhibitions of memory of information sequence on network •Sigmoid activation function • Flow in both directions	• Difficulty in training and number of parameters are large (Lipton, Berkowitz, & Elkan, 2015) • Time varying patterns and sequential can be modelled simultaneously (Lipton et al., 2015)	•Filtering and control (Medsker & Jain, 1999) • Dynamic system identification (Medsker & Jain, 1999) • Forecasting (Medsker & Jain, 1999)
Hopfield (Hopfield, 1984)	•Symmetric two-layer recurrent network •Sigmoid activation function • Non-linear associative memory	• Good for noisy and incomplete data • Except bipolar and binary input other input are useless.	•Intelligent computation (Tang, Tan, & Yi, 2007)• Optimization (Hoskins & Himmelblau, 1988)
Kohonen (self-organizing map, SOM) (Kohonen, 1989)	• Self-organizing • 2 layer network • Unsupervisely trained	• Number of clusters can be optimized on its own• Not an incremental network (Dokur, Ölmez, Yazgan, & Ersoy, 1997) • A few numbers of clusters are not good for it • Can organize large-scale data (Recknagel, 2013)	•Data mapping (Basheer & Hajmeer, 2000)•Pattern recognition (Basheer & Hajmeer, 2000)• Classification (Basheer & Hajmeer, 2000)
Grossberg(Adaptive resonance theory, ART) (Carpenter & Grossberg, 2016)	Recurrent network with 2 layer • Unsupervisely trained • Feed forward and feedback weight adjustments	• Fast training and continuous plasticity (Crestani & Pasi, 2013) • Because of representing clusters by nodes, network is susceptible of degradation and failure upon damage • Small clusters can be broken by large problems (Wunsch II, Hasselmo, Venayagamoorthy, & Wang, 2003)	•Classification (Basheer & Hajmeer, 2000)•Pattern recognition (Basheer & Hajmeer, 2000)
Counter propagation (Hecht-Nielsen, 1988)	•Combination of Kohonen (in hidden layer) and Grossberg (in output layer) networks •Sigmoid activation function • Trained by unsupervised-supervised hybrid learning	• Faster than MLP in training (Kasabov, 1996) • Network optimization is time expensive and difficult (Ballabio, Vasighi, Consonni, & Kompany-Zareh, 2011) • Due to unsupervised learning the performance is better compared to BP(Taylor, 2006)	•Function approximation (Zupan & Gasteiger, 1991) •Pattern recognition (Zupan & Gasteiger, 1991) •Classification(Zupan & Gasteiger, 1991)
Convolutional neural networks (CNNs) (Rumelhart et al., 1985)	•Feed-forward multi-channel input •Preserves spatial dependency • Pooling operations and successive convulsion	• Large-scale problems can be handled (Kasabov, 1996) • Limited semantic generalization (Hosseini, Xiao, Jaiswal, & Poovendran, 2017) • Reduced memory size (Zhang, Wang, Tao, Gong, & Zheng, 2017) • Mathematically more complex than MLPs (Caterini & Chang, 2018) • Lower chance of over-fitting and more training (Zhang et al., 2017)	•Image processing (McCann, Jin, & Unser, 2017)•Classification (McCann et al., 2017)
Deep neural networks (DNNs)	• More than one hidden layer • Processes data hierarchically (Cios, 2018) • Usually supervised or semi-supervised training • In fully supervised DNN, backpropagation with ramp activation function is used (Cios, 2018)	• Capable of large-scale data processing problems (Caterini & Chang, 2018) • More details (features) can be extracted in training due to hierarchical data processing (Cios, 2018) • Cautions should be made in unsupervised learning applications with modified inputs (Cios, 2018)	• Classification (Caterini & Chang, 2018) • Image processing (Caterini & Chang, 2018) • Multivariate regression (Du & Xu, 2017)
Deep belief networks (DBNs) (Hinton, Osindero, & Teh, 2006)	• Consists of a large number of layers; each layer consisting of restricted Boltzmann machines (RBMs) (Sun, Steinecker, & Glocker, 2014) • Trained unsupervised layer-by-layer, and weights are adjusted top-down (Sun et al., 2014)	• Can discover a structure in data which is not labelled or structured (Sun et al., 2014) • Can extract high-level features (Sun et al., 2014) • Requires an additional pre-training stage to familiarize the network with data (Sun et al., 2014) • Unsupervised learning in DBNs may not properly work with networks with stochastic or randomly initialized variables (Sun et al., 2014)	• Classification and clustering(Fink, Zio, & Weidmann, 2015) • Image processing (Sun et al., 2014) • Model discrimination (Fink et al., 2015) • Monitoring and quality control (Sun et al., 2014)

Figure 3. Class 1 and Class 2 classification (Cortes & Vapnik, 1995)

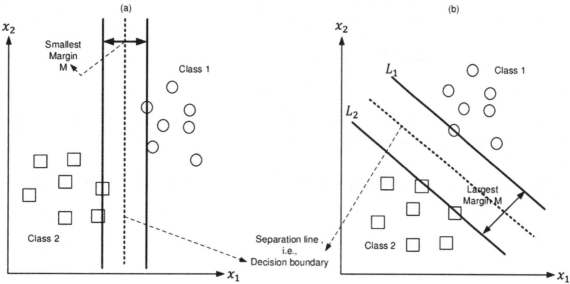

Figure 4. Transformation in feature space

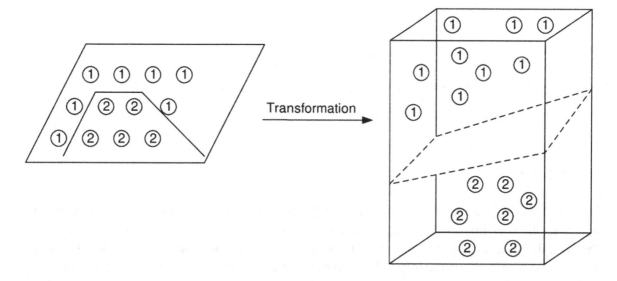

points (one circle and two squares) precisely fallen on the two lines on the two sides of the edge. These are called as the support vectors.

However, the classification of the SVM can be done in a higher dimensional space where the separation of two classes are non-linear utilizing transformation in kernel (or feature) space (sigmoid, polynomial, or/and radial basis function) delineated in Figure 4. And An outline of common kernel functions utilized in SVM is given in Table 7.

Table 7. Kernel functions of SVM

Kernel	Kernel function	Parameters
Linear	$K(x_i, x_j) = (x_i x_j)^a$	$A \in N$
Polynomial	$K(x_i, x_j) = (c + x_i x_j)^a$	$A, c \in N$
Gaussian	$K\left(x_i, x_j\right) = \exp\left[-\dfrac{x_i - x_j}{2\sigma^2}\right]$	$\sigma \in R, \sigma > 0$
Sigmoid	$K(x_i, x_j) = \tan h(\eta(x_i x_j) + \theta)$	$\eta, \theta \in R$

Figure 5. Bell-shape membership function of (a) contours and (b) distribution by fuzzy sets (Terano et al., 2014)

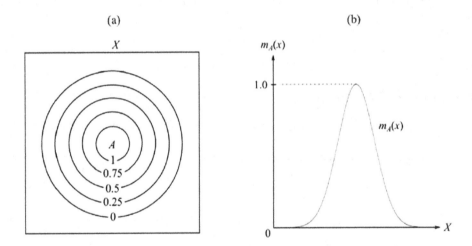

Fuzzy Logic

Zadeh (1965) first proposed Fuzzy Logic (FL) where the set theory of more than one valued logic being as a generalization. Frameworks having non-crisp boundaries are managed by it where characteristics for example being unclear/ambiguous and hazy are displayed by these frameworks (Terano, Asai, & Sugeno, 2014). Assume, in total space X, x is a member. In the crisp logic, the set A on total space (X) is defined by the characteristic function x_A where the total space is being mapped to the set {0,1}, as following (Terano et al., 2014):

$x_A: X \rightarrow \{0,1\}$

$$x \rightarrow x_A(x) = \begin{cases} 0 & x \notin A \\ 1 & x \in A \end{cases}$$

Figure 6. General framework of fuzzy logic

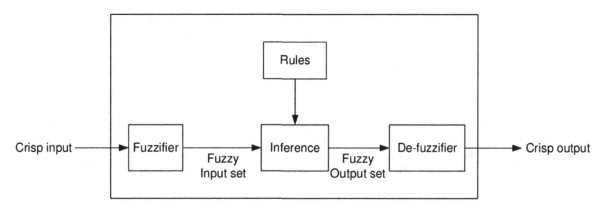

Table 8. Standard operation in FL system (Zoveidavianpoor, Samsuri, & Shadizadeh, 2012)

Fuzzy operator name	Algebraic operator name	Symbol	Description	Equation based on Algebraic	Equation based on Fuzzy
Intersection	AND	∩	Applied to two fuzzy sets A and B with the membership function $\mu_A(x)$ and $\mu_B(x)$	$\mu_{(A \cap B)} = \left\{ \mu_A\left(x\right), \mu_B\left(x\right) \right\}, x \in X$	$\mu_{(A \cap B)} = \min\left\{ \mu_A\left(x\right), \mu_B\left(x\right) \right\}, x \in X$
Union	OR	∪	Applied to two fuzzy sets A and B with the membership function $\mu_A(x)$ and $\mu_B(x)$	$\mu_{(A \cup B)} = \left\{ \mu_A\left(x\right), \mu_B\left(x\right) \right\}, x \in X$	$\mu_{(A \cup B)} = \max\left\{ \mu_A\left(x\right), \mu_B\left(x\right) \right\}, x \in X$
Complement	NOT	NOT	Applied to fuzzy sets A with the membership function $\mu_A(x)$	$\mu_A\left(x\right) = 1 - \mu_A\left(x\right), x \in X$	$\mu_A\left(x\right) = 1 - \mu_A\left(x\right), x \in X$

In this manner, if x belongs to A, the value of 1 can be taken by the characteristic function, while if it is not a part of A, the function is 0. The following relationship is equivalent in the FL in Eq. (9):

$m_A: X \rightarrow [0,1]$

$x \rightarrow m_A(x)$

Figure 7. Population based optimization algorithms (Vasant & Vasant, 2012)

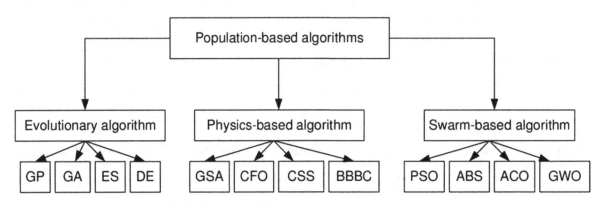

in which, the mf(membership function) is represented by m_A (Terano et al., 2014). Different notation appears in the membership function in the literature, for example, fA and µA (Zadeh, 1965). From the Eq. (9) and Eq. (10), Boolean set in the crisp logic and a domain in the FL are the mapping of space X. A continuum speaks a ''class'' by Zadeh (Zadeh, 1965) work. Figure 5 outlines a portrayal of the fuzzy sets where mf as a continuum of the level of A-ness (Terano et al., 2014) or a continuum of the mg (membership grades) . Hence, the fuzzy sets consider the crisp sets as a special case.

In the theory of fuzzy logic other membership function exist beside the bell-shape membership (Figure 5 (b)).

Evolutionary Algorithms

Numerous species over millions of years have evolved to adjust to different environments based on the Darwinian evolutionary theory. Considering the environment as a type of the problems and Evolutionary algorithm as an adaption of the population to fit the best environments, the same idea can be applied to numerical optimization. Until better solution is being achieved, the fundamental thought of evolutionary algorithm is to evolve a population of candidate solutions under a selective process analogous to the mutation, natural selection and reproduction. To generate offspring solution, parent solution is combined utilizing effective search algorithm where the offspring solution can be evaluated and may themselves produce offspring (Husbands, Copley, Eldridge, & Mandelis, 2007). Continuation of the generation prompts better solution to optimization, search and design issues. Many algorithm-like genetic algorithms, evolutionary programming, evolution programs and evolution methodologies are included by evolutionary algorithm. Both GA and DE give extraordinary performance in dealing with solutions which have variety of engineering issues. Hence, they are briefly explained in the following section.

Genetic Algorithm (GA)

As being a prediction tool, in optimization and global search issues GA aims to create high quality solution (Salcedo-Sanz, Deo, Cornejo-Bueno, Camacho-Gómez, & Ghimire, 2018). By searching through a feature space, the nearest optimal solution is being able to deduce by this model (Eberhart & Kennedy, 1995;

Vasant & Barsoum, 2009). For candidate solution (CS) a solution needs to be chosen in GA technique where evolving towards a better solution is being set by its population. A set of properties are contained in each CS and these properties can mutate and change, in this manner the evolution is progressed as a duplicate process from a population of randomly generated individuals. Calculation of the objective function is done by each generation (the population). Then in the next iteration of the algorithm, the new generation of the candidate solution is used. The algorithm stops and uses the final model when a maximum number of generations have been produced to make the prediction. In Figure 8 and Figure 9 overall optimization process are appeared. Further a flow chart of GA is given in Fig 10.

Differential Evolution (DE)

As a population-based model, DE uses a real-coded GA and a normal random generator for finding the global minimum of the objective function with an ARS (adaptive random search) (Maria, 1998). Mutation operation is mostly based on DE where for finding the optimal solution GA relies on crossover operation (Ab Wahab, Nefti-Meziani, & Atyabi, 2015). Like other evolutionary algorithms, DE consists of four stages: initialization, mutation, crossover, and selection. During the initialization step, a population/generation with a fixed number of candidate solutions (NP) using minimum and maximum values for each defined variable and a uniform random value in the range from 0 to 1 is created (Storn, 1995). The next step is to evolve the initial population in which every solution is mutated by adding the difference of two random solutions from the current population to a different selected random solution scaled by a factor F. Then, during the crossover process, diversity is created in the newly generated candidate

Figure 8. GA optimization (Velez-Langs, 2005)(Chen, 2013)

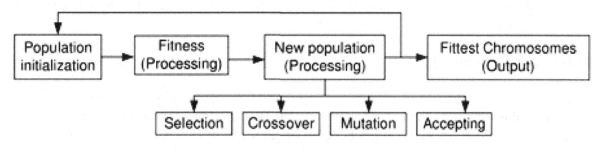

Figure 9. (a) Crossover and (b) mutation

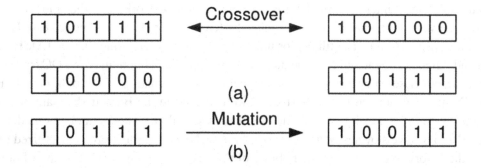

Figure 10. The flow chart of DE algorithm (Ab Wahab et al., 2015; Khademi, Rahimpour, & Jahanmiri, 2010)

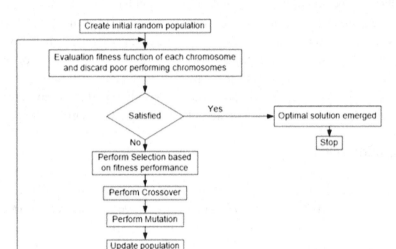

solutions by applying the crossover probability rate (CR). There are two main crossover variants for DE: exponential and binomial. Finally, in the selection step, every solution vector in the trial population is compared with the corresponding vector in the initial population and depending on the nature of the problem (minimization or maximization), the one with the lower or higher objective function value is moved to the next generation. The four-step process repeated until the stopping criteria (reaching to the maximum number of generations or obtaining the defined different tolerance between the objective function values in the current generation and the previous one) are met. Figure 4 shows different steps of the DE algorithm.

TOC Prediction Method

There is extensive application of artificial intelligence (AI)-based solution to complex engineering problems. In this section, we focus on the problems related to TOC content prediction in shale reservoir.

Sfidari et al (Sfidari, Kadkhodaie-Ilkhchi, & Najjari, 2012) firstly clustered Petro-physical data into distinct groups using Hierarchical cluster analysis and K-means clustering. For any further subdivision of the dataset no classification would be needed but rather pursues normally dependent on the special attributes pf well log estimation reflecting lithofacies and mineral reaction inside the logged interims. At that point, utilizing an intelligent model, for example, Neural Network (NN) the amount of the-TOC was assessed in every individual EF (Electro-facies). Here, 3 layered BP-NN model with Levenberg-Marquardt training algorithm was utilized for prediction in the clustered intervals and MSE was high. Ouadfeula and Aliouane (Ouadfeul & Aliouane, 2014) utilized ANN to predict the TOC from well-logs data if there should arise an occurrence of nonappearance of estimation of the bulk density log. The implanted NN model is applied to two horizontal wells drilled in the Barnett shale and it gave great outcomes that were exceptionally near the determined TOC utilizing the Schmoker's model. In their work, sonic P and S wave slowness logs, Neutron porosity, Natural gamma ray were utilized to predict TOC. From their work, it demonstrated the ability of the ANN to predict a TOC in case of nonappearance of the density log or a discontinuous of this log. Tan et al. (Ouadfeul* & Aliouane, 2015) presented three different regression algorithms (SMO-SVR, Nu-SVR and the Epsilon-SVR), four different kernel functions (Linear function, Polynomial function, Gaussian function and Multilayer perceptron) and a TOC prediction content that utilizes wireline logs in a leave-one-out cross-validation process and a packet dataset validation process. In following, the SMO-SVR, Nu-SVR and the Epsilon-SVR models are tested by comparison with respect to their TOC prediction accuracy. Both leave-one-out cross-validation and packet dataset validation demonstrate that the Epsilon-SVR model is superior to the SMO-SVR and Nu-SVR models. Rather than the RBF strategy, the SVR-derived TOC is in better agreement. Shi et al.(Tan et al., 2015)utilized MLP-NN and Fuzzy logic applied to two horizontal wells drilled in the lower Barnett shale formation to predict TOC from well logs data and to implant an intelligent framework ready to replace the Schmoke model in case of lack of measurement of the Bulk density where the utilization of ANN in the prediction of the TOC in shale reservoir was superior to the Fuzzy logic. Shi et al (Shi et al., 2016) used Artificial Neural Network (ANN) and Extreme Learning Machine (ELM) in TOC prediction where the Extreme Learning Machine (ELM) is a lot quicker than the Artificial Neural Network (ANN) model according to the training time comparison which made Extreme Learning Machine beneficial for practical use above ANN. For both ELM and ANN, DTC; GR; CNL; DEN; KTH; TH; U well logs data were used for training, testing and validation purpose to predict TOC. Zhu et al. (Zhu et al., 2018) utilized BP_Adaboost, KELM, SVM, DEN, Δlog R and Integrated hybrid neural network (IHNN) to predict TOC content from well-logs data. The author looked at the prediction models set up in 132 rock sample in the shale gas reservoir inside the Jiaoshiba zone, rather than the established models, the accuracy of the proposed IHNN method is a lot higher and thus the generalization ability of the IHNN algorithm is also very strong. Measurements of drill cutting samples had been done by Rock-Eval pyrolysis and then FL synthesized the TOC log from conventional well log data. Further Δlog$R$ method had been applied for calculating TOC and then the synthesized TOC log data have been assembled into cluster utilizing k-means algorithm. Furthermore, training ANN and SVM classifiers have been utilized to predict the source rock class membership (zones) from well-log data. In Bolandi et al. (Bolandi, Kadkhodaie, & Farzi, 2017) work, both ANN and SVM were used for classification problem of source rock zonation. In term of classification accuracy, the SVM with RBF kernel readily outperformed ANN. Tahmasebi et al (Tahmasebi, Javadpour, & Sahimi, 2017) borrowed a hybrid method from machine learning and artificial intelligence proposed for accurate prediction of the parameters. The two techniques have the capacity to be tuned quickly and to utilize the more established database to precisely portray shale reservoirs. By this way, comparing with Multiple linear regression (MLR) the hybrid machine learning (HML) strategy gave considerably more accurate prediction to the TOC and FI. Mahmoud et al. (Mahmoud et al., 2017) utilized ANN model to estimate TOC for unconventional shale reservoir in Duvernay and Barnett shale formation utilizing conventional log-data (density log, gamma ray, compressional transient time, and deep induction resistivity log). ANN method gives better TOC estimations contrasted with available strategies by two criteria, higher coefficient of determination and lower average absolute deviation than accessible methods for Duvernay shale example. Furthermore, based on the weights and biases of the optimized ANN method, a new TOC empirical correlation was extracted for the first time so that without requiring the ANN model, it can be utilized with a high accuracy to estimate the TOC based on conventional log data. For accomplishing a quantitative and qualitative source rock characterization and distribution Johnson et al.(Johnson, Rezaee, Kadkhodaie, Smith, & Yu, 2018) utilized ANN across the Broome Platform of the Canning Basin. For the training, validation and test samples of the geochemical property the R^2 values is upwards of

75%. Further by predicting with ANN is the accomplishment of more prominent resolution between geochemical data points, as well as the time and laboratory requirements is significantly decreased in their work. Three kinds of models including LSSVM, PSO-LSSVM, and ANN-BP had utilized for prediction in Wang et al. (Pan Wang, Peng, & He, 2018) work. In their work, two cases of models had been designed where one took the selected well logs (DTC, CNL, GR, U, DEN and RT) as input and the other took all available well logs as input. In view of the outcomes, the PSO-LSSVM method beat ANN-BP and LSSVM methods. To make a quantitative and qualitative correlation between TOC content and wireline data ANN and Δ log R method were utilized in Alizadeh et al. (Alizadeh, Maroufi, & Heidarifard, 2018) work. At that point, to evaluate S2 and HI factor and to distinct the kerogen types mathematical relationship between geochemical factors and ANN were utilized. By utilizing the neural network, the mean TOC values were computed had higher correlation with real TOC determined from Rock Eval analysis. The neural network data showed better agreement in carbonate intervals with TOC calculated from Rock Eval. Nezhad et al.(Nezhad, Moradzadeh, & Kamali, 2018) utilized ANN for estimation where petrophysical logs and S1, S2, S3 and TOC data of geochemical analysis were respectively utilized as input and outputs of the models. Then Sequential Gaussian Simulation (SGS) technique simulated the well-derived geochemical data. The acquired outcome showed that MLP-ANN have a high precision in estimation of S2 and kerogen type detection and SGS acts superior to the MLP-NN technique for organic geochemical parameter evaluation. The impact of the sample data was considered in Wang and Peng (Pan Wang & Peng, 2018) work on AI modeling. The simulated annealing algorithm combined with the genetic algorithm to analyze the fuzzy c-means for improving the classification accuracy of the fuzzy c-means clustering algorithm and to classify sample data and after that to acquire the high-quality data. In this study, for the prediction of the TOC content, the TOC content prediction model was built up based on the particle swarm optimization (PSO-LSSVM). In the meantime, for the contrastive examination a BP neural network model was built up. From their outcome it could be seen that TOC could be predicted all the more precisely with PSO-LSSVM model that with BPNN and LSSVM models. A correlation between TOC, S1, S2 and well logs were made by Wang et al. (H. Wang, Wu, Chen, Dong, & Wang, 2019) to determine the suitable inputs. At that point 125 core shale sample and well logging data of Shahejei Formation from Dongying Depression, Bohai Bay, China were arbitrarily split into 100 training samples and 25 validating sample for building up the six-layer CNN for predicting TOC, S1 and S2. Further, the performance of CNN was compared with Passey technique and BP. Considering the outcomes, CNN exhibited higher prediction precision in both training and validation data for TOC, S1 and S2 contrasted with BP-ANN model and Passey technique by two criteria, higher R^2 and lower NRMSE.

STRENGTHS AND WEAKNESSES OF ARTIFICIAL INTELLIGENCE TECHNIQUES

In this section, the common models will be deliberated briefly which can be unified into the identification, classification, estimation, mathematical modeling, clustering and function evaluation of a hybrid model with application. In this review script, sub-models, for example, ANNs, SVM, FL, Swarm intelligence and Evolutionary algorithm (EA) will be explained through delivering the principle theoretical structures.

Of the seven AI procedures featured in this work, it is important to inquire as to whether there is any of them that can be said to be 100% faultless and fit for use in all situations. In what is by all accounts a response to the above inquiry, Luchian et al. (2015) states that it is more useful concentrating on answering the problem as opposed to sitting around idly to locate the best method. Notwithstanding, a theorem yielded by Wolpert and Macready (1997) called the No Free Lunch Theorem for Optimization (NFLTO) states as follows: Given that all issues are thought to be equivalent in strength and irrespective of the criteria utilized for passing judgment on its performance, all techniques utilized for solving the issue have a similar act. In help of the NFLTO, Anifowose et al. (2016) opines that there is certainly not a solitary comprehensive AI approach that will adequately address all difficulties in all computing conditions and data since each of the AI methods is secured up its novel qualities and inevitable defects. Table 9 outlines the strengths and weakness of a portion of the AI strategies.

To demonstrate the effectiveness or otherwise of these AI procedures, a couple of researchers have endeavored to compare a couple of the AI systems.

SYNTHESIS OF RESULTS AND CONCLUDING REMARK

This section synthesizes the discoveries and discusses about the consequences of TOC prediction in previous studies. Figure 16 shows the distribution of AI model connected in TOC prediction in shale reservoir from 2012 to 2019. This tree has been sorted dependent on a kind of strategies gathering (single or hybrid) and publication year, and they are utilized for different obligations, for example, optimizing, developing, estimating, diagnosing and designing in the prediction of TOC in shale reservoir fields. This tree additionally portrays the application patterns for every strategy in every year. As is clear, 2017 and 2018 has the most trends for applying AI techniques in TOC prediction. Likewise, the offer of utilizing single methods (78.9%) is higher than that of the hybrid methods (21.1%), then again, the assorted variety of single methods is higher than that of the hybrid methods. If there should arise an occurrence of strategy type, MLP has the most astounding utilization among different methods (both single and hybrid methods).

Table 4 shows a list of results dependents on the chosen paper number, gathered as far as the accuracy of the AI approaches and their impacts on the TOC prediction process.

To give further bits of knowledge Table 11 has been extricated from Table 10, which introduces the productivity of every AI techniques in more prominent detail.

Considering Table 10, the utilization of LSSVM and ELM introduced the highest correlation coefficient and the lowest modeling error experienced in the prediction of the TOC content in the shale

Table 9. Demonstrates a couple of these investigates

Benchmark	ANN	FUZZY	SVM	GA
Robustness against noise	High	High	High	High
Speed of convergence	Slow	Fast	-	Slow
Prone to over fitting?	Yes, but depends on how the training is done	-	No	-
Data Requirements	Huge data required	-	Small data required	-
Self-organization	Yes	-	-	No
Ability to generalize	Yes	-	Yes	-

Figure 11. AI methods in TOC prediction

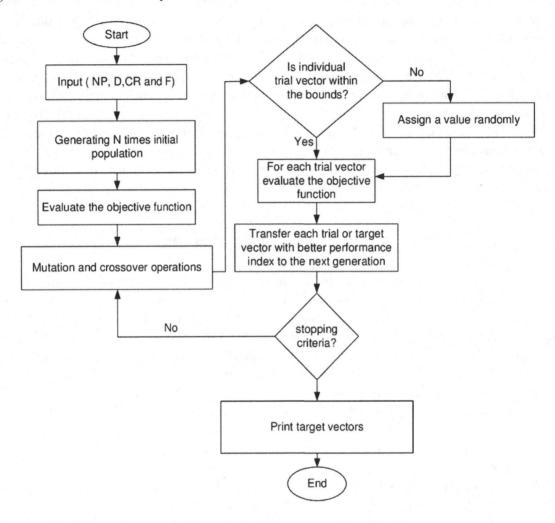

reservoir. In concentrates Referenced as 2, 10 and 11, the utilized techniques (for example LSSVM and ELM models) brought about the correlation coefficient values of about 0.9316, 0.9048 and 0.9493 for prediction of TOC. This value of correlation demonstrates the most noteworthy prediction ability of the developed approaches.

Then again, utilizing hybrid AI strategies, (for example, the PSO-LSSVM strategy) prompted an optimized and improved opportunity for the prediction of TOC content. For instance, in the investigation of Reference 2 and 11 that utilized PSO-LSSVM strategy, the outcome demonstrated a prediction accuracy with a correlation coefficient of 0.9451 and 0.9679 and in the investigation of Reference 5, the utilization of the FL and GA technique prompted an increase in the TOC content prediction contrasted with their Multiple Linear Regression (MLR) technique. That is, the FL-GA-ANN prompted an MSE magnitude of 0.08 for TOC content prediction, which was lower than that of the MLR method (at a value of 0.43).

In concentrates Referenced as 2, 9 and 15, the authors have utilized SAGA-FAC (Simulate annealing algorithm genetic algorithm-Fuzzy C mean clustering), K-means algorithm and K-means clustering and Hierarchical Cluster Analysis for the classification of the prediction method. This study demon-

Table 10. Total results of the presented studies

Paper No	Result and evaluation
1	Based on the results, CNN presented higher prediction accuracy in both training and validation data for TOC, S1 and S2 compared to available methods Passey method and BP-ANN model by two criteria, lower NRMSE and higher R^2.
2	Based on the results, TOC could be predicted more accurately with PSO-LSSVM model than with LSSVM and BPNN models, and it had a more favorable effect from visual comparison between the prediction results and the data of measured TOC, as well as error analysis (R^2, RMSE, and VAF).
3	Based on the results, MLP-ANN have a high accuracy in estimation of S2 and kerogen type detection and the obtained results indicate that SGS acts better than the MLP-NN method for organic geochemical parameter evaluation.
4	Based on results, due to higher accuracy of ANN outputs and independency to the TOC content and type of lithology, author used ANN method to estimate TOC instead of ΔlogR technique.
5	Based on the results, The PSO-LSSVM model outperforms ANN-BP and LSSVM intelligent models.
6	Considering the outcome, for the training, validation and test samples the R2 value in each of the geochemical property demonstrated is upwards of 75%. A decent connection with the laboratory measured data with correlation coefficient of 0.78 and 0.83 is demonstrated by the predicted logs, especially the TOC and S2 logs. The accuracy of the predicted S1 logs might be lower-relying upon the thermal development of the examples since the S1 isn't an in-situ property.
7	Based on the results, ANN model provides better TOC estimations compared to available methods by two criteria, lower average absolute deviation and higher coefficient of determination than available techniques for Duvernay shale example.
8	Considering the outcome, the new hybrid machine (HML) technique gave considerably more exact prediction to the TOC and FI, when contrasted and those of the MLR technique are in great concurrence with the accessible experimental data for the two properties.
9	Based on results, ANN and SVM depicts that for classification problem of source rock zonation SVM with RBF kernel readily outperformed ANN in term of classification accuracy (0.9077 and 0.9369 for ANN and SVM, respectively).
10	Based on the results, author suggest the use of the artificial neural network in the prediction of the TOC in shale gas reservoirs rather than the Fuzzy logic.
11	Based on the result, it shows that TOC prediction is easier after logging prediction has been improved. Further, by comparing the prediction models established in 132 rock samples in the shale gas reservoir within the Jiaoshiba area, it can be seen that the accuracy of the proposed IHNN model is much higher than that of the other prediction models. The mean square error of the samples, which were not joined to the established models, was reduced from 0.586 to 0.442. This shows that the generalization ability of the IHNN algorithm is also very strong. Through comprehensive analysis of the results, we can see that the SVM has a poor prediction effect for data with noise and insufficient TOC information; therefore, it is not suitable for predicting the TOC problem. Because of the mechanism of random initial weights, the precision of the BP_AdaBoost algorithm is difficult to improve further, but it can better solve the problem of inaccurate calculation of the low TOC reservoir section. In addition, we can see that the KELM algorithm has a generalization ability which is inferior to that of conventional logging curves.
12	Based on result, The ELM performed slightly better in both training and validation accuracy. However, the ANN model can also produce good results. According to the training time comparison, the ELM model is much faster than the ANN model, which indicates that ELM should be chosen as the better option if processing speed is important.
13	Based on result, the Epsilon-SVR, Nu-SVR, and SMO-SVR algorithms are tested by comparison about their TOC prediction precision. Both packet dataset validation and leave-one-out cross-validation indicate that the Epsilon-SVR algorithm is better than the Nu-SVR and SMO-SVR algorithms. In contrast to the RBF method, the SVR-derived TOC is in better agreement than the RBF-based TOC, which indicates that the SVR method is more advantageous than certain neural networks.
14	Based on the results, it is clear that the implanted neural network machine is able to provide excellent results that are very close to the calculated TOC using the Schmoker's model. Obtained results clearly show the ability of the artificial neural network to predict a Total Organic Carbon (TOC) in case of absence of the density log or a discontinuous measurement of this log.
15	Results show that a three-layered back propagation neural network model with the Levenberg–Marquardt training algorithm is a high-performance learning method for this case study. Accordingly, 7 NN model were created corresponding to the identified EF groups. Comparisons show that thermal neutron porosity (TNPHI), sonic transit time (DT), GR, CGR, SGR, K and THOR logs have strong relationships with TOC within each EF. The prediction was done in the clustered intervals and the measured MSE was as high as 0.0048.

strated that the author of paper 2 combined simulated annealing algorithm with the GA to dissect the fuzzy c-means clustering in order to classify sample information, and after that to get the high-quality information. Further, in studies referenced as 9, combination of TOC log from conventional well log information utilizing FL and ascertaining TOC applying log R method. At that point, gathering the synthesized TOC log information into cluster utilizing k-means algorithm. Additionally, the following investigation's author clustered petrophysical data into distinct groups by utilizing k-means clustering and Hierarchical cluster analysis.

Table 11. The values of the model evaluating factors

Paper No	Method	Efficiency factor	Value
1	BP-ANN	R^2	0.750 for TOC, 0.446 for S1 and 0.663 for S2 with all logs as input 0.515 for TOC, 0.384 for S1 and 0.693 for S2 with selected logs as input
		NRMSE	0.181 for TOC, 0.238 for S1 and 0.151 for S2 with all logs as input 0.123 for TOC, 0.226 for S1 and 0.1727 for S2 with selected logs as input
	CNN	R^2	0.792 for TOC, 0.740 for S1 and 0.806 for S2 with all logs as input 0.828 for TOC, 0.738 for S1 and 0.839 for S2 with selected logs as input
		NRMSE	0.119 for TOC, 0.120 for S1 and 0.124 for S2 with all logs as input 0.101 for TOC, 0.117 for S1 and 0.109 for S2 with selected logs as input
2	LSSVM	R^2	0.9316 for TOC prediction
		RMSE	0.4094 for TOC prediction
		VAF	93.4207 for TOC prediction
	PSO-LSSVM	R^2	0.9451 for TOC prediction
		RMSE	0.3383 for TOC prediction
		VAF	94.1019 for TOC prediction
	BP-ANN	R^2	0.9184 for TOC prediction
		RMSE	0.5119 for TOC prediction
		VAF	91.2551 for TOC prediction
3	MLP-NN	MSE	7.3% for training,5.6% for validation and 9.3% for testing samples in TOC prediction
4	ANN	R^2	0.89 for TOC prediction
		NRMSE	0.0135 for TOC prediction
5	ANN-BP	R^2	0.9317 for TOC prediction
		RMSE	0.0716 for TOC prediction
	LSSVM	R^2	0.9493 for TOC prediction
		RMSE	0.0658 for TOC prediction
	PSO-LSSVM	R^2	0.9679 for TOC prediction
		RMSE	0.0526 for TOC prediction
6	ANN	R^2	0.78 for TOC, 0.83 for S_2 and 0.63 for S_1
7	ANN	R^2	0.89 for TOC prediction
		AAD	0.99 for TOC prediction
8	MLR	MSE	0.43 for TOC prediction & 1.12 for FI prediction
	HML	MSE	0.08 for TOC prediction & 0.12 for FI prediction
9	SVM-RBF	R^2	0.9369 for TOC zonation
	ANN	R^2	0.9077 for TOC zonation
10	BP_Adaboost	RMAE	0.453 for well A & 0.542 for well B for TOC prediction
		MSE	0.444 for well A & 0.586 for well B for TOC prediction
		RRE	0.250 for well A & 0.355 for well B for TOC prediction
	KELM	RMAE	0.332 for well A & 0.547 for well B for TOC prediction
		MSE	0.310 for well A & 0.670 for well B for TOC prediction
		RRE	0.195 for well A & 0.523 for well B for TOC prediction
	SVM	RMAE	0.371 for well A & 0.695 for well B for TOC prediction
		MSE	0.342 for well A & 0.865 for well B for TOC prediction
		RRE	0.213 for well A & 0.485 for well B for TOC prediction
	IHNN	RMAE	0.303 for well A & 0.453 for well B for TOC prediction
		MSE	0.294 for well A & 0.442 for well B for TOC prediction

continued on the following page

Table 11. Continued

Paper No	Method	Efficiency factor	Value
		RRE	0.164 for well A & 0.284 for well B for TOC prediction
11	ANN	MAE	0.0747 for input training & 0.0677 for input testing
		RMSE	0.2734 for input training & 0.2602 for input testing
		VAF	85.69 for input training & 86.30 for input testing
		R^2	0.8749 for input training & 0.8682 for input testing
	ELM	MAE	0.0692 for input training & 0.0827 for input testing
		RMSE	0.2631 for input training & 0.1804 for input testing
		VAF	90.41 for input training & 89.18 for input testing
		R^2	0.9048 for input training & 0.9099 for input testing
12	SVR	R	0.8284 for TOC prediction
		MAE	0.7775 for TOC prediction
		RMSE	0.9868 for TOC prediction
15	BP-ANN	MSE	0.0048 for TOC prediction
	ANN	MSE	0.0073 for TOC prediction

In figure 3, we present the historical backdrop of AI strategies, characterizing a few outcomes started from different techniques to support the modeling efficiency and productiveness. In the present review article, an aggregate of 8 cutting edge research papers identified with the use of artificial intelligence (AI) methods for TOC prediction were gathered from highly cited publication, IEEE, Springer database and Science Direct and these were looked into regarding the prediction strategy, modeling techniques, and the acquired outcomes. The relatively low number of articles on account of utilizing AI strategies for TOC content prediction in the shale reservoir demonstrates a high research potential in this field.

The literature concerning the challenges and issues of the TOC content prediction in shale reservoir and application of AI strategies on prediction process have likewise been talked about. Because of a plenty of studies performed in the utilization of AI techniques, this article was not sorted into hybrid and single-based AI strategies. Be that as it may, the present assessment has been conducted utilizing past consequences of the most significant papers utilizing different datasets regarding the accuracy and sensitivity of the final prediction. In light of the combination of the outcomes, the utilization of hybrid strategy, for example, FL-GA-ANN or PSO-LSSVM prompts an improvement and optimization of the procedure of TOC content prediction in shale reservoir though the utilization of LSSVM and ELM techniques prompts the highest correlation and the lowest error for prediction of the TOC content in shale reservoir. In spite of various papers on different AI strategies in TOC content prediction in shale reservoir, there seems to have been an absence of concentrates if there should be an occurrence of getting to an comprehensive dataset, analyzing and classification of the AI techniques on account of TOC content prediction in shale reservoir.

FUTURE RESEARCH DIRECTIONS

The present review study can just incompletely make up for this requirement for future researchers to concentrate in more prominent profundity on the issues brought up in this paper. Our future perspective is to build up a multi-factor system-based AI applied to TOC content prediction techniques in shale reservoir to achieve the superior in estimating and modeling and to structure a stage which contains accurate and ground-breaking strategies for unsupervised learning on TOC content prediction information.

NOMENCLATURES

Adaptive Neuro-Fuzzy Inference System ANFIS
Artificial Neural Network ANN
Artificial Ant Colony Optimization ACO
Back Propagation Neural Network BPNN
Batch Hydrogen Production BHP
Correlation Coefficient R
Differential Evolution DE
Evolutionary Algorithm EA
Extreme Learning Machine ELM
Fuzzy Support Vector Machine FSVM
Fire Fly Algorithm FFA
Genetic Algorithm GA
Genetic Programing GP
Gray Wolf Optimization GWO
Levenberg Marquardt LM
Least Square Support Vector Machine LSSVM
Multi Layered Perceptron MLP
Monte Carlo Simulation MCS
Neuro-Fuzzy NF
Non-Dominated Sorting Genetic Algorithm NSGA
Particle Swarm Optimization PSO
Probability Distribution Functions PDF
Root Mean Square Error RMSE
Rotating Gliding Arc RGA
Self-Adaptive Gravitational Search Algorithm SAGSA
Support Vector Machines SVM
Self-Adaptive Learning Bat-Inspired Algorithm SALBIA
Teacher-Learning Algorithm TLA
Total Organic Carbon TOC

REFERENCES

Ab Wahab, M. N., Nefti-Meziani, S., & Atyabi, A. (2015). A comprehensive review of swarm optimization algorithms. *PLoS One*, *10*(5), e0122827. doi:10.1371/journal.pone.0122827 PMID:25992655

Alizadeh, B., Maroufi, K., & Heidarifard, M. H. (2018). Estimating source rock parameters using wireline data: An example from Dezful Embayment, South West of Iran. *Journal of Petroleum Science Engineering*, *167*, 857–868. doi:10.1016/j.petrol.2017.12.021

Ardabili, S. F., Mahmoudi, A., & Gundoshmian, T. M. (2016). Modeling and simulation controlling system of HVAC using fuzzy and predictive (radial basis function, RBF) controllers. *Journal of Building Engineering*, *6*, 301–308. doi:10.1016/j.jobe.2016.04.010

Autric, A. (1985). Resistivity, radioactivity and sonic transit time logs to evaluate the organic content of low permeability rocks. *The Log Analyst*, *26*(03).

Ballabio, D., Vasighi, M., Consonni, V., & Kompany-Zareh, M. (2011). Genetic algorithms for architecture optimisation of counter-propagation artificial neural networks. *Chemometrics and Intelligent Laboratory Systems*, *105*(1), 56–64. doi:10.1016/j.chemolab.2010.10.010

Basheer, I. A., & Hajmeer, M. (2000). Artificial neural networks: Fundamentals, computing, design, and application. *Journal of Microbiological Methods*, *43*(1), 3–31. doi:10.1016/S0167-7012(00)00201-3 PMID:11084225

Beers, R. F. (1945). Radioactivity and organic content of some Paleozoic shales. *AAPG Bulletin*, *29*(1), 1–22.

Bessereau, G., Carpentier, B., & Huc, A. Y. (1991). Wireline Logging And Source Rocks-Estimation Of Organic Carbon Content By The Carbolbg@ Method. *The Log Analyst*, *32*(03).

Bolandi, V., Kadkhodaie, A., & Farzi, R. (2017). Analyzing organic richness of source rocks from well log data by using SVM and ANN classifiers: A case study from the Kazhdumi formation, the Persian Gulf basin, offshore Iran. *Journal of Petroleum Science Engineering*, *151*, 224–234. doi:10.1016/j.petrol.2017.01.003

Broomhead, D. S., & Lowe, D. (1988). *Radial basis functions, multi-variable functional interpolation and adaptive networks*. Royal Signals and Radar Establishment Malvern.

Carpenter, G. A., & Grossberg, S. (2016). *Adaptive resonance theory*. Springer. doi:10.1007/978-1-4899-7502-7_6-1

Caterini, A. L., & Chang, D. E. (2018). *Deep Neural Networks in a Mathematical Framework*. Springer. doi:10.1007/978-3-319-75304-1

Charsky, A., & Herron, S. (2013). Accurate, direct Total Organic Carbon (TOC) log from a new advanced geochemical spectroscopy tool: Comparison with conventional approaches for TOC estimation. *AAPG Annual Convention and Exhibition*.

Chen, Z. (2013). *A genetic algorithm optimizer with applications to the SAGD process* (PhD Thesis). University of Calgary.

Cios, K. J. (2018). Deep Neural Networks—A Brief History. In *Advances in Data Analysis with Computational Intelligence Methods* (pp. 183–200). Springer. doi:10.1007/978-3-319-67946-4_7

Cortes, C., & Vapnik, V. (1995). Support-vector networks. *Machine Learning, 20*(3), 273–297. doi:10.1007/BF00994018

Crestani, F., & Pasi, G. (2013). *Soft Computing in Information Retrieval: Techniques and applications* (Vol. 50). Physica.

Da Silva, I. N., Spatti, D. H., Flauzino, R. A., Liboni, L. H. B., & dos Reis Alves, S. F. (2017). *Artificial neural networks*. Cham: Springer International Publishing. doi:10.1007/978-3-319-43162-8

Decker, A. D., Hill, D. G., & Wicks, D. E. (1993). Log-based gas content and resource estimates for the Antrim shale, Michigan Basin. In *Low Permeability Reservoirs Symposium*. Society of Petroleum Engineers. 10.2118/25910-MS

Delvaux, D., Martin, H., Leplat, P., & Paulet, J. (1990). Geochemical characterization of sedimentary organic matter by means of pyrolysis kinetic parameters. *Organic Geochemistry, 16*(1–3), 175–187. doi:10.1016/0146-6380(90)90038-2

Dokur, Z., Ölmez, T., Yazgan, E., & Ersoy, O. K. (1997). Detection of ECG waveforms by neural networks. *Medical Engineering & Physics, 19*(8), 738–741. doi:10.1016/S1350-4533(97)00029-5 PMID:9450258

Du, J., & Xu, Y. (2017). Hierarchical deep neural network for multivariate regression. *Pattern Recognition, 63*, 149–157. doi:10.1016/j.patcog.2016.10.003

Eberhart, R., & Kennedy, J. (1995). Particle swarm optimization. *Proceedings of the IEEE International Conference on Neural Networks, 4*, 1942–1948.

Ebtehaj, I., Bonakdari, H., Shamshirband, S., & Mohammadi, K. (2016). A combined support vector machine-wavelet transform model for prediction of sediment transport in sewer. *Flow Measurement and Instrumentation, 47*, 19–27. doi:10.1016/j.flowmeasinst.2015.11.002

Fink, O., Zio, E., & Weidmann, U. (2015). Development and application of deep belief networks for predicting railway operation disruptions. *International Journal of Performability Engineering, 11*(2), 121–134.

Ghorbani, M. A., Shamshirband, S., Haghi, D. Z., Azani, A., Bonakdari, H., & Ebtehaj, I. (2017). Application of firefly algorithm-based support vector machines for prediction of field capacity and permanent wilting point. *Soil & Tillage Research, 172*, 32–38. doi:10.1016/j.still.2017.04.009

Guangyou, Z., Qiang, J., & Linye, Z. (2003). Using log information to analyse the geochemical characteristics of source rocks in Jiyang depression. *Well Logging Technology, 27*(2), 104–109.

Guo, L., Chen, J. F., & Miao, Z. Y. (2009). The study and application of a new overlay method of TOC content. *Nat. Gas. Geosci, 20*(6), 951–956.

Hare, A. A., Kuzyk, Z. Z. A., Macdonald, R. W., Sanei, H., Barber, D., Stern, G. A., & Wang, F. (2014). Characterization of sedimentary organic matter in recent marine sediments from Hudson Bay, Canada, by Rock-Eval pyrolysis. *Organic Geochemistry, 68*, 52–60. doi:10.1016/j.orggeochem.2014.01.007

Hassoun, M. H. (1995). *Fundamentals of artificial neural networks*. MIT Press.

Hecht-Nielsen, R. (1988). Applications of counterpropagation networks. *Neural Networks*, *1*(2), 131–139. doi:10.1016/0893-6080(88)90015-9

Heidari, Z., Torres-Verdin, C., & Preeg, W. E. (2011). Quantitative method for estimating total organic carbon and porosity, and for diagnosing mineral constituents from well logs in shale-gas formations. In *SPWLA 52nd Annual Logging Symposium*. Society of Petrophysicists and Well-Log Analysts.

Heiliö, M., Lähivaara, T., Laitinen, E., Mantere, T., Merikoski, J., Raivio, K., … Tiihonen, T. (2016). Mathematical modelling. Springer.

Hester, T. C., & Schmoker, J. W. (1987). *Determination of organic content from formation-density logs, Devonian-Mississippian Woodford shale, Anadarko basin*. US Geological Survey. doi:10.3133/ofr8720

Hinton, G. E., Osindero, S., & Teh, Y.-W. (2006). A fast learning algorithm for deep belief nets. *Neural Computation*, *18*(7), 1527–1554. doi:10.1162/neco.2006.18.7.1527 PMID:16764513

Hopfield, J. J. (1984). Neurons with graded response have collective computational properties like those of two-state neurons. *Proceedings of the National Academy of Sciences of the United States of America*, *81*(10), 3088–3092. doi:10.1073/pnas.81.10.3088 PMID:6587342

Hoskins, J. C., & Himmelblau, D. M. (1988). Artificial neural network models of knowledge representation in chemical engineering. *Computers & Chemical Engineering*, *12*(9–10), 881–890. doi:10.1016/0098-1354(88)87015-7

Hosseini, H., Xiao, B., Jaiswal, M., & Poovendran, R. (2017). On the limitation of convolutional neural networks in recognizing negative images. In *2017 16th IEEE International Conference on Machine Learning and Applications (ICMLA)*, (pp. 352–358). IEEE.

Hu, H. T., Lu, S. F., Liu, C., Wang, W. M., Wang, M., Li, J. J., & Shang, J. H. (2011). Models for calculating organic carbon content from logging information: Comparison and analysis. *Acta Sedimentologica Sinica*, *29*, 1199–1205.

Huang, Z., & Williamson, M. A. (1996). Artificial neural network modelling as an aid to source rock characterization. *Marine and Petroleum Geology*, *13*(2), 277–290. doi:10.1016/0264-8172(95)00062-3

Husbands, P., Copley, P., Eldridge, A., & Mandelis, J. (2007). An introduction to evolutionary computing for musicians. In *Evolutionary computer music* (pp. 1–27). Springer.

Jarvie, D. M., Jarvie, B. M., Weldon, W. D., & Maende, A. (2015). Geochemical assessment of in situ petroleum in unconventional resource systems. In *Unconventional Resources Technology Conference* (pp. 875–894). Society of Exploration Geophysicists, American Association of Petroleum. doi:10.1007/978-1-84628-600-1_1

Johannes, I., Kruusement, K., Palu, V., Veski, R., & Bojesen-Koefoed, J. A. (2006). Evaluation of oil potential of Estonian shales and biomass samples using Rock-Eval analyzer. *Oil Shale*, *23*(2), 110–119.

Johnson, L. M., Rezaee, R., Kadkhodaie, A., Smith, G., & Yu, H. (2018). Geochemical property modelling of a potential shale reservoir in the Canning Basin (Western Australia), using Artificial Neural Networks and geostatistical tools. *Computers & Geosciences*, *120*, 73–81. doi:10.1016/j.cageo.2018.08.004

Kalantari, A., Kamsin, A., Shamshirband, S., Gani, A., Alinejad-Rokny, H., & Chronopoulos, A. T. (2018). Computational intelligence approaches for classification of medical data: State-of-the-art, future challenges and research directions. *Neurocomputing*, *276*, 2–22. doi:10.1016/j.neucom.2017.01.126

Kamali, M. R., & Mirshady, A. A. (2004). Total organic carbon content determined from well logs using ΔLogR and Neuro Fuzzy techniques. *Journal of Petroleum Science Engineering*, *45*(3–4), 141–148. doi:10.1016/j.petrol.2004.08.005

Kasabov, N. K. (1996). *Foundations of neural networks, fuzzy systems, and knowledge engineering*. Marcel Alencar.

Khademi, M. H., Rahimpour, M. R., & Jahanmiri, A. (2010). Differential evolution (DE) strategy for optimization of hydrogen production, cyclohexane dehydrogenation and methanol synthesis in a hydrogen-permselective membrane thermally coupled reactor. *International Journal of Hydrogen Energy*, *35*(5), 1936–1950. doi:10.1016/j.ijhydene.2009.12.080

King, G. E. (2010). Thirty years of gas shale fracturing: What have we learned? In *SPE Annual Technical Conference and Exhibition*. Society of Petroleum Engineers. 10.2118/133456-MS

Kohonen, T. (1989). *Self Organizing Map and associative Memory*. New York: Springer. doi:10.1007/978-3-642-88163-3

Lipton, Z. C., Berkowitz, J., & Elkan, C. (2015). *A critical review of recurrent neural networks for sequence learning*. ArXiv Preprint ArXiv:1506.00019

Mahmoud, A. A. A., Elkatatny, S., Mahmoud, M., Abouelresh, M., Abdulraheem, A., & Ali, A. (2017). Determination of the total organic carbon (TOC) based on conventional well logs using artificial neural network. *International Journal of Coal Geology*, *179*, 72–80. doi:10.1016/j.coal.2017.05.012

Maria, G. (1998). IDENTIFICATION/DIAGNOSIS-adaptive random search and short-cut techniques for process model identification and monitoring. *AIChE Symposium Series*, *94*, 351–359.

McCann, M. T., Jin, K. H., & Unser, M. (2017). Convolutional neural networks for inverse problems in imaging: A review. *IEEE Signal Processing Magazine*, *34*(6), 85–95. doi:10.1109/MSP.2017.2739299

Medsker, L., & Jain, L. C. (1999). *Recurrent neural networks: Design and applications*. CRC Press. doi:10.1201/9781420049176

Mendelzon, J. D., & Toksoz, M. N. (1985). Source rock characterization using multivariate analysis of log data. In *SPWLA 26th Annual Logging Symposium*. Society of Petrophysicists and Well-Log Analysts.

Nardon, S., Marzorati, D., Bernasconi, A., Cornini, S., Gonfalini, M., Mosconi, S., ... Terdich, P. (1991). Fractured carbonate reservoir characterization and modelling: A multidisciplinary case study from the Cavone oil field, Italy. *First Break*, *9*(12), 553–565.

Nezhad, Y. A., Moradzadeh, A., & Kamali, M. R. (2018). A new approach to evaluate Organic Geochemistry Parameters by geostatistical methods: A case study from western Australia. *Journal of Petroleum Science Engineering, 169*, 813–824. doi:10.1016/j.petrol.2018.05.027

O'Leary, D. E. (2013). Artificial intelligence and big data. *IEEE Intelligent Systems, 28*(2), 96–99. doi:10.1109/MIS.2013.39 PMID:25505373

Ouadfeul, S.-A., & Aliouane, L. (2014). Shale gas reservoirs characterization using neural network. *Energy Procedia, 59*, 16–21. doi:10.1016/j.egypro.2014.10.343

Ouadfeul, S.-A., & Aliouane, L. (2015). Total Organic Carbon Prediction in Shale Gas Reservoirs using the Artificial intelligence with a comparative study between Fuzzy Logic and Neural Network. In *14th International Congress of the Brazilian Geophysical Society & EXPOGEF* (pp. 1390–1393). Brazilian Geophysical Society.

Passey, Q. R., Creaney, S., Kulla, J. B., Moretti, F. J., & Stroud, J. D. (1990). A practical model for organic richness from porosity and resistivity logs. *AAPG Bulletin, 74*(12), 1777–1794.

Pemper, R. R., Han, X., Mendez, F. E., Jacobi, D., LeCompte, B., & Bratovich, M., ... Bliven, S. (2009). The direct measurement of carbon in wells containing oil and natural gas using a pulsed neutron mineralogy tool. In *SPE Annual Technical Conference and Exhibition*. Society of Petroleum Engineers. 10.2118/124234-MS

Peters, K. E. (1986). Guidelines for evaluating petroleum source rock using programmed pyrolysis. *AAPG Bulletin, 70*(3), 318–329.

Priddy, K. L., & Keller, P. E. (2005). *Artificial neural networks: An introduction* (Vol. 68). SPIE Press. doi:10.1117/3.633187

Recknagel, F. (2013). *Ecological informatics: Understanding ecology by biologically-inspired computation*. Springer Science & Business Media.

Rumelhart, D. E., Hinton, G. E., & Williams, R. J. (1985). *Learning internal representations by error propagation*. California Univ San Diego La Jolla Inst for Cognitive Science. doi:10.21236/ADA164453

Salcedo-Sanz, S., Deo, R. C., Cornejo-Bueno, L., Camacho-Gómez, C., & Ghimire, S. (2018). An efficient neuro-evolutionary hybrid modelling mechanism for the estimation of daily global solar radiation in the Sunshine State of Australia. *Applied Energy, 209*, 79–94. doi:10.1016/j.apenergy.2017.10.076

Schmoker, J. W. (1979). Determination of organic content of Appalachian Devonian shales from formation-density logs: Geologic notes. *AAPG Bulletin, 63*(9), 1504–1509.

Schmoker, J. W., & Hester, T. C. (1983). Organic carbon in Bakken formation, United States portion of Williston basin. *AAPG Bulletin, 67*(12), 2165–2174.

Sfidari, E., Kadkhodaie-Ilkhchi, A., & Najjari, S. (2012). Comparison of intelligent and statistical clustering approaches to predicting total organic carbon using intelligent systems. *Journal of Petroleum Science Engineering, 86*, 190–205. doi:10.1016/j.petrol.2012.03.024

Shadizadeh, S. R., Karimi, F., & Zoveidavianpoor, M. (2010). *Drilling stuck pipe prediction in Iranian oil fields: An artificial neural network approach.* Abadan, Iran: Petroleum University of Technology.

Shi, X., Wang, J., Liu, G., Yang, L., Ge, X., & Jiang, S. (2016). Application of extreme learning machine and neural networks in total organic carbon content prediction in organic shale with wire line logs. *Journal of Natural Gas Science and Engineering, 33,* 687–702. doi:10.1016/j.jngse.2016.05.060

Sondergeld, C. H., Newsham, K. E., Comisky, J. T., Rice, M. C., & Rai, C. S. (2010). Petrophysical considerations in evaluating and producing shale gas resources. In *SPE Unconventional Gas Conference.* Society of Petroleum Engineers.

Storn, R. (1995). Differential evolution-a simple and efficient adaptive scheme for global optimization over continuous spaces. Technical Report, International Computer Science Institute.

Sun, J., Steinecker, A., & Glocker, P. (2014). Application of deep belief networks for precision mechanism quality inspection. In *International Precision Assembly Seminar,* (pp. 87–93). Springer.

Tahmasebi, P., Javadpour, F., & Sahimi, M. (2017). Data mining and machine learning for identifying sweet spots in shale reservoirs. *Expert Systems with Applications, 88,* 435–447. doi:10.1016/j.eswa.2017.07.015

Tan, M., Song, X., Yang, X., & Wu, Q. (2015). Support-vector-regression machine technology for total organic carbon content prediction from wireline logs in organic shale: A comparative study. *Journal of Natural Gas Science and Engineering, 26,* 792–802. doi:10.1016/j.jngse.2015.07.008

Tang, H., Tan, K. C., & Yi, Z. (2007). *Neural networks: Computational models and applications* (Vol. 53). Springer Science & Business Media. doi:10.1007/978-3-540-69226-3

Taylor, B. J. (2006). *Methods and procedures for the verification and validation of artificial neural networks.* Springer Science & Business Media.

Terano, T., Asai, K., & Sugeno, M. (2014). *Applied fuzzy systems.* Academic Press.

Vapnik, V. (1963). Pattern recognition using generalized portrait method. *Automation and Remote Control, 24,* 774–780.

Vapnik, V. (1964). A note one class of perceptrons. *Automation and Remote Control.*

Vasant, P., & Barsoum, N. (2009). Hybrid genetic algorithms and line search method for industrial production planning with non-linear fitness function. *Engineering Applications of Artificial Intelligence, 22*(4–5), 767–777. doi:10.1016/j.engappai.2009.03.010

Vasant, P., & Vasant, P. (2012). Meta-Heuristics Optimization Algorithms in Engineering. In Business, Economics, and Finance. IGI Global.

Velez-Langs, O. (2005). Genetic algorithms in oil industry: An overview. *Journal of Petroleum Science Engineering, 47*(1–2), 15–22. doi:10.1016/j.petrol.2004.11.006

Wang, H., Wu, W., Chen, T., Dong, X., & Wang, G. (2019). An improved neural network for TOC, S1 and S2 estimation based on conventional well logs. *Journal of Petroleum Science Engineering.*

Wang, P., Chen, Z., Pang, X., Hu, K., Sun, M., & Chen, X. (2016). Revised models for determining TOC in shale play: Example from Devonian Duvernay shale, Western Canada sedimentary basin. *Marine and Petroleum Geology*, *70*, 304–319. doi:10.1016/j.marpetgeo.2015.11.023

Wang, P., & Peng, S. (2018). A New Scheme to Improve the Performance of Artificial Intelligence Techniques for Estimating Total Organic Carbon from Well Logs. *Energies*, *11*(4), 747. doi:10.3390/en11040747

Wang, P., Peng, S., & He, T. (2018). A novel approach to total organic carbon content prediction in shale gas reservoirs with well logs data, Tonghua Basin, China. *Journal of Natural Gas Science and Engineering*, *55*, 1–15. doi:10.1016/j.jngse.2018.03.029

Wei, L. Y., Saratchandran, P., & Narasimman, S. (1999). Radial Basis Function Neural Networks With Sequential Learning, Progress. In *Neural Processing* (Vol. 11). World Scientific.

Williams, R. J., & Zipser, D. (1989). A learning algorithm for continually running fully recurrent neural networks. *Neural Computation*, *1*(2), 270–280. doi:10.1162/neco.1989.1.2.270

Wunsch, D. C. II, Hasselmo, M., Venayagamoorthy, K., & Wang, D. (2003). *Advances in Neural Network Research: IJCNN 2003*. Elsevier Science Inc.

Yuan, C., Zhou, C. C., Song, H., Cheng, X. Z., & Dou, Y. (2014). Summary on well logging evaluation method of total organic carbon content in formation. *Diqiu Wulixue Jinzhan*, *29*(6), 2831–2837.

Zadeh, L. A. (1965). Fuzzy sets. *Information and Control*, *8*(3), 338–353. doi:10.1016/S0019-9958(65)90241-X

Zhang, S., Wang, J., Tao, X., Gong, Y., & Zheng, N. (2017). Constructing deep sparse coding network for image classification. *Pattern Recognition*, *64*, 130–140. doi:10.1016/j.patcog.2016.10.032

Zhu, L., Zhang, C., Zhang, C., Wei, Y., Zhou, X., Cheng, Y., ... Zhang, L. (2018). Prediction of total organic carbon content in shale reservoir based on a new integrated hybrid neural network and conventional well logging curves. *Journal of Geophysics and Engineering*, *15*(3), 1050–1061. doi:10.1088/1742-2140/aaa7af

Zoveidavianpoor, M., Samsuri, A., & Shadizadeh, S. R. (2012). Fuzzy logic in candidate-well selection for hydraulic fracturing in oil and gas wells: A critical review. *International Journal of Physical Sciences*, *7*(26), 4049–4060.

Zoveidavianpoor, M., Samsuri, A., & Shadizadeh, S. R. (2013). Prediction of compressional wave velocity by an artificial neural network using some conventional well logs in a carbonate reservoir. *Journal of Geophysics and Engineering*, *10*(4), 045014. doi:10.1088/1742-2132/10/4/045014

Zupan, J., & Gasteiger, J. (1991). Neural networks: A new method for solving chemical problems or just a passing phase? *Analytica Chimica Acta*, *248*(1), 1–30. doi:10.1016/S0003-2670(00)80865-X

Chapter 5
Bidirectional GRU–Based Attention Model for Kid-Specific URL Classification

Rajalakshmi R.
School of Computing Science and Engineering, Vellore Institute of Technology, Chennai, India

Hans Tiwari
School of Electronics Engineering, Vellore Institute of Technology, Chennai, India

Jay Patel
School of Electronics Engineering, Vellore Institute of Technology, Chennai, India

Rameshkannan R.
School of Computing Science and Engineering, Vellore Institute of Technology, Chennai, India

Karthik R.
Vellore Institute of Technology, Chennai, India

ABSTRACT

The Gen Z kids highly rely on internet for various purposes like entertainment, sports, and school projects. There is a demand for parental control systems to monitor the children during their surfing time. Current web page classification approaches are not effective as handcrafted features are extracted from the web content and machine learning techniques are used that need domain knowledge. Hence, a deep learning approach is proposed to perform URL-based web page classification. As the URL is a short text, the model should learn to understand where the important information is present in the URL. The proposed system integrates the strength of attention mechanism with recurrent convolutional neural network for effective learning of context-aware URL features. This enhanced architecture improves the design of kids-relevant URL classification. By conducting various experiments on the benchmark collection Open Directory Project, it is shown that an accuracy of 0.8251 was achieved.

DOI: 10.4018/978-1-7998-1192-3.ch005

INTRODUCTION

Nowadays, everyone relies on the web and the internet has become the primary source for seeking information for various needs ranging from education to entertainment. Especially, children prefer to use the search engine for doing their school projects and assignments. In 2012, Yvonne et. al presented their study on the information seeking behavior of young children on the search engines. To enhance the searching for learning task, Ion Madrazo Azpiazu developed a web search environment that is suitable for children and teachers and analyzed the issues faced by them (Azpiazu et. al, 2017). To understand the search behavior of children, Nevena Dragovic analyzed the query logs and proposed a method to differentiate the general queries from the children queries (Dragovic, Azpiazu, and Pera, 2010). It is evident from the above listed research works that, the Gen Z kids rely on the web for seeking information and the role of web in their daily life. However, most of the children are not monitored during their surfing time and it is important to analyse the suitability of the web page. So, we are in need of an automated system that can help to determine the kids-relevant web page. The traditional method of content based classification is not suitable, as the kids related content of the web page is highly dynamic in nature. Many approaches have been explored in the literature to determine the suitability of the web pages for children (Patel and Singh, 2016 & Gyllstrom et. al, 2010). When the web page has animated videos or if the textual content is not available in such web pages, the traditional content based methods cannot be applied for classifying the web pages. Tatiana et al. (2010) have performed a survey on information retrieval system for children. They outlined the search query, search strategy and the navigation style used by children and discussed the need for a separate page ranking algorithm for children web pages. To rank the child related web pages according to the relevance, Gyllstrom et al. (2010) suggested a link based algorithm. Zhang et al. (2006) analysed the role of URLs in finding the objectionable content, but in their approach, they have combined the content and the URLs for classifying the web page. But an effective way to find the Kids–relevant web page is to make use of the links that they visit during their browsing time. Hence, a simple URL based classifier method is suggested to address the problems found in content based classification approaches.

In this research, we have proposed a deep learning method to classify Kids-specific web page by extracting features from URLs alone. For URL classification, tokens based features are suggested in literature (Kan, 2004 & Baykan et. al, 2011). The advantage of token based approach is that, high precision can be achieved as they reflect the topic of a web page. However, in many cases, the tokens may be misspelled or shortened for making the URL fancy / funny / catchy. So, we have integrated an auto spelling correction method in this system. The URL is a sequence of tokens that are delimited by some characters like:, /, ., - etc. Also it may contain terms that are clueless to guess the topic it talks about. In some cases, the terms may be ambiguous, and may have different meaning based on the context. In traditional methods of URL classification, only the terms present in the URL are taken into account in the form of token features or n-gram features and the context of the terms are not considered. In the proposed work, in order to obtain context of the token, we have used word embedding. The URL contains a sequence of tokens and hence we applied a Recurrent Neural Network and tried to make use of sequence information also for classification of web pages. For example, consider an URL, https://www.education. com/kids-know-it/. The tokens 'education' and 'kids' are not adjacent to each to other, but if we use a Bi-directional Recurrent Neural Network, this information can be better utilized for classification. The earlier systems are limited by the hand-crafted features. In this research work, an attempt is made to learn the rich features automatically from the URL by applying Convolutional Neural Network, instead of relying on the hand crafted features.

In this research work, the problem of determining the Kids-relevant web page is studied in detail by combining the advantages of Recurrent Neural Network (RNN) and Convolutional Neural Network (CNN). This combined model is termed as Recurrent Convolutional Neural Network (RCNN). Even though RCNN model is found to be effective compared to simple RNN or CNN, all the terms in the URL are treated with equal importance in this model. But in some situations, the context may not depend on the entire sequence of tokens, but limited to a set of key terms. To give high importance to few terms and to aggregate all this information in building a better model, we have combined an attention layer with the proposed RCNN architecture. With this attention mechanism, the key terms will be assigned with the higher weight compared to the common terms. This can enhance the performance of Kids-relevant URL classifier. We have conducted various experiments on the bench mark collection ODP dataset by considering 90,560 URLs and studied the effectiveness of various deep learning architectures. We have also evaluated our approach on a real time collection of URLs that are self-collected by sending the queries to the search engine. From the experimental results, we found that attention based BGRU with CNN is the suitable method for classifying the web pages as Kids-specific or not, and we have achieved an accuracy of 82.51% in this approach. The proposed approach was compared with the existing techniques and there is a significant improvement.

The major highlights of the proposed approach are listed as follows:

- A deep learning model is proposed to classify the Kids-relevant web page based on URLs.
- This is the first attempt that considers the advantages of two different deep learning architectures namely Bidirectional Gated Recurrent Unit (BGRU) and Convolutional Neural Network (CNN) for Kids-relevant URL classification.
- Another major highlight of this work is the integration of attention mechanism with Bidirectional Gated Recurrent Unit and Convolutional Neural Network for effective classification
- The system is evaluated on a benchmark collection Open Directory Project and the comparative analysis shows significant improvement.

The remaining sections of the paper are organized as follows: The related works are presented in the Section 2, followed by the proposed methodology in Section 3. The experimental set up and the result discussion are detailed in Section 4. The concluding remarks are presented in Section 5.

BACKGROUND

Palon Jacovi et. al (2018) have done a detailed study on the application of Convolutional Neural Network for text classification. They have shown that a single filter can detect several semantics patterns in the text. Also, it is shown that the filters help not only to identify the good n-grams in the text, but also to suppress the bad n-grams. The problem of categorizing the web pages can be thought as a document classification problem. As the contents are not limited to text alone and also dynamic in nature, URL based web page classification has gained popularity in recent years and it has been studied by various researchers. Many methods (Rajalakshmi and Aravindan, 2018a & Kan, 2004 & Rajalakshmi and Xavier, 2017 & Kan and Thi, 2005 & Rajalakshmi and Aravindan, 2018b & Baykan et. al, 2011) have been suggested by extracting tokens or n-grams from the URLs and various machine learning techniques such as Naïve Bayes classifier, SVM etc. were applied for classification. By using Maximum Entropy binary classifier with n-gram (n = 4 to 8) URL features, Eda Baykan et. al (2011) tried to find the category of a webpage. Instead of designing a binary classifier, a direct multiclass classifier was preferred in to classify the web pages of all ODP categories (Rajalakshmi and Arivandan, 2018b). A supervised feature selection method was proposed for Naïve Bayes classifier with a rejection framework and the URL classifier was designed. The significance of considering the n-gram features and various feature weighting methods were explored by considering a small WebKB dataset to classify the University web pages (Rajalakshmi and Xavier, 2017). A comparative study of various feature weighting methods and the deep learning methods are studied in (Sivakumar and Rajalakshmi, 2019). However, the application of deep learning models for URL classification has not been explored much.

Saxe et. al (2017) have proposed a character level based Convolutional Neural Network to extract the features automatically to detect the malicious URLs. It is applied for the cyber security problem and they have not relied only on the URLs, but extracted features from file paths and registry keys also. All the existing methods try to select the suitable features by applying the traditional machine learning algorithms and considered the features from the URLs alone. The context of the terms in URL is not explored much and the power of deep learning techniques has not been utilized. In Rajalakshmi and Ramrag (2019), a character embedding based CNN model has been proposed to assist in health information search. To perform this task, an ensemble learning approach was suggested by extracting the features from the URLs alone and significant improvement has been achieved. In another work, Rajalakshmi, Ramraj, and Rameshkannan (2019), character level convolutional neural network has been applied and the features learnt from CNN was used to train the machine learning models such as Naive Bayes, XGB and SVM classifiers for identifying the malicious domain from DGA generated domain names. This transfer learning approach is found to be better than the other methods. But, the sequence information was not considered in this approach also. While simple convolutional kernels were used in a number of previous studies, determining the correct window size is still found to be difficult. If the window size is smaller, it results in loss of information and a larger window end up with an unnecessarily large parameter space, which results in difficulty in training.

Zhou et. al (2018) has proposed attention based approach for classifying the short text in Chinese language. They have combined the word level and character level attention for selecting the informative contents from the Chinese text. Aris et. al (2018) have suggested an attention based deep learning model for mining protein interactions and mutations in precision medicine. Yang et. al (2016) proposed a method for classifying the documents using hierarchical attention based models. Recurrent Neural Network (RNN) model analyses a text, word by word and stores the semantics of all the previous text in a fixed-sized hidden layer. Contextual information capturing is the major advantage of this model. However, one of the drawbacks of it is the presence of bias which reduces the overall effectiveness when it is capturing the semantics of an entire document, the reason being the occurrence of key components anywhere in the document instead at only the end.

In the URL also, the above problem exists as the topic class of the web page can be predicted in a better way, if the entire sequence is considered independent of its position in the URL. To overcome the limitations mentioned in the above models, Recurrent Convolutional Neural Network (RCNN) has been suggested. In the proposed approach, the combination of Recurrent Neural Network and Convolutional Neural Network has been applied to classify the URLs as kids - relevant or not. By this approach, an attempt is made to learn the token features along with their sequence and the context information. To discard the irrelevant tokens and to retain the significant URL features, the attention based mechanism is introduced with RCNN based model. The details of the proposed methodology are described in the following sections.

PROPOSED METHODOLOGY

The objective of the proposed work is to determine the topic of a web page as Kids – relevant or not. As the content based approaches are not suitable for this task, and due to the dynamic nature of web, URL based classification may be performed. In general, the URL consists of sequence of tokens. For example, consider the URL, https://www.education.com/kids-know-it/. In this URL, 'education', 'com', 'kids', 'know' and 'it' are said to be tokens. The overall architecture of the proposed system is presented in Figure 1.

The input URLs are pre-processed by tokenizing it and stop words, special character are removed, followed by Porter stemming. In general, the tokens in the URL need not be meaningful, so auto spell check feature is included. These pre-processed tokens are represented as a vector by adding an embedding layer. To learn the appropriate and rich features, Convolutional Neural Network is employed. Then, a Bidirectional GRU is used to obtain the sequence information from the URL. Finally, an attention layer is added to retain the significant features and the suitable deep learning model is built. This trained model is used for predicting the category of an unseen URL as Kids-relevant or not.

The proposed system consists of the following stages viz.,

1. Input Layer
2. Embedding layer
3. Convolutional Neural Network
4. Bidirectional Gated Recurrent Unit
5. Attention Layer
6. Output layer

Figure 1. The overview of the proposed URL based deep learning model

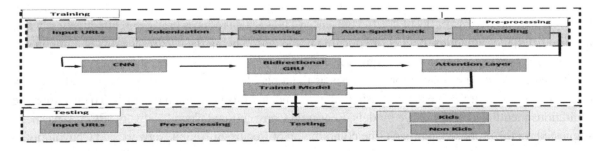

Input Layer

To make the URL suitable for input layer, the following pre-processing steps are to be performed: removal of the special characters, conversion of all the alphabetical characters to lower case, removal of stop words using porter stemmer algorithm. By this, tokens are separated and every URL is represented as

a collection of tokens. Let U = {t1, t2, t3, ….tn}. In general, the tokens of URL may not be meaningful and may be a shortened word. An auto-spell correction feature is added with the Symspell library. This library supports compound aware automatic spelling correction of multiple words in the input. By this algorithm, it is possible to correct the misspelled word. This spelling correction algorithm is million times faster through Symmetric Delete spelling correction and is the suitable choice for obtaining the correct URL token on the fly. Next, tokenization is performed followed by padding.

Embedding Layer

In traditional machine learning algorithms, tokens act as features and the context information is not considered. So to represent any URL, keeping the tokens closer to each other is important. For this, we have used Global Vector for Word Representation (GloVe), which is an unsupervised learning algorithm used for representing words as vectors. In this work, GloVe is used to get the word vector (300 dimensional vector) for the tokens in every URL after pre-processing.

The pre-processed tokens need to be represented as a fixed length vector. Let x_i denote the k-dimensional word vector that corresponds to the ith token in the URL. We have the URL input, which is of varying size. In order to get a fixed length input, we have applied padding. Hence, each URL of length n is represented in Equation (1)

$$\tag{1}$$

where x_i represents the k dimensional word vector and $+$ denotes the concatenation operator.

Convolutional Neural Network

The application of Convolutional Neural Network (CNN) for the text classification problem has been increased in recent days, because of the significant performance of it. For this URL based classification, word based convolutions are applied by using CNN alone with pre-trained embedding from GloVe. The advantage of applying CNN for this task is that, a good representation of the input URL can be learnt automatically by the convolutional filters without providing the whole collection of tokens. CNNs are also found to be fast and effective. In this work, the kernel width is fixed to 300, as we have used the 300 dimensional vector in GloVe and the length of the kernel is 3, ie. we have restricted to 3 tokens at a time. So, these convolutional filters capture the features that are similar to word n-grams, but it is done in a more compact way.

The convolution operation involves a kernel that is applied to a window of m tokens for producing a new feature. A feature C_i is generated from a window of

tokens by

$$C_i = f\left(w.x_{i:i+m-1} + b\right) \tag{2}$$

Here b is the bias term and f is the non-linear function such as hyperbolic tangent. This filter is applied to each possible window of tokens in the URL { $x_{1:m} x_{2:m+1} x_{3:m+2} \cdots x_{n-m+1:n}$ } to produce the a feature map

$$C = [C_1, C_2, C_3, \ldots C_{n-m+1}] \tag{3}$$

The max pooling operation is applied on this feature map and maximum value is taken as the feature that corresponds to this particular filter. In this way, the most important feature is captured for each feature map. These learnt features are used as input for the recurrent layer in order to capture the sequence information also.

Recurrent Neural Network

In the CNN based Model, even though CNN learns the rich token features from the URL, the context information is not captured. It extracts the most informative tokens and considers their activations. For identifying the Kids related web page, the entire sequence of tokens present in URL may be considered, as some tokens in the initial parts of the URL may be related to other tokens in subsequent parts. To achieve this, RNN based approach is proposed in this paper. In RNNs, given an URL, when looking at a token, it tries to derive the relation from the previous tokens in that URL. That is, at any time step, to compute the output of current state, the previous output and the present input are considered. That is, at each time-step, the output of the previous step along with the next word vector xi in the URL, form the inputs to the hidden layer to produce a prediction output ($\hat{y}$) and output features ht . The inputs and outputs of each single neuron in this RNN based model is given below.

$$h_t = wfh_{t-1} + wh^x x_t \tag{4}$$

$$\hat{y} = w^s f\left(h_t\right) \tag{5}$$

Here, x_t are the word vectors corresponding to the URL corpus containing T tokens and h_t is the relationship to compute hidden layer output features at time step t. wh^x is the weight matrix used to condition the input word vector. h_{t-1} is the output of non-linear function in the previous time step. $\hat{y}$ is the output probability distribution over the vocabulary at each time step t. In this way, RNN is applied to find the confidence score, by using the previous token's context score (h_{t-1}) and the last observed word vector xt, .

Bidirectional Gated Recurrent Unit

The RNN will not derive contexts from the far behind tokens, for a lengthy URLs. To overcome this issue, Gated Recurrent Unit (GRU) has been widely used. In GRU, the amount of information to be passed to next state can be controlled. The update gate is used to decide the information that is to be passed to the next node, whereas the reset gate decides about the information that are needed to be discarded. Even though, this RNN based model is able to capture the context information, it is restricted to forward direction alone. In an URL, the tokens that appear in future depend on the previous tokens. In order to capture the dependency and information in both the directions, we have used Bidirectional GRU (BGRU). In this BGRU model, the context information is captured in both the directions.

Bidirectional Gated Recurrent Unit with CNN

To combine the advantages of CNN architecture to learn the importance of token features along with the context and sequence information, we have employed Bidirectional GRU with CNN. This combination of BGRU and CNN is found to be suitable for this URL classification problem. By this approach, the dependency between tokens present in different positions can also be determined. For example, consider the URL https://www.education.com/kids-know-it/. There is a possibility that token 'education' and 'kids' may not appear adjacent to each other, and may be present in different parts in the URL. To address this, the update and reset gates are used. The role of update gate in GRU is to carry this information back and forth, whereas the role of reset gate to discard the remaining tokens that are not directly contributing to this.

Attention Based Bidirectional Gated Recurrent Unit with CNN

In an URL, some tokens present in different parts of it may be relevant and the need higher weightage among them. So in order to give more attention to those terms, we have introduced an attention layer on top of this RCNN model. The advantage of attention model is that, it did not give equal importance to all the terms; instead it gives more attention and computes the sum of weights of the key tokens that are important at each time to decide the output state.

Output Layer

The final output layer is the dense layer with the soft-max activation function. We have set the number of output neurons to be two for the task of predicting the URL as a Kids-relevant web page or not.

RESULTS AND DISCUSSION

To study the performance of the proposed approach, we have conducted various experiments with benchmark collection Open Directory Project (ODP) data set. All the experiments have been carried out on a workstation with Intel Xeon QuadCore Processor, 32 GB RAM, and Ubuntu 16.04 LTS and used Keras for implementation.

Dataset Description

The ODP dataset is a publicly available and it has been used as a benchmark data set for many web page classification tasks by various researchers. To perform the proposed Kids-specific URL classification, a total of 46280 positive samples (URLs) from Kids category have been considered. An equal number of negative samples are taken from all the remaining categories of ODP such as Adults, Arts, Business, Computers etc. to perform binary classification. In this research, 80% of URLs were considered for training and 20% was kept aside for testing. Hence, the training set consists of 74048 URLs and the remaining 18512 URLs were reserved for testing.

Selection of Hyper-Parameters

The performance of the deep learning models depends on the selection of optimal hyper parameters. The grid search technique was applied to select the suitable parameters. The learning rate was fixed to 0.001 and the drop-out probability of 0.2 was assumed. The RMSprop optimizer was applied with momentum 0.2 with a ReLU activation function. As URLs are short text, a maximum length of input was fixed as 30 and vocabulary size as 20,000. All the experiments were carried out for 75 epochs with a batch size of 128.

Experiment-1: CNN Based Model

CNN was used to learn the features automatically from the given URL in the first experiment. The model was trained for 75 epochs with the selected hyper-parameters. An accuracy of 0.7314 was achieved. However, it is not guaranteed that, each token in the URL might be correctly spelled. To make these tokens meaningful, an automatic spelling correction was added using Symspell library. The model was retrained with the autocorrected input and accuracy 0.7521 was achieved.

Experiment-2: RNN Based Model

The dependence between the adjacent tokens in the URLs needs to be considered for better classification. So, second experiment was conducted by applying RNN based approach. Among the RNN based models, two widely used variants are tried namely LSTM and GRU.

Choice of LSTM / GRU

The features that are learnt automatically using CNN serve as the rich features. To learn the long term dependency between tokens, RNN based model is preferred. As a first variant, LSTM was applied and an accuracy of 0.7254 was obtained. Also, GRU based model was trained with the same parameters mentioned above. It was observed that GRU based RNN model was comparatively faster and computationally efficient, yielding an accuracy of 0.7792. For URL classification, the classification has to be performed on the fly with less computational complexity. Hence, GRU serve as the better choice when compared to LSTM.

Bidirectional GRU based RNN

The above GRU based RNN processes the input sequence in temporal order without considering the future context. But for URL classification, the context not solely depends on past sequence. Hence, this experiment considered both past and future sequence to construct a bidirectional GRU based RNN model. An accuracy of 0.7962 was obtained.

Experiments-3 Combination of Bidirectional GRU with CNN

By applying CNN, context based rich features were extracted in experiment-1. Considering the significance of sequence information, experiment-2 was conducted using RNN. But for URL classification, these rich features can be combined with sequence information by considering the context in both directions. Hence, this experiment was conducted by combining CNN with bidirectional GRU. The context rich features generated by CNN are given as input to bidirectional GRU for further classification. This model was trained for 75 epochs and accuracy with 0.8204 was obtained.

Experiment-4 Attention based Bidirectional GRU with CNN

The above experiment using BGRU with CNN gives equal weightage to all tokens for training. From the input collection of tokens, only a few set of features may aid in identifying the correct context of the URL. Such features need to be weighted high to improve the classification accuracy. Hence, Attention mechanism was included on top of the architecture presented in Experiment 3. In this experiment, an accuracy of 0.8251 has been achieved.

Performance Analysis

The cumulative summary of all the experiments are highlighted in Table 1. It could be observed that the proposed attention based method yielded better accuracy when compared to the other methods.

The performance of the proposed approach was compared against the existing methods and the resultant observations are presented in Table 1. By applying various techniques, the problem of identifying the kids related web sites have been addressed by various researchers. Content based methods were applied in (Patel and Singh, 2016 & Zhang, Qin, and Yan, 2006). These methods may not be suitable if the contents of the webpage changes dynamically. Also these methods are time consuming and result in waste of bandwidth and the accuracy reported were in the range of 75%. Few works (Baykan et. al, 2011

Table 1. The performance of the proposed method

Methods	Accuracy
CNN	0.7521
RNN with LSTM	0.7254
RNN with Bidirectional GRU	0.7962
Bidirectional GRU with CNN	0.8204
RCNN with Attention	0.8251

& Abdallah and Iglasia, 2014), were reported for URL classification using traditional machine learning techniques like SVM, Maximum Entropy Classifier, etc. The accuracy of the all-gram features is 0.801 (Baykan et. al, 2011). But this methodology is not suitable for large scale data, as deriving n-grams (n=4 to 8) results in lot of redundant features and no feature selection method was applied. In Abdallah and Iglasia (2014), language modelling approach was applied by considering 4-grams alone. They have achieved an accuracy of 0.8109. In both the above methods, as n-grams are considered, it will increase the dimensionality of feature space and it depends on the size of training data. Also the context of the URL was not considered.

The performance of the above method solely relies on the hand engineering features and is error prone. In this research, an attempt is made using deep learning based approach for URL classification. It could be observed that the proposed attention based method was able to capture and learn the context aware URL features in an efficient way. As the bidirectional GRU is applied, the sequence information in both the directions can also be utilized for classification in addition to automatically extracting rich context information from the URL by using CNN. The attention mechanism that is combined with CNN and BGRU plays a major role in filtering the unnecessary features by giving more attention to the significant URL features. An accuracy of 0.8251 was obtained, which is a significant improvement over the existing works as shown in Table 2.

CONCLUSION

The life style of everyone is getting changed in this digital era and the usage of internet by children has increased dramatically. The content based systems are found to be less effective due to the increased growth of internet. In this research, an attention based bidirectional GRU with CNN was employed to classify the input URLs as Kids specific or not. The proposed approach extracts the context aware rich features automatically using CNN and then combines it with BGRU to maintain the sequence information in both directions. The major highlight of this work is the integration of attention mechanism on top of the BGRU with CNN architecture. With the proposed attention based deep learning model, the irrelevant features are filtered and only the context aware URL features are retained for further classification. Based on the experimental analysis performed with ODP dataset, it is shown that the performance of the proposed method was significantly better than the existing works and an accuracy of 82.5% has been achieved. This work can be improved by considering the character level embedding instead of word embedding.

Table 2. Comparative study of the proposed approach

Methods	Accuracy
All-gram features (Baykan et. al)	0.801
Language Model (Tarek Abdullah et. al)	0.8109
Proposed approach – Attention based Bidirectional GRU with CNN	0.8251

ACKNOWLEDGMENT

The authors would like to thank the management of Vellore Institute of Technology, Chennai for extending their support. The first author would like to thank the Department of Science and Engineering Research Board (SERB), Govt. of India for their financial support (Award Number: ECR/2016/00484) for this research work.

REFERENCES

Abdallah & De La Iglasia. (2014). URL based web page classification: With n-gram language models. *Proceedings of the International Joint Conference on Knowledge Discovery, Knowledge Engineering and Knowledge Management, 1*, 14 - 21.

Azpiazu, I. M., Dragovic, N., Pera, M. S., & Fails, J. A. (2017). Online searching and learning: YUM and other search tools for children and teachers. *Inf Retrieval J, 20*(5), 524–545. doi:10.100710791-017-9310-1

Baykan, E., Henzinger, M., Ludmila, M., & Weber, I. (2011). A comprehensive study of features and algorithms for URL-based topic classification. *ACM Transactions on the Web, 5*(3), 1–29. doi:10.1145/1993053.1993057

Dragovic, Azpiazu, & Pera. (2010). "Is Sven Seven?": A Search Intent Module for Children. *SIGR 2010*, 847-848.

Fergadis, A., Baziotis, C., Pappas, D., Papageorgiou, H., & Potamianos, A. (2018). Hierarchical bidirectional attention-based RNNs for supporting document classification on protein–protein interactions affected by genetic mutations. *Database*, 1–10. PMID:30137284

Gossen, T., & Nurnberger, A. (2010). *Specifics of Information Retrieval for Young Users: A Survey. In Information Processing and Management*. Elsevier.

Gyllstrom, K. Moens & Marie-Francine (2010). Wisdom of the Ages: Toward Delivering the Children's Web with the Link-based Age rank Algorithm. *Proceedings of the 19th ACM International Conference on Information and Knowledge Management, CIKM '10*, 159-168.

Jacovi, A., Shalom, O. S., & Haifa, I. (2018). Understanding Convolutional Neural Networks for Text Classification. *Proceedings of the 2018 EMNLP Workshop Blackbox NLP: Analyzing and Interpreting Neural Networks for NLP*, 56-65. 10.18653/v1/W18-5408

Kammerer, Y., & Bohnacker, M. (2012). Children's Web Search With Google: The Effectiveness of Natural Language Queries. *Proceedings of the 11th International Conference on Interaction Design and Children*, 184-187. 10.1145/2307096.2307121

Kan, M.-Y. (2004). Web page classification without the web page. In *Proceedings of the 13th International World Wide Web conference on Alternate track papers & posters (WWWAlt. '04)*. ACM. 10.1145/1013367.1013426

Kan, M.-Y., & Thi, H. O. N. (2005). *Fast webpage classification using URL features. Technical Report*. Singapore: National University of Singapore.

Patel, D., & Singh, P. K. (2016). Kids Safe Search Classification Model. *Proceedings of IEEE International Conference on Communication and Electronics Systems (ICCES)*, 1-7.

Rajalakshmi, R., & Aravindan, C. (2013). Web Page Classification using n-gram based URL Features. *IEEE Proceedings of International Conference on Advanced Computing (ICoAC 2013)*, 15–21. 10.1109/ICoAC.2013.6921920

Rajalakshmi, R., & Aravindan, C. (2018). An effective and discriminative feature learning for URL based web page classification, *International IEEE Conference on Systems, Man and Cybernetics – SMC 2018*.

Rajalakshmi, R., & Aravindan, C. (2018). *Naive Bayes Approach for URL Classification with Supervised Feature Selection and Rejection Framework. In Computational Intelligence*. Wiley; doi:10.1111/coin.12158

Rajalakshmi, R., & Ramraj, S. (2019). A deep learning approach for URL based Health Information Search. *International Journal of Innovative Technology and Exploring Engineering, 8*, 642–646.

Rajalakshmi, R., Ramraj, S., & Rameshkannan, R. (2019). *Transfer Learning Approach for Identification of Malicious Domain Names. In Security in Computing and Communications*. Springer.

Rajalakshmi, R., & Xavier, S. (2017). Experimental study of feature weighting techniques for URL based web page classification. *Procedia Computer Science, 115*, 218–225. doi:10.1016/j.procs.2017.09.128

Saxe, J., & Berlin, K. (2017). *eXpose: A Character-Level Convolutional Neural Network with Embeddings For Detecting Malicious URLs, File Paths and Registry Keys*. arXiv:1702.08568

Sivakumar, S., & Rajalakshmi, R. (2019). Comparative evaluation of various feature weighting methods on movie reviews. In H. S. Behera, J. Nayak, B. Naik, & A. Abraham (Eds.), *Computational Intelligence in Data Mining. AISC* (Vol. 711, pp. 721–730). Singapore: Springer; doi:10.1007/978-981-10-8055-5_64

Yang, Z., Yang, D., Dyer, C., He, X., Smola, A. J., & Hovy, E. H. (2016). *Hierarchical Attention Networks for Document Classification*. HLT-NAACL. doi:10.18653/v1/N16-1174

Yin, W., Kann, K., Yu, M., & Schütze, H. (2017). *Comparative Study of CNN and RNN for Natural Language Processing*. Academic Press.

Zhang, J., Qin, J., & Yan, Q. (2006). The role of URLs in objectionable web content categorization. *Proceedings of the IEEE/WIC/ACM International Conference on Web Intelligence (WI 2006)*. 10.1109/WI.2006.170

Zhou, Y., Xu, J., Cao, J., Xu, B., Li, C., & Xu, B. (2018). Hybrid Attention Networks for Chinese Short Text Classification. *Computación y Sistemas, 21*(4). doi:10.13053/cys-21-4-2847

Chapter 6
Classification of Fundus Images Using Neural Network Approach

Anoop Balakrishnan Kadan

(iD) https://orcid.org/0000-0003-4288-5065

Vimal Jyothi Engineering College, India

Perumal Sankar Subbian

Toc H Institute of Science and Technology, India

Jeyakrishnan V.

Saintgits College of Engineering, India

Hariharan N.

Adi Shankara Institute of Engineering and Technology, Ernakulam, India

Roshini T. V.

(iD) https://orcid.org/0000-0002-3437-0726

Vimal Jyothi Engineering College, India

Sravani S. Nath

Vimal Jyothi Engineering College, India

ABSTRACT

Diabetic retinopathy (DR), which affects the blood vessels of the human retina, is considered to be the most serious complication prevalent among diabetic patients. If detected successfully at an early stage, the ophthalmologist would be able to treat the patients by advanced laser treatment to prevent total blindness. In this study, a technique based on morphological image processing and fuzzy logic to detect hard exudates from DR retinal images is explored. The proposed technique is to classify the eye by using a neural network approach (classifier) to predict whether it is affected or not. Here, a classifier is added before the fuzzy logic. This fuzzy will tell how much and where it is affected. The proposed technique will tell whether the eye is abnormal or normal.

DOI: 10.4018/978-1-7998-1192-3.ch006

INTRODUCTION

There are three major complications of diabetes which lead to blindness. They are retinopathy, cataracts and glaucoma among which diabetic retinopathy (DR) is considered as the most serious complication affecting the blood vessels in the retina. DR occurs when tiny vessels swell and leak fluid or abnormal new blood vessels grow hampering normal vision. The early stage of DR is referred to as microaneurysm which appears as tiny, dark red spots or minuscule haemorrhages forming clusters with circular shape. The size varies from 10 to 100 and it ap- proximates to 1/12th diameter of an average optic disc. Haemorrhages, that appear inside deeper layers of the retina, form a round or flame shape. However, when they appear in large numbers, such a feature is considered as non-proliferative retinopa- thy. Cotton wool spots are yellowish white, fluffy lesions in the nerve fibre layer and are also called soft exudates. These spots are created as a result of swelling of the nerve fibre axons. Although soft exudates are very common in DR, hard exu- dates are typically bright, reflective and not common in DR. They appear as white or cream coloured lesions on the retina with different sizes. Each hard exudate con- sists of blood plasma and lipids leaked from blood vessels. The aim of this research is to develop a system to detect hard exudates in DR using non-dilated DR images. The exudates are identified using morphological methods and categorised into hard exudates and non-hard exudates using an adaptive fuzzy algorithm. Detection and treatment of DR at an early stage help prevent total blindness. Therefore, early detection of DR is very important because the ophthalmolo- gist would then be able to treat the patients by advanced laser treatment.

Hard exudates are one of the features of diabetic retinopathy. These are yellowish waxy spots occurs due to lipid deposits. It can be seen on posterior pole and are arranged on macular area as stars or spots. This can be illustrated in Figure 1.

They are usually deposited on retinal veins. One of the early signs of diabetic retinopathy is referred as microaneurysms. If this appear as white spots and with no blood visible in the lumen are considered as hard exudates. This can be depicted as mild and severe conditions.

Details of Learning Algorithm

What is machine learning? As Arthur Samuel [1959] has said machine learning is the science of getting computers to learn without being explicitly programmed. He tested this in checkers player. The process of machine learning is introduced in figure 5.

Figure 1. Various stages of hard exudates seen as clusters

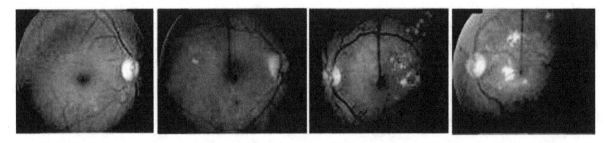

Figure 2. Images of the exudates a)mild b)moderate

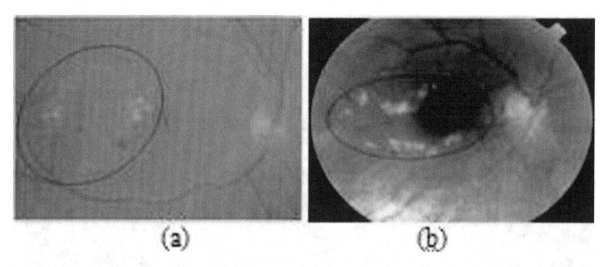

Figure 3. Images of fundus showing multiple microaneurysms (early sign of DR)

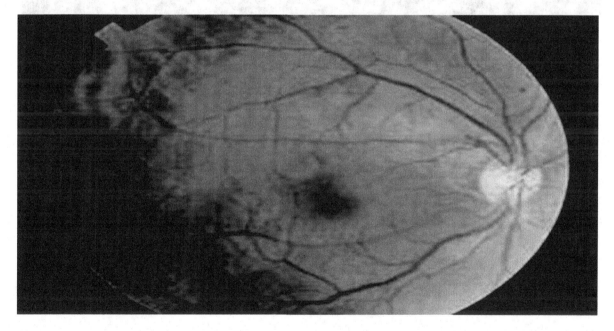

Machine learning is an application of AI (Artificial Intelligence).It provides the system the ability to learn and tackle from experiences without being explicitly code the program.Machine learning is used to learn,predict,and improvise graphically.It can be supervised learning where by knowing input and output.It could be unsupervised learning that is we dont know about output and we need to identify the patterns and make groups. The actual processing is done in machine learning algorithm.

The algorithm in this paper detects hard exudates in DR using the prin- ciples of mathematical morphology methods and fuzzy logic. At the initial stage, the exudates are identified using mathematical morphology. This stage can be di- vided into three sub-stages, namely, pre-processing, optic disc

Figure 4. Fundus image of eye (hard exudates can be seen)

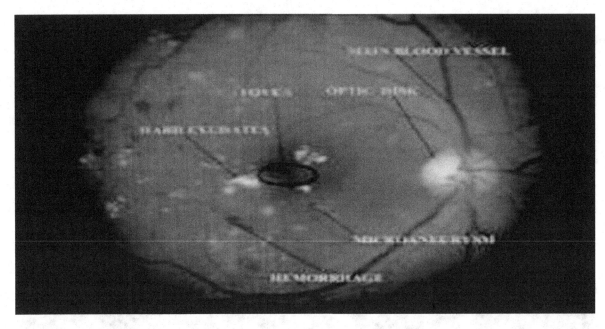

Figure 5. Process of machine learning

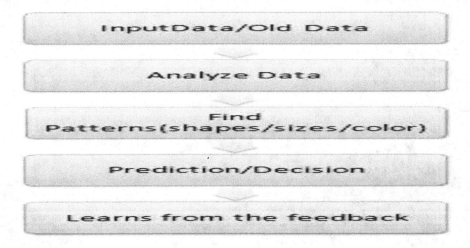

elimination and ex- udates detection. Initially, the RGB colour space in the original fundus image is converted to HSI space. Then, the median filter is applied to the intensity band of the image for noise suppression. Subsequently, the contrast limited adaptive his- togram equalisation was applied for contrast enhancement to prevent over satura- tion of the homogeneous areas in retinal image. The Gaussian function is applied for noise suppression. The colour fundus image is converted to HSI image and the I-band of the fundus image is used for further processing. Since the optic disc and exudates have high intensity values on the intensity channel, the RGB fundus image is transformed into HSI image and the intensity channel of the HSI image is taken for further processing.

Figure 6. Hard exudates on fundus image

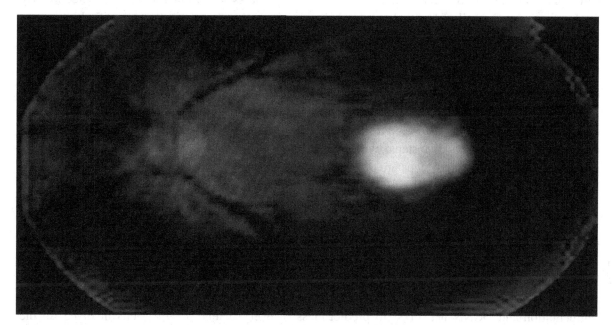

As RGB to HSI conversion is straightforward, it is not required to convert the RGB image to grey-scale as RGB to grey-scale conversion is not unique. To elimi- nate the optic disc, it is assumed that the component with the largest circular shape of a fundus image is the optic disc The second stage involves classification of eye as to detect if the eye is normal or abnormal using bayesian classifier. Later Fuzzy rules are formed using fuzzy sets derived from the RGB fundus image. These fuzzy rules are used to decide the presence of hard exudates in DR images.

In this chapter, gives details about the complications of diabetic retinopathy, definition of hard exudates, details of learning algorithm, and the ob- jective of the project and case report is further discussed. In the second section, theoretical investigations are reported. In the third section, methodology of the project is discussed and graphical representation of parameters depicted as by survey. Later on, in the fourth section existing system is studied. In the fifth section proposed work where the core idea is mentioned. In the sixth section first phase of the work is analysed with given output. Finally, conclusion and future work is further discussed. References are given.

LITERATURE SURVEY

Mrinal Haloi et al.Gaussian scale space approach, a novel method tech- nique is proposed which includes exudates detection and classification. Anisotropic diffusion filtering(preprocessing) is used to remove the noise from the images.These are done by preserving the edges. Two steps are involved in Gaussian scale space construction, this is to identify all exudates which was constructed. Morphological opera- tions (closing operations) and local thresholding techniques are applied for segmentation. In the closing operations features are enhanced. Latter, the interest map is converted to binary map. Support Vector Machines are used for classification of exudates. This is to get the information whether the exudates are soft or hard. Features of SVM, they are 22 dimensional. Exudates are checked by severity detection. By the International Council of Ophthalmology diabetic retinopathy is specifically clas- sified into many forms:none, mild, moderate, severe, proliferate. The severity of dis- eases are determined by location of exudates w.r.t fovea. Here, three datasets are in- volved that include 400 retinal images. They are DI-ARETD131 and e-ophtha EX dataset. The evaluation measures is of 96.54% and 98.35% for sensitivity and pre- diction (Haloi, Dandapat, and Sinha, 2018).

Jaeger in 1856 described diabetic macular edema recognition as round yel- low spots in whole thickness of retina. By using cascaded deep residual network technique diabetic macular edema is recognized or detected. This is done by two steps: by segmentation and classification results. In this approach pre-processing or post processing steps are omitted, instead segmentation and classification is done. Deep fully convolutional residual network (FCRN) is applied for exudate segmentation. It fuses multi-level features w.r.t fields. In exudates segmentation probability map is obtained. After exudates segmentation, cascaded deep residual networks is applied here. This network will take the location with maximum probability as the input and distinguish DME.169 fundus images(115 healthy and 54 exudates) and 82 retinal images(35 normal and 47 exudates) that of HEIMED and e-ophtha EX databases. Sensitivity of 96% and specificity of 93% (Mo, Zhang, and Feng, 2018).

Convolutional Neural Network is used for testing and training of data.U-Net (neural membranes segmentation)and DCNN networks (to predict class of every pixels) are the steps involved. In the preprocessing thresholding method, histogram equalization and normalization of data is performed in the input image. Contrast lim- ited adaptive equalization is in the preprocessing. Graphics processing unit (GPU)is of about 20 minute runtime.e-ophtha EX,DIARETDB1-V2,HEI-MED,Messidor are the images. It includes 30 images with exudates and 50 normal images from kag- gle. Images are seen as small patches (Li et. al, 2018).

To detect diabetic macular edema a novel machine learning model is pro- posed. Extraction of region (ROI) 512X512 sized images. The pixels are cropped by 48x48pixels.By data augumentation it reduces overfitting. Exudate detection model (CNN), DME classification model (6 convolutional and 3 fully connected networks) are the types of models used. In the e-ophtha dataset 47 color fundus images and in messidor dataset 1200 color fundus images (Perdomo et. al, 2016).

Automatic exudate segmentation method is proposed here for boosted exudates segmentation. This is done by Residual Nets. Authors proposed an archi- tecture that is novel end-to-end segmentation framework using ResNets (Residual nets).Automatic method for segmenting exudates in retinal images. CNN is used for automatic lesion and landmark detection.e-ophtha EX dataset (82 images with differ- ent size of images(1440x960px to 2544x1696px) and DIARETDB1 and DR2 public datasets are used here.89 color fundus images and 529 images are included (Abbasi-Sureshjani et. al, 2017). Ant colony optimization algorithm(ACO) performs better than kirsch filter. Swarm intelligence is another field of ACO. Its main purpose is edge detection, image seg- mentation, visual saliency detection and image thresholding. The evaluation mea- sures by using this proposed technique is much better than kirsch filter where sen- sitivity and specificity are of 80.8% and 99.16%.The images are normalized to improve algorithm capacity. Median filter is used for background estimation with 50x50 pixel kernel. Optic disc elimination is finalized by preprocessing (Ot, Perdomo, and Gonz, 2017).

Fuzzy Support Vector Machine (FSVM) classifier is used to detect the hard exudates in fundus images. Better discriminating power in the proposed technique than the conventional SVM. It is a novel based method. Dataset include canon CR6- 45NM retinal camera digital imaging system in JPEG format.200 retinal images are collected from diabetic retinopathy screening programmes. The criteria involved are optic disk removal, feature extraction, and classification. OD localization and OD segmentation (using morphological and edge based technique).29 features 9 for each pixel) where 25 features are law texture energy measures. FSVM classifier is divided into two: training phase and testing phase. FSVM classifier supported well than SVM classifier (Liu et. al, 2017).

A novel technique is proposed to automatically detect the exudates from DR patients retinal images. By neural network detection is done. The steps involved are preprocessing, contrast enhancement, feature extraction and learning, classification fi- nally. In the first stage of preprocessing, mean filtering is done that is used for the re- moval of noise. RGB color space is converted to lab color space and by replacing the luminosity. Contrast limited adaptive histogram equalization computes many his- tograms. Classification is done by neural network classifier where it classifies into exudates and non-exudates. Sensitivity and specificity is considered to be in better results that is96.3% and 99.8% (ManojKumar, Manjunath, and Sheshadri, 2015).

CNN approach is used in diagnosing digital fundus images and to classify its severity. The steps involved are preprocessing, training and augmentation. In pre- processing open CV software is used. Normalisation of color is implemented on images. Resized into 512x512 pixels. This is pre-trained on 10,290 images. Network was trained using stochastic gradient descent with nestrov momentum. To improve localization ability of the network augumentation is done. The evaluation measures include specificity, accuracy and sensitivity that is of 95%,75%,and 30%.CNN is used for real time classification (Deshmukh et. al, 2015).

C Agurto et al. describes for the detection and classification of different types of NPDR lesions. This includes microaneurysms, haemorrages, and exudates. This is caused due to increased amount of insulin.120 fundus images are used in this. The steps involved are preprocessing, retinal image analysis, and classification of the re- gions. In preprocessing mean-variance method is used. It will remove noise from the image using hue, saturation and intensity channels. For the blood vessel segmenta- tion Gabor wavelet and multilayer thresholding is done. Optic disc is localized using averaging filter. Morphological closing and opening operations are applied on im- ages to enhance the contrast. This is done by adaptive contrast-enhancement. Many features are used here like area, eccentricity, perimeter, mean-intensity, aspectratio, compactness, mean-HSV, mean enhanced intensity, mean gradient magnitude, mean-box gradient, third momententropy, and mean range energy. Bayesian classifier is used for classification(Gaussian mixture model).Evaluation measures include sensitivity and specificity and takes values of 97.83% and 98.36% (Agurto et. al, 2014).

A novel approach is done (by training deep CNN)with active learning. Here, dataset is split into three. Training split(8760 patches for each class),validation split(328/class) and test split(986/class).It contains 315 images with size 1440x960 px.268 images have no lesions and 47 contains exudates. In the labeled patch dataset 48x48 px contains exudates and healthy examples.This method generates masks for prediction and segments in ROI (Dashtbozorg, Mendonca, and Campilho, 2015).

M .U Akram et al. location to segmentation strategy is proposed. This strategy is used for automatic exudate segmentation in color retinal fundus images.Automatic structure removal where field view seg- mentation, main vessels segmenatation and optic disk segmentation are introduced. Thereafter location of exudates are detected. A random forest classifier is used for classification. This is done to classify the patches in fundus image whether it is exudates patches and exudates-free patches. This is to describe the texture structures.e-optha EX dataset is used. For image-level evalua- tion the database used here is DiaRetDB1 where 89 images. The resolution of the retinal fundus images is 2544x1696px.The evalua- tion results where sensitivity is of 76% (Akram et. al, 2014).

For the diagnosis of the retinopathy feature extraction is done. There is an abnormal thickness in the blood vessels where the intersection occurs. This can be found out by locating the optic disk approximately. It is then localized by using color images. Dataset of 51 images where taken for evaluating the results of the al- gorithm.5 images from local eye hospitals, 18 images from STARE database,13 im- ages from DIARETDB0 database and 15 images from DRIVE database. The steps involved are morphological (open and close)operations. Microaneurysms and haem- orrhages, blood vessels, exudates(hard and soft) are identified very accurately. Blood vessels and exudates are extracted by using open and close operations. Optic disk is detected by blood vessel extraction, exudate localization and detection, optic disk detection, microaneurysms and haemorrhages detection, and predicting the severity of diseases. The evaluation results is obtained (Patil et. al, 2016).

From local and mean entropy an algorithm is used to classify the hard exu- dates. Messidor database with total of 100 images is used for evaluating the algo- rithm. This database is publicly available. Images having the resolution of 2040x1448 pixels is in TIFF format. The steps involved are preprocessing, extraction and classi- fication.The images are classified accurately into normal and abnormal images (Balakrishnan, Venkatachalapathy, and Marimuthu, 2016).

A multiscale optimization approach is used to detect exudates in the macula region of the eye. Optical thresholding technique is used here. Two databases are used for testing purposes. UTHSCSA and MESSIDOR datasets are used here.652 images from UTHSCSA and 400 images are from MES-SIDOR sets.52 images are used for training purpose of the algorithm. No training sets are used for MESSI- DOR. The steps involved are preprocessing, amplitude-modulation and frequency modulation, parameter optimization, intensity constraint, morphology, feature extrac- tion, classification by SVM or KNN. Evaluation is done by adding up two datasets. The measures taken are sensitivity, specificity and accuracy (Welikala et. al, 2015).

C Pereira et al.optic disk is segmented by using sliding band filter. This is an automatic approach for OD segmentation using multiresolution filter. Public databases ONHSD,MESSIDOR and INSPIRE-AVR are used. The steps involved are prepro- cessing, estimation of low resolution of the optic disc, and OD segmentation. After the preprocessing stage, sliding band filter is applied. And to focus on ROI region. In segmentation it includes high resolution SBF and boundary, extraction (Pereira, Goncalves, and Ferreira, 2015).

T Jaya et al intelligent system is proposed for detection and grading of mac- ular edema. This is to assist ophthalmologists in early detection of the eye dis- ease. This is a novel method for the accurate detection of macula. It is applied by detailed feature set and Gaussian mixtures model based classifier. A hybrid classifier (Gaussian model) is introduced and a SVM for the accurate detection of macula. This will give reliable classification of retinal images in stages of macular edema. The evaluation measures obtained (Jaya, Dheeba, and Singh, 2015).

S W Franklin et al. automatic detection of exudates optic disc, blood ves- sels, blood clots are re-moved in two phases. These all are done by gradient vector flow snake algorithm and region growing segmentation algorithm. This method is applied for 850 test images. A high efficiency of 87% true exudates is obtained (Franklin and Rajan, 2014). An enhanced particle swarm optimization is another method for proposed.

It is a feature selection approach with biometric authentication for the identification of DR. It is used for preprocessing the images which are given at the input. A multi relevance vector machine is intro-duced. Here, images are classified into normal and abnormal. Evaluation results prove that it achieves good performance (Pratt et. al, 2016).

M Usman Akram et al., a dual classification approach is done. PDR (proliferative diabetic retinopathy) is a case where there is a growth of abnormal blood vessels. Independent classification is done on each feature vector. This is done by SVM (support vector machine) classifier. Dataset of 60 images are taken. The results are of good mea- sures (Usman et. al, 2014).

S Antelin Vijila et al, detected hard exudates in fundus images using cascaded correlation neural network classifier. Database used here consists of 300 retinal im- ages which are collected from the DR screening programmes from that 150 im- ages are normal fundus images. Neural network classifier has good performance. The method involves image acquisition, preprocessing, feature extraction and classifica- tion by neural network. In this histogram equalization is done for the RGB channel for image matching. TEM (Texture Energy Measures)are extracted for the image. The classifier identifies the image whether it is normal or abnormal images of fundus. For the classification CCNN or supervised learning architecture is used whether exu- dates are present or absent. Accuracy of 92.405% we get as output (Vijila and Rajesh, 2018).

Suvajit Dutta et al proposed a automated knowledge model that is by deep learning for the classifica- tion of diabetic retinopathy. The steps involved are prepro- cessing, feature extraction, fuzzy c means and neural networks. Median filter is used for removal of noise in the images. Edge detection by the use of canny edge method is highlighted. A standard clustering mechanism is used to identify member- ship in- formation from the image and FCM clustering method is applied here. Back prop- agation is used by the use of softmax layer. Image is trained by CNN method. The network is trained by the CPU support. For the densed feature images it works very well. The database used here is fundus image of human retina (kaggle.com).35000 images are used for training and testing. For the error check RMSE (Root Mean Square Error) is calculated. BNN is used for high error rate detection. DNN is having good performance rate compared to CNN (Sriman and Ivenger, 2018).

Godlin Atlas L et al detected exudates in color fundus images and char- acterized. It involves distin- guishing vein, recognize hemorrhages. and grouping of diabetic retinopathy. The database consists of 65 retinal images and characterized into normal, moderate NPDR and severe NPDR cases from STARE. The criteria are training stage, classification stage and output stage. The mean affectability is of 92.8% and mean prescient is of 92.4% respectively. Random forest classifier(RF)is used by tree-type classifiers for the classification of exudates (L, Sreeji, and Parasuraman, 2018).

T P Udhay Sankar et al proposed a technique to automatically detect and to classify the severity of diabetic retinopathy. The database includes 214 fundus im- ages which is taken from DIARETDB1.Clas- sification is done by ANN (Artificial Neural Network).Features such as area, perimeter and count from the lesions are used to classify the stages. In this proposed technique 96% of the accuracy is ob- tained (Sankar, Vijai, and Balajee, 2018).

Abhishek Vahadane et al predicted a label for the patches a deep convolu- tional neural network is used. And to predict the presence of DME,CNN rule based method is done (Vahadane et. al, 2018).

Figure 7. Block diagram

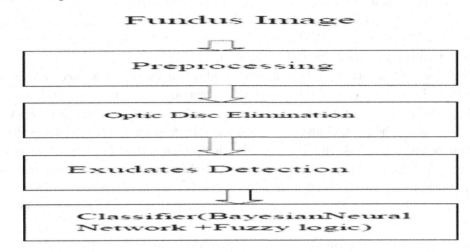

Figure 8. Plot of parameters

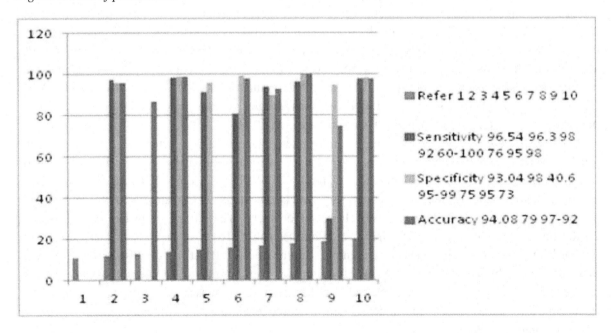

EXISTING METHODOLOGY

Study of Existing Systems

Here, the authors proposed a technique for detecting the exudates and then classifying them. Initially, hard exudates are identified by using morphological method(mathematical morphology).In this criteria it includes optic disc elimina- tion.And by using Fuzzy logic classification is done.

Figure 9. Preprocessed images a) Original fundus image b)HSI image c)Intensity band of the image d) Median filtering e)Contrast limited adaptive histogram equali- sation f)gaussian filtering

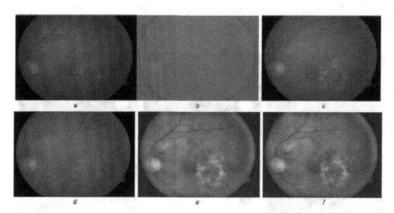

In the preprocessing stage, RGB color space is converted into HSI space after that I-band of the image is used for further processing. This is done in an original fundus image. Here, a median filter is applied for suppressing the noise that includes Gaussian function. Optic disc and exudates have high values of in- tensity. So there is no need to convert RGB to HSI and is straight forward and not unique. The second stage is about classification of exudates using fuzzy logic. This algorithm uses the values in RGB color space to form fuzzy sets and membership functions. Fuzzy output is calculated by corresponding RGB channels of a pixel in an exudates. Proposed technique is evaluated by detecting the exudates(hard exudates).The evaluation measures include sensitivity and specificity as 75.43% and 99.99% respectively.

Elimination of Optic Disc

At first, the closing operator with a flat disc shape structuring ele- ment is applied to the preprocessed image .The resultant image is binarised us- ing a thresholding technique. The new binary image consists of all the connected regions. Other than the background, the component having the largest number of pixels with circular shape contains the optic disc and therefore extracting this com- ponent separates the optic disc from all the other structures in the retinal image. If the largest connected component is the compactness. The compactness is measured by applying two thresholding techniques, namely, the P-tile method and Nilblacks method separately.

The optic disc can be considered as the largest connected component that provides high values of compactness among these two methods. In our algorithm, the optic disc is eliminated before detecting exudates as the optic disc and exudates contain similar colour and intensity. The resultant image after applying morpholog- ical closing operator with a flat disc to eliminate high contrast blood vessels.

Then, the optic disc could be identified as the largest circular connected com- ponent in the fundus image. A weight of 1.3 is used in Nilblacks method for thresh- olding. The region containing the optic disc is brighter than other regions in the retinal images. It was discovered that the optic disc occupies 2% of bright regions in fundus images with the rest being the background. This percentage is used to perform the percentile method to obtain the binary images.

The largest connected component which provides a value of high compactness among these two methods is considered as the optic disc. In this case, the binary image obtained after applying Nilblacks

Figure 10. Elimination of optic disc images a) applying morphological closing operator b)Threshold images using Nilblack's method c) Thresholded image us- ing percentile method d)large circular connected component e)Inverted binary with large circular component f)optic disc is eliminated from the preprocessed image

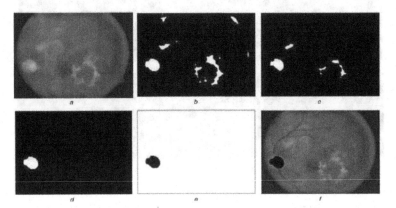

Figure 11. Output images of exudates detection stage a) applying morphological closing operator b) standard deviation of the image c)thresholded image using tri- angle method d)unwanted borders were removed e)holes are flood filled f)marker image g)morphological reconstructed image h)thresholded image i)result is super- imposed on original image

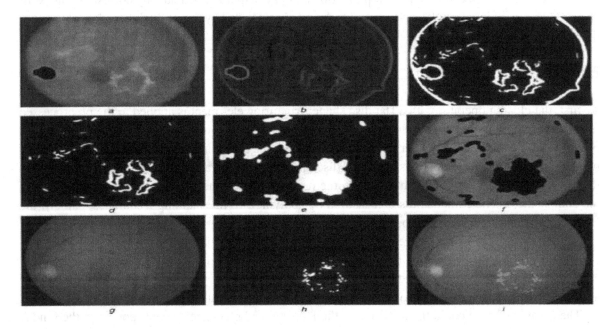

method provides a high compact- ness for the large circular component. Although the Hough transformation can also be used to isolate the optic disc in retinal images, the results are not accurate when its shape is not circular (e.g. elliptical). As such, we believe that the Hough trans- form is not a reliable method to detect the optic disc as all retinal images do not have circular optic discs.

Detection of Exudates

The next step in our strategy is to identify exudates from the image from which the optic disc was eliminated. The morphological closing operator with a flat disc shape structuring element is applied to image to remove blood vessels as both exudates and blood vessels exhibit high contrast We have applied a morphological closing operator with a radius of 16 pixels-flat disc shape structuring element to eliminate the high contrast blood vessels in fundus images before ap- plying the thresholding techniques. It is used to preserve the disc shaped objects in retinal image as the optic disc may not appear as a circular object in some retinal images. The standard deviation of the resultant image is calculated.

Classification by Fuzzy Logic for Classifying Hard Exudates

The final stage in our proposed technique is to identify the exudates as hard exudates using fuzzy logic. We use values in the RGB colour space of retinal image to form the fuzzy set and MFs. It uses the red, green and blue values of a pixel as three input values for the fuzzy inference system giving a single output. To calculate the output of given a specific rule, the fuzzy inference system provides the degree of membership to the output variable. A de-fuzzification function based on the centroid method, is used to compute the final output for identification of hard exudates.

PROPOSED SYSTEM

The proposed system is based on bayesian classification to classify the eye whether it is normal or abnormal.

Bayes Classifier

In machine learning, naive Bayes classifiers are a family of simple "probabilistic classifiers" based on applying Bayes' theorem with strong (naive) independence assumptions between the features.

Naive Bayes has been studied extensively since the 1950s. It was introduced under a different name into the text retrieval community in the early 1960s, and remains a popular (baseline) method for text categorization, the problem of judging documents as belonging to one category or the other (such as spam or legitimate, sports or politics, etc.) with word frequencies as the features. With appropriate pre- processing, it is competitive in this domain with more advanced methods including support vector machines. It also finds application in automatic medical diagnosis.

Naive Bayes classifiers are highly scalable, requiring a number of parame- ters linear in the number of variables (features/predictors) in a learning problem. Maximum-likelihood training can be done by evaluating a closed-form expression, which takes linear time, rather than by expensive iterative approximation as used for many other types of classifiers.

A Bayesian classifier is based on the idea that the role of a (natural) class is to predict the values of features for members of that class. Examples are grouped in classes because they have common values for the features. Such classes are often called natural kinds.

The idea behind a Bayesian classifier is that, if an agent knows the class, it can predict the values of the other features. If it does not know the class, Bayes' rule can be used to predict the class given (some of) the feature values. In a Bayesian classifier, the learning agent builds a probabilistic model of the features and uses that model to predict the classification of a new example. A latent variable is a probabilistic variable that is not observed. A Bayesian classifier is a probabilistic model where the classification is a latent variable that is probabilistically related to the observed variables. Classification then become inference in the probabilistic model.

CONCLUSION AND FUTURE WORK

From the base paper and comparing the results of other references we can understand that the method for classifying the images has further impro- vised.SVM classifier is a technique for image classification purpose. By comparing its results with fuzzy logic its performance measures has improved. From the report its clear that, the existing system need to be modified. Neural networks(Bayesian) can be used with fuzzy logic for classification. This is to classify the images into normal and abnormal. Bayesian gives better results in terms of accuracy and other evaluation measures.Even though CNN is best in terms of accuracy it has a issue of higher memory where in practical application we cannot use it in all time

REFERENCES

Abbasi-Sureshjani, S., Dashtbozorg, B., ter Haar Romeny, B. M., & Fleuret, F. (2017). Boosted exudate segmentation in retinal images using residual nets. Lect. Notes Comput. Sci., 10554, 210–218 doi:10.1007/978-3-319-67561-9_24

Agurto, C., Murray, V., Yu, H., Wigdahl, J., Pattichis, M., Nemeth, S., ... Soliz, P. (2014). A multiscale optimization approach to detect exudates in the macula. *IEEE Journal of Biomedical and Health Informatics*, *18*(4), 1328–1336. doi:10.1109/JBHI.2013.2296399 PMID:25014937

Akram, M. U., Tariq, A., Khan, S. A., & Javed, M. Y. (2014). Automated detection of exudates and macula for grading of diabetic macular edema. *Computer Methods and Programs in Biomedicine*, *114*(2), 141–152. doi:10.1016/j.cmpb.2014.01.010 PMID:24548898

Antelin Vijila, S., & Rajesh, R. S. (2018). Detection Of Hard Exudates In Fundus Images Using Cascaded Correlation Neural Network Classifier. *International Journal of Pure and Applied Mathematics Volume*, *118*(11), 699-706.

Balakrishnan, U., Venkatachalapathy, K., & Marimuthu, G. S. (2016). An enhanced PSO- DEFS based feature selection with biometric authentication for identification of diabetic retinopathy. *Journal of Innovative Optical Health Sciences*, *9*(6). doi:10.1142/S1793545816500206

Dashtbozorg, B., Mendonça, A. M., & Campilho, A. (2015). Optic disc segmentation using the sliding band filter. *Computers in Biology and Medicine*, *56*, 1–12. doi:10.1016/j.compbiomed.2014.10.009 PMID:25464343

Deshmukh, A. V., Patil, T. G., Patankar, S. S., & Kulkarni, J. V. (2015). Features based classification of hard exudates in retinal images. *2015 Int. Conf. Adv. Comput.Commun. Informatics, ICACCI 2015*, 1652–1655. 10.1109/ICACCI.2015.7275850

Franklin, S. W., & Rajan, S. E. (2014). Diagnosis of diabetic retinopathy by employing image processing technique to detect exudates in retinal images. *IET Image Processing*, 8(10), 601–609. doi:10.1049/iet-ipr.2013.0565

Jaya, T., Dheeba, J., & Singh, N. A. (2015). Detection of Hard Exudates in Colour Fundus Images Using Fuzzy Support Vector Machine-Based Expert System. *Journal of Digital Imaging*, 28(6), 761–768. doi:10.100710278-015-9793-5 PMID:25822397

Kumar, Manjunath, & Sheshadri. (2015). Feature extraction from the fundus images for the diagnosis of Diabetic Retinopathy. *Int. Conf. Emerg. Res. Electron. Comput. Sci. Technol.*, 240–245.

Liu, Q., Zou, B., Chen, J., Ke, W., Yue, K., Chen, Z., & Zhao, G. (2017). A location-to-segmentation strategy for automatic exudate segmentation in colour retinal fundus images. *Computerized Medical Imaging and Graphics*, 55, 78–86. doi:10.1016/j.compmedimag.2016.09.001 PMID:27665058

Mo, J., Zhang, L., & Feng, Y. (2018). AC US CR. *Neurocomputing*.

Ot, S., Perdomo, O., & Gonz, F. (2017). *Intravascular Imaging and Computer Assisted Stenting, and Large-Scale Annotation of Biomedical Data and Expert Label Synthesis*. Academic Press.

Patil, P., Shettar, P., Narayankar, P., & Patil, M. (2016). An efficient method of detecting exudates in diabetic retinopathy: Using texture edge features. *2016 Int. Conf. Adv. Comput. Commun. Informatics*, 1188–1191. 10.1109/ICACCI.2016.7732206

Perdomo, O., Otalora, S., Rodríguez, F., Arevalo, J., & González, F. A. (2016). A Novel Machine Learning Model Based on Exudate Localization to Detect Diabetic Macular Edema. Academic Press. doi:10.17077/omia.1057

Pereira, C., Gonçalves, L., & Ferreira, M. (2015). Exudate segmentation in fundus images using an ant colony optimization approach. *Inf. Sci. (Ny)*, 296(1), 14–24. doi:10.1016/j.ins.2014.10.059

Pratt, H., Coenen, F., Broadbent, D. M., Harding, S. P., & Zheng, Y. (2016). Convolutional Neural Networks for Diabetic Retinopathy. *Procedia Computer Science*, 90(July), 200–205. doi:10.1016/j.procs.2016.07.014

Sankar, U., Vijai, R., & Balajee, R. M. (2018). Detection and Classification of Diabetic Retinopathy in Fundus Images using. *Neural Networks*, 2630–2635.

Sreeji & Parasuraman. (2018). Characterization of Diabetic Retinopathy Detection of Exudates in Color Fundus Images of the Human Retina. Academic Press.

Sriman & Iyenger. (2018). *Classification of Diabetic Retinopathy Images by Using Deep Learning Models Classification of Diabetic Retinopathy Images by Using Deep Learning Models*. Academic Press.

Usman Akram, M., Khalid, S., Tariq, A., Khan, S. A., & Azam, F. (2014). Detection and classification of retinal lesions for grading of diabetic retinopathy. *Computers in Biology and Medicine*, *45*(1), 161–171. doi:10.1016/j.compbiomed.2013.11.014 PMID:24480176

Vahadane, A., Joshi, A., Madan, K., & Dastidar, T. R. (2018). Detection of diabetic macular edema in optical coherence tomography scans using patch based deep learning. SigTuple Technologies Pvt. Ltd.

Welikala, R. A., Fraz, M. M., Dehmeshki, J., Hoppe, A., Tah, V., Mann, S., ... Barman, S. A. (2015). Genetic algorithm based feature selection combined with dual classification for the automated detection of proliferative diabetic retinopathy. *Computerized Medical Imaging and Graphics*, *43*, 64–77. doi:10.1016/j.compmedimag.2015.03.003 PMID:25841182

Chapter 7
Convolutional Graph Neural Networks:
A Review and Applications of Graph Autoencoder in Chemoinformatics

J. Joshua Thomas

iD https://orcid.org/0000-0002-9992-6094

KDU Penang University College, Malaysia

Tran Huu Ngoc Tran

KDU Penang University College, Malaysia

Gilberto Pérez Lechuga

Universidad Autónoma del Estado de Hidalgo, Mexico

Bahari Belaton

Universiti Sains Malaysia, Malaysia

ABSTRACT

Applying deep learning to the pervasive graph data is significant because of the unique characteristics of graphs. Recently, substantial amounts of research efforts have been keen on this area, greatly advancing graph-analyzing techniques. In this study, the authors comprehensively review different kinds of deep learning methods applied to graphs. They discuss with existing literature into sub-components of two: graph convolutional networks, graph autoencoders, and recent trends including chemoinformatics research area including molecular fingerprints and drug discovery. They further experiment with variational autoencoder (VAE) analyze how these apply in drug target interaction (DTI) and applications with ephemeral outline on how they assist the drug discovery pipeline and discuss potential research directions.

DOI: 10.4018/978-1-7998-1192-3.ch007

INTRODUCTION

Graph neural networks (GNNs) are deep learning-centered methods that function in the graph region. Due to its substantial performance and high interpretability, GNN has been a widely applied graph analysis method recently. In the following paragraphs, we will illustrate the fundamental motivations of graph neural networks. Graphs are a kind of data structure, which models a set of objects (nodes) and their relationships (edges). Newly, researches of analyzing graphs with machine learning have been getting more and more attention because of the great communicative power of graphs, i.e. graphs can use as signification of a large number of systems across various areas including science (biomedical networks).

The motivation of GNNs roots in convolutional neural networks (CNNs) (LeCun et. al, 1998). CNN's have the ability to extract multi-scale localized spatial features and compose them to construct highly expressive representations, which led to breakthroughs in almost all machine-learning areas and started the new era of deep learning (LeCun, Bengio, and Hinton, 2015). However, CNN's can only operate on regular Euclidean data like images (2D grid) and text (1D sequence) while the data structures can regarded as instances of graphs. As we are going deeper into CNNs and graphs, we found the keys of CNNs: local connection shared weights and the use of multi-layer (LeCun, Bengio, and Hinton, 2015). However, as shown in Figure 1, it is hard to define localized convolutional filters and pooling operators, which delays the transformation of CNN from Euclidean domain to non-Euclidean domain.

Figure 1(a) Euclidean Space, 1(b) non-Euclidean space

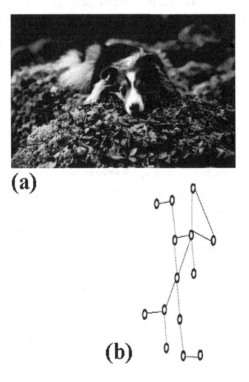

In this chapter, we try to fill this gap by comprehensive reviewing of deep learning methods on graphs. Specifically, as shown in Figure 1, we divide the existing methods into three main categories: semi-supervised methods, unsupervised methods. Concretely speaking, semi-supervised methods include Graph Neural Networks (GNNs) and Graph Convolutional Networks (GCNs), unsupervised methods are mainly composed of Graph Autoencoders (GAEs). We summarize some main distinctions of these categories in Table 1. Approximately, GNNs and GCNs are semi-supervised as they apply node attributes and node labels to train model parameters end-to-end for a specific task, while GAEs mainly focus on learning representation using unsupervised methods. Recently advanced methods use other unique algorithms that do not fall in previous categories. Besides these high-level distinctions, the model architectures also differ significantly. We will provide a comprehensive overview of these graph methods in detail. We also analyze the differences between these models and how to composite different architectures. In the end, we briefly outline the applications of these methods applied in chemoinformatics and discuss potential future directions.

The tasks for learning a deep model on graphs have considered, and that will be the contributions of this chapter:

- To apply and provide a fundamental knowledge associated with graph deep learning models for prediction, and node recommendation.
- To provide a basis for the use of graphs and nodes for chemoinformatics, a summary of autoencoders for graphs and nodes has presented.
- Applications of graph neural networks, graph convolutional networks (GCN), graph autoencoders (GAE) models, which uses in chemoinformatics, has described in detail.

The rest of the chapter has organized as follows. In the next section, we give the formal graph neural networks with benchmarks. In Section 3, recent Graph Convolutional networks (GCNs). Followed by applications in chemoinformatics explaining Graph Autoencoders (GAE) in molecule design have presented in Section 4, and 5. We worked on the application areas of these in experimental analysis with drug target interaction (DTI) using VAE in section 6. The chapter has concluded with an overview in Section 7.

Table 1. Deep learning methods on graphs and its distinctions

Category	Type	Node Attributes	Respective Domains
Graph Neural Networks (GNN)	Semi-supervised	Yes	Recurrent Neural Networks
Graph Convolutional Networks (GCN)	Semi-supervised	Yes	Convolutional Neural Networks
Graph Autoencoders (GA)	Unsupervised	Limited	Autoencoders/Variational Autoencoders
Graph Recurrent Neural Networks (GRNN)	Various	Limited	Recurrent Neural Networks

2 GRAPH NEURAL NETWORKS (GNNs)

In this section, we review the most primitive semi-supervised deep learning methods for graph data, Graph Neural Networks (GNNs) and its improvement. The origin of GNNs can dated back to the pre-deep learning era (Gori, Monfardini, and Scarselli, 2005). The idea of GNN is simple: to encode structural information of the graph, each node v_i can be represented by a low-dimensional state vector $s_i, 1 \leq i \leq N$. Motivated by recursive neural networks, a recursive definition of states is adopted (Frasconi, Gori, and Sperduti, 1998):

$$S_i = \sum_{i \in \mathcal{N}(i)} \mathcal{F}(s_i, s_j, \boldsymbol{F}_i^V, \boldsymbol{F}_j^V, \boldsymbol{F}_{i,j}^E) \tag{1}$$

$$\hat{y}_i = \mathcal{O}(s_i, F_i^V) \tag{2}$$

For graph-focused tasks, suggest adding a special node with unique attributes corresponding to the whole graph. To learn model parameters, the semi-supervised method have adopted together with other popular algorithms. After iteratively solving Eq. (1) to a stable point using Jacobi method (Powell, 1964), one step of gradient descent is performed using the Almeida-Pineda algorithm (Almeida, 1987 & Pineda, 1987) to minimize a task-specific objective function, for example, the square loss between predicted values and the ground-truth for regression tasks; then, this process is repeated until convergence. Table 1 shows the distinctions among deep learning graph methods and related domains.

In fact, GNNs and GCNs has unified into a common framework and GNNs is equivalent to GCN using identical layers to reach a stable state.

First, to ensure that Eq. (1) has a unique solution, $\mathcal{F}(.)$ has to be a reduction map (Khamsi and Kirk, 2011), which severely limits the modeling ability. Second, since many iterations are needed between gradient descend steps, GNN is computationally expensive. Because of these drawbacks and perhaps the lack of computational power (e.g. Graphics Processing Unit, GPU, is not widely used for deep learning those days) and lack of research interests, GNN was not widely known to the community.

A notable improvement to GNN is Gated Graph Sequence Neural Networks (GGS-NNs) (Li et. al, 2015) with several modifications. Most importantly, the recursive definition of Eq. (1) with Gated Recurrent Units (GRU) (Cordella et. al, 2004), thus removing the requirement of reduction map and support the usage of modern optimization techniques. Specifically, Eq. (3) is replaced by:

$$s_i^{(t)} = \left(1 - z_i^{(t)}\right) \odot s_i^{(t-1)} + z_i^{(t)} \odot \tilde{s}_i^{(t)} \tag{3}$$

where **z** is calculated by update gates, $\tilde{s}$ are candidates for updating and t is the pseudo time. Secondly, the propose networks operating in sequence to produce a sequence output, which can be applied to applications such as program verification (Brockschmidt et. al, 2015). Consider Table 2 as the notations used throughout this chapter.

Table 2. Common notations use in graphs representation

Notations	Descriptions
$G = (V, E)$	Graph
$\mathbb{R}^m$	m-dimensional Euclidean space
N, M	The number of nodes and edges
$V = \{v_1, ..., v_N\}$	The set of nodes
F^v, F^E	Attributes/Features for nodes and edges
A	Adjacency matrix
$D(i,i) = \sum_{j \neq i} A(i,j)$	The diagonal degree matrix
$L = D - A$	The Laplacian matrix
$Q \rangle Q^T = L$	The eigendecomposition of L
$P = D^{-1} A$	The transition matrix
$\mathcal{N}_k(i), \mathcal{N}(i)$	k-step and 1-step neighbors of vi
H^l	The hidden representation of the lth layer
f_l	The number of dimensions of H^l
$\rho(\bullet)$	Some non-linear activation
$X_1 \odot X_2$	Element-wise product
$\ominus$	Learnable parameters

GNNs and its extensions have many applications. For example, CommNet (Sukhbaatar and Fergus, 2016) applies GNNs to learn multi-agent communication in AI systems by regarding each agent as a node and updating the states of agents by communication with others for several time steps before taking an action. Interaction Network (IN) (Battaglia et. al, 2016) uses GNN for physical reasoning by representing objects as nodes, relations as edges and using pseudo-time as a simulation system. VAIN (Hoshen, 2017) improves CommNet and IN by introducing attentions to weigh different interactions. Relation Networks (RNs) (Santoro et. al, 2017) propose using GNN as a relational reasoning module to augment other neural networks and show promising results in visual question answering problems.

GRAPH CONVOLUTIONAL NETWORKS (GCNS)

Besides GNNs, Graph Convolutional Networks (GCNs) are another class of semi-supervised methods for graphs. Since GCNs usually can be trained with task-specific loss via back-propagation like standard CNNs, we focus on the architectures adopted. We will first discuss the convolution operations, then move to the readout operations and improvements. We summarize the main characteristics of GCNs surveyed in this paper in Table 3.

Convolution Procedures

Spectral Methods

For CNN's, convolution is the most fundamental operation. However, standard convolution for image or text has applied to graphs because of the lack of a grid structure (Shuman et. al, 2013). Bruna et al. (2013) first introduce convolution for graph data from spectral domain using the graph Laplacian matrix L (Belkin and Niyogi, 2002), which plays a similar role as the Fourier basis for signal processing (Shuman et. al, 2013). Specifically, the convolution operation on graph G is defined as,

$$u_1 * u_2 = Q\left((Q^T u_1) \odot (Q^T u_2)\right) \quad (4)$$

where u_1, $u_2 \in \mathbb{R}^N$ are two signals defined on nodes and Q are eigenvectors of L. Then, using the convolution theorem, filtering a signal u can be obtained as:

$$uQ' \ominus Q^T u \quad (5)$$

where u' is the output signal, $\ominus = \ominus(\wedge) \in \mathbb{R}^{N x N}$ is a diagonal matrix of learnable filters and $\wedge$ are eigenvalues of L. Then, a convolutional layer is defined by applying different filters to a different input and output signals as follows:

Table 3. Comparison of graph neural networks (GNNs)

Method	Convolutional	Readout	Scalability	Multiple Graphs
DCGN(16)	Spatial	First order +Diffusion	No	-
MoNet(17)	Spatial	First-order	Yes	General Framework
GATs(18)	Spatial	First-order	Yes	Attention
R-GCNs(19)	Spatial	First-order	Yes	Edge Features
PinSage(20)	Spatial	Random-wald	Yes	-
FastGCN(21)	Spatial	First-order+sampling	Yes	Inductive setting
Chen et al. (22)	Spatial	First-order+sampling	Yes	-

$$u_j^{l+1} = \rho \left(\sum_{i=1}^{f1} Q \ominus_{i,j}^l Q^T u_i^l \right) j = 1, \ldots, f_{l+1} \tag{6}$$

where l is the layer, $u_j^i \in \mathbb{R}^{\mathcal{N}}$ is the jth hidden representation for nodes in the lth layer $\ominus_{i,j}^i$ are learnable filters. The idea of Eq. (6) is similar to conventional convolutions: passing the input signals through a set of learnable filters to aggregate the information, followed by some non-linear transformation. By using nodes features F[V] as the input layer and stacking multiple convolutional layers, the overall architecture is similar to CNN's. Theoretical analysis shows that such definition of convolution operation on graphs can mimic certain geometric properties of CNNs, which we refer readers to for a comprehensive survey (Bronstein et. al, 2017).

However, directly using Eq. (6) requires O(N) parameters to be learned, which may not be feasible in practice. In addition, the filters in spectral-domain may not be localized in the spatial

$$diag\left(\ominus_{i,j}^l\right) = \mathcal{K}\alpha_{l,i,j} \tag{7}$$

where $\mathcal{K}$ is a fixed interpolation kernel and $\alpha_{l,i,j}$ are learnable interpolation coefficients. The authors also generalize this idea to the setting where the graph is not given but constructed from some raw features using either a supervised or an unsupervised method (Krizhehvsky, Sutskever, and Hinton, 2012). However, two fundamental limitations remain unsolved. First, since the full eigenvectors of the Laplacian matrix are needed during each calculation, the time complexity is at least O(N[2]) per forward and backward pass, which is not scalable to large-scale graphs. Second, since the filters depend on the eigenbasis Q of the graph, parameters cannot shared across multiple graphs with different sizes and structures. Let us look at the readout operations in convolutional operations.

Readout Operations

Using convolution operations, useful features for nodes have learnt to solve many node-focused tasks. However, to tackle graph-focused tasks, information of nodes need to be aggregated form a graph-level representation. In literature, it called the readout or graph coarsening operation. This problem is non-trivial because stride convolutions or pooling in conventional CNNs cannot be directly used due to the lack of a grid structure. Order invariance. A critical requirement for the graph readout operation is that the operation should be invariant to the order of nodes, i.e. if we change the indices of nodes and edges using a bijective function between two vertex sets, representation of the whole graph should not change. For example, whether a drug can treat certain diseases should be independent of how the drug is represented as a graph. Note that since this problem is related to the graph isomorphism problem that is known to be NP (Cordella et. al, 2004). The next paragraph we can discuss the applications of GNNs in drug molecular design.

Figure 2. Graph convolutional neural network in molecule

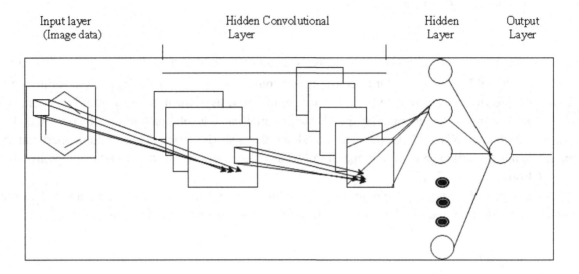

Figure 3. Encoder, latent space, decoder in VAE

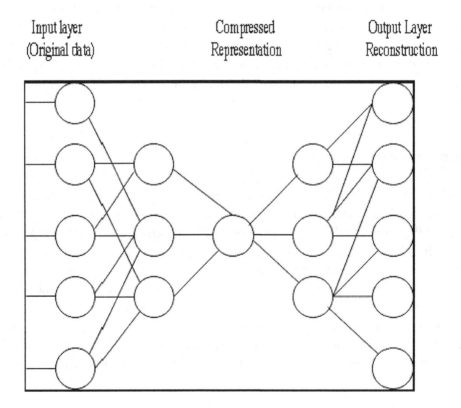

APPLICATIONS IN CHEMOINFORMATICS

In this section, we give details about the chemoinformatics applications of the proposed methodologies mentioned in the previous sections.

Computer-Aided Drug Design

In computer-aided drug design, traditional machine learning algorithms have a long history in the field of cheminformatics, notably in their contribution to quantitative structure activity relationship (QSAR) applications. In QSAR, the output has predicted is usually the biological activity of a compound. Usually regression models are used, and the input data are molecular descriptors, which are precomputed physicochemical properties of the molecule, designed from chemistry domain knowledge. Early work in QSAR applications used linear regression models, but these were quickly supplanted by Bayesian neural networks, (Soon, Hariharan, and Snyder, 2013) followed by RFs (Syetnik et. al, 2003) and SVMs (Du et. al, 2008). Practitioners in the field have historically favored models that allow for variable selection so that an informed chemist can determine if selected features made sense. In addition, models that allowed assessment of uncertainty of output predictions were also preferred. The field of QSAR is vast, and we refer readers to the following list of reviews for key historical technical developments (Tropsha, 2010). For the purpose of this review, we will limit the scope of discussion to the performance of deep neural networks DNN based QSAR models and appropriate comparisons to traditional machine learning models.

As these methods enabled the training of deeper and more complex neural network architecture, overfitting also became more of an issue, which led to the development of the dropout algorithm. In dropout, for each epoch of the training process, a fixed proportion of neurons have randomly selected, and temporarily excluded from the model. The net effect of dropout is that it simulates many different architectures during training, which prevents co-dependency among neurons and reduces overfitting (Srivastava et. al, 2014). While the architecture of modern DNNs vary widely, a popular configuration is rectilinear unit ReLU-based neural networks. When coupled with dropout and early stopping, such ReLU networks have often been enough to regularize the model (i.e., prevent overfitting) (Vincent et. al, 2008).

GRAPH AUTOENCODERS (GAEs)

Autoencoder (AE) and its variations are widely used for unsupervised learning (Krizhevsky, Sutskever, and Hinton, 2012), which are suitable to learn node representations for graphs without supervised information. In this section, we will first introduce graph autoencoders and then move to graph variational autoencoders and other improvements.

Autoencoders

The use of AEs for graphs originated from Sparse Autoencoder (SAE) (MacQueen, 1967). The basic idea is that, by regarding adjacency matrix or its variations as the raw features of nodes, AEs can be leveraged as a dimension reduction technique to learn low-dimensional node representations. Specifically, SAE adopts the following L2 reconstruction loss:

$$\min_{\ominus} \mathcal{L}_2 = \sum_{i=1}^{\mathcal{N}} P\left(i,:\right) - \hat{P}\left(i,:\right)_2 \tag{8}$$

$$\hat{P}\left(i,:\right) = \mathcal{G}h_i h_i = \mathcal{F}\left(P\left(i,:\right)\right), \tag{9}$$

where P is the transition matrix, $\hat{P}$ is the reconstructed matrix, $h_i \in \mathcal{R}^d$ is the low-dimensional representation of node v_i, $\mathcal{F}(.)$ is the encoder, $\mathcal{G}(.)$ is the decoder, $d \ll \mathcal{N}$ is the dimensionality and $\ominus$ are parameters. Both encoder and decoder are multi-layer perceptron with many hidden layers. In other words, SAE tries to compress the information of P (i,:) into low-dimensional vectors *hi* and reconstruct the original vector. SAE also adds another sparsity regularization term. After getting, the low-dimensional representation h_i k-means is applied for the node clustering task, which proves empirically to outperform non deep learning baselines (Wang, Cui, and Zhu, 2016). However, since the theoretical analysis is incorrect, the mechanism underlying such effectiveness remains unexplained. Structure Deep Network Embedding (SDNE) (Barabasi, 2016) fills in the puzzle by showing that the L2-reconstruction loss in Eq. (9) actually corresponds to the second-order proximity, i.e. two nodes share similar latten representations if they have similar neighborhoods, which is well studied in network science such as in collaborative filtering or triangle closure (Tang et. al, 2015). Motivated by network embedding methods, which show that the first-order proximity is also important (Kipf and Welling, 2016), SDNE modifies the objective function by adding another term similar to the Laplacian Eigenmaps (Belkin and Niyogi, 2002):

$$\min_{\ominus} \mathcal{L}_2 + \alpha = \sum_{i=1}^{\mathcal{N}} A\left(i,j\right) \| h_i - h_j \|_2 \tag{10}$$

i.e. two nodes also need to share similar latten representations if they are directly connected. The authors also modified the L2- reconstruction loss by using the adjacency matrix and assigning different weights to zero and non-zero elements.

Variational Autoencoders

As opposed to previous autoencoders, Variational Autoencoder (VAE) is another type of deep learning method that combines dimension reduction with generative models. VAE was first introduced into modeling graph data in (Diederik and Welling, 2014), where the decoder is a simple linear product:

$$pA/H = \prod_{i,j=1}^{\mathcal{N}} \sigma(h_i h_j^T) \tag{11}$$

where h_i are assumed to follow a Gaussian posterior distribution $q\left(h_i | \mathrm{M}, \mathfrak{L}\right) = \mathcal{N}\left(h_i | \mathrm{M}, (\mathrm{i},:)\right)$, diag $(\Sigma (\mathrm{i},:)))$ or the encoder of mean and variance matrices, the authors adopt GCN in (Wang et. al, 2016):

$$M = GCN_M\left(F, A\right), \log \pounds = GCN_\pounds\left(F^V, A\right) \tag{12}$$

Then, the model parameters can be learned by minimizing the variational lower bound:

$$\mathcal{L} = \mathbb{E}_{q\left(H|F^V, A\right)}\left[\log p(A \mid H)\right] - KL\left[q\left(H|F^V, A\right) \| p\left(H\right)\right] \tag{13}$$

However, since the full graph needs to be reconstructed, the time complexity is O(N^2). Motivated by SDNE and G2G, DVNE (Kipf and Welling, 2016) proposes another VAE for graph data by also representing each node as a Gaussian distribution. Unlike previous works that adopt KL-divergence as the measurement, DVNE uses Wasserstein distance (Diederik and Welling, 2014) to preserve the transitivity of the node's similarities. Similar to SDNE.

EXPERIMENT ANALYSIS

The experimental setting uses variational autoencoders (VAE) to determine drug-target interaction (DTI) prediction for repositioning drugs. Improvement in DTI prediction accuracy could save lot of time, effort and money invested for drug discovery and drug repositioning experiments. We propose auto-encoder (AE) based approaches to improve prediction accuracy. Extensive cross-validation experiments on four benchmark datasets using standard evaluation metrics (AUPR and AUC) show that the proposed algorithm improves the predictive performance and outperforms recent state-of-the-art computational methods by a large margin.

Results shows in Table 4 that the proposed technique in the other five competing datasets in 5-fold cross-validation experiments in terms of AUC=0.927, Sensitivity=0.886, Specificity=0.864, and G-mean=0.874. Figure 4 to Figure 7 has shown the experimental plot on truth versus prediction in terms of drug property generation.

Table 4. Drug target interaction using variable autoencoder discovery on selected datasets

Dataset	Mean(cv scores)	Std(cv scores)	CV scores	K-Fold	Avg=AUC
dataset_dgc.txt	664	444	516	5	0.940
e_admat_dgc	664	443	516	5	0.892
gpcr_admat_dgc	95	222	93	5	0.857
ic_admat_dgc	204	209	289	5	0.959
nr_admat_dgc	26	53	13	5	0.635

Figure 4. Result of DTI-1

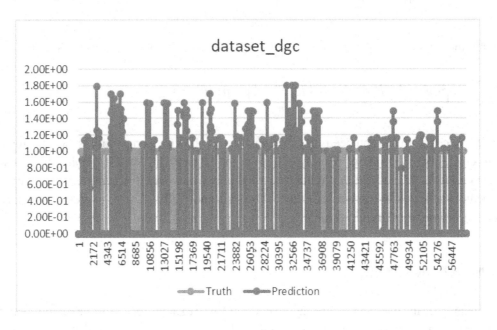

Figure 5. Result of DTI-2

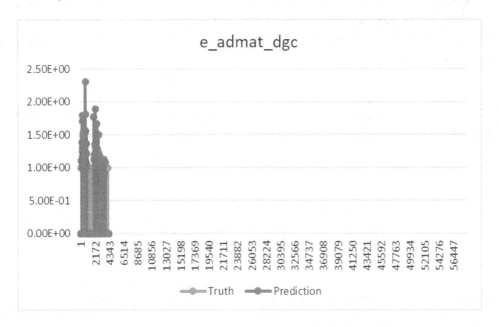

Figure 6. Result of DTI-3

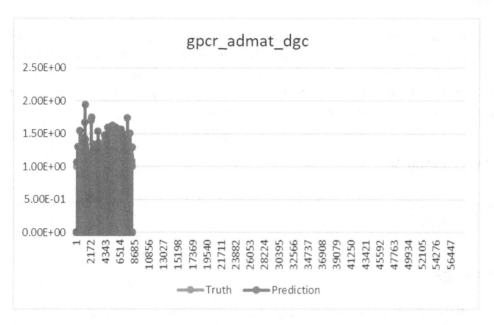

Figure 7. Result of DTI-4

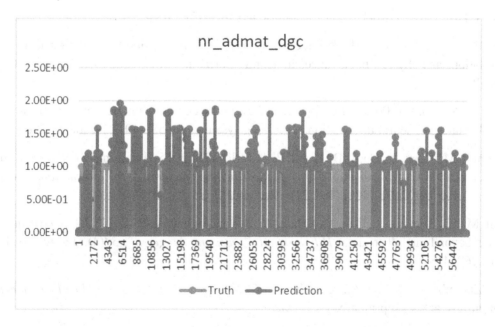

CONCLUSION AND DISCUSSION

Drug-target interaction prediction is a crucial task in genomic drug discovery. Many computational techniques has proposed in the literature. In this work, we presented a novel variational autoencoder to understand the latent space in predicting the drug-target interactions; it is a graph-regularized version of the traditional algorithm, which incorporates multiple Graph Laplacians over the drugs and targets into the framework for an improved interaction prediction.

ACKNOWLEDGMENT

Fundamental Research Grant Scheme (FRGS) supports this work under the project number FRGS/1/2019/ICT02/KDUPG/02/1.

REFERENCES

Almeida, L. B. (1987). A learning rule for asynchronous perceptrons with feedback in a combinatorial environment. In *Proceedings, 1st First International Conference on Neural Networks* (Vol. 2, pp. 609-618). IEEE.

Barabási, A. L. (2016). *Network science.* Cambridge University Press.

Battaglia, P., Pascanu, R., Lai, M., & Rezende, D. J. (2016). Interaction networks for learning about objects, relations and physics. In Advances in neural information processing systems (pp. 4502-4510). Academic Press.

Belkin, M., & Niyogi, P. (2002). Laplacian eigenmaps and spectral techniques for embedding and clustering. In Advances in neural information processing systems (pp. 585-591). Academic Press.

Brockschmidt, M., Chen, Y., Cook, B., Kohli, P., & Tarlow, D. (2015). Learning to decipher the heap for program verification. In *Workshop on Constructive Machine Learning at the International Conference on Machine Learning (CMLICML) (Vol. 21).* Academic Press.

Bronstein, M. M., Bruna, J., LeCun, Y., Szlam, A., & Vandergheynst, P. (2017). Geometric deep learning: Going beyond euclidean data. *IEEE Signal Processing Magazine, 34*(4), 18–42. doi:10.1109/MSP.2017.2693418

Bruna, J., Zaremba, W., Szlam, A., & LeCun, Y. (2013). *Spectral networks and locally connected networks on graphs.* arXiv preprint arXiv:1312.6203

Chen, J., Ma, T., & Xiao, C. (2018). *Fastgcn: fast learning with graph convolutional networks via importance sampling.* arXiv preprint arXiv:1801.10247

Chen, J., Zhu, J., & Song, L. (2017). *Stochastic training of graph convolutional networks with variance reduction.* arXiv preprint arXiv:1710.10568

Cordella, L. P., Foggia, P., Sansone, C., & Vento, M. (2004). A (sub) graph isomorphism algorithm for matching large graphs. *IEEE Transactions on Pattern Analysis and Machine Intelligence*, *26*(10), 1367–1372. doi:10.1109/TPAMI.2004.75 PMID:15641723

Diederik, P. K., & Welling, M. (2014). Auto-encoding variational bayes. *Proceedings of the International Conference on Learning Representations (ICLR)*.

Du, H., Wang, J., Hu, Z., Yao, X., & Zhang, X. (2008). Prediction of fungicidal activities of rice blast disease based on least-squares support vector machines and project pursuit regression. *Journal of Agricultural and Food Chemistry*, *56*(22), 10785–10792. doi:10.1021/jf8022194 PMID:18950187

Frasconi, P., Gori, M., & Sperduti, A. (1998). A general framework for adaptive processing of data structures. *IEEE Transactions on Neural Networks*, *9*(5), 768–786. doi:10.1109/72.712151 PMID:18255765

Gori, M., Monfardini, G., & Scarselli, F. (2005, July). A new model for learning in graph domains. In *Proceedings 2005 IEEE International Joint Conference on Neural Networks*, 2005 (Vol. 2, pp. 729-734). IEEE. 10.1109/IJCNN.2005.1555942

Hoshen, Y. (2017). Vain: Attentional multi-agent predictive modeling. In Advances in Neural Information Processing Systems (pp. 2701-2711). Academic Press.

Kearnes, S., McCloskey, K., Berndl, M., Pande, V., & Riley, P. (2016). Molecular graph convolutions: Moving beyond fingerprints. *Journal of Computer-Aided Molecular Design*, *30*(8), 595–608. doi:10.100710822-016-9938-8 PMID:27558503

Khamsi, M. A., & Kirk, W. A. (2011). *An introduction to metric spaces and fixed point theory* (Vol. 53). John Wiley & Sons.

Kipf, T. N., & Welling, M. (2016). *Variational graph auto-encoders.* arXiv preprint arXiv:1611.07308

Krizhevsky, A., Sutskever, I., & Hinton, G. E. (2012). Imagenet classification with deep convolutional neural networks. In Advances in neural information processing systems (pp. 1097-1105). Academic Press.

LeCun, Y., Bengio, Y., & Hinton, G. (2015). Deep learning. *Nature*, *521*(7553), 436.

LeCun, Y., Bottou, L., Bengio, Y., & Haffner, P. (1998). Gradient-based learning applied to document recognition. *Proceedings of the IEEE*, *86*(11), 2278–2324. doi:10.1109/5.726791

Li, Y., Tarlow, D., Brockschmidt, M., & Zemel, R. (2015). *Gated graph sequence neural networks.* arXiv preprint arXiv:1511.05493

MacQueen, J. (1967, June). Some methods for classification and analysis of multivariate observations. In *Proceedings of the fifth Berkeley symposium on mathematical statistics and probability* (*Vol. 1*, No. 14, pp. 281-297). Academic Press.

Monti, F., Boscaini, D., Masci, J., Rodola, E., Svoboda, J., & Bronstein, M. M. (2017). Geometric deep learning on graphs and manifolds using mixture model cnns. In *Proceedings of the IEEE Conference on Computer Vision and Pattern Recognition* (pp. 5115-5124). IEEE. 10.1109/CVPR.2017.576

Pineda, F. J. (1987). Generalization of back-propagation to recurrent neural networks. *Physical Review Letters*, *59*(19), 2229–2232. doi:10.1103/PhysRevLett.59.2229 PMID:10035458

Powell, M. J. (1964). An efficient method for finding the minimum of a function of several variables without calculating derivatives. *The Computer Journal, 7*(2), 155–162. doi:10.1093/comjnl/7.2.155

Santoro, A., Raposo, D., Barrett, D. G., Malinowski, M., Pascanu, R., Battaglia, P., & Lillicrap, T. (2017). A simple neural network module for relational reasoning. In Advances in neural information processing systems (pp. 4967-4976). Academic Press.

Scarselli, F., Gori, M., Tsoi, A. C., Hagenbuchner, M., & Monfardini, G. (2008). The graph neural network model. *IEEE Transactions on Neural Networks, 20*(1), 61–80. doi:10.1109/TNN.2008.2005605 PMID:19068426

Schlichtkrull, M., Kipf, T. N., Bloem, P., Van Den Berg, R., Titov, I., & Welling, M. (2018, June). Modeling relational data with graph convolutional networks. In *European Semantic Web Conference* (pp. 593-607). Springer. 10.1007/978-3-319-93417-4_38

Shuman, D. I., Narang, S. K., Frossard, P., Ortega, A., & Vandergheynst, P. (2013). The emerging field of signal processing on graphs: Extending high-dimensional data analysis to networks and other irregular domains. *IEEE Signal Processing Magazine, 30*(3), 83–98. doi:10.1109/MSP.2012.2235192

Soon, W. W., Hariharan, M., & Snyder, M. P. (2013). High-throughput sequencing for biology and medicine. *Molecular Systems Biology, 9*(1), 640. doi:10.1038/msb.2012.61 PMID:23340846

Srivastava, N., Hinton, G., Krizhevsky, A., Sutskever, I., & Salakhutdinov, R. (2014). Dropout: A simple way to prevent neural networks from overfitting. *Journal of Machine Learning Research, 15*(1), 1929–1958.

Sukhbaatar, S., & Fergus, R. (2016). Learning multiagent communication with backpropagation. In Advances in Neural Information Processing Systems (pp. 2244-2252). Academic Press.

Svetnik, V., Liaw, A., Tong, C., Culberson, J. C., Sheridan, R. P., & Feuston, B. P. (2003). Random forest: A classification and regression tool for compound classification and QSAR modeling. *Journal of Chemical Information and Computer Sciences, 43*(6), 1947–1958. doi:10.1021/ci034160g PMID:14632445

Tang, J., Qu, M., Wang, M., Zhang, M., Yan, J., & Mei, Q. (2015, May). Line: Large-scale information network embedding. In *Proceedings of the 24th international conference on world wide web* (pp. 1067-1077). International World Wide Web Conferences Steering Committee. 10.1145/2736277.2741093

Tropsha, A. (2010). Best practices for QSAR model development, validation, and exploitation. *Molecular Informatics, 29*(6-7), 476–488. doi:10.1002/minf.201000061 PMID:27463326

Veličković, P., Cucurull, G., Casanova, A., Romero, A., Lio, P., & Bengio, Y. (2017). *Graph attention networks*. arXiv preprint arXiv:1710.10903

Vincent, P., Larochelle, H., Bengio, Y., & Manzagol, P. A. (2008, July). Extracting and composing robust features with denoising autoencoders. In *Proceedings of the 25th international conference on Machine learning* (pp. 1096-1103). ACM. 10.1145/1390156.1390294

Wang, D., Cui, P., & Zhu, W. (2016, August). Structural deep network embedding. In *Proceedings of the 22nd ACM SIGKDD international conference on Knowledge discovery and data mining* (pp. 1225-1234). ACM. 10.1145/2939672.2939753

Zhuang, C., & Ma, Q. (2018, April). Dual graph convolutional networks for graph-based semi-supervised classification. In *Proceedings of the 2018 World Wide Web Conference* (pp. 499-508). International World Wide Web Conferences Steering Committee. 10.1145/3178876.3186116

Chapter 8
Deep Learning:
A Recent Computing Platform for Multimedia Information Retrieval

Menaga D.

B. S. Abdur Rahman Crescent Institute of Science and Technology, Chennai, India

Revathi S.

B. S. Abdur Rahman Crescent Institute of Science and Technology, Chennai, India

ABSTRACT

Multimedia application is a significant and growing research area because of the advances in technology of software engineering, storage devices, networks, and display devices. With the intention of satisfying multimedia information desires of users, it is essential to build an efficient multimedia information process, access, and analysis applications, which maintain various tasks, like retrieval, recommendation, search, classification, and clustering. Deep learning is an emerging technique in the sphere of multimedia information process, which solves both the crisis of conventional and recent researches. The main aim is to resolve the multimedia-related problems by the use of deep learning. The deep learning revolution is discussed with the depiction and feature. Finally, the major application also explained with respect to different fields. This chapter analyzes the crisis of retrieval after providing the successful discussion of multimedia information retrieval that is the ability of retrieving an object of every multimedia.

INTRODUCTION

The count of people using smart devices has been raised significantly with the speedy development of the mobile market. The immense growth in the field of networks, computers, software engineering, storage devices and display devices has made multimedia application an emerging and promising area of research. Various computing resources, like hardware encoder/decoder, are employed recently in modern smart devices, such as tablets, Smartphone and so on, so that the experience of the mobile users can be improved (Kim et al., 2017, Chen et al., 2015). Hence, the multimedia applications, such as game applications, video player applications, music player applications, and so on, are used by the users

DOI: 10.4018/978-1-7998-1192-3.ch008

without any restrictions in the resources and CPU usage. It is important to construct effective multimedia information processing, analysis applications, and access, for maintaining different processes, like retrieval, search, summarization, classification, recommendation, and clustering of multimedia information (Smolensky,1986, Howard *et al.*, 2017). The purpose is to satisfy the information requirements of different users in online social multimedia environments. One of the techniques for processing multimedia information is deep learning, which addresses the conventional as well as current research problems. Therefore, the ultimate aim is to use deep learning to determine the multimedia-related troubles in the future. Multimedia Information Retrieval is a common system made of Visual Retrieval, Audio Retrieval, Text Retrieval, and Video Retrieval systems. So that, every kind of digital document may be examined and searched through the elements of language appropriate to its nature, and extend the search condition. Such method is known as the Content-Based Information Retrieval (CBIR), which is the core of MIR. This new concept of content-based information handling requires to be integrated with many traditional semantics. It directs on the processing tools and searching is valid for new multimedia documents of the content-based management. MIR presents improved information, and every kind of digital document can be retrieved and analyzed by the appropriate elements. The approach of MIR directly holds the real content of documents and also consists of semantic aspects.

Organization of this chapter: The introduction provides the brief explanation about multimedia information retrieval. Then, the literature review discusses the various deep learning techniques for multimedia information retrieval. Afterthat, the various methods of deep learning are discussed and the supervised and unsupervised deep learning have been explained. The applications of deep learning are provided under Applications. Finally, the summarization of the chapter is provided in conclusion.

LITERATURE REVIEW

Deep learning is defined as a technique that automatically detects significant patterns in the data. For deep learning, data is important, from which the learning algorithm discovers and learns the data properties. Both the quality and the quantity of the dataset tend to degrade the performance of prediction and learning. However, the techniques based on deep learning are proven to be promising for extracting learning patterns and features even if the data is complex. Deep learning can be considered as methods that are based on data-driven artificial intelligence and are used to frame the relationship between the input given and the output to be generated. Moreover, deep learning has unique features, like feature learning, model training, and model construction. Deep learning can also be considered as representation learning approaches, having several levels of representation that are attained through non-linear modules, where the representation at a level is transformed into a higher level or abstract level. Hence, it is possible to learn complex functions with the utilization of these transformations. Learning the representations of data via the abstract levels is the basic idea of DL. The major advantage of DL is its ability to extract the features directly from the original data such that the complexity of feature engineering can be avoided.

The two properties of DL are:

- Numerous layers containing nonlinear processing units
- Feature presentation on every layer throughthe learning carried out either in supervised or unsupervised manner

To representveryexpressive abstraction; deep learning networks are executed using stacked autoencoders. These abstractions can signify huge set of functions than shallow networks. A significant ability for learning tasks comprising complicated models is providing remarkable representative power that offers unidentified feature coherences of input signals. The benefits of DL are summarized below:

- Compared to shallow artificial neural networks deep learning seems effective as it requires less computational units than the shallow artificial neural networks to perform the same function.
- Without the interaction or guidance of users, it can extract the features automatically
- In many cases, deep learning gives improved precision than the traditional artificial neural networks.
- By approximating or reducing huge complex datasets into extremely perfect analytical and transformative output, DL significantly facilitates human-centered smart systems, and has shown the considerable improvement in automatic feature extraction
- The existing model related to pattern recognition extracts hand-crafted features from the images before using trained classifier. By training with unlabelled data, the deep learning systems automatically extract the features, and then, it categorizes the image with an effective classifier by applying those automatically extracted features
- One of the major benefits of DL is that it can lessen the complexity in handcrafted feature engineering by learning useful feature representations from the raw data automatically.

DL was first proposed to speech separation in two conference papers by Wang and Wang in 2012, and afterward, a journal version is extended in 2013 (Yao *et al.*, 2018, Wang & Chen, 2018).The deep learning techniques have made a breakthrough for processing and analyzing data and they are rated one of the promising techniques in the 2013 MIT technology review. Deep learning techniques are mostly applied in the field of scientific and business fields and the primary invention of deep learning systems, especially, DistBelief(Dean *et al.*, 2012, Liu *et al.*, 2018) is launched by the Google in 2011.With an enormous quantity of data, DistBelief, which is a mixture of data parallelism and model parallelism, cantrain large-scale models using large number of free parameters. By making use of computing clusters, the software approach, DistBelief, was introduced.DistBelief is effective in training huge models using large amount of data by integrating data parallelism and model parallelism. For model parallelism, the huge deep learning model is divided into small blocks, where each block is allocated to a computer for training. In particular, for the fully-connected networks, like stacking auto-encoder and deep belief network, DistBelief has to transfer data between the computers to train the deep learning models, providing huge deal of communication.

Since 2000, the neural networks with deep architectures have gained attention due to its achievements in image and speech recognition. The Imagenet classification that is performed using deep convolutional neural networks (Krizhevsky *et al.*, 2012)has attained improved results in 2012 ImageNet Challenge by adapting a network comprised of three fully connected layers and five convolutional layers, along with 60 million parameters(Cheng *et al.*, 2017). Deep learning methods are approved by most of the researchers and have attained considerable accuracy (Dediu *et al.*, 2017, Jia, X. 2017) in recent ImageNet Large Scale Visual Recognition Challenge (ILSVRC) contests (Jia, X. 2017, Weston *et al.*, 201).In the 1980s(Fukushima & Miyake, 1982, Cao *et al.*, 2018), the advanced framework for deep learning was constructed on ANNs, and in 2006(Cao *et al.*, 2018), the effect of deep learning methods became noticeable. According to MIT Technology Review (Wu *et al.*, 2015),Deep Learning (DL) has been accepted as one of the ten breakthrough technologies in 2013.ConvNets have been used in segmentation, detection, object recognition from images, and so on,(LeCun*et al*., 2015) since 2000.The mainstream computer-vision and machine-learning communities mostly forsaken the ConvNets till the ImageNet (LeCun *et al*., 2015) competition was held in 2012(LeCun *et al*., 2015).In 1986, the first description modeling of Deep Belief Network (DBN) was published by Vojt (Vojt, 2016),andit was termed as "harmonium"(Vojt, 2016)simultaneously. For mobile vision applications, Google Inc. introduced a class of effective deep learning models, called MobileNets(Liu *et al*., 2018, Balouji*et al*., 2018).For minimizing the model size and latency during the execution, MobileNets try to construct smaller and faster deep convolutional neural network models using the resolution multiplier and the width multiplier. Due to the effectiveness of MobileNets, they are used to implement mobile AR systems. For recognizing dissimilar portions of machines, the models of MobileNets are employed to develop an energy-efficient and powerful vision-based image recognition technique in the AR system.

Deep learning plays a major role in big data solutions as it can extract valuable information from complex systems. Since 2006(LeCun*et al*., 2015, Vanderbruggen& Cavazos, 2017), deep learning is considered as one of the most interesting areas of research among machine learning techniques. In 2011 (Wu *et al*., 2015), Google developed the Google Brain projects with the introduction of Google X projects (Wu *et al*., 2015).Google developed the software that is based on deep learning, for analyzing millions of photos that are taken from YouTube videos so as to identify the objects, like human and cat faces, from the videos. The technology of the project is broadly used in Google+ by applying it in speech recognition system of the Android Operating Systems, and photo-search. Microsoft produced one of the best photograph classifiers,named project Adam, which enables practical computer vision, high-quality speech recognition, and email spam blocking. In 2007, Hinton planned to pre-train one layer at a moment through Restricted Boltzmann Machine (RBM) and then, it is fine-tuned using backpropagation algorithm. Thus, it forms the first advanced pre-training method used in DL that learns in unsupervised manner. Hochreiter's group utilized the deep learners to investigate the effects that occur due to the toxic defects and won the "Tox21 Data Challenge"(LeCun*et al*., 1998), in 2014.CNN was utilized in image recognition for getting better visual pattern for the images, earlier in 2011 and later in May 2012, this approach was found meaningful in image segmentation.

For character recognition, face recognition and traffic sign recognition, which are carried out using image and speech signals, DL introduced various formats, like LeNet, GoogLeNet (Balouji*et al*., 2018, Krizhevsky *et al*., 2012)and AlexNet(Krizhevsky *et al*., 2012, Vanderbruggen& Cavazos, 2017).To develop the research and to design various DL models, companies, such as VirusTotal and Reversing Labs, generate various streams of attacks. Reversing Labs provide access to large stream of attacks for detecting suspicious activities.

Zechao Li and Jinhui Tang (Li & Tang 2015) introduced a distance metric learning algorithm, named weakly-supervised deep metric learning (WDML), under the deep learning framework for community-contributed image retrieval. This method was applied to image retrieval and the experimentaion was performed to analyze its effectiveness. This method was effective and promising. It could be applied to search-based image annotation/tagging. Xueyi Zhao *et al*. (Zhao et al., 2015)developed a joint learning-to-rank method, named Deep Latent Structural SVM (DL-SSVM), which jointly learned the DNN and latent structural SVM to effectively model the interaction relationships at feature-level and ranking-level. This method obtained the promising results in the information retrieval application. Pengcheng Wu *et al*. (Wu et al., 2013) introduced a framework of online multimodal deep similarity learning (OMDSL), which optimally integrate multiple DNNs pretrained with stacked denoising autoencoder. The experimentation was performed to analyze the performance of this method for multimodal image retrieval tasks, in which the encouraging results validate the effectiveness of this technique. However, this technique was rather generic for any multimedia retrieval tasks.

VARIOUS METHODS OF DEEP LEARNING

This section briefly explains the various methods of deep learning for knowledge computing.Table 1 shows the various deep learning methods with their merits and demerits.

Deep Neural Network

Recently, Deep Neural Networks (DNNs) have attained significant attention and are being used in various applications, for achieving significant improvement in the accuracy.DNN is a feed-forward neural network and consists of few hidden layers that are framed between the input unit and output unit. The complexity of input data is significantly reduced by adapting machine learning techniques by making relevant patterns of learning algorithms more focussed for functioning. Feature identification and extraction play important roles in DNN to enhance the performance. However, it is hard and costly regarding time and knowledge to concern this feature engineering approach based on domain knowledge and the data type.

The basic idea of neural network is to learn with the objective of finding optimal parameters so as to solve a certain task. It is necessary to initialize the network parameters before training the network. Even though the values of the parameters are chosen in random manner, initially, usage of few heuristics may offer optimal values for the parameters. By providing the training data to the network, it performs the learning. For producing a better result, the training set is analyzed to adjust the network frequently. When the network attains the expected performance for the given training data, the network is said to be trained.

DNNs are made up of interrelated artificial neurons with layered association of Multilayer Perceptrons(MLPs), and it is useful to model complex non-linear relationships. The object is considered as the layered primitive composition in the compositional models of DNN. Other layers assemble the

Table 1. Deep learning methods

Methods	Description	Advantages	Disadvantages
Deep Neural Network (DNN)	A *DNN is a neural network* with more than two layers.	learn high-level features from data in an incremental manner. This eliminates the need of domain expertise and hard core feature extraction.	It requires very large amount of data in order to perform better than other techniques. It is extremely expensive to train due to complex data models.
Deep Belief Network (DBN)	DBN is a DNN model, which has no difference with MLP from the network structure, but DBN uses greedy layerwise algorithm based on RBM to initial weight matrix of DBN while MLP initials weight matrix randomly.	It can be viewed as a composition of simple, unsupervised networks. This composition leads to a fast, layer-by-layer unsupervised training procedure.	The approximate inference based on mean field approach is slower compared to a single bottom-up pass as in DBN.
Deep Convolutional Neural Network (DCNN)	It is a DNN model that can use *Backpropagation* (BP) algorithm directly.	High accuracy	High computational cost. Require large training data.

features from the lower layers and replace the complicated data with smaller units. Also, deep architecture contains various fundamental techniques. The performance of multiple architectures cannot be compared when they are experimented using dissimilar datasets. For learning a complex relationship among multiple non-linear transformations, DNN utilized an MLPlayer with extra two hidden layers. In particular, DNN is used in various multimedia applications. They offer classifiers providing improved accuracy for extracting important information using raw data. Deep network contains various layers followed by the preceding layer. Every layer in DNN forms a simple function of the preceding layer. The initial layer contains original input data and the final layer produces the output. While using the input data, every layer continuously forma complex functions to provide the output.DNN have attained promising success for large vocabulary continuous speech recognition (LVCSR) tasks for performing state-of-the-art Gaussian Mixture Model/Hidden Markov Model (GMM/HMM) gaining large variety of small and large vocabulary tasks.

Stacked RBMs are used for initializing the weights of DNN, also called as multilayer network. It is responsible for providing a universal model, which can solve different tasks. Pooling, convolution and fully connected layers are the recent DNN architectures used for digit recognition. The representative features extracted from conceptual abstractions are free from human interference by comparing to that selected manually if the given data is used to train the DNN parameters. In gear fault diagnosis, several researches have used these approaches to identify the features perfectly and adaptively, and then, with minimal tuning, the classification of fault/damage is done automatically.

The ranking scores are predicted using forward propagation algorithm based on the extracted features given as the input to the DNN. However, deep neural networks are broadly utilized as front-end feature extractors and in several end-to-end speech processing systems. The incompatible conditions in the testing and the training data lead to the vulnerability of DNNs and thereby, degrade its performance, although DNNs are trained using huge databases for learning the variabilities in the input feature space (Wu *et al.*, 2015).

The output layer of the deep neural network contains neuron functions, which are given as the input to the next layer. By allocating the weights, followed by the summation function, the neuron is significant to determine the strength of the connections. The output generated from the neuron may contain a weight 0 in the summation function of the following neuron. Meanwhile, the output generated may include the weight having higher value for other neurons so as to improve the activation. Here, two things to be remembered are:

- A deep neural network is capable of representing any non-linear prediction space, irrespective of its complexity.
- The resultant output produced by the model depends on the neuron weights assigned.

As DNN learns a hierarchical data representation independently, it does not require novel feature extractors to solve each problem.

For each training situation, DNNs can be properly trained by back-propagating expressions of a cost function that measures the discrepancy between the target outputs and produced the actual outputs. While using the softmax output function, the natural cost function I is the cross-entropy between the target probabilities f and the outputs of the softmax, m:

$$I = -\sum_{X} f_x \log m_x$$

To train the DNN classifier, the target provided takes the value as one or zero.

DNNs learn and discover a good combination of features for complex tasks, which require a lot of human effort. DNN has been used in multimedia applications and has the ability to work on a very large dataset, such as ImageNet dataset with 1.2 million images and 1000 categories.

Deep Belief Network

One of the types of DNN is Deep Belief Network (DBN), which contains many layers that are connected between the layers but not between units. Without any supervision, DBN can reconstructs its input based on the set of training samples. The layers function as feature detectors and then, the classification is performed in DBN based on supervised learning. DBN is comprised of simple unsupervised networks, such as auto encoders and Restricted Boltzmann machines (RBMs),where each hidden layer of a network forms the visible layer of the following network. An RBM contains generative energy-based and undirected model having visible input and hidden layer, in which connections are obtained among the layers and not within the layers. The connections between the peak two layers are undirected and symmetric.

Both layers contain visible and hidden neurons indicating the input and the output layer. The visible neurons are retained using the previous layer, for which these neurons are hidden. The interconnections are made between the visible neurons and the hidden ones.An important characteristic of DBN is that there is no relation between the visible and the hidden neurons and also between bothneurons. From the input data, the RBN themselves canextract and detect the features. To form a multilayer network, numerous layers of RBMs are stacked to each other. From previous RBM layer, every layer uses the hidden neurons. Various layers involved in the deep architecture help to extract deep hierarchical data representations.RBM layers are responsible for performing feature detection, whereas the classification is executed by adopting multilayer perceptron in the last layer. The input to the MLP layer is nothing but the hidden neurons of the previous RBM layer. Thus, the architecture is the combination of probalistic neurons and deterministric neurons in the feature extraction and the classification phases, respectively.

DBN is termed as a generative graphical model for learning a representation that can rebuild the training data with high probability.DBN contains one visible layer and several hidden layers. The statistical relationship can be obtained from hidden layers which are placed between upper layer and lower layer where the higher layer is more complicated. Greedy layer wise training is adopted in deep belief network for training the hidden layers in the bottom-up fashion.

Figure1 shows the DBN architecture, which contains RBM as well as MLP layers. However, RBMs use unsupervised learning and MLPs use supervised learning. Finally, a two-phase training process is obtained. The pre-training process, called first phase, separates the RBM layer used to perform unsupervised training .The second method, known as gradientdescent method contains MLP and RBM layers. The training process, known as learning, can be executed by standard backpropagation algorithm.

RBM consist of energy based method useful for discriminative or else generative model for labelled as well as unlabelled data, contains single layer of hidden units and not contains interior layer of visible and hidden neurons. Following equation shows the mean squared error calculated at the output of each neuron,

Figure 1. Architecture of DBN

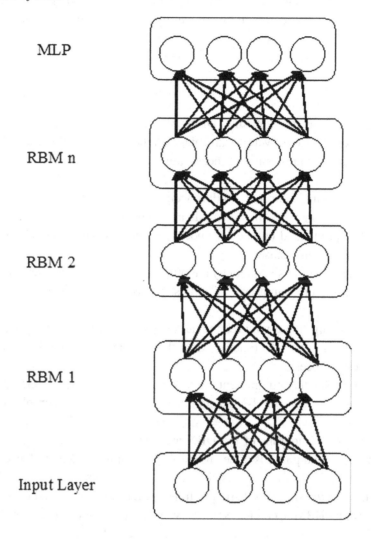

$$I_m = \frac{1}{m_s}(e_s^m)^2$$

$$I_m = \frac{1}{n_s}\sum_{x=1}^{n_s}(g_x^m - f_x^m)^2$$

where n_s is the total neuron present in the outputlayer, e_s^m is the error, g_x^m denotes the output, and f_x^m denotes the desired output. When the expected output and the target output remain same, mean square error becomes zero.

Measuring the network considerations on the entire dataset may be helpful to compute the average error for all input patterns, which will gain by computing the mean squared error,

$$I_{avg} = \frac{1}{m} \sum_{m=1}^{m} I_m$$

Especially in the case of the BP algorithm, DBNs were the primary projected in deep architecture to fine-tune initial network parameters, weights, and biases, rather than using the NN with random variables. The training, as well as the pre-training process, are given below:

- The networks are initialized through random weights, biases and additional parameters
- The input data, which signifies the potentials in its visible neurons, to initialize the first layer of RBM. Then, for a predefined number of epochs, the unsupervised training is carried out in this layer to iterate the training dataset.
- The succeeding layer acquires its input by adopting sampling potentials produced from the hidden neurons present in the preceding layer. The unsupervised training is adopted on this layer using training data samples.
- To repeat the preceding step it requires the number of layers. For each repetition the samples are generated upwards the network. Finally, when the first layer of MLP is arrived, the pretraining phase completed its process.
- Fine tuning through supervised gradient descend begin the training is concluded once it arrives a predefined number of epochs or else reaching the target error rate is completed successfully.

As the MLP network, the neurons of the DBN are interrelated in the similar manner. Hence, the training of DBN in the second phase is done similar to the training of MLP. Hence, the training phase of the DBN follows the initialization process of weights and biases of a deep MLP using the values generated through unsupervised probabilistic pre-training. DBN is comprised of a several RBMs such that the hidden layer of an RBM is connected to the visible layer of the subsequent RBM.DBN follows downward directed connections such that each layer is connected to its lower layer; however, the first two layers are undirected.

Therefore, DBN can be considered as a hybrid model, where the initial two layers are undirected graphical model, and the other models are directed generative model. Here, various layers are trained in a layerwise greedy way and the fine-tuning is done with respect to desired output. Still, the process of training is computationally challenging. Deep Belief Neural Network (DBNN), which is kind of DBN, is a probabilistic generative graphical model that contains numerous layers of stochastic and latent variables.

DBN is a typical deep architecture and it can be used for dimensionality reduction of images and text documents and language modelling. Also, it is used for efficient image identification.

Deep Convolutional Neural Network

Deep Convolutional Neural Network (DCNN) is another type of deep learning. An effective network has the capability to extract deep features of objects. By extracting the texture information by the filters at the low-layer and the semantic information using high-layer filters, DCNN developed multi-feature fusion that is being considered as a recent trend.

Another type of feed-forward neural network is CNN, and is used commonly for analyzing visual imagery. CNNs employ several MLPs for pre-processing. CNN, also known as space invariant or shift invariant artificial neural networks (SIANN), has a shared-weights architecture with translation invariance characteristics.

At present, DCNN are widely used in various platforms, like CPU, GPU, etc. The embedded devices cannot meet the real-time performance on CPU. The subsampling layers, like pooling layer, convolutional layer and fully-connected layer are the three layers of CNN. In order to decrease the dimension, subsampling operation is performed, where the layer of convolution uses convolution operation for sharing the weight. Without the considerations of manually designed features, DCNN can learn the features from the input data for the recognition or detection purpose. Various complex functions can be learned more precisely using DCNN compared to shallow networks. Therefore, DCNN can offer more sophisticated deep representations rather than hand-crafted features.

Based on the given training dataset, DCNN is used for the purpose of detection or recognition. Usually, DCNN model consists of multiple processing layers for learning dissimilar features. Comparing the hierarchy features in deep representation is more discriminative and effective. For this reason, numerous applications are attained using state-of-art. Due to its powerful capability, DCNN plays a very important role in learning. In recent years, effective intermediate regularization strategies and activation functions are proposed to recover the deep model of optimization.

In addition convolution neural network achieved the state of-the-art outcomes in phoneme recognition. CNN is significantly reduced the parameter involvement made by convolutional operations. Especially, convolutional deep belief networks (CDBNs) are used in spectrograms to facilaite the unsupervised acoustic feature learning that aimed at minimizing thereconstruction errors. Additionally, it is regularized using the penalty termnamed sparsity so that to perform the effective audio classification. In the fully connected neural network, the individual neuron present in the layer is connected with the neurons in the next layer and in addition, it is interesting to note that the neurons present within a layer is independent from each other.

CNNs are considered as spatially structured information. In the earlier period, CNNs have revolutionized the pattern recognition community and computer vision. Here, so many layers are available, and the parameters considered here are 100 million. These parameters operate to its best to obtain the patterns from a complex image to offer a better pattern than is obtained manually. The architecture of the convolutional layer is understood better through presenting an image in the input layer of the network. The initial step of the network is regarding the extraction of the features that is brought about using the convolutional and sub-sampling layers, which consist of the feature maps. While extracting the feature in the convolutional layer, the specific feature is obtained through feeding the input image through a filter and it is quite interesting to note that the filtering is progressed through adjusting the weights, which is tuned using the back propagation algorithm. The filter aims at highlighting the potential of a pixel with respect to the surrounding pixels. In the second step, the classification is performed using the extracted features. Thus, it is well known that the individual layers are engaged in performing their own functions of feature extraction and classification. The sub-sampling layer follows the convolutional layer and this arrangement continues and terminates with the subsampling layer based on the depth of the network. After the last sub-sampling layer, the fully connected layer follows, which forms the output layer of the convolutional neural network. Thus, it is well known that the CNNs find major applications in the areas of pattern recognition and particularly, in the visual domain.

Thus, a typical CNN consists of a numerous feature maps that engage themselves in extracting the local feature based on the weights irrespective of their position in the previous layer. The neurons present in a module are constrained to possess the same weights even though their receptive fields are different. The receptive field is nothing but the local area belonging to the previous layer linked with the respective neuron in such a way that the function of a weighted sum is similar to the convolution1. The individual convolutional layer engages itself in computing the local average or maximization of receptive fields of the neurons present in the convolutional layer as a result the resolution is minimized and the sensitiveness with respect to the local variations is reduced. The weigh sharing concept in CNN adds more value to the CNN in such a way that the training parameters employed are reduced. The incorporation of the domain knowledge in pattern recognition using the CNN requires training using the backpropagation algorithm in addition to the deep learning behaviour of CNN. The weight sharing in the CNNs is facilitated using the convolution operation in the convolutional layer, and at the same time, the dimensional reduction is facilitated using the subsampling layer. The weight sharing in the convolutional layer is given as,

$$g_x = h(\sum_v s_{vx} \otimes u_v + l_x)$$

where, g_x indicates the xth output of the convolutional layer, s_v specify the convolutional kernel with the vth input map u_v. The discrete convolution operator is denoted as, $\otimes$ and the bias is denoted as, l_x. The non-linear activation is indicated as, h, which is always a scaled hyperbolic tangent function.

In general, the dimension of the feature map is reduced with the use of sub sampling layer. This can be performed using the implementation of the max pooling operation or the average pooling operation. Then, the fully-connected layers of large number and the softmax layer are placed as the top layer of the recognition and the classification. Recently, the convolutional neural networks are applied in the field of speech recognition, language processing, and so on with great success. The artificial neurons that are present in the convolutional neural networks (CNNs) normally differ from all the other types of the deep learning methods as this method involves in the extraction of the features from only a small portion of the input image that is usually called as receptive fields. Thus, this type of feature extraction encourages the visual mechanisms of the living organisms, where the cells that are present in the visual cortex acts more sensitive to the smaller portion of the visual field. In the same way, various convolutional filters are used to convolute the image that is present in the convolutional layer by shifting the corresponding fields in step by step manner. In the model, each small portion that is obtained from the image, the same parameters are shared by the convolutional filters, and thus the number of the hyper parameters is reduced in large amount. The pooling layer makes in use of the max, mean, or the other statistics that are available in the features of various locations to reduce the variance of the image, and as a result, obtains the essential features. CNN acts as one of the important deep learning methods, in which the multiple layers are trained most robustly and thus, found to be more effective.

The computer vision applications, namely object detection, video surveillance, and the image classification are carried out with the widely used DCNNs. The computational complexity and the huge data moment of the DCNN reduce the performance and the efficiency of the application that blocks the use of DCNN only in embedded devices, like intelligent vehicles and in smart phones. DCNN can be used in the analysis of medical images due to the better performance in the field of natural language processing and the natural image processing. It can also be used in applications related to object segmentation, detection, and recognition. CNNs are used in medical imaging, such as lung nodule classification, 3D knee cartilage segmentation, and in the diagnosis of Alzheimer's disease.

DCNNs are the most well-known architecture for visual analysis. It models the high-level abstractions in images by employing deep architectures composed of multiple non-linear transformations. In CNNs, features are extracted at various levels of abstracts and the system has been allowed to learn complex functions, which directly map raw sensory input data to the output, without relying on hand-engineered features using domain knowledge. Also, DCNN models have been used to improve the image retrieval workflow.

DEEP LEARNING: SUPERVISED LEARNING VS. UNSUPERVISED LEARNING

The classification algorithms of deep learning are similar with the algorithms used in machine learning, which may be either supervised or unsupervised.

Supervised Learning

In supervised learning, the accurate prediction of the given input is facilitated through the establishment of the relationship between the input and the output. When a training input is given, the supervised learning algorithm analyzes the data and generates an inferred function termed as a regression function or a classifier. Supervised Approach, which is an automatic learning approach, generates the rules automatically using the learning database that contains the instances of the cases dealt already. Therefore, the aim of the supervised algorithm is to generalize the unknown inputs and it is selective to learn from the data already managed by the experts. Thus, through the inferred function is generated through the analysis of the given training data that insists the supervised learning as the better classification algorithm. The deep learning strategies utilize supervised classification to transform the input to its intermediate data form similar to that of the principal components, and later establish the layered structures, thereby, minimizing the data redundancy. The popularity of the deep learning methods exists in the conversion of the data into its compact form. Thus, the accuracy of classification using the supervised learning depends on training a data sample using the data source that is already classified correctly by the domain experts. The afore-mentioned techniques are employed in MultiLayer Perceptron (MLP) or feed forward models. The characteristics of the MLP include:

- The complex issues are solved through the effective learning, which is brought about through the hidden neurons present in the network.
- The layer is capable of distinguishing the neuronal activity that exhibits the nonlinear nature.
- The connectivity of the network is enhanced through the availability of the interconnection among the neurons in the network.

In Supervised learning, the weights in the interconnecting link is adjusted based on the error, whereas in unsupervised learning, information corresponding to the set of neurons are utilized. On the other hand, in case of the reinforcement learning, the reinforcement function is employed to change the parameters corresponding with the local weight. Additionally, the concept of machine learning deals with the automated extraction of the meaningful patterns from the data. In case of machine learning, data contributes a major role and the role of the learning algorithm is regarding the extraction of the significant information and properties buried in the data. Above all, the performance of learning and prediction is based on the quality and quantity of the dataset.

Unsupervised Learning

Learning of deep learning methods can also be done in unsupervised manner. In unsupervised learning, deep learner studies the structure of the data and its values, in addition to the underlying data distribution. Revealing the data patterns, which can be utilized for the activity recognition at higher levels, is the major purpose of the unsupervised learning approaches. Here, the actual or the target response is unknown. Unsupervised learning approach requires building a reference model identifying normal and abnormal situations (Weston *et al.*, 2012). Unsupervised classification processes the input data, making decisions without any labelled responses. Due to the existence of large unlabeled data in the current scenario, unsupervised learning is much benefited. For the better representations, DNNs perform mappings and its features can be extracted from various network layers; this reduces the dimensionality of the data. For mapping the input data to the feature space, unsupervised classification employs representation learning. DNNs are capable of learning non-linear mappings that convert the data into other representations, to make unsupervised learning easier and effective.

As the datasets given as the input to deep learning is unlabeled, it is unfeasible to verify if the outcome is correct or not. However, the result attained may be an outcome that is unexpected and is a broader desired goal, or may offer a complex statistical function that result in extracting intended values. Hence, learning the similarities in an unsupervised manner without the requirement of any labels for tuning the learner is of great interest in the vision community. Therefore, it is possible to adopt even larger datasets without any restrictions in the cost. Moreover, it can learn and organize the data without generating an error signal.

APPLICATIONS

Multimedia is the integration of graphics, video, image, document, animation, drawings, audio, and so on. Among these, image, video, and document are the most significant multimedia content. This section describes the retrieval of these multimedia contents using deep learning methods. Table 2 shows the different deep learning methods used in Multimedia Information Retrieval.

Image Retrieval

In recent years, image retrieval based on deep learning methods has receive more attention because the traditional image retrieval based on content and text has not been able to meet the user requirements. The CNN extracts the image features by continuously learning all the images in the image database.

Table 2. Deep learning methods used in Multimedia Information Retrieval

Authors	Method	Purpose	Advantages	Disadvantages
(Pang et al., 2015)	DCNN	Video Retrieval	obtains best performances on two challenging TV-Series datasets	Time consuming
(Dong et al., 2016)	deep Boltzmann machine	Video Retrieval	Encouraging results are obtained when applying the deep features for cross-modal retrieval,	not applicable for hand-crafted features
(Krizhevsky & Hinton, 2011)	Deep autoencoders	Image Retrieval	more accurate matching	quadratic time complexity
Fang Zhao *et al.* (Zhao et al., 2015)	deep semantic ranking based hashing	Image Retrieval	High ranking performance	High computational complexity
(Wu et al., 2013)	online multimodal deep similarity learning	Image Retrieval	Obtains promising results for multimodal similarity search.	generic for any multimedia retrieval tasks
(Lusci et al., 2013)	recursive neural network approaches	Chemoinformatics	build aqueous solubility predictors	This model model with contracted rings has weaker predictive capabilities
(Mitchell, 2014)	Machine learning methods	Chemoinformatics	kNN is an excellent and simple approach for problems with local data	QSAR and QSPR models reveal correlation between descriptors and properties, but do not by themselves prove mechanistic hypotheses.
(Lo et al., 2018)	machine learning techniques	Chemoinformatics	capable of processing big data at high volume,	High computational complexity
(Sugathadasa, et al., 2018)	Deep Learning	Document Retrieval	better accuracy levels	complexities and difficulties
(Balaneshinkordan, et al., 2018)	deep neural architecture	Document Retrieval	significant improvements of retrieval accuracy	Time consuming

The high-level features of deep learning network are more efficient semantic features, which express the information presented in the image. The procedure of extorting the image features by CNN is the study, extraction and abstraction of the image layer by layer. The extraction of more features of the network architecture gives the more abstract description of the image; hence it can be more contribute to image retrieval. The content-based image retrieval is separated into three stages such as, based on the features of image semantic, artificial notes, and vision character of an image. Based on neural networks, there are several methods for the content-based image retrieval. The major attractive factor behind the neural networks in CBIR is the adaptive learning. The self-organizing quality of neural networks is used for supporting an image retrieval method. Content-based image retrieval (CBIR) is a technology which in principle assists for organizing the records of digital pictures with the visual content. A relevance feedback (RF) is a major advance made in the technology of user interaction for the image retrieval. An image retrieval system is created to provide a personal collection which is focused on the features such as flexibility of browsing, display methodology, and personalization. The methods of Text-based image retrieval are used for the applications of conventional database. Image retrieval also categorized into two type's namely exact and relevant image retrieval. Exact image retrieval also referred as image recognition which requires matching on every image accurately, whereas the relevant image retrieval is based on the contents and depending upon the final values of the features, there is flexible scale of relevance. Text-based image retrieval system was used for the applications of conventional database. This is used for the business purpose and applications but the volume and usage of digital images forms the accuracy issues for the text-based image retrieval methods. Latest methods which are developed for the image retrieval considered the texture, shapes, and color of an image object. In the present decades, more region-based methods for image retrieval are proposed which are not depending on the strong segmentation.

Document Retrieval

Now a day, deep learning methods are widely used in document retrieval since they offer significant performance improvement in several branches, such as text recognition and handwritten character recognition. The recurrent neural network with long short-term memory (LSTM) and the CNN are the most triumphant deep learning methods in document retrieval. Document retrieval is the simple task in Information Retrieval (IR). In IR technique, the content is specified as a key word and has several documents. Every document is specified as a bag of words. The cosine similarity is determined among the document and tf-idf vectors of the query, which is considered as a matching score. The conventional technique works well in some cases but it suffers from mismatch problem. The semantic matching among the document and query is important to assist the user to determine the relevant information effectively. Deep learning methods are productively employed to conduct semantic matching in web search, and major improvement in relevance has been obtained. In Legal Document Retrieval by Deep Learning and Document vector embeddings, Document retrieval is about getting every correct document to the correct people, instantaneously. It is a combination of both the security and search criteria. The process of domain-specific information retrieval has been ongoing research and well-known in the field of processing natural language. Several researchers have included the various methods for outperforming the technical as well as domain specificity and offer an established model for different domains of interest. The major block in these retrieving is the serious combination of domain experts, which makes the whole process to be unwieldy and time-consuming. Here, three models have developed which are compared against a fair standard, generated via the on line repositories provided, especially for the legal domain. The three various models incorporated the representations of vector space of the legal domain, where the generation of document vector was completed in two different mechanisms. The ensemble model was built to show a higher accuracy level significantly, which certainly proves the requirements for incorporation of the domain-specific semantic similarity which calculates into the process of information retrieval. This also shows the influence of different distribution of the similarity measures, against different dimensions of document vector, which can lead to improve in the process of legal information retrieval. Document Retrieval is the process of creating a significance list of ranked documents in response to the request of an inquirer by comparing its request with a created index of the documents in the system. A document retrieval system is consisting of three modules such as document processor, matching function, and query analyzer. There are several theoretical models on which the document retrieval systems are based on Language Model, Boolean, Probabilistic, and Vector Space.

Video Retrieval

Video retrieval has received increasing attention due to the massive increase of online videos. In contradiction of image, videos have complex and different visual patterns with high-level semantic content between frames and low-level visual content in every frame, which makes the video retrieval more challenging. Due to the quick development of deep learning, various techniques depends on deep learning are employed for accurate and efficient video retrieval. In deep learning, the high-level semantic features are obtained by combining low-level visual features. CNNs are the essential part of the proficient video retrieval method because they are the flexible image representation tools with strong generalization capabilities. Due to the victory of deep learning methods in image recognition, various research works use the deep learning architectures with hash function for efficient video retrieval. Also, quick video retrieval by deep neural networks is receiving more attention. Newly, with the vast growth of online videos, research of fast video retrieval has received the rising attention. As an expansion of image hashing methods, usual video hashing methods are mostly based on the features of hand-crafted and transform the features of real-value into binary hash codes. Since video presents complex visual information than images, which extracts the features from videos which is much more demanding than that from the images. Therefore, semantic features of high-level are used to signify the essential videos rather than low-level hand-crafted methods. A deep convolutional neural network is developed to extract a binary hash function and the high-level semantic features then it is integrated into this framework for achieving an end-to-end optimization. Mainly, this also merges the triplet loss function which conserves the classification loss function, relative similarity and difference of videos. Experiments are performed on the two public datasets and the outcome shows the superiority of this method compared with the other methods of state-of-the-art video retrieval. Video retrieval is an insignificant expansion of text retrieval, but it is more complex. Most of the data is of sensory origin such as image, video and sound; hence the methods from the computer vision and digital signal processing are essential to remove the related explanation. Also, the significant and precious text data obtained from the audio analysis, much information is captured in the visual stream. Thus, a vast corpse of research in machine-driven video labeling has examined the purpose of visual content, with or without text.

CONCLUSION

Deep learning methods have improved the ability for recognizing, classifying, detecting and describing in a single word. Nowadays, deep learning is emerged as a significant method due to the ability of deep learning in the process of handling multimedia information. In this book chapter, the features and explanation of the deep learning is discussed. In addition the revolution of the deep learning for compensating the inaccuracies in conventional neural networks is clarified. Furthermore, the various methods of deep learning like, DCNN, DBN, and DNN for computing knowledge is described in detail. The applicability of the deep learning for both unsupervised and supervised tasks is comparatively discussed in the end. Finally, the suitability and application of deep learning for various fields are concluded and discussed.

REFERENCES

Balaneshinkordan, S., Kotov, A., & Nikolaev, F. (2018). *Attentive Neural Architecture for Ad-hoc Structured Document Retrieval*. CIKM. doi:10.1145/3269206.3271801

Balouji, E., Gu, I. Y., Bollen, M. H., Bagheri, A., & Nazari, M. (2018). A LSTM-based deep learning method with application to voltage dip classification. In *Proceedings of 18th International Conference on in Harmonics and Quality of Power (ICHQP)* (pp.1-5). Academic Press. 10.1109/ICHQP.2018.8378893

Cao, C., Liu, F., Tan, H., Song, D., Shu, W., Li, W., ... Xie, Z. (2018). Deep Learning and Its Applications in Biomedicine. *Genomics, Proteomics & Bioinformatics*, 16(1), 17–32. doi:10.1016/j.gpb.2017.07.003 PMID:29522900

Chen, T., Rucker, A., & Suh, G. E. (2015, December). Execution time prediction for energy-efficient hardware accelerators. In *Proceedings of the 48th International Symposium on Microarchitecture* (pp. 457-469). ACM. 10.1145/2830772.2830798

Cheng, Y., Wang, D., Zhou, P., & Zhang, T. (2017). *A survey of model compression and acceleration for deep neural networks.* arXiv preprint arXiv:1710.09282

Dean, J., Corrado, G., Monga, R., Chen, K., Devin, M., Mao, M., . . . Ng, A. Y. (2012). Large scale distributed deep networks. In Advances in neural information processing systems (pp. 1223-1231). Academic Press.

Dediu, A.-H., Martín-Vide, C., Mitkov, R., & Truthe, B. (2017). Statistical Language and Speech Processing. In *Proceedings of 5th International Conference, SLSP 2017* (pp. 23–25). Academic Press.

Dong, Z., Jia, S., Wu, T., & Pei, M. (2016). Face Video Retrieval via Deep Learning of Binary Hash Representations. *Proceedings of the Thirtieth AAAI Conference on Artificial Intelligence (AAAI-16),* 3471-3477.

Fukushima, K., & Miyake, S. (1982). Neocognitron: A self-organizing neural network model for a mechanism of visual pattern recognition. In *Competition and cooperation in neural nets* (pp. 267–285). Berlin: Springer. doi:10.1007/978-3-642-46466-9_18

Howard, A. G., Zhu, M., Chen, B., & Kalenichenko, D. (2017). *Mobilenets: Efficient convolutional neural networks for mobile vision applications.* arXiv preprint arXiv:1704.04861

Jia, X. (2017, May). Image recognition method based on deep learning. In *Control And Decision Conference (CCDC), 2017 29th Chinese* (pp. 4730-4735). IEEE. 10.1109/CCDC.2017.7979332

Kim, Y. G., Kim, M., & Chung, S. W. (2017). Enhancing Energy Efficiency of Multimedia Applications in Heterogeneous Mobile Multi-Core Processors. *IEEE Transactions on Computers,* 66(11), 1878–1889. doi:10.1109/TC.2017.2710317

Krizhevsky, A., & Hinton, G. E. (2011). Using Very Deep Autoencoders for Content-Based Image Retrieval. *Proceedings of 19th European Symposium on Artificial Neural Networks.*

Krizhevsky, A., Sutskever, I., & Hinton, G. E. (2012). Imagenet classification with deep convolutional neural networks. In Advances in neural information processing systems (pp. 1097-1105). Academic Press.

LeCun, Y., Bengio, Y., & Hinton, G. (2015). Deep learning. *Nature, 521*(7553), 436.

LeCun, Y., Bottou, L., Bengio, Y., & Haffner, P. (1998). Gradient-based learning applied to document recognition. *Proceedings of the IEEE,* 86(11), 2278–2324. doi:10.1109/5.726791

Li, Z., & Tang, J. (2015). Weakly Supervised Deep Metric Learning for Community-Contributed Image Retrieval. *IEEE Transactions on Multimedia, 17*(11), 1989–1999. doi:10.1109/TMM.2015.2477035

Liu, J., Pan, Y., Li, M., Chen, Z., Tang, L., Lu, C., & Wang, J. (2018). Applications of deep learning to MRI images: A survey. *Big Data Mining and Analytics, 1*(1), 1–18. doi:10.26599/BDMA.2018.9020001

Lo, Y., Rensi, S.E., Torng, W., & Altman, R.B. (2018). *Machine learning in chemoinformatics and drug discovery.* Academic Press.

Lusci, A., Pollastri, G., & Baldi, P. (2013). Deep Architectures and Deep Learning in Chemoinformatics: The Prediction of Aqueous Solubility for Drug-Like Molecules. *Journal of Chemical Information and Modeling*, *53*(7), 1563–1575.

Mitchell, J. B. O. (2014). Machine learning methods in chemoinformatics. *Wiley Interdisciplinary Reviews. Computational Molecular Science*, *4*(5), 468–481.

Pang, L., Zhu, S., & Ngo, C. (2015). Deep Multimodal Learning for Affective Analysis and Retrieval. *IEEE Transactions on Multimedia*, *17*(11), 2008–2020. doi:10.1109/TMM.2015.2482228

Smolensky, P. (1986). *Information processing in dynamical systems: Foundations of harmony theory (No. CU-CS-321-86)*. Colorado Univ at Boulder Dept of Computer Science.

Sugathadasa, K., Ayesha, B., Silva, N., Perera, A.S., Jayawardana, V., Lakmal, D., & Perera. M., (2018). Legal Document Retrieval Using Document Vector Embeddings and Deep Learning. *Intelligent Computing*, 160-175.

Vanderbruggen, T., & Cavazos, J. (2017). Large-scale exploration of feature sets and deep learning models to classify malicious applications. In Resilience Week (RWS), 2017 (pp. 37-43). IEEE. doi:10.1109/RWEEK.2017.8088645

Vojt, J. (2016). *Deep neural networks and their implementation*. Academic Press.

Wang, D., & Chen, J. (2018). Supervised speech separation based on deep learning: An overview. *IEEE/ACM Transactions on Audio, Speech, and Language Processing*, *26*(10).

Weston, J., Ratle, F., Mobahi, H., & Collobert, R. (2012). Deep learning via semi-supervised embedding. In *Neural Networks: Tricks of the Trade* (pp. 639–655). Berlin: Springer. doi:10.1007/978-3-642-35289-8_34

Wu, D., Wang, J., Cai, Y., & Guizani, M. (2015). Millimeter-wave multimedia communications: Challenges, methodology, and applications. *IEEE Communications Magazine*, *53*(1), 232–238. doi:10.1109/MCOM.2015.7010539

Wu, P., Hoi, S. C. H., Xia, H., Zhao, P., Wang, D., & Miao, C. (2013). Online Multimodal Deep Similarity Learning with Application to Image Retrieval. *Proceedings of the 21st ACM international conference on Multimedia*, 153-162. 10.1145/2502081.2502112

Wu, Z. Y., El-Maghraby, M., & Pathak, S. (2015). Applications of deep learning for smart water networks. *Procedia Engineering*, *119*, 479–485. doi:10.1016/j.proeng.2015.08.870

Yao, S., Zhao, Y., Zhang, A., Hu, S., Shao, H., Zhang, C., ... Abdelzaher, T. (2018). Deep Learning for the Internet of Things. *Computer*, *51*(5), 32–41. doi:10.1109/MC.2018.2381131

Zhao, F., Huang, Y., Wang, L., & Tan, T. (2015). *Deep Semantic Ranking Based Hashing for Multi-Label Image Retrieval*. Computer Vision and Pattern Recognition.

Zhao, X., Li, X., & Zhang, Z. (2015). Multimedia Retrieval via Deep Learning to Rank. *IEEE Signal Processing Letters*, *22*(9), 1487–1491. doi:10.1109/LSP.2015.2410134

Chapter 9
Deep Learning Techniques and Optimization Strategies in Big Data Analytics:
Automated Transfer Learning of Convolutional Neural Networks Using Enas Algorithm

Murugan Krishnamoorthy
https://orcid.org/0000-0002-6751-380X
Anna University, India

Bazeer Ahamed B.
https://orcid.org/0000-0003-1559-8386
Balaji Institue of Technology and Science, India

Sailakshmi Suresh
Anna University, India

Solaiappan Alagappan
Anna University, India

ABSTRACT

Construction of a neural network is the cardinal step to any machine learning algorithm. It requires profound knowledge for the developer in assigning the weights and biases to construct it. And the construction should be done for multiple epochs to obtain an optimal neural network. This makes it cumbersome for an inexperienced machine learning aspirant to develop it with ease. So, an automated neural network construction would be of great use and provide the developer with incredible speed to program and run the machine learning algorithm. This is a crucial assist from the developer's perspective. The developer can now focus only on the logical portion of the algorithm and hence increase productivity. The use of Enas algorithm aids in performing the automated transfer learning to construct the complete neural network from the given sample data. This algorithm proliferates on the incoming data. Hence, it is very important to inculcate it with the existing machine learning algorithms.

DOI: 10.4018/978-1-7998-1192-3.ch009

INTRODUCTION

Artificial Intelligence (AI), a hot topic among the computer society these days. This revolutionary domain indirectly depends on Deep Learning to formulate the structure of the artificial neural network, the brain. Deep learning is process and a way to automate Predictive Analytics. Traditional machine learning algorithms are linear and are stacked in a hierarchy of increased abstraction and complexity. AutoML alleviates human exertion by computerizing the layout of ML algorithms (Afridi, Ross, and Shapiro, 2018). It is prevalent for the implementation of deep learning framework. But this perception incurs exalted computational cost. To reconcile this issue, we resolve to Transfer neural techniques that employs comprehension from preceding tasks to accelerate design of neural networks. We broaden probe routines to enable simultaneous practice over various tasks and then transit the probe strategy to new tasks. This proposal deduces the coupling time of a task training by significant degrees on many tasks.

The system controller is modelled over generic engineering composition and parameters, along with task-related decisions encrypted in the task implantation (Ahamed and Ramkumar, 2016). For any given task, the parameters of the corresponding task controller are reloaded and new implantations are randomly activated for the new task. The parameters of the controller are synchronized with the new task implantations. By implantation for new tasks, the application that biases towards process actions that excelled well on other comparable tasks is learnt by the controller. This is the performance of transfer controller.

Designing these deep learning models is a difficult task on its own and it is not too farfetched, that it is a process of trial and error, as there is no fixed methodology to design a model that is guaranteed to perform well. Thus the focus of this implementation is to provide a modular and extensible framework that can automatically design high performing deep learning models.

BACKGROUND STUDY

Neural Networks and Domain Specific Language

Neural networks a set of logic and knowledge based approach sequenced, modelled based on the brain of human (Ahamed and Yuvaraj, 2018). They recognize by interpreting patterns, sensory data through machine perception. Commercial applications technologies generally focused on solving complex pattern or signal processing problems such as speech, handwriting, oil exploration data analysis, facial recognition and weather predictions. A Domain Specific Language (DSL), computer programing restricted expressiveness focused on a specific domain. DSLs provides significant gain in Application productivity, creativity developers, portability and performance. DSLs offer pre-defined abstractions represent concepts from application domain. A programmer uses one or more of the DSLs write the programs using specific domain constructs and notations. In additional ability to use domain knowledge to apply static & dynamic optimizations to a program (Cessac et. al, 2016). DSL specifically targeted, machine learning, abstractions to define neural networks, capture high level information used to increased productivity, performance and expose parallelism. It moves the programmers approach from a low level detailing that are not the focus of the system in development, lets them target on work the solution for the problem at hand.

Transfer Leaning and Structural Learning

A neural network gains knowledge when trained on a data set using a set of parameters. The knowledge refers to the weights, connections and other hyper parameters which would produce the desired results for the neural network and the data set (Liu et. al, 2019). There will be a myriad set of parameters and combinations for each problem, called as the parameter space. Selecting these parameters manually can be laborious because the user will have to select the variables from the large parameter space by trial and error. The user will also have to spend hours or days training the network which may not yield the desired results. Transfer learning is a machine learning method in which the knowledge gained by a neural network for one task is transferred to another network that performs a similar task. The network can be fine-tuned to accomplish the new task (Jaafra et. al, 2018). Due to the transfer of weights, the network does not need to be trained from scratch. This reduces the time it takes to build and train the network. The design of the neural network architecture is a complex task that requires a wide range of manual configurations and expertise. To address the problem, several algorithms and analysis under the topic of Structural Learning were developed, to learn architecture and parameters automatically. It is an alternative learning method to transfer learning that decides the structure of a neural network. The optimal structure will be decided in the process of learning. Structural learning networks learn the appropriate network architecture for the learning task instead of having a fixed architecture design and parameters (Hu et. al, n.d.).

Starting from a simple network model, as the learning iterates over several epochs, the network starts to grow by adding and removing neurons necessary for the task. It will learn the parameters and their dependencies and also finds the connections that are best for the network during the training period. Most of the applications of structural learning algorithms are to find the optimal structure of 'Bayesian networks'. There are several other algorithms and methods proposed structural learning of deep neural networks (Joglekar et. al, 2019).

Neural Architecture Search

Characterizer is used to represent/characterize a dataset. The characterizer extracts the features of a given dataset and computes the DCN using dataset difficulty estimation (Liu et. al, 2019). **Trainer:** The trainer implements algorithms like architecture searches, structural learning networks or just implements state-of-the-art neural network architectures. It is the job of the trainer to train and evaluate the neural network. **Lifelong Database of Datasets:** The LDD consists of datasets, their DCN and their corresponding pre-trained, optimal neural network architectures. The corresponding network architectures are found by using Trainers. When the user loads a new dataset, the framework calculates its DCN, finds the most similar dataset from the LDD and returns its neural network. **Transfer Learner:** The neural network architecture found in the previous step is fed to the Transfer Learner, which reuses the network weights and architecture, and trains the network on the user's dataset.

Neural Architecture Search (NAS) is a method of searching for the optimal architecture in the neural network search space. NAS can be done using brute force algorithms, evolutionary algorithms, reinforcement learning and probability based methods. Training just one large neural network takes considerable time (Liu, 2017). NAS requires huge computations as the search algorithm has to select an architecture, train & validate it on the dataset and move on to the next, before finding an optimal architecture. NAS is computation intensive as it has to train multiple neural network architectures before convergence. NAS is

Figure 1. Architecture of the framework based on transfer learning

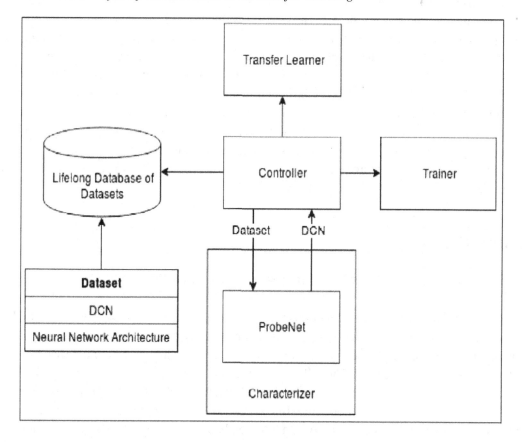

a search algorithm at its core, and hence it is not guaranteed to find the global optimum. However, results obtained by using NAS have already outperformed previous state-of-the-art neural network architectures.

Machine learning/ deep learning resulted in development of specialized frameworks to design neural networks, train and use them in production environment. These methods try to find a neural network that best suits the dataset by designing architectures that are more likely to give high accuracies and training them on the dataset. OptiML is a domain specific language for Machine learning and OptiML is developed at Stanford University's Pervasive Parallelism Laboratory (Mundt et. al, 2019). DeepDSL also converts the program to an IR with the help of symbolic gradient, optimizes the code and finally generates a Java source code that can run on any CUDA enabled platforms. DeepDSL programs are also efficient and its runtime performance and memory consumption are significantly better than Caffe and Tensorflow. It has some feature which includes automatically loading the saved parameters and continuing the training from where it stopped at the previous execution.

Meta-QNN is a method for meta modelling of neural networks using reinforcement techniques. Q-learning is chosen as reinforcement algorithm, epsilon-greedy search is used to switch between exploratory and exploitative actions of the reinforcement agent and experience replays are used to store the past experiences. ***DeepArchitect*** is a Domain Specific Language that allows the user to define the search space for NAS. The DSL allows any choice based NAS algorithm to be implemented in a modular and extensible fashion. ***ProxylessNAS*** is a method of modelling the architecture search space as a neural network, with each choice being represented as a path in the network. Path binarization is used to minimize the cost of training, as it represents the paths as O or 1, leading to only one path being active and trained at any instant. Each back propagation step includes weight updation and architecture learning (Musa, Elamin, and Elhassan, 2017). *Source Selection* can be automated by an information theoretic zero-shot method, which ranks the source convolutional neural networks based on a measure of transferability. Ranking the CNNs based on transferability is shown to achieve high correlation when compared with the accuracies obtained after transfer learning. *Net2Net* allows the user to transfer knowledge to wider and deeper networks with methods called Net2WiderNet and Net2DeeperNet respectively (Pham et. al, 2018). This is a general overview of above discussed learning paradigms that can be applied to different scenarios based on need and requirements to satisfy the given problem statement. This can be adapted after the initial analysis about the project domain.

EXPERIMENTAL STUDY

Dynamic Approach for Constructing the Neural Network

DeepDSL outperforms benchmarking programs from the current mainstream. However, DeepDSL is not user friendly and only showcases the optimization and efficiency. Hence this project proposes a DSL that provides a user friendly API with simple constructs for defining neural networks (Zhao and Huang, 2018, with its backend as DeepDSL. The following constructs had been implemented:Input layer, Fully connected layer, Convolution layer, Max pooling layer, Flattening layer, Relu, Softmax Activations and Mnistdataset. Here Input layer has 3 nodes, the first node with value 1, other two nodes with X1 and X2 as inputs, there is no computation performed at Input layer, hence the outputs nodes remains same, which are fed into the consecutive Layer. From this output, convolution implementations are performed:max pooling and flattening. Rectified Linear takes real-valued input and thresholds at zero, replaces negative values with zero. This is the overall working of deepDSL.

The Constructs of our DSL are similar to Python's Keras functional API (Figure 2). The python code written by the user generates the DeepDSLScala code when executed. The corresponding DeepDSL code is shown in Figure 2.

Figure 2. DSL code implementing the training neural network on MNIST dataset

```
1   from py2deepdsl import *
2
3   layers = [
4               Input('mnist', shape=(1, 28, 28), batchSize=512),
5               Convolv(kernelSize=5, numKernels=20),
6               MaxPool(kernelSize=2),
7               Convolv(kernelSize=5, numKernels=20),
8               MaxPool(kernelSize=2),
9               Flatten(numDims=4, cuts=1),
10              Full(numNodes=500, activation='relu'),
11              Full(numNodes=18, activation='softmax' )
12          ]
13
14  model = Model(layers=layers)
15  model .compile(decay=0.0005, momentum=0.1, learnrate=0.01, loss='categorical_crossentropy', epochs=50)
```

Construction of the Neural Network using Enas Algorithm

Defining layers manually is suboptimal as it is not guaranteed that it is found the models that give high accuracy. The user has to try out different architectures before finding an architecture that performs well. A framework can be made to automate this process (Weng et. al, 2019). Neural Architecture Search, Structural learning networks and Transfer learning are some concepts that can be used here. A framework is proposed that takes only a dataset as input and automatically finds the best neural network architecture. The framework would store many datasets and their corresponding architectures. When the user gives a new dataset, the framework chooses one of the stored architectures by finding a dataset which is most similar in characteristics to the user's dataset.

ENAS algorithm is a very quick and efficient learning technique that always assures greater accuracy. ENAS is abbreviated as an Efficient Neural Architecture Search. It automatically starts off by framing a set of building blocks that helps in architecture generation. This algorithm makes use of a controller called recurrent neural network, which is responsible for sampling some of the building blocks and connecting them to provide a complete architecture. Because of these features it is considered the state of the art algorithm when combined with transfer learning.

Figure 3, we can observe the code grabs the useful components using the ENAS algorithm and the basic building blocks can be generated easily when compared to the simple generation. Once the architecture search algorithm uses both ENAS and Auto-ML the search becomes far more efficient as the neural network can be generated using a simple Graphical Processing Unit in a very minimalamount of

Figure 3. Constructing the neural network using enas algorithm on the Mnist dataset

```
1   package deepdsl.derivation
2   import deepdsl .analysis._
3   import deepdsl.ast.(Lmdb, Mnist _)
4   import deepdsl .derivation.MemoryAnalysis._
5   import deendsl. lang.
6   import deepdsl. layer ._
7   import deepdsl.run._
8   import org.junit.Test
9
10  class TestNetworkNew (
11      val path = "deepdsl/gen"
12      private def synet(batch size: Int, learn_rate: Float, momentum: Float, decay: Float, test_iter: Int, mame: String)
13      {
14          val N = batch size
15          val dataset = List(N, 1, 20, 20)
16          val K = 10
17          val dataset = Mnist(dim)
18          val y = T._new("v", List(N))
19          val x = T.new("x", dim)
20          val cv0 = CudaLayer.convolv("cv0", 5, 20)
21          val mp0 = CudaLayer.max_pool(2)
22          val cv1 = CudaLayer.convolv("cv1", 5, 20)
23          val mp1 = Cudalayer.max_pool(2)
24          vao f10 = Layer. flatten(4, 1)
25          val fc0 = Layer .full("fc0", 500)
26          val relu = CudaLayer.relu(2)
27          val fc1 = Layer.full("fc1", 10)
28          val softmax = CudaLayer .softeax
29          val network = softmax o fc1 o relu o fc0 o f10 o mp1 o cv1 o mp0 o cv0
30          val printin(typeof(network))
31          val xCuda = x.asCuda
32          val yCuda = y.asIndicator(k).asCuda
33          val loss = (Layer.log_loss(yCuda) o network)(xCuda)
34          val accuracy = network(xCuda)
35          val param = loss.freeParam.toList
36          val solver = train(name, train_iter, test_iter, learn_rate, momentum, decay, 0)
37          val loop = Loop(loss, accuracy, dataset, (x, y), param, solver)
38          val runtimememory(loop.train.lst)
39          parameterMemory(param, momentum)
40          CudaCompile(path). print (loop)
41      }
42  @Test
43  def testMyNet = synet(512, 0.01f, 0.1f, 0.0005f, 50, 1, "MyNet") }
```

time (Wistuba and Pedapati, 2019). This approach could be a break-through for the machine learning engineers in developing a neural network that can be of high efficiency while applying it to artificial intelligence.

From Figure 4, we can observe that the enas algorithm runs multiple times with the same hidden layer and learns from the mistakes done in the previous iterations. This is an automatic construction process for an efficient neural network. This network is constructed in the backend without the user's manipulation. Hence it is an optimised method of constructing a neural network that can dynamically be generated on the basis of the user's input.

Learning Graph Analysis

Figure 5 Describes the different learning rates that are possible when applying different machine learning algorithms. It tells about the amount of precision loss that takes place in various algorithms over the period of time.

Figure 6 distinguishes the performance between static and dynamic learning. From the graph, it is evident that dynamic learning tends to have a higher start when compared to static learning. The sample user data given for the machine to learn is responsible for the higher start. This dynamic approach can be made possible with the implementation of ENAS algorithm.

Different Architectures like Lenet-5, VGG-16, Overfeat were implemented using this DSL and evaluated on the MNIST dataset. In doing this, it is shown that our DSL is able to provide enough constructs to implement most of the CNNs. However, advanced neural networks like Resnet and Inception require more constructs like residual (skip) connections to be implemented. From Table 1, it is observed that around 53% of DeepDSL's code are hidden by DSL, thus reducing code in the same programs. The DSL

Figure 4. The neural network constructed by the Enas algorithm

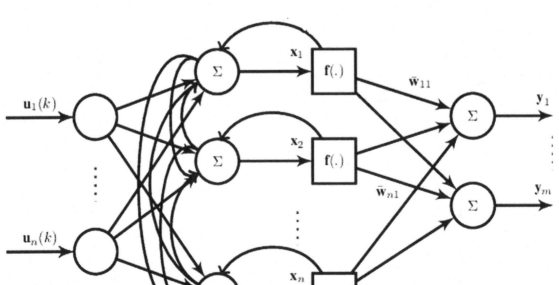

Figure 5. Loss obtained over a period of time for different learning rates

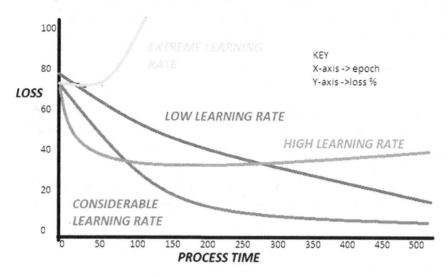

Figure 6. Performance comparison between dynamic and static learning where the former has a better start due to prior user data knowledge

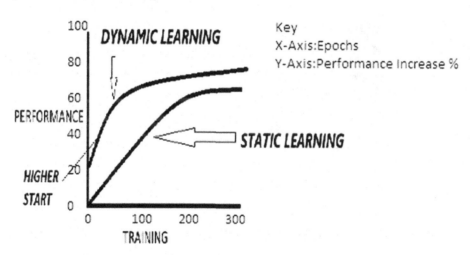

Table 1. Lines of code for implementing deep neural networks that train on MNIST dataset

Network	Our DSL	DeepDSL	% decrease
Lenet - 5	13	29	55.17
VGG - 16	24	49	51.02
OverFeat	18	39	53.84

programs take an average of 0.017 seconds for generating the DeepDSL source code, regardless of the neural networks implemented. The runtime performance can be expected to be identical to DeepDSL, as our DSL only generates the source code for DeepDSL.

Implementation Graph Analysis

The Figure 7 graph depicts the assessment accuracy that takes place in the initial iterations. Here it is observed that the assessment accuracy increases gradually over the learning time and the loss gained in the initial stages is very low because the user data is very similar to the input data.

The Figure 8 graph depicts the assessment accuracy that takes place in the iterations after the learning gradually increases. Now it is observed that the assessment accuracy is almost a hundred percent and the loss generated may have increased slightly. But the correctness of the output is very high.

Figure 7. Assessment accuracy calculated over multiple epochs at the initial stages

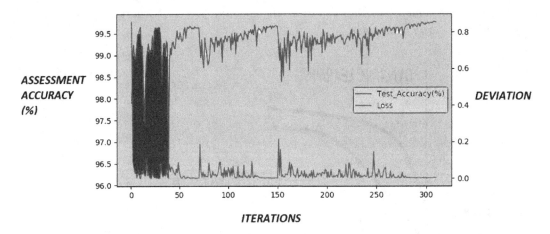

Figure 8. Assessment accuracy calculated over multiple epochs at the consecutive stages

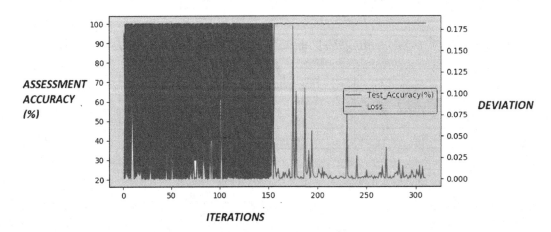

CONCLUSION

Development of this approach would include extending the domain of function to contain more exemplar objects. This incurs excessive computational cost. To resolve this issue we initiate transfer learning and this is implemented using controllers. This in hand diminishes the time for converging many records. Various transfer-based approach is applied across practicalities and configurations. Some preceding over prior distribution structures, obtained from NLP is used for domains where image related processing is involved. The controller that is part of transfer learning is made more robust to quantification noise, and to generalise the resulting learning model applicable for complex sample predictions. A series of analysis have been made to build up concrete vision in achieving dynamic approach towards neural network simulation. This project has not only looked into the theoretical aspects of functioning, but has also implemented it from the coding aspect in order to practically make this of avail. This system will enable in the development of dynamic networks based on user input. This is indeed a leap from the current existing structures. This combined approach of ENAS and Auto-ML with transfer learning to generate neural networks could be the future of artificial intelligence.

REFERENCES

Afridi, M. J., Ross, A., & Shapiro, E. M. (2018). On automated source selection for transfer learning in convolutional neural networks. *Pattern Recognition*, *73*, 65–75. doi:10.1016/j.patcog.2017.07.019 PMID:30774153

Ahamed, B. B., & Ramkumar, T. (2016). An intelligent web search framework for performing efficient retrieval of data. *Computers & Electrical Engineering*, *56*, 289–299. doi:10.1016/j.compeleceng.2016.09.033

Ahamed, B. B., & Yuvaraj, D. (2018, October). Framework for Faction of Data in Social Network Using Link Based Mining Process. In *International Conference on Intelligent Computing & Optimization* (pp. 300-309). Springer.

Cessac, B., Kornprobst, P., Kraria, S., Nasser, H., Pamplona, D., Portelli, G., & Viéville, T. (2016, October). ENAS: A new software for spike train analysis and simulation. *Bernstein Conference*.

Choi, K., Fazekas, G., & Sandler, M. (2016). *Automatic tagging using deep convolutional neural networks*. arXiv preprint arXiv:1606.00298

Elsken, T., Metzen, J. H., & Hutter, F. (2019). Neural Architecture Search: A Survey. *Journal of Machine Learning Research*, *20*(55), 1–21.

Gopalakrishnan, K., Khaitan, S. K., Choudhary, A., & Agrawal, A. (2017). Deep Convolutional Neural Networks with transfer learning for computer vision-based data-driven pavement distress detection. *Construction & Building Materials*, *157*, 322–330.

Jaafra, Y., Laurent, J. L., Deruyver, A., & Naceur, M. S. (2018). *A review of meta-reinforcement learning for deep neural networks architecture search*. arXiv preprint arXiv:1812.07995

Joglekar, M. R., Li, C., Adams, J. K., Khaitan, P., & Le, Q. V. (2019). *Neural Input Search for Large Scale Recommendation Models*. arXiv preprint arXiv:1907.04471

Liu, C., Chen, L. C., Schroff, F., Adam, H., Hua, W., Yuille, A. L., & Fei-Fei, L. (2019). Auto-deeplab: Hierarchical neural architecture search for semantic image segmentation. In *Proceedings of the IEEE Conference on Computer Vision and Pattern Recognition* (pp. 82-92). IEEE.

Liu, H. (2017). *Large-Scale Machine Learning over Graphs* (Doctoral dissertation). Carnegie Mellon University.

Mundt, M., Majumder, S., Murali, S., Panetsos, P., & Ramesh, V. (2019). Meta-learning Convolutional Neural Architectures for Multi-target Concrete Defect Classification with the COncrete DEfect BRidge IMage Dataset. In *Proceedings of the IEEE Conference on Computer Vision and Pattern Recognition* (pp. 11196-11205). IEEE.

Musa, R. Y. M., Elamin, A. E., & Elhassan, E. M. (2017). *Implementation of artificial neural networks and fuzzy logic for hypovolemia monitoring in the operation theatre* (Doctoral dissertation). Sudan University of Science and Technology.

Pham, H., Guan, M. Y., Zoph, B., Le, Q. V., & Dean, J. (2018). *Faster discovery of neural architectures by searching for paths in a large model*. Academic Press.

Weng, Y., Zhou, T., Liu, L., & Xia, C. (2019). Automatic Convolutional Neural Architecture Search for Image Classification Under Different Scenes. *IEEE Access: Practical Innovations, Open Solutions*, 7, 38495–38506. doi:10.1109/ACCESS.2019.2906369

Wistuba, M., & Pedapati, T. (2019). *Inductive Transfer for Neural Architecture Optimization*. arXiv preprint arXiv:1903.03536

Zhao, T., & Huang, X. (2018). Design and implementation of DeepDSL: A DSL for deep learning. *Computer Languages, Systems & Structures*, 54, 39–70. doi:10.1016/j.cl.2018.04.004

KEY TERMS AND DEFINITIONS

Deep Architect: A domain-specific language that allows the user to define the search space for NAS. The DSL allows any choice based NAS algorithm to be implemented in a modular and extensible fashion.

Deep Learning (DL): A part of machine learning with its algorithms, to the structure and working of the brain called artificial neural networks; a knowledge process and a way to automate Predictive Analytics.

Domain-Specific Language (DSL): A computer programing-restricted expressiveness focused on a specific domain. DSL specifically targeted, machine learning, abstractions to define neural networks, capture high level information used to increased productivity, performance and expose parallelism.

Meta-QNN: The method for meta modelling of neural networks using reinforcement techniques.

Net2Net: System that allows the user to transfer knowledge to wider and deeper networks with methods called Net2WiderNet and Net2DeeperNet, respectively.

Neural Architecture Search (NAS): The method of searching for the optimal architecture in the neural network search space.

ProxylessNAS: The method of modelling the architecture search space as a neural network, with each choice being represented as a path in the network.

Structural Learning: Networks that learn the appropriate network architecture for the learning task instead of having a fixed architecture design and parameters.

Chapter 10
Dimensionality Reduction With Multi-Fold Deep Denoising Autoencoder

Pattabiraman V.
https://orcid.org/0000-0001-8734-2203
Vellore Institute of Technology, Chennai, India

Parvathi R.
Vellore Institute of Technology, Chennai, India

ABSTRACT

Natural data erupting directly out of various data sources, such as text, image, video, audio, and sensor data, comes with an inherent property of having very large dimensions or features of the data. While these features add richness and perspectives to the data, due to sparsity associated with them, it adds to the computational complexity while learning, unable to visualize and interpret them, thus requiring large scale computational power to make insights out of it. This is famously called "curse of dimensionality." This chapter discusses the methods by which curse of dimensionality is cured using conventional methods and analyzes its performance for given complex datasets. It also discusses the advantages of nonlinear methods over linear methods and neural networks, which could be a better approach when compared to other nonlinear methods. It also discusses future research areas such as application of deep learning techniques, which can be applied as a cure for this curse.

INTRODUCTION

Dimensionality Reduction in Big data

Big Data generally refers to"Complex" data that is unmanageable to store, process and derive insights out of it using the infrastructure/technology/tools that are currently available at our disposal. Hence, Big data has become more of a relative terminology because of the fact that what is "big data" today shall

DOI: 10.4018/978-1-7998-1192-3.ch010

become "small data" over a period of time as we see cheaper storage costs and increasing computing power and easy availability of volumes of natural data. To solve real world problems using big data, we face multitude of challenges such as high Dimensionality, Scalability and transparency of algorithms, Data visualization, Real time analysis and computational complexity in data processing, etc.

Natural data inherently has very large dimensions which makes the algorithms using them prohibitively expensive in terms of computation. For example, a single grayscale image of a handwritten digit of size 28x28 pixels has to be represented as 728 vector values to represent each pixel (in this case each pixel is a dimension) and hence each image is dimensionally represented with 728 values. If we have to train a model to classify image of a digit, then we are talking about tens of thousands of examples to train and test. In the case of a document classification problem, each word which is occurring in the document is a dimension and this is complicated more with millions of documents. High dimensional natural data source comes with high volume of raw data along with thousands of features and in addition complicates the learning process from the data. Hence reducing the dimensions without losing the content and context of the data becomes a very important data processing step in Big Data analytics since it reduces the computational complexity to learn, minimizes storage requirements and makes raw data easier to visualize and interpret. Moreover, Dimensionality reduction is the solution for multiple other downstream problems such as classification and visualization and hence a key foundational problem to be addressed earlier in the cycle of Machine learning and Predictive analytics using Big data. Though there are many dimensionality reduction techniques used in practice and are in research, they are primarily divided into two categories Linear and Non-linear methods. This classification is based on whether the transformation function used in performing the dimensionality reduction is linear or not. Essentially the dimensionality reduction process projects raw data from high dimensional space to lower dimensional space (learned/extracted features) using this transformation function.

Non-Linear Methods of Dimensionality Reduction

Linear methods, such as PCA (Principal component analysis), though popular, presents very obvious features after transformation due the simplicity of the raw data being handled. Linear techniques assume and tend to fit the data and its features over a straight line and most real world complex datasets are not that simple. In complex datasets, multi dimensionality is key a attribute and Linear DR methods tend to lose the meaning inside such complexities. Non-linear DR methods do not assume that data lies in a linear fit or subspace and tend to be more robust and scalable in application using natural datasets such as images, audio and documents. Since the focus of the paper is on natural data sets, we will not focus on all linear techniques except PCA (for the purpose of benchmarking) and only analyze select nonlinear DR techniques and compare and discuss methods that are more suitable for such datasets. We will also not consider many variants and add-ons (such as Factor analysis, Principal curves, etc) which just align a mixture of linear models with the basic method. We will also not consider methods which are purely used in supervised mode such as Linear discriminant analysis and methods which are based on clustering techniques such as Self-organizing maps.

This chapter analyse the following twelve nonlinear techniques: (1) Kernel PCA,(2) Isomap, (3) Maximum Variance Unfolding, (4) diffusion maps, (5) Locally Linear Embedding,(6) Laplacian Eigenmaps, (7) Hessian LLE, (8) Local Tangent Space Analysis, (9) Sammon mapping,(10) multilayer autoencoders, (11) Locally Linear Coordination, and (12) manifold charting.

Neural Network Based Dimensionality Reduction Methods

Dimensionality reduction methods such as PCA (Linear) or ISOMAP, MDS, LLE (Nonlinear) may fall short in extracting useful features from complex datasets whereas Neural networks, influenced by the function of human brain, tend to learn features in a hierarchical/layered architecture generating patterns beyond nearest neighbors in the data. With Input and Output data driving the design of source and target layers, key design consideration is the number of neurons in the hidden layer and hence does not require knowledge about the data or parameters which is required in other methods. This advantage enables unsupervised learning suited for natural datasets and also automatic extraction of features independent of human intervention in machine learning. Deep Neural network Learning architectures are designed with multiple hidden layers and have the capability to generalize the input data by preserving the global properties (e.g. properties that describe image as a whole and not part of the image) and also enable automatic extraction of features. The nonlinear function used (in most cases a Sigmoid function) automatically fine tunes the weights to minimize the cost function (to reduce the reconstruction error) that transforms the data from high dimensional space to a lower dimensional space.

Though Neural networks are used for the purpose of Dimensionality reduction over the past decade, deep learning architectures have gained lot of mind share in the last couple of years and are used in many real world applications like computer vision, text analytics, voice analytics, etc. Using deep learning architecture for a key big data problem i.e. Dimensionality reduction, is a less explored area but initial studies have shown lot of promise and potential. In order to understand the intricacies of the behavior of various dimensionality reduction methods, the authors intend to study key nonlinear methods including a single-layer neural network based method and a deep learning method. This paper lays the foundation for the comparative study of techniques and proposes the methods and metrics used to empirically compare the performance of those techniques.

Principle Component Analysis

A detailed study by Maaten et al (2009) compare linear and nonlinear dimensionality reduction methods in using artificial and natural datasets, observe and conclude that nonlinear methods perform well on selected artificial datasets but do not clearly outperform the simpler PCA technique on natural datasets. The authors also think development of techniques where the objective/transformation function can be optimized more (such as neural network based autoencoders) will gain more traction and focus. Sorzano et al (2014) categorize the DR techniques by methods based on Statistics and Information theory, Dictionaries and Projections in their paper. Hinton et al in (2006) describe how neural networks can be used for Dimensionality reduction and explain an effective way to initialize the weights using autoencoders that learn low-dimensional features performing better than PCA for a variety of natural datasets. Chen et al (2010) discuss about how a standard stacked denoising autoencoders(SDAs) which are based on multi-layer deep neural network architecture can be extended to learn representations on text data. These extended or marginalized SDAs perform much better than classic SDAs and show better accuracy and computational efficiency in training time. In general, autoencoders project the input data to output and are generally used as a pre-training exercise to determine the best weights which can be used in neural networks instead of randomly initializing them as in traditional methods. As the input is easy to learn, normally a noise or corruption is induced which enables the autoencoders to learn better as it tries to denoise the input. Their approach marginalizes the noise and does not require an optimization algorithm to learn parameters. They claim that the simplicity, faster training time and the ability to scale for dealing with high dimensional data make mSDA a promising pre-training method in machine learning. Krizhevsky et al discuss in their paper (Chen et al, 2012), a deep learning convoluted neural net solution to classify using a subset of the ImageNet dataset which consists of 1.2 million training images with 1000 different categories for classification.The authors claim to have trained the largest convolution neural network which produced the best ever accuracy ever reported on this very high dimensional dataset. They have also optimized the code for GPU implementation and methods such as dropout to improve the training time and accuracy. They trained the network for 90 iterations through the training set of 1.2 million images for about 6 days on two 3GB GPUs.

Figure 1 shows a taxonomy of techniques for dimensionality reduction. Dimensionality reduction subdivided into convex and non-convex techniques. Convex techniques optimize an objective function that does not contain any local optima, whereas non-convex techniques optimize objective functions that do contain local optima.

PCA Approaches

There are three approaches to achieve PCA as shown in Figure 2.

Approach_1 (High Dimension Dataset, int k)

Input: High Dimensional dataset output: k Principal Components Step 1: Standardize the dataset by scaling and mean subtraction Step 2: Determine the value of reduced dimension k. Step 3: Obtain the covariance matrix C of the given dataset Step 4: Perform Eigen Decomposition on the Covariance matrix

Figure 1. Taxonomy of dimensionality reduction techniques

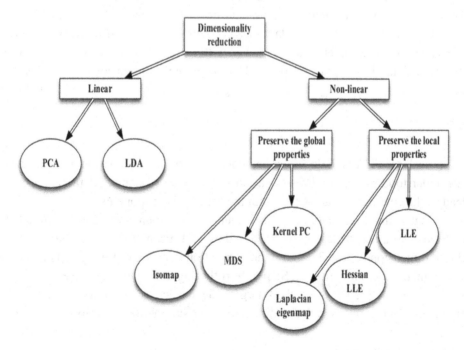

Figure 2. Approaches of Principle Component Analysis

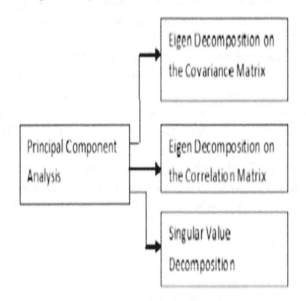

C and obtain the n Eigen Values and their corresponding Eigen Vectors. Step 5: Sort the Eigen Values in decreasing order and obtain the k largest Eigen vectors Step 6: Stack the k largest Eigen Vectors into a matrix M Step 7: Return M The second step is to perform the Eigen decomposition on the covariance matrix. The covariance matrix is a square matrix where each element in the matrix represents the covariance between the features in the corresponding row and column. The Eigen-vectors and Eigen-values represent the essence of PCA. The Eigenvectors represent the new feature space and Eigen values explain their magnitude. The Eigen vectors will have to be sorted in decreasing order of Eigen values after which k principal components have to be chosen such that k < n where n is the total features available. The dimension of the matrix with k principal components stacked together will be n x k. The final step will be a matrix multiplication of the original data matrix of dimension X x n where x is the total number of observations and n is the number of features. This will result in a transformed matrix of size X x K where x is the original number of observations and k is the reduced dimension which is less than original n. The transformed matrix is the projection of the original matrix on a lesser dimensional feature space.

Approach 2

The second approach for PCA is to do Eigen decomposition on the correlation matrix. The correlation matrix can be understood as a normalized covariance matrix. For financial datasets correlation matrix is used instead of the covariance matrix to obtain the principal components.

Approach_2(high Dimension dataset, int k) Input: High Dimensional dataset output: k Principal Components Step 1: Standardize the dataset by scaling and mean subtraction Step 2: Determine the value of reduced dimension k. Step 3: Obtain the correlation matrix Cr of the given dataset Step 4: Perform Eigen Decomposition on Cr matrix. Step 5: Sort the Eigen Values in decreasing order and obtain the k largest Eigen vectors Step 6: Stack the k largest Eigen Vectors into a matrix M Step 7: Return M Normalization is the first step where the scaling and mean subtraction is performed because performing PCA without normalization will lead to insane results. Correlation matrix is obtained by obtaining the correlation coefficient like that of Pearson's correlation coefficient between corresponding row and column elements. The formula for obtaining the correlation can be found in eq. (4). The Eigen decomposition on the correlation matrix will yield the Eigen pairs which is then sorted on decreasing order of Eigen values to obtain k ($<$ n) principal components. The k principal components are then used to project the original dataset into a lower dimensional sub space.

Approach 3

The third approach to doing PCA is to do a Singular value decomposition of the given dataset. SVD is a matrix factorization technique of the form U S V where U and V are orthogonal matrices and S is a diagonal matrix with non negative real values.

Approach_3(high Dimension dataset, int k) Input: High Dimensional dataset output: k Principal Components Step 1: Standardize the dataset by scaling and mean subtraction Step 2: Determine the value of reduced dimension k Step 3: Factorize the matrix to get U S V^t Step 4: Stack the k largest Eigen Vectors from U corresponding to sorted diagonal elements from S in decreasing order into a matrix M Step 5: Return M Eigen vectors with highest k Eigen values are picked for construction of the transformed matrix. The k Eigen values capture the desired variance and the Eigen vectors corresponding to dropped Eigen values are those that represent less information.

1.4.2 Choosing the k Value in PCA

The percentage of variance explains how good the approximation as compared to that of original data

Mean Square Projection Error

$$\frac{\sum_{i}^{n} = n \left| X_i - X_{projected} \right|}{n} \tag{1}$$

where, X_i is the ith sample of X, $X_{projected}$ is the approximation of X_i obtained with PCA and n is the total number of samples.

Total Variation:

The total variation in a given dataset can be defined as follows

$$\sum_{i}^{n} = 1 \frac{\left| x_i \right|^2}{n} \tag{2}$$

where, X_i is the ith sample of X, n is the total number of samples.

Ratio of Mean Square Projection Error to Total Variation

$$\frac{\sum \left| X_i - X_{projected} \right|^2}{\sum_{i=n}^{n} \left| x_i \right|^2} \leq 0.01 \tag{3}$$

where, X_i is the ith sample of X, $X_{projected}$ is the approximation of X_i obtained with PCA and n is the total number of samples. The constant on the right is 1-variance intended to be captured

Determining k with SVD

For a given k

$$1 - \frac{\sum S_{jj}}{\sum S_{jj}} \leq 0.01 \tag{4}$$

where, S_{ii} are the diagonal elements of S matrix obtained from SVD.

$$1 - \frac{\sum S_{jj}}{\sum S_{jj}} \geq 0.99 \tag{5}$$

PCA tries to minimize the mean squared projection error which is given by eq. (1). The total variation of the original dataset is given by eq. (2). One approach for choosing k is to make the ratio of mean squared projection error to that of total variance less than or equal to a defined constant. This constant is nothing but 1-total variance that is intended to be captured with this reduced dimension as shown in eq. (8). The variance goal is to capture 99% from the original dataset in eq. (3). As stated in the manifold hypothesis real life data are likely to concentrate on lower dimension as they are highly correlated. Hence lesser number of components tends to capture most of the original variance. So PCA has to be run with k = 1, k = 2, k = 3 and so on till a smallest k value for which the above mentioned ratio in eq. (3) is lesser than or equal to 0.01 holds good when 99% of variance is intended to be captured. This procedure is very inefficient as it is very time consuming to reach the final k value starting from first principal component. Another better approach is to perform SVD on the covariance matrix where it yields U, S and V. The S matrix is a square matrix with non negative real values across the diagonal and the non-diagonal elements are zeroes. For a given value of k the eq. (4) has to be ensured which is same as eq. (5). This approach is computationally efficient because as singular value decomposition is performed only once unlike the previous approach where PCA has to be performed for every k value.

In Figure 3, (Hinton et al, 2006), describes the classification of the chosen techniques based on their properties such as the broader category they belong to, if the convexity of the optimization function's ability to find the global optimum (for Neural network and Deep autoencoders this may not be always guaranteed because they can be stuck in the local optimum), basic parameters (that influence the optimization function directly) to be optimized and the dimensionality reduction technique's computational complexity.

CHARACTERIZATION OF THE TECHNIQUES

General Properties

In Figure 3, four general properties of 13 dimensionality reduction techniques are listed (1) the parametric nature of the mapping between the high-dimensional and the low-dimensional space, (2) the main free parameters that have to be optimized, (3) the computational complexity of the main computational part of the technique, and (4) the memory complexity of the technique.

Using the four general properties of the techniques for dimensionality reduction, the most important four observations are: (1) most nonlinear techniques for dimensionality reduction do not provide a parametric mapping between the high-dimensional and the low-dimensional space, (2) all nonlinear techniques require the optimization of one or more free parameters, (3) when D < n (which is true in most cases), nonlinear techniques have computational is advantages compared to PCA, and (4) a number of nonlinear techniques suffer from a memory complexity that is square or cube with the number of data points n. From these observations, it is observed that the nonlinear techniques enforce significant demands on computational resources, as compared to PCA. Attempts to decrease the computational and/or memory complexities of nonlinear techniques have been proposed for, e.g., Isomap (Zhange et al, 2015; Nick et al, 2015), MVU, and Kernel PCA (Anissa et al, 2015).

Autoencoders (Hinton and Salakhutdinov, 2006) are artificial neural networks used for learning efficient codings. The aim of an autoencoder is to learn a compressed representation (encoding) for a set of data. An autoencoder is often trained using one of the many back propagation variants (Conjugate Gradient Method, Steepest Descent, etc.) Though often reasonably effective, there are fundamental problems with using backpropagation to train networks with many hidden layers. Once the errors get backpropagated to the first few layers, they are minuscule and quite ineffectual. This causes the network to almost al-

Figure 3. Classification of dimensionality reduction techniques

Technique	Parametric	Parameters	Computational	Memory
PCA	yes	none	$O(D^3)$	$O(D^2)$
Class. scaling	no	none	$O(n^3)$	$O(n^2)$
Isomap	no	k	$O(n^3)$	$O(n^2)$
Kernel PCA	no	$\kappa(\cdot,\cdot)$	$O(n^3)$	$O(n^2)$
MVU	no	k	$O((nk)^3)$	$O((nk)^3)$
Diffusion maps	no	σ,t	$O(n^3)$	$O(n^2)$
LLE	no	k	$O(pn^2)$	$O(pn^2)$
Laplacian Eigenmaps	no	k,σ	$O(pn^2)$	$O(pn^2)$
Hessian LLE	no	k	$O(pn^2)$	$O(pn^2)$
LTSA	no	k	$O(pn^2)$	$O(pn^2)$
Sammon mapping	no	none	$O(in^2)$	$O(n^2)$
Autoencoders	yes	net size	$O(inw)$	$O(w)$
LLC	yes	m,k	$O(imd^3)$	$O(nmd)$
Manifold charting	yes	m	$O(imd^3)$	$O(nmd)$

ways learn to reconstruct the average of all the training data. Though more advanced backpropagation methods (such as the Conjugate Gradient Method) help with this to some degree, it still results in very slow learning and poor solutions. This problem is remedied by using initial weights that approximate the final solution. The process to find these initial weights is often called pretraining. A pretraining technique developed by Geoffrey Hintonn (2006) for training many-layered deep autoencoders involves treating each neighboring set of two layers like a Restricted Boltzmann Machine for pretraining to approximate a good solution and then using a backpropagation technique to fine-tune. The computational complexity of autoencoders is dependent on n (the matrix size), w (the number of weights in the neural network) and i (the number of iterations). The memory usage is dependent on w weights. Therefore, if the weights and iterations are large, autoencoders can have very high complexity and memory usage.

Diffusion Maps (Yaginuma et al, 1996; Wang et al, 2012) are based on defining a Markov random walk on the graph of the data. The technique defines a system of coordinates with an explicit metric that reflects the connectivity of a given data set and that is robust to noise. This diffusion metric is a transition probabilities of a Markov chain that evolves forward in time and is very robust to noise, unlike the geodesic or Euclidean distance.

Though diffusion maps perform extremely well with clean, well-sampled data, problems arise with the addition of noise, or when the data exists in multiple submanifolds. Although diffusion maps are similar to Isomap, they integrate over all paths through the graph instead of only considering shortest paths. This makes them less sensitive to short-circuiting than Isomap.

Summarization of Techniques

Figure 5 summarizes the parameters that have to be optimized, the computational complexity of each method and the memory complexity of the method (Maaten et al, 2009). In Table 1, n is the matrix size, k is the nearest neighbors, p is the ratio of nonzero elements in a sparse matrix to the total number of elements, w is the number of weights in a neural network and i is the number of iterations. LLE, HLLE and LTSA are more computationally efficient than MDS and Isomap, with approximately similar memory usage. Of all the technique, autoencoders has the highest complexity as it takes a long time to converge if the numbers of weights are high (Zhao et al, 2015).

In Figure 4 list the non-linear methods based on how they preserve the properties of data (Kalmanovich et al, 2014). Global preservation techniques describe the data as a whole. For example, the Autoencoder method describes an image as a whole rather than parts/patches of the image. One disadvantage in this is that a change in one part of the image will affect the resulting global property and hence affects data comparison because all global properties has to match for image comparison to be classified as same. Whereas, techniques using local preserves properties of a part/patch of the data/image. Multiple local properties are used to define and classify a whole image but not all the local properties need to match for a comparison to be the same. The third category as the name suggests is an ensemble of techniques used in Global and Local property preservation techniques.

With the easy availability of very large, high-dimensional data sets the authors believe that non-linear, deep learning neural network based techniques for dimensionality reduction is a lesser researched area using very large natural datasets. There is a gap in understanding the pros and cons of available dimensionality reduction techniques against the newly evolving deep learning techniques. Using a commonly available dataset such as MNIST handwritten digits as a baseline and comparing - a linear technique like PCA, a nonlinear technique like ISOMAP, a simple shallow neural network and a deep learning

Figure 4. Non-linear methods

Preserve Global Properties	Preserve Local Properties	Ensemble of Global and Local properties
Kernel PCA (Kernel based)	Local Linear Embedding (Reconstruction of Weights)	Local Linear Coordination(LLC)
MDS, ISOMAP, Diffusion Maps (Distance Preservation)	LTSA, HESSIAN LLE (Local Tangent Space)	Manifold Charting
MVU (Unfolding)	Laplacian Eigenmaps (Neighborhood Laplacian)	
Autoencoders(Neural Networks)		
Stacked Denosing Autoencoders, Convoluted Neural networks (Deep Neural Networks)		

Figure 5. Comparison of dimensionality reduction techniques

Technique	Based on	Convexity of the Optimization function	Parameters to Optimize	Computational Complexity
PCA	Statistics and Information Theory	Yes	None	$O(D^3)$
ISOMAP	Projections/k-Nearest neighbors	Yes	k	$O(N^3)$
LLE	Projections/k-Nearest neighbors	Yes	k	$O(pN^2)$
Shallow Neural network	Statistics and Information Theory/Iterative	No	net size	$O(iNw)$
Deep Autoencoders	Statistics and Information Theory/Iterative	No	net size	$O(iNwL)$

architecture like autoencoders (Kalmanovich et al, 2014) would throw more light on the advantages and disadvantages of using the techniques for such a dataset and propel advanced research in this area. Efficient Neural Architecture Search (ENAS) (Pham et al, 2018), a fast and inexpensive approach for automatic model design. In ENAS, a controller learns to discover neural network architectures by searching for an optimal subgraph within a large computational graph. The controller is trained with policy gradient to select a subgraph that maximizes the expected reward on the validation set. Meanwhile the model corresponding to the selected subgraph is trained to minimize a canonical cross entropy loss. Thanks to parameter sharing between child models, ENAS is fast: it delivers strong empirical performances using much fewer GPU-hours than all existing automatic model design approaches, and notably, 1000x less expensive than standard Neural Architecture Search.

Application of Deep learning in Big Data analytics for high dimensional data still is largely unexplored. Future research areas include adapting existing approaches (CNN or mSDA) or develop novel solutions like using other Deep architectures like Deep Belief Network, Recurrent Neural Network (RNN), etc for solving the dimensionality reduction problem. Scalability/Performance of learning algorithms and Accuracy of the predicted output will be the two important metrics which will drive the development of new novel ideas. In this paper we discussed the importance of curing the curse of dimensionality in big data analytics and various methods which are currently being deployed on different type of datasets. Past research indicates that nonlinear dimensionality reduction techniques are still not capable of outperforming traditional approach like PCA. Recent research results have shown deep learning methods (such as CNN and mSDA) used to reduce dimensions, show better accuracy and the ability to scale in large non-linear natural data sets like video, audio and text. Extending and enhancing existing dimensionality reduction algorithms so that they are compatible in a distributed computing environment and using the Graphic processing unit (GPU) for complex computational requirements are other trends we are observing for curing the curse of dimensionality. Due to the digital initiatives taken by governments, organizations and society, data sets are becoming larger and more complex, specifically in terms of dimensionality of the data, high number of features means longer computational times for training and learning, interest levels in the theme of dimensionality reduction is ever increasing as a means to speed up machine learning times, simplify problems such as classification, cognitive computing, etc. and optimize performances for various techniques and algorithms.

REFERENCES

Anissa, B., Naouar, B., Arsalane, Z., & Jamal, K. (2015, March). Face recognition: comparative study between linear and non linear dimensionality reduction methods. In *2015 International Conference on Electrical and Information Technologies (ICEIT)* (pp. 224-228). IEEE. 10.1109/EITech.2015.7162932

Chen, M., Xu, Z., Weinberger, K., & Sha, F. (2012). *Marginalized denoising autoencoders for domain adaptation*. arXiv preprint arXiv:1206.4683

Hinton, G. E., & Salakhutdinov, R. R. (2006). Reducing the dimensionality of data with neural networks. *Science, 313*(5786), 504-507.

Kalmanovich, A., & Chechik, G. (2014). *Gradual training of deep denoising auto encoders*. arXiv preprint arXiv:1412.6257

Krizhevsky, A., Sutskever, I., & Hinton, G. E. (2012). Imagenet classification with deep convolutional neural networks. In Advances in neural information processing systems (pp. 1097-1105). Academic Press.

Lecun, Y., Cortes, C., & Burges, C. J. C. (2004). *The mnist database of handwritten digits.* Retrieved from http://yann.lecun.com/ exdb/mnist/index.html

Nick, W., Shelton, J., Bullock, G., Esterline, A., & Asamene, K. (2015, April). Comparing dimensionality reduction techniques. In *Southeast Con 2015* (pp. 1–2). IEEE. doi:10.1109/SECON.2015.7132997

Pham, H., Guan, M. Y., Zoph, B., Le, Q. V., & Dean, J. (2018). *Efficient neural architecture search via parameter sharing.* arXiv preprint arXiv:1802.03268

Sorzano, C. O. S., Vargas, J., & Montano, A. P. (2014). *A survey of dimensionality reduction techniques.* arXiv preprint arXiv:1403.2877

Van Der Maaten, L., Postma, E., & Van den Herik, J. (2009). Dimensionality reduction: A comparative. *Journal of Machine Learning Research*, *10*(66-71), 13.

Vincent, P., Larochelle, H., Lajoie, I., Bengio, Y., & Manzagol, P. A. (2010). Stacked denoising autoencoders: Learning useful representations in a deep network with a local denoising criterion. *Journal of Machine Learning Research*, *11*(Dec), 3371–3408.

Wang, J., He, H., & Prokhorov, D. V. (2012). A folded neural network autoencoder for dimensionality reduction. *Procedia Computer Science*, *13*, 120–127. doi:10.1016/j.procs.2012.09.120

Yaginuma, Y., Kimoto, T., & Yamakawa, H. (1996, June). Multi-sensor fusion model for constructing internal representation using autoencoder neural networks. In *Proceedings of International Conference on Neural Networks (ICNN'96)* (Vol. 3, pp. 1646-1651). IEEE. 10.1109/ICNN.1996.549147

Zhang, K., Liu, J., Chai, Y., & Qian, K. (2015, May). An optimized dimensionality reduction model for high-dimensional data based on restricted Boltzmann machines. In *The 27th Chinese Control and Decision Conference (2015 CCDC)* (pp. 2939-2944). IEEE. 10.1109/CCDC.2015.7162428

Zhao, J. (2015). *Stacked what-where auto-encoders.* arXiv preprint arXiv:1506.02351

Chapter 11
Fake News Detection Using Deep Learning:
Supervised Fake News Detection Analysis in Social Media With Semantic Similarity Method

Varalakshmi Konagala
KLH University (Deemed), India

Shahana Bano
K. L. University, Vijayawada, India

ABSTRACT

The engendering of uncertain data in ordinary access news sources, for example, news sites, web-based life channels, and online papers, have made it trying to recognize capable news sources, along these lines expanding the requirement for computational instruments ready to give into the unwavering quality of online substance. For instance, counterfeit news outlets were observed to be bound to utilize language that is abstract and enthusiastic. At the point when specialists are chipping away at building up an AI-based apparatus for identifying counterfeit news, there wasn't sufficient information to prepare their calculations; they did the main balanced thing. In this chapter, two novel datasets for the undertaking of phony news locations, covering distinctive news areas, distinguishing proof of phony substance in online news has been considered. N-gram model will distinguish phony substance consequently with an emphasis on phony audits and phony news. This was pursued by a lot of learning analyses to fabricate precise phony news identifiers and showed correctness of up to 80%.

DOI: 10.4018/978-1-7998-1192-3.ch011

INTRODUCTION

Nowadays' phony news is making various issues from snide articles to a created news and plan government purposeful publicity in certain outlets. Counterfeit news and absence of trust in the media are developing issues with enormous consequences in our general public. Obviously, deceptive story is "fake news "but lately blathering social media's discourse is varying its definition. Some of them currently utilize the term to expel the realities counter to their favored perspectives. The importance of disinformation within American political discourse was the subject of weighty attention, particularly following the American president election. The term 'fakes news' wound up normal speech for the issue, especially to depict authentically off base and deceiving articles distributed for the most part to profit through page views. In this paper, it is seeked to make a model that can decisively envision the likelihood that a given article (Anderson et al, n.d.)

Face book has been at the epicenter of much critique following media attention. They have already implemented a feature to flag fake news on the site when a user see's it ; they have also said publicly they are working on to distinguish these articles in an automated way. Certainly, it is not an easy task. A given calculation must be politically impartial – since phony news exists on the two finishes of the range – and furthermore give equivalent equalization to authentic news sources on either end of the range. That can precisely. In addition, the question of legitimacy is a difficult one. However, in order to solve this problem, it is necessary to have an understanding on what Fake News is. Afterward, it is expected to investigate how the systems in the fields of AI, characteristic language handling help us to recognize counterfeit news.

EXISTINGSYSTEM

Deep learning is progressively being recognized as an essential tool for artificial intelligence research in many suitable applications of different areas. Deep learning models are mostly used in image recognition and speech recognition (Ahamed et al, 2016). However, the research community applied deep learning algorithms to find out the solutions for different problems in varied alternative fields (Ahamed et al, 2018). A deep learning algorithm is approximately classified into four types: 1.Q-learning, 2.Recurrent Neural Network (RNN), 3.Convolution Neural Network (CNN) and 4.Deep Neural Network (DNN). These functionalities quickly evolve with many packages together such as; Theano, Tensorflow, CNN, Caffee, and Keras, etc. The objective of traffic flow prediction is to give such traffic flow information in a visualized manner. The design of DNN is used to estimate the traffic conditions, exploitation time period, and transportation from a large amount of data. The recommended DNN model aims to differentiate the non-congested conditions through the provision of multivariate analysis. The stacked auto-encoder is employed to find out the general traffic flow options with a trained layer that works in a greedy manner. The authors of (Ahamed et al, 2018; Choi et al, 2014) have proposed most effective stacked auto-encoder method, which is applied in order to predict traffic flow features. In this, the feature functionality has been calculated based on the spatial and chronological connection square measure instinctively. The preliminary issues proposed by Poincare and Hilbert analyses that, deep learning permits the nonlinear functions for efficient modelling (Hornet et al, 2017; Lemann eta l, 2017) The Kolmogorov Arnold illustration theorem gives the hypothetical motivation for deep learning analysis (Mukherjee et al, 2013). According to this, any continuous operate of n variables outlined by F(y) is shown in the below manner.

$$F(Y) = \sum \text{Pk}\left(\sum_{i=1}^{m} \text{qij}(\text{yi})\right) \tag{1}$$

Where pk and qij are the ceaseless capacities and qij is an aggregate premise that does not rely upon F. This outcome infers that any nonstop capacity can delineate the abuse tasks of summation and execution sythesis. In a neural system, work on n factors can be spoken to with 2n+1 actuation units and one shrouded layer (Conroy et al, 2015; Ott et al, 2011). In the course of recent years, profound learning has pulled in an a significant number of analysts to formalize the applications. For street data, the traffic stream example is prepared so as to remove intentional data by abusing multilayered structure through a profound algorithmic program (Ott et al, 2011). So as to perform relatedactivities and produce various examples inside the traffic stream, a model named misuse stacked auto-encoder has bee

Deep learning initially inspired by information communicated in the biological nervous system. Deep learning models are assembled by multiple layers, which include both the visible layers and hidden layers. Visible layers contain input and output, where hidden layers are designed to extract features from feed forward operations (Shojaee et la, 2013) back propagation based on the gradient to

train neural networks. Deep learning showcases good learning capability the increasing size of the dataset. Thus deep learning has got rapid growth in applications. Deep learning models such as multilayer perceptions (MLP), convolution neural network (CNN), recurrent neural network (RNN), generative adversarial networks (GAN), have been widely applied in computer vision, natural language processing, and audio generation, etc. (Wang et al, 2012). Q-learning is a commonly used model free approach which can be used for building a self-playing PacMan agent. It revolves around the notion of updating Q values which denotes value of doing action a in states. The value update rule is the core of the Q-learning algorithm. The Figure1 describes the work flow of deep conventional neural network

Figure 1.

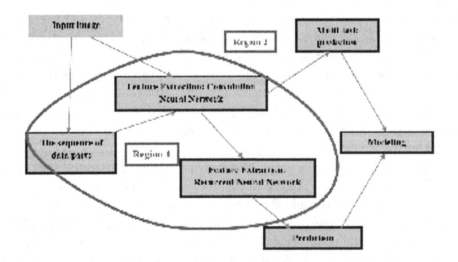

PARALLEL CONVOLUTION NEURAL NETWORKS (P-CNN)

A parallel convolution neural network, also known as P-CNN, has been widely applied in many areas and has shown outstanding capability in processing grid-like data. Examples include 1-D time series samples with regular time intervals and images which can be contemplation as 2-D grid pixels. In the mid-20th century, neurophysiologists tried to understand how the brain responds to images and discovered that some neurons in the brains of cats and monkeys are highly sensitive to edges in small regions in visual fields. Thus, as an artificial intelligence model, P-CNN is fundamentally supported by neuron science (Xie et al, 2012). A recent study of Ma et al. considers traffic data as 2-D images, one dimension of time, one dimension of location, and demonstrates better accuracy with P-CNN on the speed prediction and compared with CNN (Shojaee et al, 2013).

There exists an enormous group of research on the theme of AI strategies for misleading recognition; its majority has been concentrating on characterizing on the web audits and openly accessible online networking posts. Especially since late 2016 during the American Presidential decision, the topic of deciding 'counterfeit news' has likewise been the subject of specific consideration inside the literature (Wang et al, 2012). Frameworks a few methodologies that appear to be encouraging towards the point of impeccably characterize the deceptive articles. They note that straightforward substance related n-grams and shallow grammatical features (POS) labeling have demonstrated inadequate for the grouping task, frequently neglecting to represent significant setting data. Or maybe, these strategies have been indicated valuable just pair with progressively complex techniques for examination. Profound Language structure examination utilizing Probabilistic Setting Free Sentence structures (PCFG) have been demonstrated to be especially significant in blend with n-gram methods can accomplish 85%-91% precision in misdirection related order undertakings utilizing on the web audit corpora. Ahamed et. al. said that noxious records can be effectively and immediately made to help the spread of phony news, for example, social bots, cyborg clients, or trolls. The current calculations for recognition of phony news are it is possible that i). News Substance Based or ii). Social Setting Based. News substance put together methodologies center with respect to removing different highlights in phony news content, including information based and style based. Social setting based methodologies expect to use client social commitment as assistant data to help recognize counterfeit news (Xie et al, 2012).Another related work was finished by Kang et al. who assessed impacts of individual factors and said that metadata and picture type components are the most grounded affecting elements in believability appraisal. They reviewed 183 individuals through MTurk and completed an investigation through different charts to be specific Likert scale, Hinton guide, and warmth map. They included 11 factors, notwithstanding, did not think about close to home elements.

THE PROPOSED MODEL

Propagation Path Construction and Transformation given a news story propagating on social media, initially to construct its propagation path by identifying the users who engaged in propagating the news. Then, its propagation path denoted as a variable-length multivariate time series. $p(\text{ai}) = (...(\text{xj},t),...)$ is constructed by extracting user characteristics from relevant user profiles,the dataset composition on news spread via tweeter is described in Figure 2.

Figure 2. Dataset composition on news spread via Tweeter

In this paper a model is build based on the count vectorizer or a tfidf matrix (i.e) word tallies relatives to how often they are used in other artices in your dataset) can help . Since this problem is a kind of text classification, implementing a Naive Bayes classifier will be best as this is standard for text-based processing. The actual goal is in developing a model which was the text transformation (count vectorizer vs tfidf vectorizer) and choosing which type of text to use (headlines vs full text). Now the next step is to extract the most optimal features for count vectorizer or tfidf-vectorizer, this is done by using a n-number of the most used words, and/or phrases, lower casing or not, mainly removing the stop words which are common words such as "the", "when", and "there" and only using those words that appear at least a given number of times in a given text dataset.

Data Pre-Processing

Before speaking to the information utilizing n-gram and vector-based model, the information should be exposed to specific refinements like stop-word expulsion, tokenization, a lower packaging, sentence division, and accentuation evacuation. This will enable us to diminish the size of real information by expelling the immaterial data that exists in the information. Conventional information pre-preparing capacity to evacuate accentuation and non-letter characters for each archive; at that point brought down the letter case in the report. What's more, a n-gram word based tokenizer was made to cut the surveys content dependent

STOP WORD REMOVAL

Stop words are insignificant words in a language that will create noise when used as features in text classification. These are words commonly used in a lot sentences to help connect thought or to assist in the sentence structure. Articles, prepositions and conjunctions and some pronouns are considered stop words. The common words such as, a, about, an, are, as, at, be, by, for, from, how, in, is, of, on, or, that, the, these, this, too, was, what, when, where, who, will, etc. Those words were removed from each document, and the processed documents were stored and passed on to the next step.

STEMMING

After tokenizing the data, the next step is to transform the tokens into a standard form. Stemming, simply, is changing the words into their original form, and decreasing the number of word types or classes in the data. For example, the words "Running," "Ran" and "Runner" will be reduced to the word "run." The stemming process is to make classification faster and efficient. Furthermore, Porter stemmer, which is the most commonly, used stemming algorithms due to its accuracy.

FEATURES EXTRACTION

There are large number of terms, words, and phrases in documents that lead to a high computational burden for the learning process. Furthermore, irrelevant and redundant features can hurt the accuracy and performance of the classifiers. Thus, it is best to perform feature reduction to reduce the text feature size and avoid large feature space dimension. Two features extraction methods, namely, Term Frequency (TF) and Term Frequency-Inverted Document Frequency (TF-IDF). These methods are described in the following.

TERM FREQUENCY (TF)

Term Frequency will represent each term in our vector with a measurement that illustrates how many times the term/features occurred in the document. Count Vectorizer class from scikit-learn, a Python module to produce a table of each word mentioned, and its occurrence for each class. Count Vectorizer learns the vocabulary from the documents and then extracts the words count features. Next, then created a matrix with the token counts to represent our documents. The News site with the most URLs in our dataset is indicated in Table 1.

Table 1. The news sites with the most URLs in our dataset

Site	%	Site	%
youtube.com	4.319	wordpress.com	0.754
nytimes.com	3.145	nypost.co	0.625
theguardian.com	2.904	thehill.com	0.619
huffngtonpost.com	1.964	latimes.com	0.616
blogspot.com	1.202	newsmax.com	0.336
foxnews.com	1.262	dailycaller.com	0.367
indiatimes.com	1.458	reddit.com	0.38

TF-IDF

The Term Frequency-Inverted Document Frequency (TF-IDF) is a weighting metric often used in information retrieval and natural language processing. It is a statistical metric used to measure how important a term is in a document over a dataset. A term importance increases with the number of times a word appears in the document; however, this is counteracted by the frequency of the word in the corpus.

Let D denote a corpus, or set of documents.

Let d denote a document, $d \in$; to define a document as a set of words w. Let(d) denote the number of times word w appears in document d. Hence, the size of document d is

$$|d|=\Sigma(d)w\in d. \tag{2}$$

The normalized Term Frequency (TF) for word w with respect to document d is defined as follows:

$$(w)d=nw(d)/|d| \tag{3}$$

The Inverse Document Frequency (IDF) for a term w with respect to document corpus D, denoted $IDF(w)$ D is the logarithm of the total number of documents in the corpus divided by the number of documents where this particular term appears, and computed as follows:

$$I(w)D=1+log(|D|/\{d:D|w\in d\}|) \tag{4}$$

TF-IDF for the word w with respect to document d and corpus D is calculated as follows:

$$TF-I(w)d,D=TF(w)d\times IDF(w)D \tag{5}$$

So for example, let say a document with 200 words and need the TF-IDF for the word "people". Assuming that the word "people" occurs in the document 5 times then TF = 5/200 = 0.025. Now to calculate the IDF; let's assume that 500 documents and "people" appears in 100 of them then IDF (people) = 1 + log (500/100) = 1.69. Then TF-IDF (people) = 0.025 × 1.69 = 0.04056.

SEMANTIC SIMILARITY MEASUREMENT

Wordnet is a lexical database spearheaded by George A. Miller, which is available in English. It consists of words, specifically nouns, verbs, adjectives, and adverbs. Words that are synonymous are grouped into synsets. Synsets are connected through semantic and lexical relations. The relationships between the words are categorized as follows:

- Synonymy is a symmetric relation; it is between words that equivalents to each other.
- Antonymy (opposing-name) relationship between words with opposite meaning such as "wet" and "dry."
- Hyponymy (sub-name) is the most important relation among synsets; it connects abstract synsets with each other such as "bed" and "furniture; "bed" is a hyponym of "furniture"
- Meronymy (part-name) is a part-whole relationship, for example, "leg" and "chair" or "hand" and "arm". The parts are inherited "downward".
- Troponymy (manner-name) is similar to hyponymy, but it is for the verbs

- Similarity Between Words

The semantic similarity between two words $w1$ and $w2$, denoted $(w1, w2)$, will be calculated as follows:

$$(w1,2)=f(w1,w2) \times fH(w1,w2) \tag{6}$$

Where:

- $(w1,w2)$ is the path length between two synsets corresponding to $w1$ and $w2$, respectively.
- $(w1,w2)$ is the depth measure between two synsets corresponding to $w1$ and $w2$, respectively.

The path length function takes two words and returns the measurement of the length of the shortest path in the lexical database. All values are normalized to range from one to zero. The following formula is used to calculate the path length:

$$(w1,w2)= e- \alpha ldist(w1,w2) \tag{7}$$

EXPERIMENTAL EVALUATION

In the experiment, two public datasets, i.e., LIAR and BuzzFeed News4 to evaluate the performance of our algorithm. LIAR is one of the largest fake news datasets, containing over 12,800 short news statements and labels collected from a fact-checking website politifact.com. BuzzFeed dataset contains 1,627 news articles related to the 2016 U.S. election from Facebook. Twitter's advanced search API with the titles of news to collect related news tweets. After eliminating duplicate news and filtering out the news with no verified user's tweets. Finally obtain 332 news for LIAR and 144 news for BuzzFeed. For each news tweet, the unverified users' engagements are also collected using web scraping. Observed that users tend to explicitly express negative sentiments (using words like "lie", "fake") when they think a news report is fake. Thus, the sentiments as their opinions. As for likes and retweets, treat them as positive opinions. Note that if a user has very few engagement records, the user's credibility cannot be accurately estimated

Online news can be collected from different sources, such as news agency homepages, search engines, and social media websites. However, manually determining the veracity of news is a challenging task, usually requiring annotators with domain expertise who performs careful analysis of claims and additional evidence, context, and reports from authoritative sources. Generally, news data with annotations can be gathered in the following ways: Expert journalists, Fact-checking websites, Industry detectors, and Crowdsourced workers. However, there are no agreed upon benchmark datasets for the fake news detection problem. To evaluate the performance of algorithms for fake news detection problem, various evaluation metrics have been used. In this subsection, the most widely used metrics for fake news detection. Most existing approaches consider the fake news problem as a classification problem that predicts whether a news article is fake or not. These metrics are commonly used in the machine learning community and enable us to evaluate the performance of a classifier from different perspectives.

Specifically, accuracy measures the similarity between predicted fake news and real fake news. Precision measures the fraction of all detected fake news that are annotated as fake news, addressing the important problem of identifying which news is fake. However, because fake news datasets are often skewed, a high precision can be easily achieved by making fewer positive predictions. Thus, recall is used to measure the sensitivity, or the fraction of annotated fake news articles that are predicted to be fake news. F1 is used to combine precision and recall, which can provide an overall prediction performance for fake news detection. Note that for P recision, Recall, F1, and Accuracy, the higher the value, the better the performance. which measures the overall performance of how likely the classifier is to rank the fake news higher than any true news

By formulating this as a classification problem, following metrics has been defined. True Positive (TP): when predicted fake news pieces are actually annotated as fake news; True Negative (TN): when predicted true news pieces are actually annotated as true news; False Negative (FN): when predicted true news pieces are actually annotated as fake news; False Positive (FP): when predicted fake news pieces are actually annotated as true news

$$\text{Precision} = \frac{|TP|}{|TP| + |FN|} \quad (8)$$

$$\text{Recall} = \frac{|TP|}{|TP| + |FN|} \quad (9)$$

$$\text{F1} = 2 \cdot \frac{\text{P recision} \cdot \text{Recall}}{\text{P recision} + \text{Recall}} \quad (10)$$

$$\text{Accuracy} = \frac{|TP| + |TN|}{|TP| + |TN| + |FP| + |FN|} \quad (11)$$

- Function words are words with little lexical meaning, which are usually used to express a grammatical relationship with other words (e.g., the, she, of).
- Content words are the opposite, in the sense that they stand on their own by carrying specific purpose or meaning (not necessarily in connection to other words), such as, flew and mountain.

$$\bullet \quad \text{FD} = \frac{\sum(n_0 + n_1 + 1 - r) - n_0(n_0 + 1)/2}{n_0 n_1} \quad (12)$$

The Fake news comparison with different datasets is indicated in Table 2.

The Fake news detection in social media is compared in detection deadline(minutes) with the number of Retweetes which are shown in the Figure 3.

The semantic measurement achieved rather good results. It is able to identify near-duplicated content with up to 65% of the text changed. In reality, the majority of near-duplicated contents are less than 25% different from the original contents. This model's cross-validated accuracy score is 81.7%, true positive score is 92.6%, and its AUC score is 95%. Thus, to believe that our semantic measurement approach will be able to classify near-duplicate correctly in real-world data.

Table 2. Fake news comparison with different datasets

Datasets	Fake news datasets	Buzzfees data sets
# News	332	144
# True news	182	67
# Fake news	150	77
# Tweets	2589	1007
# Verified users	550	243
# Unverified users	3767	988
# Likes	5713	1277
# Retweets	10434	2365

Figure 3.

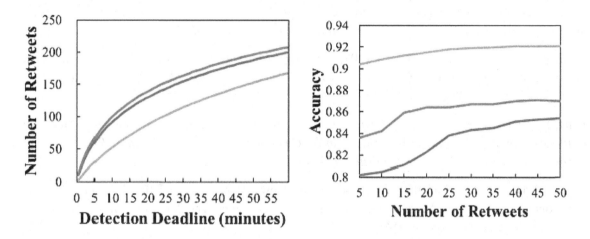

CONCLUSION

In recent years, deceptive content such as fake news and fake reviews have increasingly become a dangerous prospect, for online users. Fake reviews have affected consumer and stores alike. The use of hired writers to produce fake reviews to boost sales is also growing. It has become difficult for consumers to recognize good products from bad ones based on reviews. Most of the popular fake news stories were more widely shared on Face book than the most popular mainstream news stories, fake news are a closely related phenomenon as both consist of writing and spreading false information or beliefs. The problem of detecting opinion spam using n-gram analysis which solely relies on the text of the fake content N-gram models were able to detect fake reviews, fake news, and fake essays with an almost exact efficiency. With results the semantic similarity metrics to detect near-duplicated content. Experimental results showed that semantic similarity measurement could detect near duplicated deceptive content similar to the ones available on online reviews websites. As for future work, it is planned to incorporate the features of news contents and user profiles into our current fake news detection model.

REFERENCES

Ahamed, B. B., & Ramkumar, T. (2016). An intelligent web search framework for performing efficient retrieval of data. Computers & Electrical Engineering, 56, 289–299. doi:10.1016/j.compeleceng.2016.09.033

Ahamed, B. B., & Ramkumar, T. (2018). Proficient Information *Method for Inconsistency Detection in Multiple Data Sources. Academic Press.*

Ahamed, B. B., & Yuvaraj, D. (2018, October). Framework for Faction of Data in Social Network Using Link Based Mining Process. In International Conf*erence on Intelligent Computing & Optimization (pp. 300-309). Sp*ringer.

Anderson, M., & Anderson, M. (2017). 88% Of Consumers Trust Online Reviews As Much As Personal Recommendations. Search Engine L*and. Available at:* http://searchengineland.com/88-consumers-trust-online-reviews-much-personal-recommendations-195803

Choi, Y. (2014). Keystroke patterns as prosody in digital writings: A case study with deceptive reviews and essays. Empirical Me*thods on Natural Language Processing (EMNLP), 6.*

*Conro*y, N. J., Rubin, V. L., & Chen, Y. (2015). Automatic deception detection: Methods for finding fake news. Proceedin*gs of the Association for Information Science and Technology, 52(1), 1–4.* doi:10.1002/pra2.2015.145052010082

Feng, S., Banerjee, R., & Choi, Y. (2012). Syntactic stylometry for deception detection. Procee*dings of the 50th Annual Meeting of the Association for Computational Linguistics: Short Papers-Volume 2, Association for Computational Linguistics, 171–175.*

Horne, B. D., & Adali, S. (2017). This Just In: Fake News Packs a Lot in Title, Uses Simpler, Repetitive Content in Text Body, More Similar to Satire than Real News. The *2nd International Workshop on News and Public Opinion at ICWSM.*

Lemann, N. (2017). Solving the Problem of Fake News. *The New Yorker.* Available at: http://www.newyorker.com/news/news-desk/solving-the-problem-of-fake-news

Li, J., Ott, M., Cardie, C., & Hovy, E. (2014). Towards a general rule for identifying deceptive opinion spam. *Proceedings of the 52nd Annual Meeting of the Association for Computational Linguistics,* 1566–1576. 10.3115/v1/P14-1147

Mukherjee, A., Venkataraman, V., Liu, B., & Glance, N. (2013). *Fake Review Detection: Classification and Analysis of Real and Pseudo Reviews.* UIC-CS-03-2013. Technical Report.

Ott, M., Choi, Y., Cardie, C., & Hancock, J. T. (2011). Finding Deceptive Opinion Spam by Any Stretch of the Imagination. In *Proceedings of the 49th Annual Meeting of the Association for Computational Linguistics: Human Language Technologies* (Vol. 1, pp. 309–319). Stroudsburg, PA, USA: Association for Computational Linguistics. Retrieved from http://dl.acm.org/citation.cfm?id=2002472.2002512

Shojaee, S., Murad, M. A. A., Azman, A. B., Sharef, N. M., & Nadali, S. (2013, December). Detecting deceptive reviews using lexical and syntactic features. In *Intelligent Systems Design and Applications (ISDA), 2013 13th International Conference on* (pp. 53-58). IEEE. 10.1109/ISDA.2013.6920707

Wang, G., Xie, S., Liu, B., & Yu, P. S. (2012). Identify online store review spammers via social review graph. *ACM Transactions on Intelligent Systems and Technology, 3*(4), 61. doi:10.1145/2337542.2337546

Xie, S., Wang, G., Lin, S., & Yu, P. S. (2012, April). Review spam detection via time series pattern discovery. In *Proceedings of the 21st International Conference on World Wide Web* (pp. 635-636). ACM. 10.1145/2187980.2188164

Chapter 12
Heuristic Optimization Algorithms for Power System Scheduling Applications:
Multi–Objective Generation Scheduling With PSO

Anongpun Man-Im
Asian Institute of Technology, Thailand

Weerakorn Ongsakul
Asian Institute of Technology, Thailand

Nimal Madhu M.
Asian Institute of Technology, Thailand

ABSTRACT

Power system scheduling is one of the most complex multi-objective scheduling problems, and a heuristic optimization method is designed for finding the OPF solution. Stochastic weight trade-off chaotic mutation-based non-dominated sorting particle swarm optimization algorithm can improve solution-search-capability by balancing between global best exploration and local best utilization through the stochastic weight and dynamic coefficient trade-off methods. This algorithm with chaotic mutation enhances diversity and search-capability, preventing premature convergence. Non-dominated sorting and crowding distance techniques efficiently provide the optimal Pareto front. Fuzzy function is used to select the local best compromise. Using a two-stage approach, the global best solution is selected from many local trials. The discussed approach can schedule the generators in the systems effectively, leading to savings in fuel cost, reduction in active power loss and betterment in voltage stability.

DOI: 10.4018/978-1-7998-1192-3.ch012

INTRODUCTION

Electric Power System is one of the most complex systems considering the ever-volatile nature of demand and the newly transformed deregulated market structure. Optimal operation of the system is desirable and essential from both the financial as well as sustainability point of views. The application of optimization algorithms in power system scheduling is one of the most explored areas in power systems research. One of the major reasons for the same is the availability of numerous optimization algorithms. The introduction of heuristic algorithms provided an elegant platform where any system, despite their complex nature, could be optimized. The other reason being the flexibility of the methods, including the ability to handle multiple objective functions, constraints, etc. With the popularity of heuristic approaches, quite many applications have been identified in the field of scheduling.

The introduction of new entities into the power sector, starting from renewable power generation, has made the modelling aspect of the system quite complex. The uncertain nature of generation sources like Solar Photovoltaics and Wind Energy Systems, further complicate the process and increase the computational time and effort. Deregulation of electricity market, coupled with the introduction of demand response, demand forecast error etc. have not been kind to the complexity of the problem. These factors are the reason why power system scheduling and optimization is the topic selected for discussion here, for it is one of the most complicated scheduling processes.

Based on the orientation of interests of invested entities, power system optimal scheduling cannot be solved as a single objective problem. For example, the net profit maximization in a microgrid will include the maximization of profit of both, the seller and the buyer, which are innately contradictive in nature. Hence, the result shall be the best compromise solution point, where all the interested parties stay satisfied. The optimal scheduling problem discussed here include opposing objectives and hence, a multi-objective formulation is adopted.

Stochastic weight trade-off chaotic mutation based non-dominated sorting particle swarm optimization (SWTCM_NSPSO) is a newly devised iteration to the famous optimization algorithm, PSO. The said method shall be applied to solve a optimal power flow (MO-OPF) problem, considering multiple objectives including generator fuel cost, voltage stability, and active power loss. The optimal power flow (OPF) problem is a large-scale, highly constrained nonlinear, and non-convex multi-objective optimization problem. The aim of the OPF solution algorithm is to optimize the selected objective functions which satisfy power balance constraint and generation and transmission limit constraints [Abou El Ela, et.al, (2010), Deb, K. (2001), Jabr, R. A., & Pal, B. C. (2009), Niknam, T., et.al, (2011), Sayah, S., & Zehar, K. (2008), Wood, A. J. et.al, (1984)]. The considered objectives in this problem are justifying the financial perspective, alongside stability and efficiency concerns, too. The algorithm shall be tested on standard and famous test systems, compared with major competitions, and the results, hence obtained, analyzed to see how the formulation of the method allows in the identification of a better operating point considering all the said perspectives.

BACKGROUND

Many mathematical techniques are used to solve the simple OPF, formulated as single objective optimization problems such as quadratic programming [Grudinin, N. (1998)], linear programming [Al-Muhawesh, T. A., & Qamber, I. S. (2008)], non-linear programming [Habibollahzadeh, H., et.al, (1989)], the interior point method [Yan, X., & Quintana, V. H. (1999)], Newton approach [Sun, D. I. et.al, (1984)], the mass interaction and gravitation method based on Newton's law [Duman, S. et.al, (2012)], and Krill herd algorithm including chaotic method [Mukherjee, A., & Mukherjee, V. (2015)]. An OPF problem considering the operation cost, the constraints of valve point loading effect and prohibited zones, is solved using the Shuffle Frog Leaping algorithm, incorporated with Simulated Annealing (SA) method to improve the local exploitation for the best solution [Niknam, T. et.al, (2012)]. Invasive Weed Optimization combined with the chaotic mutation (CIWO) is also employed to optimize the non-convex optimization problem focusing on the generator fuel cost considering valve-point loading effect, prohibited zones, and different fuel types as the non-convex OPF problem [Ghasemi, M., et.al, (2014)]. Lifetime operating expense as well as the investment cost are optimized by using the hybrid of Binary Enhanced PSO (BEPSO) and Modified Differential Evolution (MED), as a single objective optimization problem [Ahmadigorji, M., & Amjady, N. (2014)]. Another algorithm used to solve OPF problem is vortex search algorithm, which used piecewise quadratic cost curve for generators [Aydin, O., et.al, (2017)]. Valve point loading is also considered in the objective function. However, these techniques appear short-handed when used to solve the non-convex, multi-objective optimization problems.

Various methods, developed recently, to solve the multi-objective OPF problem have provided better solutions compared to single objective formulations. Decoupled Quadratic Load flow together with Enhance Genetic Algorithm is used for solving the multi-objective OPF (MO-OPF) problems minimizing fuel cost, voltage stability index, and power loss [Kumari, M. S., & Maheswarapu, S. (2010)], where the optimal Pareto-front set is realized by Strength Pareto Evolutionary. Multi-objective harmony search algorithm [Sivasubramani, S., & Swarup, K. S. (2011)] is used to obtain the optimum Pareto front for a multi-objective problem by the fast non-dominate sorting and crowding distance techniques in harmony search method. To improve the convergence rate and quality of solution, the teaching learning-based optimization, combined with quasi-oppositional based learning is found effective [Mandal, B., & Roy, P. K. (2014)]. Four different objectives, including generator fuel cost, voltage stability index, power loss, and emission, are optimized using the said approach. The multi-objective evolutionary algorithm based on decomposition [Medina, M. A., et.al, (2014)] is developed by using the modified artificial bee colony algorithm and a teaching-learning algorithm and used to minimize the total generator fuel cost, active power loss and voltage stability index. The non-dominated sorting multi-objective gravitational search algorithm [Bhowmik, A. R., & Chakraborty, A. K. (2014)] is introduced for solving different OPF problems and it used non-dominated sorting and crowding distance method to manage the Pareto optimal front.

Imperialist competitive algorithm [Ghasemi, M., et.al, (2014)] is the kind that utilizes the competition between the groups of particles to solve multi-objective OPF problem. Reducing emission level and generator fuel cost considering the prohibition zones, valve-point loading effect and multiple fuel types is a mammoth of a MO problem, which is solved using hybrid PSO and Shuffle Frog Leaping algorithm. The method is designed to increase the search performance from the diversified solutions. Modified Imperialist Competitive Algorithm utilizes the Imperialist Competitive algorithm and fuzzy grouping method to enhance the global best exploration [Ghasemi, M., et.al, (2014)]. An improved Genetic Algorithm that uses a two-part crossover and uniform mutation is used to optimize the reactive power dispatch minimizing active power loss and maximizing L-index level [Devaraj, D. (2007)]. JAYA algorithm, with certain modifications, is used recently to solve a MO-OPF problem, considering four objective functions [Elattar, E. E., & El Sayed, S. K. (2019)]. The approach is formulated in the presence of renewable energy sources in the system.

Swarm intelligence is a very successful and popular group of optimization algorithms. Particle swarm optimization (PSO), coupled with the diversity preserving technique and dynamic velocity control [Hazra, J., & Sinha, A. K. (2010)], is used to enhance the efficiency and to provide a well-distributed Pareto front. PSO is also used to determine economic operating situations in the presence of FACTS devices, considering multiple objectives and the control variables [Naderi, E., et.al, (2019)]. The popularity of PSO is due to flexibility and ease in adapting the algorithm to suit the solution method. The multi-objective krill herd algorithm [Roy, P. K., & Paul, C. (2014)] is developed and used to minimize the total generator fuel cost and voltage deviation and maximize the voltage stability. Considering a dynamic load demand for a span of 24 hrs. with multiple conflicting objectives in an optimization problem, an improved artificial bee colony algorithm using the chaos queues method [Liang, R.-H., et.al, (2015)] is found to alleviate the search process getting trapped in local optima and also to be enhancing the performance. Multi-objective electromagnetism-like algorithm (MEMA) [Jeddi, B., et.al, (2016)] is developed by using the adaptive local parameter control, for balancing the exploration between local and global solutions. Social Spider Optimization is another nature-inspired algorithm, a modified version of which, is found to provide faster convergence and better search capability, when used to solve a MO-OPF problem [Nguyen, T. T. (2019)].

Hybrid algorithms are also used for the solving the MO-OPF problems. The hybrid of Enhance grey wolf and Dragonfly algorithms [C., Shailaja., & T., Anuprasath. (2019)] is used to optimize a triple objectives OPF problem and is tested on a renewable powered hybrid microgrid, using Weibull distribution to forecast the renewable output. Hybrid of Moth Swarm and Gravitational Search algorithms are combined to solve a bi-objective OPF problem considering the variable nature of wind-based power generation [C., Shailaja., & T., Anuprasath. (2019)]. A different formulation is used when the system exhibits multiple characteristics, like AC-DC interconnected systems. Prominent optimization algorithms could be used on such systems, provided the modelling of the system is carried out aptly. A simplified OPF solving algorithm for solving such a hybrid system, involving HVDC connections, discussed by Renedo, J., et.al, (2019).

Though deep and machine learning approaches [Wang, X. Z., et.al, (2016), Zeng, P., et.al, (2019)] have been used for emergency energy management of power systems, their application to power flow related studies is quite less. Generation dispatch\scheduling is one of the key areas in the field that AI approach is being used for. Relaxed deep learning is used for real-time economic generation dispatch and control [Yin, L., et.al, (2018)]. Though classified as a dispatch strategy, the solution can give the same outcome as that of OPF. Deep learning based artificial dispatcher is discussed by Tomin, N. V. et.al, (2018), that combines the intelligence of the dispatcher and the speed of the automated devices, so that the best of both can be availed. There is also the argument that such data-driven methods can identify patterns effectively and make predictive solutions, that might not be a feasible one for power flow studies. The system must be compliant to such a solution, with all the associated constraints satisfied. In order to verify the feasibility of the obtained solution, a conventional OPF algorithm may be needed.

MAIN FOCUS OF THE CHAPTER[1]

Issues, Controversies, Problems

With multi-objective non-convex problems, the basic PSO algorithm often face the problem of premature convergence. This happens when the algorithm gets trapped in the local optima, rather than migrating to the global solution, because the cognitive and social acceleration coefficients, along with the velocity momentum, become less interrelated to one another. Stochastic weight trade-off method can handle non-convex problem very well due to the balancing between global best and local best exploitation process. A stochastic weight trade-off particle swarm optimization (SWT_PSO) [Chalermchaiarbha, S., & Ongsakul, W. (2013)] is used for solving the single objective economic dispatch non-convex problem effectively. Chaotic mutation method is able to solve the problem of premature convergence and enhance the exploitation ability, both in terms of searching performance and convergence speed [Cai, J., et.al, (2007); Cai, J., et.al, (2009); He, D., et.al, (2011)]. Therefore, the combination between stochastic weight trade-off and chaotic mutation algorithm could be suitable for solving the non-convex multi-objective problem. In each trial of the algorithm, non-dominated sorting and crowding distance methods are used to obtain the optimal Pareto front, and the local best compromise solution from the Pareto front is selected by the fuzzy-based mechanism.

The multi-objective optimal power flow problem considered in this chapter is focused on minimizing the generator fuel cost and active power loss, alongside maximizing the voltage stability, quantified using, L-index. For this, a stochastic weight trade-off and chaotic mutation based non-dominated sorting particle swarm optimization (SWTCM_NSPSO) method is used and the detailed formulation shall be discussed. The SWTCM_NSPSO algorithm applies the trade-off stochastic weight method and dynamistic coefficients trade-off mechanisms on the PSO-velocity updating function for balancing exploration process of the global and local best utilization. In order to overcome the issue of premature convergence, the mechanisms of lethargy and freak control factors are utilized. In addition, this also incorporates the chaotic weight mutation method to the inertial weight factor to enhance the search capability in the diversified space, while avoiding getting trapped in the local minima. To provide better pareto front solutions, the non-dominated sorting and crowding distance evaluation methods are incorporated with the said algorithm to increase efficient operations of sharing and sorting among swarm members. To ensure consistency, the algorithm is run multiple trials. Two stages of non-dominated sorting, crowding distance, and the best compromise selecting process are utilized to choose the global best solution from many local best trial solutions. The results are demonstrated on IEEE 30 and 118-bus systems.

FORMULATION OF THE OPF PROBLEM[2]

Objective Functions

There are three objectives to minimize including the generator fuel cost, L- index, and transmission system loss.

Objective 1: Generator fuel cost minimization.

$$Minimize \, C_F = \sum_{i=1}^{N_{GEN}} \left\{ a_i P_{Gi}^2 + b_i P_{Gi} + c_i \right\} \tag{1}$$

Objective 2: Voltage stability maximization

The voltage stability margin of system can be computed by minimizing L-index at all the load buses within the interval [0-1]. The system will be safe when the L-index is close to 0. If the L-index increases to the maximum value of one, the voltage collapse will be concerned [Man-Im, et.al, (2015); Duman, S., et.al, (2012); Lee, K. Y., & El-Sharkawi, M. A. (2008)]. L-index of each load bus is defined as in (2).

$$L_j = \left| 1 - \sum_{i=1}^{N_{GEN}} F_{ji} \frac{V_{Gi}}{V_{Lj}} \right| \quad j = 1,..,N_L \tag{2}$$

Matrix (F) is computed by (3) where [Y_{LL}] and [Y_{LG}] are submatrices of the Y_{BUS} matrix.

$$[F] = -[Y_{LL}]^{-1}[Y_{LG}] \tag{3}$$

The voltage stability of whole system can be described in terms of a global indicator L-index (L_{max}) as:

$$L_{max} = \max \left\{ L_j \right\} \tag{4}$$

To be against the voltage collapse point, L_{max} should be minimized as:

$$Minimize \, L_{max} = \max \left\{ L_j \right\} \tag{5}$$

Objective 3: Transmission system loss minimization.

The total active power loss can be calculated using the bus voltage magnitudes and voltage angles from the power flow solution as:

$$Minimize \, P_{loss} = \sum_{l=1}^{N_{line}} g_l \left[V_i^2 - V_j^2 - 2V_i V_j \cos\left(\delta_i - \delta_j\right) \right] \tag{6}$$

Multi-Objective OPF Formulation

Here, the multi-objective OPF problem can be formulated as:

$$Minimize \left\{ f_{obj1}, f_{obj2}, f_{obj3} \right\} = \left\{ C_F, L_{max}, P_{loss} \right\} \tag{7}$$

$$\textit{Subject to } g\left(s,u\right) = 0 \qquad\qquad (8)$$

$$h\left(s,u\right) \leq 0 \qquad\qquad (9)$$

The vector of dependent variables consists of active power output at slack bus, load bus voltage magnitudes, reactive power outputs, and transmission line loadings expressed as:

$$s = \left[P_{G1}, V_{L1}...V_{LN_L}, Q_{G1}...Q_{GN_{GEN}}, S_{L1}...S_{LN_{line}} \right]^T \qquad\qquad (10)$$

The control variables' vector consists of active power output at PV bus excluding at the slack bus, generator terminal voltages, transformer tap settings, and shunt VAR compensations as:

$$u = \left[P_{G2}...P_{GN_{GEN}}, V_{G1}...V_{GN_{GEN}}, T_1...T_{N_{Tr}}, Q_{C1}...Q_{CN_C} \right]^T \qquad\qquad (11)$$

Technical Constraints

1. Equality Constraints

$$P_i = P_{Gi} - P_{Di} = V_i \sum_{j=1}^{N_{BUS}} V_j \left[G_{ij} \cos\left(\delta_i - \delta_j\right) + B_{ij} \sin\left(\delta_i - \delta_j\right) \right],$$

$$i = 1, 2, ..., N_{BUS}, \qquad\qquad (12)$$

$$Q_i = Q_{Gi} - Q_{Di} = V_i \sum_{j=1}^{N_{BUS}} V_j \left[G_{ij} \sin\left(\delta_i - \delta_j\right) - B_{ij} \cos\left(\delta_i - \delta_j\right) \right]$$

2. Inequality Constraints

Generation Constraints:

$$P_{Gi}^{min} \leq P_{Gi} \leq P_{Gi}^{max}, \quad i \in N_{GEN},$$
$$Q_{Gi}^{min} \leq Q_{Gi} \leq Q_{Gi}^{max}, \quad i \in N_{GEN}, \qquad\qquad (13)$$
$$V_{Gi}^{min} \leq V_{Gi} \leq V_{Gi}^{max}, \quad i \in N_{GEN}$$

Transformer Tap constraints

$$T_i^{min} \leq T_i \leq T_i^{max}, \ \ i \in N_T \tag{14}$$

Shunt VAR compensator constraints:

$$Q_{Ci}^{min} \leq Q_{Ci} \leq Q_{Ci}^{max}, \ \ i \in N_C \tag{15}$$

Voltage magnitude constraints:

$$V_{Li}^{min} \leq V_{Li} \leq V_{Li}^{max}, \ \ i \in N_L \tag{16}$$

Transmission line loading constraints:

$$S_{li}^{min} \leq S_{li}, \ \ i \in N_{line} \tag{17}$$

To handle the inequality constraint violations, the dependent variables including P_{Gl}, V_L, Q_G, and S_L are added to an objective function as quadratic penalty terms. In this penalty function, the square of inequality constraint violations is multiplied with penalty coefficients and augmented into the objective function. Therefore, this augmented objective function is able to minimize the infeasible solutions [37-38]:

$$Minimize \ f_j = f_{obj,j} + \left(\lambda_P \times \left(P_{G1} - P_{G1}^{lim} \right)^2 \right) + \lambda_V \times \sum_{i=1}^{N_L} \left(V_{Li} - V_{Li}^{lim} \right)^2$$
$$+ \lambda_Q \times \sum_{i=1}^{N_{GEN}} \left(Q_{Gi} - Q_{Gi}^{lim} \right)^2 + \lambda_S \times \sum_{i=1}^{N_{line}} \left(S_{Li} - S_{Li}^{lim} \right)^2 ; j = 1, 2 \ldots N_{obj} \tag{18}$$

The limit value of dependent variable s^{lim} is given as:

$$s^{\lim} = \begin{cases} s^{max} \ if \ s > s^{max} \\ s^{min} \ if \ s < s^{min} \end{cases}, s^{lim} = \left[P_{Gi}^{\lim}, V_{Li}^{\lim}, Q_{Gi}^{lim}, S_{Li}^{lim} \right] \tag{19}$$

PROPOSED APPROACH[3]

Stochastic Weight Tradeoff Chaotic Mutation Based NSPSO (SWTCM_NSPSO)

Particle swarm optimization (PSO) is an evolutionary computation technique modeled based on the social behaviors of bird flocking or fish schooling. A population of particles, like the flock of birds, moves in the multi-dimensional search space regulated by its location and velocity. During the movement, the velocity of each particle is adjusted in each searching process while its position is updated. PSO can utilize the experience of each particle and its neighbors to observe the better position [Niknam, T., et.al, (2012); Medina, M. A., et.al, (2014); Bhowmik, A. R., & Chakraborty, A. K. (2014)]. The velocity and position updating functions of PSO are described in (20)-(21), where $k=1, 2, ..., k_{max}$, $i=1, 2...n$, and $d=1, 2...D$. *pbest* is the best previous position of particle and *gbest* is the best particle among all particles.

$$v_{id}^{k+1} = \varpi v_{id}^k + c_1 r_1 \left(pbest_{id}^k - x_{id}^k \right) + c_2 r_2 \left(gbest_{id}^k - x_{id}^k \right) \tag{20}$$

$$x_{id}^{k+1} = x_{id}^k + v_{id}^{k+1} \tag{21}$$

However, the PSO algorithm has some limitation if applied directly to solve the multi-objective optimization problem. Since a particle is updated by using only its personal best and global best information, there is no sharing of its experience with the other particles. In addition, the velocity updating function of PSO is sensitive to cognitive parameter (c_1) and social parameter (c_2) which are incoherently generated. Hence, the local best and global best reached may not be optimum in the multi-objective problem [Ongsakul, W., & Vo, D. N. (2013); Kapse, S. P., & Krishnapillai, S. (2018)]. Moreover, the particles may be far away from the local optimum when c_1 and c_2 are too large or over dependent upon the own and neighbor experiences of each particle. If both c_1 and c_2 are too small, the experiences of own particle and its neighbors are of little effect leading to the premature convergence problem [Chalermchaiarbha, S., & Ongsakul, W. (2013)].

A stochastic weight trade-off chaotic mutation based non-dominated sorting particle swarm optimization (SWTCM_NSPSO) is proposed to solve the MO-OPF problem. SWTCM_NSPSO features include the balance between global best exploration and local best exploitation processes, combination and non-dominated sorting concept, and crowding distance assignment. The mechanisms are described as follows.

1. Balance of Global Best Searching and Local Best Utilization

$$v_{id}^{k+1} = \eta^k \times \varpi(k) r_2 sign(r_3) v_{id}^k + (1 - r_2) c_1(k) r_1 \left(pbest_{id}^k - x_{id}^k \right). \tag{22}$$

$$+ (1 - r_2) c_2(k)(1 - r_1) \left(gbest_{id}^k - x_{id}^k \right) \tag{23}$$

The velocity and position updating equations from (20) is modified as in (22). To coherently generate between c_1 and c_2, the r_1 and $1 - r_1$ are used to balance the cognitive and social components. These stochastic weights will incorporate with the experiences of individual particle and its neighbors when the velocity of particle updates. Momentum of the previous velocity term affects the efficiency of searching global best and the position update. The small value of the previous velocity momentum would influence the cognitive and social accelerated components to control the performance of position update. Therefore, r_2 and $1 - r_2$ are stochastically generated for trade-off between the previous velocity term, the cognitive and social elements. On the other hand, if the momentum is too large, the particles may be driven away from the global regions and difficult to change their directions into the optimum position. As a result, the direction of particle's position may not lead to the global optimum regions. The lethargy factor is used to improve the reverse behavior of particles into the global best regions. This factor involves with the *sign(r₃)* value defined as in (23).

$$If\ r_4 > P_{frk},\ sign\left(r_4\right) = 1, P\left(r_4\right) = 0 \tag{24}$$

$$If\ r_4 < P_{frk},\ sign\left(r_4\right) = -1, P\left(r_4\right) = 1 \tag{25}$$

$$\varpi\left(k\right) = \left(\varpi_{min} - \varpi_{max}\right)\frac{k}{k_{max}} + \varpi_{max}, k = 1, 2 \dots, k_{max} \tag{26}$$

For the increasing the global search capability, the previous velocity term is modified as (24)-(25). The P_{ltg} and P_{frk} are represented to avoid the particles from the trapping in the local optimum regions avoiding the premature convergence problem. Consequently, the modified previous velocity momentum in (22) uses $\varpi\left(k\right).r_2.sign\left(r_3\right)$ .as the weighting control factor, where $\varpi(k)$ is modified by using the gradual reducing method given in (26), to avoid the driving away from global optimum solution and to support the local searching capability for a candidate solution.

$$\eta^{k+1} = \phi \times \eta^k \times \left(1 - \eta^k\right), 0 \le \eta^k \le 1 \tag{27}$$

The chaos characteristic is a deterministic dynamic system, unpredictable, and nonlinear phenomenon. For the proposed SWTCM_NSPSO, the chaotic mutation is applied into the inertia weight factor to enhance the search capability in the diversified search space. The simplest chaotic behavior is the Logistic map given in (27), where $\varphi = 4$ and $\eta^0 \notin \left\{0, 0.25, 0.5, 0.75, 1.0\right\}$. To improve the local searching performance, the cognitive and social accelerated coefficients are designed to decrease linearly as (28)-(29).

$$c_1\left(k\right) = \left(c_{1,min} - c_{1,max}\right)\frac{k}{k_{max}} + c_{1,max}, k = 1, 2 \dots, k_{max} \tag{28}$$

$$c_2\left(k\right) = \left(c_{2,min} - c_{2,max}\right)\frac{k}{k_{max}} + c_{2,max}, k = 1, 2 \dots, k_{max} \tag{29}$$

2. Combination and Non-Dominated Sorting Concept

The combination method is utilized for sharing the individual experience of a particle with the others. In this method, the velocities and positions of '*n*' particles are updated to become their '*n*' offspring particles. The first '*n*' particles will combine with the offspring particles to form a new population of 2*n* particles. The non-dominated sorting solution is applied to sort these 2*n* particles into different non-domination levels. The classification concept of non-domination is shown in Fig. 1 [Shi, Y., & Eberhart, R. (1998); Srinivas, N., & Deb, K. (1994); Wartana, I. M. (2015)]. In Fig. 1, particles in front 1 are the best non-dominated set dominating other particles. The remaining particles from front 1 are sorted by non-dominated solution again to classify the next levels of non-dominated solution.

3. Crowding Distance Assignment

To maintain the best distribution on the non-dominated set, the crowding distance is calculated for each individual particle in each front set. The crowding distance method makes use of the density of neighbors, close to a specific point, on the non-dominated front. The density is estimated by average value of distance between an individual point/particle and its neighbors, as shown in Fig 2. The best *n* particles are selected from the non-dominated front lists based on their crowding distance in the descending order.

Figure 1. Non-Dominated Sorting Concept [Shi, Y., & Eberhart, R. (1998); Srinivas, N., & Deb, K. (1994); Wartana, I. M. (2015)]

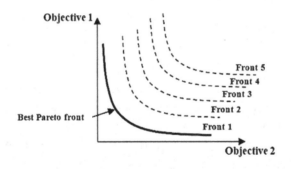

Figure 2. Crowding distance calculation [Shi, Y., & Eberhart, R. (1998); Srinivas, N., & Deb, K. (1994); Wartana, I. M. (2015)]

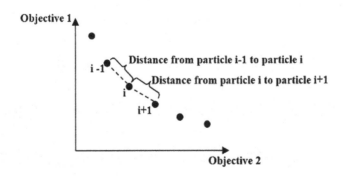

The selected *n* best particles would lead toward the optimum region in the search space as *pbest* and the best value among the set of *pbest* is denoted as *gbest* [Shi, Y., & Eberhart, R. (1998); Srinivas, N., & Deb, K. (1994); Wartana, I. M. (2015)]. The schematic of the combination of non-dominated sorting and crowding distance approaches is shown in Fig. 3.

Procedure for SWTCM_NSPSO

Step 1: The power output of each conventional unit, generator bus voltages, transformer tap settings, and reactive power of shunt VAR compensators are set as decision variables in a position as in (30). The initial iteration counter *k* is set to 0. The initial positions (x_{id}^0) of all particles are generated by randomly selecting in limit of decision variables. The velocities (v_{id}^0) of particles are randomly initialized within a range of [$v_{id,min}, v_{id,max}$] defined as in (31).

$$x_i = \left[P_{Gi}^2, \ldots, P_{Gi}^{N_{GEN}}, V_{Gi}^1, \ldots, V_{Gi}^{N_{GEN}}, T_i^1, \ldots, T_i^{N_{Tr}}, Q_{Ci}^1, \ldots, Q_{Ci}^{N_C} \right], .i=1,2,\ldots,n. \tag{30}$$

$$v_{id,max} = x_{id,max} - x_{id,min} \quad v_{id,min} = -v_{id,max} \,.. \tag{31}$$

Step 2: The objective functions (1), (5), and (6) are evaluated for each particle.

Step 3: Non-domination sorting algorithm sorts all particles and stores them in the non-dominated list.

Step 4: The *n* particles of non-dominated list are selected as pbest^k set.

Step 5: The global best set ($gbest^k$) is defined by randomly selecting from the top part (e.g. top 5%) of the non-dominated solution list.

Step 6: The updating functions in (21)-(22) are used to update all current particles. The updated particles are assigned as the offspring particles and calculate the objective values for each offspring particle from the objective functions. To handle the inequality constraints, the velocity and position of

Figure 3. Schematic of combination of non-dominated sorting and crowding distance method approach

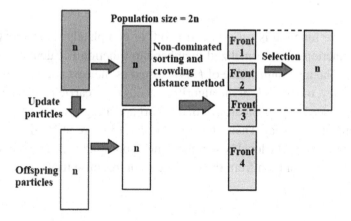

particles need to be within their limits. If the velocity and position parameters violate their limits, their respective values will be set as:

$$\text{If } v_{id}^k > v_{id,max}, \quad v_{id}^k = v_{id,max}$$
$$\text{If } v_{id}^k < v_{id,min}, \quad v_{id}^k = v_{id,min} \tag{32}$$

$$\text{If } x_{id}^k > x_{id,max}, \quad x_{id}^k = x_{id,max}$$
$$\text{If } x_{id}^k < x_{id,min}, \quad x_{id}^k = x_{id,min} \tag{33}$$

Step 7: The current P_i^k .nd offspring particles are combined into $2n$ population. All these particles are re-sorted by the non-domination criterion and crowding distance of each particle in each front is assigned.

Step 8: The particles in each front of non-dominated solution are re-arranged by considering descending order of crowding distance.

Step 9: The best n particles are selected from the $2n$ population based on priority lists of non-dominated solution.

Step 10: If the maximum iteration is met, stop. Otherwise, increase the iteration counter $k = k+1$, and return to step 3.

Selecting Compromised Solutions

After obtaining the Pareto-optimal front, a fuzzy-based mechanism is proposed to identify the best compromise solution as a decision-making function. The function for selecting compromise solutions are expressed in (34)-(35) [Sakawa, M., et.al, (1987); Carlsson, C., & Fullér, R. (1996); Farina, M., & Amato, P. (2004)].

$$f^j = \frac{\sum_{i=1}^{N_{obj}} f_i^j}{\sum_{j=1}^{m} \sum_{i=1}^{N_{obj}} f_i^j} \tag{34}$$

In (34), the objective function is varied from 1 to 0 or completely satisfactory to unsatisfactory in a linear decreasing function. The normalized membership function is calculated in (35) for each non-dominated solution j. The maximum value of f^j is selected as the best compromise trial solution.

To ensure consistency, many trials of the algorithm needs to be carried out. The non-dominated solution and crowding distance assignment are applied to sort and assign crowding distant for the local best compromise solutions of each trial. Then, the Eq. (34) and (35) are utilized again to select the global best compromise solution from the local best compromise solution front. The schematic of the selecting the global best compromise solution from the local best compromise trial solutions is shown in Fig. 4.

Figure 4. The schematic of the selection the global best compromise solution from many local best trials

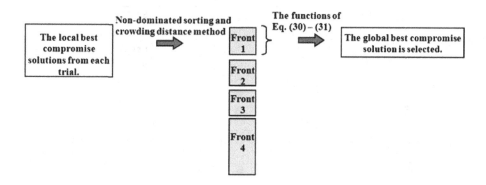

NUMERICAL SOLUTIONS AND RECOMMENDATIONS

For the OPF problem, the IEEE 30 and IEEE 118 bus are used as test systems with 100 MVA base. The IEEE 30 bus system consists of six generators at bus 1, 2, 5, 8, 11 and 13, four transformers with tap ratio in the transmission line 6–9, 6–10, 4–12 and 27–28 and reactive power injection at bus 10, 12, 15, 17, 20, 21, 23, 24 and 29. The single line diagram of IEEE 30 bus test system is illustrated in Appendix A. The active power limit and reactive power limit are presented in Appendix A. All bus voltage limits are within the range [0.95-1.1] p.u. and tap ratio settings are within the range [0.95-1.1] p.u. The limit of reactive power of shunt VAR compensator is [0-0.05] p.u. The IEEE 118 bus test system consists of 54 generators and 9 on load tap change transformers as shown in Appendix B. The software is written in MATLAB 8.1.0 and executed on an Intel(R) Core (TM) i5 processer personal computer with 2.0 GB RAM.

The SWTCM_NSPSO parameter settings are $\varpi^{max} = 1.3$, $\varpi^{min} = 1.1$, $P_{ltg} = 0.06$, $P_{frk} = 0.06$, the maximum and minimum acceleration coefficients are 2.8 and 2.4, respectively. The population size and iterations are 100 and 1000, respectively. For NSPSO parameters [Wartana, I. M. (2015)], the maximum and minimum inertia weights are 1.0 and 0.4, respectively. The acceleration coefficients c_1 and c_2 are set to 2. For NSGAII, the crossover and mutation operators are set to 20 [Wartana, I. M. (2015)]. For the consistency test, the algorithms run 50 trials. There are four different simulation cases on the IEEE 30 bus system (Case I -III) and one case on the IEEE 118 bus system as (Case IV):

Case I   Multi-objective minimization between the generator fuel cost and the L-index
Case II   Multi-objective between L-index and active power loss minimization
Case III   Multi-objective among generator fuel cost, L-index and active power loss minimization
Case IV   Multi-objective among generator fuel cost, L-index and active power loss minimization
for IEEE 118 bus test system

Selection of Global Best Solution

In Figs. 5-6, the local best solutions obtained from 50 trials for different methods are shown for Cases I - III, respectively. For each solution method, the fuzzy method in (34) - (35) is used to select the global best compromise solution from 50 local best trial solutions. Evidently, SWTCM_NSPSO can find a better global best compromise solution than SWT_NSPSO (Stochastic Weight Trade-off, NSPSO), NSPSO, NS_CPSO, and NSGA II (Non-dominated sorting Genetic Algorithm).

Figure 5. The global best compromise solution of multi-objective minimization for 50 trials in Case I

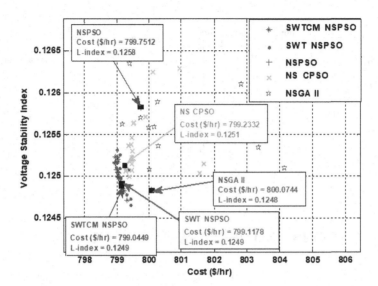

Figure 6. The global best compromise solution of multi-objective minimization for 50 trials in Case II

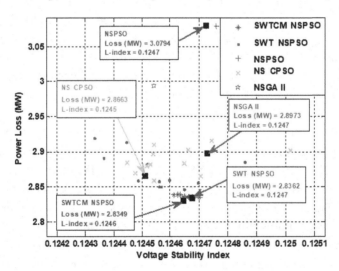

In Fig. 7, the global best compromise solution selected from 50 local best trial solutions for Case III is illustrated. All global best compromise multi-objective clearly indicates that the proposed SWTCM_NSPSO algorithm provide better cluster and better global trade-off solutions than the SWT_NSPSO, NS_CPSO, NSPSO, and NSGA II as shown in Fig 7 (a), (b), (c), and (d), respectively.

The global best compromise solution selected from 50 local best trial solutions for 118 bus test system in Case IV is illustrated in Fig. 8. All global best compromises multi-objective of SWTCM_NSPSO of Fig. 8 (d) indicate that the proposed algorithm is able to provide lower global best trade-off solutions than the NSGA II, NSPSO, NS_CPSO, and SWT_NSPSO as shown in Fig. 8 (a), (b), and (c) respectively.

Figure 7. The global best compromise solution of multi-objective minimization for 50 trials in Case III

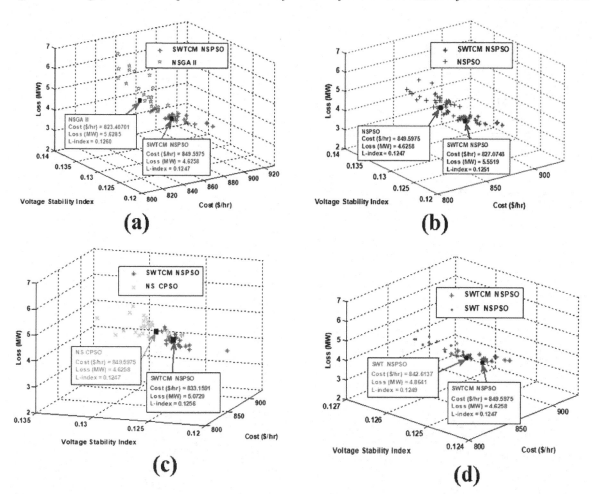

Global Best Compromise Numerical Solution

1. Multi-Objective Between Fuel Cost, L-Index, And Active Power Loss Minimization

The algorithm is tested in the backdrop of IEEE 30-bus test system, minimizing the fuel cost, active power loss and maximizing the voltage stability. All the objective functions are optimized simultaneously, and the global best solutions given in Table I. The formulated algorithm, SWTCM_NSPSO can provide the better solution than those of all compared methods. The three-dimensional Pareto front of SWTCM_NSPSO remarkably provide the well- distributed than NSGA II, NSPSO, and NS_CPSO algorithms represented in Fig. 12 (a), (b), (c), respectively. SWTCM_NSPSO has better cluster and provides a lower pareto optimal front than SWT_NSPSO as shown in Fig. 12 (d).

Figure 8. The global best compromise solution of multi-objective minimization for 50 trials in Case IV

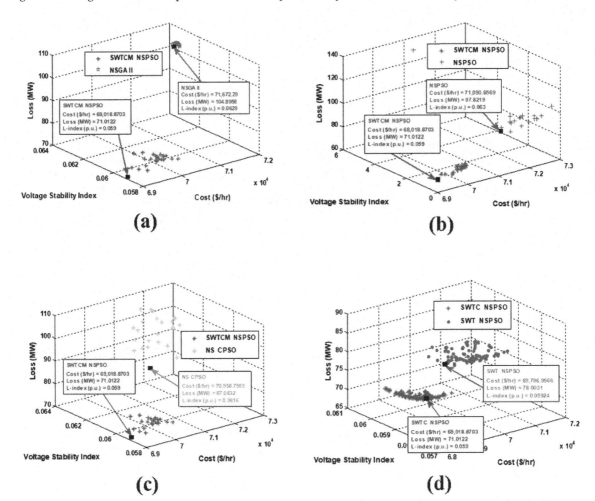

2. SWTCM_NSPSO Applied to IEEE 118 Bus Test System

While testing SWTCM_NSPSO on an IEEE 118-bus test system, it is observed that the method provided better solution compared with the other methods using the same test data, as shown in Table 2. The three-dimensional Pareto front from SWTCM_NSPSO remarkably provides a well-distributed and lower front than NSGA II, NSPSO, NS_CPSO, and SWT_NSPSO algorithms illustrated in Fig. 13 (a), (b), (c) and (d) respectively.

In all the cases, SWTCM_NSPSO algorithm outperform other algorithms in solving the multi-objective OPF problem. The features that are attributed to the said algorithm increases the performance by improving the search capability, properly balancing between the global solution search and local best result utilization, and by being able to better share the individual characteristics and experiences among population. Therefore, the discussed optimizer could find a better trade-off trial solution from a well distributed Pareto front.

Figure 9. Comparison between the global best solutions of considering all objective functions

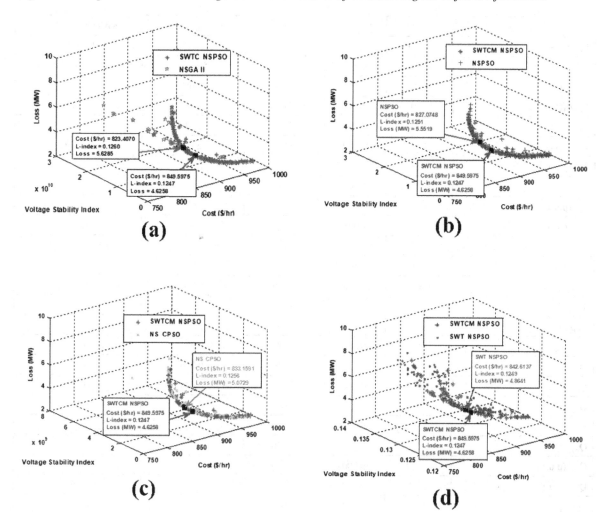

FUTURE RESEARCH DIRECTIONS

Based on the type of system to be scheduled, the features added to the optimization algorithm can vary. Also, depending on the application, the processing time need should also be acceptable. Based on the time period, the discussed algorithm can be applied from short term scheduling like, half hour ahead to day ahead scheduling of power systems. Hence, research can be focused on developing algorithms and equipping them with more/less features suitable according to the nature of system to be scheduled. Also, from the power system perspective, the incorporation of renewable energy forecasting can be incorporated into the discussion. Including emission equivalent as an additional objective function component could reduce the use of fossil fuel-based sources and prioritize renewable energy use.

Table 1. The global best solution between fuel cost, l-index, and active power loss minimization

Parameter	NSGAII	NSPSO	NS_CPSO	SWT_NSPSO	SWTCM_NSPSO
Pg_1 (MW)	130.805	123.291	119.212	112.178	111.677
Pg_2 (MW)	45.925	55.534	50.969	58.706	53.990
Pg_3 (MW)	30.427	30.942	31.843	35.597	39.434
Pg_4 (MW)	35.000	35.000	35.000	31.749	34.546
Pg_5 (MW)	24.136	25.643	27.547	27.214	28.025
Pg_6 (MW)	22.735	18.541	23.902	22.821	20.354
Vg_1 (p.u.)	1.099	1.100	1.100	1.100	1.100
Vg_2 (p.u.)	1.084	1.090	1.090	1.091	1.093
Vg_3 (p.u.)	1.057	1.079	1.080	1.071	1.080
Vg_4 (p.u.)	1.067	1.091	1.082	1.090	1.093
Vg_5 (p.u.)	1.100	1.100	1.100	1.098	1.097
Vg_6 (p.u.)	1.099	1.100	1.100	1.098	1.100
$Tap_{(6-9)}$	0.993	1.100	1.029	1.034	1.010
$Tap_{(6-10)}$	0.972	0.900	0.900	0.910	0.906
$Tap_{(4-12)}$	1.030	0.984	1.003	0.997	0.994
$Tap_{(27-28)}$	0.939	0.947	0.977	0.959	0.965
Q_{C10} (p.u.)	0.056	0.050	0.050	0.036	0.028
Q_{C12} (p.u.)	0.027	0.000	0.050	0.045	0.038
Q_{C15} (p.u.)	0.028	0.000	0.050	0.048	0.049
Q_{C17} (p.u.)	0.043	0.000	0.000	0.021	0.026
Q_{C20} (p.u.)	0.019	0.000	0.050	0.015	0.005
Q_{C21} (p.u.)	0.029	0.000	0.050	0.016	0.021
Q_{C23} (p.u.)	0.010	0.050	0.000	0.047	0.050
Q_{C24} (p.u.)	0.039	0.023	0.050	0.044	0.048
Q_{C29} (p.u.)	0.025	0.000	0.050	0.010	0.010
Cost ($/hr)	823.407	827.075	833.159	842.644	**849.598**
L-index	0.126	0.125	0.126	0.125	**0.125**
Loss (MW)	5.629	5.552	5.073	4.864	**4.626**

CONCLUSION

An optimization algorithm for power system scheduling is developed with certain features, that can enhance the performance of the said algorithm making it efficient and robust. The algorithm developed is SWTCM_NSPSO. It is developed to solve the complex and non-convex, multi-objective optimization problem of OPF. The simulation results and the inference drawn from them indicate remarkable improvement in search capability, with the use of stochastic weight trade-off and dynamistic coefficients trade-off mechanisms, while balancing both global search and local utilization, simultaneously. The algorithm is successful at avoiding premature convergence issues due to the incorporation of chaotic

Figure 10. Comparison between the global best solutions from various methods for IEEE 118-bus

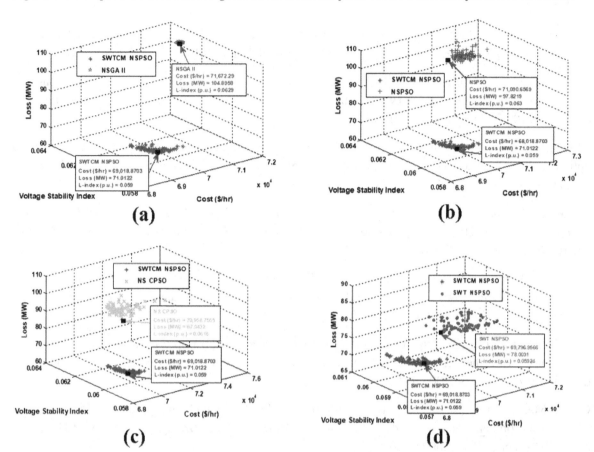

Table 2. The global solutions for IEEE 118-bus

	NSGA II	NSPSO	NS_CPSO	SWT_NSPSO	SWTCM_NSPSO
Cost ($/hr.)	71,672.290	71,090.657	70,958.756	69,796.957	**69,018.870**
Loss (MW)	104.896	97.822	87.043	78.003	**71.012**
L-index	0.063	0.063	0.062	0.059	**0.059**

mutation, freak and lethargy factors. Non-dominated sorting concept and crowding distance technique are used to obtain the optimal pareto front. The MO-OPF solution provided by SWTCM_NSPSO is better than other prominent algorithms.

ACKNOWLEDGMENT

The authors are grateful to the King HRD Scholarship, Energy Conservation and Promotion Fund, Ministry of Energy of Thailand for their partial financial support.

REFERENCES

Abou El Ela, A. A., Abido, M. A., & Spea, S. R. (2010). Optimal power flow using differential evolution algorithm. *Electric Power Systems Research*, *80*(7), 878–885. doi:10.1016/j.epsr.2009.12.018

Ahmadigorji, M., & Amjady, N. (2014). A new evolutionary solution method for dynamic expansion planning of DG-integrated primary distribution networks. *Energy Conversion and Management*, *82*, 61–70. doi:10.1016/j.enconman.2014.03.008

Al-Muhawesh, T. A., & Qamber, I. S. (2008). The established mega watt linear programming-based optimal power flow model applied to the real power 56-bus system in eastern province of Saudi Arabia. *Energy*, *33*(1), 12–21. doi:10.1016/j.energy.2007.08.004

Aydin, O., Tezcan, S. S., Eke, I., & Taplamacioglu, M. C. (2017). Solving the Optimal Power Flow Quadratic Cost Functions using Vortex Search Algorithm. *IFAC-PapersOnLine*, *50*(1), 239–244. doi:10.1016/j.ifacol.2017.08.040

Bhowmik, A. R., & Chakraborty, A. K. (2014). Solution of optimal power flow using nondominated sorting multi objective gravitational search algorithm. *International Journal of Electrical Power & Energy Systems*, *62*, 323–334. doi:10.1016/j.ijepes.2014.04.053

Cai, J., Ma, X., Li, L., & Haipeng, P. (2007). Chaotic particle swarm optimization for economic dispatch considering the generator constraints. *Energy Conversion and Management*, *48*(2), 645–653. doi:10.1016/j.enconman.2006.05.020

Cai, J., Ma, X., Li, Q., Li, L., & Peng, H. (2009). A multi-objective chaotic particle swarm optimization for environmental/economic dispatch. *Energy Conversion and Management*, *50*(5), 1318–1325. doi:10.1016/j.enconman.2009.01.013

Carlsson, C., & Fullér, R. (1996). Fuzzy multiple criteria decision making: Recent developments. *Fuzzy Sets and Systems*, *78*(2), 139–153. doi:10.1016/0165-0114(95)00165-4

Chalermchaiarbha, S., & Ongsakul, W. (2013). Stochastic weight trade-off particle swarm optimization for nonconvex economic dispatch. *Energy Conversion and Management*, *70*, 66–75. doi:10.1016/j.enconman.2013.02.009

Deb, K. (2001). *Multi-Objective Optimization using Evolutionary Algorithms*. John Wiley & Sons.

Devaraj, D. (2007). Improved genetic algorithm for multi-objective reactive power dispatch problem. *European Transactions on Electrical Power*, *17*(6), 569–581. doi:10.1002/etep.146

Duman, S., Güvenç, U., Sönmez, Y., & Yörükeren, N. (2012). Optimal power flow using gravitational search algorithm. *Energy Conversion and Management*, *59*, 86–95. doi:10.1016/j.enconman.2012.02.024

Duman, S., Sonmez, Y., Guvenc, U., & Yorukeren, N. (2012). Optimal reactive power dispatch using a gravitational search algorithm. *IET Generation, Transmission & Distribution*, *6*(6), 563–576. doi:10.1049/iet-gtd.2011.0681

Elattar, E. E., & ElSayed, S. K. (2019). Modified JAYA algorithm for optimal power flow incorporating renewable energy sources considering the cost, emission, power loss and voltage profile improvement. *Energy*, *178*, 598–609. doi:10.1016/j.energy.2019.04.159

Farina, M., & Amato, P. (2004). A fuzzy definition of "optimality" for many-criteria optimization problems. *IEEE Transactions on Systems, Man, and Cybernetics. Part A, Systems and Humans*, *34*(3), 315–326. doi:10.1109/TSMCA.2004.824873

Ghasemi, M., Ghavidel, S., Akbari, E., & Vahed, A. A. (2014). Solving non-linear, non-smooth and non-convex optimal power flow problems using chaotic invasive weed optimization algorithms based on chaos. *Energy*, *73*, 340–353. doi:10.1016/j.energy.2014.06.026

Ghasemi, M., Ghavidel, S., Ghanbarian, M. M., Gharibzadeh, M., & Vahed, A. A. (2014). Multi-objective optimal power flow considering the cost, emission, voltage deviation and power losses using multi-objective modified imperialist competitive algorithm. *Energy*, *78*, 276–289. doi:10.1016/j.energy.2014.10.007

Ghasemi, M., Ghavidel, S., Rahmani, S., Roosta, A., & Falah, H. (2014). A novel hybrid algorithm of imperialist competitive algorithm and teaching learning algorithm for optimal power flow problem with non-smooth cost functions. *Engineering Applications of Artificial Intelligence*, *29*, 54–69. doi:10.1016/j.engappai.2013.11.003

Grudinin, N. (1998). Reactive power optimization using successive quadratic programming method. *IEEE Transactions on Power Systems*, *13*(4), 1219–1225. doi:10.1109/59.736232

Habibollahzadeh, H., Luo, G., & Semlyen, A. (1989). Hydrothermal optimal power flow based on a combined linear and nonlinear programming methodology. *IEEE Transactions on Power Systems*, *4*(2), 530–537. doi:10.1109/59.193826

Hazra, J., & Sinha, A. K. (2010). A multi-objective optimal power flow using particle swarm optimization. *European Transactions on Electrical Power*, *21*(1), 1028–1045. doi:10.1002/etep.494

He, D., Dong, G., Wang, F., & Mao, Z. (2011). Optimization of dynamic economic dispatch with valve-point effect using chaotic sequence based differential evolution algorithms. *Energy Conversion and Management*, *52*(2), 1026–1032. doi:10.1016/j.enconman.2010.08.031

Jabr, R. A., & Pal, B. C. (2009). Intermittent wind generation in optimal power flow dispatching. *IET Generation, Transmission & Distribution*, *3*(1), 66–74. doi:10.1049/iet-gtd:20080273

Jeddi, B., Einaddin, A. H., & Kazemzadeh, R. (2016). A novel multi-objective approach based on improved electromagnetism-like algorithm to solve optimal power flow problem considering the detailed model of thermal generators. *International Transactions on Electrical Energy Systems*, *27*(4), e2293. doi:10.1002/etep.2293

Kapse, S. P., & Krishnapillai, S. (2018). An Improved Multi-Objective Particle Swarm Optimization Based on Utopia Point Guided Search. *International Journal of Applied Metaheuristic Computing*, *9*(4), 71–96. doi:10.4018/IJAMC.2018100104

Kumari, M. S., & Maheswarapu, S. (2010). Enhanced Genetic Algorithm based computation technique for multi-objective Optimal Power Flow solution. *International Journal of Electrical Power & Energy Systems*, *32*(6), 736–742. doi:10.1016/j.ijepes.2010.01.010

Lee, K. Y., & El-Sharkawi, M. A. (2008). *Modern heuristic optimization techniques: Theory and applications to power systems*. Piscataway, NJ: IEEE Press. doi:10.1002/9780470225868

Liang, R.-H., Wu, C.-Y., Chen, Y.-T., & Tseng, W.-T. (2015). Multi-objective dynamic optimal power flow using improved artificial bee colony algorithm based on Pareto optimization. *International Transactions on Electrical Energy Systems*, *26*(4), 692–712. doi:10.1002/etep.2101

Man-Im, A., Ongsakul, W., Singh, J. G., & Boonchuay, C. (2015). *Multi-objective optimal power flow using stochastic weight trade-off chaotic NSPSO. In 2015 IEEE Innovative Smart Grid Technologies - Asia*. ISGT ASIA; doi:10.1109/ISGT-Asia.2015.7387120

Mandal, B., & Roy, P. K. (2014). Multi-objective optimal power flow using quasi-oppositional teaching learning based optimization. *Applied Soft Computing*, *21*, 590–606. doi:10.1016/j.asoc.2014.04.010

Medina, M. A., Das, S., Coello Coello, C. A., & Ramírez, J. M. (2014). Decomposition-based modern metaheuristic algorithms for multi-objective optimal power flow – A comparative study. *Engineering Applications of Artificial Intelligence*, *32*, 10–20. doi:10.1016/j.engappai.2014.01.016

Mukherjee, A., & Mukherjee, V. (2015). Solution of optimal power flow using chaotic krill herd algorithm. *Chaos, Solitons, and Fractals*, *78*, 10–21. doi:10.1016/j.chaos.2015.06.020

Naderi, E., Pourakbari-Kasmaei, M., & Abdi, H. (2019). An efficient particle swarm optimization algorithm to solve optimal power flow problem integrated with FACTS devices. *Applied Soft Computing*, *80*, 243–262. doi:10.1016/j.asoc.2019.04.012

Nguyen, T. T. (2019). A high performance social spider optimization algorithm for optimal power flow solution with single objective optimization. *Energy*, *171*, 218–240. doi:10.1016/j.energy.2019.01.021

Niknam, T., Rasoul Narimani, M., Jabbari, M., & Malekpour, A. R. (2011). A modified shuffle frog leaping algorithm for multi-objective optimal power flow. *Energy, 36*(11), 6420–6432.

Niknam, T., Narimani, M. R., & Azizipanah-Abarghooee, R. (2012). A new hybrid algorithm for optimal power flow considering prohibited zones and valve point effect. *Energy Conversion and Management*, *58*, 197–206. doi:10.1016/j.enconman.2012.01.017

Ongsakul, W., & Vo, D. N. (2013). *Artificial intelligence in power system optimization*. Boca Raton, FL: CRC Press, Taylor & Francis.

Renedo, J., Ibrahim, A. A., Kazemtabrizi, B., García-Cerrada, A., Rouco, L., Zhao, Q., & García-González, J. (2019). A simplified algorithm to solve optimal power flows in hybrid VSC-based AC/DC systems. *International Journal of Electrical Power & Energy Systems*, *110*, 781–794. doi:10.1016/j.ijepes.2019.03.044

Roy, P. K., & Paul, C. (2014). Optimal power flow using krill herd algorithm. *International Transactions on Electrical Energy Systems, 25*(8), 1397–1419. doi:10.1002/etep.1888

Sakawa, M., Yano, H., & Yumine, T. (1987). An Interactive Fuzzy Satisficing Method for Multiobjective Linear-Programming Problems and Its Application. *IEEE Transactions on Systems, Man, and Cybernetics, 17*(4), 654–661. doi:10.1109/TSMC.1987.289356

Sayah, S., & Zehar, K. (2008). Modified differential evolution algorithm for optimal power flow with non-smooth cost functions. *Energy Conversion and Management, 49*(11), 3036–3042. doi:10.1016/j.enconman.2008.06.014

Shailaja, C., & Anuprasath, T. (2019). Internet of medical things-load optimization of power flow based on hybrid enhanced grey wolf optimization and dragonfly algorithm. *Future Generation Computer Systems, 98*, 319–330. doi:10.1016/j.future.2018.12.070

Shailaja, C., & Anuprasath, T. (2019). Optimal power flow using Moth Swarm Algorithm with Gravitational Search Algorithm considering wind power. *Future Generation Computer Systems, 98*, 708–715. doi:10.1016/j.future.2018.12.046

Shi, Y., & Eberhart, R. (1998). A modified particle swarm optimizer. In *1998 IEEE International Conference on Evolutionary Computation Proceedings. IEEE World Congress on Computational Intelligence* (Cat. No.98TH8360) (pp. 69–73). IEEE. 10.1109/ICEC.1998.699146

Sivasubramani, S., & Swarup, K. S. (2011). Multi-objective harmony search algorithm for optimal power flow problem. *International Journal of Electrical Power & Energy Systems, 33*(3), 745–752. doi:10.1016/j.ijepes.2010.12.031

Srinivas, N., & Deb, K. (1994). Muiltiobjective Optimization Using Nondominated Sorting in Genetic Algorithms. *Evolutionary Computation, 2*(3), 221–248. doi:10.1162/evco.1994.2.3.221

Sun, D. I., Ashley, B., Brewer, B., Hughes, A., & Tinney, W. F. (1984). Optimal Power Flow by Newton Approach. *IEEE Transactions on Power Apparatus and Systems, PAS-103*(10), 2864–2880. doi:10.1109/TPAS.1984.318284

Tomin, N. V, Kurbatsky, V. G., & Negnevitsky, M. (2018). *The Concept of the Deep Learning-Based System "Artificial Dispatcher" to Power System Control and Dispatch.* ArXiv, abs/1805.05408

Wang, X. Z., Zhou, J., Huang, Z. L., Bi, X. L., Ge, Z. Q., & Li, L. (2016). A multilevel deep learning method for big data analysis and emergency management of power system. In *Proceedings of 2016 IEEE International Conference on Big Data Analysis, ICBDA 2016.* IEEE. 10.1109/ICBDA.2016.7509811

Wartana, I. M. (2015). A multi-objective problems for optimal integration of the DG to the grid using the NSGA-II. In *2015 International Conference on Quality in Research (QiR)* (pp. 106–110). Academic Press. 10.1109/QiR.2015.7374906

Wood, A. J., & Wollenberg, B. F. (1984). *Power generation, operation, and control.* New York: Wiley.

Yan, X., & Quintana, V. H. (1999). Improving an interior-point-based OPF by dynamic adjustments of step sizes and tolerances. *IEEE Transactions on Power Systems*, *14*(2), 709–717. doi:10.1109/59.761902

Yin, L., Yu, T., Zhang, X., & Yang, B. (2018). Relaxed deep learning for real-time economic generation dispatch and control with unified time scale. *Energy*, *149*, 11–23. doi:10.1016/j.energy.2018.01.165

Zeng, P., Li, H., He, H., & Li, S. (2019). Dynamic Energy Management of a Microgrid Using Approximate Dynamic Programming and Deep Recurrent Neural Network Learning. *IEEE Transactions on Smart Grid*. doi:10.1109/TSG.2018.2859821

APPENDIX

IEEE 118-Bus system Data and Diagram

Figure 11. IEEE 118-Bus system
Source: https://al-roomi.org/power-flow/118-bus-system (Accessed last on 16-May-2019)

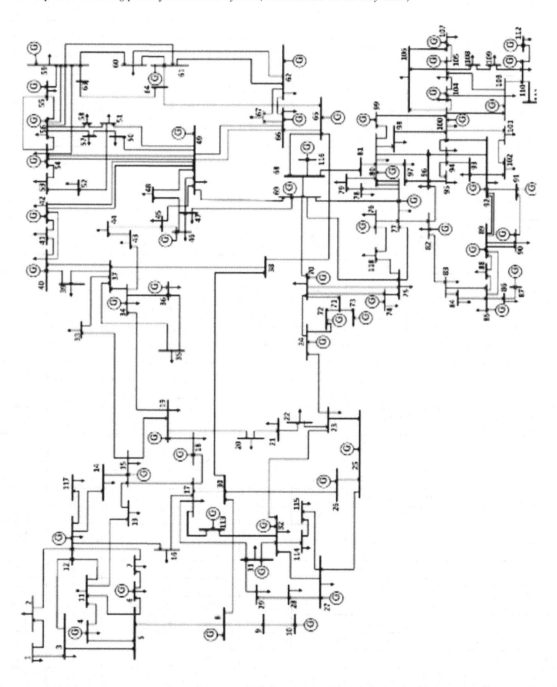

Table 3. IEEE 118 Bus Data and Generator Cost Functions

Bus No.	Unit Cost Coefficients			Pmax (MW)	Pmin (MW)	Qmax (MVAR)	Qmin (MVAR)	Vmax (p.u.)	Vmin (p.u.)
	a (MBtu)	b (MBtu/ MW)	c (MBtu/ MW²)						
4	31.67	26.2438	0.069663	30	5	300	-300	1.1	0.95
6	31.67	26.2438	0.069663	30	5	50	-13	1.1	0.95
8	31.67	26.2438	0.069663	30	5	300	-300	1.1	0.95
10	6.78	12.8875	0.010875	300	150	200	-147	1.1	0.95
12	6.78	12.8875	0.010875	300	100	120	-35	1.1	0.95
15	31.67	26.2438	0.069663	30	10	30	-10	1.1	0.95
18	10.15	17.8200	0.012800	100	25	50	-16	1.1	0.95
19	31.67	26.2438	0.069663	30	5	24	-8	1.1	0.95
24	31.67	26.2438	0.069663	30	5	300	-300	1.1	0.95
25	6.78	12.8875	0.010875	300	100	140	-47	1.1	0.95
26	32.96	10.7600	0.003000	350	100	1000	-1000	1.1	0.95
27	31.67	26.2438	0.069663	30	8	300	-300	1.1	0.95
31	31.67	26.2438	0.069663	30	8	300	-300	1.1	0.95
32	10.15	17.8200	0.012800	100	25	42	-14	1.1	0.95
34	31.67	26.2438	0.069663	30	8	24	-8	1.1	0.95
36	10.15	17.8200	0.012800	100	25	24	-8	1.1	0.95
40	31.67	26.2438	0.069663	30	8	300	-300	1.1	0.95
42	31.67	26.2438	0.069663	30	8	300	-300	1.1	0.95
46	10.15	17.8200	0.012800	100	25	100	-100	1.1	0.95
49	28	12.3299	0.002401	250	50	210	-85	1.1	0.95
54	28	12.3299	0.002401	250	50	300	-300	1.1	0.95
55	10.15	17.8200	0.012800	100	25	23	-8	1.1	0.95
56	10.15	17.8200	0.012800	100	25	15	-8	1.1	0.95
59	39	13.2900	0.004400	200	50	180	-60	1.1	0.95
61	39	13.2900	0.004400	200	50	300	-100	1.1	0.95
62	10.15	17.8200	0.012800	100	25	20	-20	1.1	0.95
65	64.16	8.3391	0.010590	420	100	200	-67	1.1	0.95
66	64.16	8.3391	0.010590	420	100	200	-67	1.1	0.95
69	6.78	12.8875	0.010875	300	80	99999	-99999	1.1	0.95
70	74.33	15.4708	0.045923	80	30	32	-10	1.1	0.95
72	31.67	26.2438	0.069663	30	10	100	-100	1.1	0.95
73	31.67	26.2438	0.069663	30	5	100	-100	1.1	0.95
74	17.95	37.6968	0.028302	20	5	9	-6	1.1	0.95
76	10.15	17.8200	0.012800	100	25	23	-8	1.1	0.95
77	10.15	17.8200	0.012800	100	25	70	-20	1.1	0.95
80	6.78	12.8875	0.010875	300	150	280	-165	1.1	0.95
82	10.15	17.8200	0.012800	100	25	9900	-9900	1.1	0.95
85	31.67	26.2438	0.069663	30	10	23	-8	1.1	0.95
87	32.96	10.7600	0.003000	300	100	1000	-100	1.1	0.95
89	6.78	12.8875	0.010875	200	50	300	-210	1.1	0.95

continued on the following page

Table 3. Continued

Bus No.	Unit Cost Coefficients			Pmax (MW)	Pmin (MW)	Qmax (MVAR)	Qmin (MVAR)	Vmax (p.u.)	Vmin (p.u.)
	a (MBtu)	b (MBtu/ MW)	c (MBtu/ MW^2)						
90	17.95	37.6968	0.028302	20	8	300	-300	1.1	0.95
91	58.81	22.9423	0.009774	50	20	100	-100	1.1	0.95
92	6.78	12.8875	0.010875	300	100	9	-3	1.1	0.95
99	6.78	12.8875	0.010875	300	100	100	-100	1.1	0.95
100	6.78	12.8875	0.010875	300	100	155	-50	1.1	0.95
103	17.95	37.6968	0.028302	20	8	40	-15	1.1	0.95
104	10.15	17.8200	0.012800	100	25	23	-8	1.1	0.95
105	10.15	17.8200	0.012800	100	25	23	-8	1.1	0.95
107	17.95	37.6968	0.028302	20	8	200	-200	1.1	0.95
110	58.81	22.9423	0.009774	50	25	23	-8	1.1	0.95
111	10.15	17.8200	0.012800	100	25	1000	-100	1.1	0.95
112	10.15	17.8200	0.012800	100	25	1000	-100	1.1	0.95
113	10.15	17.8200	0.012800	100	25	200	-100	1.1	0.95
116	58.81	22.9423	0.009774	50	25	1000	-1000	1.1	0.95

Chapter 13
Multiobjective Optimization of a Biofuel Supply Chain Using Random Matrix Generators

Timothy Ganesan
Royal Bank of Canada, Canada

Pandian Vasant
Universiti Teknologi PETRONAS, Malaysia

Igor Litvinchev
ⓘ https://orcid.org/0000-0002-1850-4755
Nuevo Leon State University, Mexico

ABSTRACT

As industrial systems become more complex, various complexities and uncertainties come into play. Metaheuristic-type optimization techniques have become crucial for effective design, maintenance, and operations of such systems. However, in highly complex industrial systems, conventional metaheuristics are still plagued by various drawbacks. Strategies such as hybridization and algorithmic modifications have been the focus of previous efforts to improve the performance of conventional metaheuristics. This work tackles a large-scale multi-objective (MO) optimization problem: biofuel supply chain. Due to the scale and complexity of the problem, the random matrix approach was employed to modify the stochastic generator segment of the cuckoo search (CS) technique. Comparative analysis was then performed on the computational results produced by the conventional CS technique and the improved CS variants.

INTRODUCTION

Real-world industrial optimization often revolves around systems which have various complexities and uncertainties. Therefore heavy computational rigor becomes required when faced with these problems. This is when metaheuristic techniques become indispensable (Ganesan *et al.*, 2016; Ganesan *et al.*, 2018a;

DOI: 10.4018/978-1-7998-1192-3.ch013

Yang, 2013). A few examples of such complexities are: multiobjective (MO), non-convex, highly nonlinear, interlinked variables and multivariate. All these issues existing in a single problem have the capability to overwhelm the computational technique (conventional metaheuristics) - resulting in weak optimization capability. Thus, conventional metaheuristics are often improved via hybridization or other algorithmic enhancements (Ganesan *et al.*, 2015; Ganesan *et al.*, 2018b; Hong *et al.*, 2016; Dong *et al.*, 2016). As for optimization problems which are MO, the following frameworks have been introduced in the past:

- Strength Pareto Evolutionary Algorithm (SPEA-2) (Zhao *et al.*, 2016)
- Weighted sum approach (Naidu *et al.*, 2014)
- Normal-Boundary Intersection (NBI) (Ahmadi *et al.*, 2015; Ganesan et al., 2013)
- Non-Dominated Sorting Genetic Algorithm (NSGA-II) (Mousavi *et al.*, 2016)
- Epsilon-constraint method (Bouziaren and Brahim Aghezzaf, 2018)

Scalarization and NBI approaches involve the aggregation of multiple target objectives. This effectively transforms the MO problem into a single objective one - reducing its complexity to a high degree and thus making it easier to solve. Although other techniques like non-dominated sorting, SPEA and epsilon-constraint approaches are equally effective for solving triple-objective MO problems, the weighted sum approach (scalarization technique) was used in this work since it was easier to work with. This is in the sense that scalarization approaches are readily compatible when used with a variety of metaheuristics as compared to other methods (e.g. nondominated sorting methods). Once the objective function is aggregated, the problem could be solved using a variety metaheuristic as a single objective problem. This makes the weighted sum approach a very attractive option since a plethora of metaheuristic techniques could be implemented alongside it. On the other hand, the epsilon-constraint method could become tedious when dealing with problems having more than two objectives since the problem has to be solved multiple times with varying epsilon constraints - making it a computationally expensive approach.

In recent works, Cuckoo Search (CS) has been seen to be highly effective in solving MO supply chain problems as compared to other heuristics (e.g. bee colony optimization, genetic algorithm, particle swarm optimization and artificial fish swarm) (Elkazzaz et al., 2018; Liang and Sun, 2019, Srivastav and Agrawal, 2015). Therefore CS approach was utilized in conjunction with the weighted sum approach to tackle the biofuel supply chain problem in this work.

Supply chain problems are large-scale problems with complex interlinked variables. This sort of problem characteristics closely resemble structures often encountered in the nuclei of heavy atoms - e.g. platinum, gold or rhodium. Such structures are said to have the property of universality. Eugene Wigner developed an effective technique (using random matrices) for modeling complex systems endowed with universality (Che, 2017). Ever since then, random matrix theory (RMT) has been used extensively for modeling large complex structures with highly interlinked components in various fields: solid state physics (Verbaarschot, 2004; Beenakker, 2015), quantum chromodynamics (Akemann, 2017), quantum information theory (Collins and Nechita, 2016), transport optimization (Krbálek and Seba, 2000), Big Data (Qiu and Antonik, 2017) and finance (Zhaoben et al., 2014). Since supply chain networks share many key characteristics with some of the previously mentioned systems, these networks may naturally contain the property of universality.

In the past work, metaheuristic techniques have been effectively applied to solve the biofuel supply chain problem (Tan *et al.*, 2017). Although effective in a bi-objective scenario, the performance of the approach may not be as stable in a triple-objective problem (large-scale) as encountered in this work

- producing a research gap. To account for the increase in complexity due to the additional objective function, the RMT framework was used to improve the conventional CS technique by modifying the stochastic generator component. Instead of employing the conventional Gaussian stochastic generator, this component was replaced with a RMT-based generator. The resulting four RMT-based CS algorithms were implemented on the biofuel supply chain problem: Gaussian Unitary Ensemble CS (GUE-CS), Gaussian Orthogonal Ensemble CS (GOE-CS), Gaussian Symplectic Ensemble CS (GSE-CS) and Poisson-based CS (Poisson-CS).

This paper is organized as follows: Section 2 provides the literature review and Section 3 presents the problem formulation of the MO biofuel supply chain model. In Section 4 the conventional CS approach is presented while an overview of RMT and its role in the development of stochastic generators is described in Sections 5 and 6. Section 7 presents the analyses on the computational results followed by the final section; conclusions and recommendations for future work.

LITERATURE REVIEW

Present day supply chain optimization challenges decision makers on a global scale due to its highly complicated nature as well as its large-scale structure. Over the years various cutting edge tools have been implemented for modeling supply chains (Seuring, 2013; Brandenburg *et al.*, 2014; Ahi and Searcy, 2013). These efforts are then followed by the application of optimization techniques - to efficiently aid the decision making process (Ogunbanwo *et al.*, 2014; Mastrocinque *et al.*, 2013). In this spirit, fuel supply chain networks have recently become a field of interest by decision makers and practitioners in various industries. This can be seen in the optimization work found in Lin *et al.*, (2014) which aimed to minimize the annual biomass-ethanol production costs in a fuel supply chain. The supply chain problem in that work was a large-scale model consisting of stacking, in-field transportation, preprocessing, biomass harvesting, transportation, packing and storage, to ethanol production and distribution. The authors used a mixed integer programming technique to reduce the cost of production in a biorefinery (by approximately 62%). Similarly in Zhang *et al.*, (2013) a switchgrass-based bioethanol supply chain located in North Dakota, U.S. was modeled and optimized. In the work of Lin *et al.*, (2014), mixed integer linear programming was employed to optimize the model - where the authors obtained an optimal usage of marginal land for switchgrass production. This efforts were tailored for sustainable and economical harvest of bioethanol. Optimization of a large-scale sustainable dual feedstock bioethanol supply chain in a stochastic environment was done in Osmani and Zhang, (2014). The optimization was carried out while taking into consideration the biomass purchase price, sales price, supply and demand. The work used a sample average approximation algorithm as a decomposition technique with a mixed integer linear programming approach. Other works using mixed integer linear/nonlinear programming approaches in a fuel supply chain optimization context could be seen in Osmani and Zhang, (2013) and Gao and You, (2015). An example of a study that does not employ a mixed integer approach for fuel supply chain optimization is Marufuzzaman *et al.*, (2014). The solution procedure employed in that work was a combined approach of Lagrangian relaxation and L-shaped techniques. The numerical experiments performed in Marufuzzaman *et al.*, (2014) provided interesting information on carbon regulatory mechanisms and uncertainties encountered in biofuel supply chains. In Castillo-Villar, K.K., (2014) and De Meyer *et al.*, (2014), a general review is given on metaheuristics applied to bioenergy supply chains.

Cuckoo search (CS) technique has been highly effective in optimizing real-world supply chains. For instance in the work of Mattos *et al.*, (2017), a series of metaheuristics including CS was applied to a supply chain (consumer-packaged goods industry). Rigorous comparative studies was done on the performance as well as the results generated by the techniques employed in that work. A similar case could be found in Abdelsalam and Elassal, (2014) - where CS was employed among other metaheuristics to a joint economic lot-sizing problem. The problem involved a multi-layered supply chain consisting of multiple retailers and a single manufacturer/supplier. The results showed that the CS technique favors the centralized policy as opposed to a decentralized one for safety stock. Another interesting implementation of CS is seen in the work of Srivastav and Agrawal, (2017). In that work, a MO lot-size reorder point backorder inventory problem was tackled using CS. The MO problem (three objective functions) consisted of the following targets (annual): expected number of stocked out units, total relevant cost and expected number of stocked-out occasions. An efficient Pareto curve between cost and service levels was constructed using the CS technique.

BIOFUEL SUPPLY CHAIN MODEL

The fuel supply chain model employed in this work was developed in Tan *et al.*, (2017). In that work only two objective functions were considered: profit (PR) and social welfare (SW). The environmental benefits objective was incorporated into the SW function. In this work, the environmental benefits was isolated from the SW function and taken as an independent objective function (denoted *Env*). Therefore the fuel supply chain model in this chapter consists of three objective functions to be maximized along with associated inequality constraints (see equations (6) - (15)). The objective functions are shown in equations (1) - (5):

$$PR = P(1-EC) \times \sum_t q_t$$
$$- \left\{ FCp + \sum_t \left[GC \cdot q_t + \sum_i \left(SC \cdot IQ_{i,t} + \sum_k SQ_{i,k,t} \cdot PP_i \right) + Y_{1t} \cdot extraY_1 + Y_{2t} \cdot extraY_2 \right] \right\} \quad (1)$$

$$SW = ACS \cdot (1-EC) \sum_t q_t + GT - GS \cdot (1-EC) \sum_t q_t \quad (2)$$

$$Env = AC \cdot \left[CET \cdot (1-EC) \cdot \sum_t q_t - (CEcb - CEtp) \right] \quad (3)$$

such that,

$$CEcb = 2\sum_{i,k,t} PQ_{i,k,t} \cdot \sum_{i,k} \left[\frac{CEncb_{i,k} \cdot Dcb_{i,k}}{LCcb_{i,k}} \right] + \left(\sum_{i,k,t} PQ_{i,k,t} \cdot \sum_{i,k} CEicb_{i,k} Dcb_{i,k} \right) \tag{4}$$

$$CEtp = 2\sum_{i,k,t} SQ_{i,k,t} \cdot \sum_{i,k} \left[\frac{CEntb_{i,k} \cdot Dbp_{i,k}}{LCtp_{i,k}} \right] + \left(\sum_{i,k,t} PQ_{i,k,t} \cdot \sum_{i,k} CEicb_{i,k} Dcb_{i,k} \right) \tag{5}$$

The constraints for the biofuel supply chain model are given below:

$$q_t \leq q_{max} \tag{6}$$

$$IQ_{i,t} \geq SIlb_i \tag{7}$$

$$\sum_i IQ_{i,t} \leq IQ_{max} \tag{8}$$

$$Q_{min} \leq \sum_t q_t \leq Q_{max} \tag{9}$$

$$HV_{min} \leq \sum_i HV_i \cdot BR_{i,t} \leq HV_{max} \tag{10}$$

$$\sum_i SQ_{i,k,t} \geq SQ_{min\,i,k} \tag{11}$$

$$\sum_i PQ_{i,k,t} \leq PQ_{max} \tag{12}$$

$$\sum_i PQ_{i,k,t} \leq AQ_{max,i,t} \tag{13}$$

$$WR_{i,k,t} \leq \left[\frac{1 - MCori_{i,t}}{1 - MC_{\max.i,t}} \right] \tag{14}$$

$$\sum_{i,t} SQ_{i,k,t} \cdot PP_{i,k,t}$$
$$\geq \left[FCb_k + \sum_{i,t} SQ_{i,k,t} \cdot \left(AP_{i,k,t} + \frac{TCcb_{i,k} \cdot Dcb_{ik}}{LCcb_{i,k}} \right) \frac{1}{WR_{i,k,t}} + \sum_{i,t} SQ_{i,k,t} \cdot \frac{TCtp_{i,k} Dbp_k}{LCtp_{ik}} \right] \cdot \left(1 + ER_k \right) \tag{15}$$

such that,

$$i \in [1,2],\ k \in [1,10],\ t \in [1,12] \tag{16}$$

The decision parameters are: q_t, $IQ_{i,t}$, $SQ_{i,k,t}$, $PP_{i,k,t}$, $PQ_{i,k,t}$ and $BR_{i,t}$. Detailed parameter settings of the biofuel supply chain model used in this work is available in Tan *et al.*, (2017).

CUCKOO SEARCH

Similar to swarm intelligence techniques, CS is a population-based stochastic search and optimization algorithm (Mareli and Twala, 2017; Joshi *et al.*, 2017). CS was originally inspired by brood parasitism often found among some species of cuckoo birds. The parasitism occurs when the cuckoo birds lay their eggs in the nests of other bird species (non-cuckoo birds). In a CS algorithm, a search pattern corresponds to a nest - where an individual attributed to a search pattern is represented by a cuckoo egg. Thus the cuckoo egg symbolizes a potential solution candidate to the optimization problem - which will be tested by the fitness function. Then the solution will be accounted for in subsequent iterations to see if it is fit (fulfilling the fitness criteria). Otherwise the solution (egg) would be discarded and another candidate solution would be considered. This way the solution to the optimization problem would be iteratively improved as the technique explores the search space. The stochastic generator of the CS technique is based on the heavy-tailed random walk probability distribution, Lévy flights. The equation for the iterative candidate solution i and iteration t for the CS algorithm is given as:

$$y_i^{t+1} = y_i^t + \beta \cdot Levy\left(\lambda \right) \tag{17}$$

such that the Lévy distribution is given as follows:

$$Levy(\lambda) = t^{\lambda} \tag{18}$$

where t is the random variable, $\beta > 0$ is the relaxation factor (which is modified based on the problem at hand) and $\lambda \in (1,3]$ is the Lévy flight step-size. With $t \geq 1$, λ is related to the fractal dimension and the Lévy distribution becomes a specific sort of Pareto distribution. The CS algorithm is based on a few fundamental philosophies. For instance each cuckoo bird lays a single egg at one time and randomly places the egg in a selected nest. The second being: via fitness screening, the best egg (candidate solution) is carried forward into the next iteration. The worst solutions are discarded from further iterations. The nests represent the objective space (or the optimization problem landscape). The parameter setting for the CS technique used in this work is shown in Table 1 while its respective algorithm is given in Algorithm 1:

Algorithm 1: Cuckoo Search (CS)

```
Step 1: Initialize algorithmic parameters; yᵢ, β, λ, N
Step 2: Define parameters in the constraints and decision variable
Step 3: Via Lévy flights randomly lay a cuckoo egg in a nest
Step 4: Define fitness function based on solution selection criteria
Step 5: Screen eggs and evaluate candidate solution
        IF: fitness criteria is satisfied
                Select candidate solution (egg) to be considered in the next
iteration, n+1
        ELSE: fitness criteria is not satisfied
                Discard candidate solution (egg) from further iterations
Step 6: Rank the best solutions obtained during fitness screening
Step 7: If the fitness criterion is satisfied and t= Tₘₐₓ halt and print
solutions,else proceed to Step 3
```

RANDOM MATRIX THEORY

Random Matrix Theory (RMT) is a robust mathematical technique used to describe the behavior of complex systems. Due to its applicability to a vast range of systems, RMT is known to exhibit universality – a property of global symmetries shared by many systems within a certain symmetry class. In some sense RMT is a generalization of conventional statistical systems that often consists of matrices with fixed eigenvalues. In RMT, the eigenvalues themselves are statistically variant fitting into a probability distribution. This way RMT deals with the statistical behavior of the eigenvalues of random matrices.

Table 1. CS Settings

Parameters	Values
Total Number of Eggs (N)	20
Number of nests, *nests*	4
Lévy flight step-size, λ	1.5
Relaxation factor, β Maximum number iteration, T_{max}	0.8 300

On the other hand, the random matrices have stochastic entries which are described by a distinct probability distribution function. Therefore in RMT there exists two probability distributions describing: the random matrix entries and the eigenvalue spread. The nearest neighbor spacing probability distribution (Schweiner et al., 2017) of eigenvalues is given by Wigner's Surmise:

$$P(s) = A_i s^i \exp(-B_i s^2)$$ (19)

where s is the eigenvalue spacing, A_i and B_i are constant parameters. The normalized spacing, s and the mean spacing $\langle s \rangle$ is as follows:

$$s = \left[\frac{\lambda_{n+1} - \lambda_n}{\langle s \rangle} \right] \text{ such that } \langle s \rangle = \langle \lambda_{n+1} - \lambda_n \rangle$$ (20)

where λ_n is the nth eigenvalue sequentially such that $\lambda_1 < \ldots < \lambda_n < \lambda_{n+1}$. The first type of random matrices are those that are modeled based on complex quantum systems (which have chaotic classical counterparts). The index i represents systems falling into this type of RMT theory - whereby $i = 1, 2$ and 4 denotes the Gaussian Orthogonal Ensemble (GOE) (Krishnan et al., 2017), Gaussian Unitary Ensemble (GUE) (Arguin et al., 2017) and Gaussian Symplectic Ensemble (GSE) (Rehemanjiang et al., 2016) spacing distributions respectively (Schierenberg et al., 2012). These spacing distribution are given as follows:

i.   i. Gaussian Orthogonal Ensemble (GOE)

$$P_1(s) = \frac{\pi}{2} s \exp(-\frac{\pi}{4} s^2)$$ (21)

ii.   ii. Gaussian Unitary Ensemble (GUE)

$$P_2(s) = \frac{32}{\pi^2} s^2 \exp(-\frac{4}{\pi} s^2)$$ (22)

iii.   iii.   Gaussian Symplectic Ensemble (GSE)

$$P_4(s) = \frac{2^{18}}{3^6 \pi^3} s^4 \exp(-\frac{64}{9\pi} s^2)$$ (23)

The second type of random matrix is employed to model complex quantum systems which have integrable classical counterpart (non-chaotic). The spacing distribution for such random matrices usually obey the Poisson process:

$$P_o(s) = \exp(-s)$$ (24)

These ensembles describe the probability density functions governing the random matrix entries. The constants, A_i and B_i are selected such that the following averaging properties are respected:

$$\int_0^\infty ds P_i(s) = 1 \tag{25}$$

$$\int_0^\infty ds P_i(s) s = 1 \tag{26}$$

RANDOM MATRIX GENERATORS

Conventional metaheuristics are equipped with stochastic generators also known as the random generator component of the algorithm. This component randomly initializes the search of the metaheuristic, positioning the start point of the search process in the objective space. The technique then iteratively improves the quality of the solution as the search progresses. Previous works have been done where different types of stochastic generators were experimented and their impacts on the performance of certain metaheuristics were evaluated (Ganesan et al., 2018; Ganesan et al., 2016a; Ganesan et al., 2016b). In those works, it was observed that the changes in the type of stochastic generators do influence the results of the optimization efforts.

RMT could be considered as a generalization of conventional statistical systems. RMT was initially founded and used to solve problems involving systems with high levels of complexity - where the eigenstates of the systems are non-stationary and conventional stochastic techniques breakdown. Examples of such systems are: the behavior of heavy nuclei (Firk and Miller, 2009), energy flows in molecules (Leitner, 2005), stability of large ecosystems (Gibbs et al., 2017) and properties of a gas of charged particles (Coulomb gas) (Cugliandolo, 2017).

In essence RMT deals with complex systems with a network of many interacting components. Similar problems have been found in real-world optimization – where the problems are large-scale and often contain many interacting parameters which are correlated in a complicated way. The natural extension to the conventional metaheuristics which enables it to deal with large-scale complex problems would be the generalization of its stochastic generator using RMT (creating a random matrix generator). In this spirit, the probability distribution function which randomizes the metaheuristics' initialization is modified using RMT. The proposed algorithmic technique for creating a random matrix generator is as follows:

Algorithm 2: Random Matrix Generator

Step 1:	Generate random eigenvalue spacings, s from a Poisson/GUE/GOE/GSE
Step 2:	Determine the average eigenvalue spacing, $\Delta\lambda$
Step 3:	Set initial eigenvalue, λ_0
Step 4:	Set initial n x n matrix, H_{ij}

Step 5:   Determine consequent eigenvalues, λ_i

$$\lambda_{i+1} = \lambda_i + \Delta\lambda$$

Step 6:   Determine n x 1 eigenvector, E_i:

$$E_i = \sum_j H_{ij} + \lambda_i$$

Step 7:   Generate random variables from a Gaussian probability distribution function endowed eigenvector as the variance, $\sigma^2 = E_i$:

$$P_i(x) = \frac{1}{\sqrt{2\pi E_i^2}} \exp\left(-\frac{(x-\mu)^2}{2E_i^2}\right)$$

RESULTS AND ANALYSIS

In this work, the objective functions of the MO biofuel supply chain problem was combined into a single function using the weighted sum approach. This procedure effectively transforms the MO problem into a single-objective optimization problem which can be solved for different weight values. The summing property for the weights are given as follows:

$$\sum_{i=1,..,m} w_i = 1 \text{ such that } w_i \in (0,1) \tag{27}$$

where the index i represents the individual weights and m is the maximum number of objectives (which is equivalent to the maximum number of weights). Due to the stochastic nature of the algorithms employed in this work, the methods were executed multiple times (3 executions) and the best solution was sampled. 28 variations of the weights were considered to construct the Pareto frontier - at which the individual solutions were classified as best, worst and median. The individual solutions were measured and ranked using the hypervolume indicator (HVI) (Jiang *et al.*, 2015; Bringmann and Friedrich, 2013). The HVI effectively measures the dominance levels of solutions to a MO optimization problem. While using the HVI, the nadir point is commonly employed as a reference (or basis) during measurement. Hence the nadir point is considered as the most non-dominant point - where its exact value is used consistently on all the results obtained in this work. Considering the nadir point, the HVI is computed and scaled as follows:

$$HVI = \left[\frac{(x_1 - 10^6)(x_2 - 10^4)(x_3 - 10^3)}{10^{16}}\right] \tag{28}$$

where x_1, x_2 and x_3 are individual candidate solutions. The ranked weighted individual solutions obtained using the CS approach is provided in Table 2. The entire frontier constructed using the CS approach is shown in Figure 1:

Using the Poisson-CS approach, the resulting ranked individual solutions is given in Table 3 while its associated Pareto frontier is depicted in Figure 2.

Table 4 and Figure 3 provides the ranked individual solutions and the Pareto frontier obtained using the GSE-CS algorithm.

The ranked individual solutions as well as their respective weights for the GOE-CS and GUE-CS are given in Tables 5 and 6. Figures 4 and 5 depicts the solutions representing the entire Pareto frontier.

In addition, the HVI was used to measure the overall level of dominance for the entire Pareto frontier generated by each technique employed in this work. Figure 6 shows these degrees of dominance:

Figure 6 shows that the most dominant frontier was obtained using the GOE-CS followed by the conventional CS technique. Interestingly, the other three techniques improved with random matrix generators produced the least dominant frontiers - GUE-CS, Poisson-CS and GSE-CS respectively.

The most dominant individual solution was achieved by the GOE-CS technique followed by the Poisson-CS and CS techniques (see Tables 5, 3 and 2). The least dominant individual solutions were obtained using the GSE-CS and GUE-CS respectively (see Tables 4 and 6). To a high degree the dominance

Table 2. Ranked individual solutions for the CS technique

Description		Best	Median	Worst
weights	w_1	0.3	0.2	0.6
	w_2	0.2	0.6	0.3
	w_3	0.5	0.2	0.1
Objective functions	PR	513,600,000	511,207,000	513,417,000
	SW	1,018,670	1,021,820	1,020,790
	Env	142,326	101,600	70,408.1
Iterations	t	52	44	49
Metric	HVI	7,307.18	5,193.35	3,594.96

Table 3. Ranked individual solutions for the Poisson-CS technique

Description		Best	Median	Worst
weights	w_1	0.4	0.4	0.3
	w_2	0.4	0.5	0.4
	w_3	0.2	0.1	0.3
Objective functions	PR	245,476,000	442,101,000	282,918,000
	SW	1,006,110	1,004,330	1,004,940
	Env	462,609	6,895.43	1,117.03
Iterations	t	2	198	10
Metric	HVI	11,241.33264	258.5735346	3.282591965

Figure 1. Comparative Pareto frontier from the CS technique

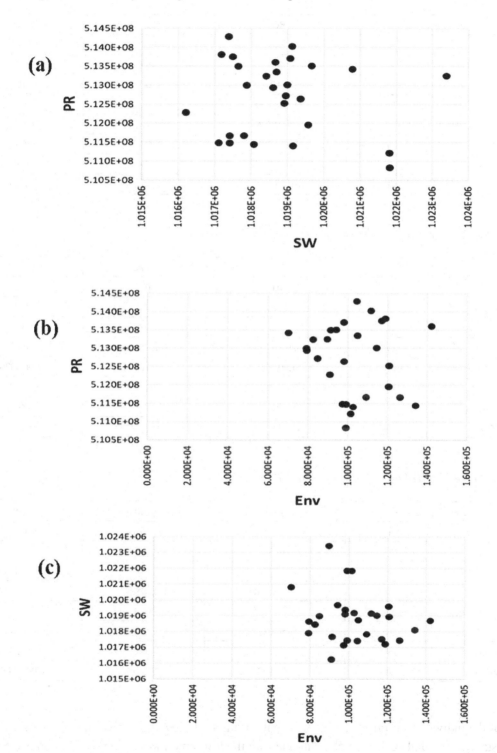

Table 4: Ranked individual solutions for the GSE-CS technique

Description		Best	Median	Worst
weights	w_1	0.2	0.3	0.5
	w_2	0.5	0.6	0.2
	w_3	0.3	0.1	0.3
Objective functions	PR	457,778,000	307,741,000	353,240,000
	SW	1,004,270	1,004,690	1,004,450
	Env	36,541.3	2,741.15	1,050.19
Iterations	t	215	27	78
Metric	HVI	1,614.146034	53.12461162	1.758080756

Table 5. Ranked individual solutions for the GOE-CS technique

Description		Best	Median	Worst
weights	w_1	0.6	0.2	0.1
	w_2	0.2	0.2	0.7
	w_3	0.2	0.6	0.2
Objective functions	PR	320,196,000	311,556,000	314,295,000
	SW	1,004,690	1,004,800	1,004,820
	Env	405,964	200,519	141,623
Iterations	t	47	35	40
Metric	HVI	12,857.6503	6,163.962109	4,382.82702

Table 6. Ranked individual solutions for the GUE-CS technique

Description		Best	Median	Worst
weights	w_1	0.5	0.4	0.2
	w_2	0.3	0.2	0.7
	w_3	0.2	0.4	0.1
Objective functions	PR	337,985,000	365,898,000	304,589,000
	SW	1,004,570	1,004,440	1,004,660
	Env	156,623	17,765	1,158.42
Iterations	t	64	95	25
Metric	HVI	5,215.785325	608.3501587	4.783774438

levels of the individual solutions were consistent with that of the entire Pareto frontier. For example in both instances the GOE-CS and CS techniques are the top three most dominant techniques. Similarly the GSE-CS, GUE-CS and the Poisson-CS came in lower in terms of dominance in both respects. It could be observed that the techniques that managed to focus their individual solutions at the optimal

Figure 2. Pareto frontier from the Poisson-CS technique

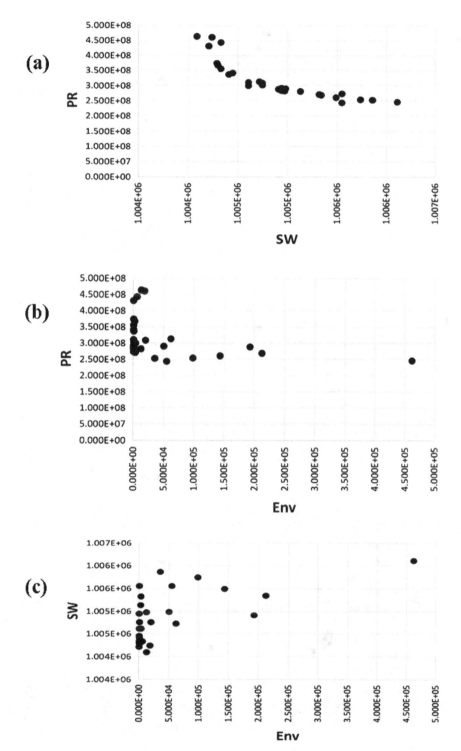

Figure 3. Pareto frontier from the GSE-CS technique

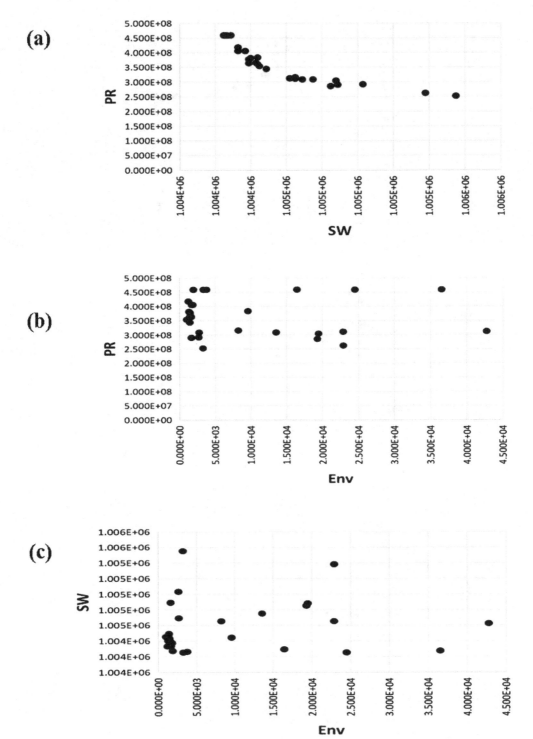

region of the objective space (as indicated in Figure 4) have a higher overall level of dominance. Besides GOE-CS, the conventional CS technique generates many individual solutions at that region (refer to Figure 1). Other techniques tend to generate solutions at other suboptimal regions in the objective space. For instance the Poisson-CS technique (in Figure 2) generates solutions at very low values of the *Env,* objective function while the GSE-CS technique (in Figure 3) generates scattered individual solutions which are non-uniformly distributed. On the other hand, the GUE-CS (in Figure 5) produces a relatively uniform distribution of solutions in the objective space - however these solutions are not located in the optimal region.

It is important to note that the Poisson-CS seems to behave in a contradictory way when the dominance of its individual solutions are compared with the dominance of the entire Pareto frontier. The Poisson-CS can be seen to have a high level of individual solution dominance (second to the GOE-CS; 11,241.33) but an extremely weak frontier dominance; ranking second last to the GSE-CS approach (see Figure 6). It is possible that the Poisson-CS approach seems to be highly incompatible with the problem at hand in the 'No Free Lunch Theorem' sense (Whitley, 2014). Such incompatibility could be observed in the anomalous solutions generated by the technique (as indicated in Figure 2).

It may be that in this work one of the risks of modifying the stochastic generator has been identified. Since the stochastic generator is a core component in metaheuristics, modifying it changes the very nature of algorithm. This could significantly boost the technique's performance or it could negatively impact the technique by worsening its optimization performance - as observed in the case of the Poisson-CS technique in this work. The overall computational time taken for all the techniques utilized in this work to generate the entire Pareto frontier is shown in Figure 7:

The execution times of all the techniques in Figure 7 are observed to be consistent with the frontier dominance values (see Figure 6). The techniques generating the most dominant frontiers (GOE-CS, CS and GSE-CS) spent less time searching through the objective space as compared to the Poisson-CS as well as GUE-CS approaches. Due to their efficiency in reaching the optimal region in the objective space, execution time for these techniques are short.

In this work, the solutions produced by the all the techniques were found to be feasible as none of the constraints were violated. The algorithmic complexity of the techniques employed are fairly similar since no additional computational steps were added into the existing CS approach. The only difference is that the stochastic generators are replaced with different types of RMT-based distributions (Poisson, GUE, GOE and GSE). No premature convergence was observed during the execution of the techniques in this work. The fitness criteria specified in all the techniques were respected during program execution. All techniques implemented throughout this work performed stable computations.

CONCLUSION AND RECOMMENDATIONS

In this work, the GOE-CS technique outperformed all other approaches. From the analysis of the results of the computational experiments, it can be observed that the RMT-based stochastic generators could significantly affect the optimization performance of the CS method. The overall Pareto dominance produced by the GOE-CS was 34.276% higher than the conventional CS. The improved performance of the GOE-CS is reflected in its computational efficiency (20.931% faster convergence). Thus it can be seen that the RMT-based improvement to the conventional CS approach is very suitable to be employed in highly complex environments such as the MO biofuel supply chain problem.

Figure 4. Pareto frontier from the GOE-CS technique

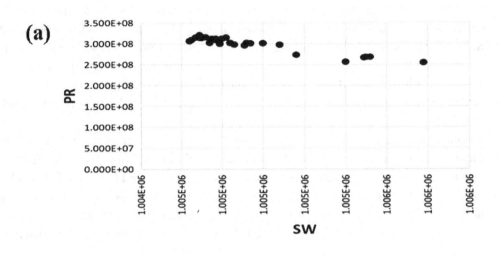

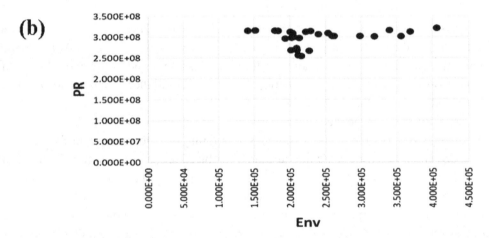

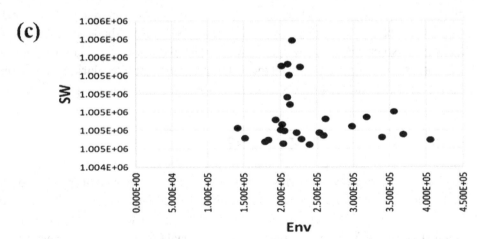

Figure 5. Pareto frontier from the GUE-CS technique

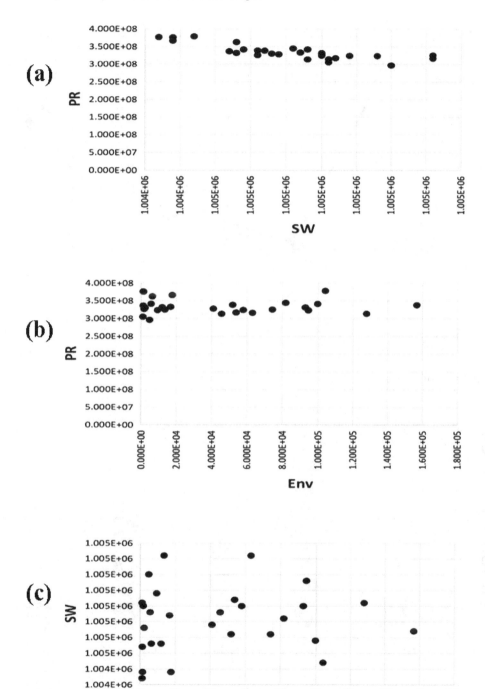

Figure 6. Degrees of dominance of the all the Pareto frontiers

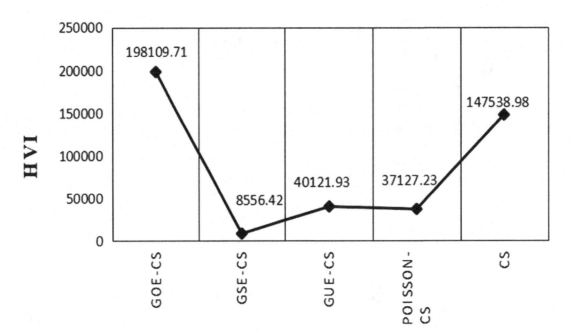

Figure 7. Degrees of dominance of all the all the Pareto frontiers

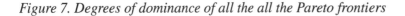

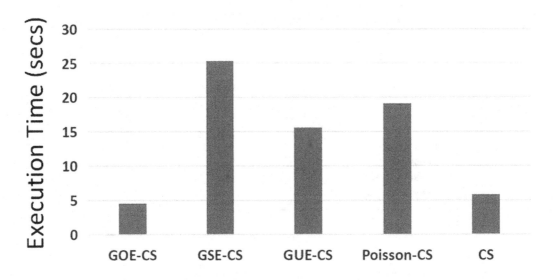

Although the GOE-CS performed better than the conventional CS, some RMT-based techniques was also observed to negatively impact algorithmic performance - as observed in the results produced by the Poisson-CS approach. Therefore further tests involving RMT-based stochastic generators could be conducted in future works. For instance, numerical experiments on the performance of RMT-based stochastic generators on other metaheuristics could be carried out - e.g. particle swarm optimization

(Mousavi et al., 2016), differential evolution (Ganesan et al., 2015), bat algorithm (Singh et al, 2015) and fish swarm algorithm (Luan et al., 2016). In addition, research could also be done on methods to counter the effects of the unsatisfactory performance encountered by some RMT-based techniques (like the Poisson-CS).

References

Abdelsalam, H. M., & Elassal, M. M. (2014). Joint economic lot sizing problem for a three—Layer supply chain with stochastic demand. *International Journal of Production Economics*, *155*, 272–283. doi:10.1016/j.ijpe.2014.01.015

Ahi, P., & Searcy, C. (2013). A comparative literature analysis of definitions for green and sustainable supply chain management. *Journal of Cleaner Production*, *52*, 329–341. doi:10.1016/j.jclepro.2013.02.018

Ahmadi, A., Kaymanesh, A., Siano, P., Janghorbani, M., Nezhad, A. E., & Sarno, D. (2015). Evaluating the effectiveness of normal boundary intersection method for short-term environmental/economic hydrothermal self-scheduling. *Electric Power Systems Research*, *123*, 192–204. doi:10.1016/j.epsr.2015.02.007

Akemann, G., (2017). Random matrix theory and quantum chromodynamics. Stochastic Processes and Random Matrices. *Lecture Notes of the Les Houches Summer School, 104*, 228.

Beenakker, C. W. J. (2015). Random-matrix theory of Majorana fermions and topological superconductors. *Reviews of Modern Physics*, *87*(3), 1037–1066. doi:10.1103/RevModPhys.87.1037

Bouziaren, S. A., & Brahim Aghezzaf, B. (2018). An Improved Augmented epsilon-Constraint and Branch-and-Cut Method to Solve the TSP with Profits. *IEEE Transactions on Intelligent Transportation Systems*, *20*(1), 195–204. doi:10.1109/TITS.2018.2808179

Brandenburg, M., Govindan, K., Sarkis, J., & Seuring, S. (2014). Quantitative models for sustainable supply chain management: Developments and directions. *European Journal of Operational Research*, *233*(2), 299–312. doi:10.1016/j.ejor.2013.09.032

Bringmann, K., & Friedrich, T. (2013). Approximation quality of the hypervolume indicator. *Artificial Intelligence*, *195*, 265–290. doi:10.1016/j.artint.2012.09.005

Castillo-Villar, K. K. (2014). Metaheuristic algorithms applied to bioenergy supply chain problems: Theory, review, challenges, and future. *Energies*, *7*(11), 7640–7672. doi:10.3390/en7117640

Che, Z. (2017). Universality of random matrices with correlated entries. *Electronic Journal of Probability*, 22.

Collins, B., & Nechita, I. (2016). Random matrix techniques in quantum information theory. *Journal of Mathematical Physics*, *57*(1), 015215. doi:10.1063/1.4936880

Corney, J. F., & Drummond, P. D. (2004). Gaussian Quantum Monte Carlo Methods for Fermions and Bosons'. *Physical Review Letters*, *93*(26), 260401. doi:10.1103/PhysRevLett.93.260401 PMID:15697955

De Meyer, A., Cattrysse, D., Rasinmäki, J., & Van Orshoven, J. (2014). Methods to optimise the design and management of biomass-for-bioenergy supply chains: A review. *Renewable & Sustainable Energy Reviews, 31*, 657–670. doi:10.1016/j.rser.2013.12.036

Dong, N., Fang, X., & Wu, A. G. (2016). A Novel Chaotic Particle Swarm Optimization Algorithm for Parking Space Guidance. *Mathematical Problems in Engineering.*

Elkazzaz, F., Mahmoud, A., & Maher, A. (2018), Cuckoo Search Algorithm for Multi-objective Supply Chain Problem. In *MATEC Web of Conferences* (Vol. 189, p.06001). EDP Sciences.

Ganesan, T., Aris, M. S., & Elamvazuthi, I. (2018b). *Multiobjective Strategy for an Industrial Gas Turbine: Absorption Chiller System. In Handbook of Research on Emergent Applications of Optimization Algorithms* (pp. 531–556). IGI Global. doi:10.4018/978-1-5225-2990-3.ch023

Ganesan, T., Aris, M. S., & Vasant, P. (2018a). Extreme Value Metaheuristics for Optimizing a Many-Objective Gas Turbine System. *International Journal of Energy Optimization and Engineering, 7*(2), 76–96. doi:10.4018/IJEOE.2018040104

Ganesan, T., Elamvazuthi, I., & Vasant, P. (2015). Multiobjective design optimization of a nano-CMOS voltage-controlled oscillator using game theoretic-differential evolution. *Applied Soft Computing, 32*, 293–299. doi:10.1016/j.asoc.2015.03.016

Ganesan, T., Vasant, P., & Elamvazuthi, I. (2013). Normal-boundary intersection based parametric multi-objective optimization of green sand mould system. *Journal of Manufacturing Systems, 32*(1), 197–205. doi:10.1016/j.jmsy.2012.10.004

Ganesan, T., Vasant, P., & Elamvazuthi, I. (2016). *Advances in Metaheuristics: Applications in Engineering Systems.* CRC Press. doi:10.1201/9781315297651

Gao, J., & You, F. (2015). Shale gas supply chain design and operations toward better economic and life cycle environmental performance: MINLP model and global optimization algorithm. *ACS Sustainable Chemistry & Engineering, 3*(7), 1282–1291. doi:10.1021/acssuschemeng.5b00122

Hong, Y. Y., Beltran, A. A., & Paglinawan, A. C. (2016). A Chaos-Enhanced Particle Swarm Optimization with Adaptive Parameters and Its Application in Maximum Power Point Tracking. *Mathematical Problems in Engineering.*

Jiang, S., Zhang, J., Ong, Y. S., Zhang, A. N., & Tan, P. S. (2015). A simple and fast hypervolume indicator-based multiobjective evolutionary algorithm. *IEEE Transactions on Cybernetics, 45*(10), 2202–2213. doi:10.1109/TCYB.2014.2367526 PMID:25474815

Joshi, A. S., Kulkarni, O., Kakandikar, G. M., & Nandedkar, V. M. (2017). Cuckoo Search Optimization-A Review. *Materials Today: Proceedings, 4*(8), 7262–7269.

Krbálek, M., & Seba, P. (2000). The statistical properties of the city transport in Cuernavaca (Mexico) and random matrix ensembles. *Journal of Physics. A, Mathematical and General, 33*(26), L229–L234. doi:10.1088/0305-4470/33/26/102

Liang, H., & Sun, L. (2019). Improve cloud manufacturing supply chain note-enterprises optimize combination of the Cuckoo Search. *Concurrency and Computation: Practise and Experience*, *31*(10), e4764. doi:10.1002/cpe.4764

Lin, T., Rodríguez, L. F., Shastri, Y. N., Hansen, A. C., & Ting, K. C. (2014). Integrated strategic and tactical biomass–biofuel supply chain optimization. *Bioresource Technology*, *156*, 256–266. doi:10.1016/j. biortech.2013.12.121 PMID:24508904

Luan, X. Y., Li, Z. P., & Liu, T. Z. (2016). A novel attribute reduction algorithm based on rough set and improved artificial fish swarm algorithm. *Neurocomputing*, *174*, 522–529. doi:10.1016/j.neucom.2015.06.090

Mareli, M., & Twala, B. (2017). *An adaptive Cuckoo search algorithm for optimisation.* Applied Computing and Informatics.

Marufuzzaman, M., Eksioglu, S. D., & Huang, Y. E. (2014). Two-stage stochastic programming supply chain model for biodiesel production via wastewater treatment. *Computers & Operations Research*, *49*, 1–17. doi:10.1016/j.cor.2014.03.010

Mastrocinque, E., Yuce, B., Lambiase, A., & Packianather, M. S. (2013). A multi-objective optimization for supply chain network using the bees algorithm. *International Journal of Engineering Business Management*, *5*, 38. doi:10.5772/56754

Mattos, C. L., Barreto, G. A., Horstkemper, D., & Hellingrath, B. 2017, June. Metaheuristic optimization for automatic clustering of customer-oriented supply chain data. In *Self-Organizing Maps and Learning Vector Quantization, Clustering and Data Visualization (WSOM), 2017 12th International Workshop on* (pp. 1-8). IEEE. 10.1109/WSOM.2017.8020025

Mousavi, S. M., Sadeghi, J., Niaki, S. T. A., & Tavana, M. (2016). A bi-objective inventory optimization model under inflation and discount using tuned Pareto-based algorithms: NSGA-II, NRGA, and MOPSO. *Applied Soft Computing*, *43*, 57–72. doi:10.1016/j.asoc.2016.02.014

Naidu, K., Mokhlis, H., & Bakar, A. H. A. (2014). Multiobjective optimization using weighted sum artificial bee colony algorithm for load frequency control. *International Journal of Electrical Power & Energy Systems*, *55*, 657–667. doi:10.1016/j.ijepes.2013.10.022

Ogunbanwo, A., Williamson, A., Veluscek, M., Izsak, R., Kalganova, T., & Broomhead, P. (2014). Transportation network optimization. In *Encyclopedia of Business Analytics and Optimization* (pp. 2570–2583). IGI Global. doi:10.4018/978-1-4666-5202-6.ch229

Osmani, A., & Zhang, J. (2013). Stochastic optimization of a multi-feedstock lignocellulosic-based bioethanol supply chain under multiple uncertainties. *Energy*, *59*, 157–172. doi:10.1016/j.energy.2013.07.043

Osmani, A., & Zhang, J. (2014). Economic and environmental optimization of a large scale sustainable dual feedstock lignocellulosic-based bioethanol supply chain in a stochastic environment. *Applied Energy*, *114*, 572–587. doi:10.1016/j.apenergy.2013.10.024

Pan, I., & Das, S. (2016). Fractional order fuzzy control of hybrid power system with renewable generation using chaotic PSO. *ISA Transactions*, *62*, 19–29. doi:10.1016/j.isatra.2015.03.003 PMID:25816968

Plerou, V., Gopikrishnan, P., Rosenow, B., Amaral, L. A. N., Guhr, T., & Stanley, H. E. (2002). Random matrix approach to cross correlations in financial data. *Physical Review. E, 65*(6), 066126. doi:10.1103/PhysRevE.65.066126 PMID:12188802

Qiu, R. C., & Antonik, P. (2017). *Smart grid using big data analytics: a random matrix theory approach.* John Wiley & Sons. doi:10.1002/9781118716779

Seuring, S. (2013). A review of modeling approaches for sustainable supply chain management. *Decision Support Systems, 54*(4), 1513–1520. doi:10.1016/j.dss.2012.05.053

Shi, J., Zhang, W., Zhang, Y., Xue, F., & Yang, T. (2015). MPPT for PV systems based on a dormant PSO algorithm. *Electric Power Systems Research, 123*, 100–107. doi:10.1016/j.epsr.2015.02.001

Singh, K., Vasant, P., Elamvazuthi, I., & Kannan, R. (2015). PID tuning of servo motor using bat algorithm. *Procedia Computer Science, 60*, 1798–1808. doi:10.1016/j.procs.2015.08.290

Sottinen, T., & Tudor, C. A. (2006). On the Equivalence of Multiparameter Gaussian Processes. *Journal of Theoretical Probability, 19*(2), 461–485. doi:10.100710959-006-0022-5

Srivastav, A., & Agrawal, S. (2017). *Multi-objective optimization of slow moving inventory system using cuckoo search.* Intelligent Automation & Soft Computing.

Tan, Q., Wang, T., Zhang, Y., Miao, X., & Zhu, J. (2017). Nonlinear multi-objective optimization model for a biomass direct-fired power generation supply chain using a case study in China. *Energy, 139*, 1066–1079. doi:10.1016/j.energy.2017.08.050

Verbaarschot, J. 2004, December. The supersymmetric method in random matrix theory and applications to QCD. In AIP Conference Proceedings (Vol. 744, No. 1, pp. 277-362). AIP. doi:10.1063/1.1853204

Whitley, D. (2014). Sharpened and focused no free lunch and complexity theory. In *Search Methodologies* (pp. 451–476). Boston, MA: Springer. doi:10.1007/978-1-4614-6940-7_16

Wigner, E. P. (1993). Characteristic vectors of bordered matrices with infinite dimensions I. In *The Collected Works of Eugene Paul Wigner* (pp. 524–540). Berlin: Springer. doi:10.1007/978-3-662-02781-3_35

Yang, X. S. (2013). *Optimization and metaheuristic algorithms in engineering. In Metaheuristic in Water Geotechnical and Transport Engineering* (pp. 1–23). Waltham: Elsevier.

Zhang, J., Osmani, A., Awudu, I., & Gonela, V. (2013). An integrated optimization model for switchgrass-based bioethanol supply chain. *Applied Energy, 102*, 1205–1217. doi:10.1016/j.apenergy.2012.06.054

Zhao, F., Lei, W., Ma, W., Liu, Y., & Zhang, C. (2016). An Improved SPEA2 Algorithm with Adaptive Selection of Evolutionary Operators Scheme for Multiobjective Optimization Problems. *Mathematical Problems in Engineering.*

Zhaoben, F., Ying-chang, L., & Zhidong, B. (2014). *Spectral Theory of Large Dimensional Random Matrices and Its Applications to Wireless Communications and Finance Statistics: Random Matrix Theory and Its Applications.* World Scientific.

Zhou, C., Hou, C., Wei, X., & Zhang, Q. (2014). Improved hybrid optimization algorithm for 3D protein structure prediction. *Journal of Molecular Modeling, 20*(7), 2289. doi:10.100700894-014-2289-2 PMID:25069136

APPENDIX

Biofuel Supply Chain Parameters

AC abatement cost of carbon dioxide [yuan/kg]

$CEicb_{ik}$ increment of carbon dioxide emissions with loading each additional ton of biomass fuel per kilometer when broker k collects biomass fuel i [kg/t and km]

$AQmax_{i,t}$ maximum available quantity of local biomass fuel i in month t [t/month]

ACS average electricity consumer surplus [yuan/kWh]

$CEitp_k$ increment of carbon dioxide emissions with loading each additional ton of fuel per kilometer when broker k transports biomass fuel to biomass power plant [kg/t and km]

$CEncb_{ik}$ carbon dioxide emissions per kilometer when broker k collects biomass fuel I with no-load conveyance [kg/km]

$CEntp_k$ carbon dioxide emissions per kilometer when broker k transports biomass fuel to biomass power plant with no load conveyance [kg/km]

CET carbon dioxide emissions of thermal power plant for unit power generation [kg/kWh]

Dcb_{ik} average transport distance when broker k collecting biomass fuel i [km]

Dtp_k transport distance between broker k and biomass power plant [km]

E efficiency of biomass power plant [decimal fraction]

EC electricity consumption rate of biomass power plant [decimal fraction]

$extraY1$ first extra cost of excessive biomass power plant fuel inventory [yuan/month]

$extraY2$ second extra cost of excessive biomass power plant fuel inventory [yuan/month]

ER_k expected return of broker k [decimal fraction mass/year]

FCb_k fixed cost of broker k [yuan/year]

FCp fixed cost of biomass power plant [yuan/year]

GC unit generation cost of biomass power plant [yuan/kWh]

GS government subsidies to biomass power generation [yuan/kWh]

GT government tax revenues from biomass power plant [yuan/year]

HV_i heat value of biomass fuel i [kJ/kg]

HVe heat value of electricity [kJ/kWh]

$HVmax$ maximum heat value of mixed fuel [kJ/kg]

HV_{min} minimum heat value of mixed fuel [kJ/kg]

$IQ_{i,0}$ inventory quantity of biomass fuel i at the beginning of month 1 [tonnes]

$CEcb$ carbon dioxide emissions during collecting biomass fuel [kg]

$CEtp$ carbon dioxide emissions during transporting biomass fuel to biomass power plant [kg]

EIC extra inventory cost of biomass power plant [yuan]

$IQ_{i,t}$ inventory quantity of biomass fuel i at the end of month t [tonnes]

PP_i purchase price of biomass fuel i from brokers [yuan/t]

$PQ_{ik,t}$ purchase quantity of biomass fuel i by broker k in month t [t]

q_t electricity generation of biomass power plant in month t [kWh/month]

R_t conversion rate from biomass fuel to electricity in month t [kg/kWh]

IQ_{max} maximum inventory quantity of biomass power plant [t]

IL rate of inventory loss [decimal fraction/month]

$LCcb_{ik}$ load capacity of conveyance when broker k collects biomass fuel i [t]

$LCtp_{ik}$ load capacity of conveyance when broker k transports biomass fuel i to biomass power plant [t]

$MCmax_i$ maximum moisture content of biomass fuel i required by biomass power plant [decimal fraction mass]

$MCorii_t$ original moisture content of biomass fuel i in month t [decimal fraction mass]

$MCaft_{ik}$ moisture content of biomass fuel i after processing by broker k [decimal fraction mass]

P on-grid price of biomass power plant [yuan/kWh]

$PQ_{max,\,k}$ maximum purchasing quantity of biomass fuel by broker k [t/month]

q_{max} maximum monthly electricity generation quantity of biomass power plant [kWh/month]

Q_{max} maximum annual electricity generation quantity of biomass power plant [kWh/year]

Q_{min} minimum annual electricity generation of biomass power plant [kWh/year]

$RIub_1$ first upper bound of reasonable fuel inventory [t]

$RIub_2$ second upper bound of reasonable fuel inventory [t]

$SIlb_i$ lower bound of safety inventory for biomass fuel i [t]

SC unit storage cost of biomass power plant [yuan/month]

$SQmin_{ik}$ minimum supply quantity of biomass fuel i from broker

$TCcb_{ik}$ average unit transportation cost of broker k when collecting biomass fuel i [yuan/ km]

$TCtp_{ik}$ average unit transportation cost of broker k when transporting biomass fuel i to biomass power plant [yuan/km]

$WR_{ik,t}$ ratio of the weight of biomass fuel i after processing to the weight before processing by broker k in month t [decimal fraction mass]

$AP_{ik,t}$ average price of broker k buying biomass fuel i in month t [yuan/t]

$BC_{i,t}$ biomass fuel i consumption in month t [t]

$BR_{i,t}$ blending ratio of biomass fuel i in mixed fuel in month t [decimal fraction mass]

CER carbon dioxide emissions reduction [kg]

CET_{eq} carbon dioxide emissions of thermal power plant for power generation equal to biomass power plant [kg]

CEB carbon dioxide emissions of biomass power plant [kg]

$SQ_{ik,t}$ supply quantity of biomass fuel i by broker k in month t [t]

VCp total variable cost of biomass power plant [yuan/year]

$Y1t$ binary variable to determine whether the inventory is over $RIub1$ at the end of month t

$Y2t$ binary variable to determine whether the inventory is over $RIub2$ at the end of month t

PR Profits (yuan)

SW Social Welfare (yuan)

Env Environmental Benefit (kg/power station)

Random Matrix Theory and CS

$P1(s)$ Probabilistic Spacing Distribution for Gaussian Orthogonal Ensemble (GOE)

$P2(s)$ Probabilistic Spacing Distribution for Gaussian Unitary Ensemble (GUE)

$P3(s)$ Probabilistic Spacing Distribution for Gaussian Symplectic Ensemble (GSE)

Po(*s*) Probabilistic Spacing Distribution for Poisson Distribution

s Eigenvalue Spacing distribution

λ Eigenvalue

$\Delta\lambda$ Eigenvalue Interval

Ei Eigenvector

Hij Initial Matrix

σ^2 Statistical variance

μ Statistical Mean

wi Weights for the weighted sum method

*T*max Maximum limit of function evaluations

m Maximum number of objective functions

*HV*I Hypervolume Indicator

β Relaxation factor

iter Number of algorithm iterations

t Random Variable

yti Candidate solution

Levy(λ) Lévy Distribution

N Total Number of Eggs

Chapter 14
Optimized Deep Learning System for Crop Health Classification Strategically Using Spatial and Temporal Data

Saravanan Radhakrishnan
Vellore Institute of Technology, India

Vijayarajan V.
Vellore Institute of Technology, India

ABSTRACT

Deep learning opens up a plethora of opportunities for academia and industry to invent new techniques to come up with modified or enhanced versions of standardized neural networks so that the customized technique is suitable for any specialized situations where the problem is about learning a complex mapping from the input to the output space. One such situation lies in a farm with huge cultivation area, where examining each of the plant for any anomalies is highly complex that it is impractical, if not impossible, for humans. In this chapter, the authors propose an optimized deep learning architectural model, combining various techniques in neural networks for a real-world application of deep learning in computer vision in precision farming. More precisely, thousands of crops are examined automatically and classified as healthy or unhealthy. The highlight of this architecture is the strategic usage of spatial and temporal features selectively so as to reduce the inference time.

INTRODUCTION

There are numerous types of neural networks being invented and introduced on a daily basis. While such new neural network models can be designed and evaluated quickly, configuring them in a way to get the best out of them is quite challenging. That is why "configuring neural network models" is often termed as a "dark art." The reasons for the lack of guidance can be attributed partly to the fact that many of the

DOI: 10.4018/978-1-7998-1192-3.ch014

techniques in machine learning space quickly lose relevance as faster and higher power hardware with superior architecture replace older hardware at a rapid rate. Another prime reason is that there can never be one best algorithm that works best for all cases as it is not possible to analytically evaluate the optimal configuration for a given problem and data set. It is always possible to tweak the configurations to make improvements to speed of learning, right-fitting of the model, accuracy of inference, etc.

Moreover, data for neural networks will be from several different sources. For example, in precision farming, data will come from multiple sensors, cameras, etc. Some of these might be complex data like multispectral images. Many neural network models can't handle highly complex data. Others may not accurately capture the relationships between different variables. Hence there is a need to create a neural network system that would take simple and complex data as input and the system should be capable of working around the missing variables.

There are also some newer neural network architectures that can take multiple, heterogeneous inputs and extract features on their own and share the "learnings" with downstream sub-systems, thereby facilitating creation of an optimal learning system. Developing such deep learning systems working on heterogeneous data is very challenging since each data type may need distinct pre-processing steps and feature engineering. Hence it is still very much an open area of research and is very often heavily dependent on the specific problem on hand.

BACKGROUND

As evidenced by the detailed survey captured in (Radhakrishnan & Vijayarajan V., 2019), even as there are various researches happening in Deep Learning in the context of Farming 4.0, the economic viability of its application is still very less. The literature survey further provides research direction to optimize deep learning applications for monitoring crop health so as to make this technology useful to farmers. Hence the domain considered for this research work of optimizing deep learning system is "Precision Floriculture" in Green House cultivation where the produce is cut flowers.

That said, there are various researches being carried out to employ Deep Learning to classify plants based on their botanical parts like leaf, flower, etc. Han et al. (Han, Seng, Joseph, & Remagnino, 2017) investigated the use of deep learning to extract discriminatory features from images of leaves by learning and use them as classifiers to identify plant species. Their results demonstrate that compared to using hand crafted features of leaf images, learning the features using CNNs do provide better feature representations.

Gurnani et al. (Gurnani, n.d.) developed a deep learning framework to categorize flowers by doing transfer learning from two famous CNN architectures called GoogleNet which was pre-trained on ILSVRC2014 dataset and AlexNet which was pre-trained on ILSVRC2012 dataset and found their accuracies to be 47% and 43% respectively. By the way, ILSVRC stands for ImageNet Large Scale Visual Recognition Competition. In this study they confirmed the popular claim by researchers that the performance of the neural network will be commensurate with the depth of the network. This claim is further ascertained by Liu et al. (Liu, Yang, Cheng, & Song, 2018) who designed a very deep leaf classification model using a ten-layer CNN based on LeNet architecture to classify 32 species of plants and achieved an accuracy rate of 87.92%.

Further, the same LeNet architecture was used by Amara et al. (Amara, Bouaziz, & Algergawy, 2017) to build a deep neural network to detect two common banana diseases called banana sigatoka and banana speckle from banana leaves. Unlike other earlier experimental setups, they have used images captured under challenging conditions such as illumination, complex background, different images resolution, size, pose and orientation. The key take away from their work is that better accuracy of more than 90% is achievable using color images opposed to lower accuracy of about 85% using grey scale images. The authors achieved best performance with a train-test data split of 80%-20%.

Jeon et al. (Jeon & Rhee, 2017) proposed a deep learning method to classify leaves. They demonstrated that a variant of GoogleNet model with a network depth of 22 layers of inception modules achieved a recognition rate of more than 94%. Similarly for classification of plant species using leaf features, Tan et al. (Tan, Chang, Abdul-kareem, Yap, & Yong, 2018) proposed a model called D-Leaf for feature extraction and compared the same with pre-trained and fine-tuned AlexNet models. The features extracted from these models were classified using various machine learning classifiers. The best performance achieved was using ANN for classification with a result of about 95%.

Hiary et al. (Hiary, Saadeh, Saadeh, & Yaqub, 2018) improved classification accuracy by employing a 2-step deep learning model in which first step dealt with segmenting the flower using Fully Convolutional Network (FCN) thereby reducing the surrounding clutter and the second step involved a CNN classifier initialized using the trained FCN which itself was initialized from the VGG-16 model that provided the best result of about 97% for classifying flower images from ImageNet dataset.

Previous studies reveal that many variants of convolutional neural network models take multiple data types including images as inputs, extract features from the images and classify the images very well as trained. Yet there seems no good strategy for cases where there are different sets of secondary data that can be included to increase the classification accuracy and speed of inference. In such cases where secondary data can also be included, the data would become enormously large demanding very high computational and storage power. Hence the decision of augmenting additional input data can be made progressively. For example, secondary data may be augmented based on the confidence score of the model for a particular class thereby reducing the space and time complexity. If the difference between the probabilities of the outputs is not significantly high, then the classifier model with augmented data (other input data relevant to the class) can further be employed to improve the confidence score. As a result, there is clearly a need to create an optimization technique that leverages the spatial and temporal features to improve efficiency and accuracy of Deep Neural Networks. It is worthwhile to invent an optimization strategy combining multiple proven neural network models to progressively improve the efficiency and accuracy of Neural Networks based on earlier results and their confidence scores to include more spatial and temporal data as necessary.

Thus, to summarize, the mission is to build an optimized Deep Learning System that starts with a simple classification using ***select spatial data*** (features of flowers) and based on confidence scores of the prediction outcomes of this relatively simpler base Convolutional Neural Network model, the system should move on to employing specific additional models to use ***additional spatial data*** (features from leaves) in an attempt to ascertain the crop health. The aim is to put the classification inference speed ahead of the classification accuracy. This is achieved by using simpler CNN that uses only spatial features of flower to distinguish healthy crops from unhealthy crops. Only when the confidence score is low in this step, will the algorithm proceed to use more spatial features, this time from leaves. Further, only if the algorithm is NOT able to ascertain that the crop is healthy (or classifies it as unhealthy) using these spatial features the algorithm proceeds to use temporal data. This way the system evolves the classification by augmenting **newer temporal data** into the model.

ASSUMPTIONS AND CONSTRAINTS

There are some key assumptions made and constraints defined while designing this architecture. These provide a foundation to base the research work. The constraints are not true limitations of the system – they are there only to provide clarity to the scope of the research work. Relaxing a constraint will mandate a modification to the architecture.

1. While there are so many ways in which the crop stress gets manifested, this work considers only the symptoms showing up in the flowers as primary and considers the difference in green wavelength reflectance showing up on the leaves as secondary.
2. Wilting, malformed shapes, double-face or drooping of flowers and yellowing of leaves are the anomalies used to categorize a crop as unhealthy. The rationale for this is that most of the causal factors of an unhealthy crop will manifest as these anomalies. Table 1 lists some of the major anomalies in cut-flowers and their causal factors.

3. The scope has been confined to only gerbera flowers of light pink colour so that the training data can be limited. To make the system colour agnostic, varieties of colours may be included for training, but data size needs to be proportionately large.
4. The RGB (also called true color image wherein each pixel is represented as varying intensities in 3 channels, one each for Red, Green and Blue colors) and NIR images (Near-InfraRed images captured using special sensors that are extremely sensitive instruments, optimized to measure the absorbance of samples at specific wavelength regions from 780nm to 1300nm which lies just outside the visible spectrum) are captured at defined schedule for learning and inference.

Table 1. Common anomalies and their important causal factors

Anomaly	Causal factor	Remark
Double-faced Gerbera flower	Nutrient imbalance	Two-facedness is a physiological disorder caused by imbalance of nutrients.
Wilted flower / Malformed flower	Unsuitable Temperature and Humidity	The favourable temperature is 10-25°C and optimum humidity is 70 – 80%
	Pest infestation	Pests like thrips & mites make flowers malformed. Thrip infestation is the prime reason for distorted shapes in the flowers of gerbera crop
	Water Stress	Excess or insufficient water in soil will cause flower wilting
Flower bent	Malnutrition	Loss of cell turgidity due to under nutrition (Eg: insufficient Calcium)
	Unsuitable Temperature and Humidity	Harsh weather causes drooping of flowers

5. The images for training and inference are obtained directly from above the crop and thus only leaves and flowers need to be seen in the images.

6. Classification results are required only once, though inference will be run for 3 consecutive days as elaborated in detail in *Inference Methodology* section.

7. The finer details on the implementation of any standard neural networks (like CNN) used as sub-systems are not discussed elaborately and only the non-standard changes (aka customizations) in the implementation are elaborated. It is assumed that the readers of this chapter already have a good understanding of the workings of standard neural networks.

DATA COLLECTION AND PREPARATION SCHEME FOR TRAINING

In order to train the system with spatio-temporal features impacting crop health, training data was collected from a one-acre farm cultivating about 20,000 Gerbera crops as follows.

1. RGB-NIR Images are collected at 9AM daily for 1000 crops for 3 consecutive days. Data from across days must be from same crops and next days' data must be collated with corresponding data from the previous days. The rationale for capturing this data at same time is that ambient variables like air temperature and humidity conditions around the crops play a major role in determining the morphology of the leaves and flowers. Moreover, restricting data only for 3 days is due to the similar fact that the morphological changes to the flower and leaves are kept to a reasonable limit.

2. Data Augmentation: Using the famous technique called "*data augmentation*", more data gets generated from available data. In this case, 2000 random images from the image data store are duplicated and rotated to random angles and some flipped vertically and/or horizontally, thus making the image data store size to 5000. Other common techniques like warping and scaling are not employed to generate more data, because these transformation operations will change the morphology of flower images and may lead to inaccuracies in classification.

3. Labelling and Creation of ground truth: Each of the images now goes through a laborious process of labelling using tools like LabelBox or Pascal VOC. In this case, there are only two labels per image, viz, Flower and Leaf. Thus, the label data store is created for the image data store containing 5000 RGB images.

4. Use FCN (Fully Convolutional Networks, explained later in this chapter) to create mask using segmentation of the flower from each RGB image and applying the same in the image's corresponding NIR plane to remove the pixels representing the flowers. The removal of these pixels corresponding to flowers leaves the NIR plane only with the leaves pixels. This step is important to accurately calculate the NDVI (Normalized Difference Vegetative Index) of the crop. The FCN method is elaborated in the next sections.

5. Using the Red and NIR bands of the RGB-NIR images, NDVI images are created. NDVI is calculated on a per-pixel basis as the normalized difference between the red and near infrared bands from an image:

$$NDVI = (NIR - RED) / (NIR + RED)$$

where, NIR is the near infrared band value for a cell and RED is the red band value for the cell. NDVI can be calculated for any image that has a red and a near infrared band. The biophysical interpretation of NDVI is the fraction of absorbed photo-synthetically active radiation. Healthy leaves absorb most of red and blue but reflect only some green. On the contrary, healthy leaves reflect lot more Infrared and less red and blue compared to sick or dead leaves. Moreover, since it is a ratio of two bands, NDVI helps compensate for variation in illumination within an image owing to slope and variations in images due to factors like time of day when the images were acquired. Therefore, NDVI proves helpful to compare images over time and spot changes in crop health. This will be used as a temporal feature in this classification system.

6. Similar to NDVI, the Blue and NIR bands of the RGB-NIR images were used to create SI-NDVI images (Single Image NDVI) using the below formula:

SI-NDVI = (NIR - BLUE) / (NIR + BLUE)

where, NIR is the near infrared band value for a cell and BLUE is the blue band value for the cell. Beisel et al., in their work (Beisel et al., 2018), elaborated how single-image normalized difference vegetation index (SI-NDVI) can be helpful in early detection of plant stress.

7. Then, for each NDVI and SI-NDVI image, NDVI histogram is constructed and statistical data are calculated as follows and stored in a 1x4 vector.

   ○ Mean = Sum of all pixel values / total number of pixels in the image
   ○ Variance (S^2) = average squared deviation of pixel values from *mean*
   ○ Standard deviation (S) = square root of the *variance*
   ○ Percentage of pixels that lie in the interval: $- S < x < + S$

This 1x4 vector for NDVI is augmented with 1x4 vector of SI-NDVI to create 1x8 vector, called as VI vector. Once this step is complete, it becomes clear on how to present the NDVI and SI-NDVI data to the input layer of the neural network.

8. Normalizing and Standardizing: All the numerical data in VI vector are min-max scaled to the range [0, 1] and are then concatenated into a single feature vector (FV) to form the input into the multi-layer perceptron model.

Formatting the data correctly is one of the key aspects to the success of a Deep Learning System. The authors recommend segregating the data for training, validation and testing with a 50%, 25%, 25% split respectively.

STANDARD NETWORKS AS SUBSYSTEMS

Before discussing the overall architecture and methodology, brief explanation of the three standard neural networks used as sub-models in the system, standard techniques like one-hot encoding and the rationale for using them are discussed in the next sections. Not all the nitty-gritties and internal configurations of each of these standard neural networks are purposefully omitted since these are now becoming trivia of neural networks and would also be specific to real world scenarios and their data sets. What is more important is the overall architecture involving novel techniques in data collection and preparation scheme and efficient interplay of these models to make best use of the spatial and temporal data during the inference phase.

MULTI-LAYER PERCEPTRON (MLP) AND RATIONALE FOR INCLUSION

Multi-Layer Perceptron is a type of Feed Forward Artificial Neural Network that should contain one input layer, one output layer and one or more hidden layers. The primary difference between a linear perceptron and multi-layer perceptron is that linear perceptron will not be able to distinguish non-linearly separable data but MLP can do so due to the presence of multiple layers and non-linear activations. MLP uses back-propagation for training. Authors selected to use MLP with two hidden layers and sigmoid activations for 1x11 feature vector containing numeric data (NDVI stats, SI-NDVI stats, soil moisture, temperature and humidity) since it is the simplest deep learning model best suited for binary classification when the inputs are purely numeric data. The concept of using multi-layer perceptron for time-series analysis of NDVI using remote sensing data to monitor temporal changes in vegetation was discussed by Stepchenko et al. in their paper (Stepchenko & Chizhov, 2015). This serves as an inspiration to use multi-layer perceptron for observing changes in NDVI and SI-NDVI in the leaves over a period of 3 days in this experiment.

CONVOLUTIONAL NEURAL NETWORKS (CNN) AND RATIONALE FOR INCLUSION

Convolutional Neural Networks are very different from many other networks as they involve layers to convolve, which unlike normal layers, all nodes are not connected to all other nodes. Each node only focuses only on cells in their neighbourhood, thus trying to identify features like edges and corners. Therefore CNNs are best suited for image classifications. Hence the authors decided to use the *plain vanilla* CNN for the base model which takes RGB image as input for binary classification. The hidden layers of the CNN model used for this binary classification contain a series of three convolutional, nonlinear and pooling layers followed by a fully connected layer. ReLu is the activation function for this model and *max pooling*, the most common pooling technique is used for pooling layer with pool size of 3 x 3 pixels.

FULLY CONVOLUTIONAL NETWORK (FCN - SEMANTIC SEGMENTATION) AND RATIONALE FOR INCLUSION

Semantic Segmentation is a technique of classifying each pixel in an image into an object class. In other words, this technique assigns a label for each pixel. When convolution is used to classify an input image, it gets downsized as it goes through convolution and fully connected layers and outputs a predicted label. In the process of convolution, when going deeper, intricate features are obtained at the cost of spatial information. On the contrary, shallow layers tend to have more local information. Combining both will enhance the result. This is the key concept behind Fully Convolutional Networks (FCN) that serves as the basis for semantic segmentation. This technique is clearly explained in the work (Shelhamer, Long, & Darrell, 2017) by Shelhamer et al. In this chapter, semantic segmentation is used to identify the pixels pertaining to flowers in the RGB image so that these pixels will be zeroed out in the replicated RGB image and NIR image. This removal of pixels belonging to flowers from the images ensures that NDVI and SI-NDVI are calculated rightfully only for the leaves.

TRANSFER LEARNING AND RATIONALE FOR INCLUSION

Transfer learning is a technique to reduce training burden for new models by reusing the learning done by another model. The effectiveness of transfer learning depends on the applicability of low level features learned by the pre-trained model to the new models. For example, a model trained to classify birds will be more effective when retrained to classify animals than when retrained to classify vehicles. While retraining a new model, weights of one or more of the early convolutional layers of the network will be reused and last few layers will need to be retrained thus accelerating the training time drastically. For the problem on hand, transfer learning is used to retrain the FCN and downstream CNN from the base CNN trained for binary classification. Detailed of this retraining is presented later in this chapter.

OTHER MODEL ARCHITECTURES AND RATIONALE FOR NOT USING THEM

One common approach to the scenario of multi-class classification that the authors are proposing a new model architecture is to use a binary relevance method like One-Vs-Rest (OVR) or One-Vs-All, where in the strategy would be to fit one classifier per class so that deeper insights can be arrived about the plant from the perspective of that particular class. For example, an OVR classifier for "pest-infested versus other abnormality" would give greater knowledge of pest-infestations on the plant. This way multiple labels with varying probabilities can be assigned to each class. Similarly, there are certain architectures making use of OVR and ensemble techniques, wherein the results from the individual models are merged to predict multiple classes. But in all these architectures, there are many shortcomings for the problem on hand. As such there is no possibility of giving additional and appropriate inputs depending on the confidence score of the classifier. The relevance of these inputs will greatly improve if they happen to multiple data types like numeric and image, but these cannot be fed to the models. Moreover, there is no possibility of including temporal data for classification.

The authors are defining the architecture for this problem wherein there are heterogeneous set of input data, like image (RBG), statistical data derived from the histogram of the NDVI image, all going into a downstream model with concatenation to predict crop anomaly.

ARCHITECTURE OF THE COMPLETE SYSTEM

Here authors present the overall architecture of the system. As show in figure 1, there are four virtual layers in the system. The first layer takes in input data from outside world. These primary inputs to the system are RGB and NIR images.

The next layer is also input layer, but this represents the secondary data derived / inferred from one of the neural networks or another process within the system and will be used by another neural network in the system. The label data-store which get generated by using a labelling tool, the masks that get

Figure 1. Overall architecture of the complete system

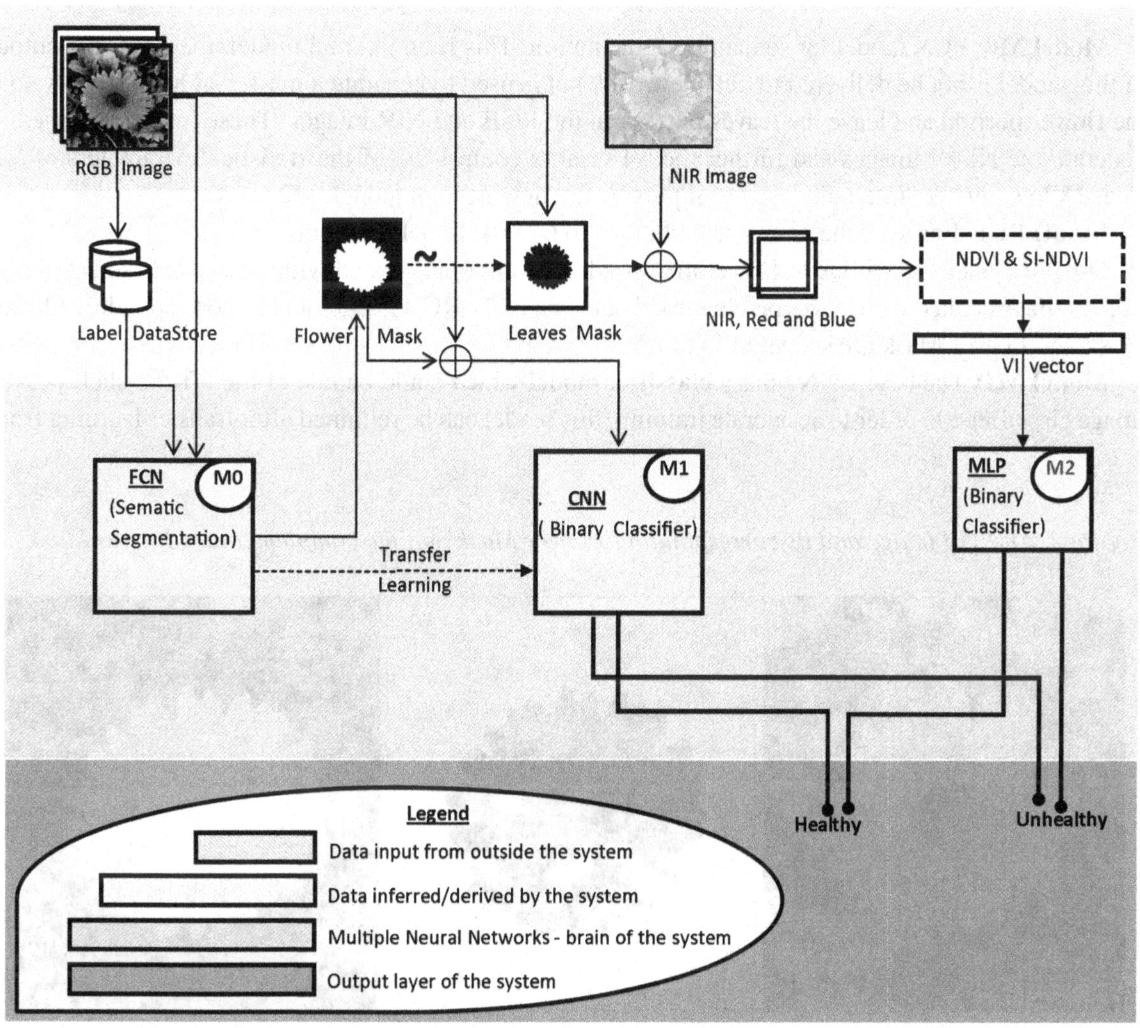

generated using the RGB images, leaves images that get generated applying the mask onto the RGB and NIR images, Vegetative Index vector that created using NDVI and SI-NDVI calculators and morphological defect categorization data that get generated by one of the neural network models are all part of the secondary input data.

The third virtual layer in the system is the most crucial layer that contains all the neural network models working in tandem. It is a known fact that deep neural networks are much more powerful than shallow networks, but training them is that much harder. Moreover, there will be significant processing time during inference as well. The beauty of this architecture lies in the fact that it is a system of networks stitched together using multiple sub-models, each tailored to perform specific subtask and share data with other sub-models, communicate with each other on the way to determining the crop health. Interesting thing to note is that all the sub-models will not be used for all the inference instances. For example, an image of a crop might only go through the first CNN model during an inference and when the image is classified as that of a "healthy" crop, it will not go through further models at all. More details on this are provided in the "Training methodology" and "Inference methodology" sections.

Each of the neural network models in this layer is described below.

Model M0: FCN model for semantic segmentation. This is an internal model, meaning, the output of this model is not be delivered to outside world, but is used to generate a mask that helps to carve out the flower portion and leave the leaves portion in the RGB and NIR images. These images are used to generate the NDVI images and further the VI vectors comprising of the statistical parameters of VI. These VI vectors are internally used as inputs by the downstream model, M2.

Input: RGB Image of the crop – scaled down to 64X64. Label data-store.

Output: Pixels pertaining to flower identified. Flower Mask created with flower pixels zeroed out. Leaves Mask created with leaves pixels zeroed out. One of the RGB images and its corresponding Flower Mask and Leaves Mask are shown in Figure 2.

Model M1: The base CNN binary classifier model which could be one of the off-the-shelf proven image classifiers. In order to accelerate training, this model can be retrained after transfer learning from

Figure 2. An RGB image and its corresponding Flower Mask and the complementary Leaves Mask

M0 using learning rate of 0.001 and batch size of 10. The only design consideration is that the output must be a sigmoid classifier so that the confidence score (probability) of the classification is known. The next model will be used during inference only based on this probability. The idea is the health of the horticultural crop will reflect in the morphology of the flower which is the ultimate produce of horticulture. Only when the binary image classifier is unable to classify the crop (read perfect flower) as "healthy" with high confidence score or when it is able to classify the crop health as "unhealthy" with high confidence score, will the next parameters be used to predict the crop health and further the causal factors attributed to the unhealthy crop (if found so).

Input: RGB Image of the crop after applying the flower mask so leaves are removed from the image – scaled down to 64X64.

Output: Binary probabilistic classification of Healthy crop or Unhealthy crop.

Model M2: This is the base MLP binary classifier model which could again be one of the off-the-shelf proven classifiers based on numeric inputs. Based on the classification confidence score by the earlier CNN model only, this subsequent model will be used during inference. The idea is the health of the horticultural crop will also reflect in the reflectance of visible and NIR light by leaves. Leaves contain a chemical compound called chlorophyll which strongly absorbs the red and blue wavelengths in the visible light spectrum of the radiation but strongly reflects green and NIR wavelengths. Higher the NDVI, healthier the plant is. NDVI approaches zero as the plant gets unhealthier. Hence VI vector is fed as input to this classifier. Only when the binary classifier predicts the crop as "unhealthy", will the crop be shortlisted for further observation on the next 2 days.

Input: VI vector containing mean, variance, standard deviation and pixels percentage within one sigma of NDVI and SI-NDVI images.

Output: Binary probabilistic classification of Healthy crop or Unhealthy crop.

The last layer, obviously, the output layer shows the outputs from the various neural networks that are sub-models in the system. Outputs from M1 and M2 are predictions of crop health as "healthy" or "unhealthy". Output form M0 is used internally. The true innovation is that the system uses the right information for binary classification, like using only the flowers section for CNN image classifier looking for morphological anomalies in flowers and using only the leaves section for MLP classifier looking for reflectance (pixel intensities) anomalies of certain wavelengths in leaves.

TRAINING METHODOLOGY

Step 1: First step after collecting RGB-NIR images for 3 consecutive days at a particular time each day, is to construct a label data-store. Using a labelling tool, the flowers and background (leaves) are labelled in the RGB images and stored in the label data-store.

Step 2: Next step is curating and categorizing the images as that of healthy and unhealthy plants by experts after downsizing them to 64x64.

Step 3: Then the process moves on to constructing an FCN (M0) to classify each pixel in the input RGB image as either "flower" or "leaves". Since this is a special CNN, off-the-shelf models trained to do binary classification of the image can be retrained after removing the final fully connected layers and adding upsampling / deconvolution layers. By using this semantic segmentation technique, the pixels pertaining to flowers and those pertaining to leaves in the RGB image are identified.

Step 4: Each RGB image is duplicated and the pixels corresponding to the spatial location of leaves are zeroed out in this duplicated image. Similarly the pixels corresponding to flowers are made as 1. This binary image serves as the "flowers mask". Meaning, when applied on its corresponding RGB image only the pixels corresponding to flowers will retain their pixel intensities and all other pixels will become zero values. The binary image thus created is complemented – meaning all zeroes become ones and vice versa. This new mask called "leaves mask" is now applied on RED, BLUE and NIR planes so that only leaves portion of the images will be used rightfully for the NDVI and SI-NDVI calculations.

Step 5: Next step is constructing a Convolutional Neural Network (M1) for binary classification. Depending on the real world problem, this could again be one of the proven off-the-shelf CNN for binary image classification. The input image is fed through three convolution layers and followed by that two fully connected (FC) layers, and output one predicted label for the input image which is either healthy or unhealthy. All the RGB images containing healthy crop depicted by flower without any anomaly are grouped as "healthy" and all images containing flowers with anomalies are grouped as "unhealthy". Training helps the model learn and classify RGB images of crops with *any* anomaly in the morphology of the flower as *"unhealthy"* crop; all else as *"healthy"* crop. The output layer of this model needs to be sigmoid layer since what is needed is the confidence score of the two classes as opposed to true binary classification as either "healthy" or "unhealthy". The purpose of this score is explained later in "Inference Methodology" section.

Step 6: Next, using the RED and BLUE planes of RGB image and NIR image, the NDVI and SI-NDVI of the leaves are calculated. Then the mean, standard deviation, variance and percentage of pixels within 1 sigma standard deviation are calculated for each NDVI and SI-NDVI image. These statistical parameters are maintained as Vegetative Index (VI) vector.

Step 7: Preserve the VI vectors belonging to healthy crops and unhealthy crops separately. Train a simple Multi-layer perceptron (M2) to do binary classification using the VI vectors as input.

Step 8: The model (M2) needs to be trained once each day using the corresponding data collected during the three consecutive days, day 1 (d-2), day 2 (d-1) and day 3 (d). It is pretty obvious that the corresponding model of the previous day can be used to do "transfer learning" and retrain the new model for that day. Moving in the temporal dimension, the previously obtained VI vector needs to be appended to current data. For example, when training the model for day 2, that day's VI vector appended to the day1's VI vector, thereby providing temporal data to the system. Similarly, when training the model for day 3, that day's VI vector also gets appended to the VI vector containing first day and second day data. In deep learning, LSTM (Long Short-Term Memory), GRU (Gated Recurrent Units) or any other variant of RNN (Recurrent Neural Network) will be used to model networks needing connection to temporal sequences. For the problem on hand, RNNs will be overkill since these parameters are modelled much easier. So, the outcome of this step is 3 temporal variants for model M2: $(M2)_{d-2}$, $(M2)_{d-1}$ and $(M2)_d$

Step 9: So, by end of the training, M0, M1 and three variants of M2 will be available. Among these, the latter 4 models are trained to predict one of the two classes, of course using different inputs:
  ◦ Healthy
  ◦ Unhealthy

INFERENCE METHODOLOGY

This section provides an overview of the inference methodology. The inference objective is to categorize thousands of crops as healthy or unhealthy. To be specific, the objective is to arrive at the percentage of unhealthy crops and to identify those needing immediate attention. Capturing RGB and NIR images of all crops for 3 days and continuously processing them all using the deep learning inference system is a cumbersome process. To strike right balance between load on the system and accuracy of prediction, three temporal checkpoints separated by an interval of 24 hours are identified: 9.00AM for 3 days. The unhealthy crops identified on first day need to be monitored on next day and if there's improvement in the health (read classified as healthy), the same will be removed from the lot to be monitored for the next (third) day. The final set of "unhealthy" plants is identified during the inference on the third day.

Here is the sequence of events during each of the inference processes.

Inference: Day 1 @ 9.00 AM

Step 1: The entire process starts with collecting RGB-NIR images of the crops to be analysed for health. Care is to be taken to restrict to one flower per crop. Let us say there are 1000 crops considered for monitoring on a particular day. RGB-NIR images of these crops are captured as the first step.

Step 2: Each of the RGB image is sent to the deep learning system. The RGB image will be passed as input to the FCN (M1) which identifies the pixels corresponding to the flower. This data will be passed on to a module that creates a mask of same size as the image and will place 1 for all pixels identified as flower and 0 for all other pixels. This is called "Flower Mask".

Step 3: This flower mask is then applied on the RGB image so that all the pixels in the RGB image corresponding to flowers are kept intact while other pixels are zeroes out.

Step 4: The RGB image which now contains only the flower is fed to the binary image classifier (M0) which predicts the health of the crop based on the morphology of the flower. The idea is that any issues with the crop will have an impact on the produce of the crop. If the CNN image classifier predicts the crop as healthy with a confidence score (read probability) of 0.75 or above, then the image (and hence the crop) will be removed from that day's monitoring. In this case, the system moves on to picking the next RGB image and do all the processes explained in the previous steps.

Step 5: If the classifier predicts the crop as healthy with a score below 0.75 or it predicts the crop as unhealthy with a score of 0.75 or above, then the system generates a complementary mask by inverting the ones to zeros and vice versa in the flower mask, thus generating what is called a "leaves mask".

Step 6: This mask is then applied on the NIR image so that all the pixels in the NIR image corresponding to flowers are zeroes out, thus leaving the pixel values corresponding to the leaves intact.

Step 7: The resultant NIR image (containing only leaves pixels) are passed on to NDVI calculator module. The NDVI image and SI-NDVI image for this crop thus obtained are used to generate statistical parameters like mean, standard deviation, variance and percentage of pixels within 1 sigma standard deviation are calculated for each NDVI and SI-NDVI image. These statistical parameters are maintained as Vegetative Index (VI) vector.

Step 8: Then the base Multi-layer Perceptron $(M2)_{d-2}$ for First Day which takes VI vector as input and does binary classification gets invoked. The binary classification is to categorize the plant as either healthy or unhealthy based on the NIR reflectance of the crop. Only when the plant is categorized as "unhealthy" by this model, there comes the need to keep a close tab on it. The idea is to observe the change in NDVI and SI-NDVI before concluding if the plant is healthy or otherwise. In order to do that, temporal data of 2 temporal points are required. In this experimental setup, the authors decided the temporal points are 9AM on the next two days.

Step 9: If the MLP classifier $(M2)_{d-2}$ predicts the crop as healthy, then the all the data pertaining to the crop (RGB-NIR image, Mask, NDVI data, etc.) are removed from the system and the system moves on to picking the next RGB image and do all the processes explained in the previous steps.

Step 10: Once the system completes processing all the images for that day, what will be left is a subset of images pertaining to crops to be monitored the next day.

Inference: Day 2 @ 9.00 AM

Step 1: The entire process for the second day starts with collecting RGB and NIR images for that subset of crops left for temporal monitoring from the previous day. Then the system processes the next steps for each image in this subset.

Step 2: Similar to the process explained in the Day 1 procedure, leaves mask is generated and subsequently the NIR image with only leaves get generated.

Step 3: Again, as explained in the Day 1 procedure, VI vector gets generated and is appended with Day 1 VI vector.

Step 4: Then the Multi-layer Perceptron $(M2)_{d-1}$ for Second Day which now takes the VI vector (containing data for day 1 and day 2) as input and does binary classification gets invoked.

Step 5: If the MLP classifier $(M2)_{d-1}$ predicts the crop as healthy, then the all the data pertaining to the crop (RGB-NIR image, Mask, NDVI data, etc.) are removed from the system and the system moves on to picking the next RGB image and do all the processes explained in the previous steps. The idea is that the crop shortlisted for close monitoring is recovering or recovered and there is no need to include this plant in the final set of "unhealthy plants".

Inference: Day 3 @ 9.00 AM

Step 1: The entire process for the third (last) day starts with collecting RGB and NIR images for that subset of crops left for temporal monitoring from the previous day. Then the system processes the next steps for each image in this subset.

Step 2: Similar to the process explained in the Day 1 procedure, leaves mask is generated and subsequently the NIR image with only leaves get generated.

Step 3: Again, as explained in the Day 1 procedure, VI vector gets generated and is appended with Day 2 VI vector.

Step 4: Then the Multi-layer Perceptron $(M2)_d$ for Third Day which now takes the VI vector (containing data for day 1, day 2 and day 3) as input and does binary classification gets invoked.

Step 5: If the MLP classifier $(M2)_d$ predicts the crop as healthy, then the all the data pertaining to the crop (RGB-NIR image, Mask, NDVI data, etc.) are removed from the system and the system moves on to picking the next RGB image and do all the processes explained in the previous steps.

Step 6: The plants now left is the final set of "unhealthy plants".

RESULTS AND DISCUSSION

The plants left in the final set determined by the system as "unhealthy" are examined by experts to confirm if they are truly "unhealthy". In this experiment, the authors observed that the system was able to predict unhealthy plants with about 75% accuracy. The loss and accuracy plots during training and validation are shown in the Figures 2 and 3.

Of the predicted 443 plants only 274 plants are truly "unhealthy". This means, the *precision score* (True Positive / Actual Results) is 61% (274/443), which is not quite good. However, in this case, *recall score* (True Positive / Predicted Results) is more important, since the system **should** identify as much unhealthy crops as possible. Even if it incorrectly includes slightly more healthy plants into this category in an attempt to identify all the "unhealthy" crops, it is still OK. The system was able to "catch" 274 of the 322 "unhealthy" plants. This means a recall score of 85% (274/322) which is quite impressive. Table 2 shows the confusion matrix.

Last but not the least, as shown in Table 3, the F1 score (2 X ((Precision X Recall) / (Precision + Recall)) of 71% and Accuracy (True Positive + True Negative / Total) of 78% are fine indicators that the system does a reasonably good job of classification.

Figure 3. Plot of Model Accuracy on Training and Validation Datasets

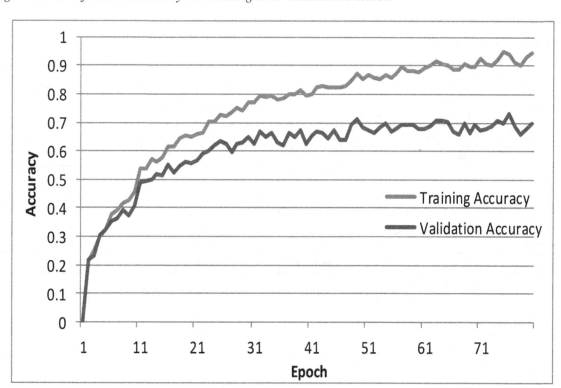

Figure 4. Plot of Model Loss on Training and Validation Datasets

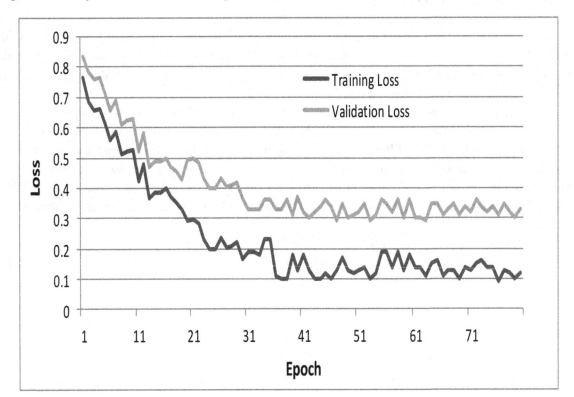

Table 2. Confusion matrix of the system

n = 1000		Predicted		Total
		Healthy	**Unhealthy**	
Actual	**Healthy**	509	169	678
	Unhealthy	48	274	322
Total		557	443	1000

Table 3. Performance metrics of the classification system

Precision	0.61851	F1 Score	0.71634
Recall	0.850932	Accuracy	0.783

Error Analysis, Shortcomings, and Further Scope of Work

From the results, the authors observed that 169 of the 217 misclassifications were False negatives (78%) and 48 were False positives (22%). In other words, the system misclassified lot more healthy crops as unhealthy crops than the other way. Careful analysis of the misclassification revealed that most of the errors (about 30%) were due to the short-circuiting optimization in the system. It is possible to increase the confidence score threshold of the CNN model (M1) so it would further let the image go through other models in the system and this would improve the classification and reduce this type of error. But the downside to this will be that the classification time will increase which would make it impractical to classify thousands of flowers every day in the farm. This necessitates tuning the system in a way as to find the right balance between speed and accuracy when deployed in a farm.

It was also observed that the system misclassified most images that were included in the inference that came from a different distribution. This distribution contained images captured at a different season. This gave insight into how the system performs on images collected at a different season when the overall outlook of the farm changes. the inference accuracy will be impacted. The proposed model suffers from this shortcoming which leads to further research direction of recalibrating the trained models periodically as and when the deployed system deteriorates over a period of time.

CONCLUSION

The authors have developed an architecture that can assimilate multiple types of data from farm to categorise the crop issues despite some incomplete information like pest population and soil nutrition. If the objective was to classify only the morphological anomaly of the flower like bent, wilted or double-faced, then the same could be achieved by training a CNN to perform multi-class classification with RGB images of various flowers with morphologically anomalies. But the objective was to start with a simple binary classification using select features and based on confidence scores of the prediction outcomes of this Convolutional Neural Network model move on to use ***additional spatial data*** to improve the classification confidence and further evolve the classification by augmenting ***newer temporal data*** into the model thus progressively using more spatial and temporal data as needed. This was achieved by the fact that most crops get determined as healthy either by the first basic CNN binary image classifier that uses flower morphology and hence do not go through the remaining models thus avoid taxing the system. This short-circuiting proves very useful in farms where thousands of crops need to be monitored on a daily basis.

REFERENCES

Amara, J., Bouaziz, B., & Algergawy, A. (2017). *A Deep Learning-based Approach for Banana Leaf Diseases Classification*. Academic Press.

Beisel, N. S., Callaham, J. B., Sng, N. J., Taylor, D. J., Paul, A. L., & Ferl, R. J. (2018). Utilization of single-image normalized difference vegetation index (SI-NDVI) for early plant stress detection. *Applications in Plant Sciences*, 6(10), e01186. doi:10.1002/aps3.1186 PMID:30386712

Gurnani, A. (n.d.). *Flower Categorization using Deep Convolutional Neural Networks*. Academic Press.

Han, S., Seng, C., Joseph, S., & Remagnino, P. (2017). *How deep learning extracts and learns leaf features for plant classification*. Academic Press. doi:10.1016/j.patcog.2017.05.015

Hiary, H., Saadeh, H., Saadeh, M., & Yaqub, M. (2018). *Flower classification using deep convolutional neural networks*. Academic Press. doi:10.1049/iet-cvi.2017.0155

Jeon, W., & Rhee, S. (2017). *Plant Leaf Recognition Using a Convolution Neural Network*. Academic Press.

Liu, J., Yang, S., Cheng, Y., & Song, Z. (2018). Plant Leaf Classification Based on Deep Learning. *2018 Chinese Automation Congress (CAC)*, 3165–3169. 10.1109/CAC.2018.8623427

Radhakrishnan, S., & Vijayarajan V. (2019). *Farming 4.0*. doi:10.4018/978-1-5225-9199-3.ch017

Shelhamer, E., Long, J., & Darrell, T. (2017). Fully Convolutional Networks for Semantic Segmentation. *IEEE Transactions on Pattern Analysis and Machine Intelligence*, *39*(4), 640–651. doi:10.1109/TPAMI.2016.2572683 PMID:27244717

Stepchenko, A., & Chizhov, J. (2015). NDVI Short-Term Forecasting Using Recurrent Neural Networks. *Environment. Technology. Resources. Proceedings of the International Scientific and Practical Conference*. 10.17770/etr2015vol3.167

Tan, J. W., Chang, S., Abdul-kareem, S., Yap, H. J., & Yong, K. (2018). *Deep Learning for Plant Species Classification using Leaf Vein Morphometric*. doi:10.1109/TCBB.2018.2848653

Chapter 15

Protein Secondary Structure Prediction Approaches:
A Review With Focus on Deep Learning Methods

Fawaz H. H. Mahyoub
https://orcid.org/0000-0003-4094-7023
School of Computer Sciences, Universiti Sains Malaysia, Malaysia

Rosni Abdullah
School of Computer Sciences, Universiti Sains Malaysia, Malaysia

ABSTRACT

The prediction of protein secondary structure from a protein sequence provides useful information for predicting the three-dimensional structure and function of the protein. In recent decades, protein secondary structure prediction systems have been improved benefiting from the advances in computational techniques as well as the growth and increased availability of solved protein structures in protein data banks. Existing methods for predicting the secondary structure of proteins can be roughly subdivided into statistical, nearest-neighbor, machine learning, meta-predictors, and deep learning approaches. This chapter provides an overview of these computational approaches to predict the secondary structure of proteins, focusing on deep learning techniques, with highlights on key aspects in each approach.

INTRODUCTION

Proteins constitute most of the dry mass of the cell. They are not just the building blocks of the cells; they also perform most of the functions of the cells. Proteins act as antibodies, antifreeze molecules, elastic fibres, signal integrators, enzymatic catalysis, toxins, hormones, transmembranal, and so on (Bruce et al., 2015). Majority of these functions are dependent on the 3D structure of proteins (Bruce et al., 2015). Accurate prediction of this 3D structure from the protein sequence is a very intricate task in computa-

DOI: 10.4018/978-1-7998-1192-3.ch015

tional biology (Yang et al., 2018). Since the rapid expansion in the fields of genomics and proteomics; particularly, the DNA and protein sequencing technologies, there has been an enormous accumulation of protein sequence data. However, predicting the 3D structures of protein from its sequence data remains a key challenge facing bioinformatics (Jiang, Jin, Lee, & Yao, 2017). A proffered approach to resolving this prediction difficulty involves breaking down the problem into smaller structural problems, in the hope that their solutions will eventually result in a solution of predicting the 3D structure of proteins.

A number of these structural problems can be symbolized as 1D vectors along the protein sequence. Hence, they can be categorized as 1D structural features. Commonly used 1D structural features of protein are secondary structures (local conformations of the backbone of protein) (Voet & Voet, 2011), backbone torsion angles (rotation angles in the protein's backbone) (Voet & Voet, 2011), residue depth (the distance of an amino acid residue in the protein sequence from the adjacent solvent molecule) (Chakravarty & Varadarajan, 1999), residue accessible surface area (solvent accessibility) (Pedersen et al., 1991), residue contact number (the count of spatially-close amino acid residues within a cut-off space) (Pollastri, Baldi, Fariselli, & Casadio, 2002), and half-sphere exposure (orientation-dependent contact numbers) (Hamelryck, 2005).

This chapter focuses mainly on predicting the secondary structure of proteins. This is imperative as precisely predicting the secondary structures of proteins is crucial for several 3D protein structure related predictions (Hanson, Yang, Paliwal, & Zhou, 2017; Heffernan, Yang, Paliwal, & Zhou, 2017). The prediction of secondary structures has an extensive background, starting by the early work on the secondary structures of the backbone of proteins (Pauling & Corey, 1951a, 1951b; Pauling, Corey, & Branson, 1951), but it is only with the application of modern deep learning techniques and the growth of resolved protein structures that we seem to be approaching the theoretical limit of 3-state prediction accuracy (88-90%) (Rost, 2001; Yang et al., 2018).

The purpose of this chapter is to review the various predicting approaches of the secondary structure of proteins with emphasis on deep learning methods. The paper begins with a brief overview of proteins and their structure levels, followed by sections presenting the approaches utilized for the prediction of the secondary structure of proteins.

BACKGROUND

Proteins

Proteins are the centre of many biological activities, including transporting molecules (Klingenberg, 1981), responding to stimuli (Yoshida, Sanematsu, Shigemura, Yasumatsu, & Ninomiya, 2005), and catalysing metabolic reactions necessary for life possible (Margolis, 2008). Furthermore, proteins act as chemical go-betweens to sustain internal communication, as regulators to turn genes on and off, and as storages to store nutrients and energy-rich molecules for later use (Zvelebil & Baum, 2007). Most of the proteins are globular. Globular proteins are simpler to crystallize because of their chemical character-istics. Conversely, non-globular proteins such as fibrous and membrane proteins are frequently defined by numerous repeated amino acid sequences with less distinctive chemical characteristics (Yoo, Zhou, & Zomaya, 2008).

Protein Structure Levels

The structure of protein comprises four levels (*primary structure, secondary structure, tertiary structure, and quaternary conformation*), as shown in Figure 1. The **primary structure** is composed of the amino acid sequence ordered in the polypeptide chain. The **secondary structure** is the first level of protein folding, in which parts of the chain fold to form generic structures that are found in all proteins. The **tertiary structure** is produced by the additional combination, folding and packing together of these elements to ultimately provide 3D conformation that is exclusive to the protein. Many functional proteins are formed of more than one protein chain, in which case the individual chains are called protein subunits. The subunit composition and arrangement in such multi-subunit proteins is called the **quaternary conformation**. The structure adopted by a protein chain, and thus its function, is controlled entirely by its amino acid sequence, however, the rules that determine how a protein chain of a given sequence folds up are poorly comprehended (Zvelebil & Baum, 2007). The prediction of the 3D structure of proteins from a linear sequence of amino acids has proven difficult. Thus, the study of more predictable protein structural features that are valuable to the prediction of 3D structure of proteins (e.g. secondary structure) has been performed by many researchers (Hanson, Paliwal, Litfin, Yang, & Zhou, 2018).

Figure 1. Graphic illustrations of different levels of protein (Campbell et al., 2007)

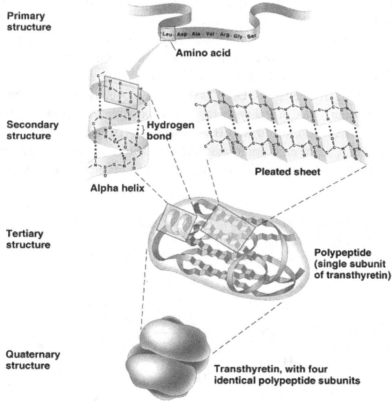

Amino Acids

Proteins are made up of 20 types of naturally existing amino acids. Each amino acid comprises a central alpha-carbon atom, a carboxyl group and an amino group on both ends, and a variable side-chain (see Figure 2). The side chain of the amino acid can affect the physicochemical characteristics of the amino acid such as mass, polarity, acidity, hydrophobicity, and electron charge. The functional properties of proteins are almost entirely due to side chain interactions (Zvelebil & Baum, 2007). The physicochemical features of amino acids significantly impact the secondary structures of proteins, and can be utilized for the prediction of protein secondary structures (Hanson et al., 2018). The 20 amino acids can be classified into eight groups based on the similarity of their physicochemical features, specifically, hydrophobic, hydrophilic; polar, non-polar; small, large; charged, uncharged (Pok, Jin, & Ryu, 2008). These eight characteristic physicochemical features can be applied to encode each amino acid residue and to obtain correlative data with respect to the creation of protein secondary structure. The hydrophobic, hydrogen bond and charge physicochemical features have the most considerable effect on the secondary structures of protein, hence they are often the most utilized physicochemical features in PSSP (Qu, Sui, Yang, & Qian, 2011).

Protein Secondary Structure

Comparison of the protein structural levels shows that the protein secondary structure plays the most critical role in the study of proteins. It comprises the primary fold of the polypeptide chain. Thus, the spatial structure of the protein is based on its secondary component. The secondary structure of the protein denotes the local conformations of the amino acid polypeptide due to interactions of the polypeptide backbone (Voet & Voet, 2011). Precisely, there are several methods of classifying the secondary structure of proteins, such as DSSP (Kabsch & Sander, 1983), STRIDE (Frishman & Argos, 1995), and DEFINE (Richards & Kundrot, 1988). Nonetheless, DSSP is the most frequently utilized technique in predicting the secondary structure of proteins. In reality, there are eight possible secondary structure conformations in a given protein: 3-turn helix (G), 4-turn helix (H), 5-turn helix (I), β-strand (E), β-bridge (B), bend (S), turn (T), and no structure (C). The eight conformations of protein secondary structure are further simplified into three states by the following transformation: G, H and I are altered into H (α-helix), B and E are

Figure 2 The general structure of an amino acid (Zvelebil & Baum, 2007)

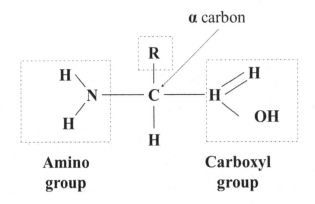

converted into E (β-strand), whereas the others are transformed into C (coil). The diverse classification approaches for these eight classes significantly affects the predicted results (Y. Zhang & Sagui, 2015).

Hence, it is almost necessary to assess the accuracy of a set of predictions to determine the most accurate method available and also to identify successful improvements in developing and tuning parameters for new methods. Alternative measures have been proposed, some looking at the level of individual residues such as Q_3 accuracy for 3-state secondary structure and Q_8 accuracy for 8-state secondary structure, others focusing on complete helices and strands such as SOV_3 and SOV_8 (Zemla, Venclovas, Fidelis, & Rost, 1999) for 3- and 8-state secondary structures, respectively.

SECONDARY STRUCTURE PREDICTION APPROACHES

The prediction of the secondary structure of proteins has always been an issue in bioinformatics (Yang et al., 2018). Several methods were proposed for the prediction of the secondary structure of proteins. These methods can be roughly subdivided into: **statistical**, **nearest-neighbour**, **machine learning**, **meta-predictors**, and **deep learning** approaches, see Figure 3. This subdivision illustrates how the methods have developed over time, and how new structural information has been combined with advances in computer technology. Statistical methods are developed according to the probability that an amino acid will produce a specific secondary structure. Nearest-neighbour methods apply pre-existing knowledge of resolved protein structures to a particular section of the target protein sequence. Machine learning methods train a learning algorithm to acquire structure-sequence relationships, which can subsequently

Figure 3. Illustration of protein secondary structure prediction approaches with their representative methods

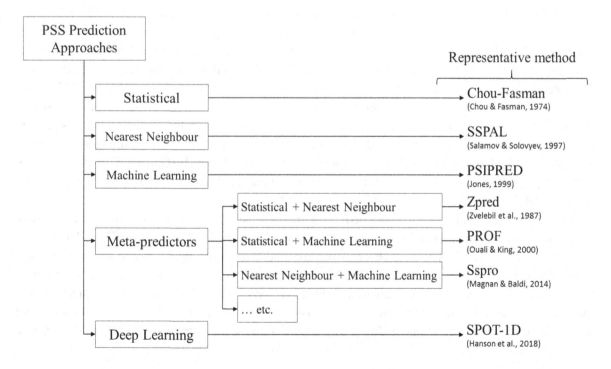

be implemented to predict the secondary structure states of the target protein sequence. Meta-predictors methods combine a set of complementary techniques to improve the general accuracy of the prediction. Deep learning methods are the cutting-edge and influential machine learning techniques for predicting protein secondary structure. A more comprehensive explanation and overview of this subdivision is presented below.

Statistical Approach

Statistical methods utilize parameters derived from the sequence analyses of recognized protein structures to form statistical rules, given the probability that an amino acid will produce a specific secondary structure state. However, early statistical methods suffered from lack of data because of the few experimentally unravelled 3D structures obtainable at the protein data bank. However, this is currently not a problem for globular proteins using simple statistical models. For many years, the most extensively applied statistical technique has been that of Chou and Fasman (1974), which was developed in the 1970s. Later, this method is superseded by more accurate statistical methods, such as the GOR method (Garnier, Osguthorpe, & Robson, 1978), which make assignments based on stretches of amino acid residues.

The method of Chou and Fasman was originally based on an examination of 15 proteins with about 2,400 amino acids (Chou & Fasman, 1974). Later, the analysis was extended on larger data sets of 29 proteins (Chou & Fasman, 1977), 64 proteins (Chou, 1989), and 144 proteins with an aggregate of 33,118 amino acids (Kyngäs & Valjakka, 1998). This method simply assigns individual amino acids as α- or β-formers, indifferent, and α- or β-breakers. Short segments composed of formers (with the absence of many breakers) were assigned as the core of an α-helix or β-strand. The boundaries of secondary structure elements were delineated by the presence of strong breakers. The method attained a 3-state prediction accuracy of ~55%.

Garnier et al. (1978) make predictions based on stretches of amino acid residues in the protein sequence, thus, enabling the consideration of local interactions between amino acid residues. Over the years, the GOR method has been continuously enhanced by incorporating more detailed statistics and larger databases. GOR I (Garnier et al., 1978) used a dataset of 26 proteins with approximately 4,500 amino acids and reached a 3-state prediction accuracy of 56%. GOR II (Gibrat, 1986) used a larger dataset of 75 proteins containing 12,757 amino acids and reached a 3-state prediction accuracy of 57.7%. Both versions used singlet frequency information within a 17-long window to predict the secondary structure states. GOR III (Gibrat, Garnier, & Robson, 1987) used further data relating to the frequencies of pairs of amino acids within the 17-long window of better refinement 68 proteins containing 11237 amino acids. The method reached a 3-state prediction accuracy of 63%. GOR IV (Garnier, Gibrat, & Robson, 1996) employed 267 protein chains comprising 63,566 amino acids and reached 3-state prediction accuracy of 64.4%.

The evolutionary information, obtained from multiple sequence alignments using PSI-BLAST (Altschul et al., 1997), has been included in the latest version GOR V (Kloczkowski, Ting, Jernigan, & Garnier, 2002). In the GOR V, a secondary structure prediction is obtained for each separate homologous sequence. These are then combined using the sequence alignment to identify equivalent amino acid residues. The structural state prediction score is averaged over all the sequences at each position of the query sequence. The final prediction at each position is the structural state with the highest average score. This could be subsequently modified by a filter to remove short strands and helices. The GOR V used 513 non-homologous protein chains containing 84,107 amino acids and reached a 3-state prediction accuracy of 73.5%.

In summary, statistical methods were employed to correlate structural and sequence features with the aim of forming statistical rules for the prediction of the secondary structure of proteins. The initial effort involved the correlation of the content of specified amino acids with that of an α-helix. This concept was extended for the correlation of the contents of all amino acids with those of α-helix and β-strand conformations. Furthermore, the information theory has been utilized to consider the local interactions between amino acids within a resizable window. The evolutionary information offered by multiple sequence alignments was also considered in the prediction process. Statistical methods are the earliest approach for predicting the secondary structure of proteins, and formed the basis for many subsequent approaches. Furthermore, they are easy to use and provide results that are easy to interpret. However, the accuracy is still relatively low. The statistical methods 3-state prediction accuracy has reached as high as 73.5%. Table 1 tabulates the performance accuracy of selected statistical methods.

Nearest-Neighbour Approach

The statistical prediction methods involve analysing recognized protein structures domiciled at the protein data bank to determine individual amino acid or amino acid pairing preferences, and prescribing a technique that combines these into a prediction. In contrast, nearest-neighbour methods directly apply the raw data of the observed protein structure domiciled in the protein data bank to a specified section of the target protein sequence. The approach adopts the principle that proteins with analogous sequences share the same fold and applies it at the level of short stretches of sequence. Furthermore, it assumes that even in a set of non-homologous proteins, short stretches of similar sequence could occupy the same secondary structure state.

The basic procedure of nearest-neighbour methods is as follows. First, for an individual segment of the target protein sequence, the best gapless alignments are retrieved from the data bank containing the recognized proteins. This often involves the implementation of a scoring scheme developed specifically for the task. Then, a set of the highest-scoring alignments are utilized to predict the structural state of the central amino acid for each segment. The prediction mainly involves taking the most commonly found states of the aligned amino acid, although it may also include weighted scores.

Despite the availability of many substitution-scoring matrices used in sequence alignment, most of nearest-neighbour secondary structure prediction methods frequently derived their own scoring schemes (Zvelebil & Baum, 2007). Early nearest-neighbour methods (Levin & Garnier, 1988; Levin, Robson, &

Table 1. Summary of the performance accuracy of selected statistical methods

Author	$Q_3\%$	$SOV_3\%$
(Chou & Fasman, 1974)	55.0	
(Garnier et al., 1978)	56.0	
(Gibrat, 1986)	57.7	
(Gibrat et al., 1987)	63.0	
(Garnier et al., 1996)	64.4	
(Kloczkowski et al., 2002)	73.5	70.8

Garnier, 1986) used their own scoring matrices so that all segments whose alignment scores exceeded a cut-off value are included in the prediction. They used a window of 7-8 amino acid residues with a score cut-off value of 3-7 and obtained the 3-state prediction accuracy of 63% and 58%, respectively. Salzberg and Cost (1992) used distance tables, which describe the numeric distance between each amino acid pairs as well as attaching weights to each retrieved segment. Their method achieved a 3-state prediction accuracy of 71.0%.

Levin (1997) updated an earlier work (Levin & Garnier, 1988) to obtain a 3-state prediction accuracy of 72.8%. The modifications include the use of the Blosum62 matrix (Henikoff & Henikoff, 1992) as a scoring system and the use of an expanded dataset of recognized protein structures. Salamov & Solovyev (1997) implemented a combination of local structural environment scores and score matrix to calculate the top 50 non-intersected discrete alignments of the target protein sequence with each protein sequence at the protein data bank to achieve a 3-state prediction accuracy of 73.5%.

In a nutshell, nearest-neighbour methods apply the annotation of recognized protein structures stored in protein structure databases to predict the secondary structure states of the target protein sequence at the level of short segments. However, the main practical issue with this method is the lack of structural information on all possible segment sequences, hence similar sequences need to be examined. The key difficulty is defining the nearest-neighbour sequences using a quantitative measure. Another problem associated with this approach is that several proteins have alternate folds, with some regions having significantly different secondary structure states under different conditions (W. Li, Kinch, Karplus, & Grishin, 2015). The 3-state prediction accuracy of nearest-neighbour methods reached as high as 73.5%. Table 2 tabulates the performance accuracy of selected nearest-neighbour methods.

Machine Learning Approach

The secondary structure prediction methods discussed so far rely on some form of carefully designed model and statistical analysis of the existing protein structure data to obtain the prediction. Machine learning methods appear to lack this element of design. They simply use protein annotation with recognized structures that are domiciled in the protein structure database to train a machine learning model, which is then used to predict the secondary structure states of the target protein sequence. The most frequently used machine learning techniques for predicting secondary structure are support vector machines, hidden Markov models, and neural networks (Yoo et al., 2008). The neural network models of Qian and Sejnowski (1988) and of Holley and Karplus (1989) were two of the early methods of machine learning for predicting the secondary structure of proteins.

Table 2. Summary the performance accuracy of selected nearest-neighbour methods

Author	$Q_3\%$	$SOV_3\%$
(Levin et al., 1986)	58.0	
(Levin & Garnier, 1988)	63.0	
(Salzberg & Cost, 1992)	71.0	
(Levin, 1997)	72.8	
(Salamov & Solovyev, 1997)	73.5	

One of the most important aspects of neural networks is the way the input data are encoded within the network (Zvelebil & Baum, 2007). Holley and Karplus (1989) constructed a neural network model to predict the state of the secondary structure of the amino acid at the centre of 17-long windows. Twenty-one bits are used to encode each of the 20 amino acids. The additional bit is utilized to indicate whether the window overlaps the N-terminal or the C-terminal of the protein sequence. The neural network architecture includes a hidden layer and an output layer with two nodes in each layer. The method obtained a 3-state prediction accuracy of 63.2%. Qian and Sejnowski (1988) used the same coding for input data with marginally dissimilar network architecture. They considered 13-long windows in the input layer and had three nodes in the output layer. They also used a cascade of neural networks to capture correlations between secondary structure predictions of adjacent amino acid residues. This method obtained a 3-state prediction accuracy of 64.3%.

Rost and Sander significantly improved the prediction accuracy by integrating the evolutionary information encoded in multiple sequence alignments into a neural network model (Rost & Sander, 1993). Instead of using 20 bits to encode each amino acid, the normalized frequencies of the 20 amino acids occurring in the equivalent column of the multiple sequence alignment are used. This method increased the 3-state prediction accuracy to >70%.

The prediction accuracy of the neural network-based methods was further improved using additional accurate evolutionary information derived from larger databases and enhanced searches (Jones, 1999). Jones developed a neural network-based secondary structure prediction model using the PSI-BLAST (Altschul et al., 1997) sequence profile as input data. This model achieved a 3-state prediction accuracy of 76.5%. Cuff and Barton combined diverse kinds of multiple sequence alignment profiles derived from the same sequences to obtain different values of 3-state prediction accuracy that ranged from 70.5% to 76.4%, depending on the data set evaluated (Cuff & Barton, 2000).

Further improvement in the prediction accuracy was achieved by combining different protein structural representations into neural networks. Wood and Hirst used the PSI-BLAST (Altschul et al., 1997) sequence profile to develop an iterative neural network model for predicting both the secondary structure and the ψ dihedral angles. The study achieved predictive values better than earlier iterations and obtained an overall 3-state prediction accuracy of 79.4% (Wood & Hirst, 2005). Yaseen and Li encoded statistical context-based scores together with the PSI-BLAST sequence profile to train a neural network model and developed a prediction method that achieved a 3-state prediction accuracy of 80.7% (Yaseen & Li, 2014). In addition to neural network models, other machine learning models have been used to develop secondary structure prediction systems such as the probabilistic networks models (Bystroff, Thorsson, & Baker, 2000; Schmidler, Liu, & Brutlag, 2000) obtained a 3-state prediction accuracy of 74.3%. Moreover, support vector machine models have been employed to predict the secondary structure of proteins (Karypis, 2006; Kim & Park, 2003), reaching a 3-state prediction accuracy of 77.8%.

In summary, machine learning methods use the annotation of the known protein structures at protein structure databases to build models for predicting the secondary structure states of the target protein sequence. Machine learning approach is potentially very powerful because it can in principle represent the relationship between some input data and the output. Furthermore, machine learning methods can be parameterized by giving test sequences and their correct secondary structure without any other information. However, these methods are fully reliant on the input windows of neighbouring amino acid residue data, implying they are incapable of wholly learning the relationship between the amino acid residues in the entire protein sequence. The 3-state prediction accuracy values of all aforementioned machine learning methods were slightly above 80%. Table 3 tabulates the performance accuracy of selected machine learning methods.

Meta-Predictors Approach

Meta-predictors methods use a mixture of previous techniques. The fundamental theory of this approach is that different types of algorithms can be combined to enhance the prediction of the secondary structure of proteins. Nearest-neighbour and machine learning methods significantly improved the prediction accuracy when a set of query derived similar fragments are available in the protein data bank, but are ineffective when such perfectly similar fragments are absent. Conversely, statistical methods fairly accurately predict the secondary structures of less comparable fragments, even in the absence of appropriate structural fragments. The meta-predictors approach involves the combination of the outputs of several complementary methods so as to enhance the overall prediction of the secondary structure of proteins.

Early meta-predictors methods combined statistical and nearest-neighbour methods (e.g., Zpred (Zvelebil, Barton, Taylor, & Sternberg, 1987)). Zpred uses the GOR method (Gibrat, 1986) to obtain the secondary structure labels for each separate homologous sequence. These are then combined using the sequence alignment to identify equivalent residues. The structural state prediction score is averaged over all the sequences at each locus of the query sequence. A residue conservation score is calculated at each alignment location according to the classification of amino acid properties introduced by Taylor

Table 3. Summary of the performance accuracy of selected machine learning methods

Author	Q_3%	SOV_3%
Neural Network Methods		
(Qian & Sejnowski, 1988)	64.3	
(Holley & Karplus, 1989)	63.2	
(Rost & Sander, 1993)	69.7	
(Jones, 1999)	76.5	78.7
(Cuff & Barton, 2000)	76.4	74.2
(Wood & Hirst, 2005)	79.4	77.5
(Yaseen & Li, 2014)	80.7	83.9
Probabilistic Network Methods		
(Asai, Hayamizu, & Handa, 1993)	54.0	
(Schmidler et al., 2000)	68.8	
(Bystroff et al., 2000)	74.3	
Support Vector Machine Methods		
(Hua & Sun, 2001)	73.5	76.2
(Ward, McGuffin, Buxton, & Jones, 2003)	74.2	68.3
(Kim & Park, 2003)	76.6	80.1
(Karypis, 2006)	77.8	75

(1986). The residue conservation score is assigned to the averaged prediction at each site of the query sequence. The final prediction at each position is the structural state with the maximum average score. The prediction accuracy of the Zpred technique exceeds that of GOR alone by 9%.

Moreover, meta-predictors methods of statistical and neural network models have been proposed, this includes PROF (Ouali & King, 2000) and YASPIN (K. Lin, Simossis, Taylor, & Heringa, 2005). PROF is formed by cascading different types of prediction, different versions of GOR technique (Garnier et al., 1996, 1978; Gibrat, 1986; Gibrat et al., 1987), and different alignment algorithms within one program using neural networks to choose the final prediction. The PROF method obtained a 3-state prediction accuracy of 76.7%. YASPIN uses a combination of neural networks and hidden Markov model methods, attaining a 3-state prediction accuracy of 77%.

Furthermore, meta-predictors methods of nearest-neighbour and neural networks model have been proposed, this includes PROTEUS (Montgomerie, Sundararaj, Gallin, & Wishart, 2006), PORTER (Mirabello & Pollastri, 2013) and SSPro (Magnan & Baldi, 2014). PROTEUS uses a set of query derived similar fragments from the protein data bank for predicting the secondary structures when homologous are obtainable in the protein data bank, and a jury of neural network-based secondary structure prediction methods when homologous are not available. PORTER combines the query derived similar fragments from the protein data bank with both the initial query sequence and equivalent PSI-BLAST profile to modify the input to a complex neural network ensemble. Similarly, SSPro combines the query derived similar fragments from the protein data bank to modify the prediction at the output level of a complex neural network.

Generally, the meta-predictors methods combine two or more complementary methods to improve the overall prediction of the secondary structure of proteins. The direct use of structural information contained in protein data bank accounts for the improved prediction of the secondary structure of proteins (Magnan & Baldi, 2014). This approach achieves a much better accuracy when homologous structures are obtainable in the protein data bank (Yang et al., 2018). However, when similar sequences are unavailable in the protein data bank, the approach performs slightly less than the previous approaches. Table 4 tabulates the performance accuracy of selected meta-predictors methods.

Deep Learning Approach

Deep learning is a subset of machine learning that enables the feasibility of the computation of multilayer neural networks (Goodfellow, Bengio, & Courville, 2016). Deep neural architectures have become popular tools in a wide variety of tasks including speech recognition (Amodei et al., 2016), image recognition

Table 4. Summary of the performance accuracy of selected meta-predictors methods

Author	Q_3%	SOV_3%
(Zvelebil et al., 1987)	66.0	
(Ouali & King, 2000)	76.7	73.7
(K. Lin et al., 2005)	77.0	73.8
(Montgomerie et al., 2006)	81.3	
(Mirabello & Pollastri, 2013)	82.2	
(Magnan & Baldi, 2014)	79.0 - 92.9	

(He, Zhang, Ren, & Sun, 2016), natural language processing (Sundermeyer, Schlüter, & Ney, 2012), and a versatile artificial intelligence instrument in bioinformatics (Jiang et al., 2017). In contrast to shallow learning models, deep learning encompasses relatively more multilayer nonlinear operational elements as its hidden layers (Schmidhuber, 2015), as shown in Figure 4. This enables the model to discover additional advanced features from raw data that are appropriate for the prediction process (Bengio & Delalleau, 2011). The pattern identification involved in the prediction of the secondary structure of proteins is highly nonlinear and complicated (Paliwal, Lyons, & Heffernan, 2015). Hence, several studies have attempted to explore the applications of deep learning in the prediction of the secondary structure of proteins because of its enormous potential and prospective effectiveness in processing bio-data.

Several deep neural networks were proposed for 3-state secondary structure problem (Heffernan et al., 2015; Qi, Oja, Weston, & Noble, 2012; Spencer, Eickholt, & Cheng, 2015) and subsequent attempts using convolutional (Busia & Jaitly, 2017; Fang, Shang, & Xu, 2018; Z. Lin, Lanchantin, & Qi, 2016; Zhou & Troyanskaya, 2014) and recurrent (Heffernan et al., 2017; Sønderby & Winther, 2014; Torrisi, Kaleel, & Pollastri, 2018) neural network architectures have achieved incremental improvement in deciphering the problem of 3- and 8-state secondary structure prediction. Moreover, convolutions combined with a Conditional Random Field (CRF) output layer (Wang, Peng, Ma, & Xu, 2016) or with recurrent neural networks (Hanson et al., 2018; Klausen et al., 2018; B. Zhang, Li, & Lü, 2018) have been utilized to improve performance on the 3- and 8-state secondary structure problem as well.

Taking inspiration from the natural language processing domain, Qi et al. (2012) created a multitask predictor to predict an array of local protein properties, which include the secondary structure of proteins, using a deep neural network (DNN) architecture. In addition to the evolutionary information captured using PSSM profiles, the study exploited a learned embedding to disseminate information across associated tasks with the aim of clearly mapping amino acid sequences into a feature space. This method achieved a 3-state prediction accuracy of 80.3%. Instead of using a learned embedding, physiochemical properties are used by Spencer et al. (2015) and Heffernan et al. (2015) to capture similarities information among amino acid types. Spencer et al. (2015) applied a deep belief network model to 3-state secondary structure prediction. Each layer in this model is a Restricted Boltzmann Machine (RBM) (Hinton & Salakhutdinov, 2006). This method achieved a 3-state prediction accuracy of 80.7%. Heffernan et al.

Figure 4. Schematic illustration of deep neural network (Jiang et al., 2017)

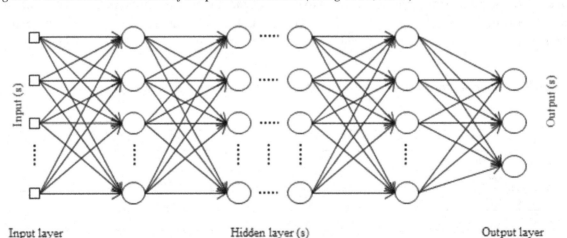

Input layer   Hidden layer (s)   Output layer

(2015) developed a multi-step iterative Stacked Spars Auto-Encoder (SSAE) deep neural network model that predicts four diverse sets of structural properties including protein secondary structure and achieved a 3-state prediction accuracy of 81.8%.

With the advent of deep learning techniques, recent efforts have focused on the prediction of 8-state secondary structures (Yang et al., 2018). The 8-state prediction is a significantly more complex procedure than the 3-state prediction (Hanson et al., 2018). Zhou and Troyanskaya (2014) developed a deep learning approach to 8-state secondary structure prediction using a multi-layer convolutional supervised Generative Stochastic Network (GSN) (Bengio, Laufer, Alain, & Yosinski, 2014) and achieved an 8-state prediction accuracy of 66.4%. To leverage the spatial structure of the data, a deep convolutional neural network (CNN) architecture was developed by Z. Lin et al. (2016) for the prediction of protein properties. This architecture used a multilayer shift-and-stitch technique (Sermanet et al., 2013) to produce fully dense per-position predictions on protein sequences and achieved 68.4% 8-state prediction accuracy. Furthermore, a multi-scale convolutional architecture with residual connections have been integrated for secondary structure prediction (Busia & Jaitly, 2017; Fang et al., 2018) and achieved an 8-state prediction accuracy of 71.4%.

Recurrent neural networks have proved more useful for sequential data (Amodei et al., 2016; Sundermeyer et al., 2012). Sønderby and Winther (2014) applied a Bidirectional Long Short-Term Memory (BLSTM) neural network model to 8-state secondary structure prediction and achieved 67.4% prediction accuracy. Heffernan et al. (2017) applied BLSTM in place of SSAE neural network architecture used in their previous multitask predictor (Heffernan et al., 2015) and improved the performance accuracy for all predicted tasks. The use of BLSTM, in addition to using the evolutionary information captured by the PSSM and HHblits profiles, further improves the 3-state prediction performance to 84.5%. Torrisi et al. (2018) employed an ensemble of Bidirectional Recurrent Neural Networks (BRNN) using sequence profiles from multiple sequence alignment generated by PSI-BLAST (Altschul et al., 1997) and HHblits (Remmert, Biegert, Hauser, & Söding, 2011) algorithms. This method achieved 73% and 84.2% for 8- and 3-state prediction, respectively.

Furthermore, a combination of convolutions with sequential models (e.g., CRF, RNN) have been utilized to improve performance on the 3- and 8-state secondary structure problem. Wang et al. (2016) combined consecutive of five convolutional layers with a CRF output layer and demonstrated convincing improvements on the prediction accuracy. Z. Li and Yu (2016) utilized a multitask learning to achieve 69.7% and 84% for 8- and 3-state predictions, respectively, using a collection of 10 independently trained models, with each consisting of a multi-scale convolutional layer followed by three layers of Bidirectional Gated Recurrent Units (BGRU). Klausen et al. (2018) employed a multitask learning using a multi-scale convolutional layer of large kernel sizes followed by two BLSTM layers and achieved 72.3% and 85.3% for 8- and 3-state prediction, respectively.

More recently, predictors of protein secondary structure have been proposed using convolutional, residual, and recurrent neural networks. Zhang et al. (2018) utilized a multi-scale convolutional layer flowed by three BGRU layers with residual connections to predict 3- and 8-state secondary structure. This method achieved 74% for 8-state prediction and 87.3% for 3-state prediction. Hanson et al. (2018) employed a multitask learning using an ensemble of nine independently trained models, each comprised of residual convolutional layers (ResNet) (He et al., 2016) and BLSTM layers. This method predicts six different sets of structural properties, including protein secondary structure, and achieved 77.1% and 87.2% for 8- and 3-state prediction, respectively.

In summary, traditional machine learning techniques, which include support vector machines, hidden Markov models and shallow neural networks are constrained by the complexity of the functions they can learn efficiently. Deep learning techniques have been proven to outperform these traditional techniques in a wide variety of areas (Amodei et al., 2016; He et al., 2016; Sundermeyer et al., 2012). The key advantage of deep learning is the ability to efficiently exploit large volume of data and high computing power. In recent times, prediction accuracy of the secondary structure of protein has been considerably enhanced, which can be attributed to the fast growth of resolved protein structures stored in protein structure databases as well as developments in deep learning methods, e.g. residual and multi-scale convolutional networks (He et al., 2016; Szegedy et al., 2015), and BRNNs (Hochreiter & Schmidhuber, 1997; Schuster & Paliwal, 1997). The 3-state prediction accuracy of deep learning methods described above has reached as high as 87%, approaching the theoretical upper limits of effective 3-state secondary structure prediction accuracy of 88-90% (Rost, 2001; Yang et al., 2018). Furthermore, deep learning methods significantly improved the prediction accuracy of 8-state secondary structure, reaching as high as 77% Q_8 accuracy. Table 5 tabulates detailed information of models architecture, data used, and performance accuracies achieved in selected deep learning-based methods.

DISCUSSION

The last few decades have witnessed significant improvements in the prediction of secondary structure. Diverse algorithms have been implemented for the prediction of the secondary structure of proteins. These algorithms have advanced from simple linear statistical models to complex machine learning models. The prediction has increasingly improved, consistently with advances in computational techniques, as well as the development and increased accessibility of solved protein structures stored in the protein data

Table 5. Summary of the models architecture, data used, and performance accuracies achieved in selected deep learning-based methods

Author	Neural Network Architecture	Ensemble	Multitask	Train Data	Test Data	Q_3%	Q_8%
(Qi et al., 2012)	DNN		✓	11,795	513	80.3	
(Zhou & Troyanskaya, 2014)	GSN		✓	5,600	513		66.4
(Sønderby & Winther, 2014)	BLSTM			5,600	513		67.4
(Spencer et al., 2015)	RBM			1,230	198	80.7	
(Heffernan et al., 2015)	SSAE		✓	5,600	1,199	81.8	
(Z. Lin et al., 2016)	CNN		✓	11,795	513		68.4
(Wang et al., 2016)	CNN; CRF			5,600	513	82.3	68.3
(Z. Li & Yu, 2016)	CNN; BGRU	✓	✓	5,600	513	84.0	69.7
(Heffernan et al., 2017)	BLSTM		✓	5,600	1,199	84.5	
(Busia & Jaitly, 2017)	CNN	✓		5,600	513		71.4
(Fang et al., 2018)	CNN			9,000	513		70.6
(Torrisi et al., 2018)	BRNN	✓		15,800	3,155	84.2	73.0
(Klausen et al., 2018)	CNN; BLSTM		✓	10,337	513	85.3	72.0
(B. Zhang et al., 2018)	CNN; BGRU	✓		11,700	513	87.3	74.0
(Hanson et al., 2018)	ResNet; BLSTM	✓	✓	10,029	1,213	87.2	77.1

banks in addition to the advancement of alignment algorithms. A minor enhancement in the prediction accuracy of secondary structure can considerably resolve several research issues and the associated software tools (Fang et al., 2018). The 3-state prediction accuracy of 55% achieved in 1974 by Chou and Fasman (1974) was increased to 70% by PHD server (Rost & Sander, 1993), to 82% by PORTER using BRNNs (Mirabello & Pollastri, 2013), and to 87% by SPOT-1D using structural features prediction by an ensemble of residual convolutional and BLSTM models (Hanson et al., 2018), see Figure 5. Besides the 3-state prediction, deep learning-based approaches were applied to predict 8-state secondary structure, reaching Q8 prediction accuracy range of 72-77%.

Concisely, the development of the prediction techniques of the secondary structure of proteins is presented in this chapter. Early methods correlate structural and sequence features to form statistical rules for prediction of the secondary structure of proteins. Subsequent methods used the annotation of the recognized protein structures stored in protein structure databases to develop prediction models of secondary structure. In present times, deep learning techniques have evolved into the most popular approach for the prediction of protein secondary structure, due to their capacity to extract significant and tiered representations from large datasets (Torrisi et al., 2018).

Recent advances including the availability of progressively larger training data sets, utilizing of different methods to leverage evolutionary information, use of multitask learning, and use of an ensemble of several independently trained models, have enhanced the secondary structure prediction accuracy. For examples, the large dataset size of 10029 proteins contributed to an improvement in the 3-state secondary structure predictions of SPIDER3 (Heffernan et al., 2017) by about 1.6% compared to the previously reported prediction accuracy when using a dataset size of 5600 proteins (Hanson et al., 2018). Using two different algorithms, PSI-BLAST (Altschul et al., 1997) and HHblits (Remmert et al., 2011), to extract evolutionary information boosted the prediction accuracy to some extent (Fang et al., 2018; Hanson et al., 2018; Torrisi et al., 2018).

Multitask learning methods used similarities among amino acid types along with the evolutionary information to perform secondary structure predictions (Heffernan et al., 2017; Z. Lin et al., 2016; Qi et al., 2012; Zhou & Troyanskaya, 2014). To capture these similarities, several secondary structure methods used the amino acid's physiochemical properties (Fang et al., 2018; Spencer et al., 2015). Other methods used a learned embedding matrix to transform the sparse one-hot encoding of each amino acid into a denser representation (Busia & Jaitly, 2017; Z. Li & Yu, 2016; Z. Lin et al., 2016; Qi et al., 2012). A combination of embedding matrix and physiochemical properties of the amino acids is also used (B. Zhang et al., 2018). Other multitask learning methods used structural features of protein such as backbone

Figure 5. The improving history of predicting protein secondary structure

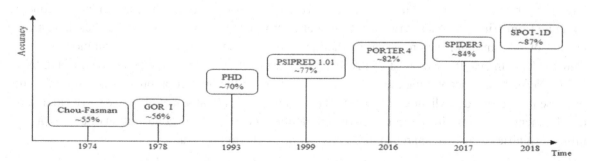

angles, solvent accessibility, and contact numbers, for prediction (Hanson et al., 2018; Klausen et al., 2018). In addition to multitasking, ensemble learning is also used to improve the prediction performance (Haas et al., 2018; Z. Li & Yu, 2016).

Generally, deep learning techniques have managed to incrementally improve performance on secondary structure problem, beginning with the use of their capacity to extract valuable and tiered representations from protein sequences. This include the use of DNN (Qi et al., 2012), convolutional GSN (Zhou & Troyanskaya, 2014), RBM (Spencer et al., 2015), and SSAE (Heffernan et al., 2015). Moreover, translation-invariant deep learning architectures are applied to extract local contextual representations from protein sequences (Busia & Jaitly, 2017; Fang et al., 2018; Z. Lin et al., 2016). Furthermore, considering non-local interactions existing in amino acid sequences, bidirectional recurrent neural networks are applied to extract local and global contextual representations (Heffernan et al., 2017; Sønderby & Winther, 2014; Torrisi et al., 2018). Furthermore, combining different types of deep learning architectures has been used for secondary structure problem, taking the advantage of their ability to capture local and/or nonlocal interactions. This include CNN and CRF (Wang et al., 2016), CNN and BGRU (Z. Li & Yu, 2016), CNN and BLSTM (Klausen et al., 2018), CNN and BGRU (B. Zhang et al., 2018), as well as ResNet and BLTSM (Hanson et al., 2018). Deep learning techniques have achieved incremental improvement in the prediction performance of 3-state secondary structure. Nonetheless, their prediction performance decreases when protein sequences with few known homologous sequences are predicted (Hanson et al., 2018). Therefore, it is crucial to develop secondary structure prediction techniques for sparse sequence profiles. Moreover, due to imbalanced dataset problem, advancement in prediction was hindered in the case of the more complex 8-state secondary structure prediction. This occurs since deep learning algorithms are typically developed to enhance the prediction accuracy by minimizing the error. Hence, the balance of classes is not considered by the deep learning techniques. However, combining deep models with different methods to resolve such class imbalance issues could be more helpful for the 8-state secondary structure problem.

CONCLUSION

This review illustrates how the prediction methods of secondary structure have developed with time, and how new structural information combined with computer technology have been incorporated into prediction models to improve their outcomes. The leading development since the inception of secondary structure prediction is the exploitation of evolutionary information that is exist in homologous proteins, as well as the use of deep learning techniques with improved capability to manipulate sequential data. However, proteins with few sequence homologs have very sparse sequence profile, and hence do not fare well. Their predictions are not very helpful to ab initio folding. Thus, the prediction of secondary structure from primary sequence rather than sequence profile remains challenging. Furthermore, a large portion of relevant information on the prediction of the secondary structure of an amino acid arises from the local interactions amongst relatively few of the directly neighbouring residues (Busia & Jaitly, 2017). Nevertheless, accounting the non-local interactions in the prediction process is essential to improve sequence-based prediction of protein structural properties (Hanson et al., 2018). Prioritizing the development of features that can enhance the prediction process over the contribution of only sequence profiles signifies a positive approach to improving the prediction accuracy.

REFERENCES

Altschul, S. F., Madden, T. L., Schäffer, A. A., Zhang, J., Zhang, Z., Miller, W., & Lipman, D. J. (1997). Gapped BLAST and PSI-BLAST: A new generation of protein database search programs. *Nucleic Acids Research*, *25*(17), 3389–3402. doi:10.1093/nar/25.17.3389 PMID:9254694

Amodei, D., Ananthanarayanan, S., Anubhai, R., Bai, J., Battenberg, E., & Case, C., … Zhu, Z. (2016). Deep Speech 2: End-to-end speech recognition in English and Mandarin. In M. F. Balcan, & K. Q. Weinberger (Eds.), *Proceedings of The 33rd International Conference on Machine Learning* (Vol. 48, pp. 173–182). New York, NY: PMLR.

Asai, K., Hayamizu, S., & Handa, K. (1993). Prediction of protein secondary structure by the hidden Markov model. *Bioinformatics (Oxford, England)*, *9*(2), 141–146. doi:10.1093/bioinformatics/9.2.141 PMID:8481815

Bengio, Y., & Delalleau, O. (2011). On the expressive power of deep architecture. Berlin: Springer Berlin Heidelberg.

Bengio, Y., Laufer, E., Alain, G., & Yosinski, J. (2014). Deep generative stochastic networks trainable by backprop. In E. P. Xing, & T. Jebara (Eds.), *Proceedings of the 31st International Conference on Machine Learning* (Vol. 32, pp. 226–234). Beijing, China: PMLR.

Bruce, A., Alexander, J., Julian, L., Martin, R., Keith, R., & Walter, P. (2015). *Molecular biology of the cell* (6th ed.). New York, NY: Garland Science.

Busia, A., & Jaitly, N. (2017). Next-step conditioned deep convolutional neural networks improve protein secondary structure prediction. *CoRR, abs/1702.0*.

Bystroff, C., Thorsson, V., & Baker, D. (2000). HMMSTR: A hidden Markov model for local sequence–structure correlations in proteins. *Journal of Molecular Biology*, *301*(1), 173–190. doi:10.1006/jmbi.2000.3837 PMID:10926500

Campbell, N. A., Reece, J. B., Urry, L. A., Cain, M. L., Wasserman, S. A., Beth, W., & Jackson, R. B. (2007). *Biology* (8th ed.). San Francisco, CA: Pearson.

Chakravarty, S., & Varadarajan, R. (1999). Residue depth: A novel parameter for the analysis of protein structure and stability. *Structure (London, England)*, *7*(7), 723–732. doi:10.1016/S0969-2126(99)80097-5 PMID:10425675

Chou, P. Y. (1989). Prediction of protein structural classes from amino acid compositions. In G. D. Fasman (Ed.), *Prediction of Protein Structure and the Principles of Protein Conformation* (pp. 549–586). Boston, MA: Springer US. doi:10.1007/978-1-4613-1571-1_12

Chou, P. Y., & Fasman, G. D. (1974). Prediction of protein conformation. *Biochemistry*, *13*(2), 222–245. doi:10.1021/bi00699a002 PMID:4358940

Chou, P. Y., & Fasman, G. D. (1977). Secondary structural prediction of proteins from their amino acid sequence. *Trends in Biochemical Sciences*, *2*(6), 128–131. doi:10.1016/0968-0004(77)90440-6

Cuff, J. A., & Barton, G. J. (2000). Application of multiple sequence alignment profiles to improve protein secondary structure prediction. *Proteins*, *40*(3), 502–511. doi:10.1002/1097-0134(20000815)40:3<502::AID-PROT170>3.0.CO;2-Q PMID:10861942

Fang, C., Shang, Y., & Xu, D. (2018). MUFOLD-SS: New deep inception-inside-inception networks for protein secondary structure prediction. *Proteins*, *86*(5), 592–598. doi:10.1002/prot.25487 PMID:29492997

Frishman, D., & Argos, P. (1995). Knowledge-based protein secondary structure assignment. *Proteins*, *23*(4), 566–579. doi:10.1002/prot.340230412 PMID:8749853

Garnier, J., Gibrat, J. F., & Robson, B. (1996). GOR method for predicting protein secondary structure from amino acid sequence. In *Computer Methods for Macromolecular Sequence Analysis* (Vol. 266, pp. 540–553). Academic Press. doi:10.1016/S0076-6879(96)66034-0

Garnier, J., Osguthorpe, D. J., & Robson, B. (1978). Analysis of the accuracy and implications of simple methods for predicting the secondary structure of globular proteins. *Journal of Molecular Biology*, *120*(1), 97–120. doi:10.1016/0022-2836(78)90297-8 PMID:642007

Gibrat, J. F. (1986). *Modelisation by computers of the 3-D Structure of Proteins* (PhD Thesis). University of Paris VI.

Gibrat, J. F., Garnier, J., & Robson, B. (1987). Further developments of protein secondary structure prediction using information theory: New parameters and consideration of residue pairs. *Journal of Molecular Biology*, *198*(3), 425–443. doi:10.1016/0022-2836(87)90292-0 PMID:3430614

Goodfellow, I., Bengio, Y., & Courville, A. (2016). *Deep learning*. Cambridge, UK: MIT Press.

Haas, J., Barbato, A., Behringer, D., Studer, G., Roth, S., Bertoni, M., ... Schwede, T. (2018). Continuous Automated Model EvaluatiOn (CAMEO) complementing the critical assessment of structure prediction in CASP12. *Proteins*, *86*(S1), 387–398. doi:10.1002/prot.25431 PMID:29178137

Hamelryck, T. (2005). An amino acid has two sides: A new 2D measure provides a different view of solvent exposure. *Proteins*, *59*(1), 38–48. doi:10.1002/prot.20379 PMID:15688434

Hanson, J., Paliwal, K., Litfin, T., Yang, Y., & Zhou, Y. (2018). Improving Prediction of Protein Secondary Structure, Backbone Angles, Solvent Accessibility, and Contact Numbers by Using Predicted Contact Maps and an Ensemble of Recurrent and Residual Convolutional Neural Networks. *Bioinformatics*. PMID:30535134

Hanson, J., Yang, Y., Paliwal, K., & Zhou, Y. (2017). Improving protein disorder prediction by deep bidirectional long short-term memory recurrent neural networks. *Bioinformatics (Oxford, England)*, *33*(5), 685–692. PMID:28011771

He, K., Zhang, X., Ren, S., & Sun, J. (2016). Deep residual learning for image recognition. *The IEEE Conference on Computer Vision and Pattern Recognition (CVPR)*.

Heffernan, R., Paliwal, K., Lyons, J., Dehzangi, A., Sharma, A., Wang, J., ... Zhou, Y. (2015). Improving prediction of secondary structure, local backbone angles, and solvent accessible surface area of proteins by iterative deep learning. *Scientific Reports*, *5*(1), 11476. doi:10.1038rep11476 PMID:26098304

Heffernan, R., Yang, Y., Paliwal, K., & Zhou, Y. (2017). Capturing non-local interactions by long short-term memory bidirectional recurrent neural networks for improving prediction of protein secondary structure, backbone angles, contact numbers and solvent accessibility. *Bioinformatics (Oxford, England)*, *33*(18), 2842–2849. doi:10.1093/bioinformatics/btx218 PMID:28430949

Henikoff, S., & Henikoff, J. G. (1992). Amino acid substitution matrices from protein blocks. *Proceedings of the National Academy of Sciences of the United States of America*, *89*(22), 10915–10919. doi:10.1073/pnas.89.22.10915 PMID:1438297

Hinton, G. E., & Salakhutdinov, R. R. (2006). Reducing the dimensionality of data with neural networks. *Science*, *313*(5786), 504–507. doi:10.1126cience.1127647 PMID:16873662

Hochreiter, S., & Schmidhuber, J. (1997). Long short-term memory. *Neural Computation*, *9*(8), 1735–1780. doi:10.1162/neco.1997.9.8.1735 PMID:9377276

Holley, L. H., & Karplus, M. (1989). Protein secondary structure prediction with a neural network. *Proceedings of the National Academy of Sciences of the United States of America*, *86*(1), 152–156. doi:10.1073/pnas.86.1.152 PMID:2911565

Hua, S., & Sun, Z. (2001). A novel method of protein secondary structure prediction with high segment overlap measure: Support vector machine approach. *Journal of Molecular Biology*, *308*(2), 397–407. doi:10.1006/jmbi.2001.4580 PMID:11327775

Jiang, Q., Jin, X., Lee, S.-J., & Yao, S. (2017). Protein secondary structure prediction: A survey of the state of the art. *Journal of Molecular Graphics & Modelling*, *76*, 379–402. doi:10.1016/j.jmgm.2017.07.015 PMID:28763690

Jones, D. T. (1999). Protein secondary structure prediction based on position-specific scoring matrices. *Journal of Molecular Biology*, *292*(2), 195–202. doi:10.1006/jmbi.1999.3091 PMID:10493868

Kabsch, W., & Sander, C. (1983). Dictionary of protein secondary structure: Pattern recognition of hydrogen-bonded and geometrical features. *Biopolymers*, *22*(12), 2577–2637. doi:10.1002/bip.360221211 PMID:6667333

Karypis, G. (2006). YASSPP: Better kernels and coding schemes lead to improvements in protein secondary structure prediction. *Proteins*, *64*(3), 575–586. doi:10.1002/prot.21036 PMID:16763996

Kim, H., & Park, H. (2003). Protein secondary structure prediction based on an improved support vector machines approach. *Protein Engineering, Design & Selection*, *16*(8), 553–560. doi:10.1093/protein/gzg072 PMID:12968073

Klausen, M. S., Jespersen, M. C., Nielsen, H., Jensen, K. K., Jurtz, V. I., Soenderby, C. K., ... Marcatili, P. (2018). NetSurfP-2.0: Improved prediction of protein structural features by integrated deep learning. *bioRxiv*.

Klingenberg, M. (1981). Membrane protein oligomeric structure and transport function. *Nature*, *290*(5806), 449–454. doi:10.1038/290449a0 PMID:6261141

Kloczkowski, A., Ting, K. L., Jernigan, R. L., & Garnier, J. (2002). Combining the GOR V algorithm with evolutionary information for protein secondary structure prediction from amino acid sequence. *Proteins, 49*(2), 154–166. doi:10.1002/prot.10181 PMID:12210997

Kyngäs, J., & Valjakka, J. (1998). Unreliability of the Chou-Fasman parameters in predicting protein secondary structure. *Protein Engineering, Design & Selection, 11*(5), 345–348. doi:10.1093/protein/11.5.345 PMID:9681866

Levin, J. M. (1997). Exploring the limits of nearest neighbour secondary structure prediction. *Protein Engineering, Design & Selection, 10*(7), 771–776. doi:10.1093/protein/10.7.771 PMID:9342143

Levin, J. M., & Garnier, J. (1988). Improvements in a secondary structure prediction method based on a search for local sequence homologies and its use as a model building tool. *Biochimica et Biophysica Acta, 955*(3), 283–295. doi:10.1016/0167-4838(88)90206-3 PMID:3401489

Levin, J. M., Robson, B., & Garnier, J. (1986). An algorithm for secondary structure determination in proteins based on sequence similarity. *FEBS Letters, 205*(2), 303–308. doi:10.1016/0014-5793(86)80917-6 PMID:3743779

Li, W., Kinch, L. N., Karplus, P. A., & Grishin, N. V. (2015). ChSeq: A database of chameleon sequences. *Protein Science, 24*(7), 1075–1086. doi:10.1002/pro.2689 PMID:25970262

Li, Z., & Yu, Y. (2016). Protein secondary structure prediction using cascaded convolutional and recurrent neural networks. In *Proceedings of the 25th International Joint Conference on Artificial Intelligence (IJCAI)* (pp. 2560–2567). AAAI Press.

Lin, K., Simossis, V. A., Taylor, W. R., & Heringa, J. (2005). A simple and fast secondary structure prediction method using hidden neural networks. *Bioinformatics (Oxford, England), 21*(2), 152–159. doi:10.1093/bioinformatics/bth487 PMID:15377504

Lin, Z., Lanchantin, J., & Qi, Y. (2016). MUST-CNN: A multilayer shift-and-stitch deep convolutional architecture for sequence-based protein structure prediction. *Thirtieth AAAI conference on artificial intelligence.*

Magnan, C. N., & Baldi, P. (2014). SSpro/ACCpro 5: Almost perfect prediction of protein secondary structure and relative solvent accessibility using profiles, machine learning and structural similarity. *Bioinformatics (Oxford, England), 30*(18), 2592–2597. doi:10.1093/bioinformatics/btu352 PMID:24860169

Margolis, R. N. (2008). The nuclear receptor signaling atlas: Catalyzing understanding of thyroid hormone signaling and metabolic control. *Thyroid, 18*(2), 113–122. doi:10.1089/thy.2007.0247 PMID:18279012

Mirabello, C., & Pollastri, G. (2013). Porter, PaleAle 4.0: High-accuracy prediction of protein secondary structure and relative solvent accessibility. *Bioinformatics (Oxford, England), 29*(16), 2056–2058. doi:10.1093/bioinformatics/btt344 PMID:23772049

Montgomerie, S., Sundararaj, S., Gallin, W. J., & Wishart, D. S. (2006). Improving the accuracy of protein secondary structure prediction using structural alignment. *BMC Bioinformatics, 7*(1), 301. doi:10.1186/1471-2105-7-301 PMID:16774686

Ouali, M., & King, R. D. (2000). Cascaded multiple classifiers for secondary structure prediction. *Protein Science, 9*(6), 1162–1176. doi:10.1110/ps.9.6.1162 PMID:10892809

Paliwal, K., Lyons, J., & Heffernan, R. (2015). A short review of deep learning neural networks in protein structure prediction problems. *Advanced Techniques in Biology & Medicine, 2015*(3). doi:10.4172/2379-1764.1000139

Pauling, L., & Corey, R. B. (1951a). Configurations of polypeptide chains with favored orientations around single bonds: Two new pleated sheets. *Proceedings of the National Academy of Sciences of the United States of America, 37*(11), 729–740. doi:10.1073/pnas.37.11.729 PMID:16578412

Pauling, L., & Corey, R. B. (1951b). The pleated sheet, a new layer configuration of polypeptide chains. *Proceedings of the National Academy of Sciences of the United States of America, 37*(5), 251–256. doi:10.1073/pnas.37.5.251 PMID:14834147

Pauling, L., Corey, R. B., & Branson, H. R. (1951). The structure of proteins: Two hydrogen-bonded helical configurations of the polypeptide chain. *Proceedings of the National Academy of Sciences of the United States of America, 37*(4), 205–211. doi:10.1073/pnas.37.4.205 PMID:14816373

Pedersen, T. G., Sigurskjold, B. W., Andersen, K. V., Kjær, M., Poulsen, F. M., Dobson, C. M., & Redfield, C. (1991). A nuclear magnetic resonance study of the hydrogen-exchange behaviour of lysozyme in crystals and solution. *Journal of Molecular Biology, 218*(2), 413–426. doi:10.1016/0022-2836(91)90722-I PMID:2010918

Pok, G., Jin, C. H., & Ryu, K. H. (2008). Correlation of amino acid physicochemical properties with protein secondary structure conformation. In *2008 International Conference on BioMedical Engineering and Informatics* (*Vol. 1*, pp. 117–121). Academic Press. 10.1109/BMEI.2008.266

Pollastri, G., Baldi, P., Fariselli, P., & Casadio, R. (2002). Prediction of coordination number and relative solvent accessibility in proteins. *Proteins, 47*(2), 142–153. doi:10.1002/prot.10069 PMID:11933061

Qi, Y., Oja, M., Weston, J., & Noble, W. S. (2012). A unified multitask architecture for predicting local protein properties. *PLoS One, 7*(3), 1–11. doi:10.1371/journal.pone.0032235 PMID:22461885

Qian, N., & Sejnowski, T. J. (1988). Predicting the secondary structure of globular proteins using neural network models. *Journal of Molecular Biology, 202*(4), 865–884. doi:10.1016/0022-2836(88)90564-5 PMID:3172241

Qu, W., Sui, H., Yang, B., & Qian, W. (2011). Improving protein secondary structure prediction using a multi-modal BP method. *Computers in Biology and Medicine, 41*(10), 946–959. doi:10.1016/j.compbiomed.2011.08.005 PMID:21880310

Remmert, M., Biegert, A., Hauser, A., & Söding, J. (2011). HHblits: Lightning-fast iterative protein sequence searching by HMM-HMM alignment. *Nature Methods, 9*(2), 173–175. doi:10.1038/nmeth.1818 PMID:22198341

Richards, F. M., & Kundrot, C. E. (1988). Identification of structural motifs from protein coordinate data: Secondary structure and first-level supersecondary structure*. *Proteins, 3*(2), 71–84. doi:10.1002/prot.340030202 PMID:3399495

Rost, B. (2001). Review: Protein secondary structure prediction continues to rise. *Journal of Structural Biology, 134*(2), 204–218. doi:10.1006/jsbi.2001.4336 PMID:11551180

Rost, B., & Sander, C. (1993). Improved prediction of protein secondary structure by use of sequence profiles and neural networks. *Proceedings of the National Academy of Sciences of the United States of America, 90*(16), 7558–7562. doi:10.1073/pnas.90.16.7558 PMID:8356056

Salamov, A. A., & Solovyev, V. V. (1997). Protein secondary structure prediction using local alignments. *Journal of Molecular Biology, 268*(1), 31–36. doi:10.1006/jmbi.1997.0958 PMID:9149139

Salzberg, S., & Cost, S. (1992). Predicting protein secondary structure with a nearest-neighbor algorithm. *Journal of Molecular Biology, 227*(2), 371–374. doi:10.1016/0022-2836(92)90892-N PMID:1404357

Schmidhuber, J. (2015). Deep learning in neural networks: An overview. *Neural Networks, 61*, 85–117. doi:10.1016/j.neunet.2014.09.003 PMID:25462637

Schmidler, S. C., Liu, J. S., & Brutlag, D. L. (2000). Bayesian segmentation of protein secondary structure. *Journal of Computational Biology, 7*(1–2), 233–248. doi:10.1089/10665270050081496 PMID:10890399

Schuster, M., & Paliwal, K. K. (1997). Bidirectional recurrent neural networks. *IEEE Transactions on Signal Processing, 45*(11), 2673–2681. doi:10.1109/78.650093

Sermanet, P., Eigen, D., Zhang, X., Mathieu, M., Fergus, R., & LeCun, Y. (2013). *Overfeat: Integrated recognition, localization and detection using convolutional networks.* ArXiv Preprint ArXiv:1312.6229

Sønderby, S. K., & Winther, O. (2014). *Protein secondary structure prediction with long short term memory networks.* ArXiv:1412.7828

Spencer, M., Eickholt, J., & Cheng, J. (2015). A deep learning network approach to ab initio protein secondary structure prediction. *IEEE/ACM Transactions on Computational Biology and Bioinformatics, 12*(1), 103–112. doi:10.1109/TCBB.2014.2343960 PMID:25750595

Sundermeyer, M., Schlüter, R., & Ney, H. (2012). *LSTM neural networks for language modeling.* INTERSPEECH.

Szegedy, C., Liu, W., Jia, Y., Sermanet, P., Reed, S., Anguelov, D., … Rabinovich, A. (2015). Going deeper with convolutions. *The IEEE Conference on Computer Vision and Pattern Recognition (CVPR).*

Taylor, W. R. (1986). The classification of amino acid conservation. *Journal of Theoretical Biology, 119*(2), 205–218. doi:10.1016/S0022-5193(86)80075-3 PMID:3461222

Torrisi, M., Kaleel, M., & Pollastri, G. (2018). Porter 5: State-of-the-art ab initio prediction of protein secondary structure in 3 and 8 classes. *bioRxiv.*

Voet, D., & Voet, J. G. (2011). *Biochemistry* (4th ed.). New York, NY: Wiley.

Wang, S., Peng, J., Ma, J., & Xu, J. (2016). Protein secondary structure prediction using deep convolutional neural fields. *Scientific Reports, 6*(1), 18962. doi:10.1038rep18962 PMID:26752681

Ward, J. J., McGuffin, L. J., Buxton, B. F., & Jones, D. T. (2003). Secondary structure prediction with support vector machines. *Bioinformatics (Oxford, England)*, *19*(13), 1650–1655. doi:10.1093/bioinformatics/btg223 PMID:12967961

Wood, M. J., & Hirst, J. D. (2005). Protein secondary structure prediction with dihedral angles. *Proteins*, *59*(3), 476–481. doi:10.1002/prot.20435 PMID:15778963

Yang, Y., Gao, J., Wang, J., Heffernan, R., Hanson, J., Paliwal, K., & Zhou, Y. (2018). Sixty-five years of the long march in protein secondary structure prediction: The final stretch? *Briefings in Bioinformatics*, *19*(3), 482–494. PMID:28040746

Yaseen, A., & Li, Y. (2014). Context-based features enhance protein secondary structure prediction accuracy. *Journal of Chemical Information and Modeling*, *54*(3), 992–1002. doi:10.1021/ci400647u PMID:24571803

Yoo, P. D., Zhou, B. B., & Zomaya, A. Y. (2008). Machine learning techniques for protein secondary structure prediction: An overview and evaluation. *Current Bioinformatics*, *3*(2), 74–86. doi:10.2174/157489308784340676

Yoshida, R., Sanematsu, K., Shigemura, N., Yasumatsu, K., & Ninomiya, Y. (2005). Taste receptor cells responding with action potentials to taste stimuli and their molecular expression of taste related genes. *Chemical Senses, 30*(suppl_1), i19–i20.

Zemla, A., Venclovas, Č., Fidelis, K., & Rost, B. (1999). A modified definition of Sov, a segment-based measure for protein secondary structure prediction assessment. *Proteins*, *34*(2), 220–223. doi:10.1002/(SICI)1097-0134(19990201)34:2<220::AID-PROT7>3.0.CO;2-K PMID:10022357

Zhang, B., Li, J., & Lü, Q. (2018). Prediction of 8-state protein secondary structures by a novel deep learning architecture. *BMC Bioinformatics*, *19*(1), 293. doi:10.118612859-018-2280-5 PMID:30075707

Zhang, Y., & Sagui, C. (2015). Secondary structure assignment for conformationally irregular peptides: Comparison between DSSP, STRIDE and KAKSI. *Journal of Molecular Graphics & Modelling*, *55*, 72–84. doi:10.1016/j.jmgm.2014.10.005 PMID:25424660

Zhou, J., & Troyanskaya, O. (2014). Deep supervised and convolutional generative stochastic network for protein secondary structure prediction. In E. P. Xing, & T. Jebara (Eds.), *Proceedings of the 31st International Conference on Machine Learning* (Vol. 32, pp. 745–753). Bejing, China: PMLR.

Zvelebil, M., Barton, G. J., Taylor, W. R., & Sternberg, M. J. E. (1987). Prediction of protein secondary structure and active sites using the alignment of homologous sequences. *Journal of Molecular Biology*, *195*(4), 957–961. doi:10.1016/0022-2836(87)90501-8 PMID:3656439

Zvelebil, M., & Baum, J. (2007). *Understanding bioinformatics*. New York, NY: Garland Science. doi:10.1201/9780203852507

Chapter 16
Recent Trends in the Use of Graph Neural Network Models for Natural Language Processing

BURCU YILMAZ

ⓘD https://orcid.org/0000-0003-3643-7450

Institute of Information Technologies, Gebze Technical University

Hilal Genc

Department of Computer Engineering, Gebze Technical University, Turkey

Mustafa Agriman

ⓘD https://orcid.org/0000-0001-6212-8825

Computer Engineering Department, Middle East Technical University, Turkey

Bugra Kaan Demirdover

Computer Engineering Department, Middle East Technical University, Turkey

Mert Erdemir

ⓘD https://orcid.org/0000-0002-8283-8952

Computer Engineering Deptartment, Middle East Technical University, Turkey

Gokhan Simsek

Computer Engineering Department, Middle East Technical University, Turkey

Pinar Karagoz

ⓘD https://orcid.org/0000-0003-1366-8395

Computer Engineering Department, Middle East Technical University, Turkey

ABSTRACT

Graphs are powerful data structures that allow us to represent varying relationships within data. In the past, due to the difficulties related to the time complexities of processing graph models, graphs rarely involved machine learning tasks. In recent years, especially with the new advances in deep learning techniques, increasing number of graph models related to the feature engineering and machine learning are proposed. Recently, there has been an increase in approaches that automatically learn to encode graph structure into low dimensional embedding. These approaches are accompanied by models for machine learning tasks, and they fall into two categories. The first one focuses on feature engineering techniques on graphs. The second group of models assembles graph structure to learn a graph neighborhood in the machine learning model. In this chapter, the authors focus on the advances in applications of graphs on NLP using the recent deep learning models.

DOI: 10.4018/978-1-7998-1192-3.ch016

1 INTRODUCTION

A graph is a powerful data structure that can express complex data, while having the capacity to embody the relationships between the entities of the data, but it comprises some challenges. A graph does not have an order to allow them to be processed in a Convolutional Neural Network or Recurrent Neural Network. It does not have a fixed size of node either. Extracting features from k-hop neighbourhood of a node while preserving the complex structure of the graph and without losing information is not an easy task. In the recent years, the success of deep learning in many domains have shed light to graph neural models. A number of models using graph deep models are proposed on many tasks.

Graph structure is proven to be useful in various domains such as social media, chemistry and biology. Another interesting domain that recently benefits from graph structure is natural language processing (NLP). Conventionally, in NLP solutions, sentences are considered as sequence of tokens. Hence, sequence based representations and sequence based deep learning approaches have been popularly applied. With the use of graph models, graph embedding and graph based deep learning solutions reveal successful results for NLP solutions.

There is a rich variety of NLP problems that benefit from graph embedding and graph deep learning models (Goldberg, & Hirst, 2017). For natural language based data, such as text or voice that is converted to text, there are several possibilities to represent text as a graph, such as capturing relationships between a document and the words or semantic or co-occurrence based relationships between words. Furthermore, such a graph can be enriched with other types of entities such as authors, subject, and relationships among them. Once a text is represented as a graph, use of graph embedding facilitates applications involving finding similarity between two texts, such as news clustering and blog post recommendation.

There are also NLP applications that make use of graph deep learning models. For example, semantic parsing involves generating formal meaning representation of the given sentences so that it can be automatically processed. Recent solutions for semantic parsing use various neural models involving graphs such that, the sentence is firstly represented as a graph and then, the graph processing neural models convert it to the desired representation. Machine translation is another popular NLP application that benefits from neural model. Machine translation is the transformation of a text in one natural language, such as English, to a text in another natural language, such as Turkish, having the same meaning. This also can be considered as a problem of transforming one sequence to another sequence. However, the recent approaches involve graph representations and graph processing neural models.

Below listed are the main objectives and contributions of this chapter:

- To the best of our knowledge, there is very limited work that presents the state-of-the-art graph deep learning models for natural language processing tasks. This survey summarizes the recent trends in the use of graph neural network models for NLP problems.
- To provide a basis for the use of graph neural network models for NLP, a summary of embedding methods for graph and nodes are given. Additionally, we present a time performance comparison on the same benchmark data set.
- Two basic graph deep learning models, Graph Convolutional Neural Network (GCN) and Graph-to-Sequence (Graph2Seq) models, which are frequently applied on NLP problems are described in detail.

The rest of the chapter is organized as follows. In the next section, we give the state of the art graph and node embedding methods with the benchmarks. In Section 3, recent GCN and Graph2Seq models are presented. In Section 4, we give the application areas of these recent models in Natural Language Processing. The chapter is concluded with and overview in Section 5.

2 GRAPH REPRESENTATION LEARNING: GRAPH AND NODE EMBEDDINGS

Graph is a very common and natural representation structure for data in various real-world applications such as social networking, natural language processing, online documents and their relationships. Finding the patterns within or between them can be very resource exhaustive due to the nature of graph operations. In order to optimize the graph operations while using in application areas such as pattern recognition and machine learning, transforming them into vector space can increase the performance. Recently, several methods have been proposed for the representation of graph and its nodes in vector space (Mikolov, Chen, Corrado, & Dean, 2013; Narayanan, Chandramohan, Chen, Liu, & Saminathan, 2016; Ou, Cui, Pei, Zhang, & Zhu, 2016). While ***node embedding*** is used for the latent vector representation of every vertex in the given graph, ***graph embedding*** is the latent vector representation of the whole graph itself. In this section, we present graph2vec (Narayanan et al., 2017) as an example to graph embedding solution, and summarize hope (Ou et al., 2016), node2vec (Tsoumakas, & Katakis, 2007) and deep-walk (Perozzi, Al-Rfou', & Skiena, 2014) as the node embedding solutions.

Graph2vec

While graph structures are being used in a wide range of scientific areas, the methods to represent graphs start to change due to needs. For example, tasks such as graph classification, clustering and the analysis of the graphs may require to transform the graph structure to vector space since machine learning has a richer toolset of approaches when it comes to vectors. Even if the embedding can be done with graph kernels, they are limited to certain features such as using shortest path etc. In their work, Narayanan et al. (2017) propose *graph2vec* method to address the limitations of the graph kernels and offer a new solution. They use unsupervised learning method to learn the nature of different sized graphs and embed them into a fixed length vector. The idea is based on the skipgram method, which is mainly related with doc2vec, proposed by Le and Mikolov (2014), which is an an extension to word2vec (Mikolov et al., 2013). Their approach provides significant improvements in the aspect of performance and accuracy on graph classification and clustering.

Additionally, Narayanan et al. (2016) propose a method for embedding rooted subgraphs of large graphs into vector space, prior to graph2vec approach. This former work relies on another approach called subgraph2vec. Their motivation is based on the usage of graph embeddings in malware detection and predicting the properties of the chemical compounds such as solubility and anti-cancer behaviour (Narayanan et al., 2017). As in graph2vec, they use unsupervised representation learning techniques and aim to outperform the graph kernels. They generally focus on building a deep learning variant of Weisfeiler-Lehman graph kernel, which is proposed as test method for graph isomorphism problem in 1970's (Shervashidze, Schweitzer, Leeuwen, Mehlhorn, & Borgwardt, 2011). The results are almost similar with the graph2vec.

HOPE

High-Order Proximity Preserved Embedding (HOPE), is a graph embedding algorithm. It focuses on preserving asymmetric transitivity (Ou et al., 2016). In general terms, transitivity can be described as follows: In a graph, if there is an edge between vertices u and v and an edge between vertices v and w, then it is likely that there is an edge between vertices u and w. This property is asymmetric in directed graphs and symmetric in undirected graphs. Thus, it is intuitive to preserve it in undirected graphs. Some studies tackle the problem of embedding in directed graphs (Narayanan et al., 2017; Perozzi et al., 2014), however none of them successfully preserve asymmetric transitivity. *HOPE* fulfils this by using Katz proximity (Katz, 1953). Katz proximity is correlated with asymmetric transitivity and higher Katz proximity indicates higher similarity.

Node2vec

Predictions over nodes and edges of graphs is an important task in network analysis. Tsoumakas et al. aim to find the most probable labels of nodes in the network (Tsoumakas, & Katakis, 2007). For node related predictions such as predicting interest of users in a social network or protein-protein interaction, using node embedding is a suitable solution. Any supervised machine learning algorithm requires a set of informative, discriminating, and independent features, which can be provided through feature vector representation for nodes and edges.

Node2vec is an algorithmic framework for learning continuous feature representations for nodes in networks. In node2vec, a mapping from the nodes to a low-dimensional space of features that maximizes the likelihood of preserving network neighbourhoods of nodes, is constructed (Grover, & Leskovec, 2016). It is a semi-supervised algorithm for scalable feature learning in networks. The algorithm extracts feature representations of nodes in a d-dimensional feature space. Second order random walk approach is used in order to generate network neighbourhood for nodes.

Additionally, Grover and Leskovec (2016) proposed a model to extract embedding of edges between nodes for link prediction. Link prediction is used in genomics, finding interaction between genes, and in social networks. In order to generate feature representations of edges, they compose the learned feature representations of the nodes.

DeepWalk

Random walk is an algorithm that provides random paths on a graph. The method is successfully used in various problems to get accurate results in the presence of missing information. *DeepWalk* is a supervised learning algorithm that uses local information obtained from truncated random walks to learn latent representations by treating walks as the equivalent of sentences (Perozzi et al., 2014). DeepWalk generates random walks for each vertex in the graph and each random walk has specific length. In addition, next step is selected uniformly among previous vertex's neighbours.

Additionally, scalable, incremental and parallelizable nature make DeepWalk suitable for a broad class of real world applications such as network classification and anomaly detection (Perozzi et al., 2014).

Experimental Analysis

In order to compare the performance of these embedding solutions, we use a textual data set (news collection), which is represented as a graph. To represent the textual data as a graph structure, we designed a graph model that keeps the named entities of the text as the nodes of the graph using the model proposed by Seker and Eryigit (2012). Each method uses a different kind of representation of graph, for example HOPE expects edge list for each graph whereas graph2vec expects edge list with additional information.

The performance analysis of HOPE under different dimensions is shown in Figure 1-a. In this experiment, we have increased the vector dimension by 4 while changing no other parameter. Here, time denotes the total execution time for 1000 news graphs. As it can be seen in Figure 1-a, as we increase dimensionality, execution time also increases, as expected.

For graph2vec method, we adjust configuration in three different parameters. The first parameter is the number of epochs. Graph2vec tool uses 10 epochs by default. For time performance analysis, the number of epochs is increased by 10 until 100. In order to see the effect of dimension, we apply graph2vec with the same number of epochs, but under different dimensions. To this aim, we choose the dimensions of 32 and 256 as lower and upper bound. The results for this analysis is shown in the Figure 1-b.

As seen in the figure, the change in the dimension (from 32 to 256) does not affect the execution time much, but the higher execution cost is brought, when the number of epochs is increased. In order to analyse the effect of dimension change better, we conducted another experiment such that the size of the dimensions is increased by 32 starting from 32 until 256. Note that the default dimension size is 128 for graph2vec. For each dimension size, we apply both 10 and 100 epochs (lower and upper bound for the analysis given in Figure 1-b). The result of this analysis is shown in Figure 1-c.

It is seen that the number of epochs is more effective than dimensions parameter on execution time performance. Thus, the number of dimensions can be used as the default for time performance consideration. On the other hand, it will be better for finding the optimal number of epochs by experimenting on similarity accuracy.

In addition to epochs and dimensions, we have conducted another experiment in order to analyse how the number of workers effects the time performance under the default configuration on epochs and dimension. Such an analysis may guide the researcher to tune the parallelization of the task in order to improve time performance. The number of workers is 4 by default in graph2vec tool. Thus, we analysed the performance from 2 to 10 workers. The result of the analysis is shown in Figure 1-d.

As it is seen in the figure, the increase in the number of workers improves the performance in general. However, for our 1000 news data graphs, having more than 6 workers start to degrade the performance slightly. Therefore, for our data set, using the default setting (which is 4 workers) or having 6 workers appear as a feasible setting.

For node2vec method, we analysed the effect of two different parameters used in the configuration. The first parameter is the size of the dimension. The effect of dimension is analysed by varying dimension sizes from 10 to 50, under the default length of walk (16), number of walks (100) and number of workers (2). The analysis results are shown in Figure 2-a. The second parameter is the length of walk. The effect of the length of walk is analysed by varying the values from 5 to 25, under the default dimension size (20), number of walks (100) and number of workers (2). The results are given in Figure 2-b. As seen in the results, for both of the parameters, the effect on time performance is not exactly linear. On the other hand, the time cost is within a certain width and the overall time cost is higher than the other three methods.

Figure 1. Experimental results for HOPE and graph2vec

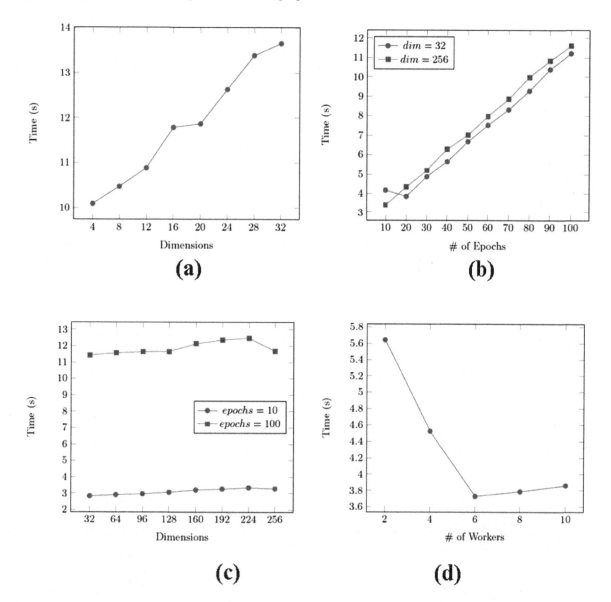

For DeepWalk, we designed our experiments to analyse the effect of two configuration parameters: dimension and walk length, as in the previous analysis. The dimension size is varied from 32 to 256 under the default values for the other settings. The results are given in Figure 2-c. For the analysis on the effect of change in walk length, the dimension size is set to 32 and the walk length is varied from 5 to 25. The results are shown in Figure 2-d. As seen in the figures, both parameters have a linear relation with the time performance, where the walk length causes a higher increase in time cost.

As the final observation, the time costs for importing these four embedding methods are given in Table 1. The import time cost is the smallest for node2vec, whereas the gap is almost 1.5 seconds for the highest import time cost of HOPE.

Figure 2. Experimental results for node2vec and DeepWalk

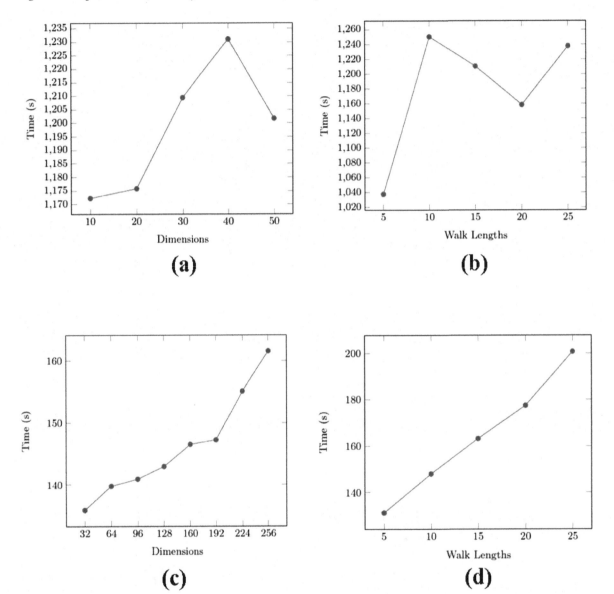

Table 1. Experimental results about import time in seconds.

Method	Import Time (in seconds)
graph2vec	8.79
HOPE	9.41
node2vec	7.82
DeepWalk	9.29

3 GRAPH DEEP LEARNING MODELS

In the last few years inspired from the recent success of deep learning models, a large number of models, Graph Convolutional Networks (GCN), Graph Attention Networks, Graph Autoencoders, Graph Generative Networks and Graph Spatial-Temporal Networks are proposed for graph data. In this section, we focus on GCN and Graph to Sequence (Graph2Seq) models mostly used in natural language processing applications, and give a summary of recent state-of-the-art proposed GCN and Graph2Seq models in general.

Graph Convolutional Neural Networks (GCN)

GCN models are like traditional Convolutional Neural Networks except that they redefine the convolution process specifically for graph data, which extract features from neighbourhood of the node. Since unstructured graph data do not have a grid structure, standart convolution operation can not be used for graphs. For each node, a node representation is extracted by composing of its features together with its neighbors features. The state-of-the art-models mostly use convolution operation for graph data in spectral and spatial domain. While Spectral GCNs use convolution filters based on graph spectral theory, convolution operation of Spatial GCNs is aggregating of feature information from its neighbours. After extracting features from nodes using convolution operation, these features are aggregated with an order invarient operation to form a graph-level representation. Because of the lack of grid structure, pooling operation in standart CNNs cannot be directly used. Sum, average or max-pooling operations are mostly used as aggregation operations. Till now, the neighborhoods of nodes are combined with equal weights. There might be a need to involve the effect of each neighbor to the model. Graph attention mechanism is used to assign larger weights to the more significant nodes in the graph. The weights are learned during the training of the neural network.

Peng et al. (2018) propose a graph neural network model called the Deep Graph-CNN to better classify long bodies of text. The model derives its embeddings based on non-consecutive words that appear within a small window and uses large scale hierarchal text classification. The embeddings can be retrieved by first converting long documents to graphs instead of viewing these documents as many words in sequences. Word co-occurrence is a method used to construct the graph. It involves building an edge between the node representations of two words that occur at the same time in a small window of texts. Once the graph is finished, any sub-graph can be considered akin to a "long distance n-gram" because it builds a correlation between these words in the same small window. A CNN model that does not involve any graphs have proven to be successful with natural language processing in earlier publications. CNNs already capture the meaning of text based on consecutive words. We can consider these consecutive words to be the equivalents of n-grams. However, the usage of the CNN alone fails to capture the meaning of text based on embeddings derived from its non-consecutive words.

Graph representation learning usually involves two methods. Generative models learn the connectivity distribution of the graph and discriminative models predict the probability of an edge existing between any two given vertices. Wang et al. (2018) propose the graph representation learning framework Graph-GAN, which uses a combination of both of these methods. The usage of both of these methods at once actually enhances the model's performance. This is because for a given vertex, the generative model tries to learn the connectivity distribution with respect to all other vertices and produces "fake" samples. These samples then fool the discriminative model, which tries to detect whether the sampled vertex is from ground truth or derived from the generative model. In other words, the signals from the discriminator guide the generator and improve its performance and the generator pushes the discriminator to better identify the differences between ground truth from generated samples. The authors evaluate the performance of the proposed model and compare its performance to those of other state-of-the-art models, which are DeepWalk, LINE, Node2vec, and Struc2vec. The Graph-GAN model outperforms all of the state-of-the-art models across the applications of link prediction, node classification, and recommendation.

Network embedding is the method of learning low-dimensional embeddings of vertices in such a way that it captures and preserves the graph structure. The words "network" and "graph" can be used interchangeably in the context of this study. Because graph structures can be complex, baseline models for network embedding are considered shallow and do not yield sufficient graph representations. Wang, Cui and Zhu (2016) propose a network embedding method to solve this problem, which they introduce a Structural Deep Network Embedding (SDNE) model. The model first uses a semi-supervised deep learning model with multiple layers of non-linear functions. This allows the model to capture the highly non-linear structure of the input graph. Then the SDNE model employs the first-order and second-order proximity at the same time to preserve the graph structure. The supervised information uses first-order proximity to preserve the local graph structure and the unsupervised information captures the global graph structure. The model preserves both the local and global graph structure by using these two proximities and it is applicable to sparse graphs. The TSNE graphs of the baseline models showing the representations of three news topics all show a lesser distinction between the three categories than that of the SDNE model. In addition, the SDNE model outperforms all of the baseline models in the applications of multi-label classification, link prediction, and visualization.

Baseline graph similarity and graph distance computations are functional but are very inefficient in practice. SimGNN involves two components (Bai et al., 2019). The first is an embedding function that extracts graph embeddings with one embedding being derived from each graph. This graph-level embedding preserves and accentuates the similarity between the graphs. The second is a node comparison method to derive node embeddings, which can be used to supplement the graph embeddings obtained by the proposed model. The combination of the graph embeddings and the node embeddings enhances the performance of the model. The proposed model returns less errors than the baseline models and achieves noticeable time reduction. However, SimGNN is not without flaws. It can process graphs with node types but it cannot process edge features. An analogy for this would be in the field of chemistry, where chemical bonds as well as elements are usually labelled and have a great effect on experimental outcome. Thus, an enhanced version of SimGNN would definitely allow the characterization of edge features as well.

Event detection models which rely on non-graph deep learning, lacks the ability to capture the non-consecutive k-grams. These non-consecutive k-grams may give significant information about event triggers in the words far apart in the sentences. Nguyen and Grishman (2018) proposed to encode input sentences as an input to the deep learning models which composed of Bidirectional Long-Short Term Memory Network (BiLSTM) and GCN together. GCNs can only capture the information in the neighbours. Although increasing the number of convolution layers can be a solution for the problem, Nguyen and Grishman (2018) proposed to employ a BiLSTM and extract new representation vectors, which is the concatenation of the forward and backward hidden vector sequences at the corresponding positions. They applied convolution over the dependency trees using the BiLSTM representation. These representations capture long range dependencies of words using fewer convolution layers in GCNs. They used pooling, feed forward and softmax layers.

Although CNNs perform success with very deep models, because of the vanishing gradient problem, most state-of-the-art GCN models do not scale well to deep architectures. Stacking multiple layers of graph convolutions leads to high complexity in back-propagation. For this reason, GCNs are mostly no more than 3 layers deep. To avoid vanishing gradient problem in CNN, ResNet includes residual connections between input and output layers. ResNets can reach more than 152 layers. An extension model that use connections between layers called DenseNet proposes to connect each layer to every other layer in a feed-forward fashion (Li, Müller, Thabet, & Ghanem, 2019). Li et al. (2019) proposed to transfer the ideas behind ResNet and DenseNet to enable much deeper GCNs that converge well and achieve superior performance. They show that adding a combination of residual and dense connections, and dilated convolutions, enables successful training of GCNs up to 56 layers deep.

Graph-to-Sequence Models

Sequence-to-sequence (Seq2Seq) models achieve excellent performance on many natural language tasks such as natural language generation, machine translation, machine summarization. The basic models mostly use encoder-decoder architectures with RNN or LSTM models. In the encoder, there is a stack of several units (RNN, LSTM or GRU cells) where each one gets a single element of the input sequence. Each cell gets the feature vectors of that element in the sequence and the previous information and propagates it to the next cell. The final hidden state encapsulates the information in the input sequence, and sends it to the decoder. In the decoder, there is a stack of cells where each cell predicts an output at a time step t. Similarly, each cell accepts a hidden state from the previous unit, and predicts the output element in the sequence. Most of the state-of-the-art models use attention mechanisms, bidirectional RNN or bidirectional LSTM to improve the performance of Seq2Seq models.

The limitation of Seq2Seq model is that the inputs are only represented as sequences. However, many data are best expressed with a more complex structure such as graphs. When the graph structured inputs are transformed into sequences, the problem becomes a sequence to sequence problem. However, because of the information loss in the conversion process, the Seq2Seq models do not perform well with graph data. For this reason, recent proposed models using graph structures as input do not transform the data and transfer the graph directly to the deep learning model.

The Graph-to-Sequence (Graph2Seq) models have a graph encoder, which embeds node embeddings, edge embeddings and graph network mostly using aggregators such as mean, LSTM and pooling aggregators, and attention mechanisms. The decoder takes the output of the graph encoder as the initial hidden state and continues similarly as it is in Seq2Seq decoder models.

Xu et al. (2018a) propose to use an end-to-end conventional encoder-decoder architecture that maps the input graph to a sequence of vectors, and then used another attention-based LSTM to decode the target sequence from these vectors. The method extracts the embeddings for forward nodes and backwards nodes in the graph, and concatenates these representations. The graph encoder neural network generates both the graph embeddings and the node embeddings. They applied a set of aggregation functions (mean, LSTM and pooling aggregators) to aggregate feature information from different number of hops away from each node. In the decoding, they used attention-based LSTM to decode the target sequence from these vectors. In their other work, Xu et al. (2018b) enhance their model by introducing syntactic graph which includes word order, dependency, and constituency features. They use a Graph2Seq model similar to the work proposed by Xu et al. (2018a) which includes a graph encoder and a sequence decoder with attention mechanism.

Beck, Haffari, and Cohn (2018) propose graph-to-sequence model that employs an encoder based on Gated Graph Neural Networks, which can incorporate the full graph structure without loss of information. The model is designed for rooted directed acyclic graphs (DAGs) where node embedding information is propagated in a top down manner. Since RNN based encoders can use backward propagation to their models too, reverse edges and self-loop edges are added to the graph. By adding the edges the graph becomes undirected which causes information loss. For this purpose, they added positional embeddings to every node. These embeddings are indexed by integer values representing the minimum distance from the root node and are learned as model parameters. The model has an encoder-decoder architecture. The encoder is a Gated Graph Neural Networks (GGNN) that gets the concatenation of node embeddings and positional embeddings as input. Attention and decoder components are similar to standard Seq2Seq models.

Marcheggiani, Bastings, and Titov (2018) propose a graph2seq model where a novel graph-state LSTM is used as an encoder. To capture non-local interaction between nodes, they allow information exchange between nodes through a sequence of state transitions. An RNN is used to model the state transition process.

4 APPLICATIONS IN NATURAL LANGUAGE PROCESSING

In this section, we give details about the natural language processing applications of the proposed methodologies mentioned in the previous sections.

Machine Translation, Abstract Meaning Representations to Text and Concersation Modelling: Seq2Seq models are mostly used in machine translation and machine summarization. Graph2seq model proposed by Beck et al. (2018) benchmark their model in two Graph2Seq tasks, generation from Abstract Meaning Representations (AMR) and Machine Translation. They reported that their approach outperforms standard Seq2Seq models in both tasks. Song, Zhang, Wang and Gildea (2018) also propose a Graph2Seq model for AMR to text generation. Their model that allows high parallelization, is more efficient and gives better performance than the baseline Seq2Seq models. Marcheggiani et al. (2018) proposed to use GCNs for machine translation. Zayats and Ostendorf (2018) proposed a model based on graph-structured bidirectional LSTM for conversation modelling. Sorokin and Gurevych (2018) used Gated GNNs to encode the graph structure of the semantic parsing for knowledge base question answering.

Visual Question Answering: Visual Question Answering (VQA) has received increasing interest in the recent years. Given an image, and a text question about the image, VQA is to give a text answer. The recent proposed models in literature use deep neural networks, which encode the photo and the text question by combining the features from the picture using very deep models using many convolutional layers and RNN or LSTM models for the text question, and produce a text based answer by using a decoder similar in Seq2Seq models. For the question, an RNN or LSTM model is constructed. These two representations are transferred into a joint space and feeding the output to a decoder similar to in Seq2Seq model.

Some of the models represent the spatial relations of the scene using a graph and use Graph2Seq models in the task. Teney, Liu and Hengel (2017) describe a deep neural network suitable for processing the question and scene graphs to infer an answer. In a scene graph, nodes represent objects in the scene, and edges represent their spatial relationships. A parse tree is constructed as the question graph, where word embeddings for each word and syntactic dependencies for edges are used.

Reasoning: Xu et al. (2018) benchmark their Graph2Seq model to test reasoning capabilities of the model. Given a set of sentences describing the relative geographical positions between objects, they aim to answer position related questions. For example, given a text such as "The garden is west of the bathroom. The bedroom is north of the hallway. The office is south of the hallway. The bathroom is north of the bedroom. The kitchen is east of the bedroom", the model will answer a question as in "How do you go from the bathroom to the hallway?". They transform the sentences to a graph using the relative geographical positions between them so that garden, bathroom, bedroom, hallway, office and kitchen will be represented by node A, node B, node C, node D, node E and node F, respectively. Then the question is transformed into finding the shortest path between two nodes. The proposed Graph2Seq model described in Section 4 is compared against an LSTM model as the baseline. The authors report that the LSTM model fails on the task, while the proposed Graph2Seq model outperforms the baseline. They also benchmark for a Natural Language Generation (NLG) task. They translate Structured Query Language (SQL) query to a natural language description of the query. They have two baselines, a Seq2Seq model and a Seq2Seq model with an attention mechanism. They get significantly better results in comparison to the baselines.

Semantic Parsing: Semantic parsing is creating a mapping from sentences to formal representations of its meaning. Xu et al. (2018b) propose a Graph2Seq model for semantic parsing. Their model which use both multiple trees and the word sequence for semantic parsing achieves competitive performance and outperforms the Seq2Seq baseline models.

Text Classification: For the text classification task, Peng et al. compare their proposed model with the state-of-the-art traditional hierarchical text classification methodologies and recent deep learning architectures as the baseline, which are Logistic Regression, Hierarchical SVM, Hierarchical Regularization, Hierarchical RNN based Models, CNNs based Models, Deep Graph-CNN Models. They analyse their model for both effectiveness and efficiency. Their approach provides promising results.

Using Graph Embeddings For Natural Language Processing: Genc and Yilmaz (2019) propose to extract embeddings for varying levels of granularities of entities such as date, month, and year embeddings using node2vec method from Snake Graph model. They also propose enrichment methodologies to transfer non-graph data with the intention of making the model learn the embeddings more accurately, which may shed light to transfer learning on graph embedding methodologies. In the experiments, they propose to use date embeddings for event detection in social media analysis. Ganguly, Gupta, Varma, & Pudi (2016) propose a method to combine both textual information and the link information to extract author representations. They validate their methodology for link prediction and clustering tasks.

5 OPEN PROBLEMS AND FUTURE DIRECTIONS

With the recent advances in deep learning models, graph based deep learning models achieved success in varying fields. But still it comprises challenges when applying deep learning models to graph data. In this section, we will state some open problems and future directions in graph based deep learning models concerning NLP tasks (Zhou et al., 2018; Zhang, Cui, & Zhu, 2018; Wu et al., 2018; Zhang, Tong, Xu, & Maciejewski, 2018).

Shallow networks: The success of deep learning lies in deep models stacking hundreds of layers to get better performance. Although in image classification the number of layers in ResNet and DenseNet exceeds hundred layers, models in NLP tasks mostly use shallow networks. Similarly, in Graph Convolutional Networks with the increase in the number of layers, the model performance drops dramatically. That's why, most of the models stuck on the shallow networks. But these shallow models may fail to discover the more complex patterns behind the graphs. Although Li et al. (2019) proposed to transfer the ideas behind ResNet and DenseNet to enable much deeper GCNs that achieve training of GCNs up to 56 layers deep while achieving better performance than shallow networks, designing deep GNN is a challenge and using these deeper graph deep models in NLP tasks will be interesting for future research.

Dynamic Graphs: Data changes over time. For example, in social networks, people may have new friends in time, that's why the graph structure representing the network has to change. That's why the graphs representing the model should have dynamic nature, where nodes, edges and their features will be different in varying time stamps. There is very limited preliminary work on this area, therefore new models should be developed to handle dynamic graphs (Ma et al., 2018; Manessi, Rozza, & Manzo, 2017).

Non-Structural Text Data: Graphs can have diverse structures like being homogenous or heterogenous, weighted or unweighted depending on the problem. When we consider NLP related tasks, there is no optimal method to represent text with graphs. Mostly words or entities represent nodes. But how the relations will be contructed is a misery (Genc, & Yilmaz, 2019). The proposed models should consider these concerns.

Other Isssues: There are also challenges related to application of deep learning models to graph data just like scalability and parallelization. There is no straight-forward way to define convolution and pooling operation for graph data (Bronstein, Bruna, LeCun, Szlam, & Vandergheynst, 2017).

CONCLUSIONS

Deep neural network based solutions are proven to have successful results in various problems. Among them, NLP stands out as one of the domains having considerable accuracy increase in the solutions. Another interesting evolvement in this direction is the use of graph representations. Hence graph embeddings and graph deep learning models are successfully employed in open up new modelling and solution possibilities in various NLP tasks and problems. In this chapter, we aim to provide an overview on the recent trends and efforts toward this direction.

ACKNOWLEDGMENT

This work is supported by TUBITAK under the project number 117E566.

REFERENCES

Bai, Y., Ding, H., Bian, S., Chen, T., Sun, Y., & Wang, W. (2019). SimGNN: A Neural Network Approach to Fast Graph Similarity Computation. In *Proceedings of the Twelfth ACM International Conference on Web Search and Data Mining*. ACM. 10.1145/3289600.3290967

Beck, D., Haffari, G., & Cohn, T. (2018). Graph-to-Sequence Learning using Gated Graph Neural Networks, In *Proceedings of the 56th Annual Meeting of the Association for Computational Linguistics*. (pp. 273–283). Academic Press. 10.18653/v1/P18-1026

Bronstein, M. M., Bruna, J., LeCun, Y., Szlam, A., & Vandergheynst, P. (2017). Geometric Deep Learning: Going beyond Euclidean data. *IEEE Signal Processing Magazine*, *34*(4), 18–42. doi:10.1109/MSP.2017.2693418

Ganguly, G. J. S., Gupta, M., Varma, V., & Pudi, V. (2016). Author2Vec: Learning Author Representations by Combining Content and Link Information. *Proceedings of the 25th International Conference Companion on World Wide Web*.

Genc, H., & Yilmaz, B. (2019). Text-based Event Detection: Deciphering Date Information Using Graph Embeddings. In Proceedings of Big Data Analytics and Knowledge Discovery (DAWAK) (Lecture Notes in Computer Science) (pp.11706-11712). Academic Press.

Goldberg, Y., & Hirst, G. (2017). *Neural Network Methods in Natural Language Processing*. Morgan & Claypool Publishers. doi:10.2200/S00762ED1V01Y201703HLT037

Grover, A., & Leskovec, J. (2016). node2vec: Scalable feature learning for networks. In *Proceedings of the 22nd ACM SIGKDD international conference on Knowledge discovery and data mining* (pp. 855-864). ACM. 10.1145/2939672.2939754

Katz, L. (1953). A new status index derived from sociometric analysis. *Psychometrika*, *18*(1), 39–43. doi:10.1007/BF02289026

Le, Q. V., & Mikolov, T. (2014). Distributed representations of sentences and documents. *Proceedings of the 31 st International Conference on Machine Learning*, 32.

Li, G., Müller, M., Thabet, A., & Ghanem, B. (2019). *Can GCNs Go as Deep as CNNs?* arXiv:1904.03751

Ma, Y., Guo, Z., Ren, Z., Zhao, E., Tang, J., & Yin, D. (2018). *Dynamic graph neural networks*. arXiv preprint arXiv:1810.10627

Manessi, F., Rozza, A., & Manzo, M. (2017). *Dynamic graph convolutional networks*. arXiv preprint arXiv:1704.06199

Marcheggiani, D., Bastings, J., & Titov, I. (2018). Exploiting Semantics in Neural Machine Translation with Graph Convolutional Networks. In *Proceedings of Annual Conference of the North American Chapter of the Association for Compuational Linguistics: Human Language Technologies (NAACL-HLT)* (pp. 486–492). Academic Press. 10.18653/v1/N18-2078

Mikolov, T., Chen, K., Corrado, G., & Dean, J. (2013). Efficient estimation of word representations in vector *space. Proceedings of the International Conference on Learning Representations (ICLR)*.

Narayanan, A., Chandramohan M., Chen, L., Liu, Y., & Saminathan S. (2016). subgraph2vec: Learning distributed representations of rooted sub-graphs from large graphs. *CoRR*.

Narayanan, A., Chandramohan, M., Venkatesan, R., Chen, L., Liu, Y., & Jaiswal S. (2017). graph2vec: Learning distributed representations of graphs. *CoRR*, abs/1707.05005.

Nguyen, T. H., & Grishman, R. (*2018*). Graph Convolutional Networks with Argument-Aware Pooling for Event Detection. *Proceedings of AAAI Conference on Artificial Intelligence.*

Ou, M., Cui, P., Pei, J., Zhang, Z., & Zhu, W. (2016). Asymmetric transitivity preserving graph embedding. In *Proceedings of the 22nd ACM SIGKDD International Conference on Knowledge Discovery and Data Mining* (pp. 1105-1114). ACM. 10.1145/2939672.2939751

Peng, H., Li, J., He, Y., Liu, Y., Bao, M., Wang, L., ... Yang, Q. (2018). Large-scale hierarchical text classification with recursively regularized deep graph-cnn. *Proceedings of the 2018 World Wide Web Conference on World Wide Web.* 10.1145/3178876.3186005

Perozzi, B., Al-Rfou', R., & Skiena, S. (2014). Deepwalk: online learning of social representations. In *Proceedings of the 20th ACM SIGKDD International Conference on Knowledge Discovery and Data Mining* (pp. 701-710). ACM.

Seker, G. A., & Eryigit, G. (2012). Initial explorations on using CRFs for Turkish named entity recognition. *Proceedings of the International Conference on Computational Linguistics (COLING).*

Shervashidze, N., Schweitzer, P., van Leeuwen, E. J., Mehlhorn, K., & Borgwardt, K. M. (2011). Weisfeiler-lehman graph kernels. *Journal of Machine Learning Research, 12,* 2539–2561.

Song, L., Zhang, Y., Wang, Z., & Gildea, D. (2018). A Graph-to-Sequence Model for AMR-to-Text Generation. In *Proceedings of the 56th Annual Meeting of the Association for Computational Linguistics (vol. 1).* Academic Press. 10.18653/v1/P18-1150

Sorokin, D., & Gurevych, I. (2018). Modeling Semantics with Gated Graph Neural Networks for Knowledge Base Question Answering. In *Proceedings of the 27th International Conference on Computational Linguistics* (pp. 3306–3317). Academic Press.

Teney, D., Liu, L., & Hengel, A. V. D. (2017). Graph-Structured Representations for Visual Question Answering. *Proceedings of IEEE Conference on Computer Vision and Pattern Recognition (CVPR).*

Tsoumakas, G., & Katakis, I. (2007). Multi label classification: An overview. *International Journal of Data Warehousing and Mining, 3*(3), 1–13. doi:10.4018/jdwm.2007070101

Wang, D., Cui, P., & Zhu, W. (2016). Structural deep network embedding. In *Proceedings of the 22nd international conference on Knowledge discovery and data mining (SIGKDD).* ACM.

Wang, H., Wang, J., Wang, J., Zhao, M., Zhang, W., Zhang, F., ... Guo, M. (2018). Graphgan: Graph representation learning with generative adversarial nets. *Proceedings of Thirty-Second AAAI Conference on Artificial Intelligence.*

Wu, Z., Pan, S., Chen, F., Long, G., Zhang, C. & Yu, P.S. (2018). *A Comprehensive Survey on Graph Neural Networks.* Academic Press.

Xu, K., Wu, L., Wang, Z., Feng, Y., Witbrock, M., & Sheinin, V. (2018a). *Graph2Seq: Graph to Sequence Learning with Attention-based Neural Networks.* arXiv:1804.00823

Xu, K., Wu, L., Wang, Z., Feng, Y., Witbrock, M., & Sheinin, V. (2018b). Exploiting Rich Syntactic Information for Semantic Parsing with Graph-to-Sequence Model. In *Proceedings of the 2018 Conference on Empirical Methods in Natural Language Processing* (pp. 918–924). Academic Press. 10.18653/v1/D18-1110

Zayats, V., & Ostendorf, M. (2018). Conversation Modeling on Reddit using a Graph-Structured LSTM. *Transactions of the Association for Computational Linguistics*, 6, 121–132. doi:10.1162/tacl_a_00009

Zhang, S., Tong, H., Xu, J., & Maciejewski, R. (2018). Graph Convolutional Networks: Algorithms, Applications and Open Challenges. In *Proceedings of International Conference on Computational Social Networks* (pp. 79-91). Academic Press. 10.1007/978-3-030-04648-4_7

Zhang, Z., Cui, P., & Zhu, W. (2018). Deep Learning on Graphs. *Survey (London, England)*.

Zhou, J., Cui, G., Zhang, Z., Yang, C., Liu, Z., Wang, L., Li, C., & Sun, M. (2018). *Graph Neural Networks: A Review of Methods and Applications*. Academic Press.

Chapter 17
Review on Particle Swarm Optimization Approach for Optimizing Wellbore Trajectory

Kallol Biswas

https://orcid.org/0000-0003-4895-4025
Universiti Teknologi PETRONAS, Malaysia

Pandian M. Vasant
Universiti Teknologi PETRONAS, Malaysia

Moacyr Batholomeu Laruccia
Independent Researcher, Malaysia

José Antonio Gámez Vintaned
Universiti Teknologi PETRONAS, Malaysia

Myo M. Myint
Universiti Teknologi PETRONAS, Malaysia

ABSTRACT

Due to a variety of possible good types and so many complex drilling variables and constraints, optimization of the trajectory of a complex wellbore is very challenging. There are several types of wells, such as directional wells, horizontal wells, redrilling wells, complex structure wells, cluster wells, and extended reach wells. This reduction of the wellbore length helps to establish cost-effective approaches that can be utilized to resolve a group of complex trajectory optimization challenges. For efficient performance (i.e., quickly locating global optima while taking the smallest amount of computational time), we have to identify flexible control parameters. This research will try to develop a review of the various (particle swarm optimization) PSO algorithm used to optimize deviated wellbore trajectories. This chapter helps to find out optimal wellbore trajectory optimization algorithms that can close the technology gap by giving a useful method. This method can generate a solution automatically.

DOI: 10.4018/978-1-7998-1192-3.ch017

INTRODUCTION

In the oil and gas industry cost minimization is a major concern for drilling engineers. From the very beginning, the advantages of drilling deviated wellbore have been very well-known to the industry. Though it is costly, this drilling makes it possible to place the well-path within productive intervals. In the beginning of the 19th century near Texon, Texas, USA the first horizontal well drilled. Before 1950 only a horizontal section of just a few tens of meters drilled during wellbore drilling, but gradually technology developed(Pratt, 2004). Directional drilling technology became a commercially-viable technology between the 1980s to 1990s. Directional drilling technology was the most preferred technology at that time, but it was quite different from today. From previous studies, it is found that the cost of drilling directional is 1.4 times costlier than the drilling of vertical well(Joshi, 2003). But in both cases, the cost of drilling is directly proportional to two factors such as the length of a wellbore and computational time. So, under all geological constraints and limitations if it is possible to reduce the length of the wellbore trajectory it will typically decrease the time to reach the desired target destination. Finally, it will reduce the overall drilling cost. At the same time, it also reduces the probability of risk(Karimpour et al., 2016). There are some reasons which made directional drilling popular since 1990(Short, 1993). Such as it increases well productivity, increases the net productive section length, it can improve the production by penetrating more fractures in a fractured reservoir, better control etcetera. From the literature review, it is found that in the early era due to lack of strong mathematical model and related optimization theories, well design strongly depends on the experiences of an engineer. There was no automated way. Due to this, the researchers did the selection and adjustment of parameters again and again. The repeated selection and adjustment are very time consuming and inefficient(Amara & Martin, 1990; Miska & Skalle, 1981; Rampersad, Hareland, & Pairintra, 1993). In 1998 Helmy(Helmy, Khalaf, Darwish, & completion, 1998) established the first nonlinear optimization theory-based practical good design method. In that method, he considered some constraints such as build-up rate, drop-off rate, casing setting depth, inclination angle, azimuth angle, kick off point, etc(Helmy et al., 1998). But the model was in 2D. After that, another optimization work of wellbore trajectory completed which was based on the 3D model(Shokir et al., 2004). But these types of traditional optimization methods used direct search methods like random search which is inefficient to find the global optima in a vast search area. If the search is gibbous these methods also show their lacking. All those methods only deal with the continuous variable. The perfect design of a wellbore trajectory during good planning may reduce the probability of borehole failure(Awal, Khan, Mohiuddin, Abdulraheem, & Azeemuddin, 2001). Thus to reduce the cost and computational time trajectory optimization of a complex wellbore is the main purpose in drilling engineering. In recent years optimization has been used frequently in the petroleum industry. There are so many AI techniques and algorithms for optimization(Vasant & DeMarco, 2015; Vasant & Vasant, 2012). It has been used for various purposes such as plant optimization, transport schedule optimization, process optimization etcetera (Atashnezhad, Wood, Fereidounpour, Khosravanian, & Engineering, 2014; Guria, Goli, & Pathak, 2014; Shokir et al., 2004). The heuristic algorithm tries to find a solution to the problem through trial and error method. They take a reasonable amount of time. Whether the solution will be acceptable and reasonable it completely depends on the type of optimization task. Usually, the heuristic algorithm does not give a guarantee to find the best or global optimal solution. Rather it can provide an acceptable solution within a reasonable amount of time. Metaheuristic means a higher level heuristic algorithm(Bianchi, Dorigo, Gambardella, & Gutjahr, 2009; Yang, 2009) which is a combination of several low-level heuristic algorithms. A modern heuristic algorithm has two key feature such as "intensification" and "diversification". If an algorithm can produce a diverse range of solutions and have the potentiality to find global optima we can mark it as an effective optimization algorithm. Furthermore, it should have the ability to explore the whole search area and to intensify its investigation radius around the neighbourhood of an acceptable solution. Heuristic algorithms have been applied to the constrained problem from the 1940s (Polya, 1945). Started with Genetic Algorithm (GA) (Gallagher, Sambridge, & Geosciences, 1994) the application of a metaheuristic algorithm in the form of a nature-inspired evolutionary algorithm (EA) escalated since the 1990s. And in many cases where those algorithms tried to solve effectively some nonlinear, non-smooth optimization challenges those performed better than the nonlinear gradient based optimizers. And this metaheuristic algorithm in the form of EA showed better and easier adaption power than others(Yang, 2010).

Wellbore trajectory length minimization is typically desirable as a way to improve the economics of drilling operations. These researches infer that criteria to optimize wellbore trajectory can be various according to specific circumstances (such as the single-well or group wells, oil drilling or scientific drilling) such as maximizing the oil production in oil drilling and the hole locating in the group well drilling. Particle swarm optimization (PSO) is a metaheuristic optimization method that makes few assumptions about the problem being optimized with the ability to search large solution spaces to findbetter solutions. It was first developed by Kennedy and Eberhart (1995) and Kennedy (1997). PSO optimizes a problem iteratively by monitoring and improving a population of candidate solutions, referred to as "particles", in terms of an objective function or fitness test (i.e. measure of quality). It does this by repeatedly adjusting the position of the particles in the search-space according to simple

mathematical formulas that determine each particle's "position" and "velocity" .How PSO and different version of PSO optimized wellbore trajectory problem will be discussed here.

BACKGROUND

As said earlier the cost of directional drilling is much higher than vertical drilling. But we can justify this method by its ability to increase the production of well. It can also reduce the overall cost of supply. In the drilling industry by collecting different data regarding the well a wellbore trajectory design is proposed. Then when drilling engineers start their drilling they try to follow the designed path or designed trajectory. But in maximum cases, it is not possible for them to follow the actual design path by point to point. In that case, there is a need for optimization of the different parameters of that wellbore trajectory. So that it can reduce the true measured depth (TMD). One point should be considered that the researchers must reach the actual target so that the researchers also need an actual path. So, if we want to reduce the overall cost and time we have to find optimized wellbore trajectory parameters and exact path. The final goal is to find out optimum directional well design parameters. But in that case, the coordinates of the reservoir and downhole target location should be available. So here measured drilling depth is the objective function. It is a function of system variables. When different algorithm tries to optimize this problem at the end they bring out some probable solution. Those solutions depend on system variables and constraints. Among those solutions, some are trapped in local optima. But those are not an effective solution. The researchers have to find out the global optima by honoring all those system variables and constraints. Among those solutions, we have to mark them through different ranks. Among different ranks, the best global solution will come out based on its effective capability. There are so many methods used to evaluate trajectories. A few of them are the minimum curvature method, angle averaging method, the radius of curvature method, tangential method etcetera. The tangential method only considers the direction angle and inclination angle. The tangent of these angles is a wellbore path. But the accuracy of this method is minimum. So some new methods were developed to calculate the trajectory(Suryanarayana, McCann, Rudolf, Rupani, & Journal, 1998; Xiushan, Zaihong, Sen, & Journal, 1997). Here in most cases, they applied the radius of curvature method to calculate the wellbore trajectory. Shokir (Shokir et al., 2004) in his paper consider a horizontal well to design the well problem.

Since 1980 radius of the curvature method has been well established(Adams & Charrier, 1985). Here a simple deviated wellbore shown in Fig 1. And the effective parameters are true vertical depths (TVD), lateral length, dogleg severity (DLS) etcetera. This well design is used to optimized through different algorithms here. We can calculate the constant of curvature between two points in space through equation (1)

$$a = \frac{1}{\Delta M}\sqrt{(\theta_1 - \theta_2)^2 \sin^4\left(\frac{(\emptyset_1 - \emptyset_2)}{2}\right) + (\emptyset_1 - \emptyset_2)^2} \ldots\ldots\ldots \quad (1)$$

where a is the curvature of the curve.

Now the radius of curvature is

$$r = \frac{1}{a} = \frac{5486.4}{\pi * T} \ldots\ldots\ldots\ldots\ldots\ldots\ldots\ldots\ldots\ldots\ldots\ldots\ldots\ldots\ldots\ldots \quad (2)$$

where T is the dogleg severity

Figure 1. Vertical plane cross-section of a generic 3D-deviated-and-partially-horizontal well trajectory (Shokir et al., 2004)

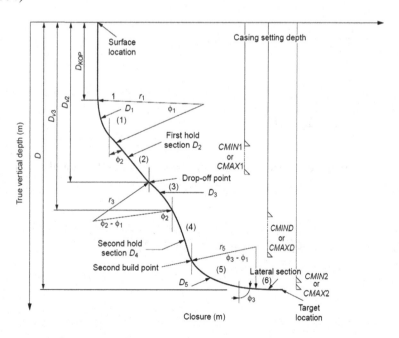

From Equations (1) and (2) the well path between two points in 3D can be calculated as a function of the radius of curvature as well as the change of inclination and direction

$$\Delta M = r * \sqrt{\left((\theta_1 - \theta_2)^2 \sin^4 \left(\frac{(\varnothing_1 - \varnothing_2)}{2} \right) + (\varnothing_1 - \varnothing_2)^2 \right)} \ \dots \tag{3}$$

So, from a general equation to calculate the well path of a horizontal well consists of seven segments, kickoff the segment, *Dkop (Kick-off point)*, three-segment for build and drop D1, D2, D3, two hold segment D4, D5, and final lateral section in the target layer *HD*, as following:

$$D_1 = r_1 * \left((\theta_1 - \theta_2)^2 \sin^4 \left(\frac{\varnothing_1}{2} \right) + (\varnothing_1)^2 \right)^{0.5} \ \dots \dots \dots \tag{4}$$

$$D_2 = (D_{v2} - D_{kop} - D_1 * \left(\frac{\sin(\varnothing_1) - \sin(\varnothing_{kop})}{(\varnothing_1 \varnothing_{kop})} \right) / \cos(\varnothing_1) \ \dots \dots \tag{5}$$

$$D_3 = r_3 * \left((\theta_4 - \theta_3)^2 \sin^4 \left(\frac{\varnothing_1 + \varnothing_2}{2} \right) + (\varnothing_1 - \varnothing_2)^2 \right)^{0.5} \ \dots \dots \tag{6}$$

$$D_4 = (D_{v3} - D_{v2} - D_3 * \left(\frac{\sin(\varnothing_2) - \sin(\varnothing_1)}{(\varnothing_1 - \varnothing_2)} \right) / \cos(\varnothing_2) \ \dots \dots \tag{7}$$

$$D_5 = r_5 * \left((\theta_6 - \theta_5)^2 \sin^4 \left(\frac{\varnothing_3 + \varnothing_2}{2} \right) + (\varnothing_3 - \varnothing_2)^2 \right)^{0.5} \ \dots \dots \tag{8}$$

where, $\varnothing_{kop}$ = inclination angle at kickoff point, which was assumed to equal zero (Adam, 1985), and $r1$, $r2$, and $r3$
can be calculated as:

$$\Delta North = \frac{\Delta MD.\left(\cos(\varnothing_1) - \cos(\varnothing_2) \right).\left(\sin(\theta_2) - \sin(\theta_1) \right)}{(\varnothing_1 - \varnothing_2).(\theta_1 - \theta_2)} \ \dots \dots \tag{9}$$

$$\Delta EAST = \frac{\Delta MD.\left(\cos\left(\varnothing_1\right) - \cos\left(\varnothing_2\right)\right).\left(\cos\left(\theta_1\right) - \cos\left(\theta_2\right)\right)}{\left(\varnothing_2 - \varnothing_1\right).\left(\theta_2 - \theta_1\right)} \quad \ldots\ldots\ldots\ldots.. \tag{10}$$

$$\Delta VERTICAL = \frac{\Delta MD.\left(\sin\left(\varnothing_2\right) - \sin\left(\varnothing_1\right)\right)}{\left(\varnothing_1 - \varnothing_2\right)} \quad \ldots\ldots\ldots\ldots\ldots\ldots\ldots \tag{11}$$

Equations (9) to (11) provide the north-south, east-west and true vertical depth (TVD) at any point along with specific curved segments of a wellbore trajectory. Equation (12) then calculates the true measured depth (TMD) of the wellbore trajectory, which is the objective function for this study:

$$\text{TMD} = D_{KOP} + D_1 + D_2 + D_3 + D_4 + D_5 + \text{HD} \ldots\ldots\ldots\ldots\ldots \tag{12}$$

USED METHODOLOGY

If the precinct of the downhole target and coordinates of wellhead are particularized, then an optimal wellbore trajectory can be designed to elect a set of geometry parameters, which in turn will satisfy both the technical constraints and geometrical constraints. This designed trajectory can escape from the intersection of certain faults, avoids shallow gas pocket. It can also elude the local optima and existing wellbore. But finding an optimum trajectory from a vast solution space is very difficult. Because space is non-linear and non-smooth. For improving the economy of the drilling operation length minimization plays an important role(Samuel, 2009). Till now so many metaheuristic algorithms used to optimize wellbore trajectory. Here the researchers will discuss how different Particle Swarm Optimization (PSO) algorithm used to optimize wellbore trajectory.

PARTICLE SWARM OPTIMIZATION

It is a metaheuristic algorithm. It also tries to give some probable solutions for a problem. It has the ability to search for a solution in a large search space. The algorithm was first proposed by Kennedy and Eberhart(Kennedy, 1997; Kennedy & Eberhart, 1995). This algorithm uses random iterations. Here swarm can be made where the particles are grouped, and it depends on the neighborhood. Particle exchange their information within the group. How particles interact computationally can be known by the help of the adjacency matrix. In matrix row represent the same types of a swarm, they are called informing particles. They communicate within themselves. But the column represents the informed particles. They contain the information gathered by the different swarm. They also hold information about the global position. So the global position can be achieved when the informing particle communicates with the informed particles. PSO first monitor and then improve the candidate solution. Through this way, it tries to optimize an objective function. PSO adjusts the position again and again according to a mathematical formula. Then from this, it tries to find out the position and velocity of particles. (Ganesan, Vasant, &

Elamvazuthy, 2012; Shi & Eberhart, 1998). Recent research shows that PSO has been applied to a much diverse application (Eberhart & Hu, 1999; Han, Huang, Jia, Wang, & Li, 2005; Xiao, Dow, Eberhart, Miled, & Oppelt, 2003; Xu, Wunsch II, & Frank, 2007). This optimization technique has in recent years been successfully applied, often in hybrid methodologies involving other optimization tools, to successfully solve varied optimization problems in the petroleum industry, for example, prediction of reservoir permeability; prediction of minimum miscibility pressure for carbon dioxide injection; parameter estimation for a polypropylene reactor . In fact, recent research has demonstrated that PSO applications include many diverse areas of potential application, such as: communication networks; robotics; signal processing; power generation, transmission and distribution systems and networks; prediction and forecasting, electronics and electromagnetics; meteorological predictions; investment decision-making; face detection and recognition, etc. For example, in the medical and pharmaceutical sectors, some PSO applications include human tremor analysis for the diagnosis of Parkinson's disease; inference of gene regulatory networks; gene clustering; and, DNA motif detection. Hence, this relatively recent tool has seen rapid and diverse uptake which testifies to its powerful and desirable performance. Here the author used the wellbore designed by Shokir(Shokir et al., 2004) to apply the PSO algorithm. Here the PSO algorithm used random candidates. GA has operators such as crossover and mutation but on the other hand, PSO does not have these types of operators. Here a particle is recognized as elements that are similar to chromosome in GA. Here each particle is assigned to an initial value. Later two vector such as velocity and position vector are assigned to each particle. Then the particles move around the search space. It tries to find out feasible solutions. It also tries to find out the next optimum candidate value. Memory is assigned for the best previous position. Later a general memory is assigned for the best position after the last iteration. By this way, it repeats the approach in the search for the best solution. When it gets a better solution, it replaces the previous value. This process will continue until it can find the global optima. But finding an actual global position is not guaranteed. (Sharma & Khurana, 2013). Here particles are grouped into swarm(Onwunalu, 2010). How particle will interact with each other this will determine by the concept of the adjacency matrix. Based on different communication topologies of neighborhood different types of PSO can be defined. In the PSO algorithm, three important components are cognitive component (φ_p), inertia component (ω) social component, (φ_g). For a two dimensional space

$$V_{i,d} = \acute{E}V_{i,d} + \varphi_p r_p \left(p_{i,d} - X_{i,d} \right) + \varphi_g r_g \left(g_d - X_{i,d} \right) \dots\dots\dots\dots\dots \quad (13)$$

where

$V_{i,d}$: Velocity of i_{th} particle and for d_{th} dimension
r_p, r_g: are random numbers uniformly distributed between 0 and 1, applied to the cognitive and social components, respectively
$p_{i,d}$: Best particle value found in the current swarm for the d_{th} dimension of i_{th} particle, up to current iteration
$X_{i,d}$: Value of the d_{th} dimension of i_{th} particle
g_d: Best global value found for the dth dimension by all particles in the current and previous swarms up to current iteration, which, at the end of the last iteration, contains the optimal values the d_{th} dimension

$$X_i + X_i + v_i \dots\dots\dots\dots \quad (14)$$

In equation (14), the value of the ith particle, Xi, for each dimension, is adjusted by the calculated velocity to provide the particle values to test in the next iteration of the model.

Here the inertia component restricts the particles within the boundaries of the problem area. The particles move towards their best previous position when cognitive components play a role. And they can achieve their best global position with the help of social components. When Non tuned PSO algorithm applied to a wellbore trajectory a minimum trajectory length has achieved.

From the result (Fig 2), it is found that the non-tuned PSO algorithm cannot achieve the minimum length. In that case, the parameters of PSO algorithm can be tuned with the help of another PSO algorithm. It is called meta optimization. After tuning the parameters of PSO new values were assigned to them. So in meta optimization, behavioral parameters of any algorithms are tuned. Meta optimization is a simple way of finding good behavioral parameters for an optimizer by applying another optimizer to tune the behavioral parameters. The search behavior of an algorithm controlled by the behavioral parameters. Flow chart of PSO shown in Fig 3. Here the swarms of first PSO algorithm is called super swarm which is used to tune and optimize another PSO algorithm. The swarm of another PSO algorithm used to optimize the wellbore trajectory. Those are called sub swarm. Super warm and subswarm are interrelated.the quality of super swarm can be tasted by subswarm. The relations between super swarm and subswarm have shown in the flow chart of PSO in FIG 2. It is a 5-dimensional problem which includes 4 behavioral parameter and unknown TMD.So in the meta optimization of this study 5 particle positions was searched. From the meta optimization result, the study has also found if the number of swarms reduced then eventually it reduces the computational time. The study has also found if the number of iteration is more it can also produce a more statistically reliable result. Later tuned PSO optimizer used to searched 65 positions in this study to find the wellbore trajectory. If we tune the PSO parameters, it can improve the efficiency of the algorithm. Here the author used meta optimization to tune the parameters of PSO(Pedersen, 2010). Meta optimization operators also help to tune the operators of GA(Mercer & Sampson, 1978). These optimized GA and PSO parameters were used by so many researchers (Keane, 1995; Meissner, Schmuker, & Schneider, 2006; Pedersen & Chipperfield, 2010). Here the author used two PSO algorithm to optimize the wellbore trajectory. They were named as super swarm and subswarm. Super swarm used to tune the PSO behavioral parameters and subswarm tries to find out the global optima. Here the author used the methodology proposed by Onwunalu(Onwunalu, 2010). The number of swarms represents the number of times particle positions are adjusted by the velocity function in each iteration of the algorithm. From Fig 4 it is found that PSO can give a minimum depth. But it is not the

Figure 2. TMD VS Iteration number

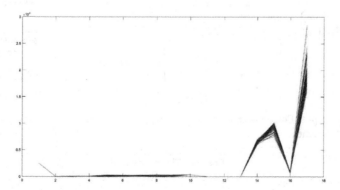

Figure 3. Flow chart of Particle Swarm Optimization(Atashnezhad et al., 2014; Onwunalu, 2010)

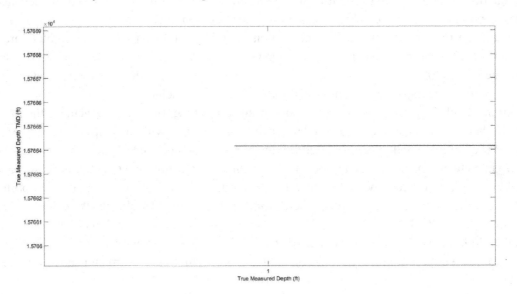

Figure 4. True measured depth after tuned PSO optimizer applied

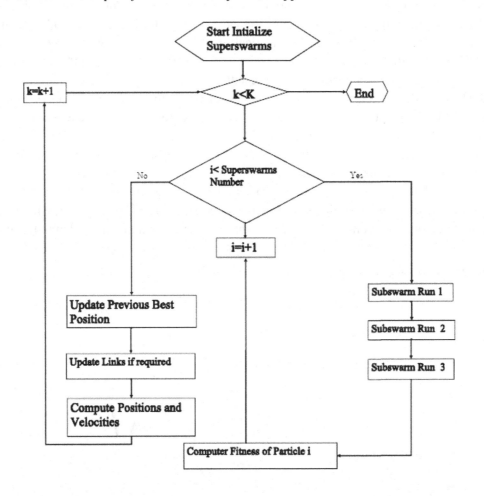

precise measured depth. If the number of swarms is lower, it will take less computation time. In the tuned PSO optimization the author used a 65 particles position and the iteration number is 200. From the result, the author shows that tuned PSO parameters give a better result than the non-tuned one. And here the convergence time is less than the tuned one. Tuned PSO parameters can show less dispersion. From the result, it is also clear that with the increase of dimension of a problem the search capability of PSO decreased. (Huang, Ding, Yu, Wang, & Lu, 2016)

For these researches, the objective function has usually been assumed to be the minimization of the total trajectory length, which forms a single objective optimization problem. However, a single objective optimization approach cannot ensure an appropriate wellbore trajectory, other factors that impact the drilling process should be taken into account. Thus, Multi-objective optimization has been used for the wellbore trajectory design issue. These researches infer that criteria to optimize wellbore trajectory can be various according to specific circumstances (such as the single-well or group wells, oil drilling or scientific drilling) such as maximizing the oil production in oil drilling and the hole locating in the group well drilling. The above researches also indicate that one essential and key factor for wellbore trajectory design is to minimize the trajectory length, as it affects the drilling time and its associated costs. However, wellbore safety is another unignorable factor on which more emphasis should be put during the whole drilling engineering procedure. Minimizing torque on the drill string considers the operating condition, and can help to avoid drilling and completion problems even failure before they occur. Minimization of the total well profile strain energy can help to guarantee a smooth trajectory and reduce some accidents such as pipe stuck in the complex well.

Multi-Objective Cellular Particle Swarm Optimization

In 1940s Von Neumann and Ulam invented Cellular automata (CA). Till today it has been used as an effective tool for scientific researcher and also recognized as an effective tool. There are several research areas where it has been used as an effective tool such as fault detection, intelligent optimization algorithms, bus and traffic route system, digital artworks generation et cetera(Lárraga & Alvarez-Icaza, 2011; Luo, Jia, Li, Wang, & Gao, 2012). Now, what are cellular automata? Actually neighboring automata provides information to uniformly arranged finite-state automata. Later these uniformly arranged finite-state automata consist a lattice. And this lattice is called cellular automaton. By utilizing a function which is called a state transit function the cellular automaton can compute their next states. The most important part of cellular automata is cellular which in turn can be recognized as cell or element. It is also the most basic part of cellular automata (CA). In cell space, there is some lattice called discrete crystal lattice. The cellular is distributed on this. Cell space refers to the set of all cell nodes distributed in the Euclidean space. In the Euclidean space, all cell nodes distributed randomly. The set of all cell nodes is called cell spaces. It can be randomly dimensional. Such as one dimensional, two dimensional, multi-dimensional. If the cell spaces are divided into different spaces then the cell can take different shapes. The isometric division is the sole way of dividing one-dimensional space. And it is the only piecewise dividing way. In the case of two-dimensional space, there are so many options such as it can be divided into square, triangle or hexagonal cell shapes. But generally at a single moment, one cell can only have a single state. But it can have multiple variables. These variables are used to describe the cell state at a time. Neighbor means those cell which is placed around the current cell and they have an influence on the behavior of the current cell. It has also an influence on the current cell when it updates the state. In the case of one-dimensional cellular automata, the neighbors can be determined on the basis of the radius. Actually, that cell which remains within the radius is called neighbors. The definition of neighbors is more complex in the case of two-dimensional cellular automata. Here based on transition rule the cell state is determined. At the same time, it is applied to all cells. Thus the whole CA system is evolved through the design space.

Figure 5 shows the flow chart of CPSO. In cellular particle swarm optimization (CPSO) a cell can be defined as a selected candidate solution. Neighborhood function determines the neighborhood for PSO. In CA according to transition rule particle exchange information with neighbor particles. After that, it updates its velocity and position. Actually, the neighboring particle with the best fitness value is substituted for the current particle. So, in turn, the construction of the neighborhood is very important. It is a key step. But it is a complex task to determine the radius of a certain particle during the construc-

Figure 5. Flow chart of CPSO(Zheng, Lu, & Gao, 2019)

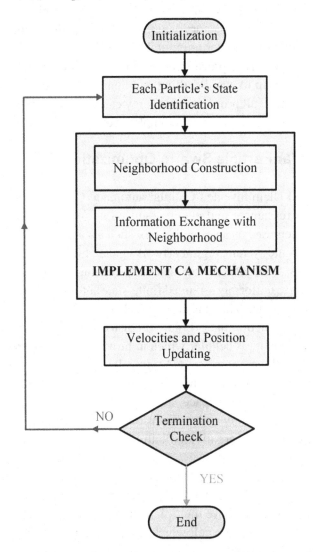

tion of the neighborhood. If the radius is small then it may miss the global optimum. If the radius is large then it may get a global optimum but there may be a slow convergence. Here more importance is given on global search. It also tries to make a balance between local exploitation and global exploration sufficiently. Here a new neighborhood function is considered. Where a 1×d matrix consists of d uniform random numbers in $(-1, 1)$ is considered. If the current particle can gains better than a particle which has global best position value ten it may give a smaller radius ratio than the considered matrix. In that case, it gives more importance to local search. Among the particles generated via the new adaptive neighborhood function, a neighbor particle with the best fitness value is substituted for the ith particle Therefore, particles in CPSO updates its velocity and position.

But it should be considered that a single solution to a problem is not practically viable. Because a problem depends on several factors. During theoretical analysis, some parameters considered as a constant. So, in that case, maximum algorithms try to find out Pareto optimal solution.

In single-objective PSO, they can be determined simply and uniquely, whereas in the multiobjective optimization there are numerous potential feasible solutions which are unable to be distinguished through fitness values. In Pareto optimal solution both dominated and non dominated solutions become separate. Such a set of Pareto optimal solutions is called a Pareto optimal set. In the first non dominated front all the solutions will have their domination count as zero. After that, it tries to reduce the count of domination by one. Through the ongoing process if it again becomes zero, then it is assigned to a separate list. So these members remain under the second non dominated the front. If it follows the above procedure then the third front is identified. This process continues until all fronts are identified. Domination constraint rule is employed during handling the constraints. Among numerous solutions, there are some solutions which have smaller overall constraint violation. These solutions may be taken as superior. When the two solutions violate the same number of constraints, the one with violation of a smaller amount is superior. In the case of selecting flight trajectory, the selection of global optimal position and particle optimal position plays an important role. They can be determined uniquely and simply in case of single objective PSO. But it is difficult during multi-objective optimization. Because there are so many solutions and it is difficult to distinguish among them through the fitness value. Here through Pareto-based dominance, the particle optimal position is chosen. It takes on the non-dominated particle between the current position and previous best position. But if the current particle position and previous particle best position do not dominate each other in that it takes a random value. Then it calculates the distance between the current particle and non inferior solutions. Then a particle which is situated at a maximum distance is taken. The whole process can be described as follows: (1) According to non-dominated ranking rule a comparison is made between the population particles and external archive particles, (2) Then the residue particles are categorized again according to the crowded distance. Among this particle, one particle will be found which has minimum crowded distance. Later this particle will be removed. One thing should be considered that in that case, the non-inferior solutions may be reached to a predetermined value. (3) when the number of particles has not reached the predetermined external archive size, all the-inferior particles are stored in the external archive. In the above external archive maintenance strategy, elitist solutions are efficiently preserved in the external archive.

RESULTS

After analyzing the optimization it is found that if the number of iteration is increased non dominated solutions are also increased. But in that case, non dominated solution may lose. The evolution is guided by the optimal position of the particle. This evolution process along with optimizing process helps the algorithm to achieve convergence. Here for the specific issue, a redundant set is provided. Particles are varied according to the problem in this redundant set. In the external archive, there are some elitist particles. These particles provide the particle for the redundant set. This set brings two advantages to optimization. Premature convergence of population to local optima is prevented by this. This is done by interfering with the population generation. Prevent the population into a premature convergence a local optimum by Increase the diversity of elite solutions by particle variation in the external archive. With the increasing of iterations, numbers of non-dominated solutions increase sharply. What is more, the global optimal position guided evolution and optimizing process could easily lead to a precocious convergence.

Finally, the radius parameter in the adaptive neighborhood function is analyzed to investigate its influence on MOCPSO performance Finally, the radius parameter in the adaptive neighborhood function is analyzed to investigate its influence on MOCPSO .performance

The redundant set brings two advantages into the optimization. Prevent the population into a premature convergence a local optimum by interfering with the population generation. 0Increasethe diversity of elite solutions by particle variation in the external archive. The NSGA-II is currently one of the most popular multi-objective genetic algorithms with a good convergence and has become a performance baseline for other multiobjective optimization algorithms.

The developed optimization algorithm has a good result in the wellbore trajectory design optimization problem, however, limitations still exist. It has several limitations. There is so many problem property information. In this algorithm, these are not utilized to improve the performance of the proposed optimization algorithm for wellbore trajectory optimization. Increasing the number of neighbors may contribute to the performance of the algorithm to a certain extent. On the other hand, it may increase the computational time and complexity simultaneously. Besides, the influence of the specific drilling equipment utilized on the objective functions was not taken into account in the formulation of the wellbore trajectory design problem.

CONCLUSION

Designing a wellbore trajectory is an important step in the oil and gas industry. Here we analyze so many metaheuristic algorithms that were used to solve wellbore trajectories. Behavioral-parameter tuning has a significant effect on the convergence of the Meta-heuristic particle swarm optimization algorithm. This is clear from the comparisons between tuned and non-tuned algorithm. This approach is well suited to drilling optimization challenges. The hybrid PSO algorithm finds the optimum solution space for the complex wellbore trajectory TMD optimization case studied more rapidly than other evolutionary algorithms, using similar population sizes, a number of iterations run, VBA coding and execution on the same computer. Wellbore trajectory design. The drilling parameters, such as inclination hold angles, azimuth angles, dogleg severity, true vertical depths, and lateral length can be processed by using the hybrid algorithm to optimize objective function TMD under the nine constraint conditions. The simulations show that CPSO has better minimum objective value, faster-running speed. We believe that using the new algorithm in actual drilling processing for wellbore trajectory control can enhance the real-time processing ability, improve drilling efficiency, and reduce drilling cost and time.

FUTURE RESEARCH

Since quantitative approach means systematic analysis of social factor via computational, statistical and mathematical technique, the researcher is more interested in this. The objective of computable research is to flourish and engage numerical models, theories and/or speculation related to the case. Here the measurement process is central. There is a fundamental connection between empirical observations of quantitative relationships. Central measurement process provides this connection. In layman's terms, this means that the quantitative researcher asks a specific, narrow question and collects a sample of numerical data from participants to answer the questions. Here we proposed PSO to be optimized with CCA (Cheetah chase algorithm.)

The methodology is summarized as follows:

1. Identify the system.
2. Collect data to describe the system: collect all related data to the well under consideration (*e.g.* geologic data, surface, and target coordinate, etc).
3. Identify system variables.
4. System constraints: constraints are all restrictions placed on the system. These constraints could take the form of either equalities or inequalities.
5. Initialization.
6. Evaluation.
7. Velocity update.
8. Solution construction.
9. CCA-based search for updating the candidate groups.
10. Application of algorithm.

The Cheetah is a giant and energetic civet that was once found all through Asia, Africa and certain places of Europe. Among the predators of Africa, Cheetahs are the most energetic predators. They are actually famous for their grotesque speed when in a chase. They can run at 60mph for a minimum span of time. The speediest animal on the earth is Cheetah. The Cheetah is one of a kind among Africa's civets principally on the grounds that they are most dynamic amid the day. They keep themselves away from rivalry for nutriment. They do not engage with rivalry with other substances like Lions and Hyenas. Because they also go out for prey at the cooler night. The Cheetah has outstanding visual perception thus chases utilizing sight by first stalking its prey from between 10 to 30 meters away, and after that pursuing it when the time is correct. The Cheetah has a thin and light body. This makes it suitable for the speediest animal. These behaviors represent unique features of the cheetah's capability to capture fast-moving prey. Cheetahs can start from 0 miles for per hour to 65 miles per hour in only 3.5 seconds. Cheetahs can achieve the best speed anyplace in the middle of 60 and 70 miles per hour, varies on the size of a cheetah. But, the fascinating thing is that cheetahs can just run that quick for 20 to 30 seconds.

Along these lines, they can't maintain that speed for long circumstances. What is the reason they can't run that quick for long? All things considered, in light of the fact that keeping up that speed for any more extended than 20-30 seconds could have an exceptionally negative impact on their organs, and the cheetah could experience the ill effects of extraordinary over-effort and over-warming. CCA was developed by Goudhaman(Goudhaman, Vanathi, & Sasikumar). The CCA is inspired by social behavior of Cheetah and its speed. The prey technique can be formulated in such a way that it is associated with the objective function to be optimized, which makes it possible to formulate new optimization algorithms.

Since PSO and CPSO both have the problem of local convergence. Sometimes this algorithm cannot go for search along the whole area, in that case, it needs an algorithm that not only gives good solutions but gives it more precisely and within least time. So, in that case, PSO needs hybridization. But the algorithm which will optimize PSO should be a faster one and should have the ability to avoid local convergence. Cheetah Chase algorithm one of them. Due to its faster speed and more convergence power, it can help PSO to optimize wellbore trajectory more precisely where the required time is less. In order to make the ants survey the overall search space, CCA is applied to update the candidate groups for the PSO which ensures highly preferable positions in the search space and increases the probability of finding a better solution. Framework of hybridization of PSO with CCA shown in Fig 6.

Figure 6. Framework of Particle swarm optimization and Cheetah chase algorithm

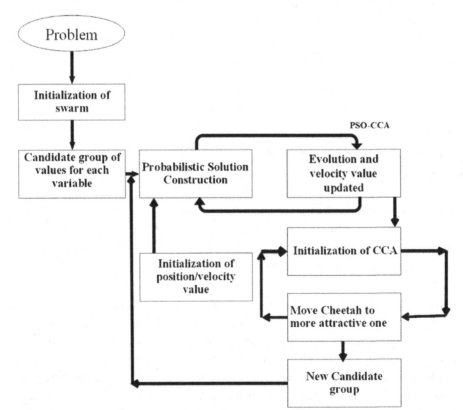

FUNDING

This research received no specific grant from any funding agency in the public, commercial, or not-for-profit sectors.

REFERENCES

Adams, N., & Charrier, T. (1985). *Drilling engineering: a complete well planning approach.* Pennwell Corp.

Amara, M., & Martin, B. (1990). *The offshore directional drilling advisor: an expert system for directional drilling optimization.* Paper presented at the SPE Annual Technical Conference and Exhibition. 10.2118/20419-MS

Atashnezhad, A., Wood, D. A., Fereidounpour, A., & Khosravanian, R. J. J. o. N. G. S. (2014). Designing and optimizing deviated wellbore trajectories using novel particle swarm algorithms. *Engineering, 21*, 1184-1204.

Awal, M., Khan, M., Mohiuddin, M., Abdulraheem, A., & Azeemuddin, M. (2001). *A new approach to borehole trajectory optimisation for increased hole stability.* Paper presented at the SPE middle east oil show. 10.2118/68092-MS

Bianchi, L., Dorigo, M., Gambardella, L. M., & Gutjahr, W. J. J. N. C. (2009). *A survey on metaheuristics for stochastic combinatorial optimization.* Academic Press.

Dalzell, J. (2013). *Conventional Natural Gas Supply Costs in Western Canada.* Canadian Energy Research Institute.

Eberhart, R. C., & Hu, X. (1999). Human tremor analysis using particle swarm optimization. *Proceedings of the 1999 Congress on Evolutionary Computation-CEC99* (Cat. No. 99TH8406). 10.1109/CEC.1999.785508

Gallagher, K., & Sambridge, M. J. C. (1994). Genetic algorithms: a powerful tool for large-scale nonlinear optimization problems. *Geosciences, 20*(7-8), 1229-1236.

Ganesan, T., Vasant, P., & Elamvazuthy, I. (2012). A hybrid PSO approach for solving non-convex optimization problems. *Archives of Control Sciences, 22*(1), 87–105. doi:10.2478/v10170-011-0014-2

Goudhaman, M., Vanathi, N., & Sasikumar, S. (n.d.). *Semantic Approach for Dynamic Shortest Path Problem (SPP) By Cheetah Chase Algorithm (CCA).* Academic Press.

Guria, C., Goli, K. K., & Pathak, A. K. J. P. S. (2014). *Multi-objective optimization of oil well drilling using elitist non-dominated sorting genetic algorithm.* Academic Press.

Han, P., Huang, Y., Jia, Z.-Z., Wang, D.-F., & Li, Y.-L. (2005). *Mixed H/spl I. bar/2/H/spl I. bar// spl infin/optimal PID control for superheated steam temperature system based on PSO optimization.* Paper presented at the 2005 International Conference on Machine Learning and Cybernetics. 10.1109/ICMLC.2005.1527082

Helmy, M. W., Khalaf, F., & Darwish, T. J. S. d. (1998). *Well design using a computer model*. Academic Press.

Huang, L., Ding, S., Yu, S., Wang, J., & Lu, K. (2016). Chaos-enhanced Cuckoo search optimization algorithms for global optimization. *Applied Mathematical Modelling, 40*(5-6), 3860–3875. doi:10.1016/j.apm.2015.10.052

Joshi, S. (2003). *Cost/benefits of horizontal wells*. Paper presented at the SPE Western Regional/AAPG Pacific Section Joint Meeting. 10.2118/83621-MS

Karimpour, K., Zarghami, R., Moosavian, M., Bahmanyar, H. J. O., Science, G., & Nouvelles, T. R. d. I. E. (2016). *New fuzzy model for risk assessment based on different types of consequences*. Academic Press.

Keane, A. J. (1995). Genetic algorithm optimization of multi-peak problems: Studies in convergence and robustness. *Artificial Intelligence in Engineering, 9*(2), 75–83. doi:10.1016/0954-1810(95)95751-Q

Kennedy, J. (1997). The particle swarm: social adaptation of knowledge. *Proceedings of 1997 IEEE International Conference on Evolutionary Computation (ICEC'97)*. 10.1109/ICEC.1997.592326

Kennedy, J., & Eberhart, R. (1995). Particle swarm optimization. In *IEEE International of first Conference on Neural Networks*. Perth, Australia: IEEE Press.

Lárraga, M. E., & Alvarez-Icaza, L. (2011). *Towards a realistic description of traffic flow based on cellular automata*. Paper presented at the 2011 14th International IEEE Conference on Intelligent Transportation Systems (ITSC). 10.1109/ITSC.2011.6082931

Luo, Y.-J., Jia, B., Li, X.-G., Wang, C., & Gao, Z.-Y. (2012). A realistic cellular automata model of bus route system based on open boundary. *Transportation Research Part C, Emerging Technologies, 25*, 202–213. doi:10.1016/j.trc.2012.06.004

Meissner, M., Schmuker, M., & Schneider, G. (2006). Optimized Particle Swarm Optimization (OPSO) and its application to artificial neural network training. *BMC Bioinformatics, 7*(1), 125. doi:10.1186/1471-2105-7-125 PMID:16529661

Mercer, R. E., & Sampson, J. (1978). Adaptive search using a reproductive meta-plan. *Kybernetes, 7*(3), 215–228. doi:10.1108/eb005486

Miska, S., & Skalle, P. J. S. o. P. E. J. (1981). *Theoretical description of a new method of optimal program design*. Academic Press.

Onwunalu, J. (2010). *Optimization of field development using particle swarm optimization and new well pattern descriptions*. Stanford University.

Pedersen, M. E. H. (2010). *Tuning & simplifying heuristical optimization*. University of Southampton.

Pedersen, M. E. H., & Chipperfield, A. J. (2010). Simplifying particle swarm optimization. *Applied Soft Computing, 10*(2), 618–628.

Polya, G. (1945). *How to solve it*. Princeton University Press.

Pratt, S. J. G. (2004). *A fresh angle on oil drilling*. Academic Press.

Rampersad, P., Hareland, G., & Pairintra, T. (1993). *Drilling optimization of an oil or gas field.* Paper presented at the SPE Eastern Regional Meeting. 10.2118/26949-MS

Samuel, R. (2009). *Ultra-Extended-Reach Drilling (u-ERD: Tunnel in the Earth)—A New Well-Path Design.* Paper presented at the SPE/IADC Drilling Conference and Exhibition. 10.2118/119459-MS

Sharma, P., & Khurana, N. (2013). Study of optimal path finding techniques. *International Journal of Advancements in Technology, 4*(2), 124–130.

Shi, Y., & Eberhart, R. (1998). *A modified particle swarm optimizer.* Paper presented at the 1998 IEEE international conference on evolutionary computation proceedings. IEEE world congress on computational intelligence (Cat. No. 98TH8360). 10.1109/ICEC.1998.699146

Shokir, E. E.-M., Emera, M., Eid, S., & Wally, A. J. O. (2004). *A new optimization model for 3D well design.* Academic Press.

Short, J. A. (1993). *Introduction to directional and horizontal drilling.* Pennwell Corporation.

Suryanarayana, P., McCann, R. C., Rudolf, R. L., & Rupani, R. A. J. O. (1998). *Mathematical technique improves directional well-path planning.* Academic Press.

Vasant, P., & DeMarco, A. (2015). *Handbook of research on artificial intelligence techniques and algorithms.* Information Science Reference. doi:10.4018/978-1-4666-7258-1

Vasant, P., & Vasant, P. (2012). Meta-Heuristics Optimization Algorithms in Engineering. In Business, Economics, and Finance. IGI Global.

Xiao, X., Dow, E. R., Eberhart, R., Miled, Z. B., & Oppelt, R. J. (2003). Gene clustering using self-organizing maps and particle swarm optimization. *Proceedings International Parallel and Distributed Processing Symposium.* 10.1109/IPDPS.2003.1213290

Xiushan, L., Zaihong, S., & Sen, F. J. O. (1997). *Natural parameter method accurately calculates well bore trajectory.* Academic Press.

Xu, R., Wunsch, I. I. D., & Frank, R. (2007). Inference of genetic regulatory networks with recurrent neural network models using particle swarm optimization. *IEEE/ACM Transactions on Computational Biology and Bioinformatics, 4*(4), 681–692. doi:10.1109/TCBB.2007.1057 PMID:17975278

Yang, X.-S. (2009). Harmony search as a metaheuristic algorithm. In *Music-inspired harmony search algorithm* (pp. 1–14). Springer. doi:10.1007/978-3-642-00185-7_1

Yang, X.-S. (2010). *Nature-inspired metaheuristic algorithms.* Luniver Press.

Zheng, J., Lu, C., & Gao, L. (2019). Multi-objective cellular particle swarm optimization for wellbore trajectory design. *Applied Soft Computing, 77,* 106–117. doi:10.1016/j.asoc.2019.01.010

Compilation of References

Ab Wahab, M. N., Nefti-Meziani, S., & Atyabi, A. (2015). A comprehensive review of swarm optimization algorithms. *PLoS One*, *10*(5), e0122827. doi:10.1371/journal.pone.0122827 PMID:25992655

Abbasi-Sureshjani, S., Dashtbozorg, B., ter Haar Romeny, B. M., & Fleuret, F. (2017). Boosted exudate segmentation in retinal images using residual nets. Lect. Notes Comput. Sci., 10554, 210–218 doi:10.1007/978-3-319-67561-9_24

Abdallah & De La Iglasia. (2014). URL based web page classification: With n-gram language models. *Proceedings of the International Joint Conference on Knowledge Discovery, Knowledge Engineering and Knowledge Management, 1*, 14-21.

Abdelsalam, H. M., & Elassal, M. M. (2014). Joint economic lot sizing problem for a three—Layer supply chain with stochastic demand. *International Journal of Production Economics*, *155*, 272–283. doi:10.1016/j.ijpe.2014.01.015

Abhinav-Vishwa, M. K., Lal, S. D., & Vardwaj, P. (2011). Clasification of arrhythmic ECG data using machine learning techniques. *International Journal of Interactive Multimedia and Artificial Intelligence*, *1*(4), 67–70. doi:10.9781/ijimai.2011.1411

Abou El Ela, A. A., Abido, M. A., & Spea, S. R. (2010). Optimal power flow using differential evolution algorithm. *Electric Power Systems Research*, *80*(7), 878–885. doi:10.1016/j.epsr.2009.12.018

Adams, N., & Charrier, T. (1985). *Drilling engineering: a complete well planning approach*. Pennwell Corp.

Afridi, M. J., Ross, A., & Shapiro, E. M. (2018). On automated source selection for transfer learning in convolutional neural networks. *Pattern Recognition*, *73*, 65–75. doi:10.1016/j.patcog.2017.07.019 PMID:30774153

Agurto, C., Murray, V., Yu, H., Wigdahl, J., Pattichis, M., Nemeth, S., ... Soliz, P. (2014). A multiscale optimization approach to detect exudates in the macula. *IEEE Journal of Biomedical and Health Informatics*, *18*(4), 1328–1336. doi:10.1109/JBHI.2013.2296399 PMID:25014937

Ahamed, B. B., & Ramkumar, T. (2018). *Proficient Information Method for Inconsistency Detection in Multiple Data Sources*. Academic Press.

Ahamed, B. B., & Ramkumar, T. (2016). An intelligent web search framework for performing efficient retrieval of data. *Computers & Electrical Engineering*, *56*, 289–299. doi:10.1016/j.compeleceng.2016.09.033

Ahamed, B. B., & Yuvaraj, D. (2018, October). Framework for Faction of Data in Social Network Using Link Based Mining Process. In *International Conference on Intelligent Computing & Optimization* (pp. 300-309). Springer.

Ahi, P., & Searcy, C. (2013). A comparative literature analysis of definitions for green and sustainable supply chain management. *Journal of Cleaner Production*, *52*, 329–341. doi:10.1016/j.jclepro.2013.02.018

Ahmadi, A., Kaymanesh, A., Siano, P., Janghorbani, M., Nezhad, A. E., & Sarno, D. (2015). Evaluating the effectiveness of normal boundary intersection method for short-term environmental/economic hydrothermal self-scheduling. *Electric Power Systems Research*, *123*, 192–204. doi:10.1016/j.epsr.2015.02.007

Ahmadigorji, M., & Amjady, N. (2014). A new evolutionary solution method for dynamic expansion planning of DG-integrated primary distribution networks. *Energy Conversion and Management*, *82*, 61–70. doi:10.1016/j.enconman.2014.03.008

Ai, D., Yang, J., Wang, Z., Fan, J., Ai, C., & Wang, Y. (2015). Fast multi-scale feature fusion for ECG heartbeat classification". *EURASIP Journal on Advances in Signal Processing*, *1*(1), 46. doi:10.118613634-015-0231-0

Akemann, G., (2017). Random matrix theory and quantum chromodynamics. Stochastic Processes and Random Matrices. *Lecture Notes of the Les Houches Summer School, 104*, 228.

Akram, M. U., Tariq, A., Khan, S. A., & Javed, M. Y. (2014). Automated detection of exudates and macula for grading of diabetic macular edema. *Computer Methods and Programs in Biomedicine*, *114*(2), 141–152. doi:10.1016/j.cmpb.2014.01.010 PMID:24548898

Al Dossary, M. A., & Nasrabadi, H. (2015). *Well placement optimization using imperialist competition algorithm.* Paper presented at the SPE reservoir characterisation and simulation conference and exhibition. 10.2118/175646-MS

Al Dossary, M. A., & Nasrabadi, H. J. J. o. P. S. (2016). Well placement optimization using imperialist competitive algorithm. *Engineering, 147*, 237-248.

Alickovic, E., & Subasi, A. (2016). Medical decision support system for diagnosis of heart arrhythmia using DWT and random forests classifier. *Journal of Medical Systems*, *40*(4), 108. doi:10.100710916-016-0467-8 PMID:26922592

Alizadeh, B., Maroufi, K., & Heidarifard, M. H. (2018). Estimating source rock parameters using wireline data: An example from Dezful Embayment, South West of Iran. *Journal of Petroleum Science Engineering*, *167*, 857–868. doi:10.1016/j.petrol.2017.12.021

Almeida, L. B. (1987). A learning rule for asynchronous perceptrons with feedback in a combinatorial environment. In *Proceedings, 1st First International Conference on Neural Networks* (Vol. 2, pp. 609-618). IEEE.

Al-Muhawesh, T. A., & Qamber, I. S. (2008). The established mega watt linear programming-based optimal power flow model applied to the real power 56-bus system in eastern province of Saudi Arabia. *Energy*, *33*(1), 12–21. doi:10.1016/j.energy.2007.08.004

Altschul, S. F., Madden, T. L., Schäffer, A. A., Zhang, J., Zhang, Z., Miller, W., & Lipman, D. J. (1997). Gapped BLAST and PSI-BLAST: A new generation of protein database search programs. *Nucleic Acids Research*, *25*(17), 3389–3402. doi:10.1093/nar/25.17.3389 PMID:9254694

Amara, J., Bouaziz, B., & Algergawy, A. (2017). *A Deep Learning-based Approach for Banana Leaf Diseases Classification.* Academic Press.

Amara, M., & Martin, B. (1990). *The offshore directional drilling advisor: an expert system for directional drilling optimization.* Paper presented at the SPE Annual Technical Conference and Exhibition. 10.2118/20419-MS

Amodei, D., Ananthanarayanan, S., Anubhai, R., Bai, J., Battenberg, E., & Case, C., ... Zhu, Z. (2016). Deep Speech 2: End-to-end speech recognition in English and Mandarin. In M. F. Balcan, & K. Q. Weinberger (Eds.), *Proceedings of The 33rd International Conference on Machine Learning* (Vol. 48, pp. 173–182). New York, NY: PMLR.

Anderson, M., & Anderson, M. (2017). 88% Of Consumers Trust Online Reviews As Much As Personal Recommendations. *Search Engine Land.* Available at: http://searchengineland.com/88-consumers-trust-online-reviews-much-personal-recommendations-195803

Anissa, B., Naouar, B., Arsalane, Z., & Jamal, K. (2015, March). Face recognition: comparative study between linear and non linear dimensionality reduction methods. In *2015 International Conference on Electrical and Information Technologies (ICEIT)* (pp. 224-228). IEEE. 10.1109/EITech.2015.7162932

Antelin Vijila, S., & Rajesh, R. S. (2018). Detection Of Hard Exudates In Fundus Images Using Cascaded Correlation Neural Network Classifier. *International Journal of Pure and Applied Mathematics Volume, 118*(11), 699-706.

Ardabili, S. F., Mahmoudi, A., & Gundoshmian, T. M. (2016). Modeling and simulation controlling system of HVAC using fuzzy and predictive (radial basis function, RBF) controllers. *Journal of Building Engineering, 6,* 301–308. doi:10.1016/j.jobe.2016.04.010

Ariadji, T., Sukarno, P., Sidarto, K. A., Soewono, E., Riza, L. S., & David, K. J. J. o. E. (2012). Optimization of Vertical Well Placement for Oil Field Development Based on Basic Reservoir Rock Properties using a Genetic Algorithm. *Science, 44*(2), 106-127.

Asai, K., Hayamizu, S., & Handa, K. (1993). Prediction of protein secondary structure by the hidden Markov model. *Bioinformatics (Oxford, England), 9*(2), 141–146. doi:10.1093/bioinformatics/9.2.141 PMID:8481815

Atashnezhad, A., Wood, D. A., Fereidounpour, A., & Khosravanian, R. J. J. o. N. G. S. (2014). Designing and optimizing deviated wellbore trajectories using novel particle swarm algorithms. *Engineering, 21,* 1184-1204.

Autric, A. (1985). Resistivity, radioactivity and sonic transit time logs to evaluate the organic content of low permeability rocks. *The Log Analyst, 26*(03).

Awal, M., Khan, M., Mohiuddin, M., Abdulraheem, A., & Azeemuddin, M. (2001). *A new approach to borehole trajectory optimisation for increased hole stability.* Paper presented at the SPE middle east oil show. 10.2118/68092-MS

Awotunde, A. A., & Sibaweihi, N. J. S. E. (2014). Consideration of voidage-replacement ratio in well-placement optimization. *Management, 6*(1), 40-54.

Aydin, O., Tezcan, S. S., Eke, I., & Taplamacioglu, M. C. (2017). Solving the Optimal Power Flow Quadratic Cost Functions using Vortex Search Algorithm. *IFAC-PapersOnLine, 50*(1), 239–244. doi:10.1016/j.ifacol.2017.08.040

Azpiazu, I. M., Dragovic, N., Pera, M. S., & Fails, J. A. (2017). Online searching and learning: YUM and other search tools for children and teachers. *Inf Retrieval J, 20*(5), 524–545. doi:10.100710791-017-9310-1

Bai, Y., Ding, H., Bian, S., Chen, T., Sun, Y., & Wang, W. (2019). SimGNN: A Neural Network Approach to Fast Graph Similarity Computation. In *Proceedings of the Twelfth ACM International Conference on Web Search and Data Mining.* ACM. 10.1145/3289600.3290967

Baker, J. M., Deng, L., Glass, J., Khudanpur, S., Lee, C. H., Morgan, N., & Shaughnessy, D. O. (2009). Developments and directions in speech recognition and understanding, part 1 [dsp education]. *IEEE Transactions on Signal Processing Magazine, 26*(3), 75–80. doi:10.1109/MSP.2009.932166

Balakrishnan, U., Venkatachalapathy, K., & Marimuthu, G. S. (2016). An enhanced PSO- DEFS based feature selection with biometric authentication for identification of diabetic retinopathy. *Journal of Innovative Optical Health Sciences, 9*(6). doi:10.1142/S1793545816500206

Balaneshinkordan, S., Kotov, A., & Nikolaev, F. (2018). *Attentive Neural Architecture for Ad-hoc Structured Document Retrieval.* CIKM. doi:10.1145/3269206.3271801

Ballabio, D., Vasighi, M., Consonni, V., & Kompany-Zareh, M. (2011). Genetic algorithms for architecture optimisation of counter-propagation artificial neural networks. *Chemometrics and Intelligent Laboratory Systems, 105*(1), 56–64. doi:10.1016/j.chemolab.2010.10.010

Ballard, D. H., & Brown, C. M. (1982). *Computer vision*. Englewood Cliffs, NJ: Prenice-Hall.

Balouji, E., Gu, I. Y., Bollen, M. H., Bagheri, A., & Nazari, M. (2018). A LSTM-based deep learning method with application to voltage dip classification. In *Proceedings of 18th International Conference on in Harmonics and Quality of Power (ICHQP)* (pp.1-5). Academic Press. 10.1109/ICHQP.2018.8378893

Bangerth, W., Klie, H., Wheeler, M. F., Stoffa, P. L., & Sen, M. K. (2006). On optimization algorithms for the reservoir oil well placement problem. *Computational Geosciences, 10*(3), 303–319. doi:10.100710596-006-9025-7

Barabási, A. L. (2016). *Network science*. Cambridge University Press.

Basheer, I. A., & Hajmeer, M. (2000). Artificial neural networks: Fundamentals, computing, design, and application. *Journal of Microbiological Methods, 43*(1), 3–31. doi:10.1016/S0167-7012(00)00201-3 PMID:11084225

Battaglia, P., Pascanu, R., Lai, M., & Rezende, D. J. (2016). Interaction networks for learning about objects, relations and physics. In Advances in neural information processing systems (pp. 4502-4510). Academic Press.

Baykan, E., Henzinger, M., Ludmila, M., & Weber, I. (2011). A comprehensive study of features and algorithms for URL-based topic classification. *ACM Transactions on the Web, 5*(3), 1–29. doi:10.1145/1993053.1993057

Beck, D., Haffari, G., & Cohn, T. (2018). Graph-to-Sequence Learning using Gated Graph Neural Networks, In *Proceedings of the 56th Annual Meeting of the Association for Computational Linguistics*. (pp. 273–283). Academic Press. 10.18653/v1/P18-1026

Beenakker, C. W. J. (2015). Random-matrix theory of Majorana fermions and topological superconductors. *Reviews of Modern Physics, 87*(3), 1037–1066. doi:10.1103/RevModPhys.87.1037

Beers, R. F. (1945). Radioactivity and organic content of some Paleozoic shales. *AAPG Bulletin, 29*(1), 1–22.

Beisel, N. S., Callaham, J. B., Sng, N. J., Taylor, D. J., Paul, A. L., & Ferl, R. J. (2018). Utilization of single-image normalized difference vegetation index (SI-NDVI) for early plant stress detection. *Applications in Plant Sciences, 6*(10), e01186. doi:10.1002/aps3.1186 PMID:30386712

Belkin, M., & Niyogi, P. (2002). Laplacian eigenmaps and spectral techniques for embedding and clustering. In Advances in neural information processing systems (pp. 585-591). Academic Press.

Bengio, Y., & Delalleau, O. (2011). On the expressive power of deep architecture. Berlin: Springer Berlin Heidelberg.

Bengio, Y., Laufer, E., Alain, G., & Yosinski, J. (2014). Deep generative stochastic networks trainable by backprop. In E. P. Xing, & T. Jebara (Eds.), *Proceedings of the 31st International Conference on Machine Learning* (Vol. 32, pp. 226–234). Beijing, China: PMLR.

Bessereau, G., Carpentier, B., & Huc, A. Y. (1991). Wireline Logging And Source Rocks-Estimation Of Organic Carbon Content By The Carbolbg@ Method. *The Log Analyst, 32*(03).

Bhowmik, A. R., & Chakraborty, A. K. (2014). Solution of optimal power flow using nondominated sorting multi objective gravitational search algorithm. *International Journal of Electrical Power & Energy Systems, 62*, 323–334. doi:10.1016/j.ijepes.2014.04.053

Bianchi, L., Dorigo, M., Gambardella, L. M., & Gutjahr, W. J. N. C. (2009). *A survey on metaheuristics for stochastic combinatorial optimization*. Academic Press.

Bojarski, Asa, Colak, & Czarkowski. (2017). Analysis and control of multiphase inductively coupled resonant converter for wireless electric vehicle charger applications. *IEEE Transactions on Transportation Electrification, 3*(2), 312-320.

Bojarski, M., Choromanska, A., Choromanski, K., Firner, B., Jackel, L., & Muller, U. (2016). *Visualbackprop: visualizing cnns for autonomous driving.* arXiv preprint arXiv:1611.05418

Bojarski, M., Yeres, P., Choromanska, A., & Choromanski, K. (2017). *Explaining how a deep neural network trained with end-to-end learning steers a car.* arXiv preprint arXiv:1704.07911

Bolandi, V., Kadkhodaie, A., & Farzi, R. (2017). Analyzing organic richness of source rocks from well log data by using SVM and ANN classifiers: A case study from the Kazhdumi formation, the Persian Gulf basin, offshore Iran. *Journal of Petroleum Science Engineering, 151*, 224–234. doi:10.1016/j.petrol.2017.01.003

Bouziaren, S. A., & Brahim Aghezzaf, B. (2018). An Improved Augmented epsilon-Constraint and Branch-and-Cut Method to Solve the TSP with Profits. *IEEE Transactions on Intelligent Transportation Systems, 20*(1), 195–204. doi:10.1109/TITS.2018.2808179

Brandenburg, M., Govindan, K., Sarkis, J., & Seuring, S. (2014). Quantitative models for sustainable supply chain management: Developments and directions. *European Journal of Operational Research, 233*(2), 299–312. doi:10.1016/j.ejor.2013.09.032

Bringmann, K., & Friedrich, T. (2013). Approximation quality of the hypervolume indicator. *Artificial Intelligence, 195*, 265–290. doi:10.1016/j.artint.2012.09.005

Brits, R., Engelbrecht, A. P., & Van den Bergh, F. (2002). A niching particle swarm optimizer. *Proceedings of the 4th Asia-Pacific conference on simulated evolution and learning.*

Brockschmidt, M., Chen, Y., Cook, B., Kohli, P., & Tarlow, D. (2015). Learning to decipher the heap for program verification. In *Workshop on Constructive Machine Learning at the International Conference on Machine Learning (CMLICML)* (*Vol. 21*). Academic Press.

Bronstein, M. M., Bruna, J., LeCun, Y., Szlam, A., & Vandergheynst, P. (2017). Geometric deep learning: Going beyond euclidean data. *IEEE Signal Processing Magazine, 34*(4), 18–42. doi:10.1109/MSP.2017.2693418

Broomhead, D. S., & Lowe, D. (1988). *Radial basis functions, multi-variable functional interpolation and adaptive networks.* Royal Signals and Radar Establishment Malvern.

Bruce, A., Alexander, J., Julian, L., Martin, R., Keith, R., & Walter, P. (2015). *Molecular biology of the cell* (6th ed.). New York, NY: Garland Science.

Bruna, J., Zaremba, W., Szlam, A., & LeCun, Y. (2013). *Spectral networks and locally connected networks on graphs.* arXiv preprint arXiv:1312.6203

Busia, A., & Jaitly, N. (2017). Next-step conditioned deep convolutional neural networks improve protein secondary structure prediction. *CoRR, abs/1702.0.*

Bystroff, C., Thorsson, V., & Baker, D. (2000). HMMSTR: A hidden Markov model for local sequence–structure correlations in proteins. *Journal of Molecular Biology, 301*(1), 173–190. doi:10.1006/jmbi.2000.3837 PMID:10926500

Cai, J., Ma, X., Li, L., & Haipeng, P. (2007). Chaotic particle swarm optimization for economic dispatch considering the generator constraints. *Energy Conversion and Management, 48*(2), 645–653. doi:10.1016/j.enconman.2006.05.020

Cai, J., Ma, X., Li, Q., Li, L., & Peng, H. (2009). A multi-objective chaotic particle swarm optimization for environmental/economic dispatch. *Energy Conversion and Management, 50*(5), 1318–1325. doi:10.1016/j.enconman.2009.01.013

Campbell, N. A., Reece, J. B., Urry, L. A., Cain, M. L., Wasserman, S. A., Beth, W., & Jackson, R. B. (2007). *Biology* (8th ed.). San Francisco, CA: Pearson.

Cao, C., Liu, F., Tan, H., Song, D., Shu, W., Li, W., ... Xie, Z. (2018). Deep Learning and Its Applications in Biomedicine. *Genomics, Proteomics & Bioinformatics*, *16*(1), 17–32. doi:10.1016/j.gpb.2017.07.003 PMID:29522900

Carlsson, C., & Fullér, R. (1996). Fuzzy multiple criteria decision making: Recent developments. *Fuzzy Sets and Systems*, *78*(2), 139–153. doi:10.1016/0165-0114(95)00165-4

Carpenter, G. A., & Grossberg, S. (2016). *Adaptive resonance theory*. Springer. doi:10.1007/978-1-4899-7502-7_6-1

Castillo-Villar, K. K. (2014). Metaheuristic algorithms applied to bioenergy supply chain problems: Theory, review, challenges, and future. *Energies*, *7*(11), 7640–7672. doi:10.3390/en7117640

Caterini, A. L., & Chang, D. E. (2018). *Deep Neural Networks in a Mathematical Framework*. Springer. doi:10.1007/978-3-319-75304-1

Cessac, B., Kornprobst, P., Kraria, S., Nasser, H., Pamplona, D., Portelli, G., & Viéville, T. (2016, October). ENAS: A new software for spike train analysis and simulation. *Bernstein Conference*.

Chakravarty, S., & Varadarajan, R. (1999). Residue depth: A novel parameter for the analysis of protein structure and stability. *Structure (London, England)*, *7*(7), 723–732. doi:10.1016/S0969-2126(99)80097-5 PMID:10425675

Chalermchaiarbha, S., & Ongsakul, W. (2013). Stochastic weight trade-off particle swarm optimization for nonconvex economic dispatch. *Energy Conversion and Management*, *70*, 66–75. doi:10.1016/j.enconman.2013.02.009

Chang, Y. Q., Bouzarkouna, Z., & Devegowda, D. (2015). Multi-objective optimization for rapid and robust optimal oilfield development under geological uncertainty. *Computational Geosciences*, *19*(4), 933–950. doi:10.100710596-015-9507-6

Charsky, A., & Herron, S. (2013). Accurate, direct Total Organic Carbon (TOC) log from a new advanced geochemical spectroscopy tool: Comparison with conventional approaches for TOC estimation. *AAPG Annual Convention and Exhibition*.

Chen, J., Ma, T., & Xiao, C. (2018). *Fastgcn: fast learning with graph convolutional networks via importance sampling*. arXiv preprint arXiv:1801.10247

Chen, J., Zhu, J., & Song, L. (2017). *Stochastic training of graph convolutional networks with variance reduction*. arXiv preprint arXiv:1710.10568

Chen, M., Xu, Z., Weinberger, K., & Sha, F. (2012). *Marginalized denoising autoencoders for domain adaptation*. arXiv preprint arXiv:1206.4683

Chen, Z. (2013). *A genetic algorithm optimizer with applications to the SAGD process* (PhD Thesis). University of Calgary.

Cheng, G., An, Y., Wang, Z., & Zhu, K. (2012). *Oil well placement optimization using niche particle swarm optimization*. Paper presented at the 2012 Eighth International Conference on Computational Intelligence and Security. 10.1109/CIS.2012.22

Cheng, Y., Wang, D., Zhou, P., & Zhang, T. (2017). *A survey of model compression and acceleration for deep neural networks*. arXiv preprint arXiv:1710.09282

Chen, H. W., Feng, Q. H., Zhang, X. M., Wang, S., Ma, Z. Y., Zhou, W. S., & Liu, C. (2018). A meta-optimized hybrid global and local algorithm for well placement optimization. *Computers & Chemical Engineering*, *117*, 209–220. doi:10.1016/j.compchemeng.2018.06.013

Chen, H. W., Feng, Q. H., Zhang, X. M., Wang, S., Zhou, W. S., & Geng, Y. H. (2017). Well placement optimization using an analytical formula-based objective function and cat swarm optimization algorithm. *Journal of Petroleum Science Engineering, 157*, 1054–1070. doi:10.1016/j.petrol.2017.08.024

Chen, T., Rucker, A., & Suh, G. E. (2015, December). Execution time prediction for energy-efficient hardware accelerators. In *Proceedings of the 48th International Symposium on Microarchitecture* (pp. 457-469). ACM. 10.1145/2830772.2830798

Che, Z. (2017). Universality of random matrices with correlated entries. *Electronic Journal of Probability*, 22.

Choi, K., Fazekas, G., & Sandler, M. (2016). *Automatic tagging using deep convolutional neural networks.* arXiv preprint arXiv:1606.00298

Choi, Y. (2014). Keystroke patterns as prosody in digital writings: A case study with deceptive reviews and essays. *Empirical Methods on Natural Language Processing (EMNLP), 6.*

Chou, P. Y. (1989). Prediction of protein structural classes from amino acid compositions. In G. D. Fasman (Ed.), *Prediction of Protein Structure and the Principles of Protein Conformation* (pp. 549–586). Boston, MA: Springer US. doi:10.1007/978-1-4613-1571-1_12

Chou, P. Y., & Fasman, G. D. (1974). Prediction of protein conformation. *Biochemistry, 13*(2), 222–245. doi:10.1021/bi00699a002 PMID:4358940

Chou, P. Y., & Fasman, G. D. (1977). Secondary structural prediction of proteins from their amino acid sequence. *Trends in Biochemical Sciences, 2*(6), 128–131. doi:10.1016/0968-0004(77)90440-6

Cios, K. J. (2018). Deep Neural Networks—A Brief History. In *Advances in Data Analysis with Computational Intelligence Methods* (pp. 183–200). Springer. doi:10.1007/978-3-319-67946-4_7

Clerc, M. (1999). The swarm and the queen: towards a deterministic and adaptive particle swarm optimization. *Proceedings of the 1999 congress on evolutionary computation-CEC99 (Cat. No. 99TH8406).* 10.1109/CEC.1999.785513

Collins, B., & Nechita, I. (2016). Random matrix techniques in quantum information theory. *Journal of Mathematical Physics, 57*(1), 015215. doi:10.1063/1.4936880

Conroy, N. J., Rubin, V. L., & Chen, Y. (2015). Automatic deception detection: Methods for finding fake news. *Proceedings of the Association for Information Science and Technology, 52*(1), 1–4. doi:10.1002/pra2.2015.145052010082

Cordella, L. P., Foggia, P., Sansone, C., & Vento, M. (2004). A (sub) graph isomorphism algorithm for matching large graphs. *IEEE Transactions on Pattern Analysis and Machine Intelligence, 26*(10), 1367–1372. doi:10.1109/TPAMI.2004.75 PMID:15641723

Corney, J. F., & Drummond, P. D. (2004). Gaussian Quantum Monte Carlo Methods for Fermions and Bosons'. *Physical Review Letters, 93*(26), 260401. doi:10.1103/PhysRevLett.93.260401 PMID:15697955

Cortes, C., & Vapnik, V. (1995). Support-vector networks. *Machine Learning, 20*(3), 273–297. doi:10.1007/BF00994018

Crestani, F., & Pasi, G. (2013). *Soft Computing in Information Retrieval: Techniques and applications* (Vol. 50). Physica.

Cuff, J. A., & Barton, G. J. (2000). Application of multiple sequence alignment profiles to improve protein secondary structure prediction. *Proteins, 40*(3), 502–511. doi:10.1002/1097-0134(20000815)40:3<502::AID-PROT170>3.0.CO;2-Q PMID:10861942

Da Silva, I. N., Spatti, D. H., Flauzino, R. A., Liboni, L. H. B., & dos Reis Alves, S. F. (2017). *Artificial neural networks.* Cham: Springer International Publishing. doi:10.1007/978-3-319-43162-8

Daamouche, A., Hamami, L., Alajlan, N., & Melgani, F. (2012). A wavelet optimization approach for ECG signal classification. *Biomedical Signal Processing and Control, 7*(4), 342–349. doi:10.1016/j.bspc.2011.07.001

Dahl, G. E., Yu, D., Deng, L., & Acero, A. (2012). Context-dependent pre-trained deep neural networks for large-vocabulary speech recognition. *IEEE Transactions on Audio, Speech, and Language Processing, 20*(1), 30–42. doi:10.1109/TASL.2011.2134090

Dalzell, J. (2013). *Conventional Natural Gas Supply Costs in Western Canada.* Canadian Energy Research Institute.

Dashtbozorg, B., Mendonça, A. M., & Campilho, A. (2015). Optic disc segmentation using the sliding band filter. *Computers in Biology and Medicine, 56*, 1–12. doi:10.1016/j.compbiomed.2014.10.009 PMID:25464343

de Albuquerque, V. H. C., Nunes, T. M., Pereira, D. R., Luz, E. J. D. S., Menotti, D., Papa, J. P., & Tavares, J. M. R. (2016). Robust automated cardiac arrhythmia detection in ECG beat signals". *Neural Computing & Applications*, 1–15.

De Meyer, A., Cattrysse, D., Rasinmäki, J., & Van Orshoven, J. (2014). Methods to optimise the design and management of biomass-for-bioenergy supply chains: A review. *Renewable & Sustainable Energy Reviews, 31*, 657–670. doi:10.1016/j.rser.2013.12.036

Dean, J., Corrado, G., Monga, R., Chen, K., Devin, M., Mao, M., . . . Ng, A. Y. (2012). Large scale distributed deep networks. In Advances in neural information processing systems (pp. 1223-1231). Academic Press.

Deb, K. (2001). *Multi-Objective Optimization using Evolutionary Algorithms.* John Wiley & Sons.

Decker, A. D., Hill, D. G., & Wicks, D. E. (1993). Log-based gas content and resource estimates for the Antrim shale, Michigan Basin. In *Low Permeability Reservoirs Symposium.* Society of Petroleum Engineers. 10.2118/25910-MS

Dediu, A.-H., Martín-Vide, C., Mitkov, R., & Truthe, B. (2017). Statistical Language and Speech Processing. In *Proceedings of 5th International Conference, SLSP 2017* (pp. 23–25). Academic Press.

Delvaux, D., Martin, H., Leplat, P., & Paulet, J. (1990). Geochemical characterization of sedimentary organic matter by means of pyrolysis kinetic parameters. *Organic Geochemistry, 16*(1–3), 175–187. doi:10.1016/0146-6380(90)90038-2

Deng, L., Li, J., Huang, J. T., Yao, K., Yu, D., Seide, F., . . . Acero, A. (2013). Recent advances in deep learning for speech research at Microsoft. *Acoustics, Speech and Signal Processing (ICASSP), 2013 IEEE International Conference on*, 8604–8608. 10.1109/ICASSP.2013.6639345

Deshmukh, A. V., Patil, T. G., Patankar, S. S., & Kulkarni, J. V. (2015). Features based classification of hard exudates in retinal images. *2015 Int. Conf. Adv. Comput.Commun. Informatics, ICACCI 2015*, 1652–1655. 10.1109/ICACCI.2015.7275850

Devaraj, D. (2007). Improved genetic algorithm for multi-objective reactive power dispatch problem. *European Transactions on Electrical Power, 17*(6), 569–581. doi:10.1002/etep.146

Diederik, P. K., & Welling, M. (2014). Auto-encoding variational bayes. *Proceedings of the International Conference on Learning Representations (ICLR).*

Ding, D. (2008). *Optimization of wellplacement using evolutionary algorithms, SPE Europec.* Paper presented at the EAGE Ann. Conf. & Exhibition, SPE.

Ding, S., Jiang, H., Li, J., Liu, G., & Mi, L. J. J. o. I. (2016). Optimization of well location, type and trajectory by a modified particle swarm optimization algorithm for the punq-s3 model. *Information, 4*(1).

Ding, S., Lu, R., Xi, Y., Wang, S., & Wu, Y. J. C. (2019). Well placement optimization using direct mapping of productivity potential and threshold value of productivity potential management strategy. *Engineering, 121*, 327-337.

Ding, S. W., Jiang, H. Q., Li, J. J., & Tang, G. P. (2014). Optimization of well placement by combination of a modified particle swarm optimization algorithm and quality map method. *Computational Geosciences, 18*(5), 747–762. doi:10.100710596-014-9422-2

Dokur, Z., Ölmez, T., Yazgan, E., & Ersoy, O. K. (1997). Detection of ECG waveforms by neural networks. *Medical Engineering & Physics, 19*(8), 738–741. doi:10.1016/S1350-4533(97)00029-5 PMID:9450258

Dong, N., Fang, X., & Wu, A. G. (2016). A Novel Chaotic Particle Swarm Optimization Algorithm for Parking Space Guidance. *Mathematical Problems in Engineering*.

Dong, X., Wang, C., & Si, W. (2017). ECG beat classification via deterministic learning". *Neurocomputing, 240*, 1–12. doi:10.1016/j.neucom.2017.02.056

Dong, Y., & Wu, Y. (2015). Adaptive cascade deep convolutional neural networks for face alignment. *Computer Standards & Interfaces, 42*, 105–112. doi:10.1016/j.csi.2015.06.004

Dong, Z., Jia, S., Wu, T., & Pei, M. (2016). Face Video Retrieval via Deep Learning of Binary Hash Representations. *Proceedings of the Thirtieth AAAI Conference on Artificial Intelligence (AAAI-16)*, 3471-3477.

Dragovic, Azpiazu, & Pera. (2010). "Is Sven Seven?": A Search Intent Module for Children. *SIGR 2010*, 847-848.

Du, H., Wang, J., Hu, Z., Yao, X., & Zhang, X. (2008). Prediction of fungicidal activities of rice blast disease based on least-squares support vector machines and project pursuit regression. *Journal of Agricultural and Food Chemistry, 56*(22), 10785–10792. doi:10.1021/jf8022194 PMID:18950187

Du, J., & Xu, Y. (2017). Hierarchical deep neural network for multivariate regression. *Pattern Recognition, 63*, 149–157. doi:10.1016/j.patcog.2016.10.003

Duman, S., Güvenç, U., Sönmez, Y., & Yörükeren, N. (2012). Optimal power flow using gravitational search algorithm. *Energy Conversion and Management, 59*, 86–95. doi:10.1016/j.enconman.2012.02.024

Duman, S., Sonmez, Y., Guvenc, U., & Yorukeren, N. (2012). Optimal reactive power dispatch using a gravitational search algorithm. *IET Generation, Transmission & Distribution, 6*(6), 563–576. doi:10.1049/iet-gtd.2011.0681

Eberhart, R. C., & Hu, X. (1999). Human tremor analysis using particle swarm optimization. *Proceedings of the 1999 Congress on Evolutionary Computation-CEC99* (Cat. No. 99TH8406). 10.1109/CEC.1999.785508

Eberhart, R., & Kennedy, J. (1995). Particle swarm optimization. *Proceedings of the IEEE International Conference on Neural Networks, 4*, 1942–1948.

Ebtehaj, I., Bonakdari, H., Shamshirband, S., & Mohammadi, K. (2016). A combined support vector machine-wavelet transform model for prediction of sediment transport in sewer. *Flow Measurement and Instrumentation, 47*, 19–27. doi:10.1016/j.flowmeasinst.2015.11.002

El Bouchti, A., Chakroun, A., Abbar, H., & Okar, C. (2017). Fraud detection in banking using deep reinforcement learning. *Seventh International Conference on Innovative Computing Technology (INTECH)*, 58-63. 10.1109/INTECH.2017.8102446

Elattar, E. E., & ElSayed, S. K. (2019). Modified JAYA algorithm for optimal power flow incorporating renewable energy sources considering the cost, emission, power loss and voltage profile improvement. *Energy, 178*, 598–609. doi:10.1016/j.energy.2019.04.159

Elhaj, F. A., Salim, N., Harris, A. R., Swee, T. T., & Ahmed, T. (2016). Arrhythmia recognition and classification using combined linear and nonlinear features of ECG signals. *Computer Methods and Programs in Biomedicine, 127*, 52–63. doi:10.1016/j.cmpb.2015.12.024 PMID:27000289

Elkazzaz, F., Mahmoud, A., & Maher, A. (2018), Cuckoo Search Algorithm for Multi-objective Supply Chain Problem. In *MATEC Web of Conferences* (Vol. 189, p.06001). EDP Sciences.

Elsken, T., Metzen, J. H., & Hutter, F. (2019). Neural Architecture Search: A Survey. *Journal of Machine Learning Research*, *20*(55), 1–21.

Emad, O., Yassine, I. A., & Fahmy, A. S. (2015). Automatic localization of the left ventricle in cardiac mri images using deep learning. *Engineering in Medicine and Biology Society (EMBC), 2015 37th Annual International Conference of the IEEE*, 683–686. 10.1109/EMBC.2015.7318454

Emerick, A. A., Silva, E., Messer, B., Almeida, L. F., Szwarcman, D., Pacheco, M. A. C., & Vellasco, M. M. B. R. (2009). *Well placement optimization using a genetic algorithm with nonlinear constraints.* Paper presented at the SPE reservoir simulation symposium. 10.2118/118808-MS

Fang, C., Shang, Y., & Xu, D. (2018). MUFOLD-SS: New deep inception-inside-inception networks for protein secondary structure prediction. *Proteins*, *86*(5), 592–598. doi:10.1002/prot.25487 PMID:29492997

Farina, M., & Amato, P. (2004). A fuzzy definition of "optimality" for many-criteria optimization problems. *IEEE Transactions on Systems, Man, and Cybernetics. Part A, Systems and Humans*, *34*(3), 315–326. doi:10.1109/TSMCA.2004.824873

Feng, S., Banerjee, R., & Choi, Y. (2012). Syntactic stylometry for deception detection. *Proceedings of the 50th Annual Meeting of the Association for Computational Linguistics: Short Papers-Volume 2, Association for Computational Linguistics*, 171–175.

Feng, F., Wang, X., & Li, R. (2014). Cross-modal retrieval with correspondence autoencoder. *Proceedings of the ACM International Conference on Multimedia*, 7–16.

Feng, Q. H., Zhang, J. Y., Zhang, X. M., & Hu, A. M. (2012). Optimizing well placement in a coalbed methane reservoir using the particle swarm optimization algorithm. *International Journal of Coal Geology*, *104*, 34–45. doi:10.1016/j.coal.2012.09.004

Fergadis, A., Baziotis, C., Pappas, D., Papageorgiou, H., & Potamianos, A. (2018). Hierarchical bi-directional attention-based RNNs for supporting document classification on protein–protein interactions affected by genetic mutations. *Database*, 1–10. PMID:30137284

Fink, O., Zio, E., & Weidmann, U. (2015). Development and application of deep belief networks for predicting railway operation disruptions. *International Journal of Performability Engineering*, *11*(2), 121–134.

Foroud, T., Baradaran, A., & Seifi, A. (2018). A comparative evaluation of global search algorithms in black box optimization of oil production: A case study on Brugge field. *Journal of Petroleum Science Engineering*, *167*, 131–151. doi:10.1016/j.petrol.2018.03.028

Forouzanfar, F., & Reynolds, A. J. J. o. P. S. (2013). Well-placement optimization using a derivative-free method. *Engineering*, *109*, 96-116.

Forouzanfar, F., Poquioma, W. E., & Reynolds, A. C. (2016). Simultaneous and Sequential Estimation of Optimal Placement and Controls of Wells With a Covariance Matrix Adaptation Algorithm. *SPE Journal*, *21*(2), 501–521. doi:10.2118/173256-PA

Franklin, S. W., & Rajan, S. E. (2014). Diagnosis of diabetic retinopathy by employing image processing technique to detect exudates in retinal images. *IET Image Processing*, *8*(10), 601–609. doi:10.1049/iet-ipr.2013.0565

Frasconi, P., Gori, M., & Sperduti, A. (1998). A general framework for adaptive processing of data structures. *IEEE Transactions on Neural Networks*, *9*(5), 768–786. doi:10.1109/72.712151 PMID:18255765

Frishman, D., & Argos, P. (1995). Knowledge-based protein secondary structure assignment. *Proteins, 23*(4), 566–579. doi:10.1002/prot.340230412 PMID:8749853

Fukushima, K., & Miyake, S. (1982). Neocognitron: A self-organizing neural network model for a mechanism of visual pattern recognition. In *Competition and cooperation in neural nets* (pp. 267–285). Berlin: Springer. doi:10.1007/978-3-642-46466-9_18

Gallagher, K., & Sambridge, M. J. C. (1994). Genetic algorithms: a powerful tool for large-scale nonlinear optimization problems. *Geosciences, 20*(7-8), 1229-1236.

Ganesan, T., Aris, M. S., & Elamvazuthi, I. (2018b). *Multiobjective Strategy for an Industrial Gas Turbine: Absorption Chiller System. In Handbook of Research on Emergent Applications of Optimization Algorithms* (pp. 531–556). IGI Global. doi:10.4018/978-1-5225-2990-3.ch023

Ganesan, T., Aris, M. S., & Vasant, P. (2018a). Extreme Value Metaheuristics for Optimizing a Many-Objective Gas Turbine System. *International Journal of Energy Optimization and Engineering, 7*(2), 76–96. doi:10.4018/IJEOE.2018040104

Ganesan, T., Elamvazuthi, I., & Vasant, P. (2015). Multiobjective design optimization of a nano-CMOS voltage-controlled oscillator using game theoretic-differential evolution. *Applied Soft Computing, 32*, 293–299. doi:10.1016/j.asoc.2015.03.016

Ganesan, T., Vasant, P., & Elamvazuthi, I. (2013). Normal-boundary intersection based parametric multi-objective optimization of green sand mould system. *Journal of Manufacturing Systems, 32*(1), 197–205. doi:10.1016/j.jmsy.2012.10.004

Ganesan, T., Vasant, P., & Elamvazuthi, I. (2016). *Advances in Metaheuristics: Applications in Engineering Systems.* CRC Press. doi:10.1201/9781315297651

Ganesan, T., Vasant, P., & Elamvazuthy, I. (2012). A hybrid PSO approach for solving non-convex optimization problems. *Archives of Control Sciences, 22*(1), 87–105. doi:10.2478/v10170-011-0014-2

Ganguly, G. J. S., Gupta, M., Varma, V., & Pudi, V. (2016). Author2Vec: Learning Author Representations by Combining Content and Link Information. *Proceedings of the 25th International Conference Companion on World Wide Web.*

Gao, J., & You, F. (2015). Shale gas supply chain design and operations toward better economic and life cycle environmental performance: MINLP model and global optimization algorithm. *ACS Sustainable Chemistry & Engineering, 3*(7), 1282–1291. doi:10.1021/acssuschemeng.5b00122

Garnier, J., Gibrat, J. F., & Robson, B. (1996). GOR method for predicting protein secondary structure from amino acid sequence. In *Computer Methods for Macromolecular Sequence Analysis* (Vol. 266, pp. 540–553). Academic Press. doi:10.1016/S0076-6879(96)66034-0

Garnier, J., Osguthorpe, D. J., & Robson, B. (1978). Analysis of the accuracy and implications of simple methods for predicting the secondary structure of globular proteins. *Journal of Molecular Biology, 120*(1), 97–120. doi:10.1016/0022-2836(78)90297-8 PMID:642007

Genc, H., & Yilmaz, B. (2019). Text-based Event Detection: Deciphering Date Information Using Graph Embeddings. In Proceedings of Big Data Analytics and Knowledge Discovery (DAWAK) (Lecture Notes in Computer Science) (pp.11706-11712). Academic Press.

Ghasemi, M., Ghavidel, S., Akbari, E., & Vahed, A. A. (2014). Solving non-linear, non-smooth and non-convex optimal power flow problems using chaotic invasive weed optimization algorithms based on chaos. *Energy, 73*, 340–353. doi:10.1016/j.energy.2014.06.026

Ghasemi, M., Ghavidel, S., Ghanbarian, M. M., Gharibzadeh, M., & Vahed, A. A. (2014). Multi-objective optimal power flow considering the cost, emission, voltage deviation and power losses using multi-objective modified imperialist competitive algorithm. *Energy*, *78*, 276–289. doi:10.1016/j.energy.2014.10.007

Ghasemi, M., Ghavidel, S., Rahmani, S., Roosta, A., & Falah, H. (2014). A novel hybrid algorithm of imperialist competitive algorithm and teaching learning algorithm for optimal power flow problem with non-smooth cost functions. *Engineering Applications of Artificial Intelligence*, *29*, 54–69. doi:10.1016/j.engappai.2013.11.003

Ghorbani, M. A., Shamshirband, S., Haghi, D. Z., Azani, A., Bonakdari, H., & Ebtehaj, I. (2017). Application of firefly algorithm-based support vector machines for prediction of field capacity and permanent wilting point. *Soil & Tillage Research*, *172*, 32–38. doi:10.1016/j.still.2017.04.009

Gibrat, J. F. (1986). *Modelisation by computers of the 3-D Structure of Proteins* (PhD Thesis). University of Paris VI.

Gibrat, J. F., Garnier, J., & Robson, B. (1987). Further developments of protein secondary structure prediction using information theory: New parameters and consideration of residue pairs. *Journal of Molecular Biology*, *198*(3), 425–443. doi:10.1016/0022-2836(87)90292-0 PMID:3430614

Giuliani, C. M., & Camponogara, E. (2015). Derivative-free methods applied to daily production optimization of gas-lifted oil fields. *Computers & Chemical Engineering*, *75*, 60–64. doi:10.1016/j.compchemeng.2015.01.014

Goldberg, Y., & Hirst, G. (2017). *Neural Network Methods in Natural Language Processing*. Morgan & Claypool Publishers. doi:10.2200/S00762ED1V01Y201703HLT037

Goodfellow, I., Bengio, Y., & Courville, A. (2016). *Deep learning*. Cambridge, UK: MIT Press.

Gopalakrishnan, K., Khaitan, S. K., Choudhary, A., & Agrawal, A. (2017). Deep Convolutional Neural Networks with transfer learning for computer vision-based data-driven pavement distress detection. *Construction & Building Materials*, *157*, 322–330.

Gori, M., Monfardini, G., & Scarselli, F. (2005, July). A new model for learning in graph domains. In *Proceedings 2005 IEEE International Joint Conference on Neural Networks*, 2005 (Vol. 2, pp. 729-734). IEEE. 10.1109/IJCNN.2005.1555942

Gossen, T., & Nurnberger, A. (2010). *Specifics of Information Retrieval for Young Users: A Survey. In Information Processing and Management*. Elsevier.

Goudhaman, M., Vanathi, N., & Sasikumar, S. (n.d.). *Semantic Approach for Dynamic Shortest Path Problem (SPP) By Cheetah Chase Algorithm (CCA)*. Academic Press.

Grover, A., & Leskovec, J. (2016). node2vec: Scalable feature learning for networks. In *Proceedings of the 22nd ACM SIGKDD international conference on Knowledge discovery and data mining* (pp. 855-864). ACM. 10.1145/2939672.2939754

Grudinin, N. (1998). Reactive power optimization using successive quadratic programming method. *IEEE Transactions on Power Systems*, *13*(4), 1219–1225. doi:10.1109/59.736232

Guangyou, Z., Qiang, J., & Linye, Z. (2003). Using log information to analyse the geochemical characteristics of source rocks in Jiyang depression. *Well Logging Technology*, *27*(2), 104–109.

Guo, L., Chen, J. F., & Miao, Z. Y. (2009). The study and application of a new overlay method of TOC content. *Nat. Gas. Geosci*, *20*(6), 951–956.

Guria, C., Goli, K. K., & Pathak, A. K. J. P. S. (2014). *Multi-objective optimization of oil well drilling using elitist non-dominated sorting genetic algorithm*. Academic Press.

Gurnani, A. (n.d.). *Flower Categorization using Deep Convolutional Neural Networks*. Academic Press.

Guyaguler, B., & Horne, R. N. (2001). *Uncertainty assessment of well placement optimization.* Paper presented at the SPE annual technical conference and exhibition. 10.2118/71625-MS

Gyllstrom, K. Moens & Marie-Francine (2010). Wisdom of the Ages: Toward Delivering the Children's Web with the Link-based Age rank Algorithm. *Proceedings of the 19th ACM International Conference on Information and Knowledge Management, CIKM '10*, 159-168.

Haas, J., Barbato, A., Behringer, D., Studer, G., Roth, S., Bertoni, M., ... Schwede, T. (2018). Continuous Automated Model EvaluatiOn (CAMEO) complementing the critical assessment of structure prediction in CASP12. *Proteins, 86*(S1), 387–398. doi:10.1002/prot.25431 PMID:29178137

Habibollahzadeh, H., Luo, G., & Semlyen, A. (1989). Hydrothermal optimal power flow based on a combined linear and nonlinear programming methodology. *IEEE Transactions on Power Systems, 4*(2), 530–537. doi:10.1109/59.193826

Hamelryck, T. (2005). An amino acid has two sides: A new 2D measure provides a different view of solvent exposure. *Proteins, 59*(1), 38–48. doi:10.1002/prot.20379 PMID:15688434

Hamida, Z., Azizi, F., & Saad, G. (2017). An efficient geometry-based optimization approach for well placement in oil fields. *Journal of Petroleum Science Engineering, 149*, 383–392. doi:10.1016/j.petrol.2016.10.055

Han, P., Huang, Y., Jia, Z.-Z., Wang, D.-F., & Li, Y.-L. (2005). *Mixed H/spl I. bar/2/H/spl I. bar//spl infin/optimal PID control for superheated steam temperature system based on PSO optimization.* Paper presented at the 2005 International Conference on Machine Learning and Cybernetics. 10.1109/ICMLC.2005.1527082

Han, S., Seng, C., Joseph, S., & Remagnino, P. (2017). *How deep learning extracts and learns leaf features for plant classification.* Academic Press. doi:10.1016/j.patcog.2017.05.015

Hanson, J., Paliwal, K., Litfin, T., Yang, Y., & Zhou, Y. (2018). Improving Prediction of Protein Secondary Structure, Backbone Angles, Solvent Accessibility, and Contact Numbers by Using Predicted Contact Maps and an Ensemble of Recurrent and Residual Convolutional Neural Networks. *Bioinformatics*. PMID:30535134

Hanson, J., Yang, Y., Paliwal, K., & Zhou, Y. (2017). Improving protein disorder prediction by deep bidirectional long short-term memory recurrent neural networks. *Bioinformatics (Oxford, England), 33*(5), 685–692. PMID:28011771

Hare, A. A., Kuzyk, Z. Z. A., Macdonald, R. W., Sanei, H., Barber, D., Stern, G. A., & Wang, F. (2014). Characterization of sedimentary organic matter in recent marine sediments from Hudson Bay, Canada, by Rock-Eval pyrolysis. *Organic Geochemistry, 68*, 52–60. doi:10.1016/j.orggeochem.2014.01.007

Hassan, W., Saleem, S., & Habib, A. (2017). Classification of normal and arrhythmic ECG using wavelet transform based template-matching technique". *JPMA. The Journal of the Pakistan Medical Association, 67*(6), 843. PMID:28585579

Hassoun, M. H. (1995). *Fundamentals of artificial neural networks.* MIT Press.

Hazra, J., & Sinha, A. K. (2010). A multi-objective optimal power flow using particle swarm optimization. *European Transactions on Electrical Power, 21*(1), 1028–1045. doi:10.1002/etep.494

Hecht-Nielsen, R. (1988). Applications of counterpropagation networks. *Neural Networks, 1*(2), 131–139. doi:10.1016/0893-6080(88)90015-9

He, D., Dong, G., Wang, F., & Mao, Z. (2011). Optimization of dynamic economic dispatch with valve-point effect using chaotic sequence based differential evolution algorithms. *Energy Conversion and Management, 52*(2), 1026–1032. doi:10.1016/j.enconman.2010.08.031

Heffernan, R., Paliwal, K., Lyons, J., Dehzangi, A., Sharma, A., Wang, J., ... Zhou, Y. (2015). Improving prediction of secondary structure, local backbone angles, and solvent accessible surface area of proteins by iterative deep learning. *Scientific Reports*, *5*(1), 11476. doi:10.1038rep11476 PMID:26098304

Heffernan, R., Yang, Y., Paliwal, K., & Zhou, Y. (2017). Capturing non-local interactions by long short-term memory bidirectional recurrent neural networks for improving prediction of protein secondary structure, backbone angles, contact numbers and solvent accessibility. *Bioinformatics (Oxford, England)*, *33*(18), 2842–2849. doi:10.1093/bioinformatics/btx218 PMID:28430949

Heidari, Z., Torres-Verdin, C., & Preeg, W. E. (2011). Quantitative method for estimating total organic carbon and porosity, and for diagnosing mineral constituents from well logs in shale-gas formations. In *SPWLA 52nd Annual Logging Symposium*. Society of Petrophysicists and Well-Log Analysts.

Heiliö, M., Lähivaara, T., Laitinen, E., Mantere, T., Merikoski, J., Raivio, K., ... Tiihonen, T. (2016). Mathematical modelling. Springer.

Heinsfeld, A. S., Franco, A. R., Craddock, R. C., Buchweitz, A., & Meneguzzi, F. (2018). Identification of autism spectrum disorder using deep learning and the ABIDE dataset. *NeuroImage. Clinical*, *17*, 16–23. doi:10.1016/j.nicl.2017.08.017 PMID:29034163

He, K., Zhang, X., Ren, S., & Sun, J. (2016). Deep residual learning for image recognition. *The IEEE Conference on Computer Vision and Pattern Recognition (CVPR)*.

Helmy, M. W., Khalaf, F., & Darwish, T. J. S. d. (1998). *Well design using a computer model*. Academic Press.

Henikoff, S., & Henikoff, J. G. (1992). Amino acid substitution matrices from protein blocks. *Proceedings of the National Academy of Sciences of the United States of America*, *89*(22), 10915–10919. doi:10.1073/pnas.89.22.10915 PMID:1438297

Hester, T. C., & Schmoker, J. W. (1987). *Determination of organic content from formation-density logs, Devonian-Mississippian Woodford shale, Anadarko basin*. US Geological Survey. doi:10.3133/ofr8720

Hiary, H., Saadeh, H., Saadeh, M., & Yaqub, M. (2018). *Flower classification using deep convolutional neural networks*. Academic Press. doi:10.1049/iet-cvi.2017.0155

Hinton, G. E., & Salakhutdinov, R. R. (2006). Reducing the dimensionality of data with neural networks. *Science*, *313*(5786), 504-507.

Hinton, G. E., Deng, L., Yu, D., Dahl, G. E., Mohamed, A. R., Jaitly, N., ... Sainath, T. N. (2012). Deep neural networks for acoustic modeling in speech recognition: The shared views of four research groups. *IEEE Signal Processing Magazine*, *29*(6), 82–97. doi:10.1109/MSP.2012.2205597

Hinton, G. E., Osindero, S., & Teh, Y.-W. (2006). A fast learning algorithm for deep belief nets. *Neural Computation*, *18*(7), 1527–1554. doi:10.1162/neco.2006.18.7.1527 PMID:16764513

Hinton, G. E., & Salakhutdinov, R. R. (2006). Reducing the dimensionality of data with neural networks. *Science*, *313*(5786), 504–507. doi:10.1126cience.1127647 PMID:16873662

Hochreiter, S., & Schmidhuber, J. (1997). Long short-term memory. *Neural Computation*, *9*(8), 1735–1780. doi:10.1162/neco.1997.9.8.1735 PMID:9377276

Holland, J. H. J. S. a. (1992). *Genetic algorithms*. Academic Press.

Holley, L. H., & Karplus, M. (1989). Protein secondary structure prediction with a neural network. *Proceedings of the National Academy of Sciences of the United States of America*, *86*(1), 152–156. doi:10.1073/pnas.86.1.152 PMID:2911565

Hong, Y. Y., Beltran, A. A., & Paglinawan, A. C. (2016). A Chaos-Enhanced Particle Swarm Optimization with Adaptive Parameters and Its Application in Maximum Power Point Tracking. *Mathematical Problems in Engineering*.

Hopfield, J. J. (1984). Neurons with graded response have collective computational properties like those of two-state neurons. *Proceedings of the National Academy of Sciences of the United States of America*, *81*(10), 3088–3092. doi:10.1073/pnas.81.10.3088 PMID:6587342

Horne, B. D., & Adali, S. (2017). This Just In: Fake News Packs a Lot in Title, Uses Simpler, Repetitive Content in Text Body, More Similar to Satire than Real News. *The 2nd International Workshop on News and Public Opinion at ICWSM*.

Hoshen, Y. (2017). Vain: Attentional multi-agent predictive modeling. In Advances in Neural Information Processing Systems (pp. 2701-2711). Academic Press.

Hoskins, J. C., & Himmelblau, D. M. (1988). Artificial neural network models of knowledge representation in chemical engineering. *Computers & Chemical Engineering*, *12*(9–10), 881–890. doi:10.1016/0098-1354(88)87015-7

Hosseini, H., Xiao, B., Jaiswal, M., & Poovendran, R. (2017). On the limitation of convolutional neural networks in recognizing negative images. In *2017 16th IEEE International Conference on Machine Learning and Applications (ICMLA)*, (pp. 352–358). IEEE.

Howard, A. G., Zhu, M., Chen, B., & Kalenichenko, D. (2017). *Mobilenets: Efficient convolutional neural networks for mobile vision applications*. arXiv preprint arXiv:1704.04861

Huang, L., Ding, S., Yu, S., Wang, J., & Lu, K. (2016). Chaos-enhanced Cuckoo search optimization algorithms for global optimization. *Applied Mathematical Modelling*, *40*(5-6), 3860–3875. doi:10.1016/j.apm.2015.10.052

Huang, Z., & Williamson, M. A. (1996). Artificial neural network modelling as an aid to source rock characterization. *Marine and Petroleum Geology*, *13*(2), 277–290. doi:10.1016/0264-8172(95)00062-3

Hua, S., & Sun, Z. (2001). A novel method of protein secondary structure prediction with high segment overlap measure: Support vector machine approach. *Journal of Molecular Biology*, *308*(2), 397–407. doi:10.1006/jmbi.2001.4580 PMID:11327775

Hu, H. T., Lu, S. F., Liu, C., Wang, W. M., Wang, M., Li, J. J., & Shang, J. H. (2011). Models for calculating organic carbon content from logging information: Comparison and analysis. *Acta Sedimentologica Sinica*, *29*, 1199–1205.

Husbands, P., Copley, P., Eldridge, A., & Mandelis, J. (2007). An introduction to evolutionary computing for musicians. In *Evolutionary computer music* (pp. 1–27). Springer.

Hutahaean, J. J., Demyanov, V., Arnold, D., & Vazquez, O. (2014). *Optimization of Well Placement to Minimize the Risk of Scale Deposition in Field Development*. Paper presented at the Abu Dhabi International Petroleum Exhibition and Conference. 10.2118/171733-MS

Isebor, O. J., Ciaurri, D. E., & Durlofsky, L. J. (2014). Generalized Field-Development Optimization With Derivative-Free Procedures. *SPE Journal*, *19*(5), 891–908. doi:10.2118/163631-PA

Isebor, O. J., Durlofsky, L. J., & Ciaurri, D. E. (2014). A derivative-free methodology with local and global search for the constrained joint optimization of well locations and controls. *Computational Geosciences*, *18*(3-4), 463–482. doi:10.100710596-013-9383-x

Jaafra, Y., Laurent, J. L., Deruyver, A., & Naceur, M. S. (2018). *A review of meta-reinforcement learning for deep neural networks architecture search*. arXiv preprint arXiv:1812.07995

Jabr, R. A., & Pal, B. C. (2009). Intermittent wind generation in optimal power flow dispatching. *IET Generation, Transmission & Distribution, 3*(1), 66–74. doi:10.1049/iet-gtd:20080273

Jacovi, A., Shalom, O. S., & Haifa, I. (2018). Understanding Convolutional Neural Networks for Text Classification. *Proceedings of the 2018 EMNLP Workshop Blackbox NLP: Analyzing and Interpreting Neural Networks for NLP*, 56-65. 10.18653/v1/W18-5408

Jadhav, S. M., Nalbalwar, S. L., & Ghatol, A. A. (2011). Modular neural network based arrhythmia classification system using ECG signal data. *International Journal of Information Technology and Knowledge Management, 4*(1), 205–209.

Jadhav, S., Nalbalwar, S., & Ghatol, A. (2014). Feature elimination based random subspace ensembles learning for ECG arrhythmia diagnosis. *Soft Computing, 18*(3), 579–587. doi:10.100700500-013-1079-6

Jaitly, N., & Hinton, G. (2011). Learning a better representation of speech soundwaves using restricted Boltzmann machines. *Acoustics, Speech and Signal Processing (ICASSP), 2011 IEEE International Conference on*, 5884–5887. 10.1109/ICASSP.2011.5947700

Jang, I., Oh, S., Kim, Y., Park, C., & Kang, H. (2018). Well-placement optimisation using sequential artificial neural networks. *Energy Exploration & Exploitation, 36*(3), 433–449. doi:10.1177/0144598717729490

Janiga, D., Czarnota, R., Stopa, J., & Wojnarowski, P. (2019). Self-adapt reservoir clusterization method to enhance robustness of well placement optimization. *Journal of Petroleum Science Engineering, 173*, 37–52. doi:10.1016/j.petrol.2018.10.005

Jansen, J. J. C. (2011). Adjoint-based optimization of multi-phase flow through porous media–a review. *Fluids, 46*(1), 40-51.

Jarvie, D. M., Jarvie, B. M., Weldon, W. D., & Maende, A. (2015). Geochemical assessment of in situ petroleum in unconventional resource systems. In *Unconventional Resources Technology Conference* (pp. 875–894). Society of Exploration Geophysicists, American Association of Petroleum. doi:10.1007/978-1-84628-600-1_1

Jaya, T., Dheeba, J., & Singh, N. A. (2015). Detection of Hard Exudates in Colour Fundus Images Using Fuzzy Support Vector Machine-Based Expert System. *Journal of Digital Imaging, 28*(6), 761–768. doi:10.100710278-015-9793-5 PMID:25822397

Jeddi, B., Einaddin, A. H., & Kazemzadeh, R. (2016). A novel multi-objective approach based on improved electromagnetism-like algorithm to solve optimal power flow problem considering the detailed model of thermal generators. *International Transactions on Electrical Energy Systems, 27*(4), e2293. doi:10.1002/etep.2293

Jeon, W., & Rhee, S. (2017). *Plant Leaf Recognition Using a Convolution Neural Network.* Academic Press.

Jesmani, M., Jafarpour, B., Bellout, M., Hanea, R., & Foss, B. (2016). *Application of simultaneous perturbation stochastic approximation to well placement optimization under uncertainty.* Paper presented at the ECMOR XV-15th European Conference on the Mathematics of Oil Recovery. 10.3997/2214-4609.201601873

Jia, X. (2017, May). Image recognition method based on deep learning. In *Control And Decision Conference (CCDC), 2017 29th Chinese* (pp. 4730-4735). IEEE. 10.1109/CCDC.2017.7979332

Jiang, Q., Jin, X., Lee, S.-J., & Yao, S. (2017). Protein secondary structure prediction: A survey of the state of the art. *Journal of Molecular Graphics & Modelling, 76*, 379–402. doi:10.1016/j.jmgm.2017.07.015 PMID:28763690

Jiang, S., Zhang, J., Ong, Y. S., Zhang, A. N., & Tan, P. S. (2015). A simple and fast hypervolume indicator-based multiobjective evolutionary algorithm. *IEEE Transactions on Cybernetics, 45*(10), 2202–2213. doi:10.1109/TCYB.2014.2367526 PMID:25474815

Joglekar, M. R., Li, C., Adams, J. K., Khaitan, P., & Le, Q. V. (2019). *Neural Input Search for Large Scale Recommendation Models.* arXiv preprint arXiv:1907.04471

Johannes, I., Kruusement, K., Palu, V., Veski, R., & Bojesen-Koefoed, J. A. (2006). Evaluation of oil potential of Estonian shales and biomass samples using Rock-Eval analyzer. *Oil Shale, 23*(2), 110–119.

Johnson, L. M., Rezaee, R., Kadkhodaie, A., Smith, G., & Yu, H. (2018). Geochemical property modelling of a potential shale reservoir in the Canning Basin (Western Australia), using Artificial Neural Networks and geostatistical tools. *Computers & Geosciences, 120*, 73–81. doi:10.1016/j.cageo.2018.08.004

Jones, D. T. (1999). Protein secondary structure prediction based on position-specific scoring matrices. *Journal of Molecular Biology, 292*(2), 195–202. doi:10.1006/jmbi.1999.3091 PMID:10493868

Joshi, S. (2003). *Cost/benefits of horizontal wells.* Paper presented at the SPE Western Regional/AAPG Pacific Section Joint Meeting. 10.2118/83621-MS

Joshi, A. S., Kulkarni, O., Kakandikar, G. M., & Nandedkar, V. M. (2017). Cuckoo Search Optimization-A Review. *Materials Today: Proceedings, 4*(8), 7262–7269.

Kabsch, W., & Sander, C. (1983). Dictionary of protein secondary structure: Pattern recognition of hydrogen-bonded and geometrical features. *Biopolymers, 22*(12), 2577–2637. doi:10.1002/bip.360221211 PMID:6667333

Kalantari, A., Kamsin, A., Shamshirband, S., Gani, A., Alinejad-Rokny, H., & Chronopoulos, A. T. (2018). Computational intelligence approaches for classification of medical data: State-of-the-art, future challenges and research directions. *Neurocomputing, 276*, 2–22. doi:10.1016/j.neucom.2017.01.126

Kalmanovich, A., & Chechik, G. (2014). *Gradual training of deep denoising auto encoders.* arXiv preprint arXiv:1412.6257

Kamali, M. R., & Mirshady, A. A. (2004). Total organic carbon content determined from well logs using ΔLogR and Neuro Fuzzy techniques. *Journal of Petroleum Science Engineering, 45*(3–4), 141–148. doi:10.1016/j.petrol.2004.08.005

Kammerer, Y., & Bohnacker, M. (2012). Children's Web Search With Google: The Effectiveness of Natural Language Queries. *Proceedings of the 11th International Conference on Interaction Design and Children*, 184-187. 10.1145/2307096.2307121

Kan, M.-Y. (2004). Web page classification without the web page. In *Proceedings of the 13th International World Wide Web conference on Alternate track papers & posters (WWWAlt. '04)*. ACM. 10.1145/1013367.1013426

Kan, M.-Y., & Thi, H. O. N. (2005). *Fast webpage classification using URL features. Technical Report.* Singapore: National University of Singapore.

Kapse, S. P., & Krishnapillai, S. (2018). An Improved Multi-Objective Particle Swarm Optimization Based on Utopia Point Guided Search. *International Journal of Applied Metaheuristic Computing, 9*(4), 71–96. doi:10.4018/IJAMC.2018100104

Karimpour, K., Zarghami, R., Moosavian, M., Bahmanyar, H. J. O., Science, G., & Nouvelles, T. R. d. I. E. (2016). *New fuzzy model for risk assessment based on different types of consequences.* Academic Press.

Karypis, G. (2006). YASSPP: Better kernels and coding schemes lead to improvements in protein secondary structure prediction. *Proteins, 64*(3), 575–586. doi:10.1002/prot.21036 PMID:16763996

Kasabov, N. K. (1996). *Foundations of neural networks, fuzzy systems, and knowledge engineering.* Marcel Alencar.

Katz, L. (1953). A new status index derived from sociometric analysis. *Psychometrika, 18*(1), 39–43. doi:10.1007/BF02289026

Keane, A. J. (1995). Genetic algorithm optimization of multi-peak problems: Studies in convergence and robustness. *Artificial Intelligence in Engineering, 9*(2), 75–83. doi:10.1016/0954-1810(95)95751-Q

Kearnes, S., McCloskey, K., Berndl, M., Pande, V., & Riley, P. (2016). Molecular graph convolutions: Moving beyond fingerprints. *Journal of Computer-Aided Molecular Design, 30*(8), 595–608. doi:10.100710822-016-9938-8 PMID:27558503

Kennedy, J., & Eberhart, R. (1995). Particle swarm optimization. In *IEEE International of first Conference on Neural Networks.* Perth, Australia, IEEE Press.

Kennedy, J., & Eberhart, R. (1995). Particle swarm optimization. In *IEEE International of first Conference on Neural Networks.* Perth, Australia: IEEE Press.

Kennedy, J. (1997). The particle swarm: social adaptation of knowledge. *Proceedings of 1997 IEEE International Conference on Evolutionary Computation (ICEC'97).* 10.1109/ICEC.1997.592326

Khademi, M. H., Rahimpour, M. R., & Jahanmiri, A. (2010). Differential evolution (DE) strategy for optimization of hydrogen production, cyclohexane dehydrogenation and methanol synthesis in a hydrogen-permselective membrane thermally coupled reactor. *International Journal of Hydrogen Energy, 35*(5), 1936–1950. doi:10.1016/j.ijhydene.2009.12.080

Khamsi, M. A., & Kirk, W. A. (2011). *An introduction to metric spaces and fixed point theory* (Vol. 53). John Wiley & Sons.

Kim, H., & Park, H. (2003). Protein secondary structure prediction based on an improved support vector machines approach. *Protein Engineering, Design & Selection, 16*(8), 553–560. doi:10.1093/protein/gzg072 PMID:12968073

Kim, J., Min, S. D., & Lee, M. (2011). An arrhythmia classification algorithm using a dedicated wavelet adapted to different subjects". *Biomedical Engineering Online, 10*(1), 56. doi:10.1186/1475-925X-10-56 PMID:21707989

Kim, Y. G., Kim, M., & Chung, S. W. (2017). Enhancing Energy Efficiency of Multimedia Applications in Heterogeneous Mobile Multi-Core Processors. *IEEE Transactions on Computers, 66*(11), 1878–1889. doi:10.1109/TC.2017.2710317

King, G. E. (2010). Thirty years of gas shale fracturing: What have we learned? In *SPE Annual Technical Conference and Exhibition.* Society of Petroleum Engineers. 10.2118/133456-MS

Kipf, T. N., & Welling, M. (2016). *Variational graph auto-encoders.* arXiv preprint arXiv:1611.07308

Klausen, M. S., Jespersen, M. C., Nielsen, H., Jensen, K. K., Jurtz, V. I., Soenderby, C. K., ... Marcatili, P. (2018). NetSurfP-2.0: Improved prediction of protein structural features by integrated deep learning. *bioRxiv.*

Klingenberg, M. (1981). Membrane protein oligomeric structure and transport function. *Nature, 290*(5806), 449–454. doi:10.1038/290449a0 PMID:6261141

Kloczkowski, A., Ting, K. L., Jernigan, R. L., & Garnier, J. (2002). Combining the GOR V algorithm with evolutionary information for protein secondary structure prediction from amino acid sequence. *Proteins, 49*(2), 154–166. doi:10.1002/prot.10181 PMID:12210997

Kohonen, T. (1989). *Self Organizing Map and associative Memory.* New York: Springer. doi:10.1007/978-3-642-88163-3

Kora, P., & Krishna, K. S. R. (2016). ECG based heart arrhythmia detection using wavelet coherence and bat algorithm". *Sensing and Imaging, 17*(1), 1–16. doi:10.100711220-016-0136-5

Krbálek, M., & Seba, P. (2000). The statistical properties of the city transport in Cuernavaca (Mexico) and random matrix ensembles. *Journal of Physics. A, Mathematical and General, 33*(26), L229–L234. doi:10.1088/0305-4470/33/26/102

Krizhevsky, A., Sutskever, I., & Hinton, G. E. (2012). Imagenet classification with deep convolutional neural networks. In Advances in neural information processing systems (pp. 1097-1105). Academic Press.

Krizhevsky, A., & Hinton, G. E. (2011). Using Very Deep Autoencoders for Content-Based Image Retrieval. *Proceedings of 19th European Symposium on Artificial Neural Networks.*

Kumar, Manjunath, & Sheshadri. (2015). Feature extraction from the fundus images for the diagnosis of Diabetic Retinopathy. *Int. Conf. Emerg. Res. Electron. Comput. Sci. Technol.*, 240–245.

Kumari, M. S., & Maheswarapu, S. (2010). Enhanced Genetic Algorithm based computation technique for multi-objective Optimal Power Flow solution. *International Journal of Electrical Power & Energy Systems, 32*(6), 736–742. doi:10.1016/j.ijepes.2010.01.010

Kumar, R., Kumar, A., & Singh, G. K. (2015). Electrocardiogram signal compression based on singular value decomposition (SVD) and adaptive scanning wavelet difference reduction (ASWDR) technique". *AEÜ. International Journal of Electronics and Communications, 69*(12), 1810–1822. doi:10.1016/j.aeue.2015.09.011

Kumar, S. S., & Inbarani, H. H. (2016). Cardiac arrhythmia classification using multi-granulation rough set approaches. *International Journal of Machine Learning and Cybernetics*, 1–16.

Kumar, S. U., & Inbarani, H. H. (2017). Neighborhood rough set based ECG signal classification for diagnosis of cardiac diseases. *Soft Computing, 21*(16), 4721–4733. doi:10.100700500-016-2080-7

Kyngäs, J., & Valjakka, J. (1998). Unreliability of the Chou-Fasman parameters in predicting protein secondary structure. *Protein Engineering, Design & Selection, 11*(5), 345–348. doi:10.1093/protein/11.5.345 PMID:9681866

Lárraga, M. E., & Alvarez-Icaza, L. (2011). *Towards a realistic description of traffic flow based on cellular automata.* Paper presented at the 2011 14th International IEEE Conference on Intelligent Transportation Systems (ITSC). 10.1109/ITSC.2011.6082931

LeCun, Y., Bengio, Y., & Hinton, G. (2015). Deep learning. *Nature, 521*(7553), 436.

Lecun, Y., Cortes, C., & Burges, C. J. C. (2004). *The mnist database of handwritten digits.* Retrieved from http://yann.lecun.com/ exdb/mnist/index.html

LeCun, Y., Bengio, Y., & Hinton, G. (2015). Deep learning. *Nature, 521*(7553), 436–444. doi:10.1038/nature14539 PMID:26017442

LeCun, Y., Bottou, L., Bengio, Y., & Haffner, P. (1998). Gradient-based learning applied to document recognition. *Proceedings of the IEEE, 86*(11), 2278–2324. doi:10.1109/5.726791

Lee, K. Y., & El-Sharkawi, M. A. (2008). *Modern heuristic optimization techniques: Theory and applications to power systems.* Piscataway, NJ: IEEE Press. doi:10.1002/9780470225868

Lemann, N. (2017). Solving the Problem of Fake News. *The New Yorker.* Available at: http://www.newyorker.com/news/news-desk/solving-the-problem-of-fake-news

Le, Q. V., & Mikolov, T. (2014). Distributed representations of sentences and documents. *Proceedings of the 31 st International Conference on Machine Learning, 32.*

Levin, J. M. (1997). Exploring the limits of nearest neighbour secondary structure prediction. *Protein Engineering, Design & Selection, 10*(7), 771–776. doi:10.1093/protein/10.7.771 PMID:9342143

Levin, J. M., & Garnier, J. (1988). Improvements in a secondary structure prediction method based on a search for local sequence homologies and its use as a model building tool. *Biochimica et Biophysica Acta, 955*(3), 283–295. doi:10.1016/0167-4838(88)90206-3 PMID:3401489

Levin, J. M., Robson, B., & Garnier, J. (1986). An algorithm for secondary structure determination in proteins based on sequence similarity. *FEBS Letters, 205*(2), 303–308. doi:10.1016/0014-5793(86)80917-6 PMID:3743779

Li, G., Müller, M., Thabet, A., & Ghanem, B. (2019). *Can GCNs Go as Deep as CNNs?* arXiv:1904.03751

Li, Y., Tarlow, D., Brockschmidt, M., & Zemel, R. (2015). *Gated graph sequence neural networks*. arXiv preprint arXiv:1511.05493

Liang, H., & Sun, L. (2019). Improve cloud manufacturing supply chain note-enterprises optimize combination of the Cuckoo Search. *Concurrency and Computation: Practise and Experience, 31*(10), e4764. doi:10.1002/cpe.4764

Liang, R.-H., Wu, C.-Y., Chen, Y.-T., & Tseng, W.-T. (2015). Multi-objective dynamic optimal power flow using improved artificial bee colony algorithm based on Pareto optimization. *International Transactions on Electrical Energy Systems, 26*(4), 692–712. doi:10.1002/etep.2101

Li, J., Ott, M., Cardie, C., & Hovy, E. (2014). Towards a general rule for identifying deceptive opinion spam. *Proceedings of the 52nd Annual Meeting of the Association for Computational Linguistics*, 1566–1576. 10.3115/v1/P14-1147

Li, L. L., & Jafarpour, B. (2012). A variable-control well placement optimization for improved reservoir development. *Computational Geosciences, 16*(4), 871–889. doi:10.100710596-012-9292-4

Lin, K., Simossis, V. A., Taylor, W. R., & Heringa, J. (2005). A simple and fast secondary structure prediction method using hidden neural networks. *Bioinformatics (Oxford, England), 21*(2), 152–159. doi:10.1093/bioinformatics/bth487 PMID:15377504

Lin, T., Rodríguez, L. F., Shastri, Y. N., Hansen, A. C., & Ting, K. C. (2014). Integrated strategic and tactical biomass–biofuel supply chain optimization. *Bioresource Technology, 156*, 256–266. doi:10.1016/j.biortech.2013.12.121 PMID:24508904

Lin, Z., Lanchantin, J., & Qi, Y. (2016). MUST-CNN: A multilayer shift-and-stitch deep convolutional architecture for sequence-based protein structure prediction. *Thirtieth AAAI conference on artificial intelligence.*

Lipton, Z. C., Berkowitz, J., & Elkan, C. (2015). *A critical review of recurrent neural networks for sequence learning.* ArXiv Preprint ArXiv:1506.00019

Liu, H. (2017). *Large-Scale Machine Learning over Graphs* (Doctoral dissertation). Carnegie Mellon University.

Liu, C., Chen, L. C., Schroff, F., Adam, H., Hua, W., Yuille, A. L., & Fei-Fei, L. (2019). Auto-deeplab: Hierarchical neural architecture search for semantic image segmentation. In *Proceedings of the IEEE Conference on Computer Vision and Pattern Recognition* (pp. 82-92). IEEE.

Liu, J., Pan, Y., Li, M., Chen, Z., Tang, L., Lu, C., & Wang, J. (2018). Applications of deep learning to MRI images: A survey. *Big Data Mining and Analytics, 1*(1), 1–18. doi:10.26599/BDMA.2018.9020001

Liu, J., Yang, S., Cheng, Y., & Song, Z. (2018). Plant Leaf Classification Based on Deep Learning. *2018 Chinese Automation Congress (CAC)*, 3165–3169. 10.1109/CAC.2018.8623427

Liu, Q., Zou, B., Chen, J., Ke, W., Yue, K., Chen, Z., & Zhao, G. (2017). A location-to-segmentation strategy for automatic exudate segmentation in colour retinal fundus images. *Computerized Medical Imaging and Graphics, 55*, 78–86. doi:10.1016/j.compmedimag.2016.09.001 PMID:27665058

Li, W., Kinch, L. N., Karplus, P. A., & Grishin, N. V. (2015). ChSeq: A database of chameleon sequences. *Protein Science*, *24*(7), 1075–1086. doi:10.1002/pro.2689 PMID:25970262

Li, Z., & Tang, J. (2015). Weakly Supervised Deep Metric Learning for Community-Contributed Image Retrieval. *IEEE Transactions on Multimedia*, *17*(11), 1989–1999. doi:10.1109/TMM.2015.2477035

Li, Z., & Yu, Y. (2016). Protein secondary structure prediction using cascaded convolutional and recurrent neural networks. In *Proceedings of the 25th International Joint Conference on Artificial Intelligence (IJCAI)* (pp. 2560–2567). AAAI Press.

Lo, Y., Rensi, S.E., Torng, W., & Altman, R.B. (2018). *Machine learning in chemoinformatics and drug discovery.* Academic Press.

Luan, X. Y., Li, Z. P., & Liu, T. Z. (2016). A novel attribute reduction algorithm based on rough set and improved artificial fish swarm algorithm. *Neurocomputing*, *174*, 522–529. doi:10.1016/j.neucom.2015.06.090

Luo, Y.-J., Jia, B., Li, X.-G., Wang, C., & Gao, Z.-Y. (2012). A realistic cellular automata model of bus route system based on open boundary. *Transportation Research Part C, Emerging Technologies*, *25*, 202–213. doi:10.1016/j.trc.2012.06.004

Lusci, A., Pollastri, G., & Baldi, P. (2013). Deep Architectures and Deep Learning in Chemoinformatics: The Prediction of Aqueous Solubility for Drug-Like Molecules. *Journal of Chemical Information and Modeling*, *53*(7), 1563–1575.

Lyons, J., & Nasrabadi, H. (2013). Well placement optimization under time-dependent uncertainty using an ensemble Kalman filter and a genetic algorithm. *Journal of Petroleum Science Engineering*, *109*, 70–79. doi:10.1016/j.petrol.2013.07.012

Ma, X., Plaksina, T., & Gildin, E. (2013). *Integrated horizontal well placement and hydraulic fracture stages design optimization in unconventional gas reservoirs.* Paper presented at the SPE Unconventional Resources Conference Canada. 10.2118/167246-MS

Ma, Y., Guo, Z., Ren, Z., Zhao, E., Tang, J., & Yin, D. (2018). *Dynamic graph neural networks.* arXiv preprint arXiv:1810.10627

MacQueen, J. (1967, June). Some methods for classification and analysis of multivariate observations. In *Proceedings of the fifth Berkeley symposium on mathematical statistics and probability* (Vol. 1, No. 14, pp. 281-297). Academic Press.

Magnan, C. N., & Baldi, P. (2014). SSpro/ACCpro 5: Almost perfect prediction of protein secondary structure and relative solvent accessibility using profiles, machine learning and structural similarity. *Bioinformatics (Oxford, England)*, *30*(18), 2592–2597. doi:10.1093/bioinformatics/btu352 PMID:24860169

Mahmoud, A. A. A., Elkatatny, S., Mahmoud, M., Abouelresh, M., Abdulraheem, A., & Ali, A. (2017). Determination of the total organic carbon (TOC) based on conventional well logs using artificial neural network. *International Journal of Coal Geology*, *179*, 72–80. doi:10.1016/j.coal.2017.05.012

Mandal, B., & Roy, P. K. (2014). Multi-objective optimal power flow using quasi-oppositional teaching learning based optimization. *Applied Soft Computing*, *21*, 590–606. doi:10.1016/j.asoc.2014.04.010

Manessi, F., Rozza, A., & Manzo, M. (2017). *Dynamic graph convolutional networks.* arXiv preprint arXiv:1704.06199

Man-Im, A., Ongsakul, W., Singh, J. G., & Boonchuay, C. (2015). *Multi-objective optimal power flow using stochastic weight trade-off chaotic NSPSO. In 2015 IEEE Innovative Smart Grid Technologies - Asia.* ISGT ASIA; doi:10.1109/ISGT-Asia.2015.7387120

Marcheggiani, D., Bastings, J., & Titov, I. (2018). Exploiting Semantics in Neural Machine Translation with Graph Convolutional Networks. In *Proceedings of Annual Conference of the North American Chapter of the Association for Compuational Linguistics: Human Language Technologies (NAACL-HLT)* (pp. 486–492). Academic Press. 10.18653/v1/N18-2078

Mareli, M., & Twala, B. (2017). *An adaptive Cuckoo search algorithm for optimisation.* Applied Computing and Informatics.

Margolis, R. N. (2008). The nuclear receptor signaling atlas: Catalyzing understanding of thyroid hormone signaling and metabolic control. *Thyroid, 18*(2), 113–122. doi:10.1089/thy.2007.0247 PMID:18279012

Maria, G. (1998). IDENTIFICATION/DIAGNOSIS-adaptive random search and short-cut techniques for process model identification and monitoring. *AIChE Symposium Series, 94*, 351–359.

Marufuzzaman, M., Eksioglu, S. D., & Huang, Y. E. (2014). Two-stage stochastic programming supply chain model for biodiesel production via wastewater treatment. *Computers & Operations Research, 49*, 1–17. doi:10.1016/j.cor.2014.03.010

Mastrocinque, E., Yuce, B., Lambiase, A., & Packianather, M. S. (2013). A multi-objective optimization for supply chain network using the bees algorithm. *International Journal of Engineering Business Management, 5*, 38. doi:10.5772/56754

Mattos, C. L., Barreto, G. A., Horstkemper, D., & Hellingrath, B. 2017, June. Metaheuristic optimization for automatic clustering of customer-oriented supply chain data. In *Self-Organizing Maps and Learning Vector Quantization, Clustering and Data Visualization (WSOM), 2017 12th International Workshop on* (pp. 1-8). IEEE. 10.1109/WSOM.2017.8020025

McCann, M. T., Jin, K. H., & Unser, M. (2017). Convolutional neural networks for inverse problems in imaging: A review. *IEEE Signal Processing Magazine, 34*(6), 85–95. doi:10.1109/MSP.2017.2739299

Medina, M. A., Das, S., Coello Coello, C. A., & Ramírez, J. M. (2014). Decomposition-based modern metaheuristic algorithms for multi-objective optimal power flow – A comparative study. *Engineering Applications of Artificial Intelligence, 32*, 10–20. doi:10.1016/j.engappai.2014.01.016

Medsker, L., & Jain, L. C. (1999). *Recurrent neural networks: Design and applications.* CRC Press. doi:10.1201/9781420049176

Meissner, M., Schmuker, M., & Schneider, G. (2006). Optimized Particle Swarm Optimization (OPSO) and its application to artificial neural network training. *BMC Bioinformatics, 7*(1), 125. doi:10.1186/1471-2105-7-125 PMID:16529661

Mendelzon, J. D., & Toksoz, M. N. (1985). Source rock characterization using multivariate analysis of log data. In *SPWLA 26th Annual Logging Symposium.* Society of Petrophysicists and Well-Log Analysts.

Mercer, R. E., & Sampson, J. (1978). Adaptive search using a reproductive meta-plan. *Kybernetes, 7*(3), 215–228. doi:10.1108/eb005486

Mikolov, T., Chen, K., Corrado, G., & Dean, J. (2013). Efficient estimation of word representations in vector *space. Proceedings of the International Conference on Learning Representations (ICLR)*.

Miotto, Wang, Wang, Jiang, & Dudley. (2017). Deep learning for healthcare: Review, opportunities and challenges. *Briefings in Bioinformatics*, 1–11.

Mirabello, C., & Pollastri, G. (2013). Porter, PaleAle 4.0: High-accuracy prediction of protein secondary structure and relative solvent accessibility. *Bioinformatics (Oxford, England), 29*(16), 2056–2058. doi:10.1093/bioinformatics/btt344 PMID:23772049

Miska, S., & Skalle, P. J. S. o. P. E. J. (1981). *Theoretical description of a new method of optimal program design.* Academic Press.

Mitchell, J. B. O. (2014). Machine learning methods in chemoinformatics. *Wiley Interdisciplinary Reviews. Computational Molecular Science, 4*(5), 468–481.

Miyagi, A., & Yamamoto, H. (2018). Well placement optimization for carbon dioxide capture and storage via CMA-ES with mixed integer support. *Proceedings of the Genetic and Evolutionary Computation Conference Companion.* 10.1145/3205651.3205706

Mohamed, A., Yu, D., & Deng, L. (2010). Investigation of full-sequence training of deep belief networks for speech recognition. INTERSPEECH, 2846–2849.

Mohamed, Dahl, & Hinton. (2009). Deep belief networks for phone recognition. *Nips workshop on deep learning for speech recognition and related applications, 1*(9), 39.

Mohamed, Yu, & Deng. (2010). Investigation of full-sequence training of deep belief networks for speech recognition. *INTERSPEECH,* 2846–2849.

Mohamed, A., Dahl, G. E., & Hinton, G. E. (2012). Acoustic modeling using deep belief networks. *IEEE Transactions on Audio, Speech, and Language Processing, 20*(1), 14–22. doi:10.1109/TASL.2011.2109382

Mohamed, A., Sainath, T. N., Dahl, G., Ramabhadran, B., Hinton, G. E., & Picheny, M. A. (2011). Deep belief networks using discriminative features for phone recognition. *IEEE International Conference on Acoustics, Speech and Signal Processing (ICASSP),* 5060–5063. 10.1109/ICASSP.2011.5947494

Mo, J., Zhang, L., & Feng, Y. (2018). AC US CR. *Neurocomputing.*

Montgomerie, S., Sundararaj, S., Gallin, W. J., & Wishart, D. S. (2006). Improving the accuracy of protein secondary structure prediction using structural alignment. *BMC Bioinformatics, 7*(1), 301. doi:10.1186/1471-2105-7-301 PMID:16774686

Monti, F., Boscaini, D., Masci, J., Rodola, E., Svoboda, J., & Bronstein, M. M. (2017). Geometric deep learning on graphs and manifolds using mixture model cnns. In *Proceedings of the IEEE Conference on Computer Vision and Pattern Recognition* (pp. 5115-5124). IEEE. 10.1109/CVPR.2017.576

Moro, S., Cortez, P., & Rita, P. (2015). Business intelligence in banking: A literature analysis from 2002 to 2013 using text mining and latent Dirichlet allocation. *Expert Systems with Applications, 42*(3), 1314–1324. doi:10.1016/j.eswa.2014.09.024

Mousavi, S. M., Sadeghi, J., Niaki, S. T. A., & Tavana, M. (2016). A bi-objective inventory optimization model under inflation and discount using tuned Pareto-based algorithms: NSGA-II, NRGA, and MOPSO. *Applied Soft Computing, 43,* 57–72. doi:10.1016/j.asoc.2016.02.014

Mukherjee, A., Venkataraman, V., Liu, B., & Glance, N. (2013). *Fake Review Detection: Classification and Analysis of Real and Pseudo Reviews.* UIC-CS-03-2013. Technical Report.

Mukherjee, A., & Mukherjee, V. (2015). Solution of optimal power flow using chaotic krill herd algorithm. *Chaos, Solitons, and Fractals, 78,* 10–21. doi:10.1016/j.chaos.2015.06.020

Mundt, M., Majumder, S., Murali, S., Panetsos, P., & Ramesh, V. (2019). Meta-learning Convolutional Neural Architectures for Multi-target Concrete Defect Classification with the COncrete DEfect BRidge IMage Dataset. In *Proceedings of the IEEE Conference on Computer Vision and Pattern Recognition* (pp. 11196-11205). IEEE.

Musa, R. Y. M., Elamin, A. E., & Elhassan, E. M. (2017). *Implementation of artificial neural networks and fuzzy logic for hypovolemia monitoring in the operation theatre* (Doctoral dissertation). Sudan University of Science and Technology.

Naderi, E., Pourakbari-Kasmaei, M., & Abdi, H. (2019). An efficient particle swarm optimization algorithm to solve optimal power flow problem integrated with FACTS devices. *Applied Soft Computing*, *80*, 243–262. doi:10.1016/j.asoc.2019.04.012

Naderi, M., & Khamehchi, E. (2017). Application of DOE and metaheuristic bat algorithm for well placement and individual well controls optimization. *Journal of Natural Gas Science and Engineering*, *46*, 47–58. doi:10.1016/j.jngse.2017.07.012

Naidu, K., Mokhlis, H., & Bakar, A. H. A. (2014). Multiobjective optimization using weighted sum artificial bee colony algorithm for load frequency control. *International Journal of Electrical Power & Energy Systems*, *55*, 657–667. doi:10.1016/j.ijepes.2013.10.022

Najafabadi, Villanustre, Khoshgoftaar, Seliya, Wald, & Muharemagic. (2015). Deep learning applications and challenges in big data analytics. *Journal of Big Data,* 2(1). doi:10.118640537-014-0007-7

Narayanan, A., Chandramohan M., Chen, L., Liu, Y., & Saminathan S. (2016). subgraph2vec: Learning distributed representations of rooted sub-graphs from large graphs. *CoRR*.

Narayanan, A., Chandramohan, M., Venkatesan, R., Chen, L., Liu, Y., & Jaiswal S. (2017). graph2vec: Learning distributed representations of graphs. *CoRR*, abs/1707.05005.

Nardon, S., Marzorati, D., Bernasconi, A., Cornini, S., Gonfalini, M., Mosconi, S., ... Terdich, P. (1991). Fractured carbonate reservoir characterization and modelling: A multidisciplinary case study from the Cavone oil field, Italy. *First Break*, *9*(12), 553–565.

Nezhad, Y. A., Moradzadeh, A., & Kamali, M. R. (2018). A new approach to evaluate Organic Geochemistry Parameters by geostatistical methods: A case study from western Australia. *Journal of Petroleum Science Engineering*, *169*, 813–824. doi:10.1016/j.petrol.2018.05.027

Nguyen, T. H., & Grishman, R. (*2018*). Graph Convolutional Networks with Argument-Aware Pooling for Event Detection. *Proceedings of AAAI Conference on Artificial Intelligence*.

Nguyen, T. T. (2019). A high performance social spider optimization algorithm for optimal power flow solution with single objective optimization. *Energy*, *171*, 218–240. doi:10.1016/j.energy.2019.01.021

Nick, W., Shelton, J., Bullock, G., Esterline, A., & Asamene, K. (2015, April). Comparing dimensionality reduction techniques. In *Southeast Con 2015* (pp. 1–2). IEEE. doi:10.1109/SECON.2015.7132997

Nik, K. N. A., Bonner, S., Connolly, J., Al Moubayed, N., & Breckon, T. (2018). On the Classification of SSVEP-Based Dry-EEG Signals via Convolutional Neural Networks. *Systems Man and Cybernetics (SMC) 2018 IEEE International Conference on*, 3726-3731.

Niknam, T., Rasoul Narimani, M., Jabbari, M., & Malekpour, A. R. (2011). A modified shuffle frog leaping algorithm for multi-objective optimal power flow. *Energy,* 36(11), 6420–6432.

Niknam, T., Narimani, M. R., & Azizipanah-Abarghooee, R. (2012). A new hybrid algorithm for optimal power flow considering prohibited zones and valve point effect. *Energy Conversion and Management*, *58*, 197–206. doi:10.1016/j.enconman.2012.01.017

Nwankwor, E., Nagar, A. K., & Reid, D. C. (2013). Hybrid differential evolution and particle swarm optimization for optimal well placement. *Computational Geosciences*, *17*(2), 249–268. doi:10.100710596-012-9328-9

O'Leary, D. E. (2013). Artificial intelligence and big data. *IEEE Intelligent Systems*, *28*(2), 96–99. doi:10.1109/MIS.2013.39 PMID:25505373

Ogunbanwo, A., Williamson, A., Veluscek, M., Izsak, R., Kalganova, T., & Broomhead, P. (2014). Transportation network optimization. In *Encyclopedia of Business Analytics and Optimization* (pp. 2570–2583). IGI Global. doi:10.4018/978-1-4666-5202-6.ch229

Ongsakul, W., & Vo, D. N. (2013). *Artificial intelligence in power system optimization*. Boca Raton, FL: CRC Press, Taylor & Francis.

Onwunalu, J. E., & Durlofsky, L. J. (2010). Application of a particle swarm optimization algorithm for determining optimum well location and type. *Computational Geosciences, 14*(1), 183–198. doi:10.100710596-009-9142-1

Onwunalu, J., & Durlofsky, L. J. (2010). *Optimization of field development using particle swarm optimization and new well pattern descriptions*. Stanford University.

Osmani, A., & Zhang, J. (2013). Stochastic optimization of a multi-feedstock lignocellulosic-based bioethanol supply chain under multiple uncertainties. *Energy, 59*, 157–172. doi:10.1016/j.energy.2013.07.043

Osmani, A., & Zhang, J. (2014). Economic and environmental optimization of a large scale sustainable dual feedstock lignocellulosic-based bioethanol supply chain in a stochastic environment. *Applied Energy, 114*, 572–587. doi:10.1016/j.apenergy.2013.10.024

Ot, S., Perdomo, O., & Gonz, F. (2017). *Intravascular Imaging and Computer Assisted Stenting, and Large-Scale Annotation of Biomedical Data and Expert Label Synthesis*. Academic Press.

Ott, M., Choi, Y., Cardie, C., & Hancock, J. T. (2011). Finding Deceptive Opinion Spam by Any Stretch of the Imagination. In *Proceedings of the 49th Annual Meeting of the Association for Computational Linguistics: Human Language Technologies* (Vol. 1, pp. 309–319). Stroudsburg, PA, USA: Association for Computational Linguistics. Retrieved from http://dl.acm.org/citation.cfm?id=2002472.2002512

Ouadfeul, S.-A., & Aliouane, L. (2015). Total Organic Carbon Prediction in Shale Gas Reservoirs using the Artificial intelligence with a comparative study between Fuzzy Logic and Neural Network. In *14th International Congress of the Brazilian Geophysical Society & EXPOGEF* (pp. 1390–1393). Brazilian Geophysical Society.

Ouadfeul, S.-A., & Aliouane, L. (2014). Shale gas reservoirs characterization using neural network. *Energy Procedia, 59*, 16–21. doi:10.1016/j.egypro.2014.10.343

Ouali, M., & King, R. D. (2000). Cascaded multiple classifiers for secondary structure prediction. *Protein Science, 9*(6), 1162–1176. doi:10.1110/ps.9.6.1162 PMID:10892809

Ou, M., Cui, P., Pei, J., Zhang, Z., & Zhu, W. (2016). Asymmetric transitivity preserving graph embedding. In *Proceedings of the 22nd ACM SIGKDD International Conference on Knowledge Discovery and Data Mining* (pp. 1105-1114). ACM. 10.1145/2939672.2939751

Padmanabhan, J., & Johnson Premkumar, M. J. (2015). Machine learning in automatic speech recognition: A survey. *IETE Technical Review, 32*(4), 240–251. doi:10.1080/02564602.2015.1010611

Paliwal, K., Lyons, J., & Heffernan, R. (2015). A short review of deep learning neural networks in protein structure prediction problems. *Advanced Techniques in Biology & Medicine, 2015*(3). doi:10.4172/2379-1764.1000139

Pan, Y., & Horne, R. N. (1998). *Improved methods for multivariate optimization of field development scheduling and well placement design*. Paper presented at the SPE Annual Technical Conference and Exhibition. 10.2118/49055-MS

Pang, L., Zhu, S., & Ngo, C. (2015). Deep Multimodal Learning for Affective Analysis and Retrieval. *IEEE Transactions on Multimedia, 17*(11), 2008–2020. doi:10.1109/TMM.2015.2482228

Pan, I., & Das, S. (2016). Fractional order fuzzy control of hybrid power system with renewable generation using chaotic PSO. *ISA Transactions*, *62*, 19–29. doi:10.1016/j.isatra.2015.03.003 PMID:25816968

Passey, Q. R., Creaney, S., Kulla, J. B., Moretti, F. J., & Stroud, J. D. (1990). A practical model for organic richness from porosity and resistivity logs. *AAPG Bulletin*, *74*(12), 1777–1794.

Patel, D., & Singh, P. K. (2016). Kids Safe Search Classification Model. *Proceedings of IEEE International Conference on Communication and Electronics Systems (ICCES)*, 1-7.

Patil, P., Shettar, P., Narayankar, P., & Patil, M. (2016). An efficient method of detecting exudates in diabetic retinopathy: Using texture edge features. *2016 Int. Conf. Adv. Comput. Commun. Informatics*, 1188–1191. 10.1109/ICACCI.2016.7732206

Pauling, L., & Corey, R. B. (1951a). Configurations of polypeptide chains with favored orientations around single bonds: Two new pleated sheets. *Proceedings of the National Academy of Sciences of the United States of America*, *37*(11), 729–740. doi:10.1073/pnas.37.11.729 PMID:16578412

Pauling, L., & Corey, R. B. (1951b). The pleated sheet, a new layer configuration of polypeptide chains. *Proceedings of the National Academy of Sciences of the United States of America*, *37*(5), 251–256. doi:10.1073/pnas.37.5.251 PMID:14834147

Pauling, L., Corey, R. B., & Branson, H. R. (1951). The structure of proteins: Two hydrogen-bonded helical configurations of the polypeptide chain. *Proceedings of the National Academy of Sciences of the United States of America*, *37*(4), 205–211. doi:10.1073/pnas.37.4.205 PMID:14816373

Paulter, N. G., Larson, D. R., & Blair, J. J. (2004). The IEEE standard on transitions, pulses, and related waveforms, Std-181-2003. *IEEE Transactions on Instrumentation and Measurement*, *53*(4), 1209–1217. doi:10.1109/TIM.2004.831470

Pedersen, M. E. H. (2010). *Tuning & simplifying heuristical optimization*. University of Southampton.

Pedersen, M. E. H., & Chipperfield, A. J. (2010). Simplifying particle swarm optimization. *Applied Soft Computing*, *10*(2), 618–628.

Pedersen, T. G., Sigurskjold, B. W., Andersen, K. V., Kjær, M., Poulsen, F. M., Dobson, C. M., & Redfield, C. (1991). A nuclear magnetic resonance study of the hydrogen-exchange behaviour of lysozyme in crystals and solution. *Journal of Molecular Biology*, *218*(2), 413–426. doi:10.1016/0022-2836(91)90722-I PMID:2010918

Pemper, R. R., Han, X., Mendez, F. E., Jacobi, D., LeCompte, B., & Bratovich, M., ... Bliven, S. (2009). The direct measurement of carbon in wells containing oil and natural gas using a pulsed neutron mineralogy tool. In *SPE Annual Technical Conference and Exhibition*. Society of Petroleum Engineers. 10.2118/124234-MS

Peng, H., Li, J., He, Y., Liu, Y., Bao, M., Wang, L., ... Yang, Q. (2018). Large-scale hierarchical text classification with recursively regularized deep graph-cnn. *Proceedings of the 2018 World Wide Web Conference on World Wide Web*. 10.1145/3178876.3186005

Perdomo, O., Otalora, S., Rodríguez, F., Arevalo, J., & González, F. A. (2016). A Novel Machine Learning Model Based on Exudate Localization to Detect Diabetic Macular Edema. Academic Press. doi:10.17077/omia.1057

Pereira, C., Gonçalves, L., & Ferreira, M. (2015). Exudate segmentation in fundus images using an ant colony optimization approach. *Inf. Sci. (Ny)*, *296*(1), 14–24. doi:10.1016/j.ins.2014.10.059

Perozzi, B., Al-Rfou', R., & Skiena, S. (2014). Deepwalk: online learning of social representations. In *Proceedings of the 20th ACM SIGKDD International Conference on Knowledge Discovery and Data Mining* (pp. 701-710). ACM.

Peters, K. E. (1986). Guidelines for evaluating petroleum source rock using programmed pyrolysis. *AAPG Bulletin, 70*(3), 318–329.

Pham, H., Guan, M. Y., Zoph, B., Le, Q. V., & Dean, J. (2018). *Efficient neural architecture search via parameter sharing.* arXiv preprint arXiv:1802.03268

Pham, H., Guan, M. Y., Zoph, B., Le, Q. V., & Dean, J. (2018). *Faster discovery of neural architectures by searching for paths in a large model.* Academic Press.

Pineda, F. J. (1987). Generalization of back-propagation to recurrent neural networks. *Physical Review Letters, 59*(19), 2229–2232. doi:10.1103/PhysRevLett.59.2229 PMID:10035458

Pitoglou. (2018). Machine Learning in Healthcare, Introduction and Real World Application Considerations. *International Journal of Reliable and Quality E-Healthcare, 7*(2), 27-36.

Plerou, V., Gopikrishnan, P., Rosenow, B., Amaral, L. A. N., Guhr, T., & Stanley, H. E. (2002). Random matrix approach to cross correlations in financial data. *Physical Review. E, 65*(6), 066126. doi:10.1103/PhysRevE.65.066126 PMID:12188802

Pok, G., Jin, C. H., & Ryu, K. H. (2008). Correlation of amino acid physicochemical properties with protein secondary structure conformation. In *2008 International Conference on BioMedical Engineering and Informatics* (Vol. 1, pp. 117–121). Academic Press. 10.1109/BMEI.2008.266

Pollastri, G., Baldi, P., Fariselli, P., & Casadio, R. (2002). Prediction of coordination number and relative solvent accessibility in proteins. *Proteins, 47*(2), 142–153. doi:10.1002/prot.10069 PMID:11933061

Polya, G. (1945). *How to solve it.* Princeton University Press.

Pouladi, B., Keshavarz, S., Sharifi, M., & Ahmadi, M. A. (2017). A robust proxy for production well placement optimization problems. *Fuel, 206*, 467–481. doi:10.1016/j.fuel.2017.06.030

Powell, M. J. (1964). An efficient method for finding the minimum of a function of several variables without calculating derivatives. *The Computer Journal, 7*(2), 155–162. doi:10.1093/comjnl/7.2.155

Pratt, S. J. G. (2004). *A fresh angle on oil drilling.* Academic Press.

Pratt, H., Coenen, F., Broadbent, D. M., Harding, S. P., & Zheng, Y. (2016). Convolutional Neural Networks for Diabetic Retinopathy. *Procedia Computer Science, 90*(July), 200–205. doi:10.1016/j.procs.2016.07.014

Priddy, K. L., & Keller, P. E. (2005). *Artificial neural networks: An introduction* (Vol. 68). SPIE Press. doi:10.1117/3.633187

Qian, N., & Sejnowski, T. J. (1988). Predicting the secondary structure of globular proteins using neural network models. *Journal of Molecular Biology, 202*(4), 865–884. doi:10.1016/0022-2836(88)90564-5 PMID:3172241

Qiu, R. C., & Antonik, P. (2017). *Smart grid using big data analytics: a random matrix theory approach.* John Wiley & Sons. doi:10.1002/9781118716779

Qi, Y., Oja, M., Weston, J., & Noble, W. S. (2012). A unified multitask architecture for predicting local protein properties. *PLoS One, 7*(3), 1–11. doi:10.1371/journal.pone.0032235 PMID:22461885

Qu, W., Sui, H., Yang, B., & Qian, W. (2011). Improving protein secondary structure prediction using a multi-modal BP method. *Computers in Biology and Medicine, 41*(10), 946–959. doi:10.1016/j.compbiomed.2011.08.005 PMID:21880310

Radhakrishnan, S., & Vijayarajan V. (2019). *Farming 4.0.* doi:10.4018/978-1-5225-9199-3.ch017

Rahman, I., Vasant, P., Singh, B. S. M., & Abdullah-Al-Wadud, M. (2016). Hybrid Particle Swarm and Gravitational Search Optimization Techniques for Charging Plug-In Hybrid Electric Vehicles. In *Handbook of Research on Modern Optimization Algorithms and Applications in Engineering and Economics* (pp. 471–504). IGI Global. doi:10.4018/978-1-4666-9644-0.ch018

Rajalakshmi, R., & Aravindan, C. (2018). An effective and discriminative feature learning for URL based web page classification, *International IEEE Conference on Systems, Man and Cybernetics – SMC 2018.*

Rajalakshmi, R., & Aravindan, C. (2013). Web Page Classification using n-gram based URL Features. *IEEE Proceedings of International Conference on Advanced Computing (ICoAC 2013)*, 15–21. 10.1109/ICoAC.2013.6921920

Rajalakshmi, R., & Aravindan, C. (2018). *Naive Bayes Approach for URL Classification with Supervised Feature Selection and Rejection Framework. In Computational Intelligence.* Wiley; doi:10.1111/coin.12158

Rajalakshmi, R., & Ramraj, S. (2019). A deep learning approach for URL based Health Information Search. *International Journal of Innovative Technology and Exploring Engineering, 8*, 642–646.

Rajalakshmi, R., Ramraj, S., & Rameshkannan, R. (2019). *Transfer Learning Approach for Identification of Malicious Domain Names. In Security in Computing and Communications.* Springer.

Rajalakshmi, R., & Xavier, S. (2017). Experimental study of feature weighting techniques for URL based web page classification. *Procedia Computer Science, 115*, 218–225. doi:10.1016/j.procs.2017.09.128

Rampersad, P., Hareland, G., & Pairintra, T. (1993). *Drilling optimization of an oil or gas field.* Paper presented at the SPE Eastern Regional Meeting. 10.2118/26949-MS

Recknagel, F. (2013). *Ecological informatics: Understanding ecology by biologically-inspired computation.* Springer Science & Business Media.

Redouane, K., Zeraibi, N., & Nait Amar, M. (2018). *Automated Optimization of Well Placement via Adaptive Space-Filling Surrogate Modelling and Evolutionary Algorithm.* Paper presented at the Abu Dhabi International Petroleum Exhibition & Conference. 10.2118/193040-MS

Remmert, M., Biegert, A., Hauser, A., & Söding, J. (2011). HHblits: Lightning-fast iterative protein sequence searching by HMM-HMM alignment. *Nature Methods, 9*(2), 173–175. doi:10.1038/nmeth.1818 PMID:22198341

Renedo, J., Ibrahim, A. A., Kazemtabrizi, B., García-Cerrada, A., Rouco, L., Zhao, Q., & García-González, J. (2019). A simplified algorithm to solve optimal power flows in hybrid VSC-based AC/DC systems. *International Journal of Electrical Power & Energy Systems, 110*, 781–794. doi:10.1016/j.ijepes.2019.03.044

Richards, F. M., & Kundrot, C. E. (1988). Identification of structural motifs from protein coordinate data: Secondary structure and first-level supersecondary structure*. *Proteins, 3*(2), 71–84. doi:10.1002/prot.340030202 PMID:3399495

Rosenwald, G. W., & Green, D. W. J. S. o. P. E. J. (1974). *A method for determining the optimum location of wells in a reservoir using mixed-integer programming.* Academic Press.

Rost, B. (2001). Review: Protein secondary structure prediction continues to rise. *Journal of Structural Biology, 134*(2), 204–218. doi:10.1006/jsbi.2001.4336 PMID:11551180

Rost, B., & Sander, C. (1993). Improved prediction of protein secondary structure by use of sequence profiles and neural networks. *Proceedings of the National Academy of Sciences of the United States of America, 90*(16), 7558–7562. doi:10.1073/pnas.90.16.7558 PMID:8356056

Roy, P. K., & Paul, C. (2014). Optimal power flow using krill herd algorithm. *International Transactions on Electrical Energy Systems, 25*(8), 1397–1419. doi:10.1002/etep.1888

Rumelhart, D. E., Hinton, G. E., & Williams, R. J. (1985). *Learning internal representations by error propagation.* California Univ San Diego La Jolla Inst for Cognitive Science. doi:10.21236/ADA164453

Sakawa, M., Yano, H., & Yumine, T. (1987). An Interactive Fuzzy Satisficing Method for Multiobjective Linear-Programming Problems and Its Application. *IEEE Transactions on Systems, Man, and Cybernetics, 17*(4), 654–661. doi:10.1109/TSMC.1987.289356

Salamov, A. A., & Solovyev, V. V. (1997). Protein secondary structure prediction using local alignments. *Journal of Molecular Biology, 268*(1), 31–36. doi:10.1006/jmbi.1997.0958 PMID:9149139

Salcedo-Sanz, S., Deo, R. C., Cornejo-Bueno, L., Camacho-Gómez, C., & Ghimire, S. (2018). An efficient neuro-evolutionary hybrid modelling mechanism for the estimation of daily global solar radiation in the Sunshine State of Australia. *Applied Energy, 209*, 79–94. doi:10.1016/j.apenergy.2017.10.076

Salzberg, S., & Cost, S. (1992). Predicting protein secondary structure with a nearest-neighbor algorithm. *Journal of Molecular Biology, 227*(2), 371–374. doi:10.1016/0022-2836(92)90892-N PMID:1404357

Samuel, R. (2009). *Ultra-Extended-Reach Drilling (u-ERD: Tunnel in the Earth)—A New Well-Path Design.* Paper presented at the SPE/IADC Drilling Conference and Exhibition. 10.2118/119459-MS

Sankar, U., Vijai, R., & Balajee, R. M. (2018). Detection and Classification of Diabetic Retinopathy in Fundus Images using. *Neural Networks*, 2630–2635.

Santoro, A., Raposo, D., Barrett, D. G., Malinowski, M., Pascanu, R., Battaglia, P., & Lillicrap, T. (2017). A simple neural network module for relational reasoning. In Advances in neural information processing systems (pp. 4967-4976). Academic Press.

Saxe, J., & Berlin, K. (2017). *eXpose: A Character-Level Convolutional Neural Network with Embeddings For Detecting Malicious URLs, File Paths and Registry Keys.* arXiv:1702.08568

Sayah, S., & Zehar, K. (2008). Modified differential evolution algorithm for optimal power flow with non-smooth cost functions. *Energy Conversion and Management, 49*(11), 3036–3042. doi:10.1016/j.enconman.2008.06.014

Sayyafzadeh, M. (2017). Reducing the computation time of well placement optimisation problems using self-adaptive metamodelling. *Journal of Petroleum Science Engineering, 151*, 143–158. doi:10.1016/j.petrol.2016.12.015

Scarselli, F., Gori, M., Tsoi, A. C., Hagenbuchner, M., & Monfardini, G. (2008). The graph neural network model. *IEEE Transactions on Neural Networks, 20*(1), 61–80. doi:10.1109/TNN.2008.2005605 PMID:19068426

Schlichtkrull, M., Kipf, T. N., Bloem, P., Van Den Berg, R., Titov, I., & Welling, M. (2018, June). Modeling relational data with graph convolutional networks. In *European Semantic Web Conference* (pp. 593-607). Springer. 10.1007/978-3-319-93417-4_38

Schmidhuber, J. (2015). Deep learning in neural networks: An overview. *Neural Networks, 61*, 85–117. doi:10.1016/j.neunet.2014.09.003 PMID:25462637

Schmidler, S. C., Liu, J. S., & Brutlag, D. L. (2000). Bayesian segmentation of protein secondary structure. *Journal of Computational Biology, 7*(1–2), 233–248. doi:10.1089/10665270050081496 PMID:10890399

Schmoker, J. W. (1979). Determination of organic content of Appalachian Devonian shales from formation-density logs: Geologic notes. *AAPG Bulletin, 63*(9), 1504–1509.

Schmoker, J. W., & Hester, T. C. (1983). Organic carbon in Bakken formation, United States portion of Williston basin. *AAPG Bulletin, 67*(12), 2165–2174.

Schneider & Handali. (2019). Personalized explanation in machine learning. *CORR Journal.*

Schuster, M., & Paliwal, K. K. (1997). Bidirectional recurrent neural networks. *IEEE Transactions on Signal Processing, 45*(11), 2673–2681. doi:10.1109/78.650093

Seker, G. A., & Eryigit, G. (2012). Initial explorations on using CRFs for Turkish named entity recognition. *Proceedings of the International Conference on Computational Linguistics (COLING).*

Senapati, M. K., Senapati, M., & Maka, S. (2014). Cardiac Arrhythmia Classification of ECG Signal Using Morphology and Heart Beat Rate. *Proc. of Fourth International Conf. on Advances in Computing and Communications (ICACC),* 60-63. 10.1109/ICACC.2014.20

Sermanet, P., Eigen, D., Zhang, X., Mathieu, M., Fergus, R., & LeCun, Y. (2013). *Overfeat: Integrated recognition, localization and detection using convolutional networks.* ArXiv Preprint ArXiv:1312.6229

Seuring, S. (2013). A review of modeling approaches for sustainable supply chain management. *Decision Support Systems, 54*(4), 1513–1520. doi:10.1016/j.dss.2012.05.053

Sfidari, E., Kadkhodaie-Ilkhchi, A., & Najjari, S. (2012). Comparison of intelligent and statistical clustering approaches to predicting total organic carbon using intelligent systems. *Journal of Petroleum Science Engineering, 86,* 190–205. doi:10.1016/j.petrol.2012.03.024

Shadizadeh, S. R., Karimi, F., & Zoveidavianpoor, M. (2010). *Drilling stuck pipe prediction in Iranian oil fields: An artificial neural network approach.* Abadan, Iran: Petroleum University of Technology.

Shadmand, S., & Mashoufi, B. (2016). A new personalized ECG signal classification algorithm using block-based neural network and particle swarm optimization. *Biomedical Signal Processing and Control, 25,* 12–23. doi:10.1016/j.bspc.2015.10.008

Shailaja, C., & Anuprasath, T. (2019). Internet of medical things-load optimization of power flow based on hybrid enhanced grey wolf optimization and dragonfly algorithm. *Future Generation Computer Systems, 98,* 319–330. doi:10.1016/j.future.2018.12.070

Shailaja, C., & Anuprasath, T. (2019). Optimal power flow using Moth Swarm Algorithm with Gravitational Search Algorithm considering wind power. *Future Generation Computer Systems, 98,* 708–715. doi:10.1016/j.future.2018.12.046

Sharma, P., & Khurana, N. (2013). Study of optimal path finding techniques. *International Journal of Advancements in Technology, 4*(2), 124–130.

Shelhamer, E., Long, J., & Darrell, T. (2017). Fully Convolutional Networks for Semantic Segmentation. *IEEE Transactions on Pattern Analysis and Machine Intelligence, 39*(4), 640–651. doi:10.1109/TPAMI.2016.2572683 PMID:27244717

Shervashidze, N., Schweitzer, P., van Leeuwen, E. J., Mehlhorn, K., & Borgwardt, K. M. (2011). Weisfeiler-lehman graph kernels. *Journal of Machine Learning Research, 12,* 2539–2561.

Shi, Y., & Eberhart, R. (1998). A modified particle swarm optimizer. In *1998 IEEE International Conference on Evolutionary Computation Proceedings. IEEE World Congress on Computational Intelligence* (Cat. No.98TH8360) (pp. 69–73). IEEE. 10.1109/ICEC.1998.699146

Shi, J., Zhang, W., Zhang, Y., Xue, F., & Yang, T. (2015). MPPT for PV systems based on a dormant PSO algorithm. *Electric Power Systems Research, 123,* 100–107. doi:10.1016/j.epsr.2015.02.001

Shi, X., Wang, J., Liu, G., Yang, L., Ge, X., & Jiang, S. (2016). Application of extreme learning machine and neural networks in total organic carbon content prediction in organic shale with wire line logs. *Journal of Natural Gas Science and Engineering, 33*, 687–702. doi:10.1016/j.jngse.2016.05.060

Shojaee, S., Murad, M. A. A., Azman, A. B., Sharef, N. M., & Nadali, S. (2013, December). Detecting deceptive reviews using lexical and syntactic features. In *Intelligent Systems Design and Applications (ISDA), 2013 13th International Conference on* (pp. 53-58). IEEE. 10.1109/ISDA.2013.6920707

Shokir, E. E.-M., Emera, M., Eid, S., & Wally, A. J. O. (2004). *A new optimization model for 3D well design*. Academic Press.

Short, J. A. (1993). *Introduction to directional and horizontal drilling*. Pennwell Corporation.

Shrivatava, P. (n.d.). *Challenges in Deep Learning*. Retrieved from https://hackernoon.com/challenges-in-deep-learning-57bbf6e73bb

Shuman, D. I., Narang, S. K., Frossard, P., Ortega, A., & Vandergheynst, P. (2013). The emerging field of signal processing on graphs: Extending high-dimensional data analysis to networks and other irregular domains. *IEEE Signal Processing Magazine, 30*(3), 83–98. doi:10.1109/MSP.2012.2235192

Singh, K., Vasant, P., Elamvazuthi, I., & Kannan, R. (2015). PID tuning of servo motor using bat algorithm. *Procedia Computer Science, 60*, 1798–1808. doi:10.1016/j.procs.2015.08.290

Singh, M. T., & Anand, R. (2014). Subjective and objective analysis of speech enhancement algorithms for single channel speech patterns of indian and english languages. *IETE Technical Review, 31*(1), 34–46. doi:10.1080/02564602.2014.890840

Sivakumar, S., & Rajalakshmi, R. (2019). Comparative evaluation of various feature weighting methods on movie reviews. In H. S. Behera, J. Nayak, B. Naik, & A. Abraham (Eds.), *Computational Intelligence in Data Mining. AISC* (Vol. 711, pp. 721–730). Singapore: Springer; doi:10.1007/978-981-10-8055-5_64

Sivasubramani, S., & Swarup, K. S. (2011). Multi-objective harmony search algorithm for optimal power flow problem. *International Journal of Electrical Power & Energy Systems, 33*(3), 745–752. doi:10.1016/j.ijepes.2010.12.031

Smolensky, P. (1986). *Information processing in dynamical systems: Foundations of harmony theory (No. CU-CS-321-86)*. Colorado Univ at Boulder Dept of Computer Science.

Sønderby, S. K., & Winther, O. (2014). *Protein secondary structure prediction with long short term memory networks*. ArXiv:1412.7828

Sondergeld, C. H., Newsham, K. E., Comisky, J. T., Rice, M. C., & Rai, C. S. (2010). Petrophysical considerations in evaluating and producing shale gas resources. In *SPE Unconventional Gas Conference*. Society of Petroleum Engineers.

Song, L., Zhang, Y., Wang, Z., & Gildea, D. (2018). A Graph-to-Sequence Model for AMR-to-Text Generation. In *Proceedings of the 56th Annual Meeting of the Association for Computational Linguistics* (*vol. 1*). Academic Press. 10.18653/v1/P18-1150

Sonka, M., Hlavac, V., & Boyle, R. (2014). *Image processing, analysis, and machine vision*. Cengage Learning.

Soon, W. W., Hariharan, M., & Snyder, M. P. (2013). High-throughput sequencing for biology and medicine. *Molecular Systems Biology, 9*(1), 640. doi:10.1038/msb.2012.61 PMID:23340846

Sorokin, D., & Gurevych, I. (2018). Modeling Semantics with Gated Graph Neural Networks for Knowledge Base Question Answering. In *Proceedings of the 27th International Conference on Computational Linguistics* (pp. 3306–3317). Academic Press.

Sorzano, C. O. S., Vargas, J., & Montano, A. P. (2014). *A survey of dimensionality reduction techniques.* arXiv preprint arXiv:1403.2877

Sottinen, T., & Tudor, C. A. (2006). On the Equivalence of Multiparameter Gaussian Processes. *Journal of Theoretical Probability, 19*(2), 461–485. doi:10.100710959-006-0022-5

Spencer, M., Eickholt, J., & Cheng, J. (2015). A deep learning network approach to ab initio protein secondary structure prediction. *IEEE/ACM Transactions on Computational Biology and Bioinformatics, 12*(1), 103–112. doi:10.1109/TCBB.2014.2343960 PMID:25750595

Sreeji & Parasuraman. (2018). Characterization of Diabetic Retinopathy Detection of Exudates in Color Fundus Images of the Human Retina. Academic Press.

Sriman & Iyenger. (2018). *Classification of Diabetic Retinopathy Images by Using Deep Learning Models Classification of Diabetic Retinopathy Images by Using Deep Learning Models.* Academic Press.

Srinivas, N., & Deb, K. (1994). Muiltiobjective Optimization Using Nondominated Sorting in Genetic Algorithms. *Evolutionary Computation, 2*(3), 221–248. doi:10.1162/evco.1994.2.3.221

Srivastav, A., & Agrawal, S. (2017). *Multi-objective optimization of slow moving inventory system using cuckoo search.* Intelligent Automation & Soft Computing.

Srivastava, N., Hinton, G., Krizhevsky, A., Sutskever, I., & Salakhutdinov, R. (2014). Dropout: A simple way to prevent neural networks from overfitting. *Journal of Machine Learning Research, 15*(1), 1929–1958.

Stepchenko, A., & Chizhov, J. (2015). NDVI Short-Term Forecasting Using Recurrent Neural Networks. *Environment. Technology. Resources. Proceedings of the International Scientific and Practical Conference.* 10.17770/etr2015vol3.167

Storn, R. (1995). Differential evolution-a simple and efficient adaptive scheme for global optimization over continuous spaces. Technical Report, International Computer Science Institute.

Sugathadasa, K., Ayesha, B., Silva, N., Perera, A.S., Jayawardana, V., Lakmal, D., & Perera. M., (2018). Legal Document Retrieval Using Document Vector Embeddings and Deep Learning. *Intelligent Computing*, 160-175.

Sukhbaatar, S., & Fergus, R. (2016). Learning multiagent communication with backpropagation. In Advances in Neural Information Processing Systems (pp. 2244-2252). Academic Press.

Sun, J., Steinecker, A., & Glocker, P. (2014). Application of deep belief networks for precision mechanism quality inspection. In *International Precision Assembly Seminar*, (pp. 87–93). Springer.

Sun, D. I., Ashley, B., Brewer, B., Hughes, A., & Tinney, W. F. (1984). Optimal Power Flow by Newton Approach. *IEEE Transactions on Power Apparatus and Systems, PAS-103*(10), 2864–2880. doi:10.1109/TPAS.1984.318284

Sundermeyer, M., Schlüter, R., & Ney, H. (2012). *LSTM neural networks for language modeling.* INTERSPEECH.

Suryanarayana, P., McCann, R. C., Rudolf, R. L., & Rupani, R. A. J. O. (1998). *Mathematical technique improves directional well-path planning.* Academic Press.

Svetnik, V., Liaw, A., Tong, C., Culberson, J. C., Sheridan, R. P., & Feuston, B. P. (2003). Random forest: A classification and regression tool for compound classification and QSAR modeling. *Journal of Chemical Information and Computer Sciences, 43*(6), 1947–1958. doi:10.1021/ci034160g PMID:14632445

Szegedy, C., Liu, W., Jia, Y., Sermanet, P., Reed, S., Anguelov, D., … Rabinovich, A. (2015). Going deeper with convolutions. *The IEEE Conference on Computer Vision and Pattern Recognition (CVPR).*

Tahmasebi, P., Javadpour, F., & Sahimi, M. (2017). Data mining and machine learning for identifying sweet spots in shale reservoirs. *Expert Systems with Applications*, *88*, 435–447. doi:10.1016/j.eswa.2017.07.015

Tan, J. W., Chang, S., Abdul-kareem, S., Yap, H. J., & Yong, K. (2018). *Deep Learning for Plant Species Classification using Leaf Vein Morphometric*. doi:10.1109/TCBB.2018.2848653

Tang, H., Tan, K. C., & Yi, Z. (2007). *Neural networks: Computational models and applications* (Vol. 53). Springer Science & Business Media. doi:10.1007/978-3-540-69226-3

Tang, J., Qu, M., Wang, M., Zhang, M., Yan, J., & Mei, Q. (2015, May). Line: Large-scale information network embedding. In *Proceedings of the 24th international conference on world wide web* (pp. 1067-1077). International World Wide Web Conferences Steering Committee. 10.1145/2736277.2741093

Tan, M., Song, X., Yang, X., & Wu, Q. (2015). Support-vector-regression machine technology for total organic carbon content prediction from wireline logs in organic shale: A comparative study. *Journal of Natural Gas Science and Engineering*, *26*, 792–802. doi:10.1016/j.jngse.2015.07.008

Tan, Q., Wang, T., Zhang, Y., Miao, X., & Zhu, J. (2017). Nonlinear multi-objective optimization model for a biomass direct-fired power generation supply chain using a case study in China. *Energy*, *139*, 1066–1079. doi:10.1016/j.energy.2017.08.050

Tariq, Fleming, Schwartz, Dunlap, Corbin, Washington, ... Wall. (2019). Works citing "Detecting Developmental Delay and Autism Through Machine Learning Models Using Home Videos of Bangladeshi Children: Development and Validation Study. *J Med Internet Res., 21*(4).

Taylor, B. J. (2006). *Methods and procedures for the verification and validation of artificial neural networks*. Springer Science & Business Media.

Taylor, W. R. (1986). The classification of amino acid conservation. *Journal of Theoretical Biology*, *119*(2), 205–218. doi:10.1016/S0022-5193(86)80075-3 PMID:3461222

Teney, D., Liu, L., & Hengel, A. V. D. (2017). Graph-Structured Representations for Visual Question Answering. *Proceedings of IEEE Conference on Computer Vision and Pattern Recognition (CVPR)*.

Terano, T., Asai, K., & Sugeno, M. (2014). *Applied fuzzy systems*. Academic Press.

Thomas, J., Comoretto, L., Jin, J., Dauwels, J., Cash, S. S., & Westover, M. B. (2018). EEG CLassification Via Convolutional Neural Network-Based Interictal Epileptiform Event Detection. *IEEE Engineering in Medicine and Biology Society (EMBC) 2018 40th Annual International Conference of the*, 3148-3151. 10.1109/EMBC.2018.8512930

Tomin, N. V, Kurbatsky, V. G., & Negnevitsky, M. (2018). *The Concept of the Deep Learning-Based System "Artificial Dispatcher" to Power System Control and Dispatch*. ArXiv, abs/1805.05408

Torrisi, M., Kaleel, M., & Pollastri, G. (2018). Porter 5: State-of-the-art ab initio prediction of protein secondary structure in 3 and 8 classes. *bioRxiv*.

Tropsha, A. (2010). Best practices for QSAR model development, validation, and exploitation. *Molecular Informatics*, *29*(6-7), 476–488. doi:10.1002/minf.201000061 PMID:27463326

Tsoumakas, G., & Katakis, I. (2007). Multi label classification: An overview. *International Journal of Data Warehousing and Mining*, *3*(3), 1–13. doi:10.4018/jdwm.2007070101

Tulshan, A., & Dhage, N. (2019). Survey on Virtual Assistant: Google Assistant, Siri, Cortana, Alexa. *4th International Symposium SIRS 2018*, Bangalore, India. 10.1007/978-981-13-5758-9_17

Usman Akram, M., Khalid, S., Tariq, A., Khan, S. A., & Azam, F. (2014). Detection and classification of retinal lesions for grading of diabetic retinopathy. *Computers in Biology and Medicine*, *45*(1), 161–171. doi:10.1016/j.compbiomed.2013.11.014 PMID:24480176

Vahadane, A., Joshi, A., Madan, K., & Dastidar, T. R. (2018). Detection of diabetic macular edema in optical coherence tomography scans using patch based deep learning. SigTuple Technologies Pvt. Ltd.

Van Der Maaten, L., Postma, E., & Van den Herik, J. (2009). Dimensionality reduction: A comparative. *Journal of Machine Learning Research*, *10*(66-71), 13.

Vanderbruggen, T., & Cavazos, J. (2017). Large-scale exploration of feature sets and deep learning models to classify malicious applications. In Resilience Week (RWS), 2017 (pp. 37-43). IEEE. doi:10.1109/RWEEK.2017.8088645

Vapnik, V. (1963). Pattern recognition using generalized portrait method. *Automation and Remote Control*, *24*, 774–780.

Vapnik, V. (1964). A note one class of perceptrons. *Automation and Remote Control*.

Vasant, P., & Vasant, P. (2012). Meta-Heuristics Optimization Algorithms in Engineering. In Business, Economics, and Finance. IGI Global.

Vasant, P., & Barsoum, N. (2009). Hybrid genetic algorithms and line search method for industrial production planning with non-linear fitness function. *Engineering Applications of Artificial Intelligence*, *22*(4–5), 767–777. doi:10.1016/j.engappai.2009.03.010

Vasant, P., & DeMarco, A. (2015). *Handbook of research on artificial intelligence techniques and algorithms*. Information Science Reference. doi:10.4018/978-1-4666-7258-1

Velez-Langs, O. (2005). Genetic algorithms in oil industry: An overview. *Journal of Petroleum Science Engineering*, *47*(1–2), 15–22. doi:10.1016/j.petrol.2004.11.006

Veličković, P., Cucurull, G., Casanova, A., Romero, A., Lio, P., & Bengio, Y. (2017). *Graph attention networks*. arXiv preprint arXiv:1710.10903

Verbaarschot, J. 2004, December. The supersymmetric method in random matrix theory and applications to QCD. In AIP Conference Proceedings (Vol. 744, No. 1, pp. 277-362). AIP. doi:10.1063/1.1853204

Vincent, P., Larochelle, H., Bengio, Y., & Manzagol, P. A. (2008, July). Extracting and composing robust features with denoising autoencoders. In *Proceedings of the 25th international conference on Machine learning* (pp. 1096-1103). ACM. 10.1145/1390156.1390294

Vincent, P., Larochelle, H., Lajoie, I., Bengio, Y., & Manzagol, P. A. (2010). Stacked denoising autoencoders: Learning useful representations in a deep network with a local denoising criterion. *Journal of Machine Learning Research*, *11*(Dec), 3371–3408.

Voet, D., & Voet, J. G. (2011). *Biochemistry* (4th ed.). New York, NY: Wiley.

Vojt, J. (2016). *Deep neural networks and their implementation*. Academic Press.

Wang, D., & Chen, J. (2018). Supervised speech separation based on deep learning: An overview. *IEEE/ACM Transactions on Audio, Speech, and Language Processing*, *26*(10).

Wang, D., Cui, P., & Zhu, W. (2016). Structural deep network embedding. In *Proceedings of the 22nd international conference on Knowledge discovery and data mining (SIGKDD)*. ACM.

Wang, D., Cui, P., & Zhu, W. (2016, August). Structural deep network embedding. In *Proceedings of the 22nd ACM SIGKDD international conference on Knowledge discovery and data mining* (pp. 1225-1234). ACM. 10.1145/2939672.2939753

Wang, G., Xie, S., Liu, B., & Yu, P. S. (2012). Identify online store review spammers via social review graph. *ACM Transactions on Intelligent Systems and Technology, 3*(4), 61. doi:10.1145/2337542.2337546

Wang, H., Wang, J., Wang, J., Zhao, M., Zhang, W., Zhang, F., ... Guo, M. (2018). Graphgan: Graph representation learning with generative adversarial nets. *Proceedings of Thirty-Second AAAI Conference on Artificial Intelligence.*

Wang, H., Wu, W., Chen, T., Dong, X., & Wang, G. (2019). An improved neural network for TOC, S1 and S2 estimation based on conventional well logs. *Journal of Petroleum Science Engineering.*

Wang, J. S., Chiang, W. C., Yang, Y. T. C., & Hsu, Y. L. (2011). An effective ECG arrhythmia classification algorithm. *Proc. of International Conf. on Intelligent Computing*, 545-550.

Wang, J., He, H., & Prokhorov, D. V. (2012). A folded neural network autoencoder for dimensionality reduction. *Procedia Computer Science, 13*, 120–127. doi:10.1016/j.procs.2012.09.120

Wang, P., Chen, Z., Pang, X., Hu, K., Sun, M., & Chen, X. (2016). Revised models for determining TOC in shale play: Example from Devonian Duvernay shale, Western Canada sedimentary basin. *Marine and Petroleum Geology, 70*, 304–319. doi:10.1016/j.marpetgeo.2015.11.023

Wang, P., & Peng, S. (2018). A New Scheme to Improve the Performance of Artificial Intelligence Techniques for Estimating Total Organic Carbon from Well Logs. *Energies, 11*(4), 747. doi:10.3390/en11040747

Wang, P., Peng, S., & He, T. (2018). A novel approach to total organic carbon content prediction in shale gas reservoirs with well logs data, Tonghua Basin, China. *Journal of Natural Gas Science and Engineering, 55*, 1–15. doi:10.1016/j.jngse.2018.03.029

Wang, S., Peng, J., Ma, J., & Xu, J. (2016). Protein secondary structure prediction using deep convolutional neural fields. *Scientific Reports, 6*(1), 18962. doi:10.1038rep18962 PMID:26752681

Wang, X. Z., Zhou, J., Huang, Z. L., Bi, X. L., Ge, Z. Q., & Li, L. (2016). A multilevel deep learning method for big data analysis and emergency management of power system. In *Proceedings of 2016 IEEE International Conference on Big Data Analysis, ICBDA 2016.* IEEE. 10.1109/ICBDA.2016.7509811

Wang, Y., & Xu, W. (2018). *Leveraging deep learning with LDA-based text analytics to detect automobile insurance fraud. In Decision Support Systems.* Elsevier.

Ward, J. J., McGuffin, L. J., Buxton, B. F., & Jones, D. T. (2003). Secondary structure prediction with support vector machines. *Bioinformatics (Oxford, England), 19*(13), 1650–1655. doi:10.1093/bioinformatics/btg223 PMID:12967961

Wartana, I. M. (2015). A multi-objective problems for optimal integration of the DG to the grid using the NSGA-II. In *2015 International Conference on Quality in Research (QiR)* (pp. 106–110). Academic Press. 10.1109/QiR.2015.7374906

Wei, L. Y., Saratchandran, P., & Narasimman, S. (1999). Radial Basis Function Neural Networks With Sequential Learning, Progress. In *Neural Processing* (Vol. 11). World Scientific.

Welikala, R. A., Fraz, M. M., Dehmeshki, J., Hoppe, A., Tah, V., Mann, S., ... Barman, S. A. (2015). Genetic algorithm based feature selection combined with dual classification for the automated detection of proliferative diabetic retinopathy. *Computerized Medical Imaging and Graphics, 43*, 64–77. doi:10.1016/j.compmedimag.2015.03.003 PMID:25841182

Weng, Y., Zhou, T., Liu, L., & Xia, C. (2019). Automatic Convolutional Neural Architecture Search for Image Classification Under Different Scenes. *IEEE Access: Practical Innovations, Open Solutions*, *7*, 38495–38506. doi:10.1109/ACCESS.2019.2906369

Weston, J., Ratle, F., Mobahi, H., & Collobert, R. (2012). Deep learning via semi-supervised embedding. In *Neural Networks: Tricks of the Trade* (pp. 639–655). Berlin: Springer. doi:10.1007/978-3-642-35289-8_34

Whitley, D. (2014). Sharpened and focused no free lunch and complexity theory. In *Search Methodologies* (pp. 451–476). Boston, MA: Springer. doi:10.1007/978-1-4614-6940-7_16

Wigner, E. P. (1993). Characteristic vectors of bordered matrices with infinite dimensions I. In *The Collected Works of Eugene Paul Wigner* (pp. 524–540). Berlin: Springer. doi:10.1007/978-3-662-02781-3_35

Williams, R. J., & Zipser, D. (1989). A learning algorithm for continually running fully recurrent neural networks. *Neural Computation*, *1*(2), 270–280. doi:10.1162/neco.1989.1.2.270

Wistuba, M., & Pedapati, T. (2019). *Inductive Transfer for Neural Architecture Optimization*. arXiv preprint arXiv:1903.03536

Wood, A. J., & Wollenberg, B. F. (1984). *Power generation, operation, and control*. New York: Wiley.

Wood, M. J., & Hirst, J. D. (2005). Protein secondary structure prediction with dihedral angles. *Proteins*, *59*(3), 476–481. doi:10.1002/prot.20435 PMID:15778963

Wu, Z., Pan, S., Chen, F., Long, G., Zhang, C. & Yu, P.S. (2018). *A Comprehensive Survey on Graph Neural Networks*. Academic Press.

Wu, D., Wang, J., Cai, Y., & Guizani, M. (2015). Millimeter-wave multimedia communications: Challenges, methodology, and applications. *IEEE Communications Magazine*, *53*(1), 232–238. doi:10.1109/MCOM.2015.7010539

Wunsch, D. C. II, Hasselmo, M., Venayagamoorthy, K., & Wang, D. (2003). *Advances in Neural Network Research: IJCNN 2003*. Elsevier Science Inc.

Wu, P., Hoi, S. C. H., Xia, H., Zhao, P., Wang, D., & Miao, C. (2013). Online Multimodal Deep Similarity Learning with Application to Image Retrieval. *Proceedings of the 21st ACM international conference on Multimedia*, 153-162. 10.1145/2502081.2502112

Wu, Z. Y., El-Maghraby, M., & Pathak, S. (2015). Applications of deep learning for smart water networks. *Procedia Engineering*, *119*, 479–485. doi:10.1016/j.proeng.2015.08.870

Xiao, X., Dow, E. R., Eberhart, R., Miled, Z. B., & Oppelt, R. J. (2003). Gene clustering using self-organizing maps and particle swarm optimization. *Proceedings International Parallel and Distributed Processing Symposium*. 10.1109/IPDPS.2003.1213290

Xie, S., Wang, G., Lin, S., & Yu, P. S. (2012, April). Review spam detection via time series pattern discovery. In *Proceedings of the 21st International Conference on World Wide Web* (pp. 635-636). ACM. 10.1145/2187980.2188164

Xiushan, L., Zaihong, S., & Sen, F. J. O. (1997). *Natural parameter method accurately calculates well bore trajectory*. Academic Press.

Xu, K., Wu, L., Wang, Z., Feng, Y., Witbrock, M., & Sheinin, V. (2018a). *Graph2Seq: Graph to Sequence Learning with Attention-based Neural Networks*. arXiv:1804.00823

Xu, K., Wu, L., Wang, Z., Feng, Y., Witbrock, M., & Sheinin, V. (2018b). Exploiting Rich Syntactic Information for Semantic Parsing with Graph-to-Sequence Model. In *Proceedings of the 2018 Conference on Empirical Methods in Natural Language Processing* (pp. 918–924). Academic Press. 10.18653/v1/D18-1110

Xu, R., Wunsch, I. I. D., & Frank, R. (2007). Inference of genetic regulatory networks with recurrent neural network models using particle swarm optimization. *IEEE/ACM Transactions on Computational Biology and Bioinformatics*, *4*(4), 681–692. doi:10.1109/TCBB.2007.1057 PMID:17975278

Yaginuma, Y., Kimoto, T., & Yamakawa, H. (1996, June). Multi-sensor fusion model for constructing internal representation using autoencoder neural networks. In *Proceedings of International Conference on Neural Networks (ICNN'96)* (Vol. 3, pp. 1646-1651). IEEE. 10.1109/ICNN.1996.549147

Yang, J., Yao, S., & Wang, J. (2018). Deep Fusion Feature Learning Network for MI-EEG Classification. *Access IEEE*, *6*, 79050–79059. doi:10.1109/ACCESS.2018.2877452

Yang, X. S. (2013). *Optimization and metaheuristic algorithms in engineering. In Metaheuristic in Water Geotechnical and Transport Engineering* (pp. 1–23). Waltham: Elsevier.

Yang, X.-S. (2009). Harmony search as a metaheuristic algorithm. In *Music-inspired harmony search algorithm* (pp. 1–14). Springer. doi:10.1007/978-3-642-00185-7_1

Yang, X.-S. (2010). *Nature-inspired metaheuristic algorithms*. Luniver Press.

Yang, Y., Gao, J., Wang, J., Heffernan, R., Hanson, J., Paliwal, K., & Zhou, Y. (2018). Sixty-five years of the long march in protein secondary structure prediction: The final stretch? *Briefings in Bioinformatics*, *19*(3), 482–494. PMID:28040746

Yang, Z., Yang, D., Dyer, C., He, X., Smola, A. J., & Hovy, E. H. (2016). *Hierarchical Attention Networks for Document Classification*. HLT-NAACL. doi:10.18653/v1/N16-1174

Yan, X., & Quintana, V. H. (1999). Improving an interior-point-based OPF by dynamic adjustments of step sizes and tolerances. *IEEE Transactions on Power Systems*, *14*(2), 709–717. doi:10.1109/59.761902

Yao, S., Zhao, Y., Zhang, A., Hu, S., Shao, H., Zhang, C., ... Abdelzaher, T. (2018). Deep Learning for the Internet of Things. *Computer*, *51*(5), 32–41. doi:10.1109/MC.2018.2381131

Yaseen, A., & Li, Y. (2014). Context-based features enhance protein secondary structure prediction accuracy. *Journal of Chemical Information and Modeling*, *54*(3), 992–1002. doi:10.1021/ci400647u PMID:24571803

Yin, W., Kann, K., Yu, M., & Schütze, H. (2017). *Comparative Study of CNN and RNN for Natural Language Processing*. Academic Press.

Yin, L., Yu, T., Zhang, X., & Yang, B. (2018). Relaxed deep learning for real-time economic generation dispatch and control with unified time scale. *Energy*, *149*, 11–23. doi:10.1016/j.energy.2018.01.165

Yoo, P. D., Zhou, B. B., & Zomaya, A. Y. (2008). Machine learning techniques for protein secondary structure prediction: An overview and evaluation. *Current Bioinformatics*, *3*(2), 74–86. doi:10.2174/157489308784340676

Yoshida, R., Sanematsu, K., Shigemura, N., Yasumatsu, K., & Ninomiya, Y. (2005). Taste receptor cells responding with action potentials to taste stimuli and their molecular expression of taste related genes. *Chemical Senses, 30*(suppl_1), i19–i20.

Yuan, C., Zhou, C. C., Song, H., Cheng, X. Z., & Dou, Y. (2014). Summary on well logging evaluation method of total organic carbon content in formation. *Diqiu Wulixue Jinzhan*, *29*(6), 2831–2837.

Zadeh, L. A. (1965). Fuzzy sets. *Information and Control*, *8*(3), 338–353. doi:10.1016/S0019-9958(65)90241-X

Zayats, V., & Ostendorf, M. (2018). Conversation Modeling on Reddit using a Graph-Structured LSTM. *Transactions of the Association for Computational Linguistics, 6*, 121–132. doi:10.1162/tacl_a_00009

Zemla, A., Venclovas, Č., Fidelis, K., & Rost, B. (1999). A modified definition of Sov, a segment-based measure for protein secondary structure prediction assessment. *Proteins, 34*(2), 220–223. doi:10.1002/(SICI)1097-0134(19990201)34:2<220::AID-PROT7>3.0.CO;2-K PMID:10022357

Zeng, P., Li, H., He, H., & Li, S. (2019). Dynamic Energy Management of a Microgrid Using Approximate Dynamic Programming and Deep Recurrent Neural Network Learning. *IEEE Transactions on Smart Grid.* doi:10.1109/TSG.2018.2859821

Zhang, J., Qin, J., & Yan, Q. (2006). The role of URLs in objectionable web content categorization. *Proceedings of the IEEE/WIC/ACM International Conference onWeb Intelligence (WI 2006).* 10.1109/WI.2006.170

Zhang, K., Liu, J., Chai, Y., & Qian, K. (2015, May). An optimized dimensionality reduction model for high-dimensional data based on restricted Boltzmann machines. In *The 27th Chinese Control and Decision Conference (2015 CCDC)* (pp. 2939-2944). IEEE. 10.1109/CCDC.2015.7162428

Zhang, S., Tong, H., Xu, J., & Maciejewski, R. (2018). Graph Convolutional Networks: Algorithms, Applications and Open Challenges. In *Proceedings of International Conference on Computational Social Networks* (pp. 79-91). Academic Press. 10.1007/978-3-030-04648-4_7

Zhang, B., Li, J., & Lü, Q. (2018). Prediction of 8-state protein secondary structures by a novel deep learning architecture. *BMC Bioinformatics, 19*(1), 293. doi:10.118612859-018-2280-5 PMID:30075707

Zhang, J., Osmani, A., Awudu, I., & Gonela, V. (2013). An integrated optimization model for switchgrass-based bioethanol supply chain. *Applied Energy, 102*, 1205–1217. doi:10.1016/j.apenergy.2012.06.054

Zhang, L. M., Zhang, K., Chen, Y. X., Li, M., Yao, J., Li, L. X., & Lee, J. I. (2016). Smart Well Pattern Optimization Using Gradient Algorithm. *Journal of Energy Resources Technology-Transactions of the Asme, 138*(1). doi:10.1115/1.4031208

Zhang, S., Wang, J., Tao, X., Gong, Y., & Zheng, N. (2017). Constructing deep sparse coding network for image classification. *Pattern Recognition, 64*, 130–140. doi:10.1016/j.patcog.2016.10.032

Zhang, Y., & Sagui, C. (2015). Secondary structure assignment for conformationally irregular peptides: Comparison between DSSP, STRIDE and KAKSI. *Journal of Molecular Graphics & Modelling, 55*, 72–84. doi:10.1016/j.jmgm.2014.10.005 PMID:25424660

Zhang, Z., Cui, P., & Zhu, W. (2018). Deep Learning on Graphs. *Survey (London, England).*

Zhao, J. (2015). *Stacked what-where auto-encoders.* arXiv preprint arXiv:1506.02351

Zhaoben, F., Ying-chang, L., & Zhidong, B. (2014). *Spectral Theory of Large Dimensional Random Matrices and Its Applications to Wireless Communications and Finance Statistics: Random Matrix Theory and Its Applications.* World Scientific.

Zhao, F., Huang, Y., Wang, L., & Tan, T. (2015). *Deep Semantic Ranking Based Hashing for Multi-Label Image Retrieval.* Computer Vision and Pattern Recognition.

Zhao, F., Lei, W., Ma, W., Liu, Y., & Zhang, C. (2016). An Improved SPEA2 Algorithm with Adaptive Selection of Evolutionary Operators Scheme for Multiobjective Optimization Problems. *Mathematical Problems in Engineering.*

Zhao, T., & Huang, X. (2018). Design and implementation of DeepDSL: A DSL for deep learning. *Computer Languages, Systems & Structures, 54*, 39–70. doi:10.1016/j.cl.2018.04.004

Zhao, X., Li, X., & Zhang, Z. (2015). Multimedia Retrieval via Deep Learning to Rank. *IEEE Signal Processing Letters*, *22*(9), 1487–1491. doi:10.1109/LSP.2015.2410134

Zheng, J., Lu, C., & Gao, L. (2019). Multi-objective cellular particle swarm optimization for wellbore trajectory design. *Applied Soft Computing*, *77*, 106–117. doi:10.1016/j.asoc.2019.01.010

Zhou, J., Cui, G., Zhang, Z., Yang, C., Liu, Z., Wang, L., Li, C., & Sun, M. (2018). *Graph Neural Networks: A Review of Methods and Applications*. Academic Press.

Zhou, C., Hou, C., Wei, X., & Zhang, Q. (2014). Improved hybrid optimization algorithm for 3D protein structure prediction. *Journal of Molecular Modeling*, *20*(7), 2289. doi:10.100700894-014-2289-2 PMID:25069136

Zhou, J., & Troyanskaya, O. (2014). Deep supervised and convolutional generative stochastic network for protein secondary structure prediction. In E. P. Xing, & T. Jebara (Eds.), *Proceedings of the 31st International Conference on Machine Learning* (Vol. 32, pp. 745–753). Bejing, China: PMLR.

Zhou, Y., Xu, J., Cao, J., Xu, B., Li, C., & Xu, B. (2018). Hybrid Attention Networks for Chinese Short Text Classification. *Computación y Sistemas*, *21*(4). doi:10.13053/cys-21-4-2847

Zhuang, C., & Ma, Q. (2018, April). Dual graph convolutional networks for graph-based semi-supervised classification. In *Proceedings of the 2018 World Wide Web Conference* (pp. 499-508). International World Wide Web Conferences Steering Committee. 10.1145/3178876.3186116

Zhu, L., Zhang, C., Zhang, C., Wei, Y., Zhou, X., Cheng, Y., ... Zhang, L. (2018). Prediction of total organic carbon content in shale reservoir based on a new integrated hybrid neural network and conventional well logging curves. *Journal of Geophysics and Engineering*, *15*(3), 1050–1061. doi:10.1088/1742-2140/aaa7af

Zhu, S., Shi, Z., Sun, C., & Shen, S. (2015). Deep neural network based image annotation. *Pattern Recognition Letters*, *65*, 103–108. doi:10.1016/j.patrec.2015.07.037

Zoveidavianpoor, M., Samsuri, A., & Shadizadeh, S. R. (2012). Fuzzy logic in candidate-well selection for hydraulic fracturing in oil and gas wells: A critical review. *International Journal of Physical Sciences*, *7*(26), 4049–4060.

Zoveidavianpoor, M., Samsuri, A., & Shadizadeh, S. R. (2013). Prediction of compressional wave velocity by an artificial neural network using some conventional well logs in a carbonate reservoir. *Journal of Geophysics and Engineering*, *10*(4), 045014. doi:10.1088/1742-2132/10/4/045014

Zupan, J., & Gasteiger, J. (1991). Neural networks: A new method for solving chemical problems or just a passing phase? *Analytica Chimica Acta*, *248*(1), 1–30. doi:10.1016/S0003-2670(00)80865-X

Zvelebil, M., Barton, G. J., Taylor, W. R., & Sternberg, M. J. E. (1987). Prediction of protein secondary structure and active sites using the alignment of homologous sequences. *Journal of Molecular Biology*, *195*(4), 957–961. doi:10.1016/0022-2836(87)90501-8 PMID:3656439

Zvelebil, M., & Baum, J. (2007). *Understanding bioinformatics*. New York, NY: Garland Science. doi:10.1201/9780203852507

About the Contributors

J. Joshua Thomas is a senior lecturer at KDU Penang University College, Malaysia since 2008. He obtained his PhD (Intelligent Systems Techniques) in 2015 from University Sains Malaysia, Penang, and Master's degree in 1999 from Madurai Kamaraj University, India. From July to September 2005, he worked as a research assistant at the Artificial Intelligence Lab in University Sains Malaysia. From March 2008 to March 2010, he worked as a research associate at the same University. Currently, he is working with Machine Learning, Big Data, Data Analytics, Deep Learning, specially targeting on Convolutional Neural Networks (CNN) and Bi-directional Recurrent Neural Networks(RNN) for image tagging with embedded natural language processing, End to end steering learning systems and GAN. His work involves experimental research with software prototypes and mathematical modelling and design He is an Associate Editor for the Journal of Energy Optimization and Engineering (IJEOE), and invited guest editor for Journal of Visual Languages Communication (JVLC-Elsevier), He has published more than 30 papers in leading international conference proceedings and peer reviewed journals.

Pinar Karagoz is currently Professor in Computer Engineering Department, Middle East Technical University (METU). She received her Ph.D. from the same department in 2003. She worked as a visiting researcher in State University of New York (SUNY) at Stony Brook. Her research interests include data mining, web usage mining, social network analysis, information extraction from the web, semantic web services, web service discovery and composition. Dr. Karagoz has authored several publications in international journals and leading conferences. Some of her papers were published in journals such as IEEE TKDE, IEEE Industrial Informatics, ACM TWEB, Information Systems Journal, SIGMOD Record, Knowledge and Information Systems, Knowledge based Systems. Some of her research were presented and published in conferences including VLDB, CIKM, ASONAM, DAWAK, ICWS. She has also taken part in the organization committee of several conferences including ICDM and VLDB.

B. Bazeer Ahamed received a Bachelor of Technology in Vel Tech Engineering College, Affiliated to Anna University, Chennai, India and Master of Computer Science Engineering in Anna University of Technology, Tiruchirapalli, India .Ph.D From Sathyabama Institute of Technology and Science, Chennai India. He has published more than 20 peer reviewed international journals and participated in several high profile conferences. At present he is working as Associate Professor in the department of Computer Science and Engineering, Balaji Institute of Technology and Science, Warangal, India. Prof.Bazeer research is mainly focused on Data Mining &Information retrieval; additionally his research includes Networks, Data bases, Big Data. He is a Member of IEEE,ISTE, IAENG, and CSTA. He chaired the several sessions at National and International Conference.

Pandian Vasant is a senior lecturer at Department of Fundamental and Applied Sciences, Faculty of Science and Information Technology, Universiti Teknologi PETRONAS in Malaysia. He holds PhD (UNEM, Costa Rica) in Computational Intelligence, MSc (UMS, Malaysia, Engineering Mathematics) and BSc (2nd Class Upper-Hons in Mathematics, UM, Malaysia) in Mathematics. He has co-authored research papers and articles in national journals, international journals, conference proceedings, conference paper presentation, and special issues lead guest editor, lead guest editor for book chapters, edited books, and keynote lecture. (218 publications indexed in SCOPUS). In the year 2009, Dr. Pandian Vasant was awarded top reviewer for the journal Applied Soft Computing (Elsevier), awarded outstanding reviewer in the year 2015 for ASOC (Elsevier) journal and Top reviewer for Sentinels of Science: Computer Science (Oct. 2015 - Sept. 2016). He has 26 years of working experience at the various universities from 1989-2017. Currently he is Editor-in-Chief of IJCO and IJEOE, Member of American Mathematical Society, MERLIN, and NAVY Research Groups.

* * *

Rosni Abdullah is a Professor in Computer Science at the School of Computer Sciences, Universiti Sains Malaysia in Penang, Malaysia. She received her Bachelors degree in Computer Science and Applied Mathematics and Masters degree in Computer Science from Western Michigan University, Kalamazoo, Michigan, U.S.A. in 1984 and 1986 respectively. She obtained her PhD in 1997 from Loughborough University, United Kingdom in the area Parallel Algorithms. She is currently the Dean of the School of Computer Sciences, Director of the National Advanced IPv6 Centre (Nav6) and Head of the Parallel and Distributed Processing Research Group. Her current research work is in the area of parallel algorithms on multicore and GPGPU architectures for bioinformatics applications.

Mustafa Agriman is currently a graduate student at Middle East Technical University Department of Computer Engineering, Turkey. He is also working as software&design engineer at Avionic Systems of Turkish Aerospace. His research focuses on graph mining, data mining, social data management and analysis.

Solaiappan Aravind is pursuing his undergraduate degree in the Department of Computer Technology, Anna University, India. His area of interests are Big data, Networking, Deep learning and Artificial intelligence .He is a keen learner and is very creative in pitching new ideas and innovative solutions.

Shahana Bano received her MS(IS) degree in Computer Science from Montessori Mahila Kalasala Vijayawada. M.Tech degree in Computer Science from K.L. College of Engineering Vaddeswaram and received her Ph.D. from KLEF deemed to be University. Currently, she is working as a Associate Professor in the Department of Computer Science &Engineering in K.L.E.F deemed to be University, Vijayawada. She has got 12 years of teaching experience She has published 25 research papers in various national and international journals and conferences. She is member of professional societies CSI.

Bahari Belaton, Ph.D., is currently a Deputy Dean (Innovation and Research) at the School of Computer Sciences, Universiti Sains Malaysia. He obtained his Ph.D. from the University of Leeds, where he worked on model-based visualization. He has been using VTK since 2002 for his Master Level course – Envisioning Information in USM.

Kallol Biswas completed my B.sc in electrical and electronics engineering from International Islamic University Chittagong. Then I joined as an assistant engineer in an engineering solution provider company and served there for almost 1.5 years. After that, I have admitted in University Teknologi Petronas in M.sc program.

Menaga D. is a full time Research Scholar in B.S.Abdur Rahman Crescent University, Chennai, Tamilnadu, India. She is working as a JRF. Her area of interest is Data mining.

Bugra Demirdover is currently a graduate student at Middle East Technical University Department of Computer Engineering, Turkey. He is working as a game developer in SNG, a mobile gaming company. His interests are data mining, artificial intelligence and machine learning. His master research focuses on applications of machine learning techniques in games.

Chitra Dhawale currently working as a Professor and Head, P. G. Department of Computer Application, P. R. Pote College of Engineering and Management, Amravati. Earlier she was associated with Symbiosis International University, Pune. To her credit so far 5 research scholars have been awarded Ph.D. under her guidance by S.G.B. Amravati and R.T.M.Nagpur University. Her research interest includes Image and Video Processing, Multi-Biometric, Cloud Security. She has published more than 60 research papers in peer reviewed International Journals and in IEEE, Springer, Elsevier, ACM conferences proceedings and 04 book chapters in IGI Global Publications. Dr. Chitra, One of the well known academician in Computer discipline has organized various National and International Conferences, Chaired Sessions and delivered invited talk in various Faculty Development Programs, Orientation, Refresher courses, National and International Conferences. She is a senior member of the IACSIT, Member of International Association of Engineers (IAENG), Hong Kong and Life Member of ISTE, New Delhi. She has been reviewing books from various prestigious publication and also reviewer for International journals. Dr. Chitra is also a motivational speaker and conducted several workshops on "Effective Research Methodology", "Research Writing Skills", "Placement Preparation", "100 techniques for speed mathematics", "Interview Techniques", "Spiritual thoughts" etc. As a part of social contribution, she is executive member of NGO "AADHAR Foundation", Amravati.

Kritika Dhawale is studying in B.Tech (ECE), Indian Institute of Information Technology, Nagpur. She has published her research papers on "Recent Trends in Deep Learning Frameworks,Challenges and Opportunities", coauthored book chapter and working on deep learning project as a part of Internship.

Rajesh Dubey is currently associated with Mohanlal Sukhadia University, Udaipur and working as a Director, National Resource Center-Biotechnology. He is an active researcher in Biotechnology and author of many books and research articles.

Mert Erdemir is currently pursuing his Master in Computer Science (MCS) degree in Computer Science Department, University of Iowa. He received his BSc degree from Department of Computer Engineering at Middle East Technical University, Turkey. His research interests are including data mining, text mining, graph mining, social data management and analysis as well as machine learning applications.

Hilal Genc is a Master's student at gebze Technical University. Her research interests include deep learning, natural language processing, and graph representation learning.

Jahedul Islam is a post graduate student at Universiti Teknologi PETRONAS (UTP). He completed his bsc from Chittagon University of Engineering and Technology. His research interest includes soft computing and metaheuristic algorithm

Murugan Krishnamoorthy received a Bachelor of Technology in Anna University, Chennai, India and Master of Computer Science Engineering in Anna University, Tiruchirapalli, India. Ph.D. from Anna University, Chennai, India. He has published more peer-reviewed international journals and participated in several high profile conferences. At present, he is working as a Teaching Fellow in the Department of Computer Technology, Anna University, Chennai, India. His research is mainly focused on Wireless security, Cryptography, and security, NGN. He Co-chaired several sessions at International Conferences.

Igor Litvinchev is a Leading Mathematician at Computing Center Russian Academy of Sciences (CC RAS), Moscow and Professor at Nuevo Leon State University (UANL), Postgraduate Program in Systems Engineering,Monterrey, Mexico. Received his M.Sc. degree from Moscow Institute of Physics and Technology (Fizteh), Moscow, Russia; Ph.D. and Dr.Sci. degrees in systems modeling and optimization from CC RAS. He has held positions at universities in Brazil, Mexico, and Norway, as well as positions at various universities and research centers in Russia. His research focuses on large-scale system modeling, optimization, and control. Dr. Litvinchev is a member of Russian Academy of Natural Sciences and Mexican Academy of Sciences.

Nimal Madhu M. received his Doctoral degree from Asian Institute of Technology (AIT), Thailand, in 2016 and Masters from Indian Institute of Technology Bombay (IITB), India, in 2012. He is currently a Post-Doctoral Research Associate at AIT Thailand. His research interest include Power System Optimization, Power System Restructuring and Deregulation, Smart Grid, Microgrids, and AI and Deep Learning Applications in Power Systems.

Fawaz Mahyoub is a Ph.D. student at the School of Computer Sciences, Universiti Sains Malaysia in Penang, Malaysia. He received the B.Sc. degree in Computer Science from Taiz University, Taiz, Yemen in 2008 and the M.Sc. degree in Computer Science from King Abdulaziz University, Jeddah, Saudi Arabia in 2014. His research interests include deep learning, data mining and computational biology.

Anongpun Man-Im received her Doctoral degree in Electric Power System Management from Asian Institute of Technology (AIT), Thailand in 2019. Currently, she is an electrical engineer at Electricity Generating Authority of Thailand (EGAT). Her research interests include power system optimization, power system integrated renewable energy, and smart grids.

Raghu N. has eight years of experience in Academic and Research. He is currently pursing Ph.D in Electronics Engineering, Jain University, Bangalore. He completed his masters in Digital Electronics and Communication from N.M.A.M.I.T, Nitte, Mangalore in 2011 and under graduation in Telecommunication Engineering from Coorg Institute of technology, Kodagu in 2009. His research interests were in RF Communication and Image Processing. He has published his research findings in various Scopus indexed Journals and International conferences. He is a member of various professional bodies like IACSIT, CBEES and IAENG.

Berihun Negash is a senior Lecturer at Universiti Teknologi PETRONAS (UTP). Before joining UTP he was a senior Lecturer at Bahir Dar University, Ethiopia. Berihun have earned his PhD in Chemical Engineering from the UTP, an MSc degree in Petroleum Engineering from Norwegian University of science and technology and a BSc in Chemical Engineering from Bahir Dar University. Berihun has published few papers on applied data analytics for petroleum engineering problems.

Weerakorn Ongsakul received the degrees of M.S. and Ph.D. from Texas A&M University. He is currently a Professor with the Department of Energy, Environment, and Climate, Asian Institute of Technology, Thailand, specialized in the power system operation and control, computer applications to power systems, parallel processing applications, artificial intelligence applications to power systems, power system restructuring and deregulation, and smart grid and micro grid.

Jay Patel is doing his Bachelor's degree in Electronics and Computer Engineering at Vellore Institute of Technology and his research interest includes pattern recognition, Internet of Things, machine learning and Deep learning.

Gilberto Pérez-Lechuga has been a teacher and lecturer in some foreign countries, lecturing on topics of his specialty, highlighting in particular the use of operations research and applied mathematics in real-world problems with industrial applications. Founder and general director of SEIIO, an international consulting firm in Industrial Engineering and Operations Research. Author, co-author and editor of 6 books and book chapters related to his specialty and author of more than 70 scientific articles in journals specialized in applied mathematics, operations research and industrial and manufacturing engineering. Currently, he is the general director of research at the Autonomous University of the Hidalgo State, Mexico. His research interests include, modeling, simulation, optimization and applications of flexible manufacturing systems, logistics models, financial engineering, transportation systems, reliability engineering and stochastic optimization by conventional methods and swarm intelligence algorithms

Karthik R. obtained his Master's degree from Anna University, India. He is currently serving as Assistant Professor in the School of Electronics Engineering, VIT University, Chennai. His research interest includes digital image processing, pattern recognition and deep learning. He has published 21 papers in peer reviewed journals and conferences.

Parvathi R. is an Associate Professor of School of Computing Science and Engineering at VIT University, Chennai since 2011. She received the Doctoral degree in the field of spatial data mining in the same year. Her teaching experience in the area of computer science includes more than two decades and her research interests include data mining, big data and computational biology.

Saravanan Radhakrishnan holds a Masters degree in Computer Science and is currently a Ph.D Research Scholar in Vellore Institute of Technology. He has 22 years of experience in Software Development and is now a Founder and Chief Technology Officer of a Technology Startup focusing on Artificial Intelligence, Internet of Things and Robotics for varied domains including Farm Automation. His research interests are in the areas of Deep Learning, Vision Computing and Internet of Things. His passion lies in creatively combining technology and nature; his fully automated roof-top garden and many of the automations in his house speaks volumes about his passion.

Ratnavel Rajalakshmi received her Bachelor's degree in Computer Science and Engineering from Bharathidasan University. She has completed her Masters and Ph.D. in Computer Science and Engineering from Anna University, Chennai. She is currently working as an Associate Professor in the School of Computing Science and Engineering, Vellore Institute of Technology, Chennai, India. Her research interests include Web Mining, Text Analytics, Pattern Recognition, Medical ImageProcessing, Machine learning and Deep learning. She has published several research articles in international conferences and reputed journals.

Rameshkannan is a full-time research scholar at School of Computing Science and Engineering, Vellore Institute of Technology, Chennai. His research interests include Text Analytics and Machine Learning

Revathi S. is working as Associate Professor in B.S.Abdur Rahman Crescent University, Chennai, Tamilnadu, India. Her area of interest are Network Security, Security of Internet of Things and Cryptography.

Gokhan Simsek is MSc. student in Middle East Technical University, Computer Engineering Department in Turkey. He has been working as software & design engineer at Avionics Systems of Turkish Aerospace.

Hans Tiwari is doing his Bachelor's degree in Electronics and Computer Engineering at Vellore Institute of Technology, Chennai, India. His field of interests includes IoT, Machine Learning and Deep Learning.

Tran Huu Ngoc Tran is pursuing Master's in Computer Science by research. She is working on chemoinformatics drug discovery problem with the department of computing at KDU Penang University College, Malaysia. Before joining, she worked as Software Engineer in Bosch -Vietnam

Pattabiraman Venkatasubbu obtained his Bachelor's from Madras University and Master's degree from Bharathidasan University. He completed his PhD from Bharathiar University, India. He has a total Professional experience of more than 17 years working in various prestigious institutions. He has published more than 35 papers in various National and International peer reviewed journals and conferences. He visited various countries namely few China, Singapore, Malaysia, Thailand and South Africa etc. for presenting his research contributions as well as to giving key note address. He is currently an Associate Professor and Program-Chair for Master's Programme at VIT University-Chennai Campus, India. His teaching and research expertise covers a wide range of subject area including Data Structures, Knowledge Discovery and Data mining, Database Technologies, Big Data Analytics, Networks and Information security, etc.

Burcu Yilmaz is an assistant professor in Institute of Information Technologies at the Gebze Technical University. She received her PhD degree in computer science from the Gebze Institute of Technology in 2010. Burcu is conducting research in data mining, machine learning, natural language processing, deep learning, graph mining, graph neural networks and social network analysis.

Index

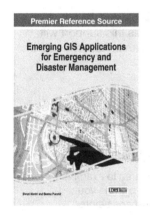
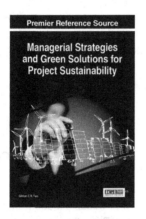

IGI Global Proudly Partners With eContent Pro International

Receive a 25% Discount on all Editorial Services

Editorial Services

IGI Global expects all final manuscripts submitted for publication to be in their final form. This means they must be reviewed, revised, and professionally copy edited prior to their final submission. Not only does this support with accelerating the publication process, but it also ensures that the highest quality scholarly work can be disseminated.

English Language Copy Editing

Let eContent Pro International's expert copy editors perform edits on your manuscript to resolve spelling, punctuaion, grammar, syntax, flow, formatting issues and more.

Scientific and Scholarly Editing

Allow colleagues in your research area to examine the content of your manuscript and provide you with valuable feedback and suggestions before submission.

Figure, Table, Chart & Equation Conversions

Do you have poor quality figures? Do you need visual elements in your manuscript created or converted? A design expert can help!

Translation

Need your documjent translated into English? eContent Pro International's expert translators are fluent in English and more than 40 different languages.

Email: customerservice@econtentpro.com   **www.igi-global.com/editorial-service-partners**

IGI Global's Transformative Open Access (OA) Model:
How to Turn Your University Library's Database Acquisitions Into a Source of OA Funding

In response to the OA movement and well in advance of Plan S, IGI Global, early last year, unveiled their OA Fee Waiver (Offset Model) Initiative.

Under this initiative, librarians who invest in IGI Global's InfoSci-Books (5,300+ reference books) and/or InfoSci-Journals (185+ scholarly journals) databases will be able to subsidize their patron's OA article processing charges (APC) when their work is submitted and accepted (after the peer review process) into an IGI Global journal.*

How Does it Work?

1. When a library subscribes or perpetually purchases IGI Global's InfoSci-Databases including InfoSci-Books (5,300+ e-books), InfoSci-Journals (185+ e-journals), and/or their discipline/subject-focused subsets, IGI Global will match the library's investment with a fund of equal value to go toward subsidizing the OA article processing charges (APCs) for their patrons.

   Researchers: Be sure to recommend the InfoSci-Books and InfoSci-Journals to take advantage of this initiative.

2. When a student, faculty, or staff member submits a paper and it is accepted (following the peer review) into one of IGI Global's 185+ scholarly journals, the author will have the option to have their paper published under a traditional publishing model or as OA.

3. When the author chooses to have their paper published under OA, IGI Global will notify them of the OA Fee Waiver (Offset Model) Initiative. If the author decides they would like to take advantage of this initiative, IGI Global will deduct the US$ 1,500 APC from the created fund.

4. This fund will be offered on an annual basis and will renew as the subscription is renewed for each year thereafter. IGI Global will manage the fund and award the APC waivers unless the librarian has a preference as to how the funds should be managed.

Hear From the Experts on This Initiative:

"I'm very happy to have been able to make one of my recent research contributions, 'Visualizing the Social Media Conversations of a National Information Technology Professional Association' featured in the *International Journal of Human Capital and Information Technology Professionals*, freely available along with having access to the valuable resources found within IGI Global's InfoSci-Journals database."

– **Prof. Stuart Palmer**,
Deakin University, Australia

For More Information, Visit: www.igi-global.com/publish/contributor-resources/open-access or contact IGI Global's Database Team at eresources@igi-global.com.

Printed in the United States
By Bookmasters